Sixth Edition

Growing Up Gifted

Developing the Potential of Children at Home and at School

Barbara Clark

Professor Emeritus

California State University, Los Angeles

Merrill
Prentice Hall

Upper Saddle River, New Jersey
Columbus, Ohio

Library of Congress Cataloging-in-Publication Data

Clark, Barbara
   Growing up gifted / Barbara Clark.—6th ed.
     p. cm.
   Includes bibliographical references (p.) and indexes.
   ISBN 0-13-094437-8
   1. Gifted children—Education—United States. I. Title.
LC3993.9.C58 2002
371.95—dc21   2001044256

Vice President and Publisher: Jeffery W. Johnston
Executive Editor: Ann Castel Davis
Editorial Assistant: Keli Gemrich
Production Editor: Linda Hillis Bayma
Production Coordination: Cliff Kallemeyn, Clarinda Publication Services
Design Coordinator: Diane C. Lorenzo
Cover Designer: Thomas Borah
Cover Art: The Stock Illustration Source, Inc.
Production Manager: Laura Messerly
Director of Marketing: Kevin Flanagan
Marketing Manager: Amy June
Marketing Coordinator: Barbara Koontz

This book was set in Garamond by The Clarinda Company. It was printed and bound by R.R. Donnelley & Sons Company. The cover was printed by The Lehigh Press, Inc.

Photo Credits: Mark Balay, p. 135; Wanda Balay, pp. 57, 88, 151, 252, 311; Carmela Brown, pp. 3, 218, 270, 300, 319, 380, 412; Barbara Clark, pp. 24, 83, 108, 140, 231, 361, 421, 446; Terry Clark, pp. 130, 154; Scott Cunningham/Merrill, p. 242; Nina Curone-Romney, p. 399; Paul DaSilva, p. 73; Chris Denes, pp. 118, 125; Chris Hoehner, p. 170; Julie Lowerre, p. 49; Anthony Magnacca/Merrill, p. 213; Toby Manzanares, pp. 167, 387, 496; Paolina Schiro, p. 285; Tom Watson/Merrill, p. 539; Zuma Bay Volleyball Club, p. 197.

Pearson Education Ltd., *London*
Pearson Education Australia Pty. Limited, *Sydney*
Pearson Education Singapore Ptd. Ltd.
Pearson Education North Asia Ltd., *Hong Kong*
Pearson Education Canada, Ltd., *Toronto*
Pearson Educación de Mexico, S.A. de C.V.
Pearson Education—Japan, *Tokyo*
Pearson Education Malaysia Pte. Ltd.
Pearson Education, *Upper Saddle River, New Jersey*

10   9   8   7   6   5   4   3

ISBN: 0-13-094437-8

To my beautiful mother, whose memory fills my days,
my son, who allowed me to live with giftedness,
my daughter, who taught me the gentleness of special gifts,
my husband, who believes in growing and miracles,
my dearest father, who loves us all,
and Emily, Allyson, Marisa, Christopher, Kimberli,
Kelly, Brianna, and Kaitlin, with special blessings for Tim,
From whom I'm learning all over again.

PREFACE

This is the sixth edition of *Growing Up Gifted*. As I began the first edition more than 20 years ago, it was my intention to write a book for my students that would include the ideas I found important in supporting my work with gifted learners. I wanted the book to be helpful to the parents of gifted students as well because I believe that parents are their first and most important teachers. Brain researchers had just begun to talk about the implications of their work for human learning, and I wanted to make that information available to those with whom I worked. The importance of early learning in human mental development was just being noted and, in some scientific circles, enriching our heredity was first being discussed. I wanted to bring these ideas into the classrooms so that all children could come closer to reaching their full potential.

As my students and I worked to bring research into practice for seven years in an experimental school setting we developed with gifted and highly gifted learners, we shared excitement and growth. Later editions of the book reflected that growth, explored new ideas, and began to be useful not only to my students but to students throughout the world. Over the years, the work of many other researchers enriched our efforts.

At this writing, the book retains parts of its original structure and yet has included knowledge and practice from so many others that it is only the vision that remains the same. Optimizing learning, synthesizing knowledge from many disciplines, and bringing together and integrating best practices from classrooms where children grow all added to the texture of the book. All of this is communicated to advocate for students whom the schools have designated as gifted learners. By sharing it, I hope that more children will grow up gifted and bring their gifts to the world.

There are three parts to the book: Part I is intended to create an understanding of who gifted learners are, how they become gifted, and what giftedness and creativity are like as one grows cognitively, socially, emotionally, and intuitively.

Part II builds on this understanding by describing school programs. How gifted learners can be supported at school and the services required to meet their needs and optimize their experiences are explored. A continuum of such services is discussed, and the options that schools can develop to serve gifted learners in the elementary, middle school, and high school programs are described. Homeschooling and global education are a part of this discussion. Evaluating programs to improve their quality, reach, and impact is explored. The methods and complexities of identifying giftedness are also found in this section.

Part III is devoted to the theories and practices of teaching gifted learners. Numerous curriculum models used to provide education for gifted learners are described. The ideas for optimizing learning that have been evolving from the 1970s are organized and shared and the Integrative Education Model, developed from translating brain research for use in the classroom, is briefly explained. Differentiating and individualizing the curriculum and the instruction, so necessary for gifted learners, are a part of the knowledge base shared in this section.

Finally, the diversity of cultures and the effect they have on the development and the expression of giftedness is explored. The impact of gender, race, ethnicity, and poverty must be carefully considered and possible avenues of intervention understood if we are to overcome any barriers that students from these cultural groups might encounter. Gifted learners who are in need because of disabilities or underachievement and those learners who are limited by their experiences with cultural diversity must be helped to reverse the loss and realize the strength and richness that such diversity can bring. Only through extending our knowledge base and increasing the number of strategies that work will we be able to meet these needs.

This book is written for the teachers at home and at school who are striving to understand a little better, reach a little higher, and achieve with excellence a little more often. At this time there is more research in the field, more programs available in the schools, more theories and practices to report, and more attention to quality evident. I have tried to bring a well-rounded sample of all this growth to you so that you can use it for the students whom you have chosen to serve. Included are activities, summaries, questions, graphics, charts, illustrations, and vignettes drawn from my experiences to aid in your understanding.

The book ends with a special epilogue that shares an experience that profoundly affected me during a trip to the newly re-established nation Kyrgyzstan. With the sharing of this experience, we come full circle to the concerns of excellence and equity explored in the first chapter. I believe that all of you who have chosen to support the growth of gifted learners will find in this book much that will aid you to be more effective and caring in your work. The information in this book provides, however, more than educational ideas; it provides a way, as my colleague in Kyrgyzstan so eloquently stated, "to survive as a country and find our leaders in our children." It is my intent to provide you with an understanding of intelligence and its nurture so that more of our children can realize their unique gifts and talents and by your efforts they may truly have the opportunity to be *growing up gifted*.

ACKNOWLEDGMENTS

I would like to thank the reviewers of this edition: Dorothy Armstrong, Grand Valley State University; Art Attell, University of Arkansas at Monticello; and Leonard Ganschow, Miami University, Ohio. They gave me some very good ideas for organization and approach that allowed me to enrich the book. I would also like to acknowledge my copyeditor, Robyn Durand, whose most helpful work clarified and strengthened my writing. As always, I am most indebted to my students, who over the years have taught me the real meaning and honor of being a *teacher*.

DISCOVER THE COMPANION WEBSITE
ACCOMPANYING THIS BOOK

The Prentice Hall Companion Website: A Virtual Learning Environment

Technology is a constantly growing and changing aspect of our field that is creating a need for content and resources. To address this emerging need, Prentice Hall has developed an online learning environment for students and professors alike—Companion Websites—to support our textbooks.

In creating a Companion Website, our goal is to build on and enhance what the textbook already offers. For this reason, the content for each user-friendly website is organized by topic and provides the professor and student with a variety of meaningful resources. Common features of a Companion Website include:

For the Professor—

Every Companion Website integrates **Syllabus Manager**™, an online syllabus creation and management utility.

- **Syllabus Manager**™ provides you, the instructor, with an easy, step-by-step process to create and revise syllabi, with direct links into Companion Website and other online content without having to learn HTML.

- Students may log on to your syllabus during any study session. All they need to know is the web address for the Companion Website and the password you've assigned to your syllabus.

- After you have created a syllabus using **Syllabus Manager**™, students may enter the syllabus for their course section from any point in the Companion Website.

- Clicking on a date, the student is shown the list of activities for the assignment. The activities for each assignment are linked directly to actual content, saving time for students.

- Adding assignments consists of clicking on the desired due date, then filling in the details of the assignment—name of the assignment, instructions, and whether it is a one-time or repeating assignment.

- In addition, links to other activities can be created easily. If the activity is online, a URL can be entered in the space provided, and it will be linked automatically in the final syllabus.
- Your completed syllabus is hosted on our servers, allowing convenient updates from any computer on the Internet. Changes you make to your syllabus are immediately available to your students at their next logon.

For the Student—

- **Topic Overviews**—outline key concepts in topic areas
- **Characteristics**—general information about each topic/disability covered on this website
- **Read About It**—a list of links to pertinent articles found on the Internet that cover each topic
- **Teaching Ideas**—links to articles that offer suggestions, ideas, and strategies for teaching students with disabilities
- **Web Links**—a wide range of websites that provide useful and current information related to each topic area
- **Resources**—a wide array of different resources for many of the pertinent topics and issues surrounding special education
- **Electronic Bluebook**—send homework or essays directly to your instructor's email with this paperless form
- **Message Board**—serves as a virtual bulletin board to post—or respond to—questions or comments to/from a national audience
- **Chat**—real-time chat with anyone who is using the text anywhere in the country—ideal for discussion and study groups, class projects, etc.

To take advantage of these and other resources, please visit the *Growing Up Gifted*, Sixth Edition Companion Website at

www.prenhall.com/clark

CONTENTS

CHAPTER 3
Being Creative: Going Beyond Giftedness   73

CHAPTER 4
Becoming Gifted   108

CHAPTER 5
Growing Up Gifted   **167**

PART II THE SCHOOL AND THE GIFTED INDIVIDUAL

CHAPTER 8
Outreach of Programs and Program Evaluation   **300**

CHAPTER 9
Finding Gifted Learners in the Schools   **319**

PART III TEACHING GIFTED LEARNERS

CHAPTER 10
Establishing the Foundation for Educating Gifted Learners   361

CHAPTER 11
Planning for Integrative Education: Using Brain Research in the Classroom   399

CHAPTER 12
Differentiating and Individualizing the Curriculum and Instruction for Gifted Learners   446

Part I

Understanding the Gifted Individual

CHAPTER 1
Discussing Issues of Excellence and Equity:
Gifted Education and Talent Development

CHAPTER 2
Discovering Who the Gifted Individuals Are

CHAPTER 3
Being Creative: Going Beyond Giftedness

CHAPTER 4
Becoming Gifted

CHAPTER 5
Growing Up Gifted

1

Discussing Issues of Excellence and Equity: Gifted Education and Talent Development

In this chapter the reader will discover:

- A discussion of the dual mission of gifted education
- A rationale for gifted education and talent development
- A discussion of the relationship between excellence and equity
- A discussion of some of the barriers to educating gifted individuals
- A discussion of some of the myths and misconceptions in gifted education
- An overview of some of the current issues in gifted education
- A Declaration of the Educational Rights of the Gifted Child

There is nothing so unequal as the equal treatment of unequal people.

—THOMAS JEFFERSON

Mary Beth had been very excited about her first day at school. Of course, she had been to school already for a year, but that really did not count. That was only kindergarten and Mary Beth knew that in kindergarten you just played—played and got acquainted with other children. Her mother said that it didn't matter what the lessons were or if you already knew everything they did in kindergarten. First grade was where you had real lessons and really learned things. Mary Beth was so anxious to learn things. As long as she could remember, clear back when she was a little girl, she loved to learn things. Her mother said that she was a natural born "interrogator." That meant that she liked to ask questions and that was a good thing she thought.

When she left the house in the morning, Mary Beth could hardly wait to get to school. Everyone noticed how happy she was. But now, as she sat at the dinner table with her family, she didn't seem happy; she seemed very quiet, which was unusual for Mary Beth.

"Well, how was the first grade? What was your favorite part of the day?" her father asked. Mary Beth didn't answer for a moment and looked very thoughtful.

"Dad, you know, Mom and I learned a lot about colors when we used to play here at home when I was a little girl. Then when I went to nursery school we learned about colors again. Last year in kindergarten everyone learned about colors. Today in first grade we spent a lot of time learning about colors. Do you think when I go to college we will still have to learn about colors?"

Obviously, Ms. Martin, Mary Beth's first grade teacher, had never heard about how unequal it is to give equal treatment to unequal people. For Mary Beth, equity would have meant giving her an equal opportunity to learn, not just doing the same thing. If she had seen the "excellent" mark in Ms. Martin's grade book for her work today, Mary Beth would question what that meant. She did not feel that she had been excellent at all.

THE DUAL MISSION OF GIFTED EDUCATION

Balancing Excellence and Equity

From its very beginning, America has championed the cause of equity. However, even with this belief as a foundation, various groups justifiably have found it necessary throughout past decades to add their voices to this call for each person's right to fulfill her or his potential. In a democracy, all people are promised that no barrier will be raised to their pursuit of health, happiness, liberty, and justice, because the fullest achievement of each must be encouraged, not only for the individual but for the benefit of all.

Although many times Americans have fallen short of our goal and have allowed skin color, religious ideals, personal beliefs, and even gender stereotypes to block the highest development of the ability of some of our citizens, we continue to pursue this ideal. In this new century, we are well-advised to continue our pursuit of equity for all. It is ironic that the most able learners should be among those who have need for equity. Herein lies the paradox. Americans love freedom and the right to pursue individual ability to its fullest, yet they resent those who have developed high levels of intelligence. They love egalitarianism and declare that none should be seen as more able than another, yet they demand high achievement in the economic and professional fields at home and in competition with other nations of the world.

Let us be sure we agree on the meaning of the terms. As Coleman, Sanders, and Cross (1997) point out, "On the surface we seem to be talking the same language, but at a deeper level there is not a match in the ideas . . . The result is that the situation remains confused and unsettled" (p. 109). When we speak of equity, it must be agreed that having *equal* opportunity does not mean having the *same* opportunity. Equity means making experiences available that are uniquely appropriate for each individual. Van Tassel-Baska (1997) states, "Equity is present when all students have equal access to potential opportunities based on reasonable standards of competence" (p. 11). Equity promises that whatever your talent or interest, whatever your skill or ability, you will have every opportunity to develop that uniqueness to its fullest extent. Offering a talented musician and a brilliant scientist the same experience is not equity; equity is offering them equal opportunities to pursue their individual paths toward excellence.

Excellence for all is the goal, however, as Van Tassel-Baska (1997) reminds us, "Excellence for all, if it means the same standards, same curriculum, same instructional emphases, becomes basically inequitable for all since it fails to recognize individual differences" (p. 11).

For years, the manner in which both excellence and equity were addressed in schools—and even the terminology used—has been obscure, contentious, and frustrating. Some educators felt strongly that national educational efforts must be focused on those children who are advanced and accelerated in their intellectual development—those now labeled gifted—to ensure their continued growth. Others just as strongly believed that such efforts must be directed to develop the intellectual talent in every child. After much discussion it has become clear that one point of view should not negate the other, because both are vitally important to America and its children. Gifted education should engage in two equally critical tasks: (1) to support and enhance the appropriate education of gifted learners, those functioning or who have the ability to function at high levels of intelligence, and (2) to support and enhance the talent in all learners so that all children may realize their fullest potential to the highest levels of their ability. In other words, the field of gifted education should support and enhance the pursuit of both excellence and equity. With such a mission, educators can ensure that gifted students continue to increase their level and range of ability as these same educators contribute to an increase in the population of gifted students through the development of the talents found in all students.

To further such a pursuit of excellence and equity, the following rationale will explore some of the ideas that create the need for gifted education as a field of study, as an area of teacher preparation, as a needed practice in our schools, and as a support for the growth of this segment of our school population.

A RATIONALE FOR GIFTED EDUCATION AND TALENT DEVELOPMENT

1. *The development of giftedness is the result of an interactive process* that involves challenges from the environment that stimulate and bring forth innate talents, capabilities, and processes. Although these innate mechanisms are most easily affected

during the early years, they require appropriate challenges throughout the individual's lifetime for high levels of actualization to occur. We either progress or regress intellectually; stability or maintenance of a fixed quantity of intelligence is not possible. Giftedness, as a label for a high level of intelligence, is a dynamic quality that can be furthered only by participation in learning experiences that challenge and extend from the point of the child's talent, ability, and interest.

2. *Our political and social system is based on democratic principles.* In a democracy, equal opportunity cannot and must not mean the *same* opportunity. As Thomas Jefferson once said, "There is nothing so unequal as the equal treatment of unequal people." The school, as an extension of those principles, purports to provide an equal educational opportunity for all children to develop their talents to the fullest potential. Because all children must, therefore, be educated at their level of development, it is then undemocratic to refuse to allow gifted children the right to educational experiences appropriate to their developed level of ability. Offering all individuals educational opportunities at only one level, with the assumption that this level will meet the needs of all, is just as unfair. For true equal opportunity, a variety of learning experiences must be available at many levels so that all children and youth can develop their talents and abilities to the level of their highest potential.

3. *When human beings are limited and restricted in their development, they suffer physical and psychological pain.* When humans are not allowed to move or reach beyond what they have previously accomplished, they often become bored, discouraged, frustrated, and angry and feel diminished as persons. To have talent, to feel a power of mind that you are never allowed to use, can be traumatic. In 1925, Terman viewed gifted children as the largest group of underachievers in education; subsequent research has shown that through the years gifted students continue to lack educational care, and possibly 85% or more are underachievers (Sisk, 1987; Whitmore, 1980). Van Tassel-Baska (2000) reported that at least 63% of students with an IQ of 130 and above are seriously underachieving, and many of these students show a record of truancy.

4. *Society gains from the advancement of all abilities and from the highest development of the talents of all of its members, whatever their strengths.* That which nurtures and actualizes each individual nourishes us as a society. To be superior to others in physical abilities (e.g., boxers, runners, skaters, tennis players) or artistic abilities (e.g., pianists, photographers, conductors, actors) is valued and rewarded in our society. Everyone accepts the idea that such athletes and artists must work or train continuously to maintain and extend their skills; they therefore earn their prestige and status. Although this is also true of intellectual ability, it is often viewed with suspicion, considered a threat by some, and assumed to be unearned by others. Those educators or parents who respond to giftedness are accused of trying to develop elitism even when appropriate educational opportunity is all they seek. Can we continue to justify elitism for some as beneficial to our society but fear it in others? Does our society have more need for physical and artistic ability than for intellectual ability? Curiously, the establishment of adequate programs for gifted students results not in the type of snobbishness feared, but in improved social relations and better attitudes of the gifted toward themselves and others.

5. *Gifted youngsters often think differently and have different interests from those of their age mates.* They usually enter school having already developed many of the basic skills, sometimes to high levels. They have areas of interest that have developed into advanced areas of content. Almost from the day they start school many gifted students begin to sense wariness or rejection because others consider them to be different. If the school does nothing, the roots of poor self-concept and disillusionment with school and society may be established. Most schools seek to develop skills for participation in society, not the re-creation of society; they tend to develop consumers of information, but seldom innovators and initiators. Re-creation, innovation, and initiation are typical traits found in gifted children and youth, resulting in a different view of the world and different educational needs.

6. *When the needs of the gifted are considered and the educational program is designed to meet these needs, these students make significant gains in achievement and their sense of competence and well-being returns.* With appropriate learning experiences, gifted students learn to work even more efficiently and effectively; they develop good problem-solving skills and see solutions from many viewpoints. They experience concepts and materials in a dynamic relationship, and they can use their vast amount of knowledge as a background for unlimited learning. Appropriate educational experiences allow them to grow, which is a right of every child.

7. *Contributions to society in all areas of human endeavor come in overweighted proportions from gifted individuals.* Society will need the gifted adult to play a far more demanding and innovative role than that expected of the more typical learner. We need a significant number of integrated, high-functioning persons to carry out tasks that will lead us to a satisfying, fulfilling future.

It is from the premises established by these seven ideas that this book will explore who gifted individuals are, how they become gifted, and what we, as educators at home or at school, can do to aid children in growing up gifted. To understand why there is such a critical need for improving education for gifted learners in our schools today, let us look further at the issues of excellence and equity and the impact this debate has had on shaping current educational decisions.

EXCELLENCE, EQUITY, AND THE GIFTED STUDENT

Unfortunately, schools are currently too often organized by age, not by assessed talents and achievements, which may not be providing the equity of opportunity students require to meet the diverse and unique needs that would allow them to develop excellence. With needs that range far beyond the age-graded curriculum in which they are commonly placed, gifted students are among the most poorly served in the school population. Attempts are made to provide services for learners who meet grade level expectations, and many special provisions and services are available for learners who are slow or disabled, whether they are placed in inclusion classrooms or special programs. However, much of the educational community believes that gifted students should be able to succeed on their own and that no challenge is needed to aid in their growth.

We now know that giftedness develops from an interactive process that involves a stimulating environment that brings forth innate capacities and talents. We either progress or regress. Just to retain their giftedness—not to mention furthering their potential—gifted students must have educational materials and experiences appropriate to their level of development. Neither we nor they can afford to inhibit their developing potential.

Our political and social system is based on democratic principles, and schools are an extension of these principles. Children who are slow or in some way educationally retarded are not asked to work with the same materials or at the same level or to progress at the same speed through the same curricula as the more typical learners. How, then, can we justify holding the gifted students to the pace and the level of the more typical student? The more intelligent individuals are, the more rapid will be the processing of their brains and the more complex their thought processes. How could the same curriculum meet such a wide range of needs? For equity of opportunity, a variety of learning experiences must be available at many levels so that all learners may better develop their potential. Each individual has the right to learn and to be provided opportunities and challenges for learning at the most appropriate level and at a pace that allows growth to proceed most efficiently toward excellence.

The Javits Act Program

The most current federal involvement in the education of gifted and talented students came with the 1988 enactment and the 1994 reauthorization of the Jacob K. Javits Gifted and Talented Students Education Act. The original authorization provided $7.9 million to be used for an Office of Gifted and Talented, for a National Center for Research and Development in the Education of Gifted and Talented Children and Youth, and for competitive grants or contracts "designed to meet the educational needs of gifted and talented students, including the training of personnel, and in the use, where appropriate, of gifted and talented services, materials, and methods for all students" (P.L. 100–297, Improving America's Schools Act, Title X, Part B, 1994, p. 319); the 1994 reauthorization boosted the amount appropriated to $9.51 million. Javits grants carry the following priorities:

1. the identification and the provision of services to gifted and talented students who may not be identified and served through traditional assessment methods (including economically disadvantaged individuals, individuals of limited-English proficiency, and individuals with disabilities)

2. to programs and projects designed to develop or improve the capability of schools in an entire State or region of the Nation through cooperative efforts and participation of state and other public and private agencies and organizations (including business, industry, and labor), to plan, conduct, and improve programs for the identification of and service to gifted and talented students, such as mentoring and apprenticeship programs. (p. 320)

By 1994, data had been collected on 75 projects that were awarded Javits Act Program grants, with 32 grants still in operation. The available outcomes are being disseminated through professional conferences and journals.

The National Research Center on the Gifted and Talented (NRC/GT), funded by the Javits Act Program, comprises four universities and 329 collaborative school districts. Since its inception, NRC/GT has produced and disseminated important research studies and other products, including practitioners' guides, video training tapes, and resource books. The Center provides national databases where researchers can deposit and gain access to data from studies of gifted and talented learners. It serves as a national repository of identification and evaluation instruments. Since 1995, the Center has been involved in long-term studies and the development of a comprehensive training package that will provide a practical set of materials for teachers to use to differentiate curriculum in classrooms with gifted learners. The Center can be reached at their website *www.gifted.uconn.edu.*

National Excellence: A Case for Developing America's Talent

A significant event that brought favorable attention to the national discussion of excellence and equity was the publication and release of the U.S. Department of Education's report *National Excellence: A Case for Developing America's Talent* (Ross, 1993). The report made a case for what was called "a quiet crisis in educating talented students" (p. 5). The crisis is described as the low achievement of gifted and talented students in the United States, compared with national criteria as well as international student achievement, the lack of concern about the quality of education being delivered to these students, the inability of regular classroom teachers to challenge these students, and the low level of funding (less than $.02 out of every $100 spent on general education students) made available for appropriate education. Of special concern is the lack of learning opportunities available to disadvantaged and minority children with outstanding talents.

Figure 1.1 *A System to Identify Gifted and Talented Students*
Source: Adapted from *National Excellence: A Case for Developing America's Talent* (p. 26) by P. O. Ross, 1993, Washington, DC: U.S. Government Printing Office.

1. Look at a variety of disciplines for outstanding students.
2. Use a variety of tests and other assessment measures to find and serve students who express high levels of ability in different ways and at different ages.
3. Ensure that all students have equal access to challenging learning opportunities and unbiased assessment.
4. Develop assessment procedures that allow varying rates of maturity and interests.
5. Seek students whose potential evidences itself in diverse and less obvious ways.
6. Consider motivational factors such as interest, drive, and passion in assessing accomplishment.

Figure 1.2 *Recommendations for Action*

Source: Adapted from *National Excellence: A Case for Developing America's Talent* (pp. 27–29) by P. O. Ross, 1993, Washington, DC: U.S. Government Printing Office.

1. Establish standards of performance in the core subjects that are high enough to challenge students of outstanding ability.
2. Establish learning opportunities that are accelerated, diverse, comprehensive, and advanced enough to meet the assessed needs of students performing at the highest levels.
3. Establish access to programs in early childhood education for children from all socioeconomic, ethnic, and racial populations that will optimize the development of their potential.
4. Establish expanded opportunities for economically disadvantaged and minority children to participate in advanced learning experiences.
5. Encourage teacher preparation, development of materials, and establishment of technical assistance that will improve educational opportunities for students with outstanding abilities.
6. Create conditions, including policies and practices, that will allow the most highly able students of the United States to compete favorably with the most highly able students anywhere in the world.

As part of the report, suggestions for a system to identify gifted and talented students were made, and recommendations for action to alleviate the crisis were discussed. Figures 1.1 and 1.2 summarize these suggestions.

INTEREST IN EDUCATING GIFTED LEARNERS

The interest in educating gifted individuals has a long history, beginning with the earliest records of human civilization. The interest in developing individual talents and gifts has varied through time, not only as to which abilities should be nurtured, but the extent to which and by whom such nurturing was provided. Figures 1.3 and 1.4 present an overview of this issue. More recent entries focus on the efforts of the United States, although gifted education is a growing concern in most countries worldwide. The 21st century has begun with great promise as the U.S. Congress debates a new authorization of the Elementary and Secondary Education Act. Amendments are being proposed that could potentially increase the amount of funding supporting gifted education to $155 million. Nationwide interest is rising, as shown by an increase in attendance at gifted conferences; the number of gifted publications, both new journals and articles in established journals in many fields, devoting space to issues of giftedness; and new resources available on the internet for teacher education focused on the gifted learner. One can only hope that this trend will continue and produce positive change in the knowledge of and priority given to this underserved population of special needs students.

Figure 1.3 *Interest in Giftedness and Talent Development over Time*

Early recorded history	Greeks, Egyptians, Romans, Chinese, and Japanese provided for the nurture of outstanding talents and abilities for the good of the state.
1400–1600	Governments in Renaissance Europe encouraged and supported the arts and creative artists. Apprentice models were used to foster outstanding abilities and gifts. Sponsorship for artists, sculptors, and musicians was provided by the church (e.g., da Vinci).
1700–1800	**Period of low interest** in America: concern grew for equity and conformity. Private tutoring was considered the birthright of male children of the aristocracy and wealthy families. Royalty and noblemen sponsored persons with notable gifts and talents in Europe (e.g., Mozart). In the U.S., Jefferson recommended using public funds for education of the brightest males.
1869	Francis Galton published *Hereditary Genius,* a study of high abilities families.
1916	**Interest rises.** Special classes for gifted students were opened in Los Angeles and Cincinnati.
1921	Lewis Terman began the famous longitudinal study of the characteristics and behaviors of gifted individuals. Included were 1500 students with IQ scores of 140 and higher whose average age was 11 years. This study resulted in the five volumes of the *Genetic Studies of Genius* (1925).
1930	**Period of low interest** began with a focus on equity throughout the country and the advent of financial chaos during the Great Depression.
1942	Leta Hollingworth published *Children Above 180 IQ,* a study of highly gifted children.
1946	**Interest rises.** The American Association for the Study of the Gifted was established as the first professional society in the field.
1954	The National Association for Gifted Children was established.
1956	J. P. Guilford suggested the importance of the study of creativity in his American Psychological Association presidential speech that also expanded the concept of intelligence.
1957	**Period of high interest.** The launch of the Russian rocket *Sputnik* brought demands for better provisions in schools for highly able students, especially those with abilities in science and math. The focus on producing excellence created the intensified growth of gifted programs and a reform of curriculum that better supported the needs of gifted students.
1958	The National Defense Education Act (P.L. 85-864) was enacted to support the development of talent, especially in math, sciences, and foreign languages. The Association for the Gifted, an affiliate of the Council for Exceptional Children, was established.
1960	**Period of low interest.** Concerns for equity diminished support for the education of gifted students.

Figure 1.3 *continued*

1965	The Elementary and Secondary Education Act (P.L. 89-10) was enacted, creating support for the development of model programs and state personnel in gifted education.
1970	The Elementary and Secondary Act (P.L. 91-230, Section 806), "Provisions related to Gifted and Talented Children," established federal recognition of the need for education of gifted and talented children. Congress requested a report on the status of programs.
1972	**Period of high interest.** Sidney Marland published *Education of the Gifted and Talented,* the report requested by Congress that established the first federal definition and data-based rationale for educating gifted and talented students.
1975	Federal Office of Gifted and Talented and grants for the field of gifted education were established with an appropriation from Congress of $2.5 million. The amount was increased gradually until, in 1980, $6.2 million was appropriated.
1981	**Period of low interest.** With the passage of the Education Consolidation and Improvement Act (P.L. 97-35), federal funds for gifted and talented students were decreased 40% and placed into a block grant with 29 other programs to be distributed at the discretion of the states. The Federal Office of Gifted and Talented was dissolved and grants canceled, suspending direct federal involvement in gifted education.
1988	**Interest rises** with the passage of the Jacob K. Javits Gifted and Talented Students Education Act (P.L. 100-297). The Federal Office for Gifted and Talented Education was reestablished with an appropriation of $7.9 million, made available for funding the office, competitive grants, and the National Research Center on the Gifted and Talented.
1993	*National Excellence: A Case for Developing America's Talent* (Ross, 1993) was released by the U.S. Department of Education.
1994	The Javits Act was reauthorized with an appropriation of $9.51 million, only to be cut in half as the control of Congress changed to a different political party and philosophy.
2000	U.S. Congress debates the reauthorization of the Elementary and Secondary Act. Possible increases in funding may be added to this legislation. Interest in Gifted and Talented Education continues high as a new millennium begins.

BARRIERS TO APPROPRIATE EDUCATION FOR GIFTED STUDENTS AND THE DEVELOPMENT OF TALENT

Elitism: A Problem or a Blessing?

It is interesting that few people would perceive themselves to be against all persons being given the opportunity to achieve the highest level of excellence of which they are capable. Yet, many think it is unfair for one person or group of people to gain

Figure 1.4 *Interest in and Support for Gifted Education in America in the Twentieth Century*

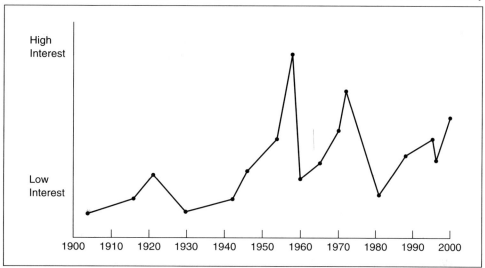

a position in which they are seen as having more ability or being more clever or "smarter" than other people. This paradox is often represented by the fear of the term *elitism*. As expressed in the report on national excellence (Ross, 1993), "These two beliefs—a distrust of the intellect and an assumption that people should be allowed to develop to their full potential—have clashed throughout American history and have muddled efforts to provide a quality education for the nation's most promising students" (p. 13).

In the past, the term elitism has often been used when referring to education for gifted individuals; the term is often used to explain why educational provisions for these students are not made. But the problem may lie in the meaning given to the word. If one means "the chosen one or the select group," as though the existence of giftedness comes only as a bestowing of riches or honor from a higher authority, we might justifiably treat such individuals as an already accomplished population who need only try and their every wish or thought would be fulfilled. Such individuals would, of course, need no help. They could get along quite well with their already fully functioning gifts. If, however, we mean "a group chosen because of some special talent, skill, or ability, which, if fostered, could become truly outstanding" (such as athletic prowess, musical talent, intellectual achievement, or business acumen), then elitism is entirely justifiable and proper for the benefit of society as a whole.

Another definition of elitism recognizes a group to which one chooses to belong out of interest, or to which one is chosen for a particular outstanding ability. Curiously, it is acceptable to be "elite" in some areas, but not in others. For example, to be a Nobel Prize Laureate is a laudatory form of elitism that is honored and promoted; to be a remarkably able mathematician is valued; and to have an elite group of such individuals in one's school or society is treasured and sought after. A powerful team in football, basketball, or any other sport is a celebrated elite group.

However, those students whose intelligence is expressed through advanced study, astute problem-solving, quick thinking, or many other attributes of gifted students are not well-tolerated by the educational system or the society it reflects.

American politicians and educators are sensitive to any issue regarding equality and often fear the term elitism. These groups are concerned that advanced and accelerated educational programs are elitist. Many educators would abandon all attempts to allow differentiated provisions for gifted students because such programs might promote elitism, even though the research (Delcourt, Loyd, Cornell, & Goldberg, 1994; Kulik & Kulik, 1982; Moos cited in Contenta, 1988) consistently shows that students who are given the opportunity to work with intellectual peers are less self-centered and have a more realistic self-concept. They also achieve at levels more consistent with their ability. It is interesting that the American public does not seem to show this same concern. According to a Gallop poll (Larsen & Griffin, 1992), the American public not only understands, but overwhelmingly agrees with the need to appropriately educate gifted children. In a discussion of the Jeffersonian tradition, Sternberg (1996) argues:

> In this tradition, people are indeed all equal in terms of political and social rights and should have equal opportunities . . . the goal of gifted education is not to favor or foster an elite, but to allow children to make full use of the differing kinds of skills they have and can develop . . . We provide for any child the education that best suits the child, and for those children who excel in a given area, of course, we want to give them the extra challenge that will propel them to the higher level of accomplishment of which they are capable. *This extra challenge is one that will require the children to use the abilities they have on tasks that are new in kind as well as more difficult than the tasks the children previously have encountered.* (p. 263) (emphasis added)

As we learn more about who the gifted learners are and how they can be nurtured, it becomes more apparent that *providing appropriately for all of society's children is the most democratic and egalitarian approach with the greatest chance for excellence and true equity for each child.*

Age-Grouped Classes

One of the major barriers to the development of appropriate educational experiences for advanced and accelerated learners is the traditional age-grouped, graded classroom. In most regular classrooms, the teacher attempts to develop a more manageable learning environment by using ability grouping to modify inappropriate age-grouping. The educational achievement in chronologically age-grouped classes can range from 4 to 8 years, depending on the grade level. Because the range of achievement can be so vast, the teacher typically plans the instructional program for the at-grade-level learner. For the very slow, below-grade-level learners, remediation programs, often mandated by the state and specifically financed, are available in most schools. For learners at the bottom 2% of the achievement scale or 2 years behind grade-level achievement, the school will provide appropriate special education modifications. These provisions are accepted and expected by both parent and educator alike.

On the other end of the scale, the school's organization may be quite different. The learners in the upper 2% of the achievement scale or 2 to 4 years ahead of grade level need as much special instruction to continue their growth as do students at the lower end, yet special resources or specially trained personnel are rarely made available. These students are too often expected to adjust to the grade-level materials and curriculum. This situation leads to unnecessary loss of ability, especially among girls and minority students, and regression toward a more average ability level is the observed outcome. However, a wealth of literature in the field of gifted education can be used to establish standards for programs that can adequately serve gifted students. The literature also contains a variety of options for delivery of services that have been shown to be successful in different settings. Knowledge of these standards and practices would make the efforts of teachers to educate gifted students more effective and more efficient, and ensure the delivery of services at a more consistently appropriate level. Although it is not easy to develop, a gifted education and talent development program that will provide the best match for the needs of the students, the expectations of the parents, the philosophy of the school administration, the resources of the community, and the resources and commitment of the school staff is attainable with knowledge and support.

Uninformed Attitudes and Beliefs of Educators and Decision Makers

Myths and misconceptions about the education of gifted learners have often become strongly held beliefs among those who are most responsible for the educational services that these students receive. Among these ideas that limit educational practices are the beliefs that:

- *"Intelligence is inherited and, therefore, does not change."* From this idea comes the often-heard phrases, "If they are really gifted, they can get by on their own," and "Gifted students should never be bored, because they can always find something to do." The facts that intelligence is developed from an interaction between genetic patterns and environmental opportunities, that it is dynamic rather than fixed, and that it is less limited than was once supposed make this attitude very problematic. Gifted students, like all students, need challenges presented to them by their educational experience at the level congruent with their ability and development. The problem for the gifted learner is that schools often do not present curriculum aimed at higher levels of thought.

- *"Giftedness can easily be measured by intelligence tests and tests of achievement."* Brain research has indicated that the brain has at least four major areas of function: physical/sensing, affective, cognitive (both linear, rational and spatial, gestalt), and intuitive. These areas combine to form a person's intelligence, and the brain seems to be nearly unlimited in its potential for development. Any of these areas of function or a combination of them can be used to express intelligence, making the concept of intelligence quite complex. Intelligence tests measure only a sample of the linear, rational ability of a person, and because intelligence can be expressed in many other ways, such a small sample cannot be viewed as an adequate measure of the universe of intelligence or the potential of any person. Although current intelligence tests give valuable estimates of abilities in the area of intelligence that can be predictive of success on school-related tasks, these tests cannot identify giftedness in many areas of intelligence or suggest an individual's potential. Identification of giftedness is a complex task and requires a variety of samples of a person's abilities from many areas of function.

- *"A good teacher can teach any student, because if good teaching is used, that is all that is needed. What is good for gifted students is good for everyone."* Although good teaching practices must be the basis for all teaching excellence, the appropriate education of gifted students does not stop with these important concepts and strategies. In addition to exemplary educational techniques that support the learning of all students, teachers of gifted students need some special abilities. They must know how to differ the pace of instruction, to accelerate or provide in-depth learning and advanced content, because these are common needs of gifted students. Teachers must know how to develop high degrees of complexity and an interrelationship in the content, as well as provide novelty and enrichment and to accept and extend intensity, divergence, and creative solutions. These special added teaching abilities are needed by teachers of gifted students, because those students have specific needs, require additional challenges, and are different both in the quantity and the quality of their educational performance.

- *"If you accelerate the curriculum for all students, you do not need programs for gifted learners."* All students must have opportunities for challenging learning experiences. However, those challenges will not be the same either in content or pace of instruction for every student. One of the commonly accepted characteristics found as the brain becomes more efficient and expresses higher levels of intelligence is the increased speed of thought processing. Gifted students learn faster and process information more quickly. It would be as unfair to ask a gifted student to slow down this process as it would be to ask a slower learner to think more quickly; neither student can do what is being asked. With the "dumbing down" that admittedly is occurring within the curriculum in many schools, some acceleration of content and pace would be a positive movement; however, to speed up the learning process to the pace of the gifted learner would be inappropriate for other learners in the regular classroom and would inhibit their chances for learning. In the vision of schools of excellence described in *National Excellence* (Ross, 1993), it is recommended that, "All children progress through challenging material at their own pace. Students are grouped and regrouped based on their interests and needs. Achieving success for all students is not equated with achieving the same results for all students" (p. 29).

- *"You really learn something when you teach it. It never hurts students to review what they have learned."* This belief has led to the practice of using gifted students as tutors for slower students in the classroom. Such activities have been used to fill the time of the student who finishes assigned work early, relieving the teacher of additional planning for such a student and simultaneously providing help to students who require extra support. This situation has been especially noticeable since the emphasis on Cooperative Learning groups as an integral part of classroom organization. Too often, in an effort to maintain the standards they require of themselves, gifted students who are placed in a heterogeneous learning group will take on the major part of the research, writing, and presentation tasks while also trying to tutor other members of the group so that the group result will not be unacceptably low to these gifted students. Although sharing with classmates is an important experience for gifted students socially, the overuse of group projects and the use of such students as tutors will prevent them from engaging in their own educational challenges. The increasing number of gifted students writing articles on their frustration with experiences in inappropriately constituted Cooperative Learning groups adequately validates the idea that there is a limit to the educational value of repeatedly reviewing materials and concepts that have already been mastered.

• *"All children are gifted."* All students are valuable, all students are important, and all students should be allowed to develop to their highest potential; however, all students are not gifted. The term *gifted* is a label to designate the students "who require services or activities not ordinarily provided by the school in order to fully develop such capabilities" (P.L. 103–382, Title XIV, p. 388, the part of the Elementary and Secondary Act known as the Javits Bill, reauthorized in 1994). The capabilities to which the law refers include high levels of intellectual, creative, artistic, leadership, or academic abilities. Obviously not all children have these needs and yet, in a misguided effort to assert the value of all children, a statement such as "all children are gifted" is mistakenly made. The problem is that such a statement can cause the unique educational provisions needed by gifted students to seem unnecessary and, therefore, not be provided.

Unbalanced Educational Reform

America's schools are, and for two decades have been, engaged in efforts to make education for the nation's children more effective, more inclusive of all populations and cultures, and more productive of quality performance. Although these goals are unquestionably desirable, their implementation must be balanced between remediating unfair practices for those who have not benefited from previous structures and practices and challenging those who have been stifled by them. "The belief espoused in school reform that children from all economic and cultural backgrounds must reach their full potential has not been extended to America's most talented students, who are underchallenged and therefore underachieve" (Ross, 1993, p. 5). Here again our focus must not be one-sided; the reform of American education requires balance between approaches that develop unused talent and those that nurture outstanding talent. Educators, students, and parents alike are becoming disenchanted with the "total" approaches: total heterogeneous grouping, total inclusion, total group instruction. Balance seems to be the necessary key.

The inclusion movement can be a most positive force in education if it is used to benefit students, not just to support an abstract principle of narrowly interpreted egalitarianism. Again, every student has a right to an equal opportunity to receive a quality educational experience; however, that should not be interpreted to be the *same* experience. The inclusion movement has drawn attention to some of the provisions necessary if learning is to be optimized for any student. It is suggested that inclusive classrooms support diverse learners and honor their diversity by establishing and maintaining a warm, accepting classroom; implementing a multilevel, multimodality curriculum; using thematic instruction, critical thinking, problem-solving, and authentic assessment; and including academic and cognitive challenges at many levels (Sapon-Shevin, 1995). Only to the extent that a classroom does have these elements in place can it accommodate diversity.

The majority of gifted students have been, and continue to be, primarily served in regular classrooms. The focus on enriching and accelerating these classrooms to include more diversity benefits gifted as well as other special-needs students. However, the regular classroom, when used as the only educational option, may not be the best placement for many special-needs students, either socially or educationally. Inclusion of students in classrooms where they are not able to benefit from the experiences being offered is of questionable value to them and often a detriment to the pace, depth, and level of instruction for other students. This is true whether the students are too far ahead of the others or behind them. Delcourt and colleagues (1994) found this to be a major problem for gifted learners. The problems of implementing the inclusive classroom today are common. Important among them is the lack of teacher preparation for inclusion, including how to work with special needs students; how to design and implement problem-based, meaning-centered curriculum; how to differentiate instruction; and how to develop the previously described conditions suggested by Sapon-Shevin (1995). Another set of problems is created by the sheer numbers of students in classes. Add to that the tremendous and growing diversity found in classrooms, and the reason why many regular classrooms are not the best placement for students whose needs have typically not been met in such classrooms becomes clear. Decisions about how much inclusion is useful must be made on an individual basis and carefully considered from the perspective of the students, both those to be included and those who are regularly in these classrooms. If all are to benefit, the question to serve as a guide is: "Where can each student best meet his or her needs?" The strongest programs for gifted students, as well as for other special-needs students, involves choice among an array of services and careful assessment of the student's needs when providing such services.

De-tracking is a movement that has attempted to correct the structuring of learning experiences that allowed mindless placement of students together in tracks over time. Some of those involved in the de-tracking movement have taken this needed correction to the level of abuse by making the idea a "moral" issue, obfuscating the important educational issue. The result has been that an effort to improve the structure and organization of instruction has often robbed teachers of the valuable tool of flexibly grouping students to structure their experiences to best meet their needs. It is far from being moral or democratic to deny advanced, appropriately paced, complex, and divergent materials and instruction to students who will lose ability, interest, and motivation without such modifications.

Nor is it reasonable to compel students with differing needs to meet the same goals or achieve the same outcomes. To insist that all teachers in every classroom can deliver diverse modifications appropriately to every student, without recognition of individual differences, is an impossible expectation. Flexible grouping will always be important so that teachers can effectively manage the many and varied needs of students within and among classrooms. As long as the practice of age-grouping is the major criterion for organizing learning, both homogeneous and heterogeneous grouping flexibly practiced and carefully planned around the assessed needs, pacing, and learning patterns of students will be necessary to ensure success for every learner.

Educators must continue to reflect on how teaching and learning can be better supported, be made more effective, and meet more of the diverse needs of students. They must be encouraged to re-form the structures and strategies used to include a higher quality of educational experiences for a wider range of abilities and talents. As they do, it will be more and more important to avoid extremes. A balance of old and new practices, social and intellectual concerns, and comfort and progress will be a positive mode to follow. That balance needs to include appropriate, challenging educational experiences for *all* students. Progress should incorporate both excellence and equity.

OTHER CURRENT ISSUES

The discussion has suggested many of the current issues now faced by the field of gifted education and talent development. For some issues, such as the name and mission of the field of gifted education and talent development, welcome breakthroughs have occurred. Others, such as the misinformation that continues to result in unfortunate attitudes and beliefs of educators and other educational decision-makers, still must be addressed more effectively. Additional issues, such as teacher preparation, minority underrepresentation, equitable identification, appropriate programming, and funding, remain current concerns even though a great deal of effort and research has been focused on these issues for several decades. Throughout this text these issues will be explored and possible solutions suggested.

The issues of excellence and equity are best resolved in balance, because in a democracy equal opportunity cannot and must not mean the *same* opportunity. Every child is unique; all children have a right to develop their own potential. *All* children must include gifted children.

A DECLARATION OF THE EDUCATIONAL RIGHTS OF THE GIFTED CHILD

Written by Barbara Clark

It is the right of a gifted child to engage in appropriate educational experiences even when other children of that grade level or age are unable to profit from the experience.

It is the right of a gifted child to be grouped and to interact with other gifted children for some part of their learning experience so that the child may be understood, engaged, and challenged.

It is the right of a gifted child to be taught rather than to be used as a tutor or teaching assistant for a significant part of the school day.

It is the right of a gifted child to be presented with new, advanced, and challenging ideas and concepts regardless of the materials and resources that have been designated for the age group or grade level in which the child was placed.

It is the right of a gifted child to be taught concepts that the child does not yet know instead of relearning old concepts that the child has already shown evidence of mastering.

It is the right of a gifted child to learn faster than age peers and to have that pace of learning respected and provided for.

It is the right of a gifted child to think in alternative ways, produce diverse products, and to bring intuition and innovation to the learning experience.

It is the right of a gifted child to be idealistic and sensitive to fairness, justice, accuracy, and the global problems facing humankind and to have a forum for expressing these concerns.

It is the right of a gifted child to question generalizations, offer alternative solutions, and value complex and profound levels of thought.

It is the right of a gifted child to be intense, persistent, and goal-directed in the pursuit of knowledge.

It is the right of a gifted child to express a sense of humor that is unusual, playful, and often complex.

It is the right of a gifted child to hold high expectations for self and others and to be sensitive to inconsistency between ideals and behavior, with the need to have help in seeing the value in human differences.

It is the right of a gifted child to be a high achiever in some areas of the curriculum and not in others, making thoughtful, knowledgeable academic placement a necessity.

It is the right of a gifted child to have a low tolerance for the lag between vision and actualization, between personal standards and developed skill, and between physical maturity and athletic ability.

It is the right of a gifted child to pursue interests that are beyond the ability of age peers, are outside the grade level curriculum, or involve areas as yet unexplored or unknown.

These are some of the rights of gifted children that deserve advocacy. If we could only be sure that the educational experiences of all gifted children honored these 15 rights, we would have the assurance that society would be blessed with a continuous supply of gifted adults, for we would have nurtured our gifted children by providing opportunities for excellence and developed the talent within all children by providing educational equity.

QUESTIONS OFTEN ASKED

1. Will grouping gifted students together result in "elitism"?

When this question is asked, elitism usually implies that the gifted students will become arrogant and snobbish and think they are better than other students. Research indicates that grouping gifted students together appropriately and flexibly in the areas in which they need advanced or accelerated work will result not only in their academic growth, but will give them a more realistic view of their abilities. Students who are always ahead of their classmates and do not have to study or are never challenged are not only in danger of becoming bored and dull, but of falsely assuming that they are superior to other students. Because they are never challenged, they do not learn good study skills and will have problems later as they try to pursue higher education. Arrogance can come from either unrealistic appraisal of their talent or from trying to cover up the feeling of being different and not understanding why others continually reject them. In either case, flexible and appropriate grouping with intellectual peers will decrease that type of elitism, not increase it.

2. Aren't all children gifted in something?

All children have enormous potential. All children are valuable and deserve opportunities to develop their talents to the highest level possible, but all children are not gifted. The term *gifted* is only a label that society gives to those who have actualized their ability to an unusually high degree or give evidence that such achievement is imminent. If we were willing to support all children to develop to their highest level, we would certainly have far more students who function in the range who are now referred to as gifted. As long as we group children together based on their age and expect them to learn from similar material at a similar pace, there will be the need to identify those who are far beyond that norm. The label *gifted* only allows us to identify those children who have needs beyond the norm and to provide more appropriately for them.

3. Why not just accelerate the material and pace for all children? Then we would not need to label any child gifted.

Whether we accelerate or slow down the educational process for all children, we will have the same problem. All children learn differently and require different material and different pacing. Forcing children who need more support and a slower pace to accelerate is just as bad as asking gifted students to slow down, wait for other students, and repeat what they have already mastered. Although the current practices of "dumbing down" textbooks, reteaching content grade after grade, and holding standards to the lowest common achievement for an age group have been criticized soundly and reforms are being made to change such practices, the need will not be met merely by raising standards or accelerating the process. A range of levels and pacing is needed if all students' needs are to be met. Flexible grouping, ongoing assessment, and varied, dynamic, and exciting strategies for teaching all children is what is most needed.

4. In a democracy, how can we justify some children getting more than others in our public schools?

We cannot nor should we just provide more for gifted students. One of the biggest problems in gifted education is that many teachers and parents believe that gifted children just need more. With that belief, teachers will assign 30 problems to an advanced math student, whereas the other students are asked to do 15. When other students read three books for an assignment, gifted students are asked to read six. Because gifted students finish assignments more quickly, they are often asked to do more—more of the same type of material. Appropriate education for gifted students would not simply have them do more; rather, they would be assigned material at their level of difficulty, pacing, and depth and be allowed to pursue inquiry beyond the known, producing unusual, complex, and creative work appropriate to their level of intellectual development. Appropriate, not just more, educational experiences are needed.

5. Considering the focus on inclusion in the regular classroom, when is it appropriate to have special programs for gifted students?

When the material and the pacing used in the classroom are not allowing gifted students to grow and learn, special provisions must be made. When there is no provision for gifted students to interact with intellectual peers, educators must plan ways in which such groupings can occur. Research indicates that these are the minimum provisions that gifted students must have if they are to continue to develop and not regress, losing ability and motivation. For many gifted students an appropriately individualized classroom can provide the differentiated materials and instruction needed; however, for gifted students whose pace and level of learning is significantly beyond their classmates, the least restrictive environment will not be the regular classroom. These students will need special classes and mentoring to grow and learn.

Society gains from the advancement of all abilities and the highest development of the talents of all of its members.

CHECKING FOR UNDERSTANDING
Follow-up Activity

Using the information in Chapter 1, write a brief Op Ed article for your local newspaper that advocates for gifted education and talent development in your area. Be sure to include: issues of excellence and equity; a rationale; and current barriers you have noted in your local area.

SUMMARY

1. Providing appropriate education for students who have been identified as gifted while finding ways to develop the talent in all children are the dual missions of the field of gifted education.

The Dual Missions of Gifted Education

2. Equity means providing equal access to opportunity and experiences that are uniquely appropriate for each individual. Equal opportunity does not mean the *same* opportunity.
3. Excellence for all as a goal assures that all children may aspire to develop their uniqueness, regardless of their skill or ability, talent or interest, to its fullest extent. This will require the recognition of individual differences.

A Rationale for Gifted Education and Talent Development

4. The development of giftedness is the result of an interactive process that involves challenges from the environment that stimulate and bring forth innate talents, capabilities, and processes throughout the individual's lifetime for high levels of actualization to result.
5. Our political and social system is based on democratic principles, and it is undemocratic to refuse to allow gifted children the right to educational experiences appropriate to their developed level of ability.
6. Both physical and psychological pain result when human beings are limited and restricted in their development.
7. Society gains from the advancement of all abilities and from the highest development of the talents of all of its members, whatever their strengths.
8. Gifted youngsters often think differently and have different interests from those of their age mates and thus require differentiated learning experiences.
9. When the needs of gifted students are considered and the educational program is designed to meet these needs, these students make significant gains in achievement and their sense of competence and well-being is enhanced.
10. Contributions to society in all areas of human endeavor are made in overweighted proportions from this population of individuals. Society will need gifted adults to play a far more demanding and innovative role than that expected of more typical learners.

Excellence, Equity, and the Gifted Student

11. The most current federal involvement in the education of gifted and talented students came with the 1988 enactment and the 1994 reauthorization of the Jacob K. Javits Gifted and Talented Students Education Act. Its provisions include funding for: the Office of Gifted and Talented, a National Center for Research and Development in the Education of Gifted and Talented Children and Youth, and competitive grants or contracts designed to meet the educational needs of gifted and talented students.
12. The publication and release of the U.S. Department of Education report *National Excellence: A Case for Developing America's Talent* (Ross, 1993) made a case for what was called "a quiet crisis in educating talented students."

Interest in Educating Gifted Learners

13. Since the earliest records of human civilization, the interest in developing individual talents and gifts has varied through time, not only as to which abilities should be nurtured, but the extent to which and by whom such nurturing was provided.

Barriers to Appropriate Education for Gifted Students and the Development of Talent

14. Even though society will benefit from the support for gifted education and talent devel-

opment, there continue to be many barriers that are erected that make appropriate educational provisions unattainable.

Elitism: A Problem or a Blessing?

15. The term *elitism* is often used to express a distrust of people who develop high levels of intelligence and is used to explain why educational provisions for these students are not supported. The problem may lie in the meaning given to the word. Appropriately defined as a group chosen based on some special talent, skill, or ability which, if fostered, could become truly outstanding (such as athletic prowess, musical talent, intellectual achievement, or business acumen), elitism is entirely justifiable and proper for the benefit of society as a whole.

Age-Grouped Classes

16. The educational achievement in chronologically age-grouped classes can range from 4 to 8 years, depending on the grade level. Because the range of achievement can be so vast, the teacher typically plans the instructional program for the at-grade-level learner.

Uninformed Attitudes and Beliefs of Educators and Decision Makers

17. Myths and misconceptions about the education of gifted learners have become strongly held beliefs among those who are most responsible for the educational services that these students receive. Among these ideas that limit educational practices are the beliefs that:

   - "Intelligence is inherited and, therefore, does not change," and related phrases such as, "If they are really gifted, they can get by on their own," and "Gifted students should never be bored, because they can always find something to do."
   - "Giftedness can easily be measured by intelligence tests and tests of achievement."
   - "A good teacher can teach any student, because if good teaching is used, that is all

that is needed. What is good for gifted students is good for everyone."
   - "If you accelerate the curriculum for all students, you do not need programs for gifted learners."
   - "You really learn something when you teach it. It never hurts students to review what they have learned."
   - "All children are gifted."

18. Efforts are underway to make education for the nation's children more effective, more inclusive of all populations and cultures, and more productive of quality performance—goals that are unquestionably desirable. However, their implementation must be balanced between remediating unfair practices for those who have not benefited from previous structures and practices and challenging those who have been stifled by them.

19. The inclusion movement can be a most positive force in education if it is used to benefit students, not just to support an abstract principle of narrowly interpreted egalitarianism.

20. Flexible grouping will always be important so that teachers can effectively manage the many and varied needs of students within and among classrooms. As long as the practice of age-grouping is the major criterion for organizing learning, both homogeneous and heterogeneous grouping flexibly practiced and carefully planned around the assessed needs, pacing, and learning patterns of students will be necessary to ensure success for every learner.

Other Current Issues

21. Issues such as teacher preparation, minority underrepresentation, equitable identification, appropriate programming, and funding remain current concerns even though a great deal of effort and research has been focused on these issues for several decades.

22. *A Declaration of the Educational Rights of the Gifted Child* are some of the rights of gifted children that deserve advocacy.

2

Discovering Who the Gifted Individuals Are

In this chapter the reader will discover:

- A definition of the terms *intelligence, giftedness, gifted individual,* and *talent development.*

- An overview of the historical development of the concept of intelligence.

- A discussion of the interactive nature of intelligence and its relationship to giftedness.

- A discussion of the importance of brain function to the concepts of intelligence and giftedness.

- Characteristics of gifted learners.

- A discussion of highly and exceptionally gifted learners.

Now that we have begun to appreciate the plasticity of our cerebral cortex, the seat of the intellectual functioning that distinguishes us as human beings, we must learn to use this knowledge. It must stimulate and guide our efforts to work toward enriching heredity through enriching the environment . . . for everyone . . . at any age.

—Marian Cleeves Diamond

Just 2 days ago Sally had been given a present by her favorite grandmother: a bag of brightly colored letters that had something on the back that made them stick to lots of things around the house. She was already getting very good at spelling all kinds of words. Mother said that not many 3-year-olds could spell so many "unusual" words. It was great fun to have everyone guess what she had spelled. This morning she was putting her words on the side of the refrigerator because her daddy could see them as he ate breakfast. She was sure he would play the word game, because he had to be right there anyway. What Sally didn't know was that as he ate her dad would be distracted by the planning he was doing for a major presentation he was making at work that day.

As her daddy sat down, Sally was ready. She took several letters from the bag and placed them on the side of the refrigerator. "What does that spell, Daddy?"

Her father looked up and said, "Honey, that doesn't spell anything. It isn't a word."

Sally put the letters back in the bag and carefully selected another handful. "What does that spell?" she asked eagerly.

Looking up impatiently her father again disclaimed, "I told you, that doesn't spell anything."

Sally was disappointed but determined as she replaced the offending letters and took two handfuls out, placing them carefully in sequence. "Now what word is that?"

Clearly annoyed, Sally's father restated, this time rather loudly, "Sally, it doesn't spell anything. That is not a word!"

Sally looked at the letters so elegantly placed across the refrigerator, thought a minute, and said with wonder, "Isn't that amazing! I can spell all those words that you don't even know yet."

Children do not understand limits in the same way adults do. But with investigations into how our brains work, how we learn, and how we develop intelligence, we are finding that there may not be the limits we thought we had. In fact, our belief systems may be the most limiting part of developing intelligence, giftedness, and talent.

INTELLIGENCE, GIFTEDNESS, AND TALENT DEVELOPMENT

Growth of intelligence depends on the interaction between our biological inheritance and our environmental opportunities to use that inheritance. High levels of intelligence or giftedness are, therefore, the result of a dynamic, stimulating, interactive process that leads to quantitative and qualitative differences in performance. How giftedness is expressed depends both on the genetic patterns of the individual and on the experiences provided by that individual's environment. The opportunities provided in the environment to develop their genetic programs allow some individuals to enhance their abilities to the point of giftedness, whereas the lack of such opportunities inhibits others in their development, some even to the level of retardation. Children are not born gifted, but with a unique and nearly unlimited potential. Clearly there is an early and continuous need for talent development.

Definitions

The following definitions of intelligence, giftedness, gifted individuals, and talent development encompass current knowledge of how intelligence develops and provide a synthesis of earlier definitions.

Intelligence is the aggregate of an individual's cognitive, affective, physical, and intuitive functioning. It is enhanced or inhibited by the interaction between the genetic pattern of individuals and the opportunities provided by the environment for individuals throughout their life span.

Giftedness is a biologically rooted concept that serves as a label for a high level of intelligence and indicates an advanced and accelerated development of functions within the brain. Such development may express itself in high levels of cognitive, affective, physical, intuitive, or a combination of abilities, such as academic aptitude, insight and innovation, creative behavior, leadership, personal and interpersonal skill, visual and performing arts or any combination thereof.

Gifted individuals are those who have developed high levels of intelligence and therefore operate or perform, or show promise of operating or performing, at high levels in any of the areas of intelligence. Because of such advanced and accelerated development, gifted individuals require services or activities not ordinarily provided by the schools so that society can ensure the growth rather than the loss of their abilities.

Talent development involves the deliberate and planned effort to provide children with an enriched and responsive learning environment both at home and at school so that all of their talents and abilities will have the opportunity to develop to maximum levels. Such appropriate stimulation will allow high levels of intelligence to develop in a variety of forms and expressions and will result in increased numbers of individuals operating or performing at the level of giftedness.

Intelligence, Giftedness, and Talent As Performance

If intelligence is used to connote only that which is measured by intelligence tests, then those who score in the upper 2% on such a test could be spoken of as gifted, as Terman suggested in 1925. However, if someone can be called gifted only when engaged in creative production and if giftedness derives from a cluster of traits—such as above-average ability, creativity, and task commitment—then there is only gifted behavior, not an intrinsic quality called giftedness, as suggested by Renzulli in 1978. If Witty (1940) is correct, then giftedness needs no referent to intelligence and can be described as possessed by those "whose performance is consistently remarkable in any potentially valuable area" (p. 516). Different still is the definition, still used in most state legislation today, that was developed in 1972 by U.S. Commissioner of Education Sidney Marland for a report to Congress on the status of the education of gifted and talented children:

> Gifted and talented children are those identified by professionally qualified persons who by virtue of outstanding abilities are capable of high performance. These are children who require differentiated educational programs and services beyond those normally provided by the regular school program in order to realize their contributions to self and society.
>
> Children capable of high performance include those with demonstrated achievement and/or potential ability in any of the following areas: 1) General intellectual aptitude, 2) specific academic aptitude, 3) creative or productive thinking, 4) leadership ability, 5) visual and performing arts. (p. 2)

The most current federal definition of gifted individuals was a part of the 1994 reauthorization of the Jacob K. Javits Gifted and Talented Students Education Act of 1988.

> The term "gifted and talented" when used in respect to students, children or youth means students, children or youth who give evidence of high performance capability in areas such as intellectual, creative, artistic, or leadership capacity, or in specific academic fields, and who require services or activities not ordinarily provided by the school in order to fully develop such capabilities. (P.L. 103-382, Title XIV, p. 388)

All of these definitions are focused in one way or another on performance as the key defining feature of intelligence and giftedness. Although observable behavior is necessary for the identification of high levels of intelligence, whether assessed by a test, a performance of skill, anecdotal reports, or other measures, such a basis for understanding giftedness is necessarily limited.

Extending the view of intelligence to include its emotional aspects, a definition of giftedness was proposed in 1991 by a group of educators known as the Columbus Group (cited in Silverman, 1993):

> Giftedness is asynchronous development in which advanced cognitive abilities and heightened intensity combine to create inner experiences and awareness that are qualitatively different from the norm. This asynchrony increases with higher intellectual capacity. The uniqueness of the gifted renders them particularly vulnerable and requires modifications in parenting, teaching, and counseling in order for them to develop optimally. (p. 3)

Asynchrony refers to the uneven rates of cognitive, emotional, and physical development found in gifted children. Their vulnerability results from the tension such a lack of synchrony creates. As Morelock (1996) observed,

> The research suggests that gifted children are special needs children because they learn differently, function differently neuropsychologically and require a different level and type of cognitive stimulation. They are also potentially socially emotional at risk. The developmental differences increase as the level of asynchrony increases. (p. 10)

One further clarification enhances the definition of giftedness. Human beings differ in ability in all human traits. Each of us is unique. However, admission of difference need not necessarily imply superiority or inferiority. People of high intelligence often cope better with the demands of today's society. But rather than consider possession of this attribute as superior, shouldn't high intelligence be viewed as being further along the way to being all a human can be? If a person taking a trip is only 40 miles from the destination while another person on the same trip is 60 miles away, is the first person superior to the second? They see different things, they discuss with a different perspective and, depending on their capability and interests, they may even end their journey at different points. Placing the two individuals in an artificial hierarchy of better or worse does not adequately differentiate their experience. Only the history of our culture can indicate which traits are requisite for human survival and actualization.

Intelligence, Giftedness, and Talent As an Integration of Brain Functions

Research data from the neurosciences suggest that a high level of intelligence is the result of advanced and accelerated growth of the major functions of the brain. Thus, the definition of intelligence should include the integration of an individual's brain functioning: cognitive, affective, physical/sensing, and intuitive (Figure 2.1). This growth is enhanced or inhibited by the interaction between the genetic pattern and the opportunities provided by the environment. Figure 2.2 shows how the major functions of the brain have been used to define the *universe of intelligence.* The concept of intelligence—and therefore giftedness as a label for high development of intelligence—can no longer be confined to cognitive function; it clearly must include all brain functions and their efficient and integrated use. Using this definition, those who are more intelligent tend to have more integrated, effective use of these functions. Figure 2.3 shows how much of the universe of intelligence is included in some of the prominent definitions of intelligence and giftedness: the federal definition, Renzulli's definition, and Gardner's definition.

It should be noted that although broadening the view of intelligence by suggesting a construct of separate intelligences, Gardner (1983) misrepresents the unifying nature of the brain process. Research indicates that the brain operates with specialized areas of function always in association and interaction, as was noted as early as the 1970s (Diamond, 1988; MacLean, 1978; Pribram, 1977; Restak, 1979). It is the associative nature of the brain that is one of its most noteworthy aspects. Therefore, the definitions of intelligence and giftedness used in this text include all areas of brain function and their expressions as interactive (referring to the constant interaction between heredity and environmental opportunities) and integrative (referring to the relationship among all areas of brain function as interrelated and interdependent).

Brain research from the mid-1960s, replicated for three decades, has shown that very intelligent or gifted learners are biologically different, not at birth but as the result of genetic patterns and environmental opportunities interacting to produce actual cellular changes in the brain (Berg & Singer, 1992; Conlan, 1993; Diamond,

Figure 2.1 *The Functions of the Brain*

The Cognitive Function (Linear and Spatial) The thinking, or cognitive, function includes the linear analytic, problem-solving, sequential, evaluative specialization of the left cortical hemisphere of the brain as well as the more spatially oriented gestalt specialization of the right cortical hemisphere. Higher intelligence requires accelerated synaptic activity and an increased density of the dendrites, which allows the establishment of complex networks of thought. Stimulating environments promote the advanced capacity to generalize, conceptualize, and reason abstractly.

The Affective Function (Emotional and Social) This is the function that is expressed in emotions and feelings, and, while affecting every part of the brain/mind system, it is primarily regulated from the limbic area by biochemical mechanisms housed there. This function more than supports thinking processes; it does, in fact, provide the gateway to enhance or limit higher cognitive function. To be meaningful, academic programs must integrate emotional growth.

The Physical Function (Sensing and Movement) This function includes movement and the entire sensorium: sight, hearing, smell, taste, and touch. The access to our world is through movement and physical sensing; our level of intellectual ability, even our view of reality, will depend on how our brain organizes and processes this information. We know that gifted learners have a heightened ability to bring in information from their environment and process this information in ways that expand their view of reality. They do, however, often define themselves by their cognitive ability. They may recognize their value through this ability alone, and they may focus more and more energy toward the pursuit of cognitive excellence. They may ignore their physical growth and development. Although we are aware of the above-average physical development of many gifted children, we must also notice how they often value and share physical pursuits far less than cognitive endeavors. It is common for gifted learners to develop a Cartesian split which, if unrecognized and left to intensify, can limit the cognitive growth they so value. Integration of the body and the mind becomes an essential part of an integrated program.

The Intuitive Function Different researchers have different ways of viewing and defining intuition. Jung, referred to intuition as one of the four basic human functions. He stated that "Intuition does not denote something contrary to reason, but something outside the province of reason" (Jung, 1933, p. 454). He considered intuition vital to understanding. Bruner (1960) discussed intuition as an important part of the education process and encouraged its training. The physicist Capra (1975) tells us that rational knowing is useless if not accompanied and enhanced by intuitive knowing. For the purposes of our discussion and the development of implementation strategies, we will expand on the work of Loye (1983) and think of intuition as occurring on at least three levels: rational, predictive, and transformational. *Rational intuition* is intuitive behavior that realigns known information in such a way that new insights emerge. *Predictive intuition* enlarges on the processes of the rational level by including new information within existing patterns or sequences and by including unknown or only suspected information within the synthesis process. An unconscious impression or information of some seemingly unknown source becomes an important part of the new patterns formed, the insights, or the profound conclusions. This type of intuitive process is responsible for many breakthrough discoveries, the

Figure 2.1 *continued*

forecasting of trends, and the intuitive leap so valued in business, diplomacy, science, economics, and personal life decisions. *Transformational intuition* seems to be using a different kind of sensing that "picks up information through a means that has defied scientific understanding" (Loye, 1983, p. 52). Ideas come suddenly, unbidden, or in a dream and what is written comes through as if from an outside source. This level of intuition can be experienced as transcendence and can be observed within the brain as a change in the rate of coherence or the correlation between brain waves from separate regions of the brain.

The function of intuition, which we all have but use in varying degrees, represents a different way of knowing. Activating intuition gives a person a sense of completeness, of true integration. This powerful tool leads to the understanding of concepts and people and to an expansion of the human reach.

> These insights tend to come suddenly and, characteristically, not when sitting at a desk working out the equations, but when relaxing in the bath, during a walk in the woods, on the beach, etc. During these periods of relaxation after concentrated intellectual activity, the intuitive mind seems to take over and can produce the sudden clarifying insights which give so much joy and delight to scientific research. (Capra, 1975, p. 31).

Many of those working to include the development of intuition in the educational setting believe that the ability to concentrate, to work at complex tasks with unusual clarity, results from the intuitive function. Identified now as a part of the function of the prefrontal cortex, intuition becomes a part of the planning, future thinking, and insight so necessary to the intelligent person.

1988, 1994; Kandel & Schwartz, 1991; Krech, 1969; Rosenzweig, 1966; Schiebel, 1993):

An increase in neuroglial cell production	Allowing more support for the neurons and a more effective and efficient neural system
A biochemical enhancement of neurons after appropriate stimulation	Allowing for more advanced and complex patterns of thought
An increase in the amount of dendritic branching	Increasing the potential for interconnections between neurons
An increase in the number of synapses and in the size of the synaptic contact	Allowing more accelerated and complex thought processes within the system

Although there is no single definition of either intelligence or giftedness in use within the educational community, current research provides a common basis for agreement that is important.

1. All individuals inherit a genotype or genetic makeup that is unique to them and, with the exception of those with brain damage, includes a brain that has vast potential for the development of intelligence.

Figure 2.2 *The Universe of Intelligence Based on Areas of Brain Function*

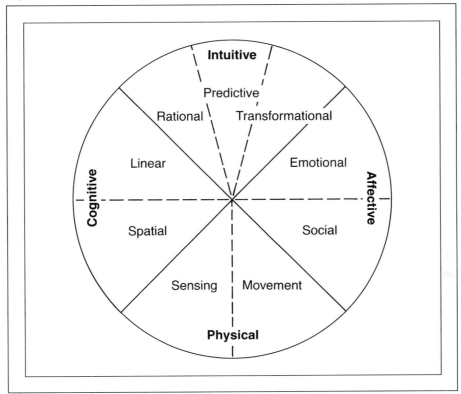

2. The concept of intelligence has become, within the past four decades, known to be dynamic, with the opportunities provided by the environment able to enhance or inhibit the development of the genotype, including the development of the brain, and thus the realization of its potential.

3. The resulting phenotypes, which are the result of genetic makeup and modifications owing to the environment, are quite different from each other and in their abilities, including the expressions of intelligence of which they are capable.

4. The concept of intelligence, therefore, has expanded to include cognitive, affective, intuitive/creative, and physical motor/sensory expressions. High levels of intelligence may be identified in any of these areas. Because the definition of intelligence can no longer be limited to cognitive or academic performance, the term *gifted* must be broadened to include this expanded definition.

5. Owing to its dynamic nature and the importance of both genetic inheritance and environmental opportunity, intelligence can no longer be thought to be in place at birth or innate and permanent in disregard of opportunity for individual development.

6. It must be acknowledged that there are individuals who, through the interaction between their genetic endowment and environmental stimulation, have enhanced the development of their intelligence more than have others, and this

Figure 2.3 *Definitions of* Intelligence *and* Giftedness *Compared With the Universe of Intelligence Based on Areas of Brain Function*

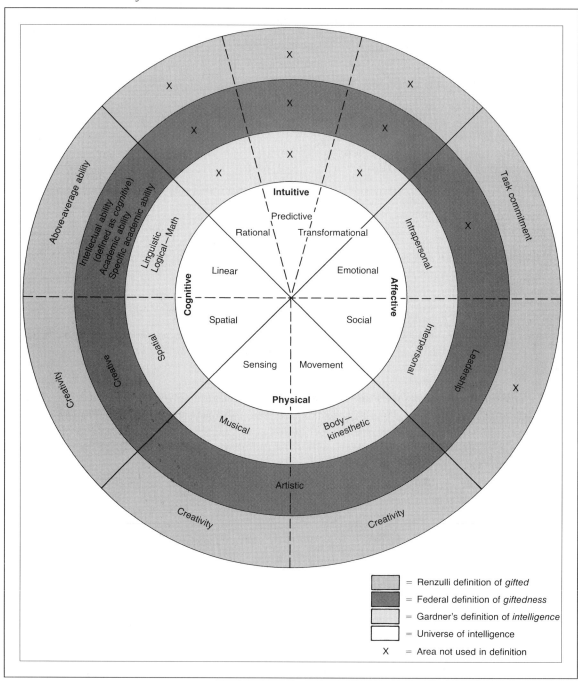

enhancement has resulted in accelerated and advanced brain function. These are the individuals who are labeled gifted.

7. The importance of the dynamic nature of this interaction suggests that if gifted individuals are to continue their intellectual development, they must be engaged in learning opportunities that challenge them and enhance their talents at their level of development or they will regress in whatever abilities and talents are not supported. Therefore, gifted individuals must have appropriate educational experience at the level of their ability and talent to be able to grow.

The incidence of students with giftedness varies from 2% to 5%, depending on the definition used. In talent development programs and in Renzulli's Schoolwide Enrichment Programs (1985), 10% to 25% of students might be included in this population.

Talent Development

Talent is a term that has been used at different times in quite disparate ways. When it was first added to the terminology in gifted education, as in "gifted and talented," it was often used as a term that allowed an extension of expressions of giftedness beyond those of an academic nature. The educational community spoke of the talented artist, musician, leader, or gymnast and sought identification procedures for these students that were far different from those used for academically able students. Some chose to use the term and the separate procedures to identify more students from the minority communities for gifted and talented programs. The implication was that minority students could not meet the testing criteria then in place—generally a single test of intelligence represented by an IQ score—and could be better identified using tests of creativity, leadership, or nonacademic performance. Because gifted programs often remained highly academic in content, the special criteria identification of minority students became a problem. Not only was the assumption that minority students could not test well academically false, the premise that students identified for creativity or other expressions of giftedness would be well-served by narrowly defined academic programs also proved to be clearly in error.

Some psychologists and educators used talent as a term to designate individuals who were not accomplished to the level of a gifted individual, but who had better-than-average potential evident. Confusion between whether reference is being made to the quality of the performance or the type of performance still plagues the use of the term talent in education today.

More recently, the term has been extended to talent development and represents a philosophical commitment on the part of some of those engaged in the education of gifted and talented individuals. Talent development does not identify persons; it indicates a belief in the need to nurture the highest capabilities within all individuals. This is a welcome clarification of the double mission of the field of gifted education and, by adding this focus on the actualization of the highest abilities of all individuals, the development of more giftedness can be ensured in our society. Many of those who are most involved in the development of talent suggest that it should become a primary concern of general education with identification and nurturing of talent potential a central goal for all children (Morelock, 1996). Others remain primarily committed to the education of the large underserved population of gifted and highly gifted individuals and welcome the efforts of those who would expand this population through search for and support of talent.

THE CONCEPT OF INTELLIGENCE

The value of understanding intelligence and its relationship to learning processes can easily be seen. Less obvious is the importance of understanding the brain's role in these processes and how such knowledge can contribute to effectively developing and educating high levels of intelligence. Wittrock (1993) suggests that educators must not ask what the brain has to do with learning; rather, we must ask (1) How can we understand the operations of the brain so that we can create more powerful lessons? and (2) How can education use the processes of the brain more effectively?

A Historical Overview of Intelligence

Although the concept of intelligence as interactive has gained wide acceptance, many still either are unaware of the data or are convinced of another view. Let us look back at how the concept of intelligence has developed over the past century (Figure 2.4).

Fixed Intelligence

More than 100 years ago, Charles Darwin (1859) began his investigation of the origin of the species. His cousin, Francis Galton (1869), had great interest in the hereditary factors that Darwin was investigating, and began asking important questions regarding the heritability of human intelligence. The importance of his investigation into intellectual differences must not be minimized because, prior to Galton, no one had investigated the individual differences of human beings. The very success of this investigation, however, locked us into a limited concept of intellectual development for nearly a century. Because Galton, influenced by Darwin, admired and pursued the heritability issue to the exclusion of environmental effects, he established a pattern that remains a part of the inquiry into intelligence to this day. This view resulted in the theory of fixed intelligence. People believed that the amount of intelligence at birth would remain intact until the day the person died. Nothing could add to or subtract from or in any way change this amount. Galton was the first to attempt an intelligence test based on scientific data. His test assumed a relationship between sensory acuity and general intelligence. Although this later proved an inadequate base for such testing, his efforts nevertheless initiated the search for functional intelligence testing. As testing for intelligence became popular, the belief prevailed that if we could find a test powerful enough, we could predict from infancy exactly what the individual would become. The seeming unreliability of infant

Figure 2.4 *A Timeline of the Development of the Concept of Intelligence as It Affects Giftedness and Talent Development*

1895	Charles Darwin (UK) began his investigation of the origin of the species.
1869	Francis Galton (UK) investigated the heritability of human intelligence and individual differences; developed the concept of fixed intelligence and the first intelligence test.
1905	Alfred Binet (France) developed intelligence scales, the concept of mental age, and intelligence quotient (IQ) to separate slow learners in schools for a special curriculum.
1921	Lewis Terman revised the Binet Intelligence Scale to establish the Stanford-Binet Intelligence Scale.
1930s–1940s	Intelligence testing became very popular, used especially by the US Army, vocational counselors, and schools.
1930–1950	Concept of predeterminism (maturation leads learning) established by G. Stanley Hall and Arnold Gesell.
1930s–1960s	Development of concepts of educability of intelligence, inconstancy of IQ, and interactive intelligence by Montessori, Wellman, Skeels and Dye, Dennis, and Hunt.
1952	Jean Piaget described the growth and development of intelligence; evolved principles of active participation in learning and stages of development; contributed to the interactive view of intelligence.
1956	J. P. Guilford's presidential speech at the American Psychological Association introduced the Structure of Intellect Model that expanded the concept of intelligence to 120 factors, including a strong focus on creativity, seen as divergent thinking.
1960s	Work done by Vygotsky in Russia in the 1920s was finally made available and challenged ideas of fixed intelligence and indicated that learning leads and directs maturation. Stressed the importance of early stimulation. Many researchers including Bruner, Hunt, Kagan, Rosensweig, and Krech established a database for interactive intelligence.
1964	Benjamin Bloom contributed to an increased awareness of the preschool years as essential to learning, the interactive intelligence theory, and the understanding of the learning process. Highlights of this work were the establishment of a database for the Headstart movement and the publication of *Taxonomy of Educational Objectives,* used as a guide in many gifted programs.
1983	Howard Gardner proposed the theory of multiple intelligences that includes linguistic, musical, logical-mathematical, spatial, bodily-kinesthetic, interpersonal, and intrapersonal intelligences.
1985	Robert Sternberg theorized a triarchic concept of intelligence that includes metaprocesses, performance processes, and knowledge-acquisition processes.
1995–date	The accumulation of evidence indicated that intelligence is multi-dimensional and is affected by an interaction between that which is inherited and the environment in which one lives.

testing was thought to be a problem of the testing procedure, not of any change in the actual intelligence.

During this period of belief in fixed intelligence, many significant events occurred. In 1905, the French government asked Alfred Binet to develop a way to separate a group of slow learners from other school children in order to create a special curriculum and methodology that would aid in their learning. Unlike those who later utilized his intelligence scales and concept of mental age, Binet did not agree with the theory of fixed intelligence or with the unitary factor of intelligence. He believed intelligence to be educable, a belief not again heard until the 1960s. Binet's articles and speeches would be considered quite radical even today. Many of the educational problems he spoke out against during his day still need change (Binet, 1969). Today in the United States, Binet is best known through a revision of his intelligence scale, originally devised by Lewis Terman of Stanford University in 1921. This test, the Stanford-Binet Intelligence Scale, originated when no one questioned the belief in fixed intelligence. Later revisions are still based on this assumption.

Testing achieved popularity during the 1930s and 1940s. For a time in America, everyone was tested for everything. There were tests for career placement, for various kinds of aptitude, for scholastic ability, for personality factors, and even for predicting success with a future marriage partner. Armies of men and thousands of school children were tested. During this period, the test became the ultimate authority. Intelligence testing was valued to the extreme that a test score placed on a school cumulative record could be used for educational decision-making without stating the availability of the protocol or even the name of the test. Parents were not permitted to know the IQ of their children, because of the prevailing belief that this number gave evidence of capacity for mental development, and such a powerful piece of information could not be trusted to the lay public. Some school districts and classrooms still are reluctant to share this information.

During this period of belief in fixed intelligence, the most extensive study of the characteristics and behaviors of gifted individuals was undertaken. Terman, working under a grant from the Commonwealth Fund of New York City, began in 1921 by choosing more than 1500 students with an average age of 11 years and IQs exceeding 140 (mean, 150). He collected extensive personal and educational data on each student. The stereotype of a gifted person at that time pictured a bespectacled, frail youngster, who was socially ill at ease, lost in a world of books and lofty thoughts, and usually isolated in some corner tenuously holding on to sanity. "Early ripe, early rot" was the motto of the day used to describe the gifted person. No clear-thinking parent would ever desire to have such a child. Any attempt to encourage this type of development was unthinkable.

Terman's data went far to dispel these myths. Although his sample was limited culturally, socioeconomically, and racially, his findings were significant in influencing those who held extreme ideas about gifted individuals. His data allow a more realistic opinion and a more accepting view of the gifted. Although conceived and mostly conducted during a period of belief in fixed intelligence, Terman's longitudinal work (lasting 30 years during his life and later updated by some of his colleagues) added to the data disputing fixed intelligence as a viable concept (Terman, 1925).

In the first half of the twentieth century, a student of Galton, G. Stanley Hall, introduced another idea about human development that was a logical outgrowth of the concept of fixed intelligence. This view of development as predetermined was made popular largely by the work of Arnold Gesell (Gesell et al., 1940), a disciple of Hall. Again, a man who made many valuable contributions to our understanding of children became instrumental in solidifying misconceptions about how children grow and develop. Predeterminism assumes that the human organism is programmed in a sequentially time-controlled way and that regardless of events or environments, the program will prevail. Maturation and learning were seen as distinct and, to some extent, separate processes, with maturation controlled by heredity and learning controlled by environmental conditions. Maturation was thought to lead necessarily to learning. This idea was carried to such an extreme that avant-garde schools viewed any attempt to guide the growth of youngsters as a grievous fault. The abuses that followed inevitably limited growth and demeaned the human beings involved. Parents were advised to allow each child to "flower" unrestrained. Permissive patterns were extolled.

Into this climate of nonintervention and nonstimulation some dissonant information began to appear. At first, people disputed, rationalized away, or simply ignored any ideas that varied from the norm. The slow acceptance of the work of Maria Montessori exemplifies the reception offered educational methodology based on opposing ideas (Standing, 1966). Although Montessori's work was highly successful, it assumed the educability of intelligence and therefore the inconstancy of the IQ. Not until decades later could the techniques and ideas of Montessori be incorporated into our educational practices. Such ideas were lost until years of evidence began to accumulate. Determined and courageous researchers and practitioners in education and psychology risked their professional reputations to share findings that were in direct conflict with the concept of intelligence as "fixed." Even today some consider this area of inquiry controversial.

Beth Wellman and colleagues at Iowa University began to question the premise of fixed intelligence. In 1938, this group began an experiment that later caused them to become part of a professional controversy (Skeels, Updegraff, Wellman, & Williams, 1938; Skodak & Skeels, 1949; Wellman, 1940). The group established a model nursery school on the grounds of an orphanage. The operation of the orphanage had been efficient in that the basic needs of the children were provided for, but little time was spent in stimulation or educational activities. The model nursery school that provided stimulation was highly successful. In fact, it seemed to change the intellectual behavior exhibited by the children in attendance. After measuring the children's progress on achievement and intelligence tests, Wellman reported her findings to the academic community in what must have been a mood of optimistic enthusiasm. In a time when information such as changes in intelligence scores and environmental intervention was received with suspicion and when women professors were themselves not taken seriously, it is small wonder that the storm of protest that followed became a humiliating experience for Wellman.

Not until years later did another team, some of whom had worked on the original project, conduct a similar study after carefully redesigning their approach to meet the criticisms of improper sampling procedures, lack of a control group, and improper research design that were used to attack the Wellman data. This study and subsequent follow-up studies finally made an impact on the academic community. The findings were intriguing. Children removed from the orphanage to a more stimulating environment (an institution for retarded girls where they received much attention, stimulation, and affection) gained more than 20 IQ points when retested, while the control group remaining at the orphanage lost between 13 and 45 IQ points (Skeels & Dye, 1959). A follow-up study (Skeels, 1966) further dramatized the findings by reporting that the experimental group had become productive, functioning adults, while the control group, for the most part, had been institutionalized as mentally retarded; few of the latter group became productive adults. Whatever one might think of the research design or sampling methods used, the results were, at the very least, provocative.

In 1960, another event occurred that again raised questions that the prevailing theory of intelligence could not answer. While observing deprived conditions in Teheran, Iran, orphanages, Dennis (1960) found 12-month-old babies who could not sit by themselves, even though maturational theories assured this behavior by 8 months of age at the latest. Some 4-year-olds could not yet walk alone, although development scales showed 1 year of age to be the appropriate time schedule. How could the maturational development of these children be so far off the norm? Do environments affect maturation after all? To answer these questions, Dennis conducted a series of experiments. The resulting data, combined with earlier data, showed the concept of fixed intelligence and its natural extension, predeterminism, to be untenable (Dennis & Dennis, 1955; Dennis & Najarian, 1957).

Interactive Intelligence

Data such as those produced by the researchers Wellman, Skodak, Skeels, and Dennis made the formulation of a new theory for looking at intelligence necessary. An important new concept of the structure of the intellect now appeared with the factor-analytic work of J. P. Guilford (1956). Guilford felt that psychology had overly restricted its view of human intelligence. His model expanded the factors seen as part of human intelligence and showed their interrelatedness. Guilford, too, discussed intelligence as educable. He drew attention to creativity as an important function of the human mental process.

Not until well into the 1960s did the challenge against fixed intelligence reach significant proportions. A veritable cadre of intelligent men and women now faced the issue. Armed with data resulting from their work, they proceeded from an examination of the dissonance between accumulating information and the old theoretic framework, through the postulation of a new theory of intelligence, to the collection of evidence to support the new hypothesis. From this point on, intelligence would be seen as educable, changeable, and dependent on the interaction between the genetic inheritance and the experiences provided by the environment. The sequence of studies that supported the new concept, difficult to assess, affected the literature and theory. Recorded here are only a few of the milestone events, because the sheer quantity of activity makes the delineation of a chronology of importance impossible.

Work done in the 1920s in Russia had just begun to reach the American academic community. The work of the Russian researcher Vygotsky, which was suppressed during his lifetime, finally became known and discussed. When data were received in Europe and finally translated for use in the United States, educators could no longer deny the possibility that learning might lead and direct the quality and speed of maturation. Vygotsky's contributions provided data for the areas of language development, educational remediation, early stimulation, and remediation of physical disability (Vygotsky, 1962).

Also from Europe, in varying quality of translation, came the work of Jean Piaget (1952), who influenced educational theory and practice to an unprecedented degree. He began his inquiry in a most unscientific manner, one that no scientist would consider sound as a research design. Without objectivity, he selected only three subjects to observe and no control group. The subjects were his own children. However, he described so clearly and in such detail what he observed that his evidence enabled him to evolve principles of growth and development. Later examination of data from a multitude of studies testing respectable numbers verified many of his principles as viable and useful.

Piaget was among the first to ask about intellectual development during the first few years of human life. Drawn from his background in marine biology, his work emphasized the principles of assimilation and accommodative interaction. He believed that intellectual growth resulted from the learner's active participation in the learning process, invariably sequenced into stages. Although he set no strict time lines on the stages of development, he considered the order unalterable, with mastery of the lower stages preceding learning in the higher stages of cognition. Piaget stated that the age at which a child passes from one stage to another depends on both the genetic endowment and the quality of the environment. He espoused one of the first interactive theories of intelligence.

The work of Benjamin Bloom (1964) made another important contribution to educational practice, particularly to the growing concern for the years of early intellectual development. A reexamination of previously published data allowed Bloom to suggest a startling hypothesis. It had long been assumed (and intelligence testing norms complied with the assumption) that humans learn in a regularly ascending line between birth and 18 years of age, after which they level off to a plateau effect until around 45, the age when a gradual decline to senility begins. Bloom used the reassessed data to show a very different pattern. Although he looked at many human characteristics, just the findings from the area of intelligence receive comment here. Between birth and 4 years of age, children accomplish 50% of the deviation in IQ that they will acquire by 18 years of age. By 6 years of age, another 30% will have been added. With the data showing 80% of the deviation in adult IQ actualized by age 6, educators developed a new awareness of preschool years as an essential time for learning. As society's concern for compensatory education also gained a following, many programs were then established to take advantage of the important early years.

The educational community began to focus on the early years of development as educators became aware of the limitations and deceptions caused by the theories of fixed intelligence and predeterminism. Reliance on these older concepts had left us with a near void in understanding how infants and young children develop intellectually. In Chapter 3 we look at the amazing and exciting knowledge that began to fill this void. Bloom made an important contribution to classroom organization for learning with the publication of his *Taxonomy of Educational Objectives, Handbook I: Cognitive Domain* (Bloom, 1956) and his work with Krathwohl and Masia (1964) in *Taxonomy of Educational Objectives, Handbook II: Affective Domain*.

For readers nearing or past the magic age of 45, let me hasten to add that subsequent studies done by the Fels Foundation (Kagan & Moss, 1962), the Berkeley Growth Studies (Bayley, 1968; Bayley & Schaefer, 1964), and the Terman data themselves (Terman & Oden, 1947) give us a very different view of the "off to senility" phenomenon. Those studies indicate that we do *not* plateau intellectually at 18 years of age; rather we continue to move either upward or gradually downward, depending on the intellectual challenges in which we engage and on our personality characteristics. Aggressive, inquiring, active, independent, sensitive people who seek new ideas and adapt comfortably to change tend to continue upward; passive, docile, dependent people who follow set patterns and seek security and repetition gradually lose intellectual facility. Data collected from the Terman studies show that growth patterns continue as people reach their 60s and 70s. Data on aging further support these possibilities.

Although it was previously believed that the plasticity of the brain was available only to the very young, in 1981 Buell and Coleman made a remarkable discovery. In their study comparing a normal aged population (ages 68 to 92), adults (ages 44 to 55), and an aged population (ages 70 to 81) showing senile dementia (SD), they found that the normal aged persons had longer and more branched dendrites than did either the adults or the SD group. These data suggest a model in which the aging cortex contains both regressing, dying neurons and surviving, growing neurons. This was the first demonstration of plasticity in the adult human brain.

As further support for Buell and Coleman's view, Diamond (1986) has shown that stimulation affects not only young rats but old ones as well to create a thickening of the thinking part of the brain. A lifetime of curiosity and activity and a love of life are important ingredients if we are to continue the stimulation of neural tissue. As Diamond states, "I found that the people who use their brains don't lose them . . . other denominators were activity, and love of life, and love of others and being loved. Love is very basic" (cited in Hopson, 1984, p. 70). Schai (cited in Ferguson, 1986a) also points to continued activity as necessary to take advantage of the plasticity of the brain. "People who led active lives when they were middle-aged remained stable or showed improvement in mental abilities after age 60. Those who didn't show marked decline" (p. 2).

The constancy of the IQ received a final blow from the work of Sontag, Baker, and Nelson (1958) and Kagan and Moss (1962). Their longitudinal studies followed 300 children from prenatal development through adulthood, with data collected at regular intervals. The results showed consistent change in IQ scores, especially at the extreme ends, with more variation evident for boys than for girls.

Jerome Bruner, J. McV. Hunt, and many others began the task of establishing and supporting a new theory of intelligence. Bruner hypothesized that the young deal with information in three ways: through action, imagery, and symbols. He believed that the preschool experience should work toward translating one into the other. Bruner (1964) stated, "The significance about the growth of the mind in the child is to what degree it depends not upon capacity but upon the unlocking of capacity" (p. 14). He saw that the process of translating or unlocking depends on interaction with the environment of the culture. He attempted to give us a method of implementation as he set forth his new theories on instruction (Bruner, 1960, 1968).

Hunt (1961) brought out the problem of the match, that is, finding the most stimulating circumstances for children at each point in their development. To him, the major challenge of our time was to discover a way to govern the encounters children have with their environment, especially during the early years of their development. With such a match of ability and experience, children could be expected to achieve a substantially higher level of intellectual capacity as adults.

Further support for this interaction theory of intelligence must be noted in the renorming of the Stanford-Binet Intelligence Scale. An analysis of the standardization results showed a dramatic rise in the IQ level, especially among the preschool population. We might assume that the higher education of parents and richer earlier environments—television, higher mobility, wider use of educational toys and books, better nutrition—have helped foster this change. Later studies indicated that the observed change is a genuine phenomenon and not a research error (Thorndike, 1975). This information is even more impelling as evidence when one considers that the new standardization population purposefully included minority representation, which had been omitted from the previous samplings.

Expanded Views of Intelligence

During the 1980s an expanded concept of intelligence, first suggested by Guilford, concerned a number of researchers and scholars. Each has added a dimension to consider in our understanding of intelligence.

In 1985, Sternberg theorized a triarchic concept of intelligence. To understand intelligence, he believes that we must view its development from three aspects: the internal world of the individual, exemplified by analytical thinking; the external world of the individual, environmental awareness; and the interaction between these two worlds that synthesizes disparate experiences in insightful ways. According to the triarchic theory, three kinds of mental processes operate: (1) metaprocesses, used to plan, monitor, and evaluate one's problem-solving; (2) performance processes, used to carry out the instructions of the metaprocesses; and (3) knowledge-acquisition processes, used to figure out how to solve problems. It is in the area of experience that Sternberg feels we fail the individual most notably, both in the development of his or her intelligence and in its identification. He refers to this experiential expression of giftedness as *synthetic intelligence* and believes that it most impacts the world. Sternberg believes that augmenting our understanding of this area will permit us to develop a more complete theory of intelligence to provide us with a base for a more useful assessment of intelligence. Such advances may further lead to more effective educational strategies.

From a somewhat different point of view Howard Gardner (1983), a Harvard University psychologist, proposed a theory of multiple intelligences that originally included seven relatively independent intelligences—linguistic, musical, logical-mathematical, spatial, bodily-kinesthetic, interpersonal, and intrapersonal. He believes that "only if we expand and reformulate our view of what counts as human intellect will we be able to devise more appropriate ways of assessing it and more effective ways of educating it" (p. 4). He is currently developing an eighth intelligence, naturalistic, that tries to capture the more unique aspects of each individual.

In the process of formulating his original theory Gardner drew from a wide range of studies on subjects including prodigies, gifted individuals, brain-damaged patients, normal children and adults, and individuals of diverse cultures. As an additional basis for this expanded view Gardner is interested in the influence of the current neurobiological data on our understanding of intelligence and its development. From these data Gardner presents evidence supporting the following conclusions: (1) there is considerable plasticity and flexibility in human growth, especially during the early months of life; (2) plasticity is modulated by genetic constraints that operate from the beginning and guide development; (3) human beings are predisposed to carry out certain specific intellectual operations whose nature can be inferred from careful observation; and (4) educational efforts must build on a knowledge of these intellectual proclivities and their points of maximum flexibility and adaptability.

Gardner's theory addresses many areas that have not previously been seen as a part of intelligence, and he brings additional clarity to the critical importance of the interaction of both genetics and environment in its development. He does, however, insist that each of his intelligences is essentially independent in function and in doing so creates a number of questionable dichotomies. For example, he suggests that discovery learning should be preferred over explicit instruction for young children and that explicit instruction is better than discovery learning for older learners. It could be, however, that a balance of both experiences is most effective for any age of learner.

Throughout the discussion of the eight intelligences, Gardner discusses the power of using one of the intelligences that is well-developed as an alternative learning mode for others not as developed. This use of the multiple intelligences supporting one another to create powerful learning comes very close to the view of integrative education developed in this text, although the area of intuitive function is not yet included in Gardner's model. Gardner shows a deep concern for optimal learning in his theoretic framework.

Because the newer data from many sources now make the fixed view of intelligence untenable, the interactive theory of intelligence seems to best describe the data available. For the development of giftedness, this theory brings into question a new area of inquiry: How do humans become gifted? In Chapter 4 we will examine the evidence in that area.

The Development of Intelligence

From the beginning of the concern for measurement of intelligence, controversy has existed regarding the origins of intelligence. Is it determined by heredity or does the environment make a difference? Was intelligence fixed or would it change over time depending on environmental experiences? Beginning in the early 1960s, the neurosciences have helped to answer such questions.

The terms *intelligence* and *intellectual ability* express many different ideas. In our discussion we have acknowledged intelligence as the result of the development and interrelationship of all functions of the human brain that can be enhanced or inhibited by the interaction between the genetic pattern and the opportunities provided by the environment. To communicate the dynamic nature of this development, Cross observes that "an animal is only as smart as it needs to be" and Diamond supports this statement by adding, "nature programs parts of the brain to sharpen up when—and only when—experience demands it" (Diamond & Hopson, 1998, p. 29).

Nature versus Nurture

As early as the 1970s, Cattell spoke of the human's "capacity to acquire new capacity" (1971, p. 8), alluding to the marvelous ability human beings have to actually change their own capacity. We can become more than we were at birth—not more in the sense of exceeding the limits of our inborn characteristics or physical structure, but most certainly more in our ability to use those characteristics and that structure. In some cases we may modify the total to become more efficient, more powerful than these limits seemingly dictated. We have not properly appreciated the ability of our organism to expand or decrease as it interacts with the environment.

High intelligence, whether expressed in cognitive abilities (such as the capacity to generalize, to conceptualize, or to reason abstractly), specific academic ability, leadership, or creative behavior expressed through visual and performing arts, results from the interaction between inherited potentialities and experiences acquired from the environment. This interaction encompasses all of the physical, mental, and emotional characteristics of the person and all of the people, events, and objects entering the person's awareness. Just as no two people have identical physical, mental, and emotional properties, neither do they have the same environment. Reality is unique to each of us. Even so simple a perception as color differs vastly among individuals. We view color differently because our own emotional pattern causes us to develop a personal meaning for each color that might change or be reinforced as our experiences with objects of each color give us additional information.

From this interactive point of view, we could not say which is more important: the inherited abilities or the environmental opportunities to develop them. A restriction on either would inhibit high levels of actualized intellectual ability. As Diamond states (1998), "The brain, with its complex architecture and limitless potential, is a highly plastic, constantly changing entity that is powerfully shaped by our experiences in childhood and throughout life . . . Our collective actions, sensations, and memories are a powerful shaper of both function and anatomy" (pp. 2–3). High levels of brain development do not occur without a high level of interaction between the inherited abilities and appropriately enriching experiences.

The Importance of Brain Function

In our definition of giftedness, a high level of intelligence is viewed as advanced and accelerated brain function. The data allowing this relationship make an exciting addition to our understanding of the development of giftedness. As early as 1977 neurobiologist T. Teyler explained,

> The fabric of the brain is set down as a result of the interaction of genetic blueprints and environmental influences. While the basic features of brain organization are present at birth (cell division is essentially complete), the brain experiences tremendous growth in

neural processes, synapse formation, and myelin sheath formation, declining around puberty. These processes can be profoundly altered by the organism's environment. Furthermore, it has been shown that brain processes present at birth will degenerate if the environmental stimulation necessary to activate them is withheld. It appears that the genetic contribution provides a framework which, if not used, will disappear, but which is capable of further development given the optimal environmental stimulation. (pp. 31–32)

To understand how some individuals become gifted and others do not, we need to become familiar with the basic structure and function of the human brain. As we seek to understand how we might nurture giftedness, such knowledge will prove invaluable.

In the 1970s it was established that at birth the human brain contains some 100 billion to 200 billion brain cells. Each neural cell is in place, ready to be developed and used for actualizing the highest levels of human potential. With a very small number of exceptions, all human infants come equipped with this marvelous, complex heritage. Such a structure will allow us to process trillions of bits of information in our lifetime. However, it is estimated that we actually use less than 5% of this capability to connect neural structures. How we use this complex system becomes critical to our development of intelligence, personality, and the very quality of life we experience as we grow (Diamond, 1998; Siegel, 1999, Teyler, 1977).

Genes cannot be thought of as causing particular attributes; rather, they have a wide range of effects in different environments. Vernon (1979) considered the nature–nurture controversy sterile and insoluble, because neither heredity nor environment can be held constant to discover its effects in isolation. Harvard biologist Stephen Jay Gould (1981) contended that, although some genes may well determine variations in human intelligence, hereditarians err by equating *heritable* with *inevitable*. Genes do not make specific bits and pieces of a body; they code for a range of forms under an array of environmental conditions. Moreover, even when a trait has been built and set, environmental intervention may still modify inherited defects. The claim that IQ is so many percent "heritable" does not conflict with the belief that enriched education can increase what we call "intelligence" (p. 156).

Even our beliefs about the absolute stability of genes must be reexamined. Genes provide us with a structure or pattern but are dependent on the environment for the particular characteristic that they will express. A signal from the environment impacts on a somatic cell and activates a regulatory gene that codes for proteins that trigger or turn on a specific somatic expression within the system (Slavkin, 1987). Whereas genes provide us with our own unique menu, the environment makes the actual selection within that range of choice.

It is misleading to think of either genes or the environment as being more important: Genes can only express themselves in an environment, and an environment has no effect except by evoking genotypes already present. Any reference to *high-IQ genes* must be seen as a misnomer. It would be equally incorrect to regard genetic endowment as "setting the limits." Siegel (1999), medical director of the Infant and Preschool Service and associate clinical professor of psychiatry at the University of California, Los Angeles, School of Medicine concludes,

An infant is born with a genetically programmed excess in neurons, and the postnatal establishment of synaptic connections is determined by both genes and experience. Genes contain the information for the general organization of the brain's structure, but experience determines which genes become expressed, how, and when. (p. 14)

The fact that development is a product of the effect of experience on the unfolding of genetic potential has now been supported by a wide range of studies over several decades (Benedersky & Lewis, 1994; Cancro, 1971; Diamond, 1988; Gunnar, 1990; Rakic, Bourgeois, & Goldman-Rakic, 1994; Rose, 1972; Rosenzweig, 1966; Siegel 1999).

As seen in the boxed feature on the following pages, the interaction between genetic and environmental contributions is complex and interdependent. Throughout this text our exploration of this interaction focuses on the environment. This one-sided focus reflects our ability as educators to influence growth and development only from the environmental realm. As educators we provide environments to deliver learning experiences, so we must be aware that decisions about those environments do, in fact, change the neurological and biological structure of our students.

Environmental interaction with the genetic program of the individual occurs whether it is planned or left to occur by chance. By conservative estimates made in the late 1950s, this interaction can result in a 20-point difference in measured intelligence; some researchers found as much as a 40-point variation (Bloom, 1964; Hunt, cited in Pines, 1979a; Skeels & Dye, 1959). For example, two individuals with approximately the same genetic capacity for developing intelligence, as a result of the environment with which they interact, could be regarded as high achieving, potentially gifted, or educably retarded. Mild retardation, constituting one of the largest categories of disabilities found among children and adults, stems in large part from a deprived environment (Tarjan, 1970). Such an environment is apparently caused by far less than optimal prenatal and perinatal conditions in interaction with deleterious factors after birth (Birch & Gussow, 1970, Diamond, 1988, 1998). We already know enough about supportive environments to prevent this type of retardation from occurring, enough to assure most of our children a level of functioning that would actualize far higher levels of intellectual ability. Yet, because of society's priorities, social dilemmas, and lack of parental training, we do not use what we know.

Those who work with gifted children must acquire an understanding of the power of this interaction between the organism and the environment. What we believe about how people become intelligent will influence the way we plan for their educational development. If we believe that individuals were born gifted, we will probably feel that we can do little to influence their development. We may believe enrichment will be sufficient for people of this ability to "get by on their own." If, however, we consider giftedness a dynamic process in which a person's innate ability is in constant and continuous interaction with the environment, and if we believe that the strength of that interaction will determine just how much ability this person will be able to develop, then we will become highly sensitive to the level and needs he or she expresses. Our awareness will allow us to support and challenge this developing intellect. Without such efforts, intellectual abilities will be wasted, and untold potential will never be realized. A discussion of how intelligence develops is far more than an academic pursuit. For our children, it is a matter of who they are and who they may become.

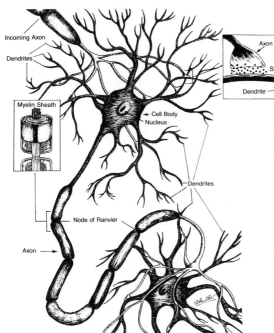

Exhibit A   *Three Interconnected Neurons*

Inside the cell body are the nucleus and the biochemical processes that maintain the life of the cell. The neuron is a tiny system for information processing that receives and sends thousands of signals. No two cells are exactly alike nor are any two brains alike. We are as different from one another as snowflakes. The dendrites are short fibers that extend from the cell body, branching out to form the pathways for receiving information from nearby nerve cells. The axon is one long nerve fiber that extends from the cell body and serves as a transmitter, sending signals that are picked up by the branches of the neighboring dendrites. The activity between neurons is carried out by the dendrites of one cell in contact with the axon of another. The end of the axon does not actually touch the dendrite of the other cell but transmits the information chemically across a region where the cells are particularly close. This junction across which impulses travel from one nerve cell to another is called the *synapse.* The transmission of a nerve impulse is an electro-chemical process. At the synapse, the

The Neuron

The nerve cell, or neuron, is the basic unit of the brain. The approximately 100 billion neurons within the brain are so small that 100,000 of them can fit into a space the size of a pinhead. Connections between neurons in the top layer of the brain (cortex) measure 10,000 miles per cubic inch. A neuron is composed of the cell body, the dendrites, and an axon (Exhibit A). If you open your hand to the fullest extent possible you will have a good representation of the nerve cell (Exhibit B). The palm of the hand is the cell body with an indentation at the center that can represent the nucleus of the cell. The extended fingers are located in the appropriate place for the dendrites and would more closely resemble dendrites if branches grew from each finger. The arm extending below the hand makes a good model of the axon that, in fact, extends from the cell body in much the same way. It is possible to use both hands as models of neurons to show the exchange of information as it occurs in the learning process and which is described in the following paragraphs.

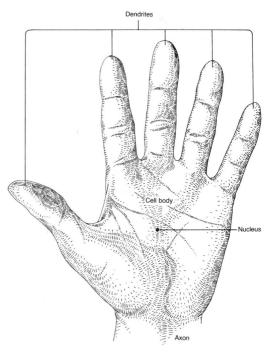

Exhibit B   *The Human Hand as Representing a Nerve Cell*

electrical impulses that travel through the cell convert into chemical signals, then back to the electrical impulses. It is this synapse that is thought to be the most likely site for neural mechanisms of learning and memory (Thompson, Berger, & Berry, 1980; Siegel, 1999).

Surrounding the neurons are special cells known as *glia*. These cells outnumber the neural cells ten to one and can be increased by stimulation from the environment (Rosenzweig, 1966; Diamond, 1988). The glial cells provide the brain with nourishment, consume waste products, and serve as packing material actually gluing the brain together. They also insulate the nerve cell, creating a myelin sheath (Exhibit A), a special coating that protects the axon and amplifies the signal leaving the cell. Myelin has an important function, in that it allows the coated axon to conduct information away from the neuron at a much faster rate than unmyelinated axons (Thompson et al., 1980). As the glial cells in the brain increase and provide more myelination, the speed of learning accelerates. The difference in myelinated and unmyelinated axons is like the difference in electrical conduction through insulated and uninsulated wiring: The speed and power of the charge increase by the presence of insulation.

The rate of glial cell production is influenced by the richness of the environment provided (Rosenzweig, 1966; Diamond, 1988). The more glia, the more accelerated will be the synaptic activity and the more powerful will be the impulse exchange from one cell to the next, allowing for faster and more complex patterns of thinking, two characteristics we find in gifted children. The speed of thought is amazing. If a nerve pathway is used often, the threshold of the synapse falls, so that the pathway operates more readily. A wave front is started that may sweep over at least 100,000 neurons a second (Brierley, 1976).

Another way to increase synaptic activity is to strengthen the neuron's cell body. Although the quantity of neural cells cannot be increased, the quality of the cells can be (Krech, 1969, 1970; Rosenzweig, 1966; Diamond, 1988). This quality enhancement allows for information to be processed more quickly and for more power to be conducted, resulting in the availability of more complex neural networks. Interaction in an enriched environment changes the chemical structure of the nerve cell, thereby strengthening the cell body.

The Organization of the Brain

The human brain is organized into four major systems with radically different structures and chemistry. Educationally this organization presents some important considerations. Two of the four brain systems have no network for verbal communication. Because the integration of total brain function is the basis for intelligence, a test that measures primarily verbal communication as its sampling of intelligence may be seen as limited.

As an aid to understanding the organization and structure of the brain, I would like to borrow from Paul MacLean (1978) an analogy he used that has helped me in my thinking and teaching. Make a fist with each of your hands so that you can see the fingernails and then place your hands together with the fingernails touching. As you look down at your hands they now form a very respectable model of the brain (Exhibit C). Wiggle your little fingers and you have identified the area through which vision enters the brain. Move your middle finger and you have located the motor area. The language area is just below the middle knuckle on the right hand (left hemisphere), though please note that it is connected to the right hemisphere (left hand) by way of the touching fingernails, which now represent the corpus callosum. This connector between the right and left hemispheres of the brain has within it more neural connections than there are in any other part of the body. Clearly the interconnection or integration of the right and left hemisphere specializations is biologically intended.

Returning to our hand-brain analogy, look at just one hand/hemisphere. Begin with the arm-wrist area, which represents the lower brain stem and the innermost areas of the cerebrum in which we find the seat of autonomic (i.e., automatic) function. This system relieves us of consciously processing each breath and each beat of our heart. Within recent years those working in the area of biofeedback have shown us that while most autonomic functions remain just that, we can, if we choose, bring the awareness of these functions to consciousness, allowing us to monitor or change the process if it has become destructive or inefficient. For example, people with high blood pressure can use biofeedback techniques to monitor and change an inappropriate distribution rate of blood, consciously helping the body to better regulate this usually automatic function (Taylor & Bongar, 1976; Taylor, Tom, & Ayers, 1981). Here we find the neural pathways for many higher brain centers. Here, too, are nuclei concerned with motor control and the communication link between the rest of the

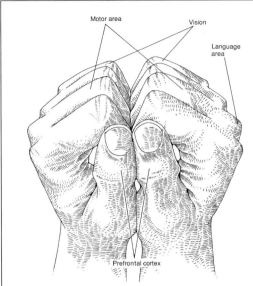

Exhibit C   *A Hand Model of the Human Brain*

gard it is of great importance to educators attempting to understand gifted development. By the release of neurotransmitters from the limbic system, the cells of the cortex are either facilitated or inhibited in their functioning. One activator for growth of function in this area is novelty (Restak, 1979). Feelings of pleasure and joy have been noted for their increased stimulation to this area (Sagan, 1977). Levels of touch and movement that are too low profoundly affect this area and may result in an increase in violent behavior (Prescott, 1979).

The exposed surface of the fingers and thumbs of both hands held together represents the third system of the brain, the convoluted mass known as the *neocortex* or the *cerebrum*. It is the largest brain system, comprising five-sixths of the total, and envelops the two previously mentioned, the lower brain stem and the midbrain, or limbic system. It is here that sensory data are processed, decisions made, and action initiated. The neocortex is necessary for language and speech. Its most overriding functions involve the reception, storage, and retrieval of information.

brain and the cerebellum located at the very base of the brain. The reticular formation is located in this area. It is, in essence, the physical basis for consciousness and plays a major role in keeping us awake and alert.

The second system of the brain is known as the limbic system (Exhibit D) or the emotional mind. It is located at midbrain and contributes significantly to the learning process. It can be symbolically viewed by partially unclenching your fist and looking at the palm of the hand. One can see the ventricles of the brain that hold the cerebrospinal fluid, as well as the mounds and depressions of the limbic system itself. Here are the biochemical systems that are activated by the emotions of the learner. Here too are the interactions that enhance or inhibit memory. This area affects such diverse functions as anxiety, rage, sentimentality, and attention span. In addition, our feelings of personal identity and uniqueness depend on this area of the brain to combine internal and external experience. It is in this limbic area that the affective feelings provide the connecting bridge between our inner and outer worlds and provide us with our construct of reality, our model of a possible world. This system is often referred to as the *gateway to higher thought,* to the cortical and neocortical functions. In this re-

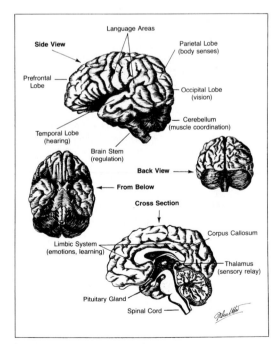

Exhibit D   *The Human Brain*

The most recently evolved section of the neocortex, the prefrontal cortex, which is represented by the thumbs in our analogy, provides for behaviors associated with planning, organizing, creating, insight, empathy, introspection, and other bases of intuitive thought (Luria, cited in Wittrock, 1980b; MacLean, 1978). It is engaged in firming up intention, deciding on action, and regulating our most complex behaviors (Restak, 1979). It is, in fact, the area that energizes and regulates all other parts: It houses our purpose.

Goodman (1978) more specifically places the following functions in the area of the prefrontal cortex, which he believes develops most fully between 12 and 16 years of age:

- *Foresight:* Ability to see patterns of change, to extrapolate from present trends to future possibilities. This process uses imagination, prediction, and behavioral planning.
- *Self-regulation:* Regulates bodily processes through insight, internal commands, and generation of visual images. This is the basis for meditation and biofeedback strategies.
- *Analytic systems thinking:* High form of creativity, complex analysis of input requiring formal logic and metaphor.
- *Holos:* Social sense, rational and emotional; the foundation of altruism.

From these perspectives we end up with four somewhat different brains in one: the smallest and oldest—the brain stem; surrounded by the larger, newer brain—the limbic system; the largest brain—the cerebrum or neocortex; and the newest, most sophisticated structure—the prefrontal cortex. Under stress the cerebrum begins shutting down, turning over more and more functions to the lower, limbic system brain. While rote learning can be continued, higher and more complex learning is inhibited (Hart, 1981). Creating opportunities for the effective operation of this total brain is our responsibility as educators and parents.

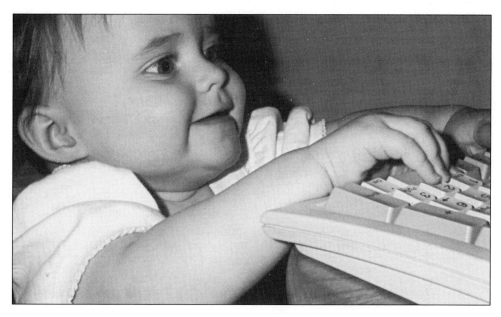

Environmental interaction with the genetic program of the individual occurs whether it is planned or left to occur by chance.

The Gifted Brain: Implications of Brain Research for Educators

There are exciting clues in brain research that can help educators at home and at school optimize learning experiences for the youngsters with whom they work. We know, for example, that the process of learning can be enhanced by increasing the strength and the speed of transmission of impulses from one brain cell to another. Through changes in teaching and learning procedures, the speed and complexity of these transmissions can be increased. These are measurable differences that show advanced and accelerated development. By the environment we provide, we change not just the behavior of children; we change them at the cellular level. In an interesting longitudinal study, Gottfried, Gottfried, Bathurst, and Guerin (1994) documented that heightened cognitive stimulation is a widespread finding among gifted children. They received more stimulation from their environment from the first year of life. As a result, they showed differences in the rate of development and in the level of performance as they grew. Frequently, early development of expressive language was observed. From these data, Morelock (1996) concluded, "Consequently, it follows that there are important differences in information processing characteristics of the young gifted brain" (p.9) In this way, gifted children become biologically different from average learners, not at birth but as a result of using and developing the wondrous, complex structure with which they were born. At birth nearly everyone is programmed to be phenomenal. Figures 2.5 and 2.6 show how the effects of environmental stimulation strengthen the brain at the cellular level, leading to enhanced ability to learn and create. Figure 2.7 summarizes what we now know about the changes we can create in the brain, the results of those changes, and what we need to do to use brain function to optimize learning.

A Summary of Brain Research for Educators

The following summary of ideas from brain research will help educators get a better idea of how changes might occur in the classroom and the impact of these changes on the learner.

The Environment

- Development of intelligence depends on the interaction between biological inheritance and environmental opportunities to use this inheritance.

- Attention and concentration rely on the impact of the environment on the brain.

- Brain development is enhanced by an environment that is stimulating and includes appropriate challenges that encourage curiosity and exploration.

- Stress produces biochemistry from the adrenal cortex that dampens cerebral cortical function. Fear, threat, anxiety, and tension make it very difficult to learn.

- The brain responds to novelty, to the unexpected, and to discrepant information. Novelty registers information independent of rewards or punishment, and such processing is more effective for learning. When asked to repeat, drill, or do reinforced repetitive activities, the brain habituates, that is, responds automatically without thought, and such practices may be counterproductive to learning

Figure 2.5 *Changes in the Cell Structure of the Brain of a Gifted Learner*

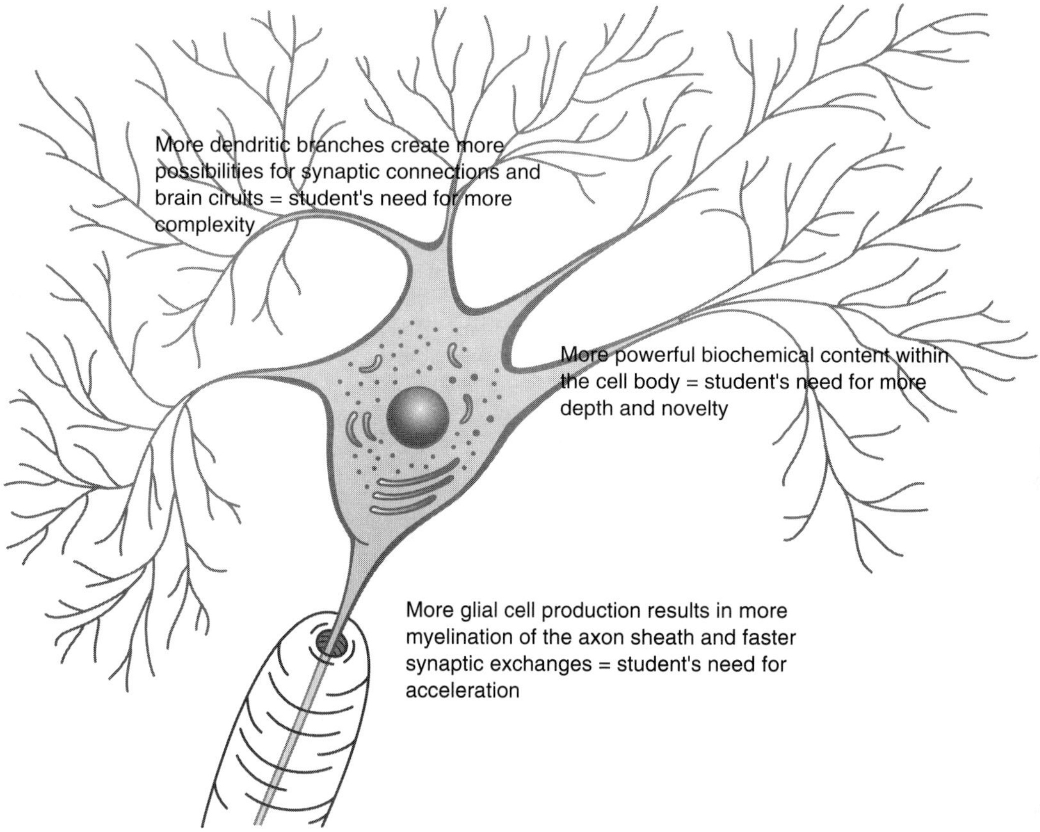

More dendritic branches create more possibilities for synaptic connections and brain ciruits = student's need for more complexity

More powerful biochemical content within the cell body = student's need for more depth and novelty

More glial cell production results in more myelination of the axon sheath and faster synaptic exchanges = student's need for acceleration

concepts. The research shows that doing something new and different is the way to gain information most effectively.

The Instruction

- The potential of brain development is essentially unlimited for most individuals.

- The dynamic nature of the brain allows intellectual growth to progress or regress, not to remain static.

- How intelligence is expressed will depend on the individual genetic pattern and anatomical structure in interaction with the support and opportunities provided by the environment.

- Individualized instructional planning is strongly indicated because each person responds uniquely to the environment.

- The use of single goals or objectives does not allow for developing patterns and relationships; bright minds require complexity.

Figure 2.6 *Biological Effects on Learning and Creating*

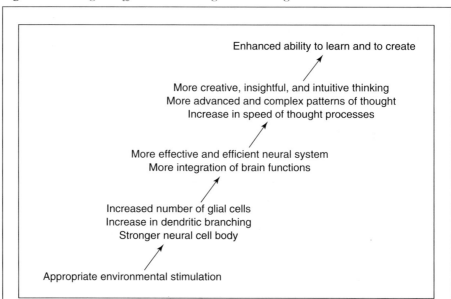

- The brain does not just process information or amplify thought, it constructs meaning. Didactic teaching is no longer justifiable; instead, teachers must create problems to solve.

- The brain attaches emotional significance to information; good learning derives from exciting teaching. Emotional responses are often more important in making cognitive decisions than are our rational processes.

- Optimal development requires the active involvement of the learner. When the learner is not actively involved, the right hemisphere generates thought not related to the external input so that the stimulation level of the learner is continuously maintained.

- Concrete experiences and active sensory stimulation are needed at both elementary and secondary levels. Written material (texts and workbooks) alone is not appropriate to teach abstract concepts.

- The processes and content of both specializations of the right and left hemispheres of the cortex need to be included in curriculum planning to take advantage of their complementary nature.

- Opportunities must be given for alternative modes of learning and expression so that the whole cortex is used for support and integration, preventing the limits to knowledge and understanding brought about by teaching each discipline as a separate specialization.

- The brain is a model builder generating models of reality. Students' minds do not just record what is taught; the brain makes inferences.

Figure 2.7 *What We Know About the Brain*

> **Stress and tension prevent good flow through in the corpus callosum and creates biochemistry in the limbic area that turns off brain cells.**
>
> **Results:**
>
> - Difficulty learning abstract and higher level concepts
> - Limited ability to integrate both hemisphere processes
> - Retention is limited
>
> **What we need to do:**
>
> - Reduce stress, anxiety, tension, fear.
> - Teach strategies for tension reduction.
> - Create an environment that is positive, productive, and encourages uniqueness and diversity of thought.
>
> **The amount of dendritic branching increases with stimulation resulting in the potential for interconnections between neurons to increase and raise the complexity of thought.**
>
> **Results:**
>
> - Unusual capacity for processing information
> - Flexible thought processes
> - Ability to synthesize comprehensively
> - Heightened capacity for seeing unusual and diverse relationships and overall gestalts.
> - Ability to generate original ideas and solutions
> - Early ability to use and form conceptual frameworks
>
> **What we need to do:**
>
> - Use all brain functions in the learning process.
> - Present a large variety of ideas at many levels, a wide range of disciplines and eras.
> - Provide instruction in the skills and structures needed for independent research.
> - Use integrated curriculum with themes and interdisciplinary content focused on relationships and connections.
> - Present learning from a variety of perspectives.
> - Encourage original applications of knowledge and understandings, including hypothesizing and predicting.
>
> **As glial cell production increases, the cell is better nourished and supported.**
>
> **Results:**
>
> - Unusually varied interests
> - Heightened self-awareness accompanied by feelings of uniqueness or difference
> - Early development of an inner locus of control and satisfaction
>
> **What we need to do:**
>
> - Create a safe learning environment, rich and varied in stimulation.
> - Provide choice throughout the curriculum and encourage products that challenge existing ideas, produce new ideas, and use a variety of techniques, materials, and forms.
> - Encourage self-initiated exploring, observing, questioning, feeling, translating, inferring, and predicting.

Figure 2.7 *continued*

- Study problems as opportunities for and encourage novel solutions.
- Value the unusual and divergent and approach areas of study in personalized, individualistic, and nontraditional ways.
- Provide inquiry and exploration into disparate and incongruent patterns of experience that lead to new, original, and reorganized knowledge.
- Encourage original interpretations or restatements of existing information, risk taking, collaboration, and multiple solutions.

The myelination of the axon is increased and the flow of energy within and between cells becomes stronger and more frequent.

Results:

- Early development of an unusual degree of curiosity
- Early ability to delay closure
- Early ability to think in different patterns, in alternatives, and in abstract terms
- Advanced cognitive and affective capacity for conceptualizing and solving societal problems
- Early ability to sense consequences, make generalizations, and visualize solutions

What we need to do:

- Provide a range of materials, including levels of difficulty and complexity, in a variety of disciplines.
- Arrange for mentors, using specialized skills and knowledge from community members.
- Compare past, present, and future events related to the study topic
- Instruct from the concrete to abstract, familiar to unfamiliar, known to unknown
- Examine topics by determining facts, concepts, generalizations, principles, and theories related to them.
- Teach the terms/language of a variety of disciplines
- Use dissonant events to solve problems

As the number of synapses and the size of the synaptic contacts increase, communication within the system becomes faster paced and more complex.

Results:

- Accelerated pace of thought and learning
- Advanced comprehension
- High level of language development and verbal ability
- Extraordinary quantity of information and unusual retentiveness.
- High level of visual and spatial ability

What we need to do:

- Assess the student's level of knowledge and skill and document content that has already been learned; teach what is not known.
- Make it possible to accomplish a range of learning in a shorter span of time by use of learning packages, peer tutoring, centers, and folders.
- Provide a wide range of levels of materials and resources.
- Provide self-paced instruction with the use of mentors or tutors, individual contracts, and/or independent study.
- Use flexible grouping based on needs and interests.

Figure 2.7 *continued*

The reticular formation, limbic system, and thalamus actively select stimuli and respond positively to novelty, to the unexpected, and to discrepant information.

Results:

- Attention and concentration rely on the impact the environment has on the brain.
- Repetition of activities creates automatic responses without thought, boredom turns the thought processes off in the cortex.

What we need to do:

- Develop a responsive learning environment that has multiple levels of materials, allows flexibility, and encourages self-direction.
- Use novelty, surprise, and dissonant events in learning experiences.
- Reduce drill and repetitive activities especially when teaching complex and abstract thought processes.

As the brain becomes more effective and more efficient, more use is made of the activity of the prefrontal cortex of the brain.

Results:

- More future planning
- Higher degree of insightful thinking
- Increased use of intuitive experiences
- An increased level of creativity is used

What we need to do:

- Model the valuing and use of intuition.
- Provide experiences in which the child can demonstrate evidence of intuitive processing.
- Use imagery, fantasy, and visualization to support the learning experience.
- Use "what if" and open-ended, future thinking strategies.
- Encourage the use of creative thinking.

The brain organizes using patterns and integrates all areas of brain function for optimal efficiency and retention.

Results:

Students taught using the integration of brain functions:
- Are more creative, try more unusual solutions, and engage in more alternative and higher level cognitive activities.
- Initiate more learning activities.
- Are more positive and enthusiastic about their learning and more highly motivated.
- Are more independent and responsible.
- Understand more deeply and retain information and concepts more effectively.

What we need to do:

- Use learning strategies that include use of all senses and integrates all areas of brain function, including the physical, the emotional/social, the intuitive, and the cognitive, both the linear and the spatial modes.

For Further Reading

Some books that provide ideas from brain research that are important for understanding the growth of intelligence and giftedness and for developing optimal learning environments and strategies include: Caine and Caine (1991, 1997), Clark (1986), Conlan (1993), Crick (1994), Diamond (1988), Diamond and Hopson (1998), Gazzaniga (1992), Gibson and Peterson (1991), Hart (1975, 1978, 1981), Howard (1994), Jensen (1998), Kandel and Schwartz (1991), Krashen (1975), Levy and Reid (1975), Ornstein (1991), Pribram (1977), Restak (1979, 1985, 1986, 1991, 1994, 2000), Sagan (1977), Samples (1976), Schiebel (1993), Siegel (1999), Sylwester, (1995), Sylwester and Cho (1993), Thompson (1993), Trefil (1997), Wills (1993), and Wittrock (1993).

CHARACTERISTICS OF GIFTED LEARNERS

As human beings develop higher levels of functioning, many unique patterns and traits emerge. For this reason educating groups of gifted individuals is not easy. They are not a homogeneous group. The more gifted a person becomes, the more unique that person may appear. Many characteristics, however, often recur in groups of gifted individuals.

Although many characteristics typical of highly gifted learners are also found among the moderately gifted, such characteristics exist in the former with a higher degree of intensity and energy. The desire to know and the capacity to create structure and organize data are noticeably greater and more efficient in the highly gifted population. However, an overly demanding view of self may result in even more difficulty developing a realistic self-concept and may lead to an unreasonably low self-esteem (Powell & Haden, 1987). Even more so than with other children, we must rely on highly gifted children to guide our parenting and teaching to approaches appropriate for them. Their unique needs leave us with no norms to follow.

As we look more closely at the characteristics and needs of gifted learners, we encounter a common problem in identifying these children. Teachers often attribute a high achiever with giftedness. Although there can be no certainty as to clear distinction in every instance, gifted children usually exhibit the ability to generalize, to work comfortably with abstract ideas, and to synthesize diverse relationships to a far higher degree. The high achiever generally functions better with knowledge and comprehension-level learning. Although high achievers get good grades and accomplish much, they lack the range and diversity of gifted students. Some need only increased opportunity; others become frustrated by more complex opportunities. A responsive learning environment is the teacher's best guide.

Gifted learners show characteristics that are different from their age peers' in each of the areas of function, although all gifted individuals have their own unique patterns of characteristics and no gifted learner exhibits every characteristic in every area. Knowing the possible range of behaviors, and the concomitant problems that result will help parents and teachers better understand and nurture these gifted individuals. Tables 2.1 to 2.4 are organized into cognitive (linear and spatial, Table 2.1), affective (emotional and social, Table 2.2), physical (movement and sensation, Table 2.3), and intuitive (Table 2.4) functions, closely approximating the functions available in the human brain. With each characteristic, there is a delineation of possible concomitant problems. This format is an extension of the work of Seagoe (1974) and incorporates her suggestions.

Table 2.1 *Giftedness Expressed by Cognitive Function*

Cognitive development rests on the understanding and integration of a vast quantity of experiences of the environment. Educational programs should provide for an array of such experiences and encourage the processes of analyzing, organizing, and evaluating, as well as those processes of a more visual, rhythmic, and holistic nature that seem to coexist within our cognitive functioning. Differentiation for gifted learners requires assessment of and planning for each child's unique characteristics, some of which may be found below.

Differentiating Characteristics	Examples of Related Needs	Possible Concomitant Problems
Extraordinary quantity of information, unusual retentiveness	To be exposed to new and challenging information of the environment and the culture, including aesthetic, economic, political, educational, and social aspects; to acquire early mastery of foundation skills	Boredom with regular curriculum; impatience with "waiting for the group"
Advanced comprehension	To be given access to challenging curriculum and intellectual peers	Poor interpersonal relationships with less able children of the same age; adults consider a gifted child "sassy" or a "smart aleck"; a dislike of repetition of already understood concepts
Unusually varied interests and curiosity	To be exposed to varied subjects and concerns; to be allowed to pursue individual ideas as far as interest takes them	Difficulty in conforming to group tasks; overextending energy levels, taking on too many projects at one time
High level of language development High level of verbal ability	To encounter uses for increasingly difficult vocabulary and concepts To share ideas verbally in depth	Perception as a "show off" by children of the same age Domination of discussions with information and questions deemed negative by teachers and fellow students; use of verbalism to avoid difficult thinking tasks
Unusual capacity for processing information	To be exposed to ideas at many levels and in large variety	Resentment of being interrupted; perceived as too serious; dislike of routine and drill
Accelerated pace of thought processes	To be exposed to ideas at rates appropriate to individual pace of learning—often accelerated	Frustration with inactivity and absence of progress
Flexible thought processes	To be allowed to solve problems in diverse ways	Perception by others as disruptive and disrespectful to authority and tradition
Comprehensive synthesis	To be allowed a longer incubation time for ideas	Frustration with demands for deadlines and for completion of each level prior to starting new inquiry

Table 2.1 *continued*

Differentiating Characteristics	Examples of Related Needs	Possible Concomitant Problems
Early ability to delay closure	To be allowed to pursue ideas and integrate new ideas without forced closure or products demanded	If products are demanded as proof of learning, will refuse to pursue an otherwise interesting subject or line of inquiry
Heightened capacity for seeing unusual and diverse relationships, integration of ideas and disciplines	To mess around with varieties of materials, ideas, opportunities for multidisciplinary learning; complexity	Frustration at being considered "off the subject" or irrelevant in pursuing inquiry in areas other than subject being considered; considered odd or weird by others
Ability to generate original ideas and solutions	To build skills in problem solving and productive thinking; to be given the opportunity to contribute to solutions of meaningful problems	Difficulty with rigid conformity; may be penalized for not following directions; may deal with rejection by becoming rebellious
Early differential patterns for thought processing (e.g., thinking in alternatives, abstract terms; sensing consequences; making generalizations; visual thinking; use of metaphors and analogies)	To be exposed to alternatives, abstractions, consequences of choices, opportunities for drawing generalizations and testing them; to solve problems by use of visual or metaphoric strategies	Rejection or omission of detail; questions generalizations of others, which may be perceived as disrespectful behavior; considers linear tasks incomplete and boring
Early ability to use and form conceptual frameworks	To use and design conceptual frameworks in information gathering and problem solving; to seek order and consistency; to develop a tolerance for ambiguity	Frustration with inability of others to understand or appreciate original organizations or insights; personally devised systems or structure may conflict with procedures or systems later taught
An evaluative approach toward self and others	To be exposed to individuals of varying ability and talent and to varying ways of seeing and solving problems; to set realistic, achievable short-term goals; to develop skills in data evaluation and decision making	Perception by others as elitist, conceited, superior, too critical; may become discouraged from self-criticism; can inhibit attempting new areas if fear of failure is too great; seen as too demanding, compulsive; can affect inter-personal relationships as others fail to live up to standards set by gifted individual; intolerant of stupidity
Unusual intensity; , persistent goal-directed behavior	To pursue inquiries beyond allotted time spans; to set and evaluate priorities	Perception by others as stubborn, willful, uncooperative

Table 2.2 *Giftedness Expressed by Affective Function*

High levels of cognitive development do not necessarily imply high levels of affective development. The same heightened sensitivities that underlie gifted intelligence can contribute to an accumulation of information about emotions that the student needs to process. The affect-based information comes from sources within and outside of the child. Gifted children need to learn that their cognitive powers applied to this material will help them to make sense of their world. Their educational program must provide opportunities to bring emotional knowledge and assumptions to awareness, and to apply verbal ability and inquiry skills in the service of affective development.

      The early appearance of social conscience that often characterizes gifted children signals an earlier need for development of a value structure and for the opportunity to translate values into social action. This can occur in the context of the society of the classroom and should then be extended into the larger world, as appropriate to the child's increasing competence and widening concerns.

Differentiating Characteristics	Examples of Related Needs	Possible Concomitant Problems
Large accumulation of information about emotions that has not been brought to awareness	To process cognitively the emotional meaning of experience; to name one's own emotions; to identify one's own and others' perceptual filters and defense systems; to expand and clarify awareness of the physical environment; to clarify awareness of the needs and feelings of others	Misinterpretation of information, affecting the individual negatively
Unusual sensitivity to the expectations and feelings of others	To learn to clarify the feelings and expectations of others	Unusual vulnerability to criticism of others; high level of need for success and recognition
Keen sense of humor—may be gentle or hostile	To learn how behaviors affect the feelings and behaviors of others	Use of humor for critical attacks upon others, resulting in damage to interpersonal relationships
Heightened self-awareness, accompanied by feelings of being different	To learn to assert own needs and feelings nondefensively; to share self with others, for self-clarification	Isolation of self, resulting in being considered aloof, feeling rejected; perceives difference as a negative attribute resulting in low self-esteem and inhibited growth emotionally and socially
Idealism and sense of justice, which appear at an early age	To transcend negative reactions by finding values to which he or she can be committed	Attempts toward unrealistic reforms and goals with resulting intense frustration (suicides result from intense depression over issues of this nature)
Earlier development of an inner locus of control and satisfaction	To clarify personal priorities among conflicting values; to confront and interact with the value systems of others	Difficulty with conformity; rejects external validation and chooses to live by personal values that may be seen as a challenge to authority or tradition
Unusual emotional depth and intensity	To find purpose and direction from personal value system; to translate commitment into action in daily life	Unusual vulnerability; difficulty focusing on realistic goals for life's work

Table 2.2 *continued*

Differentiating Characteristics	Examples of Related Needs	Possible Concomitant Problems
High expectations of self and others, often leading to high levels of frustration with self, others, and situations; perfectionism	To learn to set realistic goals and to accept setbacks as part of the learning process; to hear others express their growth in acceptance of self	Discouragement and frustration from high levels of self-criticism; difficulty maintaining good interpersonal relations as others fail to maintain high standards imposed by gifted child; immobilization of action due to high levels of frustration resulting from situations that do not meet expectations of excellence
Strong need for consistency between abstract values and personal actions	To find a vocation that provides opportunity for actualization of student's personal value system, as well as an avenue for his or her talents and abilities	Frustration with self and others leading to inhibited actualization of self and interpersonal relationships
Advanced levels of moral judgment	To receive validation for nonaverage morality	Intolerance of and lack of understanding from peer group, leading to rejection and possible isolation

Society has unique needs for the services of exceptional individuals. While we would not wish that education for the gifted focus on societal needs at the expense of the needs of these individuals, neither can education of the gifted disregard the importance of their mature social roles. Gifted students need direction in exploring all of the opportunities society has to offer them and the ways of contributing what they have to offer to society. They need conceptual frameworks to organize their experience of society (e.g., Maslow's [1968] hierarchy of needs), and they need opportunities to develop those skills that will make it possible for them to affect society. Educational programs should provide for the options, conceptual frameworks, and skills that will underlie effective social involvement of gifted students.

Differentiating Characteristics	Examples of Related Needs	Possible Concomitant Problems
Strongly motivated by self-actualization needs	To be given opportunities to follow divergent paths and pursue strong interests; to receive help in understanding the demands of self-actualization	Frustration of not feeling challenged; loss of unrealized talents
Advanced cognitive and affective capacity for conceptualizing and solving societal problems	To encounter social problems; to become aware of the complexity of problems facing society and the conceptual frameworks for problem-solving procedures	Tendency for "quick" solutions, not taking into account the complexity of the problem; young age of gifted child often makes usable alternatives suspect; older, more experienced decision makers may not take the gifted child seriously
Leadership ability	To understand various leadership steps and practice leadership skills	Lack of opportunity to use this ability constructively may result in its disappearance from child's repertoire or its being turned into a negative characteristic (e.g., gang leadership)
Solutions to social and environmental problems	To experience meaningful involvement in real problems	Loss to society if these traits are not allowed to develop with guidance and opportunity for meaningful involvement
Involvement with the metaneeds of society (e.g., justice, beauty, truth)	To explore the highest levels of human thought; to apply this knowledge to today's problems	Involvement in obscure groups with narrow, perfectionistic beliefs

Table 2.3 *Giftedness Expressed by Physical/Sensing Function*

People of highly developed intellectual ability may be unusually vulnerable to a characteristic "Cartesian split" between thinking and being: a lack of integration between mind and body. During school years, when the gifted student is experiencing large discrepancies between physical and intellectual development, the school may be unintentionally encouraging the student to avoid physical activity. If a child's intellectual peers are physically more advanced so as to make him or her feel physically inadequate, while physical peers are less intellectually stimulating and not within his or her friendship group, the usual competitive playground games may be neither inviting nor satisfying to the gifted child. If the physical development of the gifted child is to be encouraged, programs should provide experiences that develop integration between mind and body in children with nonnormative development patterns.

Differentiating Characteristics	Examples of Related Needs	Possible Concomitant Problems
Unusual quantity of input from the environment through a heightened sensory awareness	To engage in activities that will allow integration and assimilation of sensory data	Attention moving diffusely toward many areas of interest; over expenditure of energy due to lack of integration; seeming disconnectedness
Unusual discrepancy between physical and intellectual development	To appreciate own physical capacities	Results in a gifted adult who functions with a mind-body dichotomy; a gifted child who is only comfortable expressing himself or herself in mental activity, resulting in limited development both physically and mentally
Low tolerance for the lag between standards and athletic skills	To discover physical activities as a source of pleasure; to find satisfaction in small increments of improvement; to engage in non-competitive physical activities	Refusal to take part in any activities in which he or she does not excel; limiting experiences with otherwise pleasurable, constructive physical activities
"Cartesian split"—can include neglect of physical well-being and avoidance of physical activity	To engage in activities leading to mind-body integration; to develop a commitment to own physical well-being; to extend this concern to the social and political realm	Detrimental to full mental and physical health; inhibiting the development of potential for the individual

Table 2.4 *Giftedness Expressed by Intuitive Function*

This area of the human experience is involved in initiating or insightful acts and in creative activity. While this is the least well-defined area of human endeavor, it is probably the area that promises the most for the continuance and fulfillment of humankind. All other areas provide support for and are supported by this area of function. As each area evolves to high levels, more of the intuitive and creative are available.

Differentiating Characteristics	Examples of Related Needs	Possible Concomitant Problems
Early involvement and concern for intuitive knowing and metaphysical ideas and phenomena	To be given opportunities to engage in meaningful dialogue with philosophers and others concerned with these ideas, to become aware of own intuitive energy and ability; to be guided in developing and using intuitive energy and ability	Ridicule from peers; not taken seriously by elders; considered weird or strange
Open to experiences in this area; will experiment with psychic and metaphysical phenomena	To be given guidance in becoming familiar with, analyzing, and evaluating such phenomena; to be provided a historical approach	Tendency to become narrowly focused toward ungrounded belief systems
Creative approach in all areas of endeavor	To be guided in evaluating appropriate uses of creative efforts; to be encouraged to continue development of creative abilities	Perception by others as deviant; becomes bored with more mundane tasks; may be viewed as troublemaker
Ability to predict; interest in future	To be provided opportunities for exploration of "what if" questions and activities of probability and prediction	Loss of highly valuable human ability

Curiosity is an early characteristic of giftedness

HIGHLY AND EXCEPTIONALLY GIFTED INDIVIDUALS

The 3-year-old jumped off the chair onto the carpeted floor of the university classroom and stopped, wide-eyed. "Did you hear that?" he exclaimed.

"Hear what?" I asked.

"That sound," he said climbing back onto the chair. "Now listen," he demanded and proceeded to jump again to the floor.

Listening carefully, I could hear the gurgling from his stomach as he hit the floor.

"Did you hear it?" I nodded. "What *is* that?" he exclaimed excitedly.

"It's the milk you just drank," I informed him.

"Oh, wow, isn't that something?" he replied delightedly as he sat down on the floor, picked up a storybook, and began to read to my university students. This was the first time Nathaniel had been to my class of teachers of gifted learners. He was there to give them the experience of interacting with a highly gifted child. Confident and careful to be sure his audience could see all the pictures, our guest teacher obviously was enjoying himself immensely.

Having defined intelligence, giftedness, and talent development, let us now distinguish between the typical or moderately gifted (the most commonly found gifted persons), and those with unusual levels of giftedness (sometimes labeled as highly gifted individuals), and between them and the exceptionally or profoundly gifted individuals (those of rare genius). Most of our discussion in this text will relate to the moderately gifted, for highly gifted persons are as different from these individuals as the moderately gifted are from average learners. The highly gifted tend to evidence more energy than gifted individuals; they think faster and are more intent and focused on their interests and they exhibit a higher degree of ability in most of the traits we have identified with giftedness. Such children are less able to benefit from regular classroom experiences, and modifications to their educational programs need to be more comprehensive and developed to a much higher degree to meet their needs than is necessary for less gifted learners.

The exceptionally gifted learners, those who Scheibel (cited in Begley, 1993) suggests have differently wired neurons that allow more complex and efficient neural highways for transmitting information, differ even from the highly gifted learners. They seem to have different value structures, which usually allow them to cope with the dissonance they find between their perception of life and that of the average person. They tend to be more isolated by choice and more invested in concerns of a meta-nature (eg, universal problems). They seldom seek popularity or social acclaim. Typically, schools offer these students little; some educators suggest that tutoring with eminent authorities or homeschooling would be a far more productive educational plan. For further insight into highly gifted and exceptionally gifted learners, the reader may wish to consult Hollingworth (1942), Feldman and Goldsmith (1986), and the more recent work of Silverman (1990).

A continuing pressing issue is the provision of an appropriate education for highly and exceptionally gifted students. The higher the expressed intellectual ability, the more difficult will be the problem of finding a match between the school programs and the child. Or, as the Columbus Group explains, "The higher the intellectual capacity, the greater is the degree of asynchrony requiring special consideration of exceptional needs in parenting, schooling, and counseling" (Lovecky, 1994, p. 116). Although many school settings give limited priority to differentiating learning experiences for gifted students in general, even less priority is given to the highly and exceptionally gifted student. In an article decrying the dearth of true genius in our world, Begley (1993) suggests that "everywhere, as long as egalitarianism rejects the mystique of genius in favor of the notion that everyone has it in him to be an artist, there will be no successors to Picasso or Mies van der Rohe" (p. 50).

For purposes of discussion we will consider the highly gifted child to be performing two standard deviations above the average child and the exceptionally gifted child to be two standard deviations beyond the highly gifted learner. Although such a psychometric definition tells us little about the children and how they learn, it suggests that just as with the children at the opposite end of the normal curve, their learning needs will be different. Koppel (1991) explains it this way, "Think of it as the difference between a so-called precocious second grader who reads at fourth-grade level and the second grader, reading since age two, who now curls up with *The Unbearable Lightness of Being*" (p. 57).

Another area of advanced development is in the area of mobility, which may begin early and progress with unusual speed (Gross, 1999). The result, combined with the early and rapid development of speech, is that reading is likely to begin and these highly gifted children move around independently exploring their world, expressing their ideas, seeking information, and interacting fluently and meaningfully with parents, others, and their environment. Such interactions result in even more advanced and rapid intellectual growth. It has been observed that moderately gifted children waste nearly half of their time in a regular classroom and exceptionally gifted children waste almost all of their time (Hollingworth, 1942). These are the children about whom we know the least, yet they are those whose needs are most severe.

Some attention has been given to child prodigies as examples of "extreme giftedness" (Feldman, 1979, 1990; Feldman & Goldsmith, 1986; Goldsmith, 1990). These researchers define a prodigy as a child who is performing at the level of an adult professional in a cognitively demanding field before the age of 10. They suggest that the development of the prodigy's ability requires expert instruction, emotional support, strict personal discipline, and a sustained commitment to study and practice over a considerable period of time. Goldsmith (1990) finds that sustaining high levels of ability may be harder for a gifted girl because once her arena extends beyond the facilitating family, the social censure may be so strong that she neglects or even denies her giftedness. For both boys and girls, the cultural milieu seems to exert a strong influence on the actualization of high ability through the family's values, educational opportunities, and media attention.

The prodigies themselves seem to contribute to this high-level development by their persistence, passion, and commitment to their fields far in excess of what is observed in most of their age-mates (Goldsmith, 1990). "The more we understand about the processes of development and the forms in which talent may be expressed, the more able we will be to foster individual expression at every age" (p. 82).

Highly and exceptionally gifted individuals seem to be characterized by their uniqueness; each is different from others their age and from others who are highly and exceptionally gifted (McGuffog, Feiring, & Lewis, 1990). There are, however, some characteristics that seem to be common among such children. These include both marvelous traits that provide joy and fulfillment to the individuals and those that result in deep frustration and despair as they confront structures that have no space for them and attitudes that have no understanding. Figure 2.8 shares some of these characteristics found again and again in this population.

Figure 2.8 *Common Characteristics of Highly and Exceptionally Gifted Individuals*
Sources: Dahlberg, 1992; Gross, 1993; Koppel, 1991; Lovecky, 1994; Sheely & Silverman, 2000.

An extraordinary speed in processing information

A rapid and thorough comprehension of the whole idea or concept

An unusual ability to perceive essential elements and underlying structures and patterns in relationships and ideas

A need for precision in thinking and expression, resulting in need to correct errors and argue extensively

An ability to relate a broad range of ideas and synthesize commonalities among them

A high degree of ability to think abstractly that develops early

Appreciation of complexity; finding myriad alternative meanings in even the most simple issues or problems

An ability to learn in an integrative, intuitively nonlinear manner

An extraordinary degree of intellectual curiosity

An unusual capacity for memory

A long concentration span

A fascination with ideas and words

An extensive vocabulary

An ability to perceive many sides of an issue

Argumentativeness

Advanced visual and motor skills

An ability from an early age to think in metaphors and symbols and a preference for doing so

An ability to visualize models and systems

An ability to learn in great intuitive leaps

Highly idiosyncratic interpretations of events

An awareness of detail

An unusual intensity and depth of feeling

A high degree of emotional sensitivity

Highly developed morals and ethics and early concern for moral and existential issues

Unusual and early insight into social and moral issues

An ability to empathetically understand and relate to ideas and other people

An extraordinarily high energy level

A need for the world to be logical and fair

A conviction of correctness of personal ideas and beliefs

Among the learning patterns that have been shared by those in this population is one that may explain, in part, the very special nature of the learning differences (Silberstein, 1995). In explaining how his mind worked, a young adult commented:

> I seem to be much more aware than the people around me of the relationship between one event and another. Things and events have meaning and causes that to me are obvious, but other people have to work to understand. So I am always aware of relationships between events, the meaning behind events, and of the logic behind things. For me it is just present in the world; it is how my mind works. This is how I perceive and act in the world; I am not doing something when that happens. (Silberstein, 1995)

In another observation he stated, "I work a problem from the inside out. . . . I see failure as a thing you don't learn from. . . . A mistake is learning that hasn't taken place yet. Essentially what I am saying is that you can learn from anything, and if you learn it's not a failure." When asked to describe how he thinks differently, he commented, "I think what I do is think fast, and fast can give you quality. The qualitative differences are that my mind tries lots of things, and therefore can come up with a solution because I can work through lots of different answers. . . . So mere quantitative differences can lead to qualitative differences."

While discussing intuition, a most interesting pattern of thinking emerged:

> I think intuition is lots and lots of processing underneath, then it finds something close to the answer and brings it up. . . . You look for things that are shaped like the answer until you find it. I am very geometric in my thinking. To me, things are shapes even if they are ideas or arguments. To me a chain of reasoning is almost a shape. What I frequently do is look for things that are shaped the same on some concept. Therefore, while this thing about cells has a similar shape to this thing from mythology, for example, maybe there is a similarity in the argument. And then, now, let's bring them up consciously and look and see. What I'm saying is about metaphors. For me metaphors are very powerful. They are a powerful tool. I map ideas and sentences and thoughts so that I can see them and physically manipulate them. So if I have a problem, it takes on a shape, and I think "Okay, what else looks like this?" Or if I am missing information, I think, "Okay, I need some information that looks like that." (Silberstein, 1995)

After discussing his dissatisfaction with his school experiences and the boredom and damage he felt he had sustained there, he summed up his need with this statement: "Being really intelligent absolutely defines who I am. I perceive the world quite differently from most people. It is the essence of why I am who I am and not someone else."

The abilities of highly and exceptionally gifted children bring acclaim and awe from adults and age-peers alike; however, these children may find that with these abilities there are few educational settings into which they can fit comfortably and even fewer in which they can be challenged or even allowed to grow. In addition, Silverman (1995) suggests that such a high degree of asynchronous development can result in many emotional problems. The goal, as with all children, is to build a healthy, balanced life, but when these children's intellectual grasp exceeds their emotional capacity to cope with some ideas and events, frustration and depression may result. The fact of the matter is, by their very excellence, they make it hard to find others with whom to share and places in which they can belong. This is a special problem for girls. Koppel (1991) informs us that more than 50% of the gifted students in kindergarten are girls, but by junior high less than 30% are. The unpopularity of being so different, the mixed messages of fitting in yet living up to their potential, and the need to find friends "like them" take their toll. It is very clear that even in schools that have made adaptations in the curriculum and have devoted resources to gifted programs, such programs are not designed for highly and exceptionally gifted students. Modifications made for moderately gifted students do not meet the needs of these even more underserved gifted children.

Another concern is the problem of testing (Silverman, 1990). Intelligence tests are normed with the assumption that there exists a normal curve of intelligence within the population at large. Silverman believes that this assumption penalizes highly gifted children, whose scores are systematically depressed at the upper end of the curve to force-fit them to the theoretical normal distribution. Each time the tests are renormed the problem becomes worse. The ceiling effect of tests also causes reason for concern. Most tests do not have items of sufficient difficulty to fully assess the extent and strength of the abilities of highly gifted children.

Group tests present additional problems by being so easy that highly gifted children read more into the items than was intended by the test constructor. For example, a child being tested was asked, "Who discovered America?" The child thought a while and then replied, "Well some people think that it was Christopher Columbus, but I think it might have been a Viking like Leif Ericsson or maybe even . . .," and the child went on to relate a number of possible discoverers he found plausible. After presenting rationales for each of the possible candidates, the child stopped and looked puzzled. The question was repeated, "Who discovered America?" More thought and then the child decided, "I guess I'd have to say in all probability it was . . ." (an obscure explorer not often mentioned relative to the question asked). The answer was marked wrong. The "right" answer was Christopher Columbus. No credit could be given for the brilliant deductions of the child or his vast quantity of information.

Silverman (2000) believes that the best method of assessing highly gifted children is with the Stanford-Binet Intelligence Scale (Form L-M), an older form that has a higher ceiling than newer tests. The Wechsler tests, such as the WPPSI-R and the WISC-III, only go up to a score of 160, whereas the Stanford-Binet Fourth Edition only goes up to 164. She states,

> It is important to know the extent of a child's giftedness, just as it is imperative to know the extent of a child's retardation. A child with an IQ of 175 has unique needs beyond those of a child with an IQ of 145, just as a child with an IQ of 25 is significantly different from a child with an IQ of 55. A two standard deviation difference affects the child's adjustment, learning needs, and school placement. It is time we found out just how gifted our highly gifted children really are. (Silverman, 1990, p. 2)

Once identified, some of the services that have been found to provide for the needs of this unique population are special self-contained classes, special schools or programs, university-based programs, magnet schools, Governor's Schools, International Baccalaureate Programs, and special study centers. Whatever services are offered, these students must have access to acceleration, programs offering continuous progress, flexible pacing, creative and innovative methods and products, independent study, mentors, and counseling.

A high school program that has been reported as very successful in meeting the needs of the highly gifted students has a number of support systems that make such support possible. In the report (Strop, 2000), note was taken of the fact that the school was founded with the philosophy of supporting students to become their best and achieve excellence in their chosen career paths. To support these goals, a developmental counseling approach was designed to assist students with postgraduate planning that begins for each student as they enter the school. Each year another phase of the program of individualized counseling, consultation, and support groups is introduced. The other attributes of the program that are credited for its success are: the level of the principal's awareness, systematic and meaningful development of counselors and teachers, academic and affective support and flexibility that includes telescoped classes, dual credits, study groups, and mentorships. Strop comments that there is a schoolwide commitment to achievement and a celebration of flexibility. Few public high schools have been acknowledged for a program that comprehensively meets the needs of their highly gifted students as is Cherry Creek High School in Englewood, Colorado. As one highly gifted student explained, "Moving from middle school to high school was like jumping from a slow moving Chevy to a high speed Farrari. The objective was to not lose my balance" (p. 20).

As we have seen, intelligence is dynamic. As relevant as the axiom "Use it or lose it" is when applied to abilities and talents, it is critical when it focuses on the highly gifted learner. They and we have so much to lose.

In this chapter, we have begun the exploration of gifted individuals by establishing a common base of understanding of the terms and concepts that will be used throughout our discussion. The term *intelligence* is defined as the aggregate of an individual's cognitive, affective, physical, and intuitive functioning. It is enhanced or inhibited by the interaction between the genetic pattern of the individual and the opportunities provided by the environment for that individual throughout the life span. *Giftedness* is a biologically rooted concept that serves as a label for a high level of intelligence and indicates an advanced and accelerated development of functions within the brain. Such development may express itself in high levels of cognitive, affective, physical, intuitive, or a combination of abilities, such as academic aptitude, insight and innovation, creative behavior, leadership, personal and interpersonal skill, visual and performing arts, or any combination thereof. Although giftedness expresses itself in many ways, it can now be postulated from animal and human brain/mind research that individuals with high levels of intelligence—that is, gifted individuals—show measurable biological differences, not at birth, but as the result of a continuous interaction between their genetic pattern and the opportunities provided by their environment.

Gifted individuals are those who have developed high levels of intelligence and therefore operate or perform, or show promise of operating or performing, at high levels in any of the areas of intelligence. Because of such advanced and accelerated development, gifted individuals require services or activities not ordinarily provided by the schools, so that society can ensure the growth rather than the loss of their abilities. *Talent development* involves the deliberate and planned effort to provide children with a responsive learning environment both at home and at school, so that all of their talents and abilities will have the opportunity to develop to maximum levels. Such appropriate stimulation will allow high levels of intelligence to develop in a variety of forms and expressions and will result in increased numbers of individuals performing at the level of intelligence referred to as giftedness.

The interactive concept of intelligence is seen as critical to understanding the development of giftedness. An overview of the evolution of this concept was presented to aid in this understanding. Brain research, as it relates to optimal development, allows parents and educators to more effectively create stimulating interactions that may lead to high levels of intelligence. This information about how learning occurs, what stimulates and what inhibits learning, and in what ways enriched environments change the neural structure is essential to understanding and nurturing intelligence, giftedness, and the continuous development of talent.

Research in brain/mind function provides a biological basis for defining and understanding the concepts of intelligence and giftedness. Given the advances in brain research and in our understanding of the learning process, we can now discuss with more precision the nature and development of intelligence and the label for high levels of such development: giftedness.

QUESTIONS OFTEN ASKED

1. What do you mean by intelligence? Giftedness? Talented? Are they the same?

When we speak of *intelligence,* it is important to consider more than school activities or rational thinking. The more we know about the human brain, the more we notice that intelligence must include our physical ability, our emotional health, and our creative, insightful intuition along with our linear and spatial thinking. Intelligence results from the development of *all* our brain functions.

Giftedness is a biologically rooted concept that serves as a label for a high level of intelligence and indicates an advanced and accelerated development of functions within the brain. Although the terms *talent* or *talented* may be used to mean a high level of ability in any area, the terms are often used in relation to areas of performance, such as art, music, dance, or sports. *Talent development,* however, involves the deliberate and planned effort to provide all children with a responsive learning environment both at home and at school so that their abilities will have the opportunity to develop to maximum levels. This is an important concern of educators and part of the two-fold mission of gifted education.

2. Can all children become gifted?

From the data that neurobiology is providing, it is evident that nearly all children are born with very complex and unique brain structures. Although each child is different, they all seem to have extraordinary potential. I believe that, if given the opportunity to develop optimally, most children could perform at the level we now call *gifted,* and it would be probably more natural that they do so.

3. Should children know that they have been identified as gifted?

Not only should they be told, but also it is most important that they understand what giftedness means. Children who are highly intelligent know they are different, and it is important that they understand what their differences mean and how they became gifted. The lesson on giftedness in Chapter 5 (pp. 157–158) would be a good starting place.

4. Which is most important for the development of intelligence, heredity or environment?

Both are important, and current research recognizes that the interaction between them is complex and interdependent. At this time few knowledgeable scientists even try to speak of one as being more important than the other.

5. When does development of intelligence begin?

The unique genetic program of the individual begins to show the impact of the environment from conception on. The brain cells begin their development about 3 weeks after conception. From this we can see that the development of intelligence and our involvement in that development begin very early in utero.

6. Is IQ a measure of a person's intellectual capacity?

No. We have no measure of intellectual capacity. Such a measure would be possible only if intelligence did not change and were fixed from birth, rather than dynamic as it is now known to be. IQ is the score given for a measure of our performance on specific tasks, many of which we use in school-related activities. Our capacity will change depending on the opportunities we are given to develop. To obtain a reasonably adequate idea of our intellectual ability at any stage of development, we will need as many different kinds of measures and observations as possible.

7. How does knowing about the brain help us to understand and better educate gifted learners?

The more we know about how we learn, the better we will be in creating opportunities for learning. If we know that stimulation from the environment increases our brain's ability to function, then we will be concerned about providing appropriate stimulation. As we learn what activities and circumstances allow for optimal brain development, we will become far better at educating all children.

8. Why is your definition of intelligence important to how you educate a child?

If you believe that a child is born with a set amount of intelligence, then you will not be concerned with providing opportunities for optimal development; rather you will only be interested in providing information and content. You will believe that gifted children can get by on their own. If you believe that

intelligence is dynamic and dependent on the environment interacting with what is inherited, then you will be concerned about the environment you provide; you will not leave education to chance.

9. Do all gifted children have similar characteristics?

Some do; however, as we develop more of our intelligence we become more unique. The lists of characteristics describe only some of the behaviors that have been commonly observed among many, many gifted youngsters over a long period of time. No child will have them all; however, knowing how some bright children express themselves may help you understand more about the children with whom you live.

10. For educational planning, can gifted children be thought of as a homogeneous group?

No, nor can they be expected to work at the same level, pace, or depth of understanding, or have the same skills, abilities, or interests. The products they choose to give evidence of their mastery of content or skills will differ if they are allowed to select among alternatives of evaluation. Generally, the population of gifted individuals is referred to as moderately gifted (IQ range 130–144); highly gifted (IQ range 145–159); and exceptionally or profoundly gifted (IQ range $\geq$ 160). Although IQ is not a good identifier if used alone, it can give an idea of the extent of need the individual may have educationally and provide a clue to the range that the educational program may need to have available.

11. Why would anyone consider highly gifted students at-risk? They have so much going for them.

Highly gifted students become at-risk when there are no provisions made for their advanced and accelerated development. Remember, if we do not use the abilities and talents we have, we lose them. This is true at the biological level as well as at the level of behavior. Our system of education as it now is structured seldom offers learning experiences that are challenging to the highly gifted learner. To prevent a devastating loss of ability and talent we must provide appropriate educational experiences for this population.

CHECKING FOR UNDERSTANDING
Follow-Up Activity

Using the information on the brain shared in this chapter as your basis, outline a presentation that you would make to students in your classroom; parents of gifted learners at a parent meeting; or other teachers in your school or district if you were given an hour of their time.

Your goal will be to have your chosen audience understand:

- The meaning of intelligence, giftedness, and talent development
- The role of nature and nurture in the development of intelligence and giftedness
- Why the concept of interactive intelligence has replaced the idea that children are born gifted
- The importance of brain function in understanding the nature of giftedness

- Some of the common characteristics of gifted learners that result from changes in the brain when it is stimulated

To aid in their understanding you may wish to use:

1. The hand models explaining the brain and the neuron
2. Other hands-on activities (eg, use a 2.5′ × 2.5′ piece of paper to show the surface of the brain when it is not enfolded)
3. Slides or overheads of the brain
4. An opportunity for the participants to share what they know about the brain
5. A question-and-answer session to share and clarify their understanding of your goals

SUMMARY

1. Growth of intelligence depends on the interaction between our biological inheritance and our environmental opportunities to use that inheritance.

Intelligence, Giftedness, and Talent Development

2. High levels of intelligence or giftedness are the result of a dynamic, stimulating, interactive process that leads to quantitative and qualitative differences in performance.
3. How giftedness is expressed depends both on the genetic patterns of the individual and on the experiences provided by that individual's environment.
4. Intelligence is the aggregate of an individual's cognitive, affective, physical, and intuitive functioning.
5. Giftedness is a biologically rooted concept that serves as a label for a high level of intelligence and indicates an advanced and accelerated development of functions within the brain. Such development may express itself in high levels of cognitive, affective, physical sensing, or intuitive abilities, such as academic aptitude, insight and innovation, creative

behavior, leadership, personal or interpersonal skill, or visual and performing arts.
6. Gifted individuals are those who have developed high levels of intelligence and therefore operate or perform, or show promise of operating or performing, at high levels in any of the areas of intelligence. Because of such advanced and accelerated development, gifted individuals require services or activities not ordinarily provided by the schools, so that society can ensure the growth rather than the loss of their abilities.
7. Talent development involves the deliberate and planned effort to provide children with a responsive learning environment both at home and at school, so that all of their talents and abilities will have the opportunity to develop to maximum levels.
8. Most of the definitions of gifted children focus on performance and observable behavior as necessary for the identification of high levels of intelligence. Such a basis for understanding giftedness is necessarily limited.
9. A definition of giftedness proposed by a group of educators known as the Columbus Group states that giftedness is asynchronous development in which advanced cognitive abilities and heightened intensity combine to

create inner experiences and awareness that are qualitatively different from the norm. This asynchrony is believed to increase with higher intellectual capacity.

10. The universe of intelligence includes the integration of an individual's brain functioning: cognitive, affective, physical/sensing, and intuitive.

11. Gifted learners are biologically different, not at birth, but as the result of genetic patterns and environmental opportunities interacting to produce actual cellular changes in the brain.

12. Although there is no single definition of either intelligence or giftedness in use, research provides a common basis for agreement that is important.

13. *Talent development* does not identfy persons; it indicates a belief in the need to nurture the highest capabilities within all individuals.

14. The highly gifted tend to evidence more energy than gifted individuals; they think faster and are more intent and focused on their interests; and they exhibit a higher degree of ability in most of the traits we have identified with giftedness. Such children are less able to benefit from regular classroom experiences, and modifications to their educational programs need to be more comprehensive and developed to a much higher degree to meet their needs than is necessary for less gifted learners.

15. The exceptionally gifted learners, different even from the highly gifted learners, have different value structures, are more isolated by choice, and more invested in concerns of a meta-nature. Typically, schools offer these students little; some educators suggest that tutoring with eminent authorities or home-schooling would be a far more productive educational plan.

The Concept of Intelligence

16. It is important to understand the brain's role in the learning processes and how such knowledge can contribute to effectively developing and educating high levels of intelligence.

17. Over the past century, the concept of intelligence has evolved from a belief in intelligence as fixed at birth and unchangeable to a view of intelligence as interactive, that is, educable, changeable, and dependent on the interaction

between the genetic inheritance and the experiences provided by the environment.

18. During the 1980s and 1990s the concept of intelligence was expanded, first by Guilford and then by a number of researchers and scholars, including Sternberg, with his triarchic concept of intelligence, and Gardner, with his theory of multiple intelligences. Each has added a dimension to consider in our understanding of intelligence.

19. Those who work with gifted children must acquire an understanding of the brain and the power of the interaction between the organism and the environment. What we believe about how people become intelligent will influence the way we plan for their educational development.

20. There are exciting clues in brain research that can help educators at home and at school optimize learning experiences for the youngsters with whom they work.

21. By the environment we provide, we change not just the behavior of the children; we change them at the cellular level.

Characteristics of Gifted Learners

22. As human beings develop higher levels of functioning, many unique patterns and traits emerge. The more gifted a person becomes, the more unique that person may appear.

23. Knowing the possible range of behaviors and the concomitant problems that result, will help parents and teachers better understand and nurture gifted individuals.

Highly and Exceptionally Gifted Students

24. To understand how to best plan educationally, we should distinguish between the typical or moderately gifted (the most commonly found gifted persons) . . . those with unusual levels of giftedness (sometimes labeled as highly gifted individuals) and between them and the exceptionally or profoundly gifted individuals (those of rare genius).

25. Although many school settings give limited priority to differentiating learning experiences for gifted students in general, even less priority is given to the highly and exceptionally gifted student.

3 Being Creative: Going Beyond Giftedness

In this chapter the reader will discover:

- A holistic model of creativity that integrates the cognitive, affective, physical/sensing, and intuitive aspects of the human mind.

- Current views on the concept of creativity.

- Characteristics commonly found in creative people.

- Conditions that enhance and inhibit the development of creativity.

- Methods of measuring creativity.

- Ways to encourage creative behavior in the classroom and at home.

"Creativity as process is important not because the product of each moment is such a gem, but because the process is the essence of life itself."

—HAROLD H. ANDERSON

It was the most amazing thing! Amy had never thought of herself as creative. She knew she was a good student. She had been figuring out the answers to the most difficult problems her teachers had posed for the past 7 years. Her academic subjects were only occasionally even challenging, and she nearly always felt that she could really do a lot more than she was ever asked. But every time she tried to draw, the finished picture never looked like her subject. It might resemble the original, but it didn't have any life, or depth, or balance. When she painted she couldn't capture the color or texture of what she was trying to portray. She certainly wasn't musical. And when the teacher last year had said, "Just use your imagination," it didn't help her design the book cover she needed. She never even understood how people got in touch with their imaginations.

This year was different. Ms. Bourke, the history teacher, had so many beautiful and interesting displays in the room, and they were never the same week to week. After a few weeks, Amy noticed that she was using some of the designs and colors in her own work: report covers, illustrations for science, and charts for her health class. Now she could see something she liked and think of how to make it even more special to her.

Today was the most amazing, though. Ms. Bourke had passed out large lumps of clay to each student and allowed them to explore the texture of the material and just play around with it for awhile. Then she had asked the class to re-form the clay into one large shape. "Now place your hands on the clay and gently close your eyes," she had said. "For the next few minutes I'd like you to just relax and let yourself be aware of the clay under your hands. The warmth, the texture, the feel of it. Inside this mass of clay is a shape. Some form is embedded inside the clay that needs to have your help in getting out. What form can you see in your mind's eye inside your clay? Sit quietly for a minute and let the shape come into your mind."

As she sat quietly, Amy began to get the thought that there was a very handsome dog sitting inside her clay. He was just sitting there looking at her.

"In a minute I am going to ask you to gently open your eyes and remove all of the clay that surrounds the shape you saw inside and let it stand by itself. Now open your eyes and you may begin. By the way, you might be interested to know what we just did is what Leonardo da Vinci used to do when he would begin to carve a block of marble. He believed that each piece had something inside just waiting to be freed," Ms. Bourke declared.

Amy looked at her own sculpture of a handsome dog sitting in front of her, and she still marveled at how easy it had seemed to take the pieces away to free him. She could hardly believe that she had really created such a grand and special animal. Maybe she was creative after all. Oh, my!

CREATIVITY: VIEWS OF THE CONCEPT

Creativity is a very special condition, attitude, or state of being that nearly defies definition. Over the years, scholars and researchers, artists and musicians, philosophers, and educators have tried to use words to communicate this amazing phenomenon. Probably the most unexplainable part of creativity lies in the fact that, even though few agree on a definition, when we say the word, everyone senses a similar feeling. We may not be able to explain what it is rationally, but we know it just the same. When we are being creative, we are aware of its special excitement.

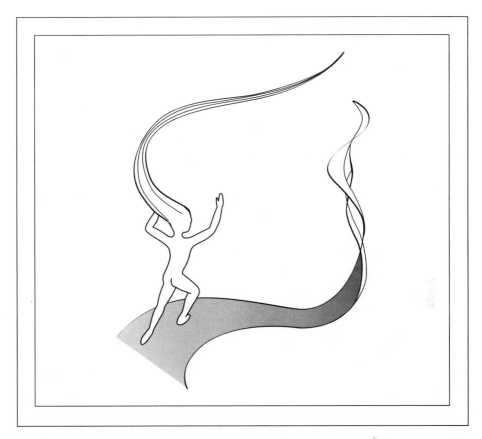

Throw your mind forward, then follow as fast as you can.
Source: Janet Kragen, 1991

A Holistic View

This chapter will define creativity holistically (see Figure 3.1) using the brain as a metaphor, as was done to define the concepts of intelligence and giftedness in Chapter 1. This holistic view focuses on creativity as the synthesis of enriched rational and spatial thought, heightened physical sensing and movement, sensitive emotional and social affect, and high intuitive consciousness. Restrict any one of these functions and you reduce creativity. Such a synthesis suggests even more: creativity may well include a spark from another dimension. This holistic view acknowledges that creativity may express the uniqueness of the person through ideas, insights, processes, acts, or products. The focus may be in one area or discipline, or may be more universal. The purpose of creativity in this model is conceptualized to recognize and bring forth that which is new, diverse, advanced, complex, or previously unknown, so that humankind can experience growth in life as fuller, richer, and more meaningful.

When viewed from this model of synthesis, different phenomena or even different types of creativity, as are now commonly described in the literature, need not

Figure 3.1 *Creativity Circle*

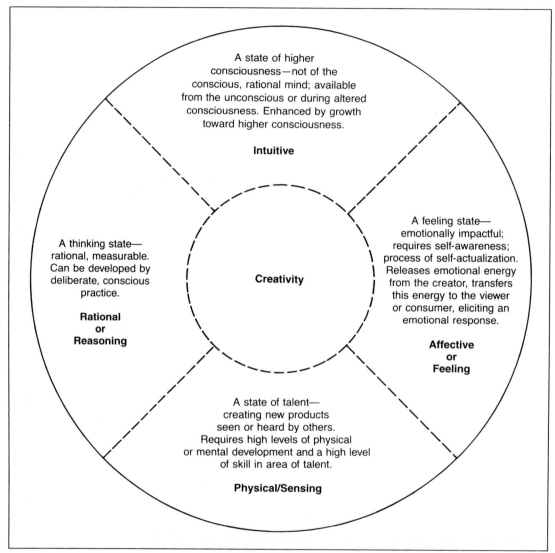

A state of higher
consciousness—not of the
conscious, rational mind; available
from the unconscious or during altered
consciousness. Enhanced by growth
toward higher consciousness.

Intuitive

A thinking state—
rational, measurable.
Can be developed by
deliberate, conscious
practice.

**Rational
or
Reasoning**

Creativity

A feeling state—
emotionally impactful;
requires self-awareness;
process of self-actualization.
Releases emotional energy
from the creator, transfers
this energy to the viewer
or consumer, eliciting an
emotional response.

**Affective
or
Feeling**

A state of talent—
creating new products
seen or heard by others.
Requires high levels of physical
or mental development and a high level
of skill in area of talent.

Physical/Sensing

be seen as contradictory but as parts of a larger whole. Some writers and researchers have used *creativity* synonymously with *giftedness;* some have limited it to feelings and affective development; some believe that creativity must be expressed in a product; and others define only the spark or insight as the entire process. A more holistic and perhaps accurate definition of creativity includes an integration of all of these ideas and allows far more understanding of the concept than the limitations of any one view. It is as though everyone who has defined or discussed creativity is correct, although their positions sound disparate. At the same time, they are incorrect, because they speak of only the part of creativity that they see or that fits their belief system. Such a limited view of creativity has caused us to recognize only a portion, an isolated part of what, in fact, is a far more complex and more integrated whole. We may have viewed and discussed only a small, exposed segment, most often the rational part, while we have only hinted at the other important facets.

Although a holistic view provides a structure that allows our discussion to take advantage of all of the research on creativity now available, regardless of the point of view of the researcher, it does not explain creativity. The mystery and wonder of how the human being creates still exists.

Creativity and Its Relationship to Giftedness

The federal definition of gifted students includes creativity as an expression of giftedness along with leadership, intellectual or academic achievement, and ability in the visual and performing arts. Sternberg and Lubart (1993) express the view that creativity is a dimension of intelligence that supplements the IQ, and they too believe that it should be seen as a type of giftedness. They suggest that creative giftedness contrasts with academic giftedness and bodily-kinesthetic giftedness. From this view, creativity involves "cognitive, stylistic, personality, motivational and environmental aspects that differ from those involved in academic giftedness" (p. 8).

Although still seeing it as a part of giftedness, Renzulli (1978, 1992) somewhat differently conceptualizes creativity as a condition for the identification of gifted behavior, when combined with motivation and above average ability. He believes that creativity can be claimed only when a product results. Runco (1992) also believes that creativity is a vital component of giftedness and suggests that children will express creativity in specific domains.

A view that creativity is an extension of giftedness comes from Feldman (cited in Piirto, 1998). He sees giftedness as the achievement of advanced mastery within a domain; creativity as extending mastery to find new meaning in the domain; and genius as remaking that domain. Limiting creativity to a cognitive view allows it to be more easily measured, researched, and taught, however it does not capture the complexity or bring understanding to the other dimensions of creativity.

Gowan (1981) discussed the relationship between giftedness and creativity by first distinguishing between personal and cultural creativity. He believed that anyone could be taught personal creativity, but that giftedness is necessary for cultural creativity—the form of creativity that produces major discoveries and ideas that significantly add to and inevitably change the future of humankind. He viewed giftedness as only the potential for creativity. Csikszentmihalyi (1995) also believes there are two types of creativity: the type found in Big *C* creative people whose works are considered eminent in their field or domain and lead to change, and the type expressed by little *c* people whose use of creativity affects only their everyday lives.

The Cognitive or Rational View of Creativity

How we define creativity will depend on our belief systems about other concepts. For example, if we believe that intelligence is defined as rational, linear thinking, and that giftedness is identified only by a high IQ or outstanding academic ability, then we would look at creativity and intelligence as separate constructs, and our investigation of creativity would focus on problem-solving, problem-finding, or some other cognitive processing model. Classic examples are Guilford's (1959) *Structure of Intellect,* Parnes' (1967) *Creative Behavior Guidebook,* Taylor's (1985) *Multiple Talents Model,* Torrance's (1966) *Tests of Creative Thinking,* and Williams' (1968) *Plank Model.* Such a belief suggests that creative people must combine, reorganize, or reshape knowledge structures to generate new understandings needed to solve problems. Such solutions are then translated into action plans to bring a creative idea into being. This is the cognitive or rational view of creativity, the view that is most researched and that has accumulated the most literature and nearly all of the testing.

In the cognitive rational view of creativity, problem-solving and divergent thinking are the central focus for the development of creativity, although from the earliest conceptualization of creativity, many researchers also included problem-finding and critical thinking (Albert & Runco, 1986; Gardner, 1993; Guilford, 1967; Renzulli, 1978; Torrance, 1964). Runco (1992) states, "The definition of creative thinking is derived from research on open-ended problem solving—such as divergent thinking—and research on problem finding . . . defined as a meaningful response to any situation . . . for finding a problem and solving it in one's own way" (p. 13).

Amabile (1989) defines the cognitive, rational view of creativity as having expertise in a given field and a high level of divergent skills. She believes these functions are necessary for all creative behavior.

Creative giftedness, as a part of Sternberg's (1985) conceptualization of giftedness, highlights the cognitive aspect by including insight, planning, and research. Gardner (1993), on the other hand, hypothesizes that creativity is a part of all of his original seven, now eight, intelligences. He believes that creativity is expressed by solving problems and devising products that may at first be novel or unusual, but that must be accepted by society before they can be considered creative. He further believes that the expression of creativity is focused on a specific domain or discipline. He concludes that it is regularly exhibited and includes devising new questions or fashioning products as well as solving problems.

In a review of the recent studies on the cognitive models of creative thought, Mumford (1998) suggests that there are two basic categories, both of which focus on problem-solving. There are those who see creative thought as an unconscious, uncontrollable phenomenon, and those who consider it a directed, controlled phenomenon that depends on using reasoning in the active manipulation of available information. In the first set of models, solution occurs after a period of preparation and incubation and relies on associations and rule systems, even though such associations may be outside of conscious awareness. The models that involve conscious reasoning stress the importance of the acquisition and manipulation of knowledge. Combination and reorganization of available information are considered the most important skills. Mumford suggests that an integrative model that incorporates both types of creative thought might be more useful at explaining the phenomenon than either view used alone.

This cognitive, rational dimension must be considered in attempting to understand the process of creativity, although it is probably the least exciting aspect.

Efforts frequently are made to measure this dimension of creativity through tests. This raises the question of just how much we can learn about creativity from tests. It is doubtful that test results can ever identify or explain the creative process.

The Affective/Emotional-Social View of Creativity

Other researchers and educators find that to investigate only the cognitive processes would restrict the understanding of creativity and its development. The majority of the studies of creativity have investigated either the cognitive view or the personality and motivation of creators. Csikszentmihalyi (1998) chooses to think of creativity as a result of the interaction between a person, a social system, and a cultural system. He believes that the affective-motivational dimension of creativity requires further study. As he states, "While most of the field has been pursuing the cognitive angle, I have been always under the impression that what counts most in creativity is curiosity, interest, and the ability to feel the joy of discovery" (p. 81). Dudek and Cote (1994) believe that creativity can occur through self-expression and personal development and may not address a problem at all.

When we shift from the realm of the rational to the realm of feeling and creativity, a whole new list of classic authorities emerge from the first studies of creativeness, including Maslow (1971), Moustakas (1967), Rogers (1959), Krishnamurti (1964), May (1959), and Fromm (1959). Maslow (1971) saw creativity as the problem of the creative person, rather than of creative products or creative behaviors. He found that the correlation between the characteristics of those evidencing creativeness and those who were healthy, self-actualizing, fully human people was nearly total. He stressed personality over achievement and the expressive quality over the problem-solving or product-making process. He considered a holistic view of creativity important. Moustakas (1967) saw creativity as experiencing life in one's own way, drawing on one's perceptions and personal resources. Rogers (1959) called it the mainstream—the tendency for human beings to actualize themselves, to become who they truly are. Krishnamurti (1964) claimed that creativity has its roots in the initiative, which comes into being only when there is deep discontent. For him, one must be wholly discontented—not complainingly, but with gaiety, joy, and love. May (1959) felt that creativity is an encounter between an intensely conscious human being and the world. For Fromm (1959), creativity is the ability to see and to respond with intense uniqueness.

A more recent contributor to the affective view of creativity, Amabile (1983, 1990) sees an affective aspect, intrinsic task motivation, as the third of her basic ingredients of creative work. In Dabrowski's (Dabrowski & Piechowski, 1977) view of creativity, life is the creative product.

Pospisil (1994) identifies fields of inquiry that impact on our understanding of the affective/emotional-social aspect of creativity, such as:

- Linguistics, with arguments that suggest that meaning and reality are formed from the interaction of the mind and the environment;

- The new physics, with ideas that are radically changing our concept of reality as old structures and beliefs give way to continuously forming new patterns and possibilities; and

- Brain research, with ideas of the dynamic nature of creativity and its physiological basis.

He believes that rational-linear thought represents only one level of reality, but he does not consider such thought as reality in the broad sense. Pospisil believes that if we are to really develop a feeling for the nature of the concept, it is necessary to explore the bases for our beliefs, assumptions, and values regarding creativity.

The Physical/Sensing View of Creativity

Creativity from the physical/sensing view is most related to the products of creativity. Art and music are examples of the expression of physical/sensing aspects of creativity, although, unfortunately, visual artists, writers, and musicians are too often seen as the only representation of creativity. By limiting creativity to a focus on creative products, we deny the possibility of private and personal expressions of creativity that may not be expressed so tangibly.

Harrington (1980) argues for the inclusion of kinesthetic and muscular modes of representation and expression in the creative process. He believes that such involvement facilitates creativity by encouraging the transformation of information into analogy and metaphor.

The Intuitive View of Creativity

The intuitive dimension of creativity may be the most intriguing, as it requires a focus on a higher level of consciousness than do the others. It focuses on the spark that enters into all the other aspects of creativity that we have been considering.

For decades people have tried to describe this dimension of creativity, including Gowan (1980), Koestler (1964), Krippner (1968), MacKinnon (1965), and Samples (1976). Each has a somewhat different view. Gowan (1980) refers to creativity as, "the first in a series of increasing operations of more and more order. Some very spectacular effects occur in these higher and rarer states . . ." (p. ix). He believes human consciousness to be Divine. Koestler (1964) believes that one relinquishes conscious control and thus liberates the mind; Krippner (1968) believes creativity to be an alternative level of awareness; and MacKinnon (1965) believes it to be a perception. Samples (1976) believes creativity produces an attitude that nurtures diversity, change, optimal involvement, and self-regulation. He feels that we must learn and relearn to honor the creativity within ourselves. From my experience, it is almost as though a person opens up, taps into, and links with the universe. The person becomes part of a unity with the higher expression, rather than a conduit for it.

Integrating the Views of Creativity

Even though a person can generally categorize aspects of creativity into one of these four different dimensions, each is actually a part of the whole. Unless all of these views and the information related to them are integrated, we may not be talking about creativity in a total sense. The researchers, scholars, and practitioners who gave rise to different perceptions of creativity add clarity to the total picture, but their views are limited as they keep the whole from being understood. Each of us as individuals has the capacity to integrate all of these dimensions of creativity holistically within ourselves.

A number of individuals have recognized the limitations of focusing on only one aspect of creativity and thus have combined several of these areas in their work. They view creativity from the full range of process and product, from skill development to expressions of personal emotion, and from the production of the arts to the use of intuition.

As early as 1972, Gowan pointed out the holistic nature of creativity. In his discussion, he grouped the investigations of creativity into the five areas: (1) cognitive, rational, and semantic; (2) personal and environmental; (3) mental health and openness; (4) Freudian and neo-Freudian; and (5) psychedelic, existential, and irrational. He viewed these subdivisions on a continuum. He presented helpful overviews of all of the areas and of their relationship to the total concept. In his later work, he expanded his involvement with the irrational aspect (Gowan, 1974, 1975, 1980):

> Creativity is a characteristic not only of individual human behavior, but also of the species in general. What is true of the development of the superior individual is also true of the developing aspects of mankind. The emergence of creative abilities is a triumph not only of individual development, but . . . the harbinger of evolutionary progress. . . . (Gowan, 1972, p. 70)

Later Gowan (1981) suggested that far more attention be paid to the development of our creative abilities. He believed that at the very least, we should study creativity directly in high school and university classes; help young children learn techniques of relaxation, stress reduction, and the incubation of creative thought; help children practice use of imagination and imagery; and encourage creative production appropriate to their developmental phase.

Another model of creativity, in which all components must work together in an integrated way, is suggested by Urban (1995). He defines creativity as "the highest form of evolution and that which leads to evolution." He echoes Maslow as he cautions us to regard creativity as a "human-bound potential or aptitude . . . linked with, dependent on, demonstrated and manifested by a person, his/her thinking, acting, and doing. This special human activity results in a new, innovative product." He introduces a six-component model of creativity that includes: (1) divergent thinking and doing; (2) general knowledge and thinking base; (3) specific knowledge base and specific skills; (4) focusing and task commitment; (5) motives and motivation; and (6) openness and tolerance of ambiguity. His use of six components moves us beyond a divergent thinking or cognitive processes approach because he believes that no one approach can be used alone, and he has constructed a more holistic structure than previous divergent thinking models. He is working toward "the dynamic balance of the unbalanced," which he suggests lies not in the middle between opposites but in the full development of both in an integrated manner.

In the early 1970s, Leonard (cited in Ferguson, 1973) proposed what was then an incredible hypothesis, that the ultimate creative capacity of the brain may be, for all practical purposes, infinite. Brain researchers currently agree that the brain is seemingly without limits to its capacity; that it cannot be filled up (Diamond, 1998). As Ferguson noted in 1973, and which continues to be reflected in the findings of today, "Emotion and intellect, freedom and discipline, reason and intuition, the precise and the gossamer, primary and secondary processes, chaos and order—all of these apparent opposites can exist in creative harmony in the human brain" (p. 295).

According to Miliora (1987), "The creative attitude requires a holistic view of reality, awareness of all levels of experience—physical, emotional, and mental, and a balance of inner and outer directedness" (p. 145). From the view of the holistic model, creativity depends on the balance among action, emotion, and cognition with the addition of insight or intuition and the ability to synthesize the components of a situation into a meaningful whole.

CHARACTERISTICS COMMONLY FOUND IN CREATIVE INDIVIDUALS

As early as 1962, Torrance compiled an extensive list of 84 characteristics found in one or more studies to differentiate highly creative persons from less creative ones. MacKinnon (1964) developed a list that characterized highly creative people in much the same way. Nearly a decade later, Maslow (1970) found that many of the characteristics on his list of self-actualizing people, whom he considered to be synonymous with creative individuals, were essentially the same. Lists from more contemporary researchers still tend to agree and mention the same characteristics (see Figure 3.2).

Researchers who talk about creativity as a rational process frequently describe creative people as independent, persistent, and highly motivated; as excited and involved. Gruber (1988) found that creative scientists engage in a wide interconnected network of projects, all sharing a strong sense of purpose, in which they are emotionally engaged. They consistently create and use images to give understanding to the interconnections evolving over time.

A somewhat different listing of characteristics was hypothesized by Renzulli (1992), with the idea that one or a combination of these factors usually found in persons viewed as creative may help us to better understand their complexity. His list includes moral courage, optimism, vision, charisma, hope, personal choice, positive feelings from hard work, a sense of power to change things, sense of destiny, sensitivity to human concerns, physical and mental energy, and a romance with a topic or discipline.

The childhood of creative people often included a lot of diversity and a great deal of freedom to explore and make decisions—they were allowed to be creative. Creatively gifted individuals are able to see problems in ways that others do not; they use divergent thinking and the processes of insight to solve problems or complete projects (Amabile, 1989; Sternberg & Lubart, 1993).

To be creative in the sense of feeling requires a special kind of perception. According to Miliora (1987), important qualities of a creative attitude are trust,

Playing pretend encourages characteristics of creativity.

curiosity, and the capacity to take risks and to be spontaneous in the moment. She conceptualizes trust as receptivity to what emerges, to change, and to the unknown, without needing to manipulate, concretize, or analyze. Trust also, she believes, needs a nonjudgmental, accepting attitude toward oneself at all levels of experience and a willingness to let go of control when appropriate. A trusting attitude about ourselves, the world, and the unknown allows change to emerge.

In the past, many people assumed that those who were highly creative were less emotionally stable, less mature, and more childlike; indeed many have equated highly creative acts with madness. In his study of the relationship of creativity to psychosis, Rothenberg (1990) has found that psychotics and highly creatives do share some types of thinking. The thinking for both transcends the common modes of logical thinking. Both combine paradoxical or antagonistic objects into a single entity and use metaphors that superimpose multiple, discrete objects. Jamison (1993) noted that another shared thought process was fluency, rapidity, and flexibility of thought, with the ability to combine ideas and categories of thought to form new and original connections. Although there are certainly distinct differences and the links are not seen as numerous or invasive, Neihart (1998) concludes, "The research suggests that differentiated emotional support should be available to students who are in pursuit of superior creative achievement" (p. 50).

Figure 3.2 *Characteristics of Creative People*

Source: The listed characteristics are from the research of Albert, 1998; Amabile, 1990; Fromm, 1959; Guilford, 1959; Heath, 1983; Koestler, 1964; Krippner, 1968; MacKinnon, 1964; Martindale, 1975; Maslow, 1959; May, 1959; Maynard, 1970; Miliora, 1987; Parnes, 1967; Rogers, 1959; Runco and Nemiro, 1994; Schaefer, 1970; Sternberg and Lubart, 1993; Taylor & Williams, 1966; Torrance, 1962; Williams, 1968.

Cognitive Rational Creative Individuals

- Self-disciplined, independent, often anti-authoritarian
- Zany sense of humor
- Able to resist group pressure, a strategy developed early
- More adaptable
- More adventurous
- Greater tolerance for ambiguity and discomfort
- Little tolerance for boredom
- Preference for complexity, asymmetry, open-endedness
- High in divergent thinking ability
- High in memory, good attention to detail
- Broad knowledge background
- Need think periods
- Need supportive climate, sensitive to environment
- Need recognition, opportunity to share
- High aesthetic values, good aesthetic judgment
- Freer in developing sex role integration; lack of stereotypical male, female identification

Affective/Emotional-Social Creative Individuals

- A special kind of perception
- More spontaneous and expressive
- Unfrightened by the unknown, the mysterious, the puzzling; often attracted to it
- Resolution of dichotomies: selfish and un-selfish; duty and pleasure; work and play; strong ego and egolessness
- Able to integrate
- More self-accepting; lack fear of own emotions, impulses, and thoughts
- Have more of themselves available for use, for enjoyment, for creative purposes; waste less of their time and energy protecting themselves
- Involved in more peak experiences, integration within the person and between the person and the world, and transcendence
- Capacity to be puzzled
- Ability to concentrate
- Ability to experience self as creative, as the originator of one's acts

- Willingness to be born every day
- Ability to accept conflict and tension rather than avoiding them
- Courage to let go of certainties, to be different, to be concerned with truth, to be certain of one's own feelings and thoughts and trust them
- Identify closely with the feelings and expectations of others
- Less repressed and defensive
- More curious
- More maturely autonomous and less dependent on views of others

Physical/Sensing Creative Individuals

- Openness to experience, new ideas
- An internal locus of evaluation
- An ability to toy with elements and concepts
- Perceiving freshly
- Concern with outside and inside worlds
- Ability to defer closure and judgment
- Skilled performance of the traditional arts
- High theoretical and aesthetic values

Intuitive Creative Individuals

- More intuitive and open to admitting turbulent inner conflicts
- Have their energy field accessible
- Have ability to tap and release unconscious and preconscious thought
- Are able to withstand being thought of as abnormal or eccentric
- Are more sensitive
- Have a richer fantasy life and greater involvement in daydreaming
- Are more enthusiastic and impulsive
- Often show abilities of synesthesia (e.g., tasting color, seeing sound, hearing smells)
- Show different brain wave patterns than the less creative, especially during creative activity
- Get excited and involved when confronted with novelty of design, music, or ideas (less creative people get suspicious and hostile)
- When given a new solution to a problem, get enthused, suggest other ideas (less creative students analyze the defect rather than explore potentials)

The creative individuals who emphasize feeling are expressive and unafraid of the unknown or the mysterious; in fact, they are often attracted to it. They are self-accepting and relatively unconcerned with others' opinions of them. They have themselves available to use for enjoying and creating. They waste little time on self-protection, even from themselves. People who express this quality of creativity are able to integrate within the person and between the person and the world. There is resolution of dichotomies such as selfish/unselfish, duty/pleasure, work/play, and so forth. They lack fear of their own emotions, impulses, and thoughts. They have the ability to be puzzled, to concentrate, and to experience themselves as creative (Maslow, 1959; Rothenberg, 1990).

In a sense, those who bring feelings into creativity have the willingness to be reborn every day. Conflict and tension are seen as opportunities, rather than as conditions to be avoided. These people have the courage to let go of certainties, to be different, to trust their inner thoughts. They model creativity and, as a result, allow others to be creative. The more they grow, the more others around them grow. This type of creative student can also be unconventional, individualistic, non-conforming, and typically viewed as "difficult," even though such behaviors may, in fact, reflect the development of creative behavior (Runco & Nemiro, 1994).

High ego-strength, attraction to complexity and unconventional ideas, moderate rebelliousness, impulsivity, openness to the unconscious, and passion for their creative efforts are identified by Albert (1998) as cross-cultural personality traits that have characterized exceptionally creative persons in western cultures through the ages. He concludes that creative activity is intrinsic to humans; it is literally built into our nature and serves us as an important tool of our adaptation.

Even those who focus on products as examples of creativity talk about intangible characteristics of the creative person such as openness to experience, an ability to play with concepts, and a tendency to perceive things in a fresh, new way. The abilities to defer closure while accepting conflict and tension, as well as a concern for aesthetic value, are identified as characteristics of those who create the physical products. Amabile (1990) found a positive relationship between intrinsic motivation and creative performance. Creative people seem to combine skilled performance with high theoretical and aesthetic values. Intuition may be the highest form of human cognition and is highly synthetic in nature.

People who express their creativity in intuitive ways use and value imagination in their thinking. Fantasy, daydreams, and dreams often help to release the creative processes. Intuition seems to express notions of deep mystery, of things that are unexplainable yet totally known. It is like soaring while being deeply grounded. Feldman (1988) has been particularly interested in the role of insight and transformation in the development of creative behavior. In some classrooms, these behaviors are seen as problematic.

Miliora (1987) comments:

> In contrast to cognition via thinking, cognition via intuition has the following characteristics: immediate and direct knowing of the totality of a situation; experiential and synthetic or holistic. It does not operate from the part to the whole as the analytical mind does. . . . For those that choose to pay attention to it, the awareness of intuition can be developed as a valuable faculty in the creative process. (pp. 139, 140)

Miliora finds imagination to be the bridge between the rational thought and feelings, with cognition via imagination preceding conceptual thinking as an important part of the creative process throughout our lives. She believes that "the capacity of images to unite physical, mental, and emotional levels of experience accounts for its potential usefulness to effect healing, growth, and learning" (p. 142).

Other characteristics associated with the intuitive form of creativity include: having an accessible energy, using the ability to release unconscious thought, having the ability to withstand being considered abnormal, being sensitive, having a rich fantasy life, enjoying great involvement in daydreaming, and being enthusiastic and impulsive. Some people who emphasize this form of creative expression in their lives say they have the ability to taste color, see sound, and hear smells. These people get excited and involved when confronted with such things as novelty of design, music, and ideas. People who are less comfortable with the intuitive aspects of creativity tend to become suspicious and hostile.

Brain wave patterns in creative people are significantly different than those of less creative individuals. Theta waves seem to be highly productive of creative thought and occur most frequently during the state of consciousness bordering on sleep. Preadolescent children exhibit far more theta-wave activity in the waking state than most adults, and this may explain children's natural tendency toward creative play, silly behavior, and fresh perceptions (Golemen, Kaufman, & Ray, 1992).

Whereas others have looked at the common characteristics of creative people in the hope of understanding what creativity is and how it can be nurtured, Gruber and Davis (1988) suggest a different approach. Following the premise that each person is unique in the combination of creative traits, they believe that the most challenging aspect of research on creativity is to construct and explain the unique combination of traits each person exhibits. They believe that any theory of creativity that is based only on examining common characteristics of creative people may be missing the way in which the interaction of the characteristics within one person creates the uniqueness of the individual and the complexity of creativity.

CONDITIONS THAT ENHANCE OR INHIBIT THE DEVELOPMENT OF CREATIVITY

Again and again in discussions of creativity, we find statements to the effect that everyone has a great deal of creativity as a child, but that very few retain it as adults. All who comment on this state of affairs go on to ask, "Why must it be so? How does it happen?"

Most writers and researchers agree that all people have the ability to be creative, at least while they are young. For decades it has been accepted that the behaviors of youth and adults have their roots in infancy and early childhood. This is also true of giftedness and creativity. We will explore optimal development in more detail in Chapter 4, but here the focus is on the nurture of creativity. To be supportive of the developing creativity in very young children, adults must understand it, value it, and encourage the expression of it. The behaviors of creative children are often unique and different and may contribute to disturbance and chaos. Being the teacher or parent of a creative child is not easy.

Nurturing Creativity at Home

Parents of creative children themselves are often creative and show self-assurance and initiative. They are comfortable with change and prefer unstructured demands. They value their own autonomy and independence but are conscientious and dependable toward their children. Such parents have more interest in cultural-intellectual pursuits than in social-civic organizations or sports. They engage in creative hobbies or play musical instruments. They read more than the average person, read more often to their children, and often take them to the library. Clearly they serve as role models for their children (Domino, 1969; Dreyer & Wells, 1966; Getzels & Jackson, 1961; Gowan, 1965; MacKinnon, 1964; Schaefer, 1970).

Creative children tend to be found in homes that are less authoritarian. The entire family stresses openness and expresses an enthusiasm for life. Parents value the expression of feelings and individual divergence. More permissive parents seem to have more spontaneous, original, self-initiating, and independent children. These children also seem less hostile, more outgoing, and friendly. Their parents allow them more freedom in decision-making and in exploring the environment. Parents of gifted and creative children prefer guidance over punishment and seldom use physical punishment (Ellinger, 1964; Nichols, 1964; Satir, 1972).

Playfulness has been cited as a quality that supports creativity both for children and adults. Imagination, make-believe, and fantasy are essential. These qualities require patient, interested, nonjudgmental listening on the part of parents as their children explore endless tales from their imagination and the impossible accomplishments of their imaginary friends (Amabile, 1989; Dansky & Silverman, 1980).

Just as with all optimal development, actualization of creativity requires environments that have psychological safety and freedom, are risk-free, and are filled with a variety of creative settings, outlets, and activities. Such environments should include materials and experiences that involve the cognitive, physical, affective, and intuitive domains. In these rich environments there must be sufficient time for both free play and playful exploration guided by an interested adult who can be responsive to the child's unique personality, interests, and pacing (Clark, 1986, 1997; Meador, 1992; Piirto, 1998).

Gardner (1993) suggests that the quality of a child's early years is crucial. From his work, he believes that individuals who ultimately make creative breakthroughs tend, from their earliest days, to be explorers and innovators, never satisfied to follow traditional paths. He uses the term "capital of creativity," which would be available to children later in their lives if they are given the opportunity to discover their world in a comfortable, exploring way.

Nurturing Creativity at School

"When students are taught in a way that enables them to encode information in a variety of ways and to capitalize on their strengths, they learn better, even for memory . . . teaching students to think creatively not only allows them to express and develop their creativity, but to learn better" (Sternberg, 1998, p. 87). These are some of the reasons that students must be taught the skills and attitudes of creativity at school.

Fantasy enhances a child's creative ability.

Amabile (1986) has found that creative production takes more than talent, personality, and cognitive ability. The most important factor seems to be the creator's love of creating. She found that the most creative individuals create for the fun and satisfaction they personally receive. Creative solutions to problems occur more often when the activity is done for pleasure than when an external reward is attached. Opportunities for creativity are reduced with supervisory restrictions, deadlines, evaluation, and reward structures. With the help of observation from famous creators, controlled experiments, and interviews with research and development (R&D) scientists, Amabile has discovered six factors that undermine creativity and interest in the creative task:

1. Expected evaluation—People who are concentrating on how their work will be evaluated are less creative than people who do not have to worry about such reviews.

2. Surveillance—People who are conscious of being watched as they are working will be less creative than people who are not aware of being monitored.

3. Reward—People who perform a task primarily to gain a tangible reward will be less creative than those who are not working principally for recognition or payment.

4. Competition—People who feel direct, threatening competition with others in their work will be less creative than those not focusing on rivalry.

5. Restricted choice—People who must perform their tasks in accordance with designated restrictions will be less creative than people given a freer choice. In interviews with R&D scientists, freedom of choice in how to approach work was the most potent feature leading to creativity.

6. Extrinsic orientation—People who are led to concentrate on all the extrinsic reasons for doing a task will be less creative than those thinking about all the intrinsic reasons. (pp. 13–14)

The focus instead needs to be on components necessary for creativity to flourish; Amabile has identified three: (1) intrinsic motivation (i.e., the desire to do something because it is important to you); (2) domain-relevant skills (i.e., skills in a specific field that were learned through formal education and experience), and (3) creativity-relevant skills (i.e., ways of thinking and working that are conducive to creativity). These components establish an environment that is more conducive to creativity than would be the use of any reward system or external pressure. Piirto (1998) reminds us that, "The most enhancing rewards for creative endeavor are in the pleasure the creator takes in doing the work itself, and in achieving the result, and not from the pay or the prize" (p. 356).

Intrinsic motivation, the first of Amabile's (1986) components, can be taught or at least modeled so that children show higher levels of intrinsic motivation after training than do untrained children. Amabile and her colleagues, Hennessey and Grossman, used videotapes showing children being interviewed by an adult sharing statements of interest, excitement, and deep involvement in some aspect of their studies. The children also talked about how they felt that high marks and teacher approval were nice but were not as important to them as enjoying their work. In addition to changing the level of intrinsic motivation for the viewers, the videotapes "immunized" the students against the negative effects of extrinsic constraints on their creativity. This work seems very promising and provides us with a simple, realistic way to accomplish an important goal—increasing intrinsic motivation within our students.

Creative individuals who have learned independence of thought and deed can become intrinsically motivated and set their own standards. The fear is that placing such children in the traditionally conformist setting of many schools may lead to inhibition of intellectual and creative growth, frustration, and often the denial and abandonment of creative potential. Researchers, teachers, and parents who value creativity find reason to be concerned.

Creative students fare somewhat better with creative teachers. However, school peers also influence learning and, in the case of creative students, their peer interactions do not seem to facilitate creative growth. In grades 2 through 6, peer sanctions operate against the most creative children. Few are credited for their contributions to the group, so they develop a tendency to work alone. In the sixth grade, highly creative children encounter open hostility, aggression, criticism, and rejection. Their peers use organized efforts to limit their scope of operation and to impose sanctions. By junior high school, creative students who are not intellectually gifted are discounted, with their ideas being considered wild and their behavior deviant and wrong. Creative boys gain more acceptance from their peers when engaging in divergent behavior than creative girls. Is it any wonder that the more creative the students, the less they like school?

In addition to intrinsic motivation, the necessity of developing a high level of skill to support the creative process has also been reported by Bailin (1988). She considers knowledge and skill of vital importance and essential to opening the way for creative achievement. High-order skills must be taught, involving critical judgment applied to flexible and changing circumstances. Such knowledge must be more than a body of facts and must include in-depth understanding of the principles and procedures of disciplines, the methods of inquiry, and the overall goals, deep issues, and controversies involved.

Drawing from the synthetic nature of creativity, Bailin (1988) links this concern for skill development to the importance of imagination. She states,

> One's skills in an area shape and constrain one's imagination and these skills themselves have an imaginative component. It is this interplay between skill and imagination which accounts for the evolution and development of traditions and thus to how creative achievement comes about. (p. 129)

Mumford (1999) strongly suggests that the production of novelty, an important part of his definition of creativity, is facilitated by knowledge of higher order cognitive systems. Sternberg and Lubart (1993) also believe that knowledge is an essential component in fostering creativity. Their research shows that knowledge helps a person produce novel work, be contrarian, and introduce novelty and fundamental abilities for creative performance. Mumford's (1998) review of recent research leads him to suggest that processes and strategies used to generate new ideas operate on knowledge. It is through the acquisition and application of such implicit and explicit structures that creative thought can become possible, he believes. To promote creativity, Mumford suggests several steps that can be taken:

- Develop base concepts with clearly articulated principles or features.
- Provide ways that students can actively work with and apply such concepts.
- Provide exercises that illustrate major models for understanding different phenomena, the principles involved in constructing such models, and the potential applications of alternative models.
- Provide students with instruction in and demonstrations of multiple, diverse, and interrelated representations and relationships as well as strategies that might be used to construct such relationships.
- Provide students with procedures to gather, appropriately structure, combine, and reorganize pertinent information.
- Provide students with standards for evaluating new ideas and identifying restrictions on or problems with their implementation.
- Provide students with real world problem-solving experiences consistent with the students' goals and interests.
- Allow students to discover strategies on their own.

Other practical suggestions that can be adapted for use in classrooms come from the research of Runco (1995):

- Use explicit instructions (e.g., "find ideas that no one else will").
- Target specific components (e.g., rather than asking students to "be creative," be specific as to "on what" and the way of recognizing an original idea).
- Do not overlook flexibility (e.g., many ways a problem can be solved).

- Use tasks and exercises for which there are no clearly defined solutions.
- Begin with the fewest demands and constraints, then later move to more constrained tasks.
- Move from open-ended tasks to those that call for discovery.

If we believe that there is a need for creative students to develop a mastery of their field, which will then allow them to move beyond the known, then schools should be about giving those tools of excellence, which would be seen as a beginning point. Schools, however, often tend to exaggerate the mastery of functions and see the mastery level as the endpoint.

As early as 1962, Torrance, who has long been a leader in the field of creativity research, found that the growth of creativity defined by test performance is not continuous, but rather increases from 3 to $4\frac{1}{2}$ years of age and then drops slightly. It begins to rise again, making a sharp drop at the fourth grade. The scores in fluency, flexibility, originality, and elaboration drop so significantly that some students have lower scores in the fifth grade than they had in the third grade. The scores begin to rise again and continue through the junior year, except for a slight drop at seventh grade (Torrance, 1964). These studies showed that as early as third grade, girls were more reluctant to think creatively than were boys. Torrance believes girls by this time have been conditioned to be more passive and accept things as they are, rather than try to manipulate or change things. He also found that contributions made by boys were more highly valued by their peers. Halpin, Payne, and Ellett (1973) found that there are other interesting and significant differences with creative adolescents between females and males, as shown in Table 3.1.

In 1981, Torrance reported interesting results from an investigation of the patterns of various cultural groups in an attempt to understand the universality of the slump in creative development at the fourth-grade level. He studied seven different cultural groups—advantaged American; disadvantaged, minority American (African-

Table 3.1 *Differences Between Creative Females and Males*

Females	Males
Liked school, especially courses in sciences, music, and art	Disliked school
Liked their teachers	Disliked their teachers and thought they were uninteresting
Regularly read news magazines and other nonrequired reading and special reports	Did little homework
Were active in dramatics and musical productions.	Disliked physical education and seldom engaged in team sports
Did not go out on dates as often	Were regarded as radical or unconventional
Were daydreamers	Often wanted to be alone to pursue their own thoughts and interests

American); primitive Western Samoan; West German; Western Australian; East Indian; and Norwegian—and came to the following conclusions:

- Cultural factors strongly influence the course of creative development, the level of creative functioning, and the type of creativity that is most evident.
- In most cultures there are discontinuities in creative development, which occur in some around the fourth grade, in others not until the sixth grade.
- Such discontinuities occur whenever the children of that culture are confronted with new stresses and demands.
- General rankings can be made among cultures of the level of creative functioning, such that children within the advantaged cultures show a higher creativity index than do children of less advantaged cultures.

Paradoxically, in addition to creating the conditions and allowing the freedom to develop, the intuitive aspects of creativity are enhanced by the absence of trying. The more one strives to succeed, the more anxious or competitive one feels and the more out of tune and insensitive one becomes. Feelings of self-confidence, self-acceptance, and self-esteem provide the basis for growth in this aspect of creativity. Emotions are inseparably involved in creative activity, inspiration, and intuition. Rationality, positive emotions, and intuition all seem to lead to creative actions.

Several components have been found to be involved in the development of the intuitive aspects of creativity. The ability to relax and reduce tension and anxiety is the first skill needed. The ability to make use of imagery and imagination also facilitate creativity and the development of higher levels of consciousness. Imagination is more than the ability to be creative, according to McKim (1980), a former Stanford University professor who taught some of the first courses on visual thinking and imagining.

> Imagination is all that you have ever learned or experienced; it is central to your every perception and act. . . . Imagination also rules what you choose to see or ignore, to like or dislike. Every moment you match your immediate experience with past experiences stored in image form. (pp. 88–89)

McKim points out that our awareness of self, our self-image, is an ability of imagination. Whereas some have attempted to treat imagination as something destructive, to be feared, McKim clearly shows it to be a necessary human ability. He concludes that only if we are familiar with and aware of our ability to imagine, only if we have active and trained imaginations, can we use this ability to enrich our reality instead of mindlessly following illusions. He believes that "those who are passively unaware of their imaginations are easy targets for promulgators of illusion" (p. 89).

Research continues to validate the importance of the school environment in establishing the conditions that lead to the expression of creativity. Creative giftedness is impacted by an interaction between the person and the environment (Csikszentmihalyi & Robinson, 1986; Mumford, Connelly, Baughman, & Marks, 1994; Tegano, Sawyers, & Moran, 1989). Safe, accepting environments that are rich and varied in stimulation and allow disagreement and controversy without hostility have been found to be most productive of behavior that underlies creativity. Situations that present incompleteness and openness, allow and encourage questions and self-expression, and foster positive change are essential. Opportunities to investigate ideas, to try out intuitive behavior, and to explore, observe, analyze, infer, predict, and find integrative elements in differences enhance the possibility of creative production (Clark, 1986). Teachers who help children learn from their mistakes, reduce anxiety in the classroom, allow rather than control, treat children with respect, and value and model creative and intuitive behavior allow the child's own creativity to emerge (Runco & Nemiro, 1994). From Renzulli's work (1992) we can add flexibility, openness to experience and new ideas, high levels of energy, optimism, enthusiasm, and a commitment to excellence, which he considers "starting material" for teachers who seek to facilitate creativity.

Conditions that Inhibit Creativity

Conditions that inhibit creativity include low self-esteem, anxiety, competition, perfectionism, authoritarianism, external reward systems, need for closure, rigid timelines, and disrespect for fantasy and daydreams; Amabile (1989) calls such conditions creativity killers. She also identifies other inhibitors such as surveillance, making children feel constantly watched; evaluation, making children worry about being judged; competition; over-control, telling children how to do everything; and pressure, placing too high expectations on children.

Krippner (1967) facetiously listed ways to prevent a child from being creative:

- Everything must be useful.
- Everything must be successful.
- Everything must be perfect.
- Everyone must like you.
- You shall not prefer solitude to togetherness.
- You must have concentrated attention.
- You must not diverge from culturally imposed sex norms.
- Do not express excessive emotional feeling.
- Do not be ambiguous.
- Do not rock the cultural boat.

Figure 3.3 summarizes conditions that facilitate and inhibit creativity.

MEASURING CREATIVITY

The criterion for selecting and evaluating creative students has usually been a high score on a test designated as a creativity measure, such as the Torrance Tests of Creative Thinking (TTCT) (Torrance, 1966); the Remote Associates Test (RAT) (Mednick & Mednick, 1967); or the Group Inventory for Finding Creative Talent (GIFT) (Rimm & Davis, 1976). If tests are to be a part of the identification, then creativity tests should be used with other data for either evaluation of individuals or

Figure 3.3 *Facilitating or Inhibiting the Development of Creativity*

Conditions That Facilitate

- Provide an environment that is rich and varied in stimulation, safe, and accepting.
- Teach with materials and methods harmonious with each other and with the teacher.
- Delineate clearly and repeatedly the aims of this type of program.
- Allow free interplay of differences.
- Make environment and materials friendly and nonthreatening, thereby allowing disagreement and controversy without hostility (this allows children to engage freely in behavior underlying creativity).
- Reduce anxiety in classroom, especially that created by the teacher.
- Handle differences as confrontations, not as conflicts.
- Find integrative elements in differences.
- Allow unifying concepts to emerge.
- Allow individuation and differentiation within the unity.
- Foster positive change in directions congruent with student's predilections in cognitive and affective areas.
- Provide situations that present incompleteness and openness.
- Allow and encourage lots of questions.
- Produce something, then do something with it.
- Grant responsibility and independence.
- Emphasize self-initiated exploring, observing, questioning, feeling, classifying, recording, translating, inferring, testing inferences, and communicating.
- Provide bilingual experiences resulting in development of greater potential creativity due to the more varied view of the world, a more flexible approach to problems, and the ability to express self in different ways that arise from these experiences.
- Allow rather than control.
- Be receptive.
- Value and model intuitive behavior.

- Give opportunities to investigate ideas of successful, eminent people who used intuitive processes.
- Give opportunities to try out intuitive behavior (e.g., in problem-solving).
- Treat the child with respect and allow freedom to explore the universe.
- Create an atmosphere with really good music, books, and pictures as a natural part of the child's world.
- Treat ideas and questions respectfully.
- Respect the child's privacy.
- Value the unusual, the divergent.
- Help the child learn by mistakes.
- Avoid sex-role stereotyping.
- Encourage self-expression.
- Teach the child to look and really *see.*
- Help the child learn to trust the senses.
- Permit the child's own creativity to emerge.

Conditions That Inhibit

- Need for success, limiting risk-taking or pursuit of unknown.
- Conformity to peer group and social pressure.
- Discouragement of exploration, using imagination, inquiry.
- Sex-role stereotyping.
- Differentiation between work and play (e.g., learning is hard work).
- Adherence to "readiness" viewpoint for learning.
- Authoritarianism.
- Disrespect for fantasy, daydreams.
- Reward systems.
- External locus of control.
- Need for closure and rigid timelines.
- Need for security and acceptance of product.
- Perfectionism.
- Low self-concept.
- Trying to be creative.
- Anxiety.
- Competition.

programs, because there is disagreement in the field about the reliability and validity, especially the predictive validity, of creativity tests. Reliability refers to the assurance that a person would have about the same score each time the test was taken. Validity refers to the idea that a test measures what it says it measures; predictive validity indicates that the score on the test can predict future accomplishments or actions. Not only is there a wide range of beliefs regarding the theory of creativity, there is the impossibility of any test representing the complexity of any of the concepts of creativity. The view of creativity that one holds determines the type of testing and the use that will be made of the results. Some suggest that the value of such testing may not be in identifying creativity, but in assessing the processes involved in creative thinking that are available to the student. Making the identification more complex are the many attributes of creativity that seem to resist measurement.

Callahan (1991) categorizes creativity tests as (1) performance- or product-oriented, for example, the Torrance Test of Creative Thinking (TTCT) (Torrance, 1966, 1990) or the Seashore Measure of Musical Talent (Seashore, Lewis, & Saetveit, 1960); (2) oriented toward measuring personality characteristics, attitudes, or values of the individual, for example, the GIFT (Rimm, 1980); or (3) as relying on biographical information. The different measures may be self-reported or rated by others, such as teachers, peers, or both.

Davis (1995) prefers to identify ways to find creativeness as formal or informal depending on whether formal testing was used or opinions of teachers, parents, and others were sought. The formal category is much the same as the first two test categories discussed by Callahan (1991). The informal category includes biographical information (Callahan's third category) as predictors of creativity, such as the existence of an imaginary playmate during childhood or involvement in theater as youth or adults. Awareness of personality traits of creative persons—positive traits such as independence, risk taking, open-mindedness; negative traits such as uncooperativeness, sloppiness with details, lack of respect for authority; and creative abilities such as fluency, sensitivity, and ability to visualize—are other possible informal guides to identification of creativity.

Creativity Tests and Measures

Performance

Among the most popular tests used in the educational setting are the performance or product measures, most notably those of divergent thinking (Hunsaker & Callahan, 1995), such as (TTCT). These tests are scored for fluency (the number of responses) and originality (the infrequency of the response statistically). Such tests are favored because they result in observable, quantifiable information thought to generalize to common situations, although such responses actually are limited to items found on the test and cannot represent the full range of creativity that might have been developed by the person taking the test.

Those studying cognitive, rational creativity also favor creativity tests that focus on problem-solving and divergent thinking. Such tests include situations that present incompleteness and openness; situations that can then be brought to closure through a process of reasoning. The process would include the use of provocative questions and would seek cleverness in evaluating the responses. These researchers and theorists prefer to view independence and responsibility as manifestations of creativity. They encourage self-initiated exploring, observing, classifying, recording, testing inferences, and abundant communicating. They focus a child's interest and attention on a task and then let the child guide the activity. The environment must be stimulating. In the end, this analysis of creativity is based on the uniqueness and variations in reasoning that they see exhibited. It is from such controlled and guided experiences that the tests of creativity are typically created.

Products

Another way of measuring creativity that has been in use for decades is the external evaluation of creative products. Assessment by experts of creative products has been found to be a valuable approach to measuring this area of creativity. Amabile (1983, 1996) studied the assessment of performance using the creative products of original writing and art and recommends consensual agreement of experts as one measure of creativity. The criteria often used for evaluation of the products of creativity are how original, inventive, or imaginative they are judged to be. Although experts who use detailed criteria most often judge creative products, the more inclusive views of creativity have added other ideas for evaluating. Amabile (1996) has developed and researched a method, the *Consensual Assessment Technique,* that relies on the agreement of judges using a definition of creativity as a guide for product evaluation, rather explicit criteria. The reliability of her product evaluation tool has been noted even when judges have had relatively little training (Plucker & Runco, 1998). Reporting on studies of performance tests, Baer (1994) found that such tests could be structured to provide reliability and stability as tests of creativity.

In addition to the more formal types of measurement of creative performance, more informal methods are being developed. Because student achievement assessment more generally has focused on techniques of authentic assessment, the use of portfolio, exhibits, open-ended tasks, and performances have also increased in the area of measuring creativity. As with any use of such products for assessment, clear standards and knowledgeable judges are required.

Although Simonov (1970) sees social consumption as the criterion for creativity in product evaluation, he believes that the longer a work survives, the closer the creator has come to "perceiving and presenting an essential truth of human existence" (p. 77).

Creative Personality Characteristics and Attitudes

Examples of tests measuring such characteristics and attitudes include Kirschenbaum's (1989) Creative Behavior Inventory and Torrance's (1988) Style of Learning and Thinking. Such measures can be obtained from teachers and others when opportunities are given to engage in activities in which creative behavior might occur. Also, self-report measures that examine affective behaviors related to creativity can be used, such as GIFT (Rimm, 1980).

Problems Measuring Creativity

Problems related to testing for creativity lie in the current questions being raised regarding the current, more complex theories of creativity. Questions have been raised regarding the reliability and validity of commonly used tests as measures of these more complex views. How the use of fluency affects originality scores is also under investigation. Such questions make it even more important to use more than one test of creativity in any decision-making procedure concerning student identification or placement.

It has not been possible to demonstrate that creativity tests are valid, Gardner (1993) contends, although he does consider creativity tests reliable. That is, they do seem to produce approximately the same rating of a person time after time, but what they are testing is not what many believe to be creativity. Nor are people regarded by those in their field as creative identified as creative by such tests.

Another measurement problem is cited by researchers who believe that there are limitations to treating divergent thinking as synonymous with creative thinking and, therefore, to using divergent thinking tests to identify creativity (Runco & Nemiro, 1994). Although it is believed that divergent thinking is involved in some creative performances, it may not be involved in every creative task nor in every domain. And yet, Fuchs-Beauchamp, Karnes, and Johnson (1993) find that most currently available standardized measures of creativity for young children emphasize divergent thinking. There are currently many theories that do not base their construct for creativity only on divergent thinking (Tardif & Sternberg, 1988), so tests of divergent thinking such as the TTCT would not, from this point of view, be testing creativity.

It has been suggested that creative thinking may be specific to a task or content domain, but does not necessarily require mastery of that domain as a goal (Plucker & Runco, 1998), which would mean that creativity could not be generalized and creative acts within one content area would be independent of activity considered creative in another area of content. With such specificity, generic tests of creativity such as the TTCT would again have questionable validity. However, it should be noted that the TTCT has been extensively researched, provides updated norms, and shows evidence of long-term predictive validity regarding adult productivity after some 20 years (Fishkin & Johnson, 1998).

For several decades, giftedness was identified on the basis of high performance on either a test of intelligence or academic achievement. Some groups of students did not seem to do well on such tests and were, therefore, not included in programs for gifted education. As the country became aware of the oversight and tried to find ways to bring diversity to such programs, some school districts began the practice of separate identification, or identification by use of alternate means of assessment. The use of creativity tests became very popular for this purpose. It was assumed that students from diverse populations would do better on creativity tests than they had on the previous criteria for identification.

There were several problems with this practice. Many of the students tested under the special criteria did no better on the creativity tests than they had on the intelligence tests. Those who did do well were placed in the programs for gifted students who had been identified by their needs for advanced or more complex material as evidenced on intelligence or achievement testing. High scores on the tests of creativity did not necessarily mean that the special criteria students had these same needs, and when no changes were made to meet their needs, they found themselves often placed more inappropriately than they had been in the regular classroom. The result was that many of these students placed in gifted programs by special criteria were overwhelmed and less able to work to their level of ability. This practice also gave the false impression that students from minority groups could not do well on intelligence or achievement testing. Instead of broadening the population served in gifted programs by broadening the screening and identification for all students, special criteria testing became as discriminatory to diverse groups as the single intelligence or achievement test had been. The current emphasis on alternative identification and the increased data on such procedures now available from the Javits projects should ensure that no student will again have to experience the problems of special criteria identification.

Hunsaker and Callahan (1995) report that schools are still having problems in the testing of creativity. In their study of 418 districts throughout the country, they found three major problems: assessment of creativity was often done by a single test; the test of creativity chosen did not match the district's stated definition; and often tests devised by teachers were used without the support of background data available in the field.

When used as one of many types of evidence of a student's special needs, creativity testing can be useful. Such tests can point to the need of some students for differentiated materials and instruction. Creativity tests can show the degree of effectiveness of the strategies used in a program to develop creative thinking. They can measure many of the skills that are found to be needed for some types of creativity. Whether a creativity test can really measure the presence or absence of skills involved in creativity or of actual creativity is debatable. Creativity is a complex concept; however, it is certain that more than cognitive skills are needed in the use of high levels of creativity. Creativity is truly a holistic concept and even the most creative individual is unlikely to behave creatively or produce creative products when they are not involved and motivated.

BEING CREATIVE

Golemen, Kaufman, and Ray (1992) support the idea that everyone has a creative spirit and deplore the fact that so many do not see themselves as creative. In describing how creativity feels, Golemen and colleagues suggest, "when creativity is in full fire, people can experience what athletes and performers call the 'white moment.' everything clicks. Your skills are so perfectly suited to the challenge that you seem to blend with it. Everything feels harmonious, unified, and effortless" (p. 44). They believe that there is too much focus on Big C creativity, defining it as limited to the achievements of geniuses. Golemen and colleagues promote two ideas for nurturing your own creativity. First, develop the habit of paying attention to your own creativity, trust it, and use it to solve your daily problems. Second,

> each day, do one thing differently from your normal routine. You might go to bed at a new time, or take a new route to work or school. Or eat something you would never dream of eating. . . . The key is not to think about how to change things or to ask, "what is the best way to change them" but rather to change things for no other reason than just for the sake of it" (p. 43).

Adding to our understanding of the experience of being creative is the work of Csikszentmihalyi (1993). Beginning in 1990, he coined the term "flow" to describe the feelings of "concentration, absorption, deep involvement, joy, a sense of accomplishment . . . using psychic energy in a harmonious pattern . . . a sense of discovery, the excitement of self-discovery . . . going beyond what one has already achieved" (pp. 176–177). The flow experience includes:

- Clear goals with immediate feedback
- Personal skills well suited to given challenges
- A merge of action and awareness
- Task concentration that suspends worries, concerns, other stimuli
- A sense of potential control
- Loss of self-consciousness
- A sense of growth and being part of a greater entity
- An altered sense of time
- A sense that the experience is worth doing for its own sake

According to Csikszentmihalyi, "A creative product is never random or arbitrary; it must be true to something deeply sensed or felt inside the person" (p. 62). He believes that if the society is to allow all of us to become creative, it must not enshrine the creative solutions of the past into permanent institutions, but give people the opportunity and support to bring forth new ideas to be evaluated, selected, and joyously implemented. "The most satisfying way to actualize the self is by building that most complex system—a good society" (p. 272).

A summary of ideas for facilitating our own creativity taken from the research of Tucker (1986) is presented in Figure 3.4.

In trying to understand the act of creating, I have interviewed a number of people who have been acknowledged for their creative products and are successfully using their creative talents in their careers. Sharing some of their comments will serve to broaden our understanding of creativity while raising new questions regarding the nature of this elusive human ability.

Little children use the intuitive aspects of the creative process when they feel safe and will share with you the kinds of things that are happening to them. Once a little boy recorded a relaxation tape for me so that I could take it home and use it to relax myself. He was inspired to do this for me because I had been sharing short relaxation exercises with music for his class as introductions to the day or to begin specific lessons. Later that evening when I listened to his tape, I was amazed to find

Figure 3.4 *Ways to Facilitate Your Own Creativity*

Source: "Breaking Through with Your Ideas" by R. Tucker, 1986. *Creative Living, 15*(3), pp. 2–8.

- Allow relaxation time or "dream space." If you want a creative mind you must allow time for it to develop.
- Discover your best time and your best space for generating ideas. Your environment can support your creativity.
- Find other creative people to be with, people who excite you and stimulate your creativity.
- Once you are with these people, draw them out; ask questions about their interests and enthusiasms.
- Break out of old routines and patterns: try things you thought you didn't like or haven't tried.
- Generate a plan or deadline that you tell to someone else, then work toward meeting your own plan.
- Develop a high level of expertise in your area of innovation. Use information from diverse resources—books, magazines, and people, including other innovators.
- Discover other people's sources of inspiration.
- Study problems as opportunities for novel solutions.
- Try your ideas out on others, first with safe people, later with those who will be more critical.

that his tape, recorded the night before, was almost a word-for-word match of the relaxation session I had done in his class that morning.

When asked from where in her physical body her creative ideas come, a writer responded, "The material comes through from the back of my head, low, near my neck." She suggested that she simply flowed with the material, writing it down as it came. Sometimes she said she was unaware of what she had written until later when she read "her" work. She shared that she really enjoyed what had been written, especially delighting in the humor of the material. She found that she is highly energized by long periods of this flow of creativity; time passes without her awareness.

When asked the same question, a sculptor expressed this dilemma: "As I began to free my creative ideas, I found that an idea would come, and as I was beginning to work with this idea another would surface. At first I used to stop the first project and begin on the second only to find that shortly a third and a fourth would come into my mind. There seemed to be a flow of ideas waiting to be noticed, and I could not work fast enough to capture them all. I was afraid that I would lose some of the ideas as I tried to complete others. Then I discovered the solution. I could store new ideas while I carried one to completion and then tap into the next when I was ready."

"Where did you store the ideas?" I asked, thinking that he would suggest some area of his head as the holding area for these creative ideas. Instead he pointed to his upper arms. After thinking about this it seemed a perfect solution. His arms were the part of his body that helped release the idea and turn it into a completed product that communicated his thought to the world.

Another friend, an internationally known conductor-composer, shared the notion that her scores and arrangements were found on awakening, fully formed in her head. She would then go immediately to her studio at the back of her home and begin the task of putting these musical patterns onto paper. She would work, sometimes for days at a time, until all of the music that she could hear was recorded on paper. Her family was used to this behavior, and they had worked out a signal that allowed her to be undisturbed when one of these creative periods was in progress. Meals were delivered to the studio, and all other day-to-day business was taken over by her husband or other members of her staff. It was not unusual for her to spend more than a week in isolation with her muse.

Conditions that produce the creative act are not always the same among those to whom I have spoken. I prefer solitude, as does my composer friend, although she can re-create internal conditions of flow when she is interrupted and can then return to a productive state. However, when asked to write on demand within a time frame, the composer shows evidence of discomfort and finds that a panic reaction begins to set in (e.g., she sweats profusely and begins to doubt her ability). Under these conditions she cannot produce.

A young musician friend who has not yet achieved the success of the other creative artists and performers mentioned here finds a different climate necessary for her productivity. She writes original music best when sitting in a very interactive, noisy environment like a live music club, the louder the better. Her product may, however, be a gentle ballad. She agrees with the others that music comes through her, not from her.

Edison, Tessla, Mozart, and Hemingway all wrote of the creative product coming through them, not from them. Conditions vary with each person as to how such conditions should be arranged and what is necessary to allow their creative spirit to flow. Only one thing seems sure in any discussion of creativity: It is a complex matter unique to each individual. The best we can do may be to model our own valuing of the creative act, provide a rich and varied environment, and allow each person the safety, support, and time to find his or her own way.

Developing Creative Behavior

One of the most integrative forms of intuition is creative behavior. It is an important area of gifted education. Schools could make important contributions toward advancing creativity, for this aspect of development is considered learned behavior and, therefore, is capable of improvement through instruction. Skills such as those measured on the Minnesota Test of Creative Thinking (MTCT) have significantly improved through special programs. If schools are to do this job, there must be a change in their focus. Cole (1969) makes the point in an interesting analogy: If people were computers, then schools would be "programming" to receive, store, retrieve, and reproduce information only. We must also "program" other processes involved in the processing, organization, efficient use, and application of information. Williams (1968) believes that all learning involves creative organization of the culture's knowledge with the individual's experience. This creativity will then produce new and unique perceptions of the culture. Although the process may differ slightly from program to program, most agree with Wallas (1926) that it must include preparation, incubation, illumination, and verification.

Treffinger (1986) proposes a model that can be used to organize the fast-growing field of strategies to improve students' creative-thinking and problem-solving abilities. The model has three levels: I, Learning Basic Thinking Tools; II, Learning and Practicing Problem-Solving Models; and III, Dealing With Real Problems and Challenges. At Level I, students learn tools for generating and analyzing ideas, both divergently (e.g., brainstorming, attribute listing) and convergently (e.g., making inferences, thinking with analogies, categorizing). All gifted programs should include this level of learning, although students of all abilities would benefit from this opportunity.

Level II gives students the opportunity to apply the basic thinking tools in complex and systematic structures. Odyssey of the Mind and Future Problem-Solving exercises are examples of Level II activities. Students must have participative experiences in learning about and practicing these models.

Solving real problems is the focus of Level III. It is suggested that students have experience with the other levels before becoming involved in this level if they are to be successful.

This three-level model of creative learning allows us to monitor the kinds of activities presented to develop creativity and to be sure that the necessary experiences are a part of our curriculum. Treffinger and others envision the teacher as becoming the facilitator, the arranger of appropriate experiences, the encourager, the skill builder. Teachers who successfully develop creativity tend to have common behaviors:

- They do more thinking activities (convergent, divergent, evaluative).
- They use fewer memory activities.
- They use evaluation for diagnosis, not judgment; rewarding correctness of spelling, punctuation, grammar, neatness, handwriting, or quantity inhibits the production of original ideas.
- They give opportunities to use knowledge creatively.
- They encourage spontaneous expression.
- They provide an atmosphere of acceptance.
- They provide a wealth of stimulation from a rich and varied environment.
- They ask provocative questions.
- They value originality.
- They encourage students to examine new ideas on their merit and not dismiss them as fanciful.
- They provide for unevaluated practice and experimentation.
- They teach skills of creative thinking, such as originality, fluency, flexibility and elaboration, deliberate idea finding, deferred judgment, forced relationships, alternative thinking, and hypothesis setting.

- They teach skills of researching, such as self-initiated exploring, observing, classifying, questioning, arranging and using information, recording, translating, inferring, testing inferences, representing experience and observations, communicating, generalizing, and simplifying.

Another clue: Creative teachers have proved more effective at teaching creativity than those who are not themselves creative.

Some strategies to develop or release creative behavior are:

Trash Archaeology. Students collect wastebaskets from at least three locations in the school at the end of the day. Treat the trash basket as an archaeological dig and reconstruct the events throughout the day in that location, noting approximate times, events, possible antecedents, and outcomes, based on materials deposited in the trash basket. (Be sure to get permission from the people whose baskets are to be explored. Some trash could be classified and reveal top secrets.)

Creative Writing Pry-Mer. As a way of initiating creative writing, write the following categories across the top of the blackboard: Characters, Goals, Obstacles, Results. Ask the students to help you list 10 items under each category; for example:

Characters	*Goals*	*Obstacles*	*Results*
1. Wonder Woman	1. Peace	1. Fire	1. A big bang
2. Abraham Lincoln	2. Moon flight	2. Stupidity	2. Elected president

When there are 10 items in each category, ask the students to take their own telephone number, drop the first three digits and, using the last four digits, match the sequence to the numbers of the items in each of the four categories (e.g., for the phone number 555-1121 the items would be Wonder Woman, peace, stupidity, a big bang). They are now to write whatever story comes to their mind using their items. Ask students to share with the class if they wish.

Coherence Corner. Direct students to sit or lie down comfortably; take 10 to 15 minutes just to relax and imagine or meditate. Afterward, return to studies renewed. Materials needed include a tape recorder; tapes of natural sounds, tranquil or classical music, or relaxation exercises; a listening post (see Figure 3.5).

Too often we do not find a climate for creativity in our schools. Where we do acknowledge it, we tend not to recognize and nurture all four dimensions. As a society, we seem to have no plan for developing creativity within people. Individuals instead are convinced that they are not creative. It is a strange paradox that, although creativity is inherently human, it is an attribute that we accept the least within ourselves. We are often frightened of our creativity and unprepared to share it with each other.

In summary, creativity is best defined as a holistic concept that includes the rational, emotional, physical, and intuitive aspects. Characteristics and conditions for

Figure 3.5 *Thinking Space/Relaxation Corner*

the nurture of intelligence, giftedness, and creativity can be drawn from each of these aspects. Integrating all of the dimensions of creativity is a dynamic process that requires synthesis. It necessitates that we draw from all our other human functions. It seems to elevate us beyond just self to link with all of the universe. It is possibly the most exciting thing with which humans can be involved, truly the highest form of human purpose.

There is a growing awareness of the difference, the contribution that an integrated approach to creativity could make in our world. For example, physics and other areas of science are talking about wholeness and oneness. Perhaps as we become more aware of how our universe operates, we will be able to see more clearly how each of us creates the universe within which we live. Creativity will not be about something someone else does—it will be about us, about each and all of us. To create is beyond giftedness; it is to become a part of the universe.

QUESTIONS OFTEN ASKED

1. Why should we consider a holistic concept of creativity?

If we continue to look at only the rational aspect of creativity, or to believe that only the products of creative acts define creativity, then we will limit our understanding of the role creativity can play in our lives. If we include both the affective and the intuitive aspects of creativity, we will discover the amazing range of ways in which each of us expresses ourself creatively. We will appreciate our capability to create and be closer to realizing our unique human potential.

2. Is everyone creative?

Everyone has the potential for developing creativity, just as we each have as yet unknown potential for developing all aspects of our intelligence.

3. How can creativity be measured?

The cognitive rational aspect of creativity can be measured by current creativity tests. The products or physical aspects can be measured by highly proficient performers and artists through a jurying process. In either case, the standards will be those agreed to by the society doing the judging. The emotional and intuitive aspects may result in a breakthrough that can be communicated and may change the culture and thereby be judged. Our daily creative behaviors are more likely to be appreciated by those close to us or more importantly by ourselves. Experiencing ourselves as creative beings is a joy in itself.

4. Why can't more people be creative?

They probably can but they choose not to for fear of being thought different, strange, unusual, silly, dumb. . . . Unfortunately, being creative in a society that values rational, material gains requires taking risks. Some may not realize how creative they could be if given the opportunity and the belief in themselves. Safe places to be creative are sorely needed, both at school and at home.

5. Can we really teach people to be creative?

We can teach some of the aspects and skills of creative behavior. We can model creative acts and attitudes. We can provide safe places for creativity to be expressed, and we can value its expression. We can take the risk of sharing our creativity. It is doubtful that we can teach someone else all there is to know about being creative, but maybe being willing to share all we know about it will be enough.

 ## CHECKING FOR UNDERSTANDING
Follow-Up Activity

The following activity can be done in a classroom with other colleagues or by yourself: Sit in a chair with a plain piece of white paper and a pencil. **Be creative.** You have 5 minutes. At the end of 5 minutes look at your creation, then rate it on a scale of 1 to 5 as to how creative you believe it is. Now notice and list all of the things that you feel allowed you to be creative in this exercise. List all of the things that inhibited you from being creative.

If you are in a classroom with others, share your list with one or two of them.

Discuss with the class or ask yourself, What did this exercise help you to understand about:

- Conditions that facilitate creativity?
- Conditions that inhibit creativity?
- The role of motivation in creativity?
- Issues involved in rating or testing creativity?
- Your definition and understanding of creativity?
- Your feelings about yourself as a creative person?

Summarize your beliefs about creativity and its nurture.

SUMMARY

1. Creativity is a highly complex human ability that is beyond giftedness and can bring forth that which is new, diverse, advanced, complex, or previously unknown, so that humankind can experience growth in life as fuller, richer, or more meaningful. It can be

enhanced or inhibited in its development depending on the opportunities provided by the environment of the home and the school.

Creativity: Views of the Concept

2. The holistic view of creativity assumes a synthesis of enriched rational and spatial thought, heightened physical sensing and movement, sensitive emotional and social affect, and high intuitive consciousness. If you restrict any one of these functions, you reduce creativity.

3. Viewing creativity holistically allows the research from all other concepts of creativity to be used to better understand the phenomenon, its attributes and its nurture.

4. Some researchers and writers believe that creativity is a component of giftedness (e.g., Marland's federal definition; Sternberg, Renzulli, and Runco), whereas some believe it is an extension of giftedness and is either a concept that uses giftedness as a beginning point or as a concept beyond, requiring higher levels of development than giftedness (e.g., Gowan, Csikszentmihalyi, and Feldman).

5. The view of creativity as cognitive and rational, focuses on problem-solving and divergent thinking and is the view that is most researched and that has accumulated the most literature and nearly all of the testing.

6. The affective/emotional-social view of creativity includes the personality and motivation research, especially intrinsic motivation, self-expression, and personal value structures.

7. Products, such as music and art, resulting from a wide range of creative human endeavors and their evaluation are the concerns of those who support the physical/sensing view of creativity.

8. The intuitive view of creativity requires a focus on a higher level of consciousness and seeks understanding of the relationship between the person who creates and a higher expression, rarer state of energy, or perhaps the universe itself.

9. From the integrative view of the holistic model, creativity depends on the balance among cognition, emotion, action resulting in products, and the insight of intuition, synthesized into a meaningful whole.

Characteristics Commonly Found in Creative Individuals

10. For several decades, researchers have compiled lists of characteristics to differentiate highly creative persons from less creative ones. Although each list reflects the concept of creativity held by the individual compiling the list, they are quite similar in the characteristics given.

11. By knowing the characteristics commonly found in creative individuals, it is thought that creativity might be better understood, identification of creative individuals easier, their needs more clearly defined, and the learning experiences to enhance their creativity more accurate in reaching their goals.

12. The possibility exists that instead of focusing on common characteristics, the task should be to construct and explain the unique combination of traits each person exhibits and in this way discover the interaction of the characteristics within one person that creates the uniqueness of the individual and the complexity of creativity.

Conditions that Enhance or Inhibit the Development of Creativity

13. To be supportive of the developing creativity in very young children, adults must understand it, value it, and encourage the expression of it.

14. Parents of creative children have been found to have traits in common and practices in the home that have been identified as enhancing to the development of creativity.

15. Factors that enhance and undermine creativity in the schools have been suggested, with intrinsic motivation, openness, and the development of high levels of knowledge cited as most critical for nurture by many researchers and external rewards, pressure to achieve, evaluation, and lack of opportunity often cited as the undermining factors.

Measuring Creativity

16. The criterion for selecting and evaluating creative students has usually been a high score on a test designated as a creativity measure.

17. If tests are to be a part of the identification, then creativity tests should be used with other data for either evaluation of individuals or programs because there is disagreement in the field about the reliability and validity, especially the predictive validity, of creativity tests.

18. Among the most popular tests used in the educational setting are the performance or product measures, most notably those of divergent thinking.

19. Another way of measuring creativity that has been in use for decades is the external evalu-

ation of creative products. Assessment by experts of creative products has been found to be a valuable approach to measuring this area of creativity as have the use of portfolio, exhibits, and other forms of authentic performance assessment.

20. Tests of creative personality characteristics and attitudes along with biographical information form another category of creativity testing.

21. Problems have been found in measuring creativity, including: use of a single test to determine creativeness, questions of reliability and validity, exclusive or overuse of divergent thinking test items, generic tests of creativity used in specific content domains, and the use of creativity testing for special criteria identification of giftedness.

Being Creative

22. Adding to our understanding of the experience of being creative is the term "flow," which is used to describe the feelings of concentration, absorption, deep involvement, joy, a sense of accomplishment, a sense of discovery, and the excitement of self-discovery, including going beyond what one has already achieved.

23. Many researchers have suggested numerous ideas for facilitating our own creativity including: allowing relaxation time; discovering your best time and your best space for generating ideas; finding other creative people to be with; and trying things you thought you did not like or have not tried.

Developing Creative Behavior

24. Schools could make important contributions toward advancing creativity, because this aspect of development is considered learned behavior and, therefore, is capable of improvement through instruction.

25. Creative teachers have proved more effective at teaching creativity than those who are not creative.

4   *Becoming Gifted*

In this chapter the reader will discover discussions and information regarding:

- The importance of early learning to the development of giftedness.
- Some of the environmental influences on intellectual development during the prenatal, perinatal, infancy, and early childhood periods.

- The concept of sensitive periods and their importance to optimal development.
- Development of a responsive learning environment for optimal intellectual growth from birth through 3 months; 4 months through 10 months; 10 months through 2 years; and 2 years through 5 years of age.
- Parenting gifted children.

A child is not an object to be molded, but rather a treasure to be unfolded.

—ANONYMOUS

The phone rang, and as Ann answered it she became concerned at the worry she could hear in her daughter's voice. "Mom, I don't know what to do!" her daughter said excitedly.

"What's happened? What is the problem?" she asked Jane as she thought immediately of her new granddaughter, Lori, only a few months old. Jane wanted to be the very best mother and had read every book she could find on the subject. She had called frequently in the past few months, often concerned about minor things that were just the result of having a first child with no basis for comparison or experience to guide her. Jane had always been a perfectionist, so Ann wasn't surprised that she overreacted to each new event in Lori's life.

"Lori just rolled over! She was on her back and now she is on her tummy! She has done that several times. The books said she shouldn't do that for several months yet. What shall I do?"

Jane replied, making it sound like she was dealing with a real tragedy.

"Stop her! Don't let her do that!" Ann exclaimed, almost sounding concerned as she tried to keep from laughing. "We can't have her ahead of the book."

Hearing the laughter in her mother's voice, Jane calmed down and asked, "Is it all right? Everyone says precocious children have so many problems. I just want her to be normal."

"Sweetheart, I'm delighted she is developing so well. You were way ahead of all of the books yourself and, although it will be a challenge to keep up, precocious children are wonderful to live with. Let her guide you. She will know what is best for herself. You just have to surround her with lots of things to experience and let her show you what she likes best. Have fun with her—it's a special time."

The potential for giftedness, or high levels of intellectual development, begins very early in a child's life. Such development relies on a rich and appropriate interaction between the child's genetic endowment and the environment in which the child grows. No child is born gifted, only with the potential for giftedness. Although all children have amazing potential, only those who are fortunate enough to have opportunities to develop their uniqueness in an environment that responds to their particular patterns and needs will be able to actualize abilities to high levels. Diamond and Hopson (1998) explain that the brain grows smarter only when environmental stimulation demands it. An environment that is confining, solitary, and lacking in challenges requires a duller brain, and nature responds by shrinking the cortex and reinvesting the energy it would take to maintain a thicker cortex elsewhere. "Nature programs parts of the brain to sharpen up when—and only when—experience demands it . . . our learning capacity is boundless and lifelong" (p. 29). As Cross (cited in Diamond & Hopson) explains, "An animal is only as smart as it needs to be" (p. 29).

The best way to provide for children as they grow so that they can make the most of their potential will always be a concern for parents and teachers. Although all children have very different personalities, preferences, and abilities, there are some general rules and strategies that have been shown to help support young children in their pursuit of who they are.

As early as 1955, Pressey admonished educators and parents to create genius. Pressey's plan for developing genius is still thought provoking today (Pressey, 1964). He studied the careers of eminent European musicians in the nineteenth century and

American athletes in the twentieth century. He suggested that the following factors are important to their development and possibly to the development of all special talent or ability:

- Excellent early opportunities for ability to develop with encouragement from family and friends
- Superior early and continuing guidance and instruction
- Frequent and continuous opportunity to practice and extend their special abilities and to progress as they are able
- Close association with others of similar ability
- Opportunities for real accomplishment within their capabilities, but with increasing challenge
- Provision for strong success experiences and recognition of these successes

Although genius may not result, we have every reason to believe that a level of giftedness may be attainable for a great many children. Although Pressey's comments grew from logical theorizing, we now have evidence to support his conclusions. The new knowledge comes from data showing us the responsiveness of the central nervous system (CNS), including the brain, to environmental demands, and from new discoveries concerning the sensitivities and propensities inherent in the CNS. Dendrites on human brain cells will shrivel and the cortex grow thinner with lack of mental activity. By increasing the level of environmental stimulation and challenge, we can increase the branching of the dendrites and cortical thickness. A thicker cortex means a smarter brain (Diamond & Hopson, 1998).

In 1971, the brain researcher Elio Maggio wrote, "Experience . . . molds neurophysiological mechanisms, even those which appear more stable and closely depending upon genetic and biochemical factors" (p. 81). After decades of research, current brain researchers concur. Experience is crucial in organizing the way the basic structures of the brain develop, especially early in life. The impact of a stimulating or boring environment has been found to be widespread throughout the regions of the brain involved in learning and remembering (Diamond & Hopson, 1998). As documented by Siegel (1999), "A wide range of studies has in fact now clarified that development is a product of the effect of experience on the unfolding of genetic potential" (p. 18). Seigel states, "Genes contain the information for the general organization of the brain's structure, but experience determines which genes become expressed, how, and when" (p. 14) . . . "Experiences can shape not only what information enters the mind, but the way in which the mind develops the ability to process that information" (p. 16).

Even before data supported these theories, clues to the importance of the earliest years as the nurturing point for eminence had been found. In 1915, Colvin stated that all the prodigies he studied were educated from the first months of their lives. Terman in 1925, Hollingworth in 1942, and Fowler in 1962 reported that they found no subjects of high ability who had not been exposed to early stimulation. Goertzel and Goertzel (1962) reported on the lives of a host of eminent people and found that, without exception, these individuals had grown up in early stimulating environments. Ausubel (1967) even contended that failure to stimulate in the early years was irreversible. Young genes display more plasticity than adult genes. Educators have long believed in early achievement, especially in speech and reading, as a sure sign of giftedness. Let us now ask a question that I find as optimistic as it is fascinating: Can early opportunity for achievement and early stimulation create giftedness? More accurately, can such opportunity allow the developing child to actualize more of the potential available that may well fall within the range of development we call *gifted*?

EARLY LEARNING: THE IMPORTANCE OF DEVELOPING POTENTIAL

In 1976, Lipsitt, Mustaine, and Zeigler compared the findings of infant studies to the phenomena then being observed in athletics: Increased knowledge of human systems and their nurture, human aspirations and motivations, and opportunities for individual performance combine to bring out higher levels of excellence year after year. The first 4 years of life are the most critical for human development. Not only is physical survival tenuous, but patterns for both the personality and the actualization of learning ability have also begun. The personality established and the type of learning opportunities available will facilitate or inhibit the development of inherited intellectual capacity. However, we have the choice: We may either plan to provide the most nourishing environment that is possible within our current knowledge, or we may allow this important interaction to occur by chance. Regardless of how we choose to approach these formative years, interaction will occur and intelligence will develop. Whether that development leads to actualization or loss of human potential depends on us.

Prior to the 1960s, relatively few studies viewed the developing infant as more than a biological entity. The earlier picture of the infant showed a reflexive organism unable to see or hear, who was only partially aware of being alive. People believed that pain, pleasure, and perception came about much later, as the neural structure completed its development. No logical person would have spoken of stimulation. For that reason parents, mostly mothers, were given instructions on bathing, feeding, and other physical concerns related to infant care. Motherhood became very clean, sterile, and convenient, as disposable bottles, disposable diapers, and ever-increasing amounts of expensive equipment made mother and child more safe and hygienic. Classes on child rearing were held, again largely for mothers, but no one considered the mental development of the new person.

Then a few researchers began to observe and publish what many intuitive mothers already knew. Infants were far more capable than anyone had believed. From the moment of birth, their world was available to them. Some researchers even began looking at the prenatal and perinatal periods of development. The findings are exciting! From 1960 to the present, we have witnessed an explosion of information about these periods and the early childhood years. We can no longer "just let children be children" without an awareness that we are inducing events that will have permanent effects on their lives. Many of our children have been fortunate; many others have not. Knowledge is now available that will allow more children to actualize their potential. It may be that most children could be functioning at the level we now call *gifted* and some will experience further reaches of development as yet unknown. Through these discoveries, we are at the threshold of our understanding about human infants; there is still much to learn.

Clues From Animal Studies

Animal studies provide answers to some very important questions. At the level of gene action and cell development it is possible to generalize animal results to humans. Comparison is less useful at the behavioral level. In the first instance, the patterns of action are the same. At their brain research laboratories at the University of California at Berkeley, Krech (1969), Rosenzweig (1966), and their colleagues sought to discover the effect experience has on learning. They questioned whether differential experience could modify the brain in measurable anatomical and chemical terms. Their initial study involved two groups of rats from the same genetic strain. One group was reared in a nonstimulating environment, in which each animal was placed in solitary confinement in a small cage situated in a dimly lit, quiet room. These rats received no attention but had unlimited access to the same standard food provided both groups. Living together in large, wire mesh cages in a well-lit, noisy, busy laboratory environmentally enriched the other group. The cages were equipped with toys, and the rats were allowed to freely explore the environment outside of the cage for 30 minutes each day. On later examination, researchers found that the brain cortexes of the rats had significantly expanded and had grown thicker and heavier than those of the deprived group!

Of greater importance, researchers found an increase in the number of glial cells (which play a vital function in the nutrition of the neurons and in the learning capability of the animal), an increase in the size of the neuronal cell bodies and their nuclei, and an increase in the diameter of the blood cell supplying the cortex. Chemical changes had also occurred. Enriched brains showed more acetyl-cholinesterase, the enzyme involved in the transsynaptic conduction of neural impulses, and cholinesterase, the enzyme found in glial cells (see Chapter 2).

Later experiments showed that, in the brains of rats sacrificed after stimulation had ceased for a period of time, the weight and size changes were no longer apparent, but the chemical changes remained. These changes correlate with changes in problem-solving ability; stimulated rats rank as superior problem-solvers.

Application to Human Infants

From animal studies we have discovered some of the effects at the cellular level that experience has on learning. We find that the cortex of the brain expands significantly and grows thicker and heavier when conditions are stimulating rather than deprived. Glial cells increase in number, and the body and the nucleus of each neural cell increase in size. Measurable chemical changes also occur within the cell that correlate with higher levels of problem-solving ability. Increases in emotional stability, curiosity, and learning ability are evident. Most thought provoking is the finding that animals with inherited superior learning ability can lose their advantage over animals from a dull strain when both are raised in restricted environments. Even superior strains that are not stimulated can be surpassed in ability by hereditarily dull strains that have been environmentally enriched. Because it would be inhumane to subject human infants to such research conditions, we take information from animal studies because the nerve cells of the rat brain are virtually identical to human brain cells and work in exactly the same primary ways (Diamond & Hopson, 1998). This is so important because the brain can be shaped by stimulation and use, by disease and trauma, and by dull routine and disuse to direct what we may become.

Researchers explored the specific factors within the environment that interact with the characteristics of human infants to promote or facilitate development, such as home qualities, patterns of mother-child or father-child interaction, and forms of communication (Clarke-Stewart, 1973; Lewis & Rosenblum, 1974; White & Watts, 1973). Although there are still many unanswered questions, a substantial amount is known about the cognitive-affective-social capabilities of infants and the mechanisms that contribute to their development.

One question continued to concern early childhood educators: Can learning—or rather the benchmarks for development—be accelerated, or is it dependent solely on maturation? Among types of learning, physical control seems most clearly affected by maturation. Haynes, White, and Held (1965) conducted an experiment on newborns in a nursery to answer the preceding question. Researchers placed mobiles in the babies' cribs, replaced plain sheets and bumpers with patterned ones, changed positions of the infants, and provided other forms of sensory enrichment. When compared with other babies, the enriched group accelerated the first major event in the developmental motor sequence, fisted swiping, by several weeks. More important, Haynes and colleagues concluded that once children operate at a higher level, they assimilate more information to allow their cognitive development to proceed even more rapidly. Techniques to accelerate infant development include those that make available more color, more complex patterns, and more accessibility to the world around them. Hunt (cited in Pines, 1979a) tells us that development does not come just from exposure to stimulating environments. The child must be allowed to cope, to interact with the environment. Acting on things, interacting with people, and having the people and the environment be responsive are critical.

For educators, these studies and similar findings mean that with early stimulation, we may reverse the effects of deprivation that have occurred over past generations. Of course, we could equally restrict an environment to the degree that a leveling effect takes place, regardless of the genetic advantage enjoyed at birth. We can no longer leave early stimulation to chance. Although genetic differences among human beings do exist, such differences are insufficient to explain different intellectual abilities. Early experience can validate or invalidate the genetic contribution to our intellectual growth.

"Long-lasting effects occur as a result of experience. The more complex the experience, 'the richer' the environment, the more complex the brain" (Restak, 1986, p. 91). Uzgiris (1989), who spent more than a decade testing infants, urges that all children be given a chance to develop the full range of their abilities, because the competencies required for the future are unknown. She believes that "intelligence, even as measured by IQ, is a dynamic function, influenced by opportunities and learning, especially during the childhood years" (p. 5). She suggests that the public be educated as to the need for support for the education of very young children.

To use the environment as a powerful interacting agent, we must know more about our children and their capabilities. Environmentally produced individual differences begin at birth, possibly before. We must provide an environment rich in opportunities and responsive to each individual. We must also allow ourselves to be effective observers in order to assure optimal growth. If even such less-complex animals as rodents show individual differences and require differential treatment and programming, and if such programming can make such critical differences, what must infants require? Do we dare to neglect the implications of these findings?

Prenatal and Perinatal Interaction

Interaction with the environment begins to affect the infant significantly during the prenatal period. Diamond and Hopson (1998) found that there is no period with a more direct and formative effect on the child's developing brain than the 9 months of pregnancy. Some researchers investigating this area of growth warn that the history of the mother governs occurrences during this period. Use of drugs, alcohol, and cigarettes by the mother prior to conception will affect her ability to conceive a healthy fetus. Her diet, health habits, anxiety, and mental health will all be reflected in her child. Poverty, poor nutrition, and violence have also been cited as having a direct physical effect on eggs and sperm even before a child is conceived (Diamond & Hopson). Even more dramatic effects can be noted during the fetal period. Researchers have shown a cause-and-effect relationship between diseases, malnutrition, and drug use by the mother and damage to the growing fetus.

Quoting research from many sources, Verny (1981) has shown the fetus to be a hearing, sensing, feeling being. By the fourth month of gestation, the unborn child can frown, squint, and grimace. By the fifth month, the child is sensitive to touch. At 4 or 5 months, the unborn child reacts to sounds and melodies; Vivaldi and Mozart cause the child to relax, Beethoven and Brahms stimulate movement. It has been reported that the fetus hears clearly from the sixth month in utero and can be seen to move in rhythm to the mother's speech. In 1980, for the first time, scientists managed to record sounds from within the amniotic sac of a mammal. Using a sheep embryo, the experiment showed that external sounds, including conversation, are clearly audible. From these and other results on fetal hearing, it is now concluded that the auditory experience of the unborn child is more significant than was previously thought (Armitage, 1980). DeCasper (cited in Diamond & Hopson, 1998) has found sound preferences in newborns, such as the mother's voice and her heartbeat. He also found that fetuses are not just listening but, more important, they are learning in the womb.

By 5 months in utero the fetus is very sensitive to light. Verny (1981) reported that when a light is shone on the mother's stomach, the child will look the other way or show a startle reaction. By the seventh or eighth month in utero, the neural circuits of the fetus are as advanced as a newborn's, and the cerebral cortex is mature enough to support consciousness. Memory may begin somewhere between the sixth and the eighth month of gestation.

Reconfirming earlier data, Chamberlain (1993) in his summary of medical-scientific evidence found that infants are highly complex and advanced even before birth. The sense of sight, taste, and hearing are in place long before birth, and the sense of smell begins as gestation ends. Rapid eye movement (REM)-style dreaming seems to occur while the infant is still in the womb.

One area of concern to many prenatal researchers involves the self-esteem and security feelings of the infant. Attitudes of the mother seem to be picked up clearly by the infant in utero by the sixth or seventh month. Some researchers feel that the mother's attitude toward the child has the single greatest effect on the well-being and future welfare of the unborn. Even when the mother pretends to be pleased with the pregnancy but deeply resents or rejects the baby, the baby knows the true feelings and reacts to them. Intense stress or prolonged discomfort in the life of the mother is deeply felt by the infant she is carrying (Verny, 1981). Glover (cited in Chapman, 2000) found that not only can anxiety in expectant mothers result in babies born smaller and earlier, but it can be damaging over the long term for children. Anxious and troubled children who often develop behavioral problems result from unrelieved anxiety experienced by the mother during the pregnancy (Huttunen & Niskanen, 1978).

Natural childbirth and use of relaxation techniques during fetal development and birth are becoming widespread. Concern has been raised over birth trauma; procedures for ensuring the infant a less painful and shocking beginning have become common (Lamaze, 1970; LeBoyer, 1975). Verny (1981) shows evidence that how children are born—how painfully, smoothly, or violently—largely determines who they become and how they will view the world around them. The only reason we may not consciously recall our birth experience may be the amnesic effect of the hormone oxytocin, which is secreted by the mother during labor and birth. We can be deeply affected by the experience without consciously remembering it.

Bonding

The intimate, emotional attachment between mother and infant, called *bonding,* may affect our ability to optimize human development. Poor bonding may contribute to psychological and social disorders throughout childhood and shows a high correlation with unsocial, unproductive adult behavior, even violence. The quality of the bonding may be determined by at least three variables: hormones, physical contact, and timing. The increase in estrogen levels experienced by the mother just before birth provides a triggering for the bonding response but is not sufficient to establish it; physical contact within moments of the birth experience seems to be required (Kennell & Klaus, 1979). Says Kennell, "The hours after birth seem to comprise a sensitive period for maternal-infant attachment" (Marano, 1981, p. 66). In ways that are physiologically measurable, bonding buffers both mother and child from the effects of stress. Breastfeeding, frequent verbalizing with the infant, holding, and rocking all are factors in good bonding.

At 1 year, mothers who have bonded spent more time supporting and caring for their babies. At 2 years, the linguistic patterns of early bonded mothers enhanced the development of complex linguistic skills. The early responsiveness of infants to their environment and their ability to interact with their parents make this an optimal period for the formation of affectional bonds. Verny (1981) contends that children who learn most quickly and seem happiest have bonded with their mothers after birth. "By joining mother and child, bonding supplies not only someone who understands and loves the baby but also an ally who can provide the infant with the stimulation he needs to expand emotionally and intellectually" (p. 153).

Bonding after birth seems to be a continuation of the bonding process begun in the womb. The last 2 or 3 months before birth are important for establishing affectional ties that can be carried into the hours and days immediately after birth. Study after study show that happy, contented women are far more likely to have bright, outgoing infants. The when and how of optimal development—the beginning of giftedness—must be seen as occurring before birth. Intelligence depends in part on the life of the unborn child.

OPTIMIZING LEARNING: DEVELOPING GIFTEDNESS (BIRTH THROUGH 2 YEARS)

A number of studies in the past decade have shown abilities of infants that are at variance with models of development previously accepted, such as that of Piaget (1952). Such previous models have seriously underestimated the abilities of infants, as Lori showed us in the opening vignette. Klaus (cited in Marano, 1981) found that newborns born to unmedicated mothers spend nearly 40 minutes of their first hour in a state of rapt attention, with their eyes bright, wide open, and capable of focusing and fixating on objects. We now know that infants are active at birth—they are perceiving, learning, and information-organizing individuals. Infants are born with depth perception, eye-hand coordination, sensory coordination, and skin sensitivity. They demonstrate, learn, remember, and show distinct preferences for certain sounds, shapes, and tastes.

Siegel (1999) reports that from the first days of life, the infant's brain is capable of creating mental models from a variety of sensory inputs. This suggests that the ability to create generalizations from experience is possible from the very beginning. Infants less than 1 month old have recognized images of objects that they have only felt in their mouths (Baillargeon, cited in Raymond, 1991b). Restak (1986) summarized by saying, "The neonate is a storer of information, can transform aspects of his world into representations, manipulate these representations, and infer that something felt in the mouth looks a certain way and no other" (p. 195).

Rovee-Collier (cited in Grunwald, 1993) found that even at $2\frac{1}{2}$ months "an infant's memory is very developed, very specific, and incredibly detailed" (p. 49). We can already see evidence by 3 months of age of the limitations the environment may be inflicting on intellectual growth. Researchers have observed that tests administered during this period can predict to a certain extent future language development, quality of interaction with the environment, and personality characteristics that help determine future learning patterns.

Psychologically, Chamberlain (1993) finds babies to be aware, expressive, and affected by their interactions with others, possessing an understanding of self from day one. By 2 days, infants recognize and mimic expressions and gestures that they cannot see themselves perform. Meltzoff and Moore (cited in Goode & Burke, 1990) found that not only do babies as early as 72 hours old copy the actions of adults, but they also mimic emotional expressions such as smiles, frowns, and looks of surprise. They express emotions, findings of which are supported by Lewis (cited in Fergusen, 1993) and his colleagues, and are strongly attracted to faces and voices, being especially partial to their parents. Touch is important in the development of the infant. Nash (1997) reports that researchers at Baylor College of Medicine have found that the brains of children who are rarely touched or engage in little play develop 20% to 30% smaller than normal for their age. Touch is indispensable for establishing normal feelings of affection and care; for attachment and for maintaining optimal physiologic function; and for preventing physiological imbalances, behavioral peculiarities, hostilities, and suppressed anger and rage. It is as necessary to normal infant development as food and oxygen (Restak, 1986).

Spelke (cited in Grunwald, 1993) suggests that at as young as 4 months of age, babies have a rudimentary knowledge of the way the world works. She believes that there is biologically programmed core knowledge not only of physics but of other cognitive skills as well. Other researchers (cited in Grunwald) concur, including Wynn, who has found a rudimentary ability to add and subtract as early as 5 months; Strauss, who finds infants of this age clearly thinking about quantities and applying numerical concepts to their world; Kuhl, who regards infants from birth to 4 months as universal linguists able to distinguish each of the 150 sounds that make up all human speech and then by 6 months able to recognize speech sounds of their native tongue; and Clifton, who discovered that experiences that infants have at 6 months can be remembered 2 years later. Such evidence indicates that infants are far more capable than has been assumed.

Dalzell (1998) reports studies indicating that infants, later classified as gifted, show a preference for novelty and precocity in domains such as verbal or mathematical. Nelson (cited in Raymond, 1991b) is linking these abilities to changes in the brain in an effort to better understand the nature of the representations and how they function. He has found patterns in the brains of infants as young as 6 months that show that they can distinguish familiar from unfamiliar experiences. Other neuroscientists are studying what happens in the brains of infants when they learn to talk or develop concepts. Studying the brain's organization and responses to learning in infants will continue to aid psychologists and educators to enrich and optimize development.

Creating a Responsive Learning Environment for Early Learning

A rich and varied environment that responds to the child's abilities, needs, and interests is referred to as a *responsive learning environment* and is the first step in optimizing learning. In the process of developing intelligence, infants and young children have a great need for such an environment. Both people and objects in the

The best rule for stimulating an infant is to maintain a responsive environment.

environment can be growth producing only if they have some meaning or use for the child. Brown and Pollitt (1996) have shown that it is a lack of environmental stimulation during 1 to 3 years of age that can lower IQ scores and learning ability. According to Jeffrey (1980), it is not the stage or sequences of development that is our most important focus, but rather the individual differences that appear with that development, differences in the ability to perform and to profit from the experiences provided.

Age is an inadequate index of neurological and physical maturation, because both are changed by the environment of the child and by that child's genetic program. Using our present knowledge, we could best provide the optimal responsive learning environment by relying on the human resources of infants to select, from a large quantity of activities provided, only those events or experiences that are uniquely stimulating to them. These would provide the best match for each infant's point in development.

Diamond and Hopson (1998) provide a description of what research from the neurosciences conclude is an enriched environment:

- Includes a steady source of positive emotional support
- Provides a nutritious diet with adequate amounts of protein, vitamins, minerals, and calories
- Stimulates all the senses (but not necessarily all at once!)
- Provides an atmosphere free of undue pressure and stress but suffused with a degree of pleasurable intensity
- Presents a series of novel challenges that are neither too easy nor too difficult for the child at his or her stage of development

- Allows for social interaction for a significant percentage of activities

- Promotes the development of a broad range of skills and interests that are mental, physical, aesthetic, social, and emotional

- Gives the child an opportunity to choose many of his or her own activities

- Gives the child a chance to assess the results of his or her efforts and to modify them

- Provides an enjoyable atmosphere that promotes exploration and fun of learning

- Above all, enriched environments allow the child to be an active participant, rather than a passive observer (pp. 107, 108)

The child in interaction with a responsive learning environment will be our best guide to optimal development.

From Birth Through 3 Months

The first 3 months of postnatal life may be the most critical for the infant's developing brain since the first trimester of intrauterine fetal life. During this period the infant has no mobility and depends on the caregiver for all intellectual stimulation. We know that the baby can see, hear, and smell, and can do all these things with discrimination. Here is a baby ready to interact with the environment, ready to learn. In too many cases this interaction is severely limited—so much so that some researchers have called this period the greatest deprivation period for human infants. Activities that have proved enriching for some infants could, in a responsive learning environment, be made available to all newborns.

The optimal environment for an infant must include attention to all of the basic needs, both physical and psychological, from the moment of birth. The needs for security, safety, nutrition, belonging, and love are basic to all infants. Only as these needs are met can the infant give any attention to self-concept and intellectual development at optimal levels. Indeed, how the basic needs are met will critically influence how self-concept and intellectual ability develop. As early as 1968, Yarrow reported that infants who are gratified much of the time and who infrequently experience tension show more capacity for handling stress than infants more often subjected to frustration. Infants in an environment characterized by frequent and exuberant expressions of positive feelings tend to develop a high degree of initiative. Other books deal in detail with how to provide for the basic needs. Although they cannot in reality be separated from intellectual growth, we artificially make that separation. Here we assume that attention to the basic needs is given, as we explore means of optimizing the growth of intellectual ability.

Researchers (cited in Goode & Burke, 1990) indicate that parenting must be very flexible and individually tailored to the unique needs of each infant. Infants vary greatly from birth in temperament, activity level, and reaction to sound, light, and touch. Strong preferences are already being shown at 6 weeks of age. Parents have for years approached the cognitive areas of learning cautiously for fear of harming their child or teaching something in the "wrong" way that would need to be unlearned at a later time. With a responsive learning environment approach, there can be no wrong way of learning. In a situation in which the child and the parent respond sensitively to each other, only growth and pleasure in learning can be the outcome.

From birth, innate programming seems to facilitate the use of language, hands, eyes, and so forth by the human infant. Unlike any other animal, the human infant has the ability to pick up logical rules. This important competency is basic and available from birth. Not only do infants notice more detail in the environment, they also actively invent rules or theories to explain what they observe. Even at 3 weeks, an infant will have complex hypotheses about the world and will react with concern if proved wrong.

Over and over in the literature on development of intellectual capacity we find reference, usually emphasized, to the importance of responding to an infant's cues or signals of distress. In times past it was thought that picking up babies when they cried would "spoil" them. The results of not attending to, ignoring, or allowing infants to "cry it out" are now viewed as far more damaging. One of the differences between institutionalized infants and home-reared infants is that institution personnel do not attend to crying behavior. The results indicate that institutionalized infants lose their sense of control over the environment and become passive, externally motivated children. This does not produce optimal intellectual growth. The quantity, timing, and degree of consistency of the caregiver's responses to the infant play important roles in developing and reinforcing the infant's belief that his or her behavior can affect the environment. This belief regarding inner locus of control, the belief that one matters in the world, seems to be learned early in life.

It is important to know that, for a few days after birth, an infant seems able to cope with only one activity at a time. Between 3 and 5 weeks, the infant can do one thing, such as nurse, while looking at another source of interest. However, when the viewed activity becomes more interesting, the first activity stops. Between 2 and 4 months, an infant will continue the first activity while involved in the second, but with less intensity, almost as though the shift can more easily be made between the two if participation in the first activity is at least superficially maintained.

This period of the infant's development is important because it holds an initiating place in the child's learning system. What first goes into the system in the way of skills, beliefs, and ideas will set up a resistance to future dissimilar patterns of learning. Initial learning is far more difficult to unlearn. In the activities outlined in Table 4.1, it must be stressed that the caregiver is the most critical factor in the child's learning.

At around 6 weeks infants can distinguish color, calculate distances as being reachable or nonreachable, and see shapes and intensity of light. Stern (1990) suggests that infants enjoy stimulating experiences in which excitation mounts, but not too fast or too high. They are bored by situations of low stimulation or sameness. Between 8 and 12 weeks, infants' capacity for interaction dramatically develops, and infants begin to smile, vocalize, and hold eye-to-eye contact.

By 3 months of age, infants begin to show curiosity, anger, pleasure, and assertiveness. They know what to expect from their mothers and are disturbed by deviation too far from the usual routine or her still face. Animation and simple playful exchanges of vocalizing and smiling with caregivers begin to establish the patterns of healthy socialization.

Not only is cognitive stimulation necessary, but also emotional involvement is shown to predict later intellectual development. Early laughter at complex events is probably one of the best predictors because it taps the motivational, attentional,

Table 4.1 *Creating a Responsive Learning Environment for Early Learning: From Birth Through 3 Months*

Caregiver Activities	Because
Respond to infant's activity and signals (e.g., awakening and looking); offer objects for baby to look at.	Establishes feeling of inner locus of control, ability of child to affect the environment.
Respond to distress signals (crying) and give attention to cause. Crying it out is definitely *not* recommended.	Establishes a code of mutual expectancy.
Breastfeed if possible, for the benefits to both the infant and the mother. If you must bottle feed, change positions for each feeding (e.g., right arm holding baby, then left). This happens naturally when breastfeeding.	Encourages development and coordination of both eyes.
Change position of crib in room.	Increases visual stimulation.
Place mobiles over crib, patterned with a variety of shapes, colors (make your own); use patterned sheets, clear bumpers; change position and surroundings of infant.	Develops visual complexity skills, nourishes growth of intelligence through heightened interaction with the environment, stimulates curiosity.
Rock infant while holding next to chest for 10-minute periods; pick up infant and place on the shoulder. Rocking chairs are most useful at this age.	Infants handled in this manner show more visual attention than other infants.
Allow bare-skin cuddling, yours and baby's; rub baby's skin with nubby towel when drying; tickle, squeeze, and pinch a little in games; give baby "feely" objects, put them in hand (e.g., velvet, silk, sponge).	Stimulates sensory development; baby learns about feeling.
Turn lights on and off for visual stimulation.	Infants are normally overly sensitive to bright sunlight; care must be taken not to create discomfort.
Provide a variety of sounds and speech patterns (musicbox, radio, variety of rhythms, voices).	These are important prelanguage experiences.
Sing songs to your baby throughout the day and end with an evening lullaby. Move baby's arms and legs to rhythm of songs on occasion.	Intimately and familiarly introduces music and rhythm; soothes baby.
Play vocal games, imitate baby's cooing, introduce real words by naming body parts and toys.	Familiar sounds are of high interest to infants; builds vocabulary, initiates conversation, establishes babies' perceived control of their lives.
Allow lots of different smells.	Stimulates olfactory sense.
Introduce the playpen or a hard, broad surface, not carpeted. It allows baby to move from room to room with you. Cover the floor with a plastic mat and turn baby loose on tummy. Keep temperature up so that baby can play without restrictive clothing (85°F). Play on floor with baby, be near; encourage movement (e.g., rolling over, creeping).	Allows intellectual stimulation.
Place baby in an infant seat or baby swing and move it from room to room as you do your chores.	Allows visual, intellectual stimulation while having security of nearness to caregiver.
Carry baby in front pack or other soft carrier when possible.	Allows parent to do chores and talk to baby while baby watches, listens, and naps next to heartbeat.

affective, and cognitive abilities of the infant. Rothbart (cited in Grunwald, 1993) has shown that insecure, shy, and inhibited babies can be changed to outgoing, confident babies by adult intervention. In the soothing process, adults help to teach babies to shift attention from negative sensations, a process adults with anxiety disorders may never have learned. Ignoring babies' fussiness is not a productive parental response.

Rocking and cuddling infants will reassure them and allow them to feel wanted and loved. Parents should also respond to babies' coos and giggles. In this way, infants learn that they can influence the world and that they really matter. The infant will learn that actions other than crying bring attention. However, one need not wait for these signals. Playing regularly with babies, enjoying them, and displaying spontaneity and affection will establish a basis for loving that will last a lifetime. Such care will allow infants to develop into trusting, loving, warm human beings.

In an interesting study, Carew (1976) reported that children prior to 2 years of age require demonstrations and modeling behaviors on the part of the caregiver. The person in charge of the infant needs to provide a variety of language patterns, visual encounters, and other sensory opportunities for the growing infant. However, such interaction should be responsive to the child. Fear of overstimulation is unnecessary as infants rarely allow themselves to be overstimulated without giving some indication to the offending adult. In this context, consider the response some thoughtless parents get when they take tired infants into restaurants or public meetings. We can all vouch for the unmistakable messages the infant is sending. The study indicated that to be most facilitative in developing a child's potential, direct guidance is advisable and necessary prior to 2 years of age, whereas opportunities for discovery and encounters within a rich environment are preferred after that age. Guidance will, of course, still be necessary.

A responsive learning environment can occur only through an aware adult who responds to signals initiated by the child. Stimulation and demonstration of language and skills are available only if the adult provides them. Be aware that 90% of all social interaction with a baby from birth to 18 months occurs during caregiving activities such as changing diapers, dressing, bathing, and feeding. These activities should be treated not as chores to get out of the way as quickly as possible but as learning opportunities and as times to communicate with the baby. Parents must be encouraged to smile and talk a lot even if they feel the baby cannot understand. These are the most important moments of the baby's life. A major factor in the success of parents of competent infants is the parents' belief that they can influence their child's mental development (Kagan, 1971). Seigel (1999) reminds us, "parenting has a direct effect on developmental outcome, even in the face of significant inherited features of physiological reactivity" (pp. 20, 21). Table 4.1 gives specific suggestions to parents for activities most appropriate to this age group.

From 4 Months Through 10 Months

Much physical activity begins from 4 months through 10 months that will remain a dominant factor throughout infancy. Societies that value and use physical affection and bodily contact in rearing their young produce relatively nonviolent adults (Restak, 1979). Among the most productive methods of providing such contact are holding, carrying, rocking, and cuddling the child. Restak considers movement and physical closeness absolute requirements for normal brain development and believes that immobility alone can create abnormal mental experiences and disturbed behavior. Understimulation can result in later hyperactivity.

During this period, interest in active exploration will also be noticeable: exploring with touch, by mouthing; with sounds, by reaching; and always visually. The amount of visual experience, the decor and colorfulness of the home, the presence of a variety of responsive play objects, and the freedom to explore the environment are seen to have a significant relationship with performance on infant testing from 5 months to 36 months. The infant enjoys people now more than before and develops obviously affectionate ties. From 4 months through 10 months can be a delightful period for both child and caregiver (Table 4.2).

Four-month-old babies have been shown to detect sight-sound correlation. In one experiment, two films were presented to the babies, one of a woman playing peek-a-boo to the camera and the other a musical showing musical instruments. Each had an appropriate accompanying sound track. The films were presented side by side in front of the infants with the sound tracks played one at a time. The infants watched the film that was appropriate to the sound track being played at each moment. Another experiment had a mother and father sitting side by side while one or the other of their voices played between them and their baby at $3\frac{1}{2}$ months of age. Again, the baby could easily identify which parent was talking and turned her attention to the appropriate parent (Restak, 1986).

From 10 Months Through 2 Years

White (1975), in his work at the Harvard Pre-School Project, has established this period as the most decisive for intellectual development. White thinks it essential to nurture balanced development in many areas, including children's interests, people (noticeably the primary caregiver), exploration of the world, and use of their own bodies (for instance, motor skills). This period will bring essential development in language, curiosity (leading to motivation), social development, and intelligence (Table 4.3).

During the 10-month to 2-year period, the baby experiences real mobility. The major driving force seems to be curiosity. At this stage, the infant's curious nature establishes roots and begins to flower into what will later be experienced by the learning child as motivation. Unreasonably applied limits and controls can cause frustration, leaving an aimless, internally unmotivated child as a result. Let us stress that allowing a baby to freely explore the environment (made safe by having dangerous items placed out of reach) is the single most important action to ensure intellectual growth. The environment need not be filled with expensive toys. Any small, manipulatable, visually detailed articles, objects to climb on, objects to move on, all easily accessible, will provide much stimulation. As the baby increasingly experiments and interacts with the environment, guidance, of course, is necessary. Whenever possible, the natural environment should be used to provide correction for the baby's misjudgments. In this way, natural consequences can themselves become teachers, and the baby can learn to change or adapt in his or her own way.

A toddler I observed waiting for a plane with his mother was engaged in exploration of the airport environment. Suddenly, as the baby was walking along a

Table 4.2 *Creating a Responsive Learning Environment for Early Learning: From 4 Through 10 Months*

Caregiver Activities	Because
Use playpen only until baby becomes mobile; if used later, only for very short periods (5 to 10 minutes).	Playpen restricts environmental interaction, limits intellectual development.
Provide toys of interest, such as mirrors (very appealing to baby now; be sure they are safe, unbreakable); stacking toys; moderately small objects for dropping, throwing, banging. Moving and pop-up toys are interesting late in this period. Be cautious about expensive "educational toys"; it is not necessary to buy toys; homemade toys, designed to baby's needs, are often far better.	Provide intellectual stimulation.
Play games with fingers and toes, stroke legs, pat back; talking and identifying parts of baby can also be added. Encourage baby to pat caregiver, touch fingers, play pat-a-cake; allow to play unrestrained by clothing.	These activities contribute to the baby's perception of self and the beginnings of cognitive experience.
Play peek-a-boo games.	Provide visual, auditory, problem-solving stimulation; encourage cognitive anticipation.
Play, talk, interact with infant during all caregiving activities.	Most important for language development and motivation.
Encourage new games invented by baby such as drop toy—caregiver picks it up—baby drops toy.	Baby develops beginnings of inner locus of control, senses an active influence on environment; increases motivation.
Play games using eyes and language in games, such as "Look at Daddy, look at Mommy, look at baby's foot, look at kitty, look at . . ." (include things above, below, to right, to left).	Promotes eye coordination and focus, language experience, coordinating sight and sound, words with things.
Take trips to the grocery store, drugstore, department store (only when baby is rested, *not* during usual nap time). While on trips, talk about what is being seen.	Alert attention to varied environments and allow enrichment of sensory experience.
Cook and talk to baby, talk at meals, encourage baby to use words (infant seats are useful on trips or to have baby nearby as you work).	An important language experience.
Look at books and talk, read to baby; use different voices or create funny faces while reading.	Symbols of language become familiar, important, a source of fun and pleasure.
Carry baby in backpack for walks and while doing chores.	Allows baby to see the world and all that you do.
Use familiar lullaby tapes at nap and bedtimes.	Provides security in routine and encourages language skills.
Introduce baby to activities set to music; musical instruments.	Enjoyable and helps familiarize baby with music and rhythms.

Early exploration is important to later development.

railing, he came to a hinged gate that opened into the area behind the counter. The hinge was fairly strong, but the child could swing the gate open a short way before it returned to a closed position on its own. The toddler pushed open the gate over and over, intent upon watching the hinge and the automatic return of the gate. He was hurting no one nor was he bothering anyone. Even if the gate had closed on his hand it would have caused little discomfort and would have provided a lesson the child would likely have incorporated into his schema for swinging doors. However, his mother saw him moving the gate and rushed to scold and spank, hurting him far more than the gate would have. Noisy crying followed, accompanied by more spanking. What should have been a useful learning experience became a power struggle ending with a frustrated, sobbing little boy commanded to sit in an overly large adult chair until his mother felt he could "behave himself."

This was in contrast to a mother I observed on a ferry one afternoon cautiously monitoring her toddler's actions while appearing unconcerned. Only when the child approached a dangerous situation, such as an open ventilation duct, did the mother move up to him to distract him to some new interest. She never interfered with his dignity nor attempted to be overly controlling. Both the mother and the little boy were enjoying the trip.

Babies are remarkably curious from 10 months to 2 years about things adults would find totally uninteresting, such as hinged doors, cellophane wrappers, tiny

Table 4.3 *Creating a Responsive Learning Environment for Early Learning: From 10 Months Through 2 Years*

Caregiver Activities	Because
Organize and design a safe physical environment that allows for a variety of sensory experiences; family living areas and outdoor areas should be available for exploration of the senses.	Gives intellectual stimulation, supports later learning, strengthens perception and problem-solving abilities.
Visual: plants, fish in bowls, pictures, patterned objects, mirrors.	
Auditory: exposure to many types of music, voices, rhythms, singing, bells, drums, shakers, music boxes, animal sounds.	
Tactile: a variety of textures to feel (soft, hard, rough, smooth), sculpture, finger food, mud play, finger paints, painting with Jell-O.	
Olfactory: bakery smells, flower smells, farm and field smells.	
Gustatory: snacks of differing tastes and textures.	
Provide a variety of toys and household objects to play with: for stringing, nesting, digging, pounding, screwing; construction toys (pieces not too small), pegboards, record players, magnets, magnetic letters, alphabet blocks, prisms, water toys, flashlights, spin tops, jigsaw puzzles, magnifying glasses, dolls, collections of small objects, toy animals, various household tools, books, and art materials.	
Play games like hide-and-seek, treasure hunts, guessing games, matching and sorting, finger games, circle games; encourage and provide materials for imitative play, such as "I do what you do."	Facilitates concept development, practice in planning and carrying out complicated projects, anticipating consequences, developing skills of problem solving.
Teach child to be aware of and name objects in the environment (including baby's own body parts). This can be done by playing games with the caregiver, giving names to objects as they are used.	Provides language experience.

pieces of dust, and plant leaves. Parents should expect fascinated repetitions and allow for them. They should be extra alert to remove dangerous items from the environment. In this way, children can begin their own self-initiated, autonomous learning.

To develop the goal-directed behavior so important to learning activity, children from 10 months through 2 years of age must experience satisfaction from their efforts, response to their actions, support for reaching out, safety, acceptance, and trust (Figure 4.1). Only as these are made a part of children's lives will they begin to explore and move cognitively toward mastery of more complex skills. If deprived of these experiences, their motivation for learning and potential for wonder and discovery are stunted. Creativity as well as competence will suffer.

As children become more mobile they need to interact with a rich environment for optimal intellectual development to occur. Accessibility to the living area

Table 4.3 *continued*

Caregiver Activities	Because
Look at scrapbooks with child, read books to child, make books familiar. Be sure to involve the child in the reading activities; help child "read" stories to dolls, other siblings, relatives.	Provides symbolic language experiences.
Make scrapbooks with the child of pictures of animals, cars, trips. These can become the child's own books.	Gives language experience.
Talk to baby during all caregiving activities: bathing, dressing, eating; use patterns of speech with baby that you use with other members of the family; short 20- to 30-second "conversations" are important.*	Helps baby to understand more complicated sentences, increases language background and experience.
Take neighborhood walks to library, stores, playgrounds, on collection excursions, out to feed birds; always discuss what is seen and experienced.	Provides a background of experiences for future concept building.
Include child in your activities whenever possible: cooking—use bowls and utensils; writing—child can write with crayons; painting—child can paint with water.	Builds self-esteem while giving the child a better understanding of your work.
Toddlers spend most of their time gaining information, building concepts, and observing.	

*When engaging children in "conversation" try to talk about what they are doing from their perspective. Try to understand their meaning for the activity and what they may be learning from it. Then try to give them something new and interesting to think about along the same lines. Allow children to initiate the activity and then respond enthusiastically, but be careful not to insist on doing it only your way.

Also use language to heighten curiosity and develop interest. Teach children vocabulary words to express their interests by engaging them at the point of interest. This will further help children see adults as valuable resources. Talk to your child even before you are sure the child understands what you are saying. It is important to use a variety of speech patterns and normal conversational intonations. Remember, you are the model. Although the act of repeating sounds the baby makes is fun and can be enjoyed by both adult and baby, the child needs good speech models and language patterns. Babytalk does not provide a useful model for children to emulate. Children do create unusual patterns for their own use. However, repetition of these patterns by the adult limits children to those unique patterns.

and outdoor areas enhances discovery and self-initiated activities by children. The caregiver must carefully prepare these areas to make them safe and filled with sensory experiences. Lots of objects and materials, not only toys but common household items and junk, all help to construct responsive learning environments. Overuse of playpens and walkers at this stage can be detrimental to intellectual development. The caregiver should continue with trips, reading, and other activities enjoyed by the child in earlier stages. Now more activities of a physical, manipulative nature should be included. Demonstration and modeling behavior by the caregiver are still important.

Bauer (cited in Raymond, 1991b) has shown that by 20 months, babies can imitate sequences they have seen 6 weeks earlier. She suggests that because babies can be shown to have recall, they must have some kind of representational tool to allow them to think about objects and people.

Figure 4.1 *A Parent's Guide to a Toddler's Responsive Learning Environment*

Sources: Adapted from *Early Learners* (pp. 16–18) by A. Hayward, 1985, Los Angeles: The Education Institute.

- *Make use of famous works of art:* Change the pictures in the child's room once a month. Have available varied pictures, posters, charts, etc. Traditional children's pictures can be mixed with reproductions of famous works of art (usually available on loan from libraries, museums, or universities). Hang some of the reproductions at the child's eye level. Hayward states, "A two-year-old child I knew would often get out of her bed at nap time and sleep on the floor underneath a picture that she adored which was taped about two and one-half feet above the floor" (p. 17).
- *Have a surprise bag:* Change the object once or twice a week. Without looking inside the bag the child puts his or her hand inside, then feels the surprise and tries to guess what it is. Begin with objects that are easy to identify and, as the child's ability to observe and analyze increases, use objects that are less readily distinguishable. Treat the child's mistakes as helpful clues and encourage risk-taking.
- *Hang educational charts:* Have charts of the alphabet, animals, the development of a seed into a plant, etc., on the wall for the child to observe and discuss. (These charts are available at educational supply stores.) Clear contact paper extends the life expectancy of pictures or paper materials that children will be handling.
- *Use child-sized bookshelves:* Place the bookshelves low enough to allow children to reach books, magazines, catalogs, department store fliers, and other reading materials that are an important part of the child's environment.
- *Use the yard as a laboratory:* The yard can be a marvelous laboratory wherein the child can observe and experiment. Such things as where puddles go, why shadows change their size and shape, how rocks can be so many different colors, etc., can be fascinating. Do some of the experiments listed in children's science books.
- *Use the community for learning:* Libraries, museums, children's theaters, concerts, tide pools, markets, and businesses all enrich the child's experience. Prepare for the "field trip" by discussing and reading about the whats and whys of the place you will be visiting. Have the child ready to look for some specific item or event when you go. Be sure to discuss the trip when you return, and allow the child to do something to record or remember the important things that were observed. An increasing number of resources and classes to help children develop important skills are now available for the toddler.

Sensitive and Critical Periods for Learning

The concept of a *sensitive period* was suggested by Bloom's (1964) hypothesis that the environment in which the individual develops will have the greatest effect on a specific characteristic in its most rapid period of change. During this period all systems—visual, mental, and motor—are ready to be used. If activated by the environment, they will be used together at peak efficiency. The time when an organizational process accelerates most rapidly is a *critical period* for the resulting organization if failure to use a process during this time results in loss of the process or function (Vygotsky, 1974).

To understand how a person's capacity for learning is affected by the early environment, especially during critical or sensitive periods, we must return to the principles of interaction. Experience affects gene production by making demands on the cell's metabolic resources in such a way that the organism is able to meet similar learning demands in the future more easily. If these demands are made early and repeatedly, they make lasting changes in the neural structure of the organism. Increased activity increases the amount of transmitter fluid produced at a synapse, the point where there is firing from one brain cell to another during thinking. Nerve cells and fibers become larger through use as does the capillary network. As we saw in Chapter 2, the thickness and weight of the entire cortex increase by environmental enrichment. There is evidence that experience does lead to maturation.

Visual Complexity

One of the first sensitive periods, visual complexity is best learned during the intellectually sensitive period from birth to 2 months. The classic study conducted by Fantz in 1961 added much to our knowledge of the learning capability of human infants. Using measures of attention, Fantz established a fact previously unknown to science: Babies see from the moment of birth. They seem to have an innate ability to perceive patterns, thereby facilitating the development of form perception. They develop their ability for perceiving complex forms to a high level of discrimination by 2 months. Given opportunities to interact with patterns of varying degrees of complexity, infants seem to prefer more complex designs. In their order of preference, the complexity of printed matter is second only to a preference for the human face. This information allowed the first sensitive period for learning to be delineated from birth to 2 months as the time when the human infant can most easily acquire form perception. It is critical that the environment provide patterns to be viewed during this sensitive learning period if the ability is to be optimally used.

When we consider the amount of visual stimulation usually available to the infant, we recognize that far more could be done to take advantage of this sensitive learning period. Most infants kept in a basket or enclosed crib are provided with only occasional changes in their field of vision. If interaction with the environment occurs from birth, repetition of this limited view must indeed be boring. For the infant reaching out visually without the ability to change body positions, the world of ruffled canopies, ceilings, pastel sheets, and occasional mobiles must be quite limiting. Fortunate is the child who during this period experiences different areas of the home, the out-of-doors, and various objects and people. The use of complexity seems to become cumulative with early experience because form and complex patterns result in a preference by the infant for more and more complex forms and patterns (Fantz, 1965). We must note that if this period is not used, the infant will still need to develop these visual skills. A delay not only retards development but also may result in less than optimal use of the child's potential.

Hearing

Brazelton and Als (1979) have shown that at birth, babies orient themselves to sound and can imitate facial gestures and synchronize their body movements to rhythm. In addition to hearing very early, babies seem to have an inborn genetic ability to elicit and respond to the meanings expressed through inflections in meaningful conversation (Restak, 1985). When the talk becomes gibberish or is just the recitation of the alphabet, babies do not respond.

Developing Language

Another sensitive period, in addition to the those mentioned for visual (form) complexity and hearing, exists for language development. Linguists have theorized that between 18 months and 4 years of age, every human has available an innate ordering device for learning language, referred to as the Language Acquisition Device (LAD) (Chomsky, 1966; McNeill, 1966). During this LAD period, the environment of the child must be rich in language experience. Never again will the child have the ability to learn language-related activities with such ease. Learning is cumulative. If we are to optimize the learning opportunities of our children, we must take advantage of those periods when learning proceeds most rapidly and efficiently (Lenneberg, 1967). Early language development is a trait often found in gifted children. In her studies of highly gifted children, Hollingworth (1942) found this to be consistently true. By 2 years of age many children have extensive vocabularies and speak in complex sentences.

> Because the experience of seeing, hearing, and forming words stimulates neural dendrites and circuits in the brain and causes the left hemisphere's language centers to grow and specialize, and because this, in turn, allows the baby to understand and speak more efficiently, the child reaps both brain stimulation and emotional development if he is bathed in communication. (Diamond & Hopson, 1998, p. 135)

Reading to early learners is an enjoyable activity that supports the ability to learn.

Young children will acquire language effortlessly if they are surrounded by language, but the kind of language they acquire, whether an instrument of clarity, precision, and imagination or only a tool to handle biological and social exchanges, will depend on the linguistic environment supplied by adults (McKenna, 1978).

By interacting with their parents, at 2 months of age infants will have learned an important skill of conversation: taking turns. Very early they are able to wait their turn and pay attention to another person (Snow cited in Patlak, 1989). Researchers such as Snow and Fernald (cited in Raymond, 1991a) have shown that, when talking to babies, adults and siblings use a special sound pattern that is similar regardless of cultural background. This responsive language is characterized by simple, concrete, rhythmic, and repetitive phrases with exaggerated and high-pitched intonations. As the babies continue to develop language of their own, Snow suggests a variety of strategies that parents and others can use to support them.

1. Affirm what the child says and expand it.

   Example—BABY: "Ball bed."
   MOTHER: "Yes, the ball went under the bed."

2. Ask a question about the baby's statement.

   Example—MOTHER: "Who rolled the ball under the bed?"

3. Expand the vocabulary by reading books with the baby.

4. Ask open-ended questions while reading.

   Example—"What is the little boy doing?" instead of "Is the little boy looking for his shoes?"

According to Vygotsky and Luria (1994), language is a mental tool that allows thinking to be more abstract, flexible, and independent from any immediate stimuli. Language builds the cognitive processes, in part by allowing the child to imagine, manipulate, and create new ideas, and by facilitating a shared experience exchanging social information with others. "Opportunities to hear and practice language will directly influence the future development of higher mental functions" (Bodrova & Leong, 1995, p. 23). Children who are developing higher levels of mental ability tend to use more complex words than the children their age (Tucker & Hafenstein, 1997).

Reading as a visual language experience is analogous to speech as an auditory language experience. Both represent receptive language, and both may present similar cognitive problems to the learner. Possibly the LAD period presents the child with an advantage in organizing visual language input (reading), as it does for other language experiences (Chukovsky, 1966; Moore, 1961, 1967).

In an attempt to understand better how the LAD period affects young children, I conducted an early reading experiment with children 2 through 4 years of age (Dunn, 1969). My goal was to discover the effectiveness of teaching 2- through 4-year-olds several basic reading skills, names of letters, letter sounds, and a few basic words by televised presentations. This was prior to *Sesame Street*. From my background in preschool television programming, I was convinced that this medium could give large numbers of children the opportunity to explore the world of symbolic language.

For 15 minutes once a week for 16 weeks, 45 mothers brought their children to the campus to watch in small groups the televised antics of a feline puppet and me. Using songs, games, and stories, we involved the children in basic reading experiences. Our 2- to 4-year-old boys and girls had IQs ranging from 74 to 134 and represented several racial and ethnic groups and socioeconomic levels.

I found the results exciting yet frustrating. All children reached mastery on all items tested. Their growth was statistically significant at the .001 level over the growth of the control group. Neither IQ nor age nor any other variable we looked at seemed to influence the results except for a slight time advantage evidenced by those children whose parents read to them. This was exciting, as it supported results of other early childhood reading experiments. The frustration came from the low expectation level that I had set as the researcher. Halfway through the experiment my concern regarding too much material presented too quickly became instead too little presented too slowly. Children began leaping ahead, and by the end of the 4-month period, over half had taken the tools offered by the program and had begun to read. I had not pretested for reading, so I could comment only briefly on this fact in the results. A follow-up study a year later showed that, of those children responding, all had continued to develop their reading skill; several had been accelerated in school placement and identified as gifted children.

Before leaving this study I would like to mention one unplanned event. Several of the mothers were unable to locate babysitters for their younger children and were allowed to bring them to the campus. One younger brother, who at the end of the experiment was 1 year, 6 months old, came every week. While the student watched the televised presentation, his younger brother could be seen through the one-way glass of the observation booth wandering about the room, sometimes watching, sometimes participating, and often seeming to be interested in play of his own design. During the posttesting, he again accompanied the family and, just out of curiosity, I asked if he would like to be tested too. He joined in with gusto. At his own private testing session I found that this child, whose chin could barely clear the table to see the cards and test items, knew several letters, could identify several letter sounds, and had a reading vocabulary of five words.

Although not reported with the experimental group, this finding made me wonder just how capable our young children are. How much could they learn if the opportunities were presented? With our group of 45, I had the pleasure of sharing a whole new world of activities. Some obtained library cards, although their mothers had to sign for them. One young man discovered that writing could be a useful tool and used his basic skills to print a note declaring his annoyance with the behavior of his little friend next door. Billboards became wonderful adventures. As one 3-year-old informed me, when she could not find anything else fun to do, she could read her baby a book.

I found with my group the same confidence and joy Fowler (1962) expresses in his earlier research on the outcome of early reading activity. I am convinced that reading is a natural, happy event if introduced during the LAD period. What we do at 6 years of age may be remedial reading. If you were to force someone to remain immobilized during the 9- through 12-month period and only allow walking activity later, around 3 or 4 years of age, it would be necessary to teach balance, left-right sequencing, how to place one foot in front of the other, shifting weight, and other incremental skills. Let us make an analogy to our approach to reading. Children I have known and those reported in the literature (Durkin, 1966; Fowler, 1962) learn with ease and pleasure during the LAD period. At 6 years of age learning to read becomes quite a different matter. We must later deliberately teach what is incidentally learned during the earlier period. Few children are allowed the opportunity to interact with symbolic language during this early period.

Professional education has done an excellent job of convincing parents that they cannot teach reading. And yet, if allowed the opportunity to play with words, if read to or shown any of the ways letters can be used to represent sounds, children find their own way to learn. In an environment that responds as the children direct, that is rich in good language experiences, children enjoy learning in their own way. Learning to read is no exception, yet some years ago educators informed parents that early learning was a waste of time. People accepted the notion that children who learned later would catch up anyway. Too many people, without looking at new data, still believe this to be true.

The work of Durkin (1966) has given us a different view of children who read early. Her research shows that children who enter school already reading have a learning advantage that continues to accelerate during the school years. By sixth grade, far from "catching up," the late readers (those learning in first grade) increasingly lagged behind the early readers in performance. Fowler (1963) found much the same to be true and linked the results of early reading to the higher intellectual development of his children. He found reading not only easily accomplished by younger children, but also felt that it enriched their play life and resulted in happier, more well-rounded children. It seems that, as Diamond and Hopson (1998) contend, early exposure to a rich language environment is more than just building a big vocabulary or complex speech; it actually structures the brain's entire cognitive mechanism and the level at which the child will interact with and understand the world.

We have long known that gifted children may read early. Could it be true that children are gifted because they read early? Could this activity and other types of stimulation set into motion structural changes in the organism that result in high-level intellectual development? The data now available support this possibility.

Discovery of other sensitive periods is necessary for optimal development to be realized. Epstein (1978) comments:

> The role of intellectual experience or learning is to select among existing networks created by the genetic apparatus during brain development. If the complete spectrum of needed experience is not available to the organism, it loses forever the possibility of having those functions that are operated by the lost networks. (p. 354)

The sensitive-period concept indicates that intensive and novel intellectual inputs to children may be most effective during brain growth stages.

Discipline

During this period of beginning mobility, the pattern for discipline will be established. As a part of creating a responsive learning environment, the way in which children are disciplined communicates the beliefs and values of their families, contributes to their understanding of appropriate ways to handle problems, and models behaviors of support and guidance or anger and fear. Methods of discipline can enhance or inhibit the curiosity, inquiry, and confidence that optimize learning. The authoritarian style of parenting has been linked to lower levels of cognitive function (Campbell & Ramey, 1995). Although each child responds differently to various methods of discipline, keep in mind that your actions teach far more than your words and that each action has long-term as well as short-term consequences.

In the past, punishment was seen as necessary to teach children proper behavior. Power and Chapieski (1986) report that physical discipline proved to be unsuccessful and limiting to the growth of cognitive ability in 14-month-old babies in both the short and long terms. In their study, babies who were physically punished were more likely to willfully grasp forbidden objects and were least likely to obey restrictions. When tested 7 months later, these babies scored lower on measures of infant development than children who received no physical discipline. Making a variety of safe objects and toys available for exploration and play lowers the need for discipline and provides opportunities for development of visual/spatial skills and problem-solving ability.

Positive guidance has proved far more productive of good behavior than punishment. Larson, Ham, and Raffaelli (1989) believe that over time any gains made by external rewards and punishments erode with rewards leading to interest only in gaining more rewards and punishment leading to frustration, dependence, and hopelessness. Only activities that elicit intrinsic motivation and sustained attention allow children to experience high levels of enjoyment and learning. Misbehavior should indicate to the caregiver that some guidance is needed. Rather than watch children make an error and then punish them, try to anticipate the error and warn them that they are approaching a decision point. We can prepare children to look ahead. We should encourage reflection, give practice in alternative thinking, and share our knowledge of the consequences.

Children must also have some alternative coping techniques. The answer to how children can develop the ability to think in consequences and alternatives, to build rationales, and to become good problem-solvers and good choosers can be found within the family. Family acceptance and the child's response to that acceptance are critical factors in developing self-esteem and intellectual potential during this period.

NURTURING GIFTEDNESS DURING EARLY CHILDHOOD (2 THROUGH 5 YEARS)

From 2 through 5 years of age, the child's mental powers show rapid growth. Speech, mobility, and increasing social involvement all add to the fast-paced intellectual development, and it is apparent that this child has outgrown the baby stage. From the work of Campbell and Ramey (1995) comes essentials for improving a young child's everyday life: encourage children to explore; praise their accomplishments; help them practice and expand their basic skills; protect them from disapproval, teasing, or punishment; and surround them with a rich, responsive language environment.

Affection and responsiveness to the child's needs show a high correlation with positive child development.

Two-year-olds may seem inflexible and are often very vocal about their demands. Their energy is abundant and their curiosity is high. Children at this age enjoy routine, because they have difficulty making up their minds.

Three-year-olds seem to feel much more secure about their world. As language and motor abilities rapidly develop and social skills increase, this age group needs caregivers to explain and model behaviors such as generosity, altruism, and care for others (Owen, 1984; Stollak, 1978). Stollak suggests that affection and responsiveness to the child's needs, a stimulating and varied environment, encouragement of exploration and independence, and fair discipline all show a high correlation with positive child development. The play materials from previous periods are useful but in different ways. Three-year-olds create, draw, pretend, and imagine, but only if allowed to and if provisions for these activities have been made. Space to explore their own way and time to "do it myself" are needed. Children at this age are now thinkers. Cognitive psychologists such as Jean Piaget (1952), Lev Vygotsky (1962), and Jerome Bruner (1960, 1964, 1968) have helped us to understand how thinking develops.

Development of the Rational Mind

Piaget (1952, 1954, 1965), an eminent Swiss psychologist honored by educational groups throughout the world, believed that there were qualitative as well as quantitative differences between the thinking of adults and children. It was not only how much they knew, but the way they knew. The mind, he believed, is always trying to balance between assimilation (bringing in new information that fits our belief system) and accommodation (changing our belief system or thought structure to allow for new information). As we grow, ever more complex structures are needed to understand our world, and we require more elaborate schemes.

Development of the thought processes involved in such schemes was thought by Piaget to occur in four discrete and qualitatively different stages. The first stage relies primarily on the senses and bodily motion to develop a few simple schemes. This stage is therefore called the *sensorimotor stage* and includes the period of infant development (birth to 18 months). The second stage, called *preoperational,* includes the years from about 2 to 7. Children now begin to develop an understanding that symbols can represent objects, that words can replace and communicate reality. During the third stage children can classify things and think with some logic; they are aware of and can formulate laws of logic. This is the stage of *concrete operations,* occurring around 7 to 11 years of age. Finally, somewhere around 12 years of age, a person reaches the stage of *formal operations*. Now future thinking, critical and alternative thinking, creative problem-solving, idealism, and comprehension of metaphors occur.

Piaget's theory uses age only as a guide, not as immutable delineations of norms of behavior. He was not interested in accelerated development; others were. Although not disputing the sequential nature of the stage theory, Webb (1974) concluded that the rate of maturation to a new stage depended on IQ. High-IQ children between 6 and 11 years of age achieved maturation in a few months, whereas normal-IQ children took a year or two. Piaget felt that the stages were developmental, not bound to age limits, proceeding sequentially one after the other. His framework allows for an understanding of the variability of learners, as it shows the differences in the structure of thought and does not view levels of intelligence merely as acquisitions of new knowledge. He looked at what was observable with the children he studied, not what was possible or even preferable. Podgoretskaya (1979) believed that what was observed did not reflect age-linked characteristics, but rather gave evidence for the types of problems that occur in the thinking process when its development is left to chance. His theory was that such defects can occur at any age if thinking is allowed to develop spontaneously and unsupported by a responsive learning environment.

Flavell (cited in Chance & Fischman, 1987) finds a problem with Piaget's stage-dependent theory. Stages imply long periods of stability followed by abrupt change, but what actually happens is that important changes occur gradually, often imperceptibly, over months or even years. Chance and Fischman also point out that by focusing on children's use of logical thought and deductive reasoning, Piaget ignored areas of thought such as creativity—a most important growth area that influences the quality of all thought and reasoning.

Clearly human growth is far more complex that can be accounted for by the concept of broad developmental stages. Not only age but also the quality of the environment affects this schedule (Chance & Fischman, 1987). For example, researchers have found that memory ability grows rapidly from birth through age 5, with its progress determined by the number of memory strategies learned by children. One such strategy is rehearsal. When trying to remember a list of items to buy at their play store, children who repeat the items and rehearse what they are to purchase remember more items than those who do not, regardless of age. Such strategies are not learned naturally as children grow. Sophisticated strategies, such as categorizing, are learned through experience, often by imitating older children or adults. It would be well to teach mnemonic strategies both at home and at school.

Young children can also learn systematic hypothesis testing if taught some simple skills of logic. Piaget (1952) believed that only children over 14 could solve scientific problems; this is true only if the children have no opportunity to play with such ideas earlier.

One of the most important skills children can learn regarding problem-solving is how to be systematic and organized. Even impulsive children can be helped to be better problem-solvers by providing instruction and encouragement in organizing their actions (Chance & Fischman, 1987).

Lev Vygotsky, a Russian psychologist, was a contemporary of Piaget who contributed to the areas of cognitive and language development and to special education (Vygotsky, 1962, 1974; Vygotsky & Luria, 1994). His theory of development was unique, although he shared many of Piaget's beliefs. It is in the areas in which they disagreed that his major contributions to our understanding of early childhood lie. His early death at 38 years of age and the political suppression of his ideas by his homeland delayed his influence on Western philosophy of child development. However, in many ways, the work of Vygotsky is closer to the findings of current research than is the work of any other theorist. Like Piaget, Vygotsky believed that all learning must be active. He too was a constructivist, acknowledging that children construct their own meaning from their experiences. However, unlike Piaget, he understood the construction of meaning to be socially mediated, not developed from interactions with physical objects alone. A child's shared performance was as valuable in the development of intelligence as was independent discovery.

For Vygotsky (1962), language played a central role in cognitive development and formed the core of a child's mental functions; for Piaget (1952), language was but a by-product of the development of the intellect. But by far the greatest difference in the thinking of these theorists was their belief about the relationship between learning and development. Piaget believed that children's ability to learn depended on and was determined by their level of development, whereas Vygotsky believed that although development can impact learning, learning not only impacts but also causes development. Consequently, all learning should be aimed at the child's emerging skills, not the existing ones. This is what he would call the *zone of proximal development*. The lower level is formed by the child's current independent performance, what the child knows and can do; the higher level by the maximum the child can reach with help and assistance. Vygotsky believed that teachers should provide activities aimed at the higher level, just beyond what children can do on their own. For gifted children, this is an especially important concept, because they move through conceptual and skill learning far more quickly than average learners. Working with their zone of proximal development allows gifted learners to continuously progress at their own rate, becoming more and more independent and able, an experience in which they seldom have the opportunity to engage.

Another belief of Vygotsky that has been validated by current research findings is that learning is most powerful when the child is emotionally engaged. Again, we see the belief that the integration of brain functions leads to more powerful learning.

Also of interest to those studying the development of giftedness is the work of Dabrowski (1972). In his theory of human development, a central theme is "developmental potential," which determines the level of development a person may reach under optimal conditions. The concept includes talents, special abilities, intelligence, and psychic overexcitabilities, defined by Piechowski, Silverman, and Falk (1985) as enhanced and intensified mental activity distinguished by characteristic forms of expression which are above common and average. The areas of mental activity to which Dabrowski refers include psychomotor, sensual, intellectual, imaginational, and emotional. Dabrowski's work provides a model that allows researchers to better understand the intellectual as well as the emotional behaviors of children at the higher levels of development (Tucker & Hafenstein, 1997).

Development of the Metaphoric Mind

What most cognitive psychologists are really describing is the development of only one of our mind styles, the linear-logical style of the left hemisphere. The descriptors they use are valid only in cultures that have placed their emphasis on linear-logical thought processes. What about our other mind, the metaphoric, intuitive, holistic mind valued by Einstein, Bruner, da Vinci, Salk, and a myriad of other creative thinkers who have changed our culture? Samples (1977) suggests a hierarchy of metaphoric modes within which students at any age have the ability to perform. Through use of these modes, students were found to develop more comfort and ability in exploring concepts, ideas, and processes in rational ways. The first, the Symbolic Metaphoric Mode, exists when either an abstract or a visual symbol is substituted for an object, process, or condition. By making the visual symbolism available, understanding can be achieved even by those who are not as adept at deriving meaning from abstract symbolism; that is, by drawing or sculpting an idea, one may understand the meaning and express it through the written word.

Next, the Synergic Comparative Mode occurs when "two or more objects, processes or conditions are compared in such a way that the both are synthesized into a greater whole as a result of the comparison" (Samples, 1977, p. 690). Herein lie the roots of holistic cyclic thought, the true beginnings of the power of the other mind. Whereas the linear-logical mind would view by seeing the differences, the holistic mind views by seeing the connections, allowing an extension or expansion of the original idea. "The petal of the flower looked like white velvet" provides two unlike objects that serve, by the connection, to extend and enhance your view of the flower.

The Integrative Metaphoric Mode exists when people experience objects, processes, or conditions directly with all of their physical and psychic being. This would require the involvement of all of the functions of the human being: feelings, rational thinking, intuitive thinking, and physical sensing in the learning process.

Finally, the Inventive Metaphoric Mode begins at any time an individual creates a new level of awareness or knowing through a self-initiated exploration of objects, processes, or conditions. Samples (1977) emphasizes the process of creating, which is to the metaphoric modes of intelligence what discovering is to the linear-logical modes.

The growth of the metaphoric, holistic mind is available throughout our lives and, when used, can be shown to result in higher feelings of self-confidence, self-esteem, and compassion; a wider exploration of traditional content and skills; and higher levels of creative invention. However, current teaching strategies, environments, and curricula neglect its use. Allowed at the beginning stages of young children's learning experiences, the acceptance of this mind style disappears as they progress in school. Samples (1977) assures us that, although his data show this disappearance, he and his colleagues have found that the metaphoric mind does not disappear. In my work I too have found that children understand and respond to any encouragement to use their other way of knowing. Both parents and teachers can, by valuing this equally important part of each child and by accepting it, encouraging it, and creating spaces for its use, allow the development of both mind styles, thereby optimizing the actualization of the child's fullest potential.

Young Gifted Children

It is important to understand average developmental patterns of infants and children so that advanced and accelerated development can be noticed. It is also important to be aware of how to optimize learning for all young children, because it is during this early period that giftedness is nurtured. Once the parent or other caregiver begins to notice exceptional ability or unusually rapid development, other concerns must be addressed. Children may begin to show abilities ahead of their same-age playmates. For example, if a 3-year-old shows abilities typical of a 4- or $4\frac{1}{2}$-year-old, or a child of 4 shows abilities typical of a 5- or 6-year-old, they may be considered gifted in those areas of ability because they are showing abilities that add $\frac{1}{4}$ to $\frac{1}{2}$ of their actual age (Robinson, 1993). Early development of language skills, including reading, is perhaps the easiest to spot; however, advanced reasoning skills, a long attention span, and an unusual amount of imagination, curiosity, or risk-taking could be signs of an accelerating neural system.

Earlier theories of child development suggested that both parents and teachers should wait until children ask for an activity. In that way, we could be sure that children were ready to learn. Now this seems far too wasteful of their resources, an unnecessary barrier to their developing potential. As we become aware of children's ability to choose only those activities or objects for which they are ready from among a variety of activities or objects, our skill in structuring a rich responsive learning environment becomes more necessary. The better we know a child, the less difficult is our task. However, we do not have to wait until we know what children need. We need only make available a large variety of objects and activities and then observe and respond as the children interact. Having available many resources, including the parent and teacher, will allow children to stretch beyond known areas, to experiment with new materials and ideas, and to develop at their own pace and in their own style.

Robinson (1993) suggests that parents of young, gifted children be prepared to deal with the following issues as the difficulty of the job of parenting a gifted child increases:

• Acceptance of your child as different; wishing that your child were "average" may seem to the child like rejection and become damaging.

- Use of developmental timetables; be careful, they are only used as *guides*. It is likely that in many areas your child will not follow the timetables of more average learners and special modifications will be necessary.

- Suggestions of family, neighbors, and friends who believe that you are pushing your child; they could limit the level and type of experiences you provide for your child.

- Consideration of your needs and those of the rest of the family, the family time available, and the family budget when meeting the needs of your gifted child. A balanced approach is important and will go far in allowing a view of life that is optimistic, energetic, and joy filled.

The Preschool Experience

During this time of rapid growth for the toddler, it is important that all modes of learning be nurtured. Many of the characteristics of giftedness may already be evident and should be supported. Throughout this chapter we have looked at how we might optimize growth for our children, and the results of that rich interaction now begin to be evident. In discussing the "brain-growth phenomenon," Diamond (Diamond & Hopson, 1998) commented that enriched environments had a positive effect on cortical thickness. Of great interest, too, is her comment, "The more startling effect, however, was the impact of *boredom:* Reduced environmental stimuli had a

The curriculum for preschool must be rich in variety and stimulating in process.

more powerful effect on cortex thinning that enhanced stimuli had on cortex thickening" (p. 150). Rather than just identifying giftedness, the activities of the years prior to and including this period can be said to produce giftedness.

After 3 years of age, an educational program with other children becomes important. The more planned educational experiences a child over age 3 has, the better that child does in intellectual, language, personal, and social development—significantly better than children placed in programs focused on free play. Gross (1999) has found that early reading, speech, and mobility among highly gifted children allows them to explore for themselves several months earlier than their age peers of average ability, while their early speech enables them to express their ideas, seek information, and interact verbally with their parents and teachers.

By age 4 children are very verbal, and teachers use high levels of this ability to identify very able children. In addition, 4-year-olds are alert, curious, attentive, and active, and can easily be engaged in the excitement of learning. At this age children show emotions that make it relatively easy for an observant teacher to provide an appropriate learning environment responsive to the child's needs and interests. Each 4-year-old seems to be a bundle of sensory-motor energy.

Four-year-olds are still living in a "me first" world. As with younger children, discovering how and at what level these children function and then challenging and supporting their growth is the primary job of their teachers both at home and at school. This Herculean task begins by simply watching the children. They will let you know everything you need to know in order to enhance and educate them.

However, some gifted children experience problems at preschool age, because preschool and kindergarten teachers are noted to often have trouble accepting the accomplishments of such advanced learners. The curriculum may be too low level and focus on skills already mastered by these children (Dalzell, 1998). Developmental theories provide the basis for many preschool programs and are often interpreted as age-related development instead of focused on the true development of the child. Gifted children often cannot find age peers who have similar interests and Dalzell notes that the preference for older playmates and the joy they find in the company of adults is difficult to satisfy in such settings. Their advanced vocabulary can make it difficult for them to relate to others and they fail to understand why other children cannot keep up with them. Too often the result is frustration and the gifted child chooses to either hide knowledge and skills or become an assistant teacher. Although gifted children need to be allowed to select meaningful activities, in many preschool programs this may not be possible.

Hoehner (cited in Clark, 1986) shares some suggestions for creating a productive, healthy social-emotional climate in the learning setting:

1. Share much of the decision-making by placing more of it in the hands of the children.

2. Include the children in resolving their arguments and differences. One procedure is to take both children aside and follow this plan:

    STEP 1: *Child A* is allowed to tell what happened without being interrupted. *Child B* is allowed to tell what happened without being interrupted. *Child A* responds to *B,* then *child B* responds to *A* until what has happened has been exhausted. (Remember: They are discussing *just what happened,* not what will happen or what might have happened.)

STEP 2: *Child A* tells what he or she wants (example: no more being hit in the shoulder by *child B*); *child B* tells what he or she wants (example: *child A* must stop pulling the ball out of *child B's* hands).

STEP 3: The teacher asks *A* if *A* can agree to what *B* wants, then asks *B* if *B* can agree to what *A* wants.

STEP 4: At agreement, the teacher excuses both children. Most often an agreement is reached, but when one is not, the teacher reconvenes the meeting to determine what they can agree on.

3. Work to extinguish or incorporate "off-the-wall" comments made by the children. For example, if there is a discussion of the Mobius strip going on and someone shouts, "John's peepee is blue," there are many viable responses the teacher can make. Smiling and saying, "Peepee or urine is not blue, but in a moment you will use blue paint to . . ." is one alternative response, or "Peepee or urine could change color to show us illness but in this Mobius you could use dark blue to show one-sidedness. . . ." The teacher might even say, "John is really feeling funny today so I'm eager to see how he uses any color, even blue, to color his Mobius pathway."

Another way of using seemingly irrelevant comments is to turn the comment into a useful question. For example, if while discussing machines one child says, "I love whales. I saw lots of whales once," the teacher might say, "Whales are quite interesting and so very big. It is fun to watch big whales move. Do you know how these big machines move?"

Always take the children from where their minds are and lovingly pull them beyond. In these examples the children were not denied their observations and their outbursts were made useful.

4. Use questions as a tool for growth. For example, if a child who has a cut hears the teacher say, "How can I help?" the child then must decide if a hug, a bandage, an ice cube, etc., is needed. The teacher then moves to help. When a child says, "I can't find anything to do," the teacher can respond with "What have you missed here today? Let's look. Do you see a center that you've forgotten? How about trying that one? How long would you say is fair? Will you let me know how it works out?"

On occasion, however, questions have a deleterious effect and must be redirected. Often when a child is revealing something sensitive in a trust group, expressing a loss or a joy, or needing to relate an experience, the child's intense look should remind the teacher *No questions, this child needs to unload this.* Patient, eye-to-eye contact helps teachers know when to ask questions.

5. Watch the child's body posture. The body can provide valuable assessment data. Small children's bodies will often reflect what is in their thoughts. Watch for slumping, skipping, head down, avoidance of eye contact, a red face, quietness, fast talking, or bubbly actions. Small children turn away from an activity if they are losing interest, and just as a child is turning to grab another child the teacher can say, "Gentle hands, use gentle hands." Recognizing these and other body actions can allow the teacher to approach the next learning opportunity better informed and can in many cases provide an early warning system.

6. Use *I* statements. As with children and adults of all ages, *I* statements empower both the teacher and the learner. When a teacher says, "You need to help me," "You need to try harder," or "You need to go out now," the statements not only are misleading but also may be untrue. What is actually being revealed is the teacher's need, and statements such as "I need you to help me," "I need you to try harder," and "I need you to go out now" set an honest emotional climate, inviting much more cooperation.

7. Promote the spontaneous spark. As the child rushes to the board with "I can do it!" do not insist on a raised hand or a *wait-your-turn* lesson. Listen, evaluate, approve, encourage, and then invite the child to carry the idea further *after* sitting back down. For example, a lecture/demonstration of the instruments of a symphony orchestra is given by a guest speaker, and then the children are invited to experience the instruments at centers around the room. Roger walks thoughtfully to the center where the drums, cymbals, bells, and baton have been placed. He picks up the baton and with great authority raps for attention from all the "musicians" in the room. He then carefully conducts a symphony of his own for the next 10 minutes. The rules of rotation and taking turns can be suspended for those 10 minutes with a nonverbal understanding between the teacher and the children. (pp. 55–56)

Vanessa Lucas, director of a child care center in Idaho, believes that the most important thing to remember in establishing a responsive learning environment for early learners is to frame all comments and instructions in the positive. Instead of saying, "Don't run inside" or "Please, don't be so loud," try saying, "Use your walking steps now, please" or "Please, use your inside voice." Although she admits that it is hard to remember sometimes, the more teachers can use positive statements, the better the climate and the more supportive the children become.

The curriculum for all preschool children must be rich in variety and stimulating in process. For those who are developing faster and show higher levels of intelligence, such variety and stimulation are even more necessary. In their experiences we can include more activities allowing self-direction, exposure to more abstract concepts, and more involvement with the tools and skills for operating in the areas of reading, mathematics, science, research, art, music, and writing and in the world in which they live. A home or classroom that seeks to optimize growth in young children will incorporate the same elements found in Chapter 9 for organizing responsive, individualized learning environments. The differences will be in timing, strategies, and the amount of support needed.

Decentralization is appropriate with centers or areas for academic and artistic activities. Choice-making can be developed and used by children as young as age 2 and gives the children a sense of competency and achievement, as it does to children further along in their learning. Even very young children can learn to manage their own choice of centers or areas in which to participate, their use of time, and other experiences leading them toward becoming independent learners. It takes more complex planning and structuring to allow the necessary freedom and independence that develop high levels of interaction for young children and ultimately produce higher levels of intelligence. However, the results are so valuable and so important to the future of the child that any parent or teacher would be well-advised to expend this extra effort.

Language patterns and vocabulary can be important teaching tools. The choice of words can make a child feel either suppressed and helpless or supported and competent. For instance, in situations in which the child is involved in an activity that is not allowed, the parent or teacher could use language allowing an alternative choice, such as "You can't do this, but you can do this," thus directing the child to a more appropriate activity. This language produces choice and allows the child to begin to develop alternative thinking skills. Set up situations where the child can be invited to explore and test hypotheses. When a child encounters an obstacle, ask "How can we do that?" If the child encounters something too risky or too scary, suggest "I'll go with you and then you can go all the way through that tunnel. Next time you can do it yourself if you want to."

Be sure to use lots of verbal reminders of the child's worth just for being who he or she is, not just when something is done well. As you pass by, say briefly "I really like you." Do be sure that you also share your negative human feelings clearly. Children notice when things are unpleasant. It would be better to state your feeling, such as "What you are doing makes me angry," rather than leaving to chance the interpretation of what is happening. You then have given the child the opportunity to change, and he or she need not misinterpret your feelings in a negative self-concept. Always with gifted children use lots of humor; they delight in it.

Gardner (cited in Chance & Fischman, 1987) reports that creativity develops rapidly in early childhood, peaking at about 7 years of age. Schools can create a climate that suppresses creativity and, through their emphasis on right answers and correct procedures, cause what will be seen as a decline of growth in this area that may not rise again until the teens. Such suppression of creativity and decline in growth need not happen, but until schools share more concern for the growth of creativity, it is likely to be stifled unless appropriate experiences are provided. According to Karnes and Johnson (1988), the creativity scores of Head Start children in a program providing enriching and stimulating experiences went up whereas the scores of Head Start children not involved in such planned stimulation dropped significantly. The difference in scores suggests that "providing children with an enriching and stimulating program is critical to the prevention of losses in creativity" (p. 5).

In Bowman's 1993 review of the research in early childhood education, she suggests goals for this age group: a climate for learning, opportunities for rewarding interpersonal relationships, acknowledgment and incorporation of the children's biological and psychological predispositions, and a focus on the development of the structures for thinking. These goals are best accomplished using informal teaching methods, such as spontaneous play with a variety of manipulatives, project work guided by the teacher, and instruction that moves from one-to-one teaching to small group work. It is also important to remember that the social climate in schools has been shown to influence school achievement. Comer (1980) showed that when teachers create an emotionally and socially responsive environment for both students and adults, the children's achievement motivation and outcomes improve.

The National Association for the Education of Young Children (NAEYC) supports the idea of "developmentally appropriate practice" for early childhood education (Willis, 1993). Such practices are intended to be responsive to the aspects of teaching and learning that change with the age and experience of the learner and provide schooling that reflects what we know about how children develop and learn and each child's own development, interests, and cultural background. It is not enough to know what is age-appropriate; one must also consider the individual child in all areas of development. This philosophy of teaching offers guidelines that reflect the complexity of the child (Figure 4.2).

The curriculum for gifted young children must play to the ages and stages of growth by always stretching just a bit beyond the normative expectations. Viewing each stage of development as an exciting opportunity for growth will allow a far more appropriate learning situation. For example, the "terrible twos" are seen as a time for testing the limits, for risk-taking; the threes begin real involvement with opportunities to build social skills; during the fours children move from "me" to others; and the fives provide endless possibilities for developing independence. A responsive learning environment allows the organic needs of the child to be met. Parke and Ness (1988) suggest that four basic tenets be kept in mind when making curricular decisions for young gifted children:

1. They have special learning needs, including a faster pace, greater depth, and differing interests from their chronological peers.

2. As with all gifted learners, the curriculum should reflect their special needs and interests.

3. The curriculum should focus on exploration, manipulation, and play.

4. They should be involved in the curricular decision-making process and learn to share responsibility for their learning.

Parke and Ness state the case for a balanced curricular approach, insisting that experiences be provided in *all* areas of development and include such activities as reading books and building castles from blocks.

Figure 4.2 *NAEYC Recommendations for a Curriculum for Young Children*

Source: Adapted from "Teaching Young Children: Educators Seek 'Developmental Appropriateness'" by S. Willis, November 1993. *ASCD Curriculum Updates.* pp. 1–8.

Does the curriculum

- Promote interactive learning and encourage the child's construction of knowledge?
- Encourage active learning and allow children to make meaningful choices?
- Foster children's exploration and inquiry, rather than focusing on "right answers" or "right ways" to complete a task?
- Lead to conceptual understanding by helping children construct their own understanding in meaningful contexts?
- Embody expectations that are realistic and attainable at this time, or could the children more easily and efficiently acquire the knowledge or skills later on?
- Encourage development of positive feelings and dispositions toward learning while leading to acquisition of knowledge and skills?
- Help achieve social, emotional, physical, and cognitive goals and promote democratic values?
- Promote and encourage social interaction among children and adults?

Academic subjects can be introduced in an integrative way—that is, by combining cognition with feeling, physical/sensing, and intuition, as described for older children in Chapter 11. The preschool curriculum presented in Tables 4.4 and 4.5 and Integrative Lessons 4.1 and 4.2 provide examples of activities to enhance integrative education.

When selecting a preschool for their gifted children, parents can improve the possibility of choosing an appropriate program by carefully observing the following:

The teachers: How do the teachers interact with the children? Do the teachers genuinely like children? Are they being authentic, showing their real feelings, letting the children know them as people? The research on programs for young children indicates that no single program can be shown to be the best. All models investigated were effective when teachers were committed to the model and dedicated to the children (Roedell, Jackson, & Robinson, 1980).

The environment: Is it nurturing for children? Is it attractive, colorful, thoughtfully organized? Is it flexible, pleasant, and inviting? Does the environment change to stay interesting? Involved, caring parents or teachers who provide

Table 4.4 *Preschool Curriculum: Ages 1–3 Years*

Caregiver Activities	Because
Provide objects for manipulation, such as blocks, bowls, and boxes.	Through touching, moving, and banging coordination is learned; relationships can be experienced.
Label your actions as you do them; label the child's actions as he or she does them; encourage talking while thinking.	Facilitates the use of language for thinking.
Model use of print showing the emotional and social meanings; encourage children to explore and experiment for themselves; encourage writing to communicate and play.	Modeling promotes and encourages reading and writing activity.
Use the children's intuitive insights and personal language to teach mathematics; promote self-confidence and autonomy for mathematical thinking; use sticks, stones, and other physical materials.	Children bring considerable mathematical experience to school with them; it should be acknowledged and used.
Teach the relationship between art and academic skills; transform their experience into artistic representations.	Enriches academic understanding and skills.
Provide intellectual peers to interact and play with.	Facilitates development of language, self-concept, and sensory-motor thinking.
Provide opportunities for drama and storytelling.	Promotes language, imagination, and the integration of thinking and emotion.
Allow children to make decisions and take increasing responsibility for learning and behavior.	Helps children develop independent thinking and action.

Table 4.5 *Preschool Curriculum: Ages 4–5 Years*

Caregiver Activities	Because
Organize an environment that allows choice and a high degree of variety and novelty. Organize so that the child can follow through on an activity to its conclusion (e.g., when writing a story, illustrate it and bind into a book; when planting seeds, water and care for plant as it grows).	Helps develop an independent, autonomous learner; inner locus of control; intellectual stimulation; sense of responsibility.
Centers or areas where children can discover basic concepts (e.g., in math or science); practice specific school skills (e.g., writing, hole punching, use of ruler); and develop awareness of themselves.	Provide intellectual stimulation, cognitive skills, problem-solving abilities.
Provide inspiration and materials for children to write their own books and poems, with the help of an encouraging adult who will write as the story/poem is dictated.	Useful in developing creativity, basic reading skills, language experience, intuitive skills.
Provide a variety of art materials, such as glue, colored paper, scissors, beans, bits of yarn, ribbon, scraps of wood, crayons, large-sized paper, marking pens, water paints, clay; materials that will stretch them beyond where they have gone (e.g., "Find something inside the clay and let it come out with your hands.").	Facilitates developing creativity, sensory skills, artistic and intuitive abilities.
Provide sharing times and social outings with other children; organize group games and cooperative activities; allow opportunities to settle differences with other children, guiding only when necessary.	Research shows that young children can increase their cooperative social interactions, ability to overcome obstacles and to talk with peers, and decrease negative behavior. This allows children to grow in social problem solving.
Make use of the community and the surrounding areas for field trips and exploration.	Develops a sense of competency, autonomy, deeper understanding and appreciation of nature.
Provide opportunities to establish a relationship with a significant adult friend.	Allows children to get another point of view on issues; acquaints them with other interests, language patterns, and vocabulary; allows them to be guided and listened to when they feel parents cannot.

ways for children to learn things that both they and the children find interesting produce the most effective environment for learning.

The activities: Are there lots of different activities at different levels of difficulty? Are there activities to challenge and stretch the children's thinking? Feelings? Intuition? Physical/sensing? Can the children go as far as they want with an activity? Are there lots of skills for the children to master creatively?

AT THE SCIENCE CENTER
Integrative Lesson 4.1 Touch Color (Chromatography)

Purpose:

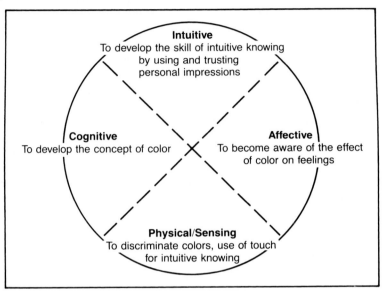

Time involved: Approximately 45 minutes

Materials needed: Plastic water glasses, round paper towel disks with strips cut out of each, set of disks with a color in the middle and no strip cut out, felt tip pens of various colors

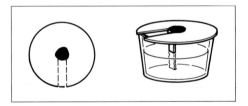

Organization preferred: Small group of children around table with teacher

Teacher role: Demonstrator, facilitator, questioner

Procedure:

1. Demonstrate how color placed on a paper towel disk separates into different designs as water is absorbed into the disk. The color will separate into its color components as this absorption takes place. Fill a clear plastic glass two-thirds full of water. Place a disk of paper toweling cut as indicated above and slightly larger than the top rim of the plastic glass flat across the top of the glass. Allow the tab attached to the disk to fall into the water. As the tab absorbs the water the color will begin to separate into lighter and lighter elements. In the discussion of this demonstration, introduce color words and discuss descriptors (blue—cool; red—hot, etc.).

2. Ask the children to experiment with various colors on paper towel disks. Encourage the children to make different mixtures of color with different felt tip pens, as well as different designs at different points on the disk's surface.
3. After each child has had an opportunity to create several disks with various designs say, "Some of the papers give you certain feelings. How do you feel when you see this color? This design?"
4. "Is there something in one of the designs specifically about you? Find it and outline it in black pen."
5. Set up a chart rack. Put slits in the form of an *x* on a tagboard hanging from the rack, then have the children relax and reach through. Ask them to determine the color of the disk on the other side.

On a different day:

6. "Each of us has a special, lovely color that gives us a special feeling. Look around the room. If you see that color move to it."

On a different day:

7. Put an item of one color in a bag. When the children are in their circle show them the bag and ask them to close their eyes and imagine something there. Ask them to open their eyes and pass the bag around the circle. Then ask them what color the item in the bag is. You may give them several color words from which to choose. Discuss and then show. Be sure to acknowledge the idea of "on target" and "off target," rather than saying the child is right or wrong.

Evaluation: Check for accuracy of knowledge of color names or other activities that use selection of colors.

Taken from a lesson by Chris Hoehner.

AT THE READING CENTER
Integrative Lesson 4.2 My Own Alphabet/Picture Cards
Purpose:

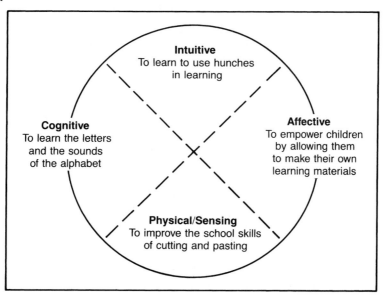

Time involved: 10 to 15 minutes or as long as the children are interested

Materials needed: Old magazines, scissors, paste, file cards with letters at the top (e.g., *A, a, B, b*)

Organization preferred: Individual activity or small group

Teacher role: Facilitator

Procedure:

1. Sit with the children and look through old magazines for small pictures of objects with a beginning sound like the letter at the top of the card. Invite them to guess when they are not sure.
2. Cut out the pictures (or allow the children to do so under your supervision) and help the children paste them on the card.
3. Ask the children to say the names of the objects as they paste them onto the card.
4. Invite a child to choose from the cards a picture that she really likes. Have the child think of that picture, seeing it in her mind. The other children are invited to guess what picture the child is seeing. Save the cards for other games.

Evaluation: Check for accuracy of letter names and sounds when playing with the cards later.

Games to play with alphabet/picture cards:

- *Scramble:* Mix up all the cards and ask the child to sort them into piles or by rows.
- *Matching Letters:* Use a large chart with the letters printed on one side. Ask the child to match the card to the letter on the chart. (Variation: place on the table two cards which have the same letter and one with a different letter. Ask the children which does not match.)
- *Alphabet Dominoes:* Use alphabet cards to play dominoes.
- *Take Away:* Place several alphabet/picture cards on a rack or table. Have the children close their eyes while you take away one card. Ask the children to open their eyes and identify which card is missing.
- *Guess My Card:* Have one child choose one card and be sure no one else can see it. Invite the other children to guess which card the child is holding. Use "on target" or "off target," rather than "right" or "wrong," to indicate the accuracy of the guess.

PARENTING GIFTED CHILDREN: TEACHERS OF THE GIFTED AT HOME

In every phase of a child's growth, parents and the home play a significant part and influence the outcome of every educational decision. The home is, in my mind, the true cradle of eminence. Whatever we find in our world that we would like to change, we must begin with parenting if we are to have a lasting impact. Some have tried to show that other influences are equally or even more important; however, they have yet to account for the powerful effects of motivation, self-image, and attitudes toward self and others—factors that find their definition in the home.

What a parent is, even before conceiving the child, profoundly influences the child's physical, emotional, social, intuitive, and cognitive abilities. What a parent does, all of the decisions and actions the parent makes, follows directly from who and what the parent is. Our society would never think of allowing damage and misuse to happen to our highways, our food, our financial arrangements, even our political and professional institutions; yet we refuse to interfere in the gross misuse

Parents need to be loyal sources of support and recognition for the abilities and talents of their children.

of our children. If we were to care for our children, all of our children, in ways we already know are enriching, then we would abundantly increase the population of children who could actualize their potential to the degree we now designate as *gifted*. Giftedness may be more "normal" than the behaviors and abilities we now accept as typical.

The family plays an important role in creating integrated growth (see Figure 4.3). Satir (1972) found that problem children come from problem families, whereas healthy, open, growing children come from nurturing families. Although her work began with therapeutic counseling for problem families, she developed a framework to guide families who seek to develop family structures that can enhance the growth of each family member. Such families produce highly functional, well-integrated children. In her ideal family, Satir summarized,

> We have adults who clearly show their own uniqueness, who demonstrate their power, who clearly show their sexuality, who demonstrate their ability to share through understanding, kindness and affection, who use their common sense, who are realistic and responsible. (p. 228)

She believed such a family to be an open system. This is in opposition to a closed system where self-worth is secondary to power and performance. In a closed system, rules are created and enforced by the boss (usually the father) who knows what is best for all, and change is resisted because there is only one way to do things—the right way. Satir believed that human beings cannot flourish in a closed system; they may barely exist. We are concerned with more than just existing; we are discussing optimizing human potential to help children become self-actualizing.

Parents of gifted children very often are gifted themselves and many of them have not yet dealt with the differences that they felt when growing up. Tolan (1992)

Figure 4.3 *Characteristics Commonly Found in Families of Gifted Children*

Source: Summarized from Baumrind, 1989; Bloom, 1982; Cornell & Grossberg, 1987; Davis & Rimm, 1994; Falbo & Cooper, 1980; Karnes, Shwedel, & Steinberg, 1984; Olszewski, Kulieke, & Buescher, 1987; Rimm & Lowe, 1988; Satir, 1972; Stanford study, 1986.

Few children in family

Gifted child oldest or only child

Early stimulation and enrichment given to children, including reading to them, encouraging language development, and exposure to a variety of experiences (e.g., museums, exhibits, and visual and performing arts)

Parents older and better educated than typical parents

Parents show high energy and love of learning

Strong work ethic and valuing of achievement modeled by parents

Parenting style authoritative, rather than authoritarian or permissive

Parents value and encourage independence in children

Parents set clear standards that are flexible and fairly administered

Parents respect the rights and dignity of children

All members of the family are encouraged to develop to the highest level of their ability as individuals

Family relationships and parent-child interactions are healthy

Parents and children share work, learning, and play

Parents involved in school-related activities

and Delisle (1998) discuss the need for parents to come to terms with this possibility and resolve any of the buried feelings such asynchronous development caused in their lives. By underappreciating the effect of their experiences as a gifted child—how they coped with the social or emotional problems, discomfort, and isolation—they may have experienced they may over-react or try to avoid similar situations being experienced by their children. As Tolan comments, "It is hard to help one's child resolve issues one has not yet resolved for oneself" (p. 9).

High levels of developed cognitive ability do not guarantee high levels of affective or emotional development. Although the capabilities exist, opportunities to develop them must be made part of the child's experience. One very early trait in the emotional growth of gifted children is their intense sense of justice and unwavering idealism. The parent of a gifted child will soon experience the futile effort of explaining why injustice so often exists. In attempting to convince my children that "the world just isn't fair," I had limited success. "If it isn't, it should be, and why aren't you [the adult] doing something about it?" they responded. Trying to discuss with a 3-year-old how one person could affect only a limited amount of inequity was frustrating for both of us. My reasons were not acceptable to my son's worldview. This sense of justice is tremendously valuable to society and beautiful in its motivating power for humanistic action.

As parents and teachers, we must guide the idealism of children so that they do not become so frustrated that they lose it early and replace it with cynicism or the sense of being powerless. Parents need to be alert to seeking alternatives with the child when seemingly inequitable solutions are posed. A real sharing of problem-solving at the child's level of understanding cannot begin too early. Classic research done in 1926 by Hollingworth pointed out that gifted children can be readily disciplined by appeals to reason, presentation of alternative views, modeling, and consistency of expressed values. With this approach, gifted children may keep their sense of justice intact.

Children need positive responses from others, starting within the family, to provide a sense of well-being and self-satisfaction. Responses received by gifted children are often less than positive and can lower their view of themselves. Statements such as "If you are so gifted, figure it out," or "Of course you don't need any help, you know everything," or "You're capable of better work than that" are unlikely to support a positive self-view.

Acknowledgment is another response often missing for gifted children. They are expected to accomplish the task, create a solution, or come up with a new idea. It is too easy to take their achievements for granted. Personal, individual recognition of their work, their originality, and their efforts is essential and should be shared by teachers and students on a regular basis. However, extreme praise by parents may cause gifted children to believe that parents expect much more of them than the parents really do. This may result in feeling pressured, especially when the child feels that the expectation cannot be met. Rimm (1996) comments, "If the expectations are too high, children will feel pressured or may resist attempts to reach such goals through oppositional behavior and underachievement" (p. 58).

Gifted children typically exhibit a high energy level and the need for less sleep, characteristics which may be disconcerting to their parents. Parents may find it helpful to engage their child in more complex activities at an earlier age (e.g., household tasks, organized play groups, sports).

Human beings need to love and to feel loved, to be in physical contact with one another, to associate with others, and to participate in groups and organizations. The family establishes a foundation of love and caring that can influence how each member views the others and operates in the world. Feeling affection is important: Shared affection is even more fulfilling for human needs. Families must provide sufficient opportunities for development of affection. Children will benefit from learning about themselves and others as loving beings. Families model this love and caring. Although gifted children may be able to analyze the problems within family patterns lacking strong love relationships, they, as much as the more typical individual, still establish patterns for themselves similar to those that the family displays. All humans must feel that they matter, that there is a group or a person with whom they can identify. Belonging is a reciprocal arrangement. It does not occur simply by proximity. There must be give and take, respect, and appreciation, as well as some degree of opportunity to share in movement toward a common goal.

Group activities, as well as respect for individual pursuits, need to be provided. On occasion, individuals attempt to meet belonging needs outside the family.

Home is the cradle of eminence.

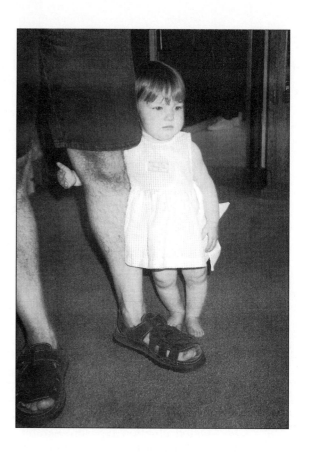

This can be a positive growth process if not used just to compensate for family deficits. Some ways of ensuring growth beyond the level of affection and belonging would include:

- Involvement in planning and carrying out family trips or activities.
- Acceptance of each person as worthy, listening to each, responding to each.
- Expression of pleasure for accomplishments of each member without comparison.
- Cooperative planning and decision-making as far as each member is able.
- Open communication among family members.
- Cooperative action, with each person's contribution seen as valuable to the whole family.
- Allowance of time to develop understanding and empathy among family members.

An important resource for parents of gifted children is the magazine from the National Association for Gifted Children, *Parenting for High Potential,* which contains news, articles on issues and concepts that parents of gifted children confront daily, and advice columns written by experts. There is an activities section especially for families. Contact the National Association for Gifted Children, 1707 L St, NW, Suite 550, Washington, DC 20036 for more information.

Development of Giftedness and Talents

In an important study, Bloom (1982) reported results that validate and extend the thesis of Pressey (1964), mentioned in Chapter 4, that giftedness and high levels of talent are created. By interviewing individuals who had attained "world class" status in a variety of fields and their parents and teachers, the conditions and determinants of their success were elicited. Just as Pressey suggested, these gifts and talents could not have been actualized without the encouragement, support, and environmental opportunities provided by the parents and teachers. Genius indeed cannot "will out" in spite of circumstances, but must be developed, perhaps even created.

> Whatever the original "gifts," [w]ithout extremely favorable supporting and teaching circumstances over more than a decade they would not have been likely to reach the levels of attainment for which they were selected . . . The most striking finding in talent development is the very active role of the family, selected teachers, and sometimes the peer group in supporting, encouraging, teaching, and training the individual at each of the major stages in his or her development. (Bloom, 1982, p. 511)

As we have seen, and Bloom confirms, data show that most human beings are born with enormous potential. However, three characteristics seem to be necessary to achieve at high levels: unusual willingness to do great amounts of work, a determination to do one's best at all cost, and the ability to learn rapidly. These traits appear to emerge from the early socialization and attitudes in the home and the early training provided by teachers. The evidence that learning rates can be altered by appropriate educational and environmental conditions suggests that very favorable learning conditions provided in the early years can markedly influence learning rate. The rate of learning is an expression of advanced and accelerated brain development, an indicator of developing intelligence.

Of major interest in the findings is the power of the parents' belief in the child. If parents believe that their child has special ability, they will hold different expectancies, allow more opportunities to develop the ability, and treat this child differently. Even if, in fact, the child is not significantly more able than others in the family, these beliefs and expectations cause parents, teachers, and the child to do things that result in the given ability reaching an outstanding level. Bloom (1982) found that only one child in each family tends to be chosen for exceptional development in a given ability—not necessarily the most able, but the one with the greatest desire to excel.

It was further discovered that it is "the values and interests of the parents that will determine which traits and qualities will be given great encouragement and further cultivation and which traits and qualities will be ignored" (Bloom, 1982, p. 520). Contrary to previously held belief, Bloom found that the children received opportunities and encouragement first, and only later were seen to possess special ability. The following factors seem to be most important in identifying and developing special ability:

- Parents who greatly value and enjoy music, arts, sports, or intellectual activity and view it as a natural part of life so that the child learns to speak its language.
- Parents who believe in the work ethic.

- A first teacher who is warm and loving, who makes lessons seem like games, instructs on a one-to-one basis, and includes parental interest.
- A second teacher who emphasizes skills and self-discipline and continues to individualize instruction.
- Access to a master teacher who opens doors.

From this study we find more evidence for the importance of early learning opportunities and encouragement to be made available. Curiously, children develop their ability because of instruction and attention, not the other way around.

It should be noted that parents are natural teachers. No one else can equal their knowledge of the child, their concern and responsiveness. With a few learning tools at their disposal, parents can play a major part in their child's early education. Attitude lends the most important ingredient to any learning situation. The child must approach learning with a spirit of adventure and playfulness. Learning should be a joy, not a punishment; a favor, not a duty. Parents can ensure this attitude if they allow the child's natural curiosity to guide the task. Falbo and Cooper (1980) found that the amount of time parents spend playing with their preschoolers is directly related to an increase in verbal intelligence test scores.

Karnes, Shwedel, and Steinberg (1984) conducted a study comparing the attitudes, values, and behavior of parents of young gifted and nongifted children in the hope that the information would help them develop an effective parent component for their preschool program for gifted learners. Many similarities existed between the groups, but the parents of the gifted children reported some interesting differences. Parents of the gifted children read to their children three times as long each day, encouraged language development, encouraged freedom, and exposed their children to a variety of experiences, including the arts, nature walks, and natural history museums. They engaged in school-related activities six times more frequently than the parents of those who were nongifted.

In a pilot study, Karnes and Shwedel (1987) reported some interesting differences in attitude and practices between fathers of young gifted children and fathers of young nongifted children. The fathers of the gifted children placed more emphasis on reading, oral language, and development of their children's fine motor skills whereas fathers of nongifted children emphasized physical activities. Fathers of the gifted children were more concerned about how their actions affected their children's self-esteem, avoiding negativistic turns of phrase, holding unconditional positive regard for their children, and encouraging their children's unusual questions. They valued and encouraged independence in their children whereas most fathers of the nongifted children felt that their children were already too independent.

A study conducted by Snowden and Christian (1999) resulted in a description of parents of young gifted children. The parents in the study were active, involved in their lives and the lives of their children, used an authoritative parenting style, were respectful of their children, balancing the needs and interests of the gifted child and those of the family unit. They provided choices and exposure to a variety of experiences that furthered the child's cognitive, social, emotional, psychomotor, and communicative development. They served as guides and mentors and provided both developmentally and individually appropriate experiences and activities. These are interesting areas of emphasis that teachers of children at home and at school may want to investigate regarding their own beliefs and practices.

A report on parental style (Stanford study, 1986) found that children of authoritarian parents are not as successful in school as are the children of parents who use a more authoritative style. In their description, authoritarian parents "attempt to shape, control, and evaluate the behaviors and attitudes of their children in accord with an absolute set of standards" (p. 3). In contrast, authoritative parents set clear standards while recognizing children's rights, expecting mature behavior, and fostering a healthy share of verbal exchange. Additionally, it was found that placing too much emphasis on either punishing or rewarding children for grades results in lower performance and less internal motivation for the student. The study found that the correlation between parenting style and success in school crosses ethnic boundaries.

Teaching is a pleasure to be shared by parents and their children. Parents need not worry if their child seems reluctant to learn at any given moment. Given flexible opportunities by parents who are open to a variety of responses, chances are that the child will learn faster than expected. If not, the child must be allowed to set the learning pace. Most important is fostering the excitement of learning. Parents can be assured that:

- Young children are capable of a great deal of learning.
- Their children will enjoy learning.
- They can be their child's most responsive teachers.
- They will enjoy sharing this experience with their child.

Siblings of Gifted Children

When one sibling is identified as gifted but another is not, families may have to overcome challenges to family unity. The situation is analogous to having one child recognized for athletic ability or artistic talent while the other child is seen as only average in these abilities. The family must clearly recognize the ability of the identified child and just as clearly recognize the abilities shown by the other child in other areas. A family that values cognitive and academic functions over other human abilities will communicate that bias to less academically able children. The human and interpersonal consequences will be difficult for all concerned.

Although care must be taken to ensure the healthy growth of intellect and self-esteem among all family members, each child need not have the same experiences. Sometimes in trying to be fair and model democratic principles, parents make the mistake of eliminating unique activities from which the gifted child could profit but which would be of no interest to or beyond the capability of other siblings. Such opportunities should not be eliminated in an effort to provide equal treatment for every child. A variety of appropriate activities can be found in which the siblings can engage; their activities need not be identical. It will be a relief to know that many of the problems encountered by the siblings of gifted children are similar to sibling problems found in any family, and no long-term effects have been found when one child is labeled gifted (Colangelo & Bower, 1987).

Our family organized a family council as an arena for solving family problems and exposing perceived inequities perpetrated by either parents or siblings. There we sought alternative solutions that could better meet the needs of all concerned. At first we held a council meeting once a week, but later we found that calling council meetings on demand of any family member better served all our needs. At the beginning, I often went to our meetings with a pre-planned solution to a problem. My goal was to convince the others—my son, my daughter, and my husband—that I was right. This approach was not useful. I soon became aware that the others often had better solutions that were far easier to carry out because all felt committed toward a plan they had helped design. All kinds of problems came before our group, from my need for neat and tidy rooms to my daughter's perceived harassment at the hands of an unaware brother. Questions of allowance, homework, bedtime, house chores, teacher attitudes, and the comfort of visiting relatives all were handled with serious and cooperative planning. Through the years, the council served to lessen the powerlessness, to increase the comfort level of family members, and generally to provide us all with excellent practice in developing our problem-solving skills, creative-thinking abilities, and feelings of caring. The family council became a meaningful way to communicate and share within the family. I highly recommend them, especially for families who live with gifted children. (See Figure 4.4 for suggestions for getting started.)

Organizing for Cooperation

As children move into the school system, where their environment and their opportunities are no longer as closely controlled by the home, parents often begin to feel powerless. They may be unaware that they have ways to influence what is happening to their child. When confronted with a situation that they know is not appropriate or that could even be damaging to their child's welfare, they may react as I did when my son was in need—trust that the school knows best and do nothing. Some parents of gifted children (fewer, I'm sure, than their public image suggests) attempt to change what is happening by complaining, attacking those they feel to be responsible, and creating only enough conflict and pressure to make everyone defensive.

There is a better way. Fortunately, both parents and school personnel want what is best for the child—at least, what they perceive to be best. The most effective way to change or correct a bad situation is, in most instances, not by direct confrontation but by an organized, knowledgeable, cooperative effort. If there must be winners and losers, too often the child is one of the losers, no matter who wins.

The first step is to organize parent groups, even before a problem arises. Parents should join with other parents of gifted children in the school or the district. Such organizations have accomplished many goals. As the child finds the school experience different than others do, parents also will find that their experiences differ from the more typical parental experiences. A review of the characteristics and unusual needs of gifted children will help parents understand why their role as a parent is often unusual. When a group of parents of gifted children organizes,

Figure 4.4 *Establishing a Family Council*

Steps:

- At first, for at least several months, set a day and time to hold the family council each week. Change the date only when absolutely necessary and be sure everyone is informed. Later, the Council can be held only on request.
- Every member of the family is a Council member and is expected to attend.
- Get the agreement of all members that the Council is a trust situation and anything discussed does not go beyond the Council; ask for individual agreement to those terms before each meeting.
- The position of Chair of the Council rotates each meeting.
- Each member is given a time to present and initiate a discussion of an issue of concern. A member may pass.
- Each member is given a time to be heard on each issue discussed. A member may pass.
- After everyone has had the opportunity to be heard and no further solutions are presented, the Chair should seek a solution by plurality vote (solution that receives the most support).
- The solution decided on will be in effect until the next Council meeting, at which time it can be reevaluated if requested. Members who are not present must abide by the solution decided on by the group present.
- Parents must be careful not to use the Council to lecture, impose their solutions, or judge other member's solutions. Get the point across by modeling, suggesting, and posing alternatives.

Benefits:

- A family council provides a forum for righting wrongs, making people aware of how their behavior affects others, appropriately expressing needs, and building good skills of communication and decision-making.
- Provides a safe place for expressing feelings and helps children find appropriate ways to express their feelings, needs, and ideas.
- Strengthens self-concept and mutual respect of family members.
- Develops a sense of responsibility and empowerment in children.
- Creates a commitment of family members to helping each other to find solutions to problems and raises the sensitivity of each to the others.
- Creates a sense of identity and belonging among family members.

they find understanding, and even relief, in their sharing of common concerns and experiences.

As a group, parents will easily find people willing to share information on educating gifted children. Such resources can inform parents regarding what is known about giftedness, the identification procedures used in their district, the gifted program in which their child participates, and answers to many questions the parents will have. Parents should learn of the many alternatives and possibilities for providing quality education both at home and at school. With a good knowledge base, parents will now be in a position to help change inadequate or unfair practices in their schools and to offer knowledgeable support to teachers. Many teachers, administrators, and school board members are anxious to make changes, try more challenging programs, or end detrimental practices. However, they do not want to go against the wishes of the community. Informed groups can also schedule field trips to enrich the learning of their children. Many educational trips that would not be accessible to single families are available to groups. Organized groups can experience: factories; museums; dress rehearsals of concerts, plays, and ballets; tours of industries, professional groups, and businesses; archaeological digs; and historical events. The possibilities are limitless, but be careful parents do not spend all their energy outside the school system, with none left for supporting and improving what is happening to their child all day, 5 days per week. It is important that parents of gifted children become involved in the school to present informed support for the practices they prefer for their children, not only showing what is wrong but presenting other alternatives and suggesting positive changes.

One note of caution: Gifted children often have gifted parents who exhibit all the same characteristics and who have some of the same independent, divergent natures. Organizing such groups may take a bit of doing; diverse opinions must be expected and allowed. However, there is much to be gained; I have found that most people who are committed to gifted education are very interesting and generous. For information on how others have organized groups of parents of gifted children, write to the ERIC Clearinghouse on Disabled and Gifted Children, Council for Exceptional Children, 1920 Association Dr, Reston, Virginia 22091.

Parent In-Service

It is as important for teachers in the home to understand the needs of gifted children and how to meet these needs as it is for teachers in the schools. A 5- to 8-week parent in-service course can help parents understand giftedness and the impact it has on their children and their school's programs. The following five sessions are outlined to provide an idea of the information that could be introduced in such a course. An outside expert or experts in the field or a knowledgeable coordinator could give the sessions, or they could be divided among interested parents to study and prepare for a presentation scheduled by the group. There are many materials available, such as this text, that could provide some of the information for the presentation.

> *Session 1: Understanding Intelligence, Creativity, and Giftedness*—This session would include: Who are gifted learners? How does someone develop high intelligence? How can giftedness be nurtured at home? At school? How can creativity be developed?

> *Session 2: The Emotional and Social Development of Gifted Learners*—The impact of giftedness on social and emotional development; development of self-esteem, values, leadership, and ethics; discipline and the gifted learner; and problems associated with growing up gifted.

Session 3: Meeting the Needs of Gifted Learners—Developing a responsive learning environment, creating program alternatives, differentiating curriculum for gifted learners, integrating all four brain functions to optimize learning, and evaluating children and programs.

Session 4: Effective Teachers at Home and at School—The nurturing home, families that produce growth, communication skills, and collaboration between home and school.

Session 5: Advocacy—Planning for advocacy with the school, student-parent-teacher interactions, legislative procedures and possibilities, and helping gifted students to be their best advocates.

Parents As Resources

Parents can cooperate with the schools in providing quality education for their gifted learners in many ways. One way is to offer their services as teachers. If the classroom is individualized and/or organized into centers, a parent can create and implement a center for a specified period of time. For example, in a school near our campus, a kindergarten teacher assesses the interests, occupations, and abilities of the parents of the children in her class each year. She invites them to share something they are especially good at with a small group of children in a learning center for 3 days. She has had language centers, construction centers, baking centers, black history centers, Cinco de Mayo centers, and numerous others. The parents have become much more involved in the classroom, provide many needed services, and enrich the learning experience for everyone. Often parents will be comfortable sharing with a few children even when they would never consider teaching the entire class.

Parents can also provide materials, help with construction when changing the classroom environment, run individualized learning labs in such subjects as reading or math, and provide transportation, additional supervision, and make arrangements for field trips. Some parents enjoy organizing other parents to make all of the above suggestions possible. It is important that teachers ask for the help they need and not waste parental talent on busy work. Parents can make important contributions to classroom learning if both the teacher and the parents take the responsibility to initiate and carry out such involvement. At the very least, parents should be involved in planning and evaluation conferences with their child and the teacher. Each of these persons has something unique to contribute to the data needed for good educational decision-making.

Parents can make a significant impact in the area of legislation. Most of the provisions for special education at the state and federal levels have been enacted because of the efforts of groups of parents. Parents must stay informed about bills and legislative action and let their elected representatives know what they want. Government officials are asked to resolve many problems. It is very easy for them to feel that the needs of gifted students, if they know of them at all, have very low priority. Teachers and other school personnel cannot influence boards of education, state superintendents, governors, and legislators with anywhere near the effectiveness that parents can. In sheer numbers, parents have the advantage. Parents have

Figure 4.5 *Suggestions for Parents*

I have found the following suggestions useful as a parent and as a teacher. Many of them came from other parents or from students, and some my children taught me. If you live with gifted children:

- Create open communication that is available from birth on. Listen, listen, listen. Listening lets your children know that you think they are valuable and careful listening lets them know that what they think is worth understanding. You become a safe and trusted friend.

    Set aside a special time for each child to have you to himself or herself, to be interested in her or him alone, to be listened to nonjudgmentally, to share ideas. Don't wait for problems or decision-making times. At our house I used the time when I tucked each child in bed, sitting down each evening for 10 to 30 minutes, with all our attention available to each other. Also try the family council described in Figure 4.4.

- Do what you like doing and include the child, as well as doing things in which the child is interested.
- Permit the children their own individuality and enjoy them for who they are, not what you would like them to be. Let them feel your acceptance of them as people.
- Respect your child and allow the child as much dignity as you would a friend.
- Allow your children to make lots of decisions, and consult them on issues affecting them whenever you believe they can understand the consequences.
- Don't confuse the IQ with the child; the child is much more.
- Help the child understand and deal with his or her belonging and conformity needs. Often, especially for girls, the pressure to conform is great, the child must feel it's really all right to be different.
- Help children with their need for perfectionism and what that does to their self-image. Serve as an example by modeling your attempts to accept your own mistakes, and show them how you keep trying.
- Help them set realistic standards and help them understand how unfair it is to hold others to their standards.

the real power in our school systems, and they must be made aware of it and use it for the benefit of the children. (See Figure 4.5 for suggestions for parents.)

This chapter has presented evidence to show the importance of optimizing the early learning periods if the child's potential is to be actualized. It seems increasingly clear that the roots of intelligence can be found not only in the genetic endowment of the individual but also within the individual's early experiences with the environment. It is doubtful that even the finest, most richly endowed brain can function at its optimum without an equally enriched environment.

Researchers are finding clues to competent functioning in the prenatal, perinatal, and postnatal periods of human development. Parenting for optimal development must include the health and living habits of the mother-to-be even prior to conception. We can no longer ignore the sensitive and critical periods for development through the fetal period and the early years of life. The use of such periods for learning may make the difference between average and gifted performance. At the

Figure 4.5 *continued*

- Arrange back-to-nature times and quiet together and apart times; show that you value reflection and daydreaming.
- Help your child set time and energy priorities. Too often the world is so exciting for these children that they seem to need to do everything at once.
- Help them appreciate individual differences, both in themselves and in others.
- Instruct by your actions more than by your words. If you want your child to be an avid reader, then you need to be one. Other interests develop this way, too.
- Don't insist that every project have closure before other things can happen. Often, what the child wanted or needed to learn from an experience occurs before the project is "finished." Sometimes other fascinating areas just have to be explored before the project can be finished properly. Otherwise, you may end up with a few finished projects and a turned-off child. Besides, this is a need that schools cannot meet. Your child will get lots of experience with closure and meeting deadlines at school.
- Be careful about supporting teachers when they are doing stupid things (e.g., a homework assignment of 50 problems all on a concept that your child mastered 2 years ago). Help the child understand the consequences of doing or not doing the task, then plan a conference with the teacher and be sure the situation is understood. If the teacher remains unreasonable, then you have a right to discuss your perception with the principal. There is little value in obedience at any cost.
- Provide a safe place by your nonjudgmental acceptance of the child. At times, your child will find being different very difficult. Neither the teacher nor the child's friends will always understand, and your child will need a place where it is safe to be who he or she is.
- Enjoy living with your child! Your life together will be a great adventure! Children are not comparable, so value each for what each offers. As parents, we are truly blessed to be able to become so intimately involved with such marvelous people, our children.

very least, we can use current information to guide our children toward becoming healthier, more intellectually able, more sensitive, and more motivated, self-directed learners. If each parent of each child were to use what is now known about nurturing human bodies and minds, how very different our world would be.

QUESTIONS OFTEN ASKED

1. Can early learning create giftedness?

It would probably be more accurate to say "develop or nurture giftedness," but yes, early learning is very important to developing high levels of intelligence.

2. How early can a baby learn?

Many researchers have reported evidence of memory being developed during the sixth and seventh month in utero. At birth most of an infant's sensory system is operable and shows levels of discrimination (e.g., responding to music heard prior to birth, mother's rhythms, and the sound of her voice). Most researchers believe that babies are aware and process information and experiences long before they can control their body movements to let us know that they are learning.

3. Can you overstimulate a baby?

Yes, but not without knowing about it. Babies share readily and loudly when they are uncomfortable with their environment. They give many subtle cues even before that. It is important that caregivers pay attention to their babies for cues and follow their lead, because each child is unique. The baby will quite dependably let you know when you have gone too far. Unfortunately, the most serious problem most babies have is understimulation or stimulation that is not directed specifically to them. That is extremely wasteful of their potential.

4. What are sensitive and critical periods for learning?

Sensitive periods are periods of growth that occur when all systems—sensory, mental, and motor—are ready to be used. If activated by the environment, they will be used together at peak efficiency (e.g., visual complexity from birth to 2 months, language acquisition between 18 months and 3 years). The time when an organizational process proceeds most rapidly is a critical period for the resulting organization. Failure to use a process during this time results in loss of the process or function (e.g., the first trimester of fetal life for physical growth and the first few months of life for the development of depth perception). If you miss a sensitive period, you miss the time for optimal learning; but if you miss a critical period, the result will be loss of function.

5. How do you discipline a gifted child?

All children respond best to guidance; however, for the gifted child it is essential. These children can be reasoned with and learn from the process quite readily. Remember that we teach mostly by our actions. If we want to teach someone how best to solve a problem, we would model the solution we want them to use in the future. That is the best reason to think carefully about rewards and punish-

ments before using them. Limits and boundaries are essential but they should be fair. As soon as the child can understand the consequences of any action, use natural consequences and alternative coping behavior as guidance. The successful parent assumes the child had good intentions but did not know the most appropriate way to carry them out.

6. How early should children be taught academic subjects such as reading and math?

Reading to children can begin before they are 1 year old. It is a most effective way to begin the development of the skills and positive attitudes needed for successful, lifelong reading. Math begins with counting—toes, fingers, buttons on Mommy's dress, and so forth. Alphabet and number songs and rhymes add to the beginning of "academic" learning as well. If you mean when should a child be sat down and forced to learn skills and drills, I would have to respond "never!" Learning can be such fun for everyone; I'll never understand why we have made it such a chore at school.

7. Don't children who learn later in school catch up to early learners?

No, they do not. Many researchers have shown that instead of "catching up," the distance between early and late learners continues to grow throughout the grades until by sixth grade, the late learner is at an incredible disadvantage. Parents are the best teachers when they allow their young children to be their guides; they have the best teacher-to-child ratio, the best overall knowledge of their child's needs, and they can allow continuous progress. Besides it's great fun!

❧ CHECKING FOR UNDERSTANDING
Follow-Up Activity

List and briefly discuss the 10 most important ideas that you would want to share with a pregnant mother about optimizing the potential of her child.

    OR

Design a brochure that could be distributed to obstetrician, pediatrician, and family physician offices containing the most important information for developing a child's potential. Be concise but clear.

❧ SUMMARY

1. The potential for giftedness begins very early in a child's life and relies on a rich and appropriate interaction between the child's genetic endowment and the environment in which the child grows.

Early Learning: the Importance of Developing Potential

2. At the level of gene action and cell development it is possible to generalize animal results to humans.
3. The cortex of the brain expands significantly and grows thicker and heavier when conditions are stimulating rather than deprived. Glial cells increase in number, and the body and the nucleus of each neural cell increase in size. There are also measurable chemical changes within the cell that correlate with higher levels of problem-solving ability.
4. The brain can be shaped by stimulation and use, by disease and trauma, and by dull routine and disuse to direct what we may become. Long-lasting effects occur as a result of experience. The more complex the experience, the richer the environment and the more complex the brain.
5. Interaction with the environment begins to affect the infant significantly during the parental period. There is no period with a more direct and formative effect on the child's developing brain than the 9 months of pregnancy.

Optimizing Learning: Developing Giftedness (Birth Through 2 Years)

6. We now know that infants are active at birth; they are perceiving, learning, and information-organizing individuals. They are aware, expressive, and affected by their interactions with others and possess an understanding of self from day one. They are born with depth perception, eye-hand coordination, sensory coordination, and skin sensitivity. They remember, and show distinct preferences for certain sounds, shapes, and tastes.
7. In the process of developing intelligence, infants and young children have a great need for a rich and varied environment that responds to their abilities, needs, and interests; this is referred to as a responsive learning environment.

8. Sensitive periods are periods of growth that occur when all systems—sensory, mental, and motor—are ready to be used and during which the environment of the individual will have the greatest effect on a specific characteristic. If activated by the environment, the systems will be used together at peak efficiency (e.g., visual complexity from birth to 2 months, language acquisition between 18 months and 3 years). The time when an organizational process proceeds most rapidly is a critical period for the resulting organization. If activated by the environment during this time, the systems will be used together at peak efficiency.
9. The way in which children are disciplined communicates the beliefs and values of their families, contributes to their understanding of appropriate ways to handle problems, and models behaviors of support and guidance or anger and fear. Methods of discipline can enhance or inhibit the curiosity, inquiry, and confidence that optimize learning.
10. It is theorized that between 18 months and 4 years of age, every human has available an innate ordering device for learning language, referred to as the Language Acquisition Device (LAD). During this LAD period, the environment of the child must be rich in language experience for never again will the child have the ability to learn language-related activities with such ease.

Nurturing Giftedness During Early Childhood (2 Through 5 Years)

11. Through the work of Piaget and his stage theories, Vygotsky and his zone of proximal development, and Dabrowski and his theory of developmental potential, we find clues and strategies for optimally developing the rational mind.
12. Although less explored, the metaphoric, intuitive, holistic mind is seen by many individuals of eminence as equally valuable to the rational mind and as essential to the development of creativity.
13. The curriculum for all preschool children must be rich in variety and stimulating in process. For those who are developing faster and who show higher levels of intelligence, such variety and stimulation are even more necessary.

14. It seems increasingly clear that the roots of intelligence can be found not only in the genetic endowment of the individual but also within the early experiences the individual has with the environment. It is doubtful that even the finest, most richly endowed brain can function at its optimum without an equally enriched environment.

Parenting Gifted Children: Teachers of the Gifted at Home

15. In every phase of a child's growth, parents and the home environment play a significant part and influence the outcome; the home is the true cradle of eminence.
16. Parents of gifted children very often are gifted themselves and many of them have not yet dealt with the differences that they felt when growing up. This may make it hard for them to help their children resolve the issues being gifted can create.
17. The family establishes a foundation of love and caring that can influence how each member views the others and operates in the world.
18. The authoritative parenting style produces children who are more successful in school and in life than does the use of the authoritarian parenting style.
19. Gifts and talents cannot be actualized without the encouragement, support, and environmental opportunities provided by the parents and teachers. Genius cannot "will out" in spite of circumstances, but must be developed, perhaps even created.
20. Parents can provide significant resources for school programs and can be important advocates for legislation and program development. Providing contact points, meetings, and conferences for parental involvement in the school program ensures both the teacher and the parents that the child's development will proceed effectively.

5

Growing Up Gifted

In this chapter the reader will discover discussions and information regarding:

- Social-emotional development and its relationship to gifted children.

- The importance of self-concept and high self-esteem.

- Moral development and gifted learners.

- The development of personality in gifted learners.

- The gifted adolescent.

The brain, with its complex architecture and limitless potential, is a highly plastic, constantly changing entity that is powerfully shaped by our experiences in childhood and throughout life . . . Our collective actions, sensations, and memories are a powerful shaper of both function and anatomy.

—MARIAN DIAMOND, 1998

Giftedness is someone you are, *not* something you do.

—JIM DELISLE, 1998

Ms. Lundi's son Ray attended this school because his mother taught here. She had a class of older students, but he really didn't see why he could not be in her class. He had been in preschool classes before and it never worked out. They always did the same things Ray had done since he could remember. Even though he usually was younger than most of the students, they never did anything that he thought was very interesting. He always ended up telling the other children what to do and how to play because they were so helpless, or he played by himself. His mother had told him that this school would be different, but he remarked that it didn't look different. There was only one other 3-year-old in his group and everyone else was 4 or 5 years old. Ray had been here for almost a week, and although he said that a lot of the activities were better than those at his other schools, he was convinced that the children were just the same. Ms. Lundi was visiting his class this morning, and she noticed that he didn't bother to talk to the other students because he was so sure they were just like all the others.

She watched as Ray walked around the room looking for something challenging to do. As he approached the science table, So-Chan looked up and invited him to join him in an experiment with static electricity. So-Chan was so excited about what he was doing that Ray joined him. Ray didn't know much about static electricity, and So-Chan seemed to know a lot "for a little kid," as Ray would say. Actually, So-Chan was about 4 years old. Ray and So-Chan discussed the experiment for a few minutes and before long both boys were engaged in the activity. For the first time, Ray had found someone his own age who understood him and whom he could enjoy. This was great!

Ms. Lundi watched the two boys as they worked together. She was glad that Ray had finally started to get acquainted. She knew how lonely he had been the past week and how unhappy he had been at the other preschools he had attended. He was such a bright child that he had never found anyone his own age who could understand him and with whom he could share his thoughts.

As the weeks went by Ray and So-Chan became inseparable, often walking hand in hand and talking as fast as they could about all kinds of things. More and more of the others in the class were invited to join them as both boys found more children who had good ideas. Ray was having a great time. He had finally discovered a group where he felt he could really belong, even more than with the older kids that he had always hung around in the past. It was a good thing they had started this school for highly gifted students.

SOCIAL-EMOTIONAL DEVELOPMENT AND GIFTEDNESS

In addition to the importance of the cognitive development of every child, social-emotional development is of increasing concern. Goleman (1995) has even developed a construct that he calls "Emotional Intelligence" (see Chapter 8 for further discussion of this construct). Events experienced with emotional intensity are most easily remembered, and repeated emotional experiences can have the greatest impact on the connections within the brain (Siegel, 1999).

Children who, by fortunate circumstances, develop more of their potential seem to meet a different set of social and emotional consequences than do more typical children. In the 1920s, it was assumed that these children were emotionally borderline neurotic or even psychotic individuals (Terman, 1925). Their advanced performance was viewed with great suspicion. A child prodigy was thought to become an adult imbecile. Parents who found their preschoolers reading would discourage such activities and encourage "playing with little friends" as an antidote. The fear that a neighbor, or worse yet a teacher, would discover precocious behavior in their child led many parents to adopt drastic and punitive actions when they observed any advanced behavior. Although attitudes have changed, some of these types of responses to advanced development still linger.

Social-Emotional Characteristics of Gifted Learners

In a climate of suspicion and rejection of advanced development, Terman (1925) began his study of gifted children at Stanford University that was mentioned in Chapter 2. Terman collected data for 35 years on the emotional and social characteristics of children whom he identified as gifted. What Terman found did not support the prevalent view of the day. The majority of children in his 140 and above IQ group were physically more attractive than the more typical children. Later studies linked this finding to better nutrition among children in his study and to the early experiences of most optimally developing children (Laycock & Caylor, 1964). Far from being the misfits and drudges people called them, the gifted youngsters in his population became leaders, organizers, football captains, and class officers. They enjoyed significantly greater popularity and their classmates viewed them positively. They showed marked superiority in moral attitudes, as measured by tests of character, and Terman found that their moral judgment developed earlier than that of the average population. These children seemed well-rounded and achieved well in most school subjects. Later data showed this population to be socially more able to adjust. As adults they suffered less from social problems such as divorce, alcoholism, and suicide than the average population. This group also had a lower prevalence of ill health and insanity and a lower mortality rate than the average population (Terman & Oden, 1947).

Terman's subjects not only completed higher levels of schooling in larger numbers than the typical population, they also received more honors and awards while doing so. Professional accomplishments were measured only among the men in the earlier reports, because women of that time period were not encouraged to seek careers. This gifted group had an outstanding record of achievement and made a far greater than average number of contributions to society. Although the limitations of this study must be noted as we view the accomplishments of the group (e.g., the overloading of participants from higher socioeconomic levels), we must recognize it as a major accomplishment in the field of gifted education. Terman himself remarked, "I take some pride in the fact that not one of the major conclusions we drew in the early 1920s regarding the traits that are typical of gifted

Social skills are learned very early.

children has been overthrown in the three decades since then" (Terman, 1954, p. 223). His profile of the gifted child has been expanded as we study broader based populations, but his statement remains essentially true.

It is as difficult to generalize the social-emotional characteristics of gifted individuals as it is their other characteristics. Indeed, social aptitudes cannot be predicted by high academic ability (Jones & Day, 1996). Discussions of generalizations of social-emotional ability bring out characteristics commonly found in the gifted population but seldom found in any one gifted individual. For the most part, given the opportunity for healthy development, the social-emotional adjustment of gifted children tends to proceed better than among the more typical population. As early as 1926, Hollingworth found a strong positive correlation between intelligence and desirable character and temperament traits.

Olszewski-Kubilius, Kulieke, and Krasney (1988) reviewed the literature on personality differences between gifted students and nongifted students and made several generalizations. Compared with their same-age peers, gifted individuals tend to exhibit lower levels of anxiety and tend to be well-adjusted, although specific personality traits may show more variation. Some evidence suggested that gifted students resemble older groups of individuals. Gifted males and gifted females are more alike than different on personality profiles. And finally, gifted achievers tend to be more responsible and show more self-control than do gifted underachievers. In general, the research indicated that gifted students appear to be more independent, intrinsically motivated, flexible, self-accepting, and psychologically well-adjusted than their nongifted peers.

Self-confidence and independence are personality traits also suggested by Davis and Rimm (1994). They comment that the generally higher levels of internal control and personal responsibility of gifted students often lead them to set high goals for themselves. However, not attaining these often unrealistic goals can result in frustration and feelings of incompetence and inadequacy. Davis and Rimm believe that this frustration occurs not because the students have produced an inferior product, but because they expected their performance to match their vision. Known as perfectionism, this common trait of gifted individuals can be very difficult to change.

The personality traits that Silverman (1994) believes are most common among gifted individuals and demonstrate their emotional complexity are sensitivity, perfectionism, intensity, and introversion. Of these, sensitivity seems to be one of the earliest and most central traits. Sensitivity may include feelings that are easily hurt, strong response to criticism, compassion for others, and even strong physical reactions to light, noise, texture, and foods.

Research studies of gender differences (Luftig & Nichols, 1991; VanTassel-Baska, 1989a) have found that the perceptions held of gifted boys differ significantly from that of gifted girls when rated by their nongifted, age peers in a heterogenous school setting. Gifted boys were given higher status than gifted girls and nongifted boys and girls. They were chosen as most popular, attractive, and creative, and more skilled at sports. Gifted girls were perceived as least popular, aloof, and bossy, placing them at-risk socially among their age peers.

When compiling studies of the social-emotional characteristics of gifted children, a generally positive profile emerges, although many of the following characteristics can create a need to which we must attend if the positive aspects are to flourish. In general, gifted individuals:

- Show better emotional adjustment than nongifted children, although some studies indicate a closer relationship to socioeconomic differences than to intellectual differences (Oram, Dewey, & Rutemiller, 1995; Ramaseshan, 1957).

- Have a high energy level that can result in emotional excitability, high sensitivity, rapid and compulsive verbalization, abundant imagination, and emotional reactions that can be extremely elevated or depressed (Piechowski, 1991).

- Are more independent and less conforming to peer opinions, more dominant, more forceful, and more competitive than typical learners (Gottfried & Gottfried, 1996; Webb, 1994).

- Show a high level of persistence, attention, curiosity, enjoyment of learning, and orientation toward mastery and challenge from early years through adolescence (Gottfried & Gottfried, 1996).

- Exhibit a tendency for excessive self-criticism and a pattern of unrealistic self-assessment of unreasonably high expectations of their performance resulting in perfectionism, the dissatisfaction with the difference between their expectations of ideal performance and assessment of their actual performance (Cross, 1997).

- Perceive themselves to have greater personal freedom than do their average classmates. They value cooperative and democratic forms of interaction, although they are less willing to compromise (Lehman & Erdwins, 1981).

- Report more positive feelings regarding themselves and others and perceive themselves to be cognitively more competent with greater confidence in their own control over successes or failures in school tasks, compared with regular age peers (Chan, 1996; Vallerand, Gagne, Senecal, & Pelletier, 1994).

- Prefer their intellectual peers to their chronological-age peers, resulting in a social preference for older children and adults. They lack interest in children of lower mental age, and choose friends among children like themselves. They relate well to adults but may have problems playing with less able playmates (Davis & Rimm, 1994; Freeman, 1994).

- Hold a high social status among their classmates, who often prefer them as companions; this is more dependent on the students' self-concept than on their level of giftedness. This factor seems to diminish at the secondary level, especially if other preferred factors of popularity (e.g., athletic ability) are not also displayed (Purkey, 1966; Cornell et al., 1990).

- Often show leadership ability and become involved in community projects and concerns. Concern for universal problems and the welfare of others begins much earlier than for more typically developing children. When involved in group leadership, they emphasize parliamentary procedure and minimize the use of more autocratic or *laissez-faire* approaches to governance (Cassel & Haddox, 1959; Roeper, 1992).

- Tend to be very idealistic, seeking what is fair and just at an early age. They are more sensitive to values and moral issues, understanding "good behavior" and "bad behavior" very early. They usually are sensitive to the feelings and rights of others and empathize with their problems. It is not unusual for gifted students to be deeply concerned about social issues—those in their school as well as those half a world away (Cox, 1926; Martinson, 1961).

Intrinsic Motivation

Lovecky (1992) adds an interesting trait to those usually mentioned with social-emotional characteristics: the need of gifted individuals for self-determination—an inner strength, a high motivation to achieve all one is capable of being, and a single-mindedness in the pursuit of their own goals. Lovecky calls this *entelechy* and refers to it as a vital force directing life and growth toward one's own destiny that allows one to pursue goals despite any obstacles. Such a trait can be seen in those who have achieved things of meaning to the society as well as to themselves.

Students who are intrinsically motivated exhibit curiosity, accept challenges willingly, are persistent with tasks that are difficult, remain task-committed, are satisfied with their efforts irrespective of the opinions of others, and are found to have lower academic anxiety (Amabile, 1989; Gottfried & Gottfried, 1996). Academic intrinsic motivation is highly correlated to school achievement and to intelligence. Flexible deadlines; elimination of overt supervision; an environment that is stimulating and safe for risk-taking and questioning; choice; and minimal competition are teacher practices that promote intrinsic motivation (Lashaway-Bokina, 2000). Gottfried and Gottfried (1996) have found that intrinsic motivation can be further encouraged if the curriculum is designed to provide the optimal level of challenge.

External rewards are highly problematic for maintaining intrinsic motivation. Edwards (1997) describes the effect of rewards as devastating. Gifted students have a higher level of internal locus of control available and are more sensitive to the environment. Lepper, Green, and Nisbett (1973) found that gifted students lose more of their power faster than do the average learners. The responsive learning environment becomes critical if the inner locus of control is to be strengthened and intrinsic motivation is to be maintained.

Competition

Clinkenbeard (1989) believes that although gifted children may have a voracious appetite for learning, they find the traditional schooling, with its norm-referenced evaluation systems and its extrinsic rewards such as gold stars, prizes, and grades, detrimental to their intrinsic motivation. The results of her study show that although competition may serve a purpose in causing immediate classroom achievement goals to be met by some students, it does not support the long-term goals of education that seek to foster individuals with the will to learn for the love of learning.

Competition may be seen as task-oriented competition, when the intent is to improve performance, and other-referenced competition, when winning or outdoing others is the intent (Tassi & Schneider, 1997). Although it has been suggested that some competition may be necessary for the motivation and the quality of performance of gifted children, the task-oriented style has been shown to be far more successful both academically and socially (Udvari & Schneider, 2000). Other-referenced competition is viewed by classmates as aggressive behavior and children using this style are disliked by the majority peer group. Ford (1989) interviewed fifth- and sixth-grade gifted students regarding their feelings about competition. Although most of the students enjoyed competition among equally matched participants, they felt that academic competition in the regular classroom "brings out the worst in everyone" (p. 132). They stated that they wished their teachers would eliminate the various contests and competitions from their classrooms. They were especially concerned that their classmates often exploited their abilities during the special projects but were unwilling to remain friends afterward.

Perfectionism

When observed as obsessive preoccupation with perfection inhibiting the gifted child from trying new experiences for fear of failing, perfectionism is a serious and limiting problem and is a characteristic often observed in many gifted learners. At the heart of perfectionism is fear—an inordinate fear of failing, the fear that unless one is perfect, one is worthless. To be gifted, for many students, is to be never less than perfect. According to Greenspon (2000) this is the fundamental problem with perfectionism, under this belief, one can never feel good enough to be acceptable as a person. "Pressing oneself to do better is healthy; feeling that one must be either perfect or worthless is not" (p. 180). For gifted learners, this fear may be confounded by the knowledge that they have extraordinary ability and a record of outstanding achievement. It may actually be possible for them to do something perfectly. Their goals are high, often unrealistically high, because they can envision an exemplary outcome. However, Greenspon does not see the wish to excel as a part of perfectionism.

The negative aspects of perfectionism may also interfere with the student's relationships with others. Not only must gifted persons meet high standards and attain specified levels of performance, but often their acceptance of other people is based on the other person's ability to meet these standards. These expectations of others can seriously interfere with interpersonal relationships, the view the gifted have of their world and, certainly, how other people view them. Unfortunately, unless someone helps gifted children to understand the dynamics of this problem and provides some alternative behaviors, it can continue throughout their lives.

The first step toward intervening in problems of perfectionism is to acknowledge and clearly affirm what appears to be occurring. For example, the response to a frustrated attempt to complete perfectly a project that is still beyond the skill of the child would be simply, "You really would like that to be finished perfectly, wouldn't you?" or "It just isn't quite the way you want it yet, is it?" From statements such as these, if open communication exists with the child, a discussion of this need usually will follow. Buffington (1987) found that not only is the perfectionist less productive but also perfectionism contributes to loneliness, relationship problems, limited self-acceptance, and moodiness. He suggests that children can be taught to deal with their perfectionism problems by:

- Learning how to mentally filter thoughts, focusing on their successes instead of their mistakes.
- Reevaluating their current standards by comparing to set criteria used by others.
- Celebrating their successes.
- Learning from their mistakes.
- Practicing making mistakes.
- Listing the advantages and disadvantages of being a perfectionist.
- Looking closely at their current level of self-acceptance and surrounding themselves with positive situations and people to improve it.

But what about children or adults who derive great pleasure from striving toward perfection? What about those who would consider their lives less fulfilling without constant pursuit of impossibly high goals? Results of a study conducted by Seigle and Schuler (2000) support the multidimensional theory of perfectionism that places it on a continuum from healthy to dysfunctional behaviors. Attributes of healthy perfectionists include:

- An intense need for order and organization
- Self-acceptance of mistakes
- High parental expectations
- Use of positive coping strategies with their perfectionist tendencies
- Absence of role models who emphasized doing one's "best"
- View of personal effort as an important part of their perfectionism

Characteristics of negative or dysfunctional perfectionists include:

- Anxiety about making errors
- Extremely high standards for self
- Perceived excessive expectations and criticisms from others
- Questioning their own judgments
- Lack of effective coping strategies
- Need for constant approval

Parker and Adkins (1995) address the dual possibilities of perfectionism, suggesting that educators too often look only at the negative aspects of this common characteristic of gifted children and adults. Although perfectionism that leads repeatedly to frustration, dissatisfaction, and low feelings of self-worth is certainly problematic and needs attention and alternative coping strategies, acknowledging the positive aspects of the pursuit of excellence seems to necessitate perseverance, high standards, extraordinary effort, and maximum use of talent.

How do the positive motivational possibilities of perfectionism turn into a negative experience? Davis and Rimm (1994) suggest that one way is the extreme praise experienced by gifted students from both their parents and their teachers which they internalize, thereby becoming dependent on such praise for their self-definition. This adds strong external pressure to the motivation to achieve at increasingly high levels just to "deserve" the praise.

Those who wish to create climates that promote psychological safety must also consider the characteristic of perfectionism often exhibited by gifted children. Psychological safety requires reduced tension and stress if children are to perform to their own satisfaction. For gifted students, external or self-imposed pressure for achievement can become unreasonable. Webb, Meckstroth, and Tolan (1982) feel that such pressure may be one of the major causes of depression among gifted youngsters. Seigle and Schuler (2000) believe that gifted perfectionists need teachers, parents, and counselors who help them focus on their present behaviors, plan realistic goals, make reasonable commitments, and accept the consequences of their behaviors. Such adults can help set priorities, model acceptance of mistakes, set high but realistic standards, encourage relaxation techniques, and teach more realistic self-evaluation skills. An environment where risk-taking is valued, in which trust is developed, and where mistakes are seen as cues to aid learning relieves students of the need to be perfect.

Social-Emotional Adjustment of Gifted Learners

Although the very nature of being different in a society that does not value difference, even positive difference, brings more adjustment problems to the individual who is gifted, the very ability that creates the problem can supply the solution. The gifted need help in learning to accept themselves as they are, to appreciate the ways in which they are both similar to and different from others. Teachers, parents, and counselors must create opportunities for gifted students to experience themselves positively and value themselves as unique persons. The positive social and emotional growth of gifted children is more related to how well the environment responds to and provides for their needs than to the different characteristics they present (Cross, 1997).

Social-emotional adjustment can be confusing for gifted children. While young, children may choose to become what their parents value, then at school they shift to perceived teacher values. How closely these are aligned will determine the energy that must be expended. Later, children discover peer values. For example, a gifted girl may discover that if she wishes to be considered feminine and gain acceptance, the perfect papers required by parents and teachers become a liability. The challenge of inquiry into unusual subjects "for girls" becomes less rewarding. For boys, the masculine ideal of athletic competence may dictate refocusing in that direction. Again, peer values may cause reordering of accepted parental and teacher values. In either case, children may decide to use their giftedness to appear not at all gifted. As we have seen from the dynamic nature of intelligence, such denial and disuse can have the long-lasting consequences of diminished intellectual development.

For highly and exceptionally gifted children, the question of social-emotional adjustment takes on an added dimension. These children have even more problems finding other children to whom they can relate. They become bored with schoolwork and they find fewer mental challenges within the school setting. Among groups of fellow students and teachers, those of lesser ability often display mediocrity and poor decision-making. Highly and exceptionally gifted children may end up feeling disrespect for the judgment and actions of those in authority (Hollingworth, 1942).

The more highly gifted the child, the greater the risk for social-emotional maladjustment and unhappiness (Hollingworth, 1942; Tannenbaum, 1983). Roedell (1984) identified eight areas of vulnerability of which to be aware so that these risks can be minimized: uneven development, perfectionism, adult expectations, intense sensitivity, self-definition, alienation, inappropriate environments, and role conflicts. She finds that the most frequent symptom among this population is lack of confidence, resulting in a helpless orientation toward perceived failure. When this interacts with heightened perfectionism, we find ineffective problem-solving and increasingly lowered self-concept. These problems can be alleviated. A study of the overall adjustment of highly gifted children noted that very low priority was given to the problems of this group. Of the 113 children tested, only 13 were seen by the school psychologist, and these 13 had been referred for the sole purpose of testing (Leaverton & Herzog, 1979). However, in special schools, where highly gifted children work with mental age peers, such children experienced fewer problems of adjustment.

As early as 1954, Barbe found that gifted children tend to choose one of three patterns for adjusting to their world. They may choose to withdraw, to isolate themselves from the group; this occurs most often when the situation offers no challenge. They may become the class clown, showing off in an effort to be accepted and to gain favorable attention; this behavior may be carried to the point that teachers and the peer group reject such attempts as being inappropriate or silly, or they may view the child as a nuisance. Finally, gifted children may seek conformity through pleasing others or by pretending not to know answers in an effort to seem like everyone else, to hide a superior intellect; this dangerous game of nonuse may result in loss of function—growth cannot be nurtured through this subterfuge. In this way, gifted children may find themselves becoming role players or what our educational system calls "underachievers." In the pages to follow we will delve into this complex problem further.

In the literature (Cross, 1997; Webb, 1994), three similar negative coping strategies used by gifted students are being researched. Blending in and underachieving are as common and problematic as previously mentioned. Drop-out rates for gifted students may now be as high as 20% of the total number of students who drop out of high school. However, suicide is a third, more extreme, coping strategy now growing in incidence and, therefore, concern. According to Cross (1997), it is the second leading cause of death among adolescents, with 10% of all adolescents making such attempts.

Positive coping strategies for the unmet social-emotional needs that giftedness can create in schools include participation in extracurricular activities, hobbies, and physical activities (Cross, 1997). Cross recommends such activities to reduce stress, to learn useful life skills, and to meet people interested in similar interests. Modeling by teachers, parents, and counselors can easily teach such strategies. Cross also suggests that it is important to create opportunities for gifted students to spend time together. The benefits, as seen in the experience of Ray at the beginning of this chapter, are to recognize that they are not alone, that it is acceptable to have serious academic pursuits and, additionally, that time spent with gifted peers can become a catalyst for future academic careers.

Many gifted students grouped by chronological age in classrooms find themselves unable to meet either their intellectual needs or their social-emotional needs. Without intellectual peers they may feel isolated and frustrated. They may even try to hide their giftedness to be more socially acceptable (Davis & Rimm, 1994). However, when gifted students are placed in classes that allow them to interact with mental peers, value their mental ability, and provide for appropriate educational challenges, their social-emotional relationships as well as their intellectual growth flourish (Higham & Buescher, 1987; Silverman 1991). Although the potential exists for highly positive development of social-emotional and moral strength among gifted children, this is a dynamic process that needs guidance. If opportunities are not provided to gifted children for positive growth and participation in real world and global issues where they believe that they can make a difference, then this very important and admirable quality of the highly intelligent can be reduced to cynicism and antisocial behavior. Newland (1976) cautions us to assure the gifted that we are concerned with their social interaction *with* others, not just their social adjustment *to* others.

THE SELF-CONCEPT OF THE GIFTED INDIVIDUAL

Two categories of self-concept have been identified: the academic self-concept, in which gifted students most often rate quite high; and the social self-concept, an area that may be very low among some gifted students (Colangelo, 1991; Davis & Rimm, 1994). Silverman (1991) found that among highly gifted students, intellectual self-concepts were much stronger than social self-concepts.

One of the first people to look at the healthy emotional development of human beings was the psychologist Abraham Maslow. Neither satisfied with the view that humans need control, nor content with the focus of most psychologists on pathology and remediation, Maslow (1971) believed "well" individuals could become even healthier. He called the pursuit toward developing one's potential *self-actualization*. Maslow identified a group of people whom he felt exhibited outstanding health, both physically and emotionally. He then collected data, coalescing the characteristics they had in common (see Figure 5.1). Although the concept of *self* was far from new (in fact, many psychologists, philosophers, and researchers had referred to it), Maslow first listed identifying characteristics that could indicate a high level of development in the social-emotional domain. Remarkably, many of these characteristics can be identified in gifted children.

In his study of self-actualizing people, Maslow (1968) conceptualized a hierarchy of human needs and used it to explain how emotional development is facilitated or inhibited. According to this hierarchy, human energy is used to provide for needs at six levels: (1) basic physical needs, (2) safety needs, (3) love and belonging needs, (4) needs for self-esteem, (5) needs for self-actualization, (6) needs for transcendence. If needs at any one level remain unmet, energies will be drained off at that level, thus inhibiting further progress and causing overemphasis on that need level. Such limitation would make attainment of the integrated person difficult. Awareness of need levels can provide parents with a model for directing family and

Figure 5.1 *Characteristics of Self-Actualization*
Source: Adapted from *The Farther Reaches of Human Nature,* by A. Maslow, 1971, New York: Viking.

1. More aware, more in touch, more perceptive, more realistically oriented.
2. More accepting of self, others, and the natural world.
3. Spontaneous, natural, authentic.
4. More autonomous and self-directed: largely free of the need to impress others or to be liked by everyone; resistant to conformity.
5. Intrinsically motivated; having meta-motivations (e.g., actualization of potentials, capacities, and talents; fulfillment of life's mission or purpose; self-knowledge; self-acceptance; growth toward unity and synergy).
6. Seeking unity, oneness, integration, increased identification with humanity.
7. Working for a cause, devoted to a task or calling, viewing work and play as one.
8. Holding universal values (beauty, justice, truth) that are important to well-being. Working toward fulfillment of meta-needs (see #5, meta-motivations).
9. Capable of rich emotional reaction and freshness of appreciation.
10. Enjoying a high frequency of peak experiences (moments of highest happiness or fulfillment) and frequent mystic, natural, or cosmic experiences.
11. Capable of deep empathy and profound relationships with others; great ability to love and to enjoy sexuality.
12. Seeking privacy on occasion for periods of intense concentration.
13. Creative, less constricted in thought processes; using a sense of humor that is not hostile.
14. More democratic in character structure.
15. Continually wondering about life: treating each day as new.

home efforts toward healthy, integrated development (Table 5.1, Self-Concept column). It is important to note that as growth occurs, individuals may be operating on several levels at the same time with more or less emphasis. Under certain circumstances and under differing conditions, one may regress or progress through the various levels of need.

The six need levels identified by Maslow may provide a framework for working with integrated development in the home, and they should also be incorporated into classroom experiences. Gifted children have tremendous potential toward self-actualization. Our society benefits from their progress toward self-actualization as do they themselves. The greatest contributions to our culture have come from individuals who developed their potential at all levels of functioning, allowing them to integrate all ways of knowing, to risk taking unknown or unpopular stands, and to implement the insights their expanding beliefs made possible. The classroom that values, encourages, and provides opportunity for diversity, self-exploration, introspection, interaction, and quiet contemplation is the classroom where self-actualization will likely be nurtured. Maslow (1971) suggests the following for developing self-actualization:

- Experience each moment fully, vividly, and with total concentration.
- Think of life as a process of choices, your choices.
- Listen to your self; trust your inner voice.
- Take responsibility for yourself.
- Dare to be different, nonconforming, real.
- Do what you do with joy, and do it well.
- Set up conditions that will allow more peak experiences; perceive the world and life positively.
- Open up to yourself, identify your defenses, and find the courage to give them up.

The goal is to have access to all of your life, all of your potential, to be who you are.

Communicating these propositions becomes the major task of educators if they desire to nurture self-actualization. Teachers must arrange learning situations so that each individual will experience these ideas. This educational opportunity becomes critical for gifted individuals with heightened awareness and greater capacity for growth.

Although the goal of self-actualization has not been actively sought in most school systems, it has for decades been a declared goal in most public schools' philosophical statements of purpose. Through the work of educators such as George Brown (1971) at the University of California, Santa Barbara, and legislators such as John Vasconcellos (1990), Chair of the California Task Force to Promote Self-Esteem and Personal and Social Responsibility, the implementation of such goals becomes more possible.

As work in the area of understanding and facilitating growth toward self-actualization has evolved, it has become apparent that the concept of *self* is central. Researchers and practitioners such as Allport, Aspy, Brookover, Combs and Snygg, Coopersmith, Jersild, Jourard, Maslow, May, Purkey, and Rogers, to name but a few, brought the concept of *self* back to psychology and education after long

Table 5.1 *Origins of Social-Emotional Development*

Period	Self-Concept (Maslow, 1968)	Moral Development (Kohlberg, 1964)	Personality Development (Erikson, 1950)
Infancy	Individuals have basic needs that form a hierarchy of growth 1. Basic physical needs (e.g., food, shelter)	Stage 1. Authority figures dictate the child's actions. Children follow moral rules to avoid punishment. During the first 5 to 8 years of life, most children find this belief reinforced regularly.	1. *Trust vs. mistrust:* Here we find the roots of inner and outer locus of control. If as infants children experience affection and consistency, they form the belief in a secure world wherein they are effective, they matter. If instead their experience is threatening, unpredictable, stressful, or apathetic, they will believe their world to be untrustworthy, unmanageable, one in which they have no control.
Childhood	2. Protection, safety, security (physical and psychological) 3. Love, a sense of belonging (as in a family, a community), and friendship 4. Respect, esteem, approval, dignity, and self-respect	Stage 2. The child gradually becomes aware of the idea of reciprocity: "If I do something for you, you will do something for me." The is concern for rewards: "What's in it for me?" Throughout both these stages, which generally continue through the primary grades, the emphasis is on external control and on concrete consequences. Stage 3. The child seeks to meet the expectations of others, being a "good" child. Being "nice" is now seen in a broader context. The ability to see situations from the position of other persons helps determine the action a child will take.	2. *Autonomy vs. shame or doubt:* Toddlers who are allowed to feel pride and success in their experiences of learning to care for themselves gain a sense of self-confidence and self-control. If continually limited, criticized, or punished, they will believe themselves to be inadequate or bad and experience shame and self-doubt. 3. *Initiative vs. guilt:* As 4- to 5-year-olds begin to explore the world beyond themselves, they discover how the world works and how they affect it. If this exploration is challenging and effective, they learn to deal with people and things in positive ways and gain a strong sense of initiative. If, however, their efforts are always criticized and punished, they will feel guilty for self-initiated actions.
Adolescence	Continuation of growth to higher levels		4. *Industry vs. inferiority:* From 6 to 11 years of age, children develop numerous skills at home, at school, and in the outside world. An evaluation of competence when

Table 5.1 *continued*

Period	Self-Concept (Maslow, 1968)	Moral Development (Kohlberg, 1964)	Personality Development (Erikson, 1950)
Adolescence			compared with peers is important at this time. Mistakes must be viewed as growth experiences if further inquiry and exploration are not to be limited.
		Stage 4. Concern for others now encompasses more of society. The law, rules of the social system, and a desire to do one's duty gain consideration. Avoidance of guilt and social disapproval motivate the child. These last two stages bring us through adolescence. Kohlberg estimated that only 10% of the adult population goes beyond this externally controlled level of development.	5. *Ego identity vs. ego diffusion:* The adolescent explores and affirms belief systems and basic values. If all the roles and beliefs found in their lives cannot be resolved into an integrated identity, the result is what Erikson calls ego diffusion.
			6. *Intimacy vs. isolation:* In late adolescence and young adulthood the focus is on developing the ability to share one's self with another and still retain the essential self. The success one has in doing this reflects the success of the previous five areas of experience.
Adulthood	5. Self-actualization; the fullest development of one's talents and capacities (see Figure 5.1)	Stage 5. The maturity of internal commitment to principles of one's own conscience develops. At this stage, responsibility, the rights of others, and human dignity are also truly understood. Avoidance of self-condemnation is now important.	7. *Generativity vs. self-absorption:* As adults with the problems of earlier stages at least partially resolved, individuals can now direct their focus toward assisting others, one's own children, social issues, etc. Unsuccessful resolution of earlier issues can result in overconcern for one's health, comfort, and psychological needs.
	6. Transcendence of self, culture, and dichotomies; primarily meta-motivated; behaving and relating to self, others, and nature at the very highest and holistic levels of human consciousness		8. *Integrity vs. despair:* As one views one's life from the perspective of age, the evaluation may reflect meaning, purpose, and satisfaction or a series of bungled attempts, unresolved efforts, and lost opportunities. The attitude of worth will be affected by this evaluation.

Table 5.1 *continued*

Levels of Social-Emotional Development (Dabrowski, 1972)	
Level I	Self-involved interests such as self-protection and survival; others seen only as involved with self, exploitative.
Level II	Externally directed, confused value structure; contradictory behaviors; fragmented view of self.
Level III	Awareness of a hierarchy of values; sense of the ideal with one's own inconsistent behavior creating inner conflict; multilevel development; sense of higher (ideal) and lower (actual) in personal values and beliefs; moral concerns.
Level IV	Self-actualization (see Maslow, Figure 5.1); inner drive for ideals; actions based on ideals and sense of responsibility; seeking self-perfection; lives ideals and gains strength from them.
Level V	Living inspired life, harmony, transcendence, oneness with humanity and nature.

abandonment by the behaviorists. (Contributions made by each person named are cited in the references at the end of this book.) As interest in the concept of *self* increased, researchers found that the view of *self* determines achievement and enhances or limits the development of a person's potential.

The *self* may be defined as a complex and dynamic system of beliefs that individuals hold to be true about themselves. The concept is organized and can be modified (Purkey, 1970). It is, in part, our own construction that is a result of the interactions we have with others. The beliefs we have about ourselves literally determine our actions and our perceptions of the world and other people. We construct our own reality from these beliefs and often operate as though our view is the only view possible (Combs & Snygg, 1959; May, 1967; Rogers, 1961). Growth of self-esteem makes the self-actualizing, integrated person possible.

With that in mind, let us look at one especially unexpected finding. Gifted individuals often have a lower self-concept than their age peers (Trotter, 1971). One reason for this could be associated with the unusually high expectations the gifted have for themselves. Parents of gifted children, sometimes accused of "pushing" their children, are actually more concerned because their children seem to push themselves unrealistically. This pressure can be far more demanding than any external pressure. The frustration of never living up to your own standards and expectations can be very self-defeating and can interfere with mental and emotional growth.

A study by Loeb and Jay (1987) provided some clearly differentiated measures of self-concept in gifted children, including gender as a variable. Their results showed that teachers and mothers of gifted students generally rated them as having fewer problems in almost all areas than did the teachers and mothers of the control students. Loeb and Jay also found that girls differ from boys on their perception of themselves as gifted. Girls were more likely to find achievement through conformity, as demanded in elementary school, congruent with a positive self-image and feelings of control over their lives. Boys, however, define their ideal male as aggressive, self-reliant, and individualistic, a pattern that does not seem to fit well into this conformity learning pattern. Later, during adolescence, the learning demands seem to reverse and the girls' pattern of "learned femininity" is not as supported by high school achievement styles. Loeb and Jay suggest defeminization of early education and redefinition of gender roles as possible modifications to aid in growth of self-esteem among both gifted girls and boys.

Contributing to the self-doubt often felt by gifted individuals is lack of recognition from others. Parents and teachers often praise and show appreciation for the performance of those who are obviously just gaining skills, although they *expect* such performance from the gifted. Because a person seems to accomplish a difficult task with ease or is able to do many things very well, others in the environment soon come to expect such behavior and seldom show appreciation for the quality of performance or effort involved. Without appropriate comments, it becomes difficult for the gifted to develop a realistic idea of the quality of their contributions. The parent or teacher who communicates only "constructive" criticism can damage the child's developing self-concept. Sharing genuine appreciation or admiration for excellence is never inappropriate.

Development of Self-Esteem

As we have seen, gifted children and youth are subject to unique stressors and are vulnerable to problems with social-emotional adjustment. According to Hoge and Renzulli (1993), although most intellectually gifted learners have no major deficits in self-esteem, there are vast numbers of case studies and individual accounts of problems in this area (Webb, 1994). Low self-esteem results in higher levels of anxiety, more frequent psychosomatic symptoms, less effectiveness, and more destructive behavior. Children with low self-esteem find it hard to believe that any personal action can have favorable outcomes. Instead, they believe themselves to be powerless and unworthy of love or attention. Children with high self-esteem more often acquire a sense of independence, exhibit exploratory behavior, assert their own rights, develop a strong inner locus of control, and express more self-trust. These traits lead them to personal happiness and more effective functioning.

The Final Report of the California Task Force to Promote Self-Esteem and Personal and Social Responsibility (Vasconcellos, 1990) reported the following key findings:

- The family is the incubator of self-esteem and the most crucial social unit in a child's life and development. The early months and years of a child's life are the most decisive in establishing a solid base for authentic, abiding self-esteem and depth of personal character.

- The parents' high self-esteem is vital to their ability to provide a healthy environment for the child. We need to extend a great effort to assist parents to develop their own self-esteem and to become more knowledgeable, capable, and effective in nurturing children's positive self-esteem and personal responsibility.

- Because children spend so much of their time in school, the environment of the school also plays a major role in the development of self-esteem. Schools that feature self-esteem as a clearly stated component of their goals, policies, and practices are more successful academically as well as in developing healthy self-esteem. (p. 5)

The quality of our lives depends on our level of self-esteem, so why do we find so many who lack adequate levels? The concept of *self* develops quite early. The following story will illustrate how information from the environment begins to affect the development of self-esteem.

A small boy about 2 years of age was sitting in a garden watching a little "bug" move slowly across the ground. The child was fascinated by the fact that the little thing had so many legs yet still was able to move without falling down. Not long ago he had a lot of trouble just managing to move around on his own two legs. He still got them mixed up occasionally. Now as he looked closely at the "bug," he noticed other strange things. There was hair all over its legs. And when he looked very closely, the "bug" really wasn't black. There were some purple and green and even some red and orange colorings on its body. The funny things that came out of its head were really neat, too.

Just then an amazing thing happened. The bug jumped. It jumped up onto a nearby leaf and, of all things, it spit threads out of its back end. The child had seen people spit, but never had he seen anything spit out of its back end. He watched this happen again and again. Then, to his disbelief, the thing walked on its *own spit!* Well, this was getting to be too much. Someone in the house was missing all of this. His mother was such a nice, fun person, and he loved her very much; yet she couldn't see and share it all with him. He knew she wouldn't be able to come out there into the garden because, actually, that was why he was there. Earlier she had suggested that he spend the morning outside because she had so much work to do. But maybe, if he was very careful, he could put his hands together like a little cup and very carefully lift the bug up and carry it into the house. Oh, he wouldn't leave it there. He would bring it right back. And he wouldn't hurt it. He just wanted her to see it, just for a minute. Happily, he picked it up and started toward the house. The door to the kitchen was pretty hard to maneuver, especially when he had to use both hands to keep the bug safe, but he managed.

As soon as he was inside he went right to his mother and held his treasure up high for her to see. What followed was not at all what he expected! As he left the house to return the "nasty, dirty, horrible, ugly spider" to its place in the garden, he thought about what she had just said. She must be right, she was always right; he knew that. Well, if she was right, then he must be wrong.

Situations such as this give little people messages about their ideas, their competence, and their image of who they are very early in life. Even children from very nurturing homes find their lives filled with individuals, groups of people, and institutions ready and very willing to show them how they are wrong—to acquaint them, often forcibly, with the "right way."

Experiences such as this begin the formation of the concept of *self*. We are born with a center core—our essence—that is unique to us and is our real self. Tiny babies have no problem communicating to us the real needs or desires they feel. Expressing the *self* is never a problem at the beginning. But, as the child in the garden discovered, it does not take long before other information causes us to doubt the messages from our center core. After enough dissonant information enters our awareness, a shell begins to build around this real center, and it is made up of all the "crummy" stuff we feel and believe about ourselves following encounters such as these.

At some point, however, it becomes far too difficult to present ourselves to the world as the "crummy" person this shell leads us to believe we are. At around 10 to

13 years of age, we begin to look around for another image to adopt. Often we completely forget the inner core of our real self and remember only the crummy shell as the definition of who we are. This second shell is formed from all of the nice and enjoyable things we find in other people. "There is someone who smiles a lot," we say. "People seem to like that, so I'll smile a lot." "That person wears clothes a certain way that others find attractive; I can do that!" And the second shell builds. Soon we have an image to present to the world that is really great; our image is filled with nice ways of doing things and an agreeable appearance. Unfortunately, this image of self is phony, and we know it. Now we must spend time and energy to keep other people far enough away that they do not see through our image. We are sure that if we let them in too close they will find out about the "real" person we are—the crummy, inept, incompetent person we know we really are— the person we know from the first shell. We now accept this shell as us. We have forgotten the beautiful, unique center core, our essence, our real self.

No matter how loving or how caring our family is, we all experience this shell-building phenomenon. Parents must find ways to recognize, accept, and support the center core. Educators can establish classrooms that allow self-discovery and support for individual and unique development. As growing people, we must keep in touch with this essence, accepting ourselves and allowing others to know us as the unique people we are. Work in this area shows us that from the earliest days of our lives and as long as we live, our awareness and understanding of who we are will have the most effect on determining the quality and direction of our existence (Briggs, 1970; Satir, 1972).

For gifted people, the pattern of shell building is intensified. Both self-imposed and external expectations are so much greater that the gifted often develop and maintain the second shell in desperation. Focus on the second shell may result in children who try to meet everyone's expectations and become "perfect" children, never allowing themselves to knowingly disappoint parents, teachers, or any other significant person. These children have an impossible task. They may try to meet their parents' needs and find that these differ from the teacher's needs; both may conflict with peer ideals and pressures. The gifted often attempt a trade-off with varying degrees of satisfaction for themselves.

Unrealistic self-expectations can result in another way of behaving. When others know a child is gifted, they may expect the child's work to have the aura of quality. Sometimes this results from a heterogeneously grouped regular classroom environment where, indeed, the work of the gifted child is outstanding compared with that of others in the room. In such cases, gifted children become used to being "best." They begin to consider everything they attempt to be exemplary. They may put forth small amounts of effort to achieve success. Many gifted children under these circumstances learn poor study habits, develop disrespect for the efforts of others, and bluff their way through educational experiences using their advanced verbal ability or their facile and nimble brain for guessing answers and outcomes. They may seldom need to develop their skills or integrate their abilities. When finally challenged to academic thought or called on for synthesis and evaluative processing, they become lost. Such sudden loss of power may cause them anger or frustration. Again, good communication of realistic expectations based on the assessed needs and abilities of the child can prevent this situation.

A young woman around 20 years of age, who was in one of my first classes at the university, came up to me after we had been discussing the common characteristics and problems associated with being gifted. Hesitantly and with much confusion, she began to relate how she personally identified with the concepts we had been discussing. She stated that she knew she could not have been gifted because she remembered always having questions when everyone else had been satisfied with the information given. She was often told that she spent too much time investigating a subject when the class needed to move on. Other students often groaned audibly at her remarks or shared insights, an occurrence that she interpreted as proof of her stupidity. She had, since junior high school, changed most of these "bad" habits and had withdrawn into her own world of interests, accepting some B's, mostly C's, and occasional D's as appropriate representation of her ability as a student. She was, however, intrigued by a number of ideas we discussed that seemed personally applicable. After sharing her bewilderment, later that evening she decided to call her parents in Pennsylvania. At our next class session she shared the news that her parents had been told when she was in the third grade that she was highly gifted, around 165 IQ, but did not mention it to her on the advice of the school personnel. Because of inadequate information about the reasons for her differences, what started as the natural curiosity and expectations of a very bright mind turned into self-doubt and self-criticism to the point that her actual performance was inhibited and her growth arrested. She later used this information to reexamine the attitudes she had developed about herself and her abilities. She began to take more risks, to become more aggressive in pursuing academic and personal knowledge. She will never compensate for the lost years, but she has made remarkable progress.

Children do not need to know their IQ score, but they must understand the behaviors associated with a high level of development. Becoming aware of the needs and responsibilities of giftedness will allow gifted children to examine their actions and the expectations they have of themselves and others. They will view their own progress more realistically and be able to clarify their beliefs and motives. These children must have adequate feedback on how others feel when their expectations are placed on them. For more effective and fulfilling interpersonal relations between the gifted child and others, the child must become aware of what may happen when others experience nonacceptance just because they do not meet the child's personal standards.

The following characteristics are commonly found in families that produce children with highly actualized potential and self-esteem:

- Parents accept their children as individuals, are loyal sources of support, and openly express acceptance.
- Parents set clear limits based on each child's ability to understand consequences; goals are clear; success is expected as a right of the child, not of the parent.
- Parental guidance is reasonable, realistic, and appropriate to each child.
- The family tends to be liberal and flexible, but not permissive.
- The family is aware of the environment and relates to the environment in a caring, protective way. Children are helped to see their part in the natural order and to respect this unity.

- Parents are relatively self-assured, are on good terms with one another; they accept the responsibility for their own actions.

- Parents lead active lives outside the family and do not rely on their families as the sole or necessarily major source of gratification and esteem.

Often gifted children, especially children who are highly and exceptionally gifted, see themselves as different, alien, and not belonging to the group. The label itself may create problems between these children and others in the classroom. By identifying with the label, these children may feel isolated and unnoticed for any reason other than their ability level. Teachers must make sure that they relate to these children in other ways, rather than only through their level of achievement. They must feel they are valuable in ways other than just their giftedness.

It is very important for teachers at home and at school to understand what is known about the brain, how it functions, and how its functioning relates to intelligence and to giftedness. It is even more important that the child is informed if this sense of not belonging is to be understood. Through knowledge of how intelligence develops, what it means to be gifted, and how that level of development affects a person's life, the child can become involved in that development. Such understanding can empower children and allow them to become partners in their own education. Besides, they find it fascinating. The following series of steps is one way to accomplish sharing information on giftedness with those who most need to know:

- STEP 1: Use the hand model of the brain outlined in Chapter 2, to explain the function of the brain and its integrative nature (see Exhibit C).

- STEP 2: Use your hands as models of neurons (see Chapter 2, Exhibit B) to explain how learning occurs in the brain.

- STEP 3: After introducing some of the known information about the brain, ask the children to choose four to six other children with whom they can work, give each group a large sheet of paper and markers, and ask the children to write down everything they know about the brain. Allow enough time for them to complete the task, approximately 20 minutes. You will be the best judge of when most have recorded all they can remember.

- STEP 4: Use a spokesperson from each group to report back to the total group. After each report, clarify any information that is unclear, extend any information that you can, and be sure to correct any information that is faulty by giving more current research. You need not say their ideas are wrong; instead, say, "We now know . . ." or "Later research has found that. . . ."

- STEP 5: Use models, slides, pictures, film, video, or any other support materials to help the students develop the concepts further. An extremely powerful tool is the use of actual brains preserved for display. We found in working with students of all ages that they were very interested in seeing the brains of various animals, comparing them, and discussing the limits each size or organization presented. The most impressive way to present such information is to allow the students to learn to dissect the material. Later, a visit from a neurobiologist or neurosurgeon can allow the children to watch an actual human brain dissection. It is a most memorable experience.

- STEP 6: Discuss how the brain changes when it is stimulated appropriately (see "The Concept of Intelligence," Chapter 2). Discuss high levels of intelligence as the result of these changes and the kinds of behavior we can observe that tell us a person is intelligent (see "Characteristics of Gifted Learners," Chapter 2).

- STEP 7: Discuss the label we have used to identify people who exhibit high levels of intelligence (i.e., gifted). Be sure to help the children understand the dynamic nature of intelligence (i.e., that we must challenge ourselves or we can lose brain power).

- STEP 8: Ask the children to identify some of the problems people who are "gifted" might face in our society. Look at possible solutions or alternative ways these problems can be handled. Identify and discuss some of the advantages a "gifted" person might have.

- STEP 9: Share with the children tools and ideas for nurturing their intelligence.

All of the above steps can be used with students of any age at home or at school with modifications. Parents will find such discussions a good base for open communication and later consideration of problems that arise from the child's experiences as a gifted child.

Schools can contribute significantly to meeting the need for human belonging. Every classroom would certainly benefit through establishment of a wealth of resources. There are no better resources than the children themselves. Gifted children often bring to the learning situation a vast quantity and diversity of knowledge and comprehension. Often they can contribute highly creative ways to apply such knowledge. The teacher loses out as much as do the children if these resources remain untapped.

To ensure a rich learning environment, teachers should establish a climate of trust within the classroom that allows each child to see each other child as a person rather than just an object. Where such a climate exists, learners can learn from each other and from the environment as well as from the teacher.

Another way teachers may promote belonging needs among gifted students is to ensure that, for at least part of the school experience, the gifted spend time with their intellectual peer group. Although there often has been resistance to such placement, especially when it means leaving the age-alike group, a study of Colangelo and Kelly (1983) advised schools to place less concern on age-peer rejection when gifted programs are implemented and more focus on acceptance by intellectual peers. When we ask gifted students to remain with their age peers as academic models in the classroom, where are their challenges for their growth? Are we so sure they wish to always be models? Wouldn't they rather belong?

Belonging does not just occur. Just as adults establish stereotypes, children easily establish categories for people. Remarks such as "He is my friend," "They are different than we are," "She is stuck-up," "They're just too stupid," and "She thinks she's so smart" represent some of the unfortunate labeling activities that form categories. People then become objects within the category, and they lose their uniqueness. Newland (1976) comments that when gifted and nongifted children are taught together, we cannot expect grouping alone to ensure knowledge and understanding of each for the other. To be effective, there must be interpersonal interaction which must be a priority for the teacher. It becomes as important to acknowledge and respect the differences between these groups as it does to look at the similarities. Newland urges that democracy not be seen as egalitarian conformity. To counter a movement toward exclusion or conformity, the teacher must take deliberate action to set up situations in which children can experience each other as unique individuals and as valuable, contributing people. When teachers do not value these activities enough to include them in their daily classroom routine, children will spend a great deal of unnecessary energy seeking fulfillment of these needs.

Consider these additional steps that can be taken to ensure high self-esteem:

- Provide in-service on educating the gifted child for *all* teachers within your school setting. The more teachers or administrators know about gifted children and their special needs, the more favorable will be attitudes and actions directed toward such children.

- Provide accessible information on alternatives for classroom organization and management. It is likely that we will continue to teach as we have been taught unless we become familiar with other approaches.

We have now developed strategies and patterns of organization that are exciting and nurturing for human growth that were not available 20 years ago. As these ideas are perfected, they must be made known to classroom teachers and building administrators.

MORAL DEVELOPMENT

For those who want to guide the development of the gifted child, moral development is another important concern. From an early age, gifted children often show evidence of moral concerns, including empathy, compassion, idealism, global concern, and advanced understanding and judgment of moral issues (Lovecky, 1997). Highly gifted children are reported as being far beyond their age peers in understanding fairness, justice, and responsibility for self and others (Gross, 1993). The level of intellectual power indicated by giftedness could be used against the person or society in general just as it could be used toward positive goals. Even if not used negatively, inadequate moral development would allow intellectual power to be inhibited by the need to be accepted and validated by others, keeping gifted individuals from contributing their innovation and re-creation needed by society.

For more than 30 years, Lawrence Kohlberg of Harvard studied, hypothesized, and tested his theories in seeking to explain how we acquire moral character. His work is important to gifted education, because he believes that maturity in the intellectual realm influences a person's maturity in moral development (Kohlberg, 1984).

Kohlberg used the phrase *moral development* to indicate the level of internalization of principles that regulate one's conduct in human relations. His focus is on reasoning about principled actions. The data he amassed came from longitudinal studies that followed 50 individuals for some 20 years. These studies of many cultures and countries are designed to show how moral development can be stimulated. His is a stage theory, asserting that all humans must pass through five stages sequentially, although not necessarily at the same age (Table 5.1, Moral Development column). He believed that the majority of adults in our culture never reach the fifth stage of principled morality. In his theory, it is important that we establish moral climates that will most benefit development in the moral area. Although some short-term benefits may arise from direct teaching of moral principles, the overall environment and the child's interactions within that environment have far more significance in later life.

Kohlberg (1984) offered an interesting conclusion resulting from his studies with members of differing cultures, social classes, races, socioeconomic groups, and both sexes. He believed that differences in moral development among groups are not related to any cultural values or beliefs, but to the amount of social participation and responsibility individuals have been allowed within those groups. The more interaction, the more maturity. The sense of participation and involvement in an overall moral environment heightens the growth of moral conduct much more than direct teaching from the family or other institutions.

Providing opportunities for role-taking is favored as a way of fostering progress through the stages. This technique allows the child to assume the viewpoint of others or to act out a situation, taking the part of one of the other participants. This can be used in the family or in the classroom. The situations can be real or imagined problems. Acting on the basis of moral reasoning is an important step for children. Sharing responsibility for decision-making and the evaluation of that decision allow moral growth. Adults who use only authority unilaterally teach a child that morality is not for everyone, thereby retarding the youth's movement to higher levels of development.

Throughout his work, Kohlberg often mentioned the establishment of a moral climate or environment. This could be the most critical factor to the child both in the home and in school. By establishing a just environment, one can teach justice. A child who experiences moral, humane behavior from others progresses in moral development. One component of this environment is discipline. The goal is to help children take responsibility for their own behavior, and to Kohlberg, authoritarian or power-assertive techniques fall short of this goal and can create uncooperative, aggressive behaviors. Warm, love-oriented discipline, making use of acceptance, understanding, frequent explanations, and reasoning, results in internalization of moral concepts and cooperative, nonaggressive behavior. Even when authoritarian discipline through fear of physical punishment succeeds in squelching overt hostility, the child's anger remains and is only temporarily suppressed. In establishing a moral environment, adults do not give up their authority; rather, they change it. Instead of authority based on fear, threat, punishment, or rewards, the basis becomes the ability to mediate conflict fairly, to guide and facilitate successful solutions to problems, and to help discover alternatives for evaluation.

Another element important to producing a positive moral climate is good, open communication. Children can be taught to communicate respectfully and clearly with others. Again, the example set by the adults in their environment will have the most impact, but there are games and strategies that can be directly taught. The family or class meeting described in Chapter 4, p. 83 can give interactive opportunities for all group or family members (see Figure 4.4).

As mentioned in Chapter 4, Dabrowski (1972) is also a theorist of emotional development who influences the research in gifted education (Miller, Silverman &

Falk, 1994; Silverman, 1994). His research has special significance for gifted learners because it is based on populations of gifted and creative individuals. Using neurological data, Dabrowski suggests that gifted and creative individuals show innate response patterns to stimuli that show unusually high levels of physical energy, sensory acuity, intellectual curiosity and drive, imagination, and empathy.

Dabrowski's theory (Piechowski, 1991) also includes a strong moral element. Focused on gifted adolescents and adults, his theory, like Kohlberg's, suggests stages of development with the final stage achieved by few (Table 5.1). His work adds validation for the holistic nature of intelligence by including emotional, imaginational, sensual, and psychomotor functions in the investigation of intellectual potential. Dabrowski's "developmental potential," the positive potential for further growth, is composed of talents, special ability intelligence, and five forms of psychic overexcitability: psychomotor, sensual, intellectual, imaginational, and emotional. Overexcitabilities or areas of supersensitivity, are described as expanded awareness, intensified emotions, and increased levels of intellectual and physical activity. Throughout life, Dabrowski believes, the development of self is accompanied by growth in moral sensitivity, integration of justice, fairness, and universal compassion.

A group of practitioners, parents, and theorists known as the Columbus Group were concerned about the movement in the field of gifted education to replace the term *gifted* with *talented*. Building from Dabrowski's work, they suggested that giftedness be conceived of as "asynchronous development in which advanced cognitive abilities and heightened intensity combine to create inner experiences and awareness that are qualitatively different from the norm" (Silverman, 1994, p. 113). They believed that this asynchrony increases with higher intellectual capacity, rendering such individuals vulnerable in their uniqueness. The group suggested that this provides a rationale for "modifications in parenting, teaching and counseling in order for them to develop optimally" (p. 113).

Paul MacLean (1978), the brain researcher whose work was reviewed in Chapter 2, believes that altruism and empathy are related to the function of the prefrontal cortex, the newest part of the human brain. He states that if these neural circuits are not brought into play at the critical time of development, they may never function properly. Providing a responsive learning environment for our children can now be seen as important to their biological, mental, and emotional growth.

According to Yarrow and Zahn-Waxler (cited in Pines, 1979b), all children seem to have the capacity for early development of altruism, but the individual differences in their development increase a great deal between 18 and 24 months of age. The most powerful factor in producing altruistic behavior is the intensity with which mothers convey the message that their children must not hurt others. In Yarrow's study, physical restraint or punishment without an explanation of how the children had hurt another did not lead to altruism but was actually counterproductive. The other factor that related to development of this trait was the mother's altruistic behavior toward the child and others in the family. In a later study (cited in Pines, 1979b), it was noted that the patterns of altruism set in this early period remained consistent at least through 7 years of age.

Webb and colleagues (1982) point out that one of the most serious problems in gifted children's early concern for moral issues is that their ability to understand the issues cognitively is often far beyond their ability to cope with the issues emotionally. Being told that they are the hope for the world, Webb and colleagues comment, puts an awesome burden on children. We must be aware of their limits in understanding as well as delight in their idealism. Silverman (1994) suggested another concern regarding the early sensitivity of gifted children. She believes that very young highly compassionate children are especially vulnerable when they express moral concerns about problems of the world. Because they have not developed effective ways to deal with strong emotional content, they may be overwhelmed by the the pain that such global problems can create and the misunderstanding of the need that they have to do something about it.

In one of the largest and most comprehensive studies of the belief systems of American children (cited in Schmidt, 1990b), researchers found that children's views of morality are influenced by many interdependent factors, with family support and poverty playing pivotal roles. The moral orientation of children seemed most related to their social background and life experiences. Older, more affluent children more often made moral judgments that were intended to serve the common good or satisfy their emotional feelings and psychological needs, whereas children from poor neighborhoods tended to make their decisions in accordance with their religious beliefs. Another finding was that a larger percentage of children of poverty felt that no adults really cared for them. Fortunately, the majority of all children did feel cared for and were family-oriented. The study found that children's sense of public responsibility was high and that they have confidence in the ability of social institutions to solve America's problems.

Gifted children develop their moral identity through those around them, their values, and their moral responses to life's situations. In the first year of life, the foundations of moral development are laid. Although some may show exceptional levels of sensitivity to justice, fairness, and the problems of others, others will be limited by the actions and development of the adults around them. Once again, we see the importance of establishing a responsive learning environment morally as well as intellectually.

Although Kohlberg and other affective educators have much to say about creating such an environment, one more element must be mentioned here. Children grow morally only as much as their self-esteem allows. Previously, this chapter considered the importance of self-esteem. Low self-esteem seems to limit growth in moral development, which in turn affects the child's view and treatment of others (Briggs, 1970; Satir, 1972). The social-emotional growth of gifted children must be considered by every parent and teacher not only because such growth can sharpen intellect but, even more important, because such growth becomes the basis for the use of that intelligence.

THE DEVELOPING PERSONALITY

Erik Erikson, another important theorist in the area of social-emotional development, also delineated stages or periods of life to express his view of a growing personality (Erikson, 1950, 1968). His eight stages encompass all ages of human life and represent periods during which experiences dictate major adjustments to the social environment and the self (Table 5.1, Personality Development column). The way each adjustment is handled affects the way the person adjusts to or handles the next stage of development. Although these experiences may be present during most of a person's life, the focus or critical stage is believed to proceed in the order shown in Table 5.1 (Erikson, 1950). Erikson's work gave us a map of clues we might look for as we strive to understand gifted children. Although the intensity with which gifted learners approach each of these stages and the resources they bring to bear on meeting the conflicts presented in each developmental period may be of a larger scope, the focus remains. If we are to optimize the development of these children, we must become aware of Erikson's points of focus.

In reporting on the relationships between family patterns and development of personality factors in gifted children, Cornell and Grossberg (1987) found that family cohesion, expressiveness, and lower family conflict are associated with better overall adjustment and more favorable cognitive development and school achievement. Cohesion is also highly correlated to fewer problems with discipline or self-control and, along with family expressiveness, is associated with high self-esteem and lower anxiety as assessed by child self-report, and with higher academic self-esteem as assessed by classroom teachers. From their data, Cornell and Grossberg point out that neither the subject matter of family activities nor the degree of structure imposed on family members is as critical to the child's adjustment as the quality of family interaction. "It would seem more important to the child's adjustment that family members interact cooperatively, with minimal conflict and maximum freedom for personal expression" (p. 64).

Izard (cited in Trotter, 1987) emphasizes the biological basis of personality in pointing out that emotions, which have a strong biological component, contribute substantially to personality and personality development. Again we are reminded that biology provides some thresholds—some limits—but, according to Lewis (cited in Trotter, 1987), within these limits the infant is affected by the moods and emotions of mother, father, siblings, uncles, grandparents, and significant others. This broader view suggests that an infant's entire social network contributes to personality development and that responsiveness from those in the environment is a critical factor in infant learning.

Attitudes of Society

The gifted individual faces another social-emotional problem while growing up—in the area of attitudes. This is a little like discussing the age-old problem of the chicken and the egg. Which came first? Do the attitudes of others result from the actions of the gifted person, or is the gifted individual's behavior the result of other people's attitudes and prejudices? A little of both is probably true.

The moral teachings of nearly all cultures contain the idea that what you give forth will be returned to you in kind: Those who view life positively will have positive experiences; those who give generously will receive generously from others;

love begets love. This seems to be quite true of attitudes of groups toward each other. Because the literature on attitudes tends to agree that attitudes are learned and therefore educable, we need to be more aware of the attitudes that we communicate toward gifted learners.

In a thought-provoking article on attitudes, Margaret Mead (1954) revealed the plight of the gifted child in the American culture of 1954. Her observations, unfortunately, are just as applicable to American culture of the twenty-first century. She observes that Americans have a narrow competitive range; like must compete with like; to be approved, all success must result from effort, abstinence, and suffering. The very term used to label children who exhibit high intellectual ability, *the gifted,* indicates that their success has been given, not earned. Therefore, giftedness is to be viewed with suspicion, if not outright hostility.

American society also tends to grade or rate attributes, rather than allow uniqueness and incomparability. Therefore, we reduce giftedness to an IQ score. By our refusal to recognize special ability in intellectual areas, we waste the ability of uncounted numbers of gifted children (Mead, 1954):

> If they learn easily, they are penalized for being bored when they have nothing to do; if they excel in some outstanding way, they are penalized as being conspicuously better than the peer group. . . . The culture tries to make the child with a gift into a one-sided person, to penalize him at every turn, to cause him trouble in making friends and to create conditions conducive to the development of a neurosis. Neither teachers, the parents of other children, nor the child's peers will tolerate a Wunderkind. (p. 213)

As a remedy for such outcomes Mead suggests:

> The more diversified, the more complex the activities within which children are encouraged to play a role the better the chance for . . . the gifted child to exercise his special talent . . . much more than rewards and praise, the gifted child needs scope, material on which his imagination can feed, and opportunities to exercise it. He needs inconspicuous access to books, museums, instruments, paints, ideas, a chance to feed himself with the accumulated heritage from the genius of other ages. He needs a chance for contact, however fleeting, perhaps only on television or in a special movie, with those who are masters in the abilities with which he has been specially endowed. And within our sternly Puritan tradition, he may well need also a special sense of stewardship for the talents which he has been given, and explicit moral sanction against selling his birthright for a mess of pottage. (p. 214)

Attitudes of Teachers and Other School Personnel

The work of Rosenthal (1968) and others showing that the level of expectation of the teacher can so easily lead to self-fulfilling prophecies gives us a clear picture of how important the teacher's attitude is to the performance of the student. Aspy (Aspy & Bahler, 1975) found the perception that teachers have of their own ability and worth is more significant in the success of their students than the student's concept of themselves. These research results readily show the power of the teacher to affect the achievement and growth of the student. The following personal experience is an example of the importance of teacher attitude to the achievement and well-being of gifted students.

After about 4 years of participation in an excellent gifted program structured and implemented following the integrative education model, a very bright young man I have known for several years began a new experience as a high school student. The "program for the gifted" at this high school provided enrichment whenever the teacher found it possible within the context of the regular class. This student found few enriching activities, but he tried to cope with the new situation as well as he could. His challenges were rare; he made his grades without much effort. In one course there was insistence on the memorization of many details, and he had to spend extra time prior to any exam so that the details could be reproduced accurately and in proper order.

After one particular exam in which the student felt he had done well, his exam was returned with the failing grade, *F*. Not used to such outcomes and feeling that something had to be wrong, as he still believed his answers were cor-

rect, he approached the teacher. A rather one-sided inquiry into the reasons for his failing mark followed, and the student became increasingly frustrated and upset as the teacher sat smiling at his discomfort. Finally, the young man demanded to know why he had failed, and the teacher's response was, "Oh, you didn't really get an *F*." At this point he showed the student an *A* recorded in his grade book with the highest mark in the class. "I just wanted to see how you would take it if you got an *F*," the teacher commented. The response he got from his student was sharp and alienating. The boy began looking for other ways to meet his needs from that moment on. His high school experience had become, with this last indignity, disappointing to say the least. He completed high school by attending university classes arranged for him by the teacher of his former gifted class.

If perception or attitude so powerfully affects students, it would be fruitful to examine the data on attitudes of school pesonnel toward the gifted. In general, over a long period of time studies have shown that the attitudes held by the majority of school personnel toward gifted individuals are not positive. The *School Staffing Survey* (1969–1970) done by the U.S. Office of Education reveals that 57.5% of school administrators in American schools stated that they had no gifted children. The Advocate Survey appended to the Marland (1972) Report to Congress described pupil personnel workers as ranging from apathetic to hostile in their attitudes toward gifted students. The negative attitudes of these groups must be changed because of their influence on the attitudes of administrators and teachers through in-service and counseling contacts (Martinson, 1972).

Although early entry to school is often sought as a solution for precocious children and such early entrants have a record of performing well academically, this practice is favored neither by school administrators nor by teachers (Hobson, 1979). A study that assessed the attitudes of kindergarten and first-grade teachers toward academically talented early entrants found that these children were ranked the lowest of all candidates to be considered for these classrooms (Jackson, Famiglietti, & Robinson, 1981). Perception improves among those who have more direct experience and among those who have had courses aimed at understanding and educating gifted children (Justman & Wrightstone, 1956). These studies indicate a lack of awareness toward the existence and needs of the gifted and suggest a need for a greater availability of gifted education courses.

Dettmer (1985) looked at the attitude differences among regular classroom teachers, teachers of the gifted (who had received training), building principals, and school psychologists on a number of questions concerning gifted students and their education. Among the statistically significant findings: All groups except for the regular classroom teachers strongly agreed that gifted students are influenced greatly by the emotional climate in the home or schoolroom; the regular classroom teachers and principals questioned the practice of omitting usual assignments or altering requirements if tests indicate that a gifted student has acquired the basic skills; principals believed that gifted children should remain with their age peers for better social adjustment, whereas teachers of the gifted disagreed. Dettmer suggests that because unsupportive attitudes or misinformation among the school staff can result in the debilitation of the education of gifted students, school districts would do well to prepare all staff members through in-service in gifted education.

Attitudes of teachers who work with the gifted are more favorable than the attitudes of those who do not. School psychologists and psychometrists experienced with the gifted favored them significantly more than did those without such experience (Weiner, 1968). In a study by Mills (1973), experience with the gifted and a background in gifted education again related to attitudes of acceptance. Younger respondents, from 10 to 29 years of age, were less sympathetic than those 30 to 39 years of age. Blacks and Hispanics were less favorable than Caucasians. The higher people rated themselves in mental ability, the more favorable they tended to be toward gifted children. Teachers of regular classes, education administrators, community leaders, and the lay public all showed significantly unfavorable attitudes toward gifted learners. Instruction and experience seem to be the most successful ways to improve attitudes. An attitude survey administered to faculty of five major universities indicated a strong positive attitude toward gifted education, with those identifying themselves as previous participants in programs for the gifted being the most positive (Weiss & Gallagher, 1980).

Lack of preparation for working with or understanding the needs of gifted students may account, in part, for the negative attitudes reported. Serious thought must be given to in-service opportunities in gifted education for all school personnel, because attitudes of teachers, principals, and counselors toward gifted students clearly affect not only the students and their performance but also the acceptance and effectiveness of the gifted program. It seems, then, that the power of attitudes in society, and specifically within the educational community, may be a prime force in furthering or denying educational opportunities for gifted children.

ADOLESCENCE: A PARTICULARLY CHALLENGING PERIOD OF GROWTH

Neuroscientists agree that the brain's greatest growth spurt ends around the age of 10. At this time the brain begins to scan and destroy the weakest synapses, preserving only those that have been transformed by experience. In this way, the patterns of the brain's functioning will be formed. By the end of adolescence, the brain will decline in plasticity but increase in power (Nash, 1997). Neurologically, the importance of the enriched environment is critical during infancy and early childhood; however, during adolescence the impact may be even greater because a boring environment has a more powerful thinning effect of the cortex than does the thickening effect of the enriched environment (Diamond & Hopson, 1998). This means that during this period of adolescence, gifted students are very susceptible to losing mental ground when not challenged.

The educational experiences of adolescents are often focused on the physical and emotional changes occurring during this period of growth, sometimes to the exclusion of academic challenges. The goals often mentioned as parts of the focus during adolescence are:

- To achieve independence.
- To discover one's identity as a person.
- To establish personal values and philosopy, both personal and social.
- To develop self-guidance, self-motivation, and self-esteem.
- To become aware of the needs of others and of how the self can contribute to meeting those needs.
- To explore and accept sexuality.
- To acknowledge intellectual power.
- To acquire life maintenance, career, and self-actualization skills.
- To develop meaningful interpersonal relationships.
- To explore reality structures by use of personal experiences.

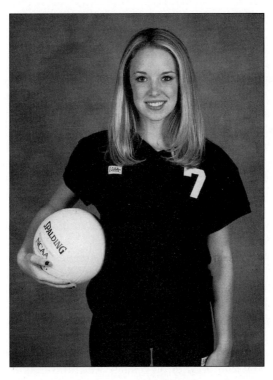

Gifted adolescents are intensely involved in intellectual, emotional, social, and physical transitions in their lives earlier than usual.

Our society seems to be organized to ignore, and often actively inhibit, the physical, mental, and emotional transitions from child to adult. In some cultures, the transition is supported by ritual or is allowed to occur naturally as a useful phase of life. But in cultures such as ours, achieving any meaningful place in the society must be delayed. Training for one's life work is continued well beyond puberty, and control of one's life is denied until well into the productive and creative phase of early adulthood. For many adolescents, such practices have forced the creation of subcultures of teenagers with values, morals, and lifestyles that seek to depart from the accepted values and traditions of the established culture. Many of the problems of this period are the result of the conflict in the youths' feelings of who they are and what society wants them to be. Many try to transform themselves—with resulting periods of introspection, drug use, and experimentation—through various identities and roles. A teenager's future may be radically altered by the ways in which identity and meaning are sought during this transition period.

The gifted, the creative, and the talented adolescents may be better equipped in many ways to meet the biological and psychological challenges of this period. Their ability to conceptualize, to see alternatives, to seek out diverse patterns and relationships, to delay closure (which allows them a higher degree of tolerance for ambiguity), and to express themselves in fulfilling ways will serve them well during this period of constant and often threatening change. But these very qualities that can lead to competence and power can bring to these youth some unique problems.

Gifted adolescents have few role models of their own age to emulate and they seldom find peer guides, which can result in a feeling of isolation. Existing guidelines for the average teenager often are not applicable to their needs. For example, the question of overload: How much is too much extracurricular activity or attempted academic coursework? Often there is a lack of challenge, no chance to push to their limits, to make mistakes, to learn to cope. Because they do so many things well, how much exploring should they do? In how many areas? When should they begin to focus? Make career choices? Specialize?

Gifted girls are especially vulnerable during this period. Society sends adolescent girls mixed messages. More than ever before, they are urged to contribute their abilities and talents to society. More careers are open for their choosing, and higher levels within those careers are beginning to accept women. At the same time, the belief in male superiority still exists in many professions and sex-role stereotyping still inhibits socialization and development at home and at school. Sex-role differences are so evident by the junior high years that girls begin to decline in achievement from the advantaged position they showed in elementary schoool (Maccoby & Jacklin, 1974). Fox (1981) tells us that these years are critical. If parents, teachers, and peers view as masculine such characteristics as assertiveness, independence, leadership, and analytic and critical thinking, then the gifted girl will be forced to choose between being gifted and being feminine. Such a choice should never have to be made.

The results of a study by Kerr, Colangelo, and Gaeth (1988) indicate some trends regarding the perception that gifted adolescents have of their own giftedness. A later study (Manaster, Chan, Watt, & Wiehe, 1994) reexamined the findings and, in some cases, found differing results. Kerr and colleagues found that gifted students generally view giftedness as being positive in its effect on themselves but negative or ambiguous for others. Manaster and coworkers questioned the effect on others because they found that the majority of their population of gifted adolescents did not sense a negative effect of their giftedness on their parents and friends, although many felt there was a negative effect from their classmates. The group studied by Kerr and colleagues saw giftedness as an advantage in terms of their personal growth and academics but strongly negative in its social implications. Again the negative social implications were not found by Manaster and coworkers and, in fact, some of the social advantages reported were high regard and opportunities for leadership. The few social disadvantages reported were involved with stereotyping. Both studies reaffirm that the gifted adolescents' view of their giftedness is multi-dimensional, with the gifted students' perception of how others view their giftedness differing from their own. Manaster and coworkers express concern that the population of gifted adolescents they studied seem dubious about the meanings of the label and do not understand their differences. Both studies agree that counselors and school psychologists need to work more closely with gifted adolescents clarifying and easing the struggle of being adolescent as well as gifted. As we know from Rogers and Maslow, the beliefs held by gifted individuals regarding their giftedness determine their actions and responses to society.

Adolescence may be the most frustrating time for youth and those who care about them, but it is also the best time for encouraging self-initiative, independence, and the growth of the creative mind. This period of reconstruction can be the beginning of personal excellence.

The Physical Transition

Not since the fetal period and the first 2 years of life does the human body have as much change occurring to its physical structure so quickly as during adolescence. The development of sex organs and new hormonal balances adds to the bewildering array of physical changes to which the youth must adjust. Unlike infancy, these changes occur with the full awareness of the young person, who can observe with both joy and frustration the whole complex process (Craig, 1980).

Male high school students who show their giftedness in visual and performing arts have been found to differ significantly from average male students in their attitudes toward physical activity (Confessore & Confessore, 1981). Whereas average youths prefer physical activities that have a strong element of daring or require them to take chances, talented youths prefer more aesthetic experiences, those that use the body as an instrument of expression. This is similar to the preference shown by the gifted female population and is the type of activity least preferred by the average males. It has been suggested that the affinity of gifted males for aesthetic experiences as a way to show their giftedness in the arts may cause others to view them as effeminate. This and their low preference for any cathartic physical activity should be viewed seriously as a clue to further study of the problem of suicide and emotional disturbance among this population.

Gifted students who have been accelerated now find themselves with a physically more mature peer group, which can lead to more pronounced feelings of difference for gifted youth, and they may retreat into activities of a cognitive nature. At this period, the proclivity for separating the activities of the mind and body is most evident, and unless opportunities are provided for integration, gifted adolescents may neglect and avoid physical pursuits. By using their verbal and rational strengths, they can achieve an understanding of the dramatic changes that are occurring, and teachers in the home and at school can address their need to integrate mind and body. The following provisions will aid in this transition:

- Experiences designed to heighten and clarify sensory awareness.
- Experiences designed to promote awareness of the student's own body and the creation of a positive body image.
- Experiences and information designed to heighten awareness of the pleasures of having a healthy body and of the means for health maintenance and growth.
- Opportunities for inquiry into the clarification of physical responses to emotions.
- Instruction and practice in techniques of relaxation and tension reduction.
- Opportunities for self-expression through movement, pantomime, and dance.
- Opportunities to develop individual physical competence and to experience the satisfaction of physical activity in ways chosen by the student from a wide range of structured and nonstructured, competitive, cooperative, and individual processes.
- Exposure to and opportunities to learn one of the disciplines devoted to mind/body integration (Yoga, T'ai-chi Ch'uan, etc.).
- Support for and assistance in making the care and development of one's own body a part of an individual lifestyle.
- Opportunities to examine the implications of current social and political policies for the health of people in the community.

The Intellectual Transition

For most adolescents, the intellectual transition marks the beginning of what Piaget calls *formal operational thought*. Most youths now become capable of reasoning with alternative hypotheses, entertaining the possible and the probable in addition to the real and the concrete. Although as many as 20% of adolescents will not show a capability for this expansion of awareness, judgment, and insight (Neimark, 1975), the gifted student has been performing many such tasks for years and is now faced with an intolerable amount of repetition and conceptual stagnation.

Schools commonly use the middle school grades to review and reintroduce concepts developed in the later elementary years. For gifted youths who have been allowed to accelerate according to their needs and abilities, such repetition is regressive. Even for those who have not had such opportunities, the repetition of known concepts can create boredom and indifference to classroom achievement. The organization of most middle schools makes personalized instruction, which was found to be highly beneficial for the gifted student during the elementary years, difficult to continue. The student is now faced with discrete time blocks and segregated subject matter as most middle schools begin the practice of educational departmentalization.

The incidence of underachievement rises during this time. Boredom with school offerings, the need to challenge parental and teacher-related values, and the desire for group acceptance combine to create the denial of academic ability. Girls, especially, succumb to the conformity needs of this period.

LeCompte (cited in Tammi, 1990) reports that 25% of the dropouts in Chicago rank in the top quarter of their classes in reading and math scores, and some are in the top 5%. She concludes that the demographics of those dropping out have changed to include the very young, the middle class, the gifted, and the bored. Her concern is that many drop-out programs are not aimed at these populations.

Learning styles differ between cognitively and academically gifted middle school students and other students on at least five variables. Gifted students are less teacher-motivated and more self-motivated; are more persistent; prefer some sound to quiet during concentrated study; prefer visual, tactile, or kinesthetic to auditory modes of learning; and prefer to learn alone (Griggs & Price, 1980). More than 80% of the highly gifted children studied by Gross (1993) reported intense social isolation in the inclusion classroom. Attempts to conform to the social and cultural expectations of the age-peer group, along with the unchallenging and repetitive curriculum, resulted in extreme and continuous intellectual and emotional frustration. The following suggestions can alleviate many of these problems:

1. Develop an academic core within the departmentalized setting by combining three periods with a team of two or three teachers. Gifted students can then be brought together for more appropriate instruction. Within such a core, flexible grouping can occur. Permitting able students to group for instruction at their level of need is far superior to the tracking plan employed by many middle school and senior high school administrators. This type of grouping recognizes that the gifted student is not gifted in every subject, allows for appropriate curricular modifications, and permits the advantages of mental peer interaction. Through the elective period choices, such a structure also allows broader exposure to students whose abilities may be in less academic areas.

2. Use mentors to provide for the acceleration and depth of interest of gifted learners. Such specialized instructors can be found among the retired community, among parents, and within the business community of any city or town.

3. Use the resources of neighboring senior high schools, junior colleges, and universities. Many universities have special provisions for middle-grade students during summers in the regular courses where credits can be accumulated on an official university transcript. Some institutions of higher education offer specially designed programs to middle-school talented and able learners in selected disciplines throughout the academic year.

When planning curriculum experiences, note that some researchers have found that educators need to be more aware of the cognitive processing differences between males and females. For example, Weiner and Robinson (1986) found not only that adolescent males have higher mathematical reasoning ability than females, but also that this ability is the single best predictor of their mathematical achievement. For adolescent females, verbal reasoning ability was the best predictor. For females learning mathematics, textbooks should place more emphasis on the conceptual approach, rather than the usual approach of deriving equations with gaps in the logical process. Teaching alternative cognitive styles also helps. Both female and male gifted students need the following provisions:

1. Exposure to the environment and the culture, including aesthetic, economic, political, educational, and social aspects.
2. Exposure to and opportunities to work with peers, adults, and other students with expertise in the student's interest areas.
3. Advanced or unusual subject matter.
4. Experience in identifying data needs, establishing data organization, and collecting data.
5. Instruction in and opportunities to develop data evaluation and decision-making skills.
6. Opportunities to identify and clarify standards of comparison and evaluation.
7. Instruction in developing original applications of knowledge and understandings, including hypothesizing and hypothesis testing.
8. Opportunities to examine and alter existing patterns physically and mentally.
9. Opportunities to evaluate personal choices in terms of available data, individual needs and goals, and choice consequences.
10. Opportunities to communicate and exchange ideas, information, and opinions in a variety of ways.
11. Opportunities to apply these ideas to real world situations.

The Social-Emotional Transition

Acceptance, belonging, and self-esteem are the areas of critical concern to the maturing adolescent. Up to this point in time, modeling, guidance, rewards, and punishments have been used to give the young person an external value structure. During adolescence most young people are attempting to develop a personal value structure, their own moral system.

Giftedness brings special advantages and disadvantages to this process. Although all adolescents can be characterized as intense and can show rapid fluctuations in emotion and widely ranging mood swings (partly a result of biochemical changes that are occurring), gifted adolescents confound this behavior by interspersing periods of unusual maturity and marvelous insight. Gifted adolescents experience conflicts between achievement and affiliation needs. Unfortunately, they may develop coping strategies to deal with anticipated peer rejection that may involve denying their talents (Moon, Kelly, & Feldhusen, 1997). This has been found to be especially true of the highly gifted and gifted females. Often the changes in programs or schools occurring at this time require that gifted students reassess their competence in relation to the new social environment (Wright & Leroux, 1997). Self-concept is now highly influenced by social comparisons, normative standards, and desire for social acceptance in relationships. In middle school, academic competence may drop as attempts at social acceptability increase. Gifted girls, in particular, may reject former alignment with gifted peers and try to hide their cognitive abilities (Leroux, 1992). Gifted females have been found to improve above the norm in their overall self-worth through high school, whereas gifted males tend to drop toward the norm (Wright & Leroux, 1997). The push/pull of special classes both supported the self-concept of gifted students involved and heightened the problem of their social acceptance; they seem to be caught between their personal values and their educational needs.

Bright adolescents appear to develop autonomy and time perspective faster than their average counterparts. For gifted students who have in the past been threatening to teachers, a new assertion of independence during this period may result in verbal or even physical confrontation. The teachers least equipped to deal with this situation are those who see their role as one of authority that must be preserved. Those teachers who are successful in guiding the gifted adolescent can admit their own inadequacies and meet the gifted student as a person, because they care more about understanding problems or miscommunications than about being in charge.

The more typical adolescent admires those who are athletic or socially gregarious. If academic success is to be given approval by his peers, the gifted boy must be athletically able, which is often an impossible task for the student who is younger and less developed than his classmates. For both boys and girls, good grades must be earned with seeming ease, because studious habits are often looked on with suspicion and penalized. For girls, intelligence is seen as too aggressive, too masculine; for boys, too feminine. These perceptions cause internal conflicts in the gifted.

Adolescents are on an emotional roller coaster, too. After in-depth study of the lives of teenagers, Csikszentmihalyi and Larson (1987) concluded that typical teenagers come down from extreme happiness or up from deep sadness within 45 minutes, compared with adults, whose happy/sad "fluxuations" can take several hours. Teenagers get the most satisfaction from meeting challenges that fit their developing skills and provide them with meaningful rewards. They like to develop new levels of expertise and accomplishment, and their success stimulates them to search for fresh challenges that are slightly harder but within reach. It is this pattern of growing ability that helps make the transition between the impulsive, egocentric activities of childhood and the world of adults. Too many teenagers use their time seeking challenges in aimless activities with friends or escape through television and computers. Such short-term pleasures deny them the personal fulfillment of more productive activity. Csikszentmihalyi and Larson suggest that adults provide models of how to choose among goals, how to persevere with patience, and how to recognize challenges and enjoy meeting them. With adult guidance, adolescents can find productive ways to achieve control over their lives and responsibility for their experiences.

Without guidance, high levels of cognitive ability can be used to meet the youths' needs in ways that will prove to be socially destructive. Too often these very able youngsters manipulate others to gain personal goals. Often the intense desire to know, to follow up on concepts, and to pursue ideas results in a social insensitivity that can lead to rejection and isolation. Large gaps between intellectual, physical, and emotional growth will need sorting out with adult help. It is important that nonjudgmental, open communication exists between teachers and students. Schools need to develop more expedient ways for the gifted to contact counselors and advisors. Too often, the intermediate and secondary systems, with their departmentalization, administrative hierarchies, and large facilities, make immediate personal contact almost impossible. By the time a counseling session has been scheduled, with the proper hall passes and classroom permission secured, students have given up on seeking help through the system. Overburdened counselors may be available only to disruptive or acting-out students. Gifted students complain that the counselor only relates to them for class scheduling or college preparation information. Some schools recognize the problem and set aside one day per week for counseling gifted students or run small counseling groups. Some have developed a crisis contact system available to all students.

In a report on the perceptions of gifted adolescents on their experiences with being labeled *gifted,* Robinson (1990) found that gifted students rarely are involved in a proactive program of individual school conferences during their initial labeling. Neither are their parents given any help in understanding the implications of the new label. This pattern persists despite the fact that when parents are more comfortable with the label they are more likely to support the students in ways that allow the students more comfort as well. According to Robinson, educational professionals need to develop practices of informing the students and their families as soon as possible of the meaning and implications of giftedness.

Gifted students can be helped to enjoy their differences, their uniqueness. They need to develop skills of individual competition, group cooperation, and trust. They need opportunities to work with students who are their intellectual peers and those with a variety of abilities. They can be taught to value their intellectual power and to use it to deal effectively with their emotions and their values. These are the students who can entertain new constructs of reality and who can envision more productive, higher levels of development for all humankind. Suggestions for working with their emotional and social transition might include the following:

- Opportunities to identify and name their own emotions, perceptual filters, and defense systems and those of others.

- Opportunities to expand and to clarify their awareness of the physical, social, and emotional environment.

- Experiences and instruction in attitudes of receptivity and suspended judgment.

- Opportunities and support for actively seeking ideas and feelings from others.

- Opportunities and instruction in constructing, clarifying, and expressing personal values.

- Opportunities to clarify short-term goals and examine them in relation to personal values and to achievability.

- Support for making personal values the foundation for career choice.

- Opportunities to develop effective community membership by participating in activities with a variety of groups, examining roles in groups and the effect of those roles, practicing open communication, examining their own functioning within groups, and improving that function.

- Opportunities to develop skills with group process, including leadership skills and use of power.

- Opportunities to develop commitment to groups and to the larger community, including goals of humankind.

The Intuitive Transition

Gifted youths have an early concern and interest in intuitive knowing. They need opportunities to converse meaningfully with philosophers and others who share their interest. Such inquiry can be made through independent study, with mentors, through group experiences led by guest experts, and through class discussions. It is important for gifted adolescents to be open to experiences in this area so that they may recognize their own intuitive energy and ability and how these qualities contribute to their cognitive and emotional growth. They need guidance in becoming familiar with analyzing and evaluating such phenomena and should be provided with both the historical approach and the current body/mind data. Because this dimension of brain function seems to be available to everyone but is found to be more active in the gifted and talented populations, guidance in evaluating appropriate uses of this type of creative effort should be available. The intuitive function is involved in initiating or insightful acts and in creative activity. It is an area that promises much for the fulfillment of humankind.

The development of an integrated person is clearly a complex process. In cases where home and school lend support in the same areas, growth will be significant. To ensure that the parent and teacher do support similar areas, each must be conscious of the environment the other creates for the child. With this knowledge, they will both be able to provide support and experiences when they are needed. A teacher can initiate this type of communication more easily than a parent. Providing deliberate contact points, meetings, and conferences for parental involvement in the school program assures both the teacher and the parent that the child's development will proceed effectively. The extra effort made to encourage parent involvement, or at least the opportunity for contact, will pay off handsomely from the educational standpoint. Many gifted programs have survived only because of loyal parent support. Many are dramatically enriched by parent participation.

This chapter has focused primarily on the social-emotional and integrative growth of gifted children and youth. The origins of social-emotional development are to be found very early in the child's interaction with the world. The child's evolving self-concept critically influences social-emotional development. Both the concept of self and moral development can facilitate or inhibit intellectual growth. For gifted children, the social-emotional aspects of growth present special problems and adolescence is a time when support must be available and challenges continued.

Our concern for optimal development and appropriate educational opportunities for gifted children requires that we consider the effect of attitudes on this process. The attitudes of both gifted people and those who work and live with them affect their development significantly. It is important to integrate growth in all of the human functions if we are to optimize the development of intelligence. Even cognitive function is limited if integration of the other areas is left to chance. Both homes and schools have an important part to play in this integration. Later chapters will present strategies to aid in making this process more effective.

In Part II, the concerns and involvement of schools in educating gifted children become the major focus. Although the information will be most useful in the classroom and administrative offices and to those educators who are concerned about educational services for gifted individuals, the parent as a cooperative, supportive resource remains a critical factor in the process of growing up gifted.

QUESTIONS OFTEN ASKED

1. Are gifted children as advanced emotionally as they are cognitively?

Sometimes, but often the development pattern will allow one area to advance and then the other. There is no guarantee that a very bright child will be socially or emotionally mature. However, gifted children can develop emotional levels rapidly because they can understand, empathize with others, and express their own feelings well when given the opportunity and a little guidance.

2. Why would gifted children have a low self-concept? They seem to have everything.

Not all do; however, it is not uncommon for gifted children to have an ideal of what they think they should be that does not match what they think they are. Often their physical ability has not caught up with their mental ability, and they cannot accomplish the things they want in the way they want. Sometimes the signals they receive from others add to this lower self-image. When they still have questions to ask and other children do not, they can interpret that to mean that they do not understand as well as others. When they say something and other children groan or say "Not that again," they may believe they have said something dumb or inappropriate. Others, assuming that gifted children know how exceptional an idea or product they are working on is, will criticize the idea or product when meaning to be helpful. Part of the low self-concept of gifted children is from just feeling different; constantly feeling different can make people doubt themselves after a while. There are many reasons, some involving outside pressure, some involving the child's pressure in-

ternally, but the result can be never meeting one's own standards, never being good enough. It is all too common among gifted children that what they see and what others see are just not the same.

3. Why do some teachers, principals, and other school personnel seem to have negative attitudes toward gifted students?

Unfortunately, studies show that this is too often true. Gifted children do not fit easily into the structure of most schools and classrooms. Because they can be 2 to 4 years ahead of the curriculum offered at any grade level, they make it very hard for a teacher of 20 to 30 other children to find appropriate curricular experiences for them. They often question and seek more information about ideas than the teacher is prepared to give. This can be seen as a challenge to the teacher's authority. They may refuse to do work that they consider boring or to repeat or practice lessons if they already understand the material. In classrooms where everyone is expected to do much the same work and cover the same material, this can be seen as a real problem. Gifted children can be demanding, challenging, intense, critical, oversensitive, highly verbal, and physically active, and they can devour material rapidly. None of these traits are in and of themselves problems, but they can present real problems for teachers who are not prepared to meet these needs. Some teachers do not know what to do with these youngsters and feel incompetent and threatened by them. For administrators, gifted children present needs for special services. This may be perceived as pressure on already tight budgets or cause special arrangements to be made that seem unnecessary. Fortunately, these attitudes often can be changed with in-service in gifted education.

4. Are most gifted children hyper-active?

Most gifted children have high levels of energy, require less sleep, and are very, very curious. These traits can resemble hyper-activity, but there is a difference. The energy of a gifted child is focused, directed, and intense. The energy of a hyperactive child is diffuse, random, and sporadic. Gifted children can attend to an activity of their interest for long periods of time; hyperactive children cannot. The brighter the child, the more the energy may look excessive.

5. Is it all right for a gifted child to be a loner?

Gifted children commonly seek times to be alone. Maslow (1971) identifies times of isolation as one of the characteristics of self-actualizing people. If, however, the child is seeking isolation as an escape from teasing, criticism, or unfair treatment, that can be a problem. Gifted children need to be taught skills of communicating with others and of understanding how to be accepting toward and accepted by others. Choosing to be alone is different from being alone because of being rejected. A consistent pattern of isolation should be questioned. All human beings need love, affection, and a sense of belonging.

6. What can I do for a child who is too much of a perfectionist?

The first thing is to acknowledge that what-ever perfectionist children perceive to be inadequate is truly their perception. My experience has been that children do not benefit from being told that something they think is awful actually is very good, even if I think it is. Instead of:

CHILD: "This is just dumb. I made a mess of it."
PARENT/TEACHER: "Oh no, it really is quite good."

which results in the child believing that you either do not see the problem, you are insincere, or you have very low standards, try:

CHILD: "This is just dumb. I made a mess of it."
PARENT/TEACHER: "I can see you are not satis-fied with the way that turned out. What would you like it to be that it isn't?"

This gives you a chance of understanding what the child sees as a problem and perhaps providing additional resources or direction.

One of the best ways to aid a child to handle perfectionism is to discuss some of the problems you have faced and the strate-gies you have used to work on your own perfectionist need. Most parents of gifted children and teachers attracted to working with them have had or are having similar problems. Children like to hear how we solve our problems that are similar to theirs.

✤ CHECKING FOR UNDERSTANDING
Follow-Up Activity

Choose one of the following issues that can lead to problems for gifted children and write an incident or a scenario that illustrates how such a problem has affected a gifted person that you know and how they resolved it. Resource people you might choose could be: you, a fam-ily member, one of your students, or one of your colleagues. You may need to interview your subject to get his or her reactions to the issue.

Issues:

Limits of perfectionism

Feelings of low self-esteem

Resolution of a moral dilemma

Negative attitudes toward giftedness held by teachers or counselors

Conflict between academic excellence and so-cial acceptance

SUMMARY

Social Emotional Development and Giftedness

1. Children who by fortunate circumstances develop more of their potential seem to meet a different set of social and emotional consequences than do more typical children.

Social-Emotional Characteristics of Gifted Learners

2. For the most part, given the opportunity for healthy development, the social-emotional adjustment of gifted children tends to proceed better than among the more typical population.
3. The personality traits that are most common among gifted individuals and demonstrate their emotional complexity are sensitivity, perfectionism, intensity, and introversion.
4. Self-confidence, independence, higher levels of internal control, and personal responsibility are also personality traits of gifted students commonly suggested by research.
5. Gifted students are often intrinsically motivated tending to exhibit curiosity, accept challenges willingly, be persistent with tasks that are difficult, remain task-committed, be satisfied with their efforts irrespective of the opinions of others, and have lower academic anxiety. Academic intrinsic motivation has been found to be highly correlated to school achievement and to intelligence.
6. Although it has been suggested that some competition may be necessary for the motivitation and the quality of performance of gifted children, the task-oriented style has been shown to be far more successful both academically and socially. Other-referenced competition is viewed by classmates as aggressive and children using this style are disliked by the majority peer group.
7. The multidimensional theory of perfectionism places it on a continuum from healthy to dysfunctional behaviors. When observed as obsessive preoccupation with perfection inhibiting the gifted child from trying new experiences for fear of failing, perfectionism is a serious and limiting problem and is an often observed characteristic of many gifted learners.

Social-Emotional Adjustment

8. The positive social and emotional growth of gifted children is more related to how well the environment responds to and provides for their needs than to the different characteristics they present.
9. The more highly gifted the child, the greater the risk for social-emotional maladjustment and unhappiness.
10. At least three patterns are used by gifted children to adjust to their world: withdrawal, isolating themselves from the group; showing off in an effort to gain favorable attention; and seeking conformity, sometime to the point of underachievement.

The Self-Concept of the Gifted Individual

11. Two categories of self-concept have been identified: the academic self-concept, in which gifted students most often rate quite high; and social self-concept, an area that may be very low among some gifted students. For highly gifted students, the intellectual self-concept may be the stronger.
12. Children with high self-esteem more often acquire a sense of independence, exhibit exploratory behavior, assert their own rights, develop a strong inner locus of control, and express more self-trust. These traits lead them to personal happiness and more effective functioning.
13. The family is the incubator of self-esteem and the most crucial social unit in a child's life and development. The early months and years of a child's life are the most decisive in establishing a solid base for authentic, abiding self-esteem and depth of personal character.
14. The parents' high self-esteem is vital to their ability to provide a healthy environment for the child.
15. Because children spend so much of their time in school, the environment of the school also plays a major role in the development of self-esteem. Schools that feature self-esteem as a clearly stated component of their goals, policies, and practices are more successful academically as well as in developing healthy self-esteem.

Moral Development

16. From an early age, gifted children often show evidence of moral concerns including empathy, compassion, idealism, global concern, and advanced understanding and judgement of moral issues. Highly gifted children are reported as being far beyond age peers in understanding fairness, justice, and responsibility for self and others.

17. The moral orientation of children seemed most related to their social background and life experiences. Gifted children develop their moral identity through those who are around them, their values, and their moral responses to life's situations.

The Developing Personality

18. Family cohesion, expressiveness, and lower levels of family conflict are associated with better overall adjustment and more favorable cognitive development, school achievement, and fewer problems with discipline or self-control.

19. American society tends to rate attributes rather than allow uniqueness and incomparability. By our refusal to recognize special ability in intellectual areas, we waste the ability of uncounted numbers of gifted children.

20. Unsupportive attitudes among the school staff can result in the debilitation of the education of gifted students. Experience with the gifted students and a background in gifted education are related to attitudes of acceptance and support.

Adolescence: A Particularly Challenging Period of Growth

21. During adolescence, the brain will decline in plasticity but increase in power, and a boring environment will have a more powerful thinning effect on the cortex than the thick-

ening effect of the enriched environment. During this period, gifted students are very susceptible to losing mental ground when not challenged.

22. The goals often mentioned as parts of the focus during the transition period of adolescence are: to achieve independence; to discover one's identity as a person; to establish personal values and a personal and social philosophy; to develop self-guidance, self-motivation, and self-esteem; to become aware of the needs of others and of how the self can contribute to meeting those needs; to explore and accept sexuality; to acknowledge intellectual power; to acquire life maintenance, career, and self-actualization skills; to develop meaningful interpersonal relationships; and to explore reality structures by use of personal experiences.

23. Gifted females are especially vulnerable during this period and may have to choose between being gifted and being feminine. They will often try to hide their cognitive abilities in favor of their desire for social acceptance.

24. Gifted males prefer more cognitive and aesthetic experiences than the physical activities having a strong element of daring preferred by average male students. This may cause them to be viewed as effeminate and less accepted by their age peers.

25. Owing to the common use of the middle school grades to review and reintroduce concepts developed in elementary years, gifted students are now faced with an intolerable amount of repetition and conceptual stagnation. This often results in boredom and indifference to classroom achievement, and the incidence of underachievement among the gifted has been seen to rise during this time.

26. Gifted youths have an early concern and interest in intuitive knowing and creative activity.

Part II

The School and the Gifted Individual

6

Developing Support Systems for Programs for Gifted Learners

In this chapter the reader will discover discussions and information regarding:

- Programs for gifted learners, yesterday and today.

- Abilities, values, and characteristics of teachers of gifted learners.

- The education necessary to be an effective teacher of gifted learners.

- How to gain the support for gifted programs from other teachers, from parents, and from the administration.

- Counselors and school psychologists as support personnel.

- Gaining the support of the community.

- Methods of educating parents to support gifted learners.

Your belief system explains only what your limits are—not what the limits are. Belief systems limit experience. Impossible things are just things you don't believe in.

—JAMES FADIMAN

Jane had been on the job for less than a month, and already it was evident that besides the administrators, who had hired her to establish provisions for gifted students, no one in the district really wanted a program for gifted students at all. Some of the faculty and administrators that she had met made it very clear that they thought such an idea was wrong; it was elitist and undemocratic. There were strong feelings of need for equity among the community and suspicion of any program that seemed to create a special group. The administration had given her a full year to lay the groundwork for a new gifted program, which at first she had thought was a luxury; now she considered it a necessity.

The previous coordinator of the program for gifted learners had not made any friends for the program. She had developed a pull-out program that segregated the gifted students for a full day twice per month. She had taken them on field trips that were the envy of all of the students in the district, and had demanded special equipment for her resource room that she insisted no other children were allowed to use. She did not meet with any of the parents or the other teachers and did not feel she had time to involve herself in district events, including faculty professional and social meetings. Because she was only "part-time," she was not required to attend such functions and could see no point in wasting her time because none of the in-service opportunities were about gifted students or "gifted issues." No one had been sorry to see her leave the district, and all were glad the gifted program had ended.

Jane began by having meetings with the parents of the gifted learners to discuss the possible options for planning a new program. She attended the faculty meetings and socials and enlisted the help of anyone interested in developing in-service opportunities. She worked with groups of administrators to get their support and to help them understand the program options she was considering. She organized several 2-day conferences throughout the district where teacher-parent-administrator teams representing schools in the district came together to learn about the nature and nurture of intelligence, new data on teaching and learning, the needs created by high intelligence, and strategies and structures for meeting these needs.

After a few months, each school chose teams to represent them at a weekend district planning conference. As part of the teaching staff, Jane invited her professor from the university where she had completed her master's degree in gifted education and others with expertise in the subject matter and creative ideas in teaching and learning to share their information in large group sessions. The conference was designed for interaction within the teams from each school and among team members with similar roles across the district. By the middle of the second day, teams were planning school programs that met their needs, and at the end of the conference a 5-year plan had been developed for each school. Jane and the district administrators who attended took the plans and worked out a district plan that would support and enhance the individual school programs. After returning to the schools, the team members became the school resources for continuing the development of their school's plan. The new data on teaching and learning were used school wide to plan structures and strategies for optimizing the learning of all students.

When programs started in the district schools the next year, Jane continued to provide ongoing in-service, support the structures devised by the school faculties, and generally support the parents, teachers, and administrators in what they had planned to do. A knowledge base and collaborative planning changed this district from one with strongly resisted provisions for gifted learners to one that would have strong programs and advocacy groups for years to come.

PROGRAMS FOR GIFTED LEARNERS YESTERDAY AND TODAY

Organizing a program that will deliver educational services to gifted learners is one of the most complex, most researched, and least clarified areas of gifted education. The administrative structure is critical to the success of the program for gifted learners. It will reflect the commitment of the school to either expand or inhibit the opportunities for learning experienced by the gifted individual. Using the knowledge that continuous stimulation is critical to optimal development and that gifted learners have unique learning needs, let us look at how we can gain support for programs to meet these needs.

Education of the Gifted Learner

As noted in Chapter 1, during several periods of American history, programs for educating gifted learners were encouraged. Terman's study during the 1920s brought on one such period. The dramatic accomplishments of the Russian space program in the late 1950s and early 1960s, which became a concern for the United States with the public launching of Sputnik, heralded another. The Marland report in 1972 alerted the nation to the fact that 57.5% of schools surveyed reported no gifted individuals among their students, at least 500,000 gifted students in the United States received no special instruction, and no gifted students were served in 21 states.

In 1978, Mitchell and Erickson updated the Marland report and found that education for gifted students had improved. The report showed that 84% of the states now had policies that provided service to gifted and talented students. However, both reports found a lack of adequate funding, trained personnel, and training opportunities; problems of identification; and lack of data on program effectiveness.

During the early 1980s, a new philosophy regarding the role of the government in education began to take form. Programs for the gifted and talented were placed into a block grant with 32 other programs and projects, with appropriations for the block sent directly to the states for administration. Some felt that the new philosophy was too biased in the direction of remedial learning and failed to foster the development of unique talents or special skills (Branscomb, 1980). Although the federal government had all but abolished its role in supporting or even encouraging the appropriate education of its most able children, national advocacy groups began to form. Through their efforts legislation once again allowed the federal government a small but important leadership role in education of gifted learners.

In April 1988, Congress passed the Jacob K. Javits Gifted and Talented Students Education Act (Title IV, Part B, of PL 100–297), which was re-appropriated (PL 103–382) in 1994. In the rationale for passing this bill it is stated in part:

- Gifted and talented students are a national resource vital to the future of the nation and its security and wellbeing.

- Unless the special abilities of gifted and talented students are recognized and developed during such student's elementary and secondary school years, much of such student's special potential for contributing to the national interest is likely to be lost.

- Gifted and talented students from economically disadvantaged families and areas, and students of limited-English proficiency are at greatest risk of being unrecognized and of not being provided adequate or appropriate educational services.

- State and local educational agencies and private nonprofit schools often lack the necessary specialized resources to plan and implement effective programs for the early identification of gifted and talented students for the provision of educational services and programs appropriate to their special needs.

- The Federal Government can best carry out the limited but essential role of stimulating research and development and personnel training, and of providing a national focal point of information and technical assistance that is necessary to ensure that our Nation's schools are able to meet the special educational needs of gifted and talented students, and thereby serve a profound national interest. (p. 3821)

The purpose of this act of Congress then became to provide financial assistance to research, demonstration projects, personnel training, and similar activities designed to identify and meet the special educational needs of gifted and talented students. The act specifically authorized for those involved in gifted and talented education:

- Pre-service and in-service training, including fellowships, for personnel.
- Model projects and exemplary programs for identification and education.
- Strengthening agencies of the state and institutions of higher education to provide leadership and assistance to local agencies.
- Programs of technical assistance and information dissemination.
- A National Center for Research and Development in the Education of Gifted and Talented Children and Youth.

To administer these activities, an Office of Gifted and Talented was established with a director and staff. During the first year, funds were appropriated and awarded to grant applicants throughout the country. Although limited in support, this recognition of the importance of gifted and talented children to our nation served as a stimulus and validation to those who would appropriately serve these students in our country.

The educational system in general is again involved in a reevaluation and in the climate of reform advocates must ensure that gifted students continue to be allowed educational experiences that are appropriate for them. As new legislation once more is being debated at the federal level, the further assistance to states to support gifted education is an exciting possibility.

Interest in the education of the gifted and talented is steadily growing worldwide. In 1975, the World Council for Gifted and Talented Children was formed and through its international conferences, journal, and newsletters, the organization is continuing to develop a worldwide network and support system of benefit to gifted children and those who work with them.

Mandating Service to Gifted Students

State mandates, funding, and administrative leadership are directly correlated to the level of services provided to gifted students, with the most critical area being mandates for appropriate services (Coleman, Gallagher, & Foster, 1994). In a survey completed in September 1998, The Council of State Directors Program for the Gifted (1999) found that 30 (69%) of the 43 states reporting had legislation mandating identification of gifted students and 26 (60%) of the states reporting mandated programs to serve them. The levels of funding accompanying these mandates vary widely from nearly $70,000,000 in Georgia to $20,000 in Rhode Island, resulting in only partial support for students identified as gifted. Many states without mandates encourage service to gifted students and may even provide money for this purpose; however, in such circumstances, neither the services nor the funds are secure, but are dependent on the economy and climate of support.

State-mandated certification is favored by a large percentage of both university program directors and practitioners (Hultgren, 1981). Of the 40 state consultants reporting, 28 (70%) favored certification requirements. Those not favoring such requirements cited lack of established professional standards or teacher competencies and the limited number of college and university teacher education programs as reasons for lack of support for certification. Some practitioners feel that such a mandate would cause inconvenience to them owing to the need to add more requirements, especially in areas in which programs in education of the gifted are largely unavailable. Administrators are often concerned about a loss of autonomy if such requirements were to become law. However, Hultgren reports that most educators feel that the advantages of having well-trained professionals far outweigh the disadvantages.

Mandating services is an important part of the process for obtaining desirable programming for gifted students (Coleman, Gallagher, & Foster, 1994). Although mandates are of limited value, when funds are not properly appropriated to establish adequate service, a state mandate creates an expectation of what local districts should be doing to appropriately educate gifted students. At the federal level, a mandate would give visibility to the need for gifted education and approval for advocates to seek appropriate service. At either level it serves as a moral and political base for parents and educators to ensure that gifted and talented students are having their unique educational needs met.

TEACHERS OF THE GIFTED: AT SCHOOL

No man can reveal to you aught but that which already lies half asleep in the dawning of your knowledge.

The teacher . . . gives not of his wisdom but rather of his faith and his lovingness. If he is indeed wise he does not bid you enter the house of his wisdom, but rather leads you to the threshold of your own mind.

(GIBRAN, 1960, P. 62)

The teacher of gifted learners is the most critical factor in optimizing their program.

The checklist shown in Figure 6.1 will provide an opportunity to assess the level of knowledge that you or groups to which you belong have regarding the education of gifted learners. It will help you to become aware of the information that is already known, beliefs that are presently held, and misconceptions that may be in the way of understanding gifted learners. This review will highlight questions and information that can be gained from the rest of this book that you or your group now find missing. This assessment could be used as a way of focusing your reading and, later, of becoming aware of what you have learned.

Almost everyone agrees that the teacher has the most significant influence on a learning environment. Many factors influence the learning of a student, but within the classroom situation, the teacher is of critical importance. As early as 1932, Anderson and Kennedy stated that the mental attitude of the teacher most influenced the atmosphere of the classroom. Gallagher, Aschner, and Jenne (1967) found that intellectual productivity in school was directly related to the teacher's style, expectations, and response patterns. In a survey of people working in gifted programs, Renzulli (1968) found that they ranked the teacher highest as a factor critical to the success of the programs. The respondents considered both selection and training of teachers as major issues. Aspy (1969) found that the high self-esteem of a teacher correlates with student success in the classroom; no other factor shows such a significant correlation. Brookover (1969) stated that the teacher's attitude toward self and others is more important to classroom success than techniques, practices, and materials. Webb (1971) showed that the way teachers behave, not what they know, is the most important issue in the transmission of the teaching-learning exchange. It

Figure 6.1 *Assessment of Knowledge of Gifted Learners*

This assessment instrument will give you an opportunity to assess the level of knowledge that you or groups to which you belong have regarding some areas in the education of gifted learners. The items will allow you to become aware of the information that is already known, beliefs that are presently held, and misconceptions that may inhibit understanding of gifted learners. Before each statement, place the number that you feel most closely represents your present position. The results are discussed at the end of this exercise. Be as open as you can. You may discover some new insights about this area.

1. I strongly agree.   2. I agree.   3. I have no opinion   4. I disagree.   5. I strongly disagree.

_____ 1. The term *gifted* can mean different things to different people and often causes confusion and miscommunication.

_____ 2. Intelligence can be developed and must be nurtured if giftedness is to occur and be maintained.

_____ 3. We seldom find very highly gifted children or the exceptionally gifted children we could call *geniuses;* therefore, we know comparatively little about them.

_____ 4. Thinking of, or speaking of, gifted children as superior people is inaccurate and misleading.

_____ 5. As schools are currently organized, it is not always possible for gifted children to receive appropriate educational experiences without special programs.

_____ 6. Equal opportunity in education does not mean having the same curriculum and activities for everyone, but rather educational adaptations to meet the specific needs of each child.

_____ 7. Gifted children, although interested in many things, usually are not gifted in everything.

_____ 8. Difficulty conforming to group tasks may be the result of the unusually varied interests or advanced comprehension of a gifted child.

_____ 9. Teachers often see gifted learners as challenging their authority, disrespectful, and disruptive.

_____ 10. Some gifted children use their high level of verbal skill to avoid difficult thinking tasks.

_____ 11. The demand for products or meeting deadlines can inhibit the development of a gifted child's ability to integrate new ideas.

_____ 12. Work that is too easy or boring frustrates a gifted child just as work that is too difficult frustrates an average learner.

_____ 13. Most gifted children in our present school system are underachievers.

_____ 14. Commonly used sequences of learning are often inappropriate and can be limiting to gifted learners.

_____ 15. Gifted children, who can be very critical of themselves, often hold lower than average self-concepts.

_____ 16. Gifted children often expect others to live up to standards they have set for themselves, with resulting problems in interpersonal relations.

_____ 17. Gifted children are more challenged and more motivated when they work with students at their level of ability.

_____ 18. Some gifted children may perform poorly or even fail subjects in which they are bored or unmotivated.

_____ 19. The ability of gifted learners to generalize, synthesize, solve problems, study in depth, engage in abstract and complex thought patterns, and think at an accelerated pace most commonly differentiates gifted from average learners; therefore, programs for gifted students should stress using these abilities.

_____ 20. The persistent goal-directed behavior of gifted children can result in others perceiving them as stubborn, willful, and uncooperative.

_____ 21. If not challenged, gifted children can waste their ability and become mediocre, average learners.

_____ 22. Gifted children often express their idealism and sense of justice at a very early age.

Figure 6.1 *continued*

_____ 23. Not all gifted children show creativity, leadership, or physical expertise.
_____ 24. People who work with, study, and try to understand gifted children have more success educating the gifted than those who have limited contact and have not educated themselves as to the unique needs of these children.
_____ 25. I would be pleased to be considered gifted, and I enjoy people who are.

The questionnaire you have just completed should give you some indication of opinions of gifted children that are supportive to their educational growth. The more "I strongly agree" answers you were able to give, the more closely your opinions match those of people who have devoted their energy to understanding gifted children. In the pages of this text, we examine these issues and others that augment our understanding of and ability to better educate gifted children.

seems apparent that those who wish to provide optimal learning situations for gifted students need to be concerned about the characteristics, values, self-concepts, and training of the teachers who implement gifted programs.

Surprisingly, only about 23 states have any requirements beyond the regular teaching credentials for teachers of the gifted. Of these, the number of required hours of training ranges from 3 to 20 semester hours, with 11 semester hours the average (Council of State Directors Program for the Gifted, 1999). Classroom teachers were reported to have an average 0 to 3 hours of training in gifted education. Even worse, few institutions, districts, or state departments of education provide pre-service or in-service experiences in gifted education. The National/State Leadership Training Institute on Gifted and Talented made one of the most impactful contributions in this area. By setting up summer institutes and national conferences, this group made people in every state aware of this critical training need and provided models and expertise for changing what was a desolate picture. Much still remains to be done, because we already know that attitudes of teachers, counselors, and administrators change favorably toward the gifted when they have participated in some gifted education. If opportunities are ever to be provided that will allow gifted children to develop their potential, then sensitive, knowledgeable teachers must be available both at school and in the home.

Abilities, Values, and Characteristics

Few educational decisions have as much influence on the gifted program as teacher selection. If we believe the lists of characteristics offered by researchers and writers in this field, then we would need to find a person who is so outstanding that few gifted programs could exist. Some believe that the teachers of gifted students must be brilliant to keep ahead of their students. Others want them to be learned and wise, with extraordinary insights and a depth of understanding of their subject or field that comes with years of living and teaching. Some would require the teacher to be an accomplished counselor, a profound philosopher, and an active community leader.

Those employed to select such a teacher must be totally overwhelmed. To complicate matters, there are teachers who have only a few of the characteristics commonly listed, but are exciting and productive in the classroom; others have many of the characteristics, but are authoritarians, without passion for their subject, who communicate little of value to their students. To compile the ideal profile, traits that seem not just desirable but most essential should be the guide. Clues to effective characteristics and attitudes can be discovered from those who work in gifted programs, from researchers, and from the students themselves.

Aspy and Roebuck (1972) investigated the relationship between teachers' classroom behavior and students' level of cognitive functioning. They found that teachers whose students attained cognitive levels beyond memory and recognition provided significantly higher levels of positive regard for their students than those whose students stayed at the lower level. These researchers concluded that insecure, insensitive, sarcastic teachers not only do not facilitate learning, but they have a marked negative effect on the quality and quantity learned, as well as on the student's self-esteem.

Lindsey (1980) presents us with a synthesis of preferred personal characteristics and teaching behaviors of the teacher who is successful in working with gifted learners:

Personal Characteristics:

- Understands, accepts, respects, trusts, and likes self, has outstanding ego strength
- Is sensitive to others, less concerned with self; supports, respects, trusts others
- Is above average intellectually; exhibits an intellectual style of conceptualizing, generalizing, creating, initiating, relating, organizing, imagining
- Is flexible, open to new ideas
- Has intellectual interests, literary and cultural
- Desires to learn, increase knowledge; has high achievement needs
- Is enthusiastic
- Is intuitive, perceptive
- Is committed to excellence
- Feels responsible for own behavior and consequences.

Personal-Professional Pre-Dispositions:

- To guide rather than to coerce or pressure
- To be democratic rather than autocratic
- To focus on process as well as product
- To be innovative and experimental rather than conforming
- To use problem-solving procedures rather than jump to unfounded conclusions
- To seek involvement of others in discovery rather than give out answers.

Teaching Behaviors:

- Develops a flexible, individualized program
- Creates a warm, safe, and permissive atmosphere
- Provides feedback
- Uses varied strategies

- Respects personal self-images and enhances positive ones; respects personal values
- Respects creativity and imagination
- Stimulates higher-order mental processes
- Respects individuality and personal integrity. (pp. 13, 14)

In a study by Kathnelson and Colley (1982), students 6 to 16 years of age involved in a special project for gifted and highly able learners were asked to record descriptions of what they would like an ideal teacher to do as a teacher and as a person. The results showed the following student responses regarding desirable characteristics:

Items Mentioned 50% of the Time

Someone who understands them.

Someone who has a sense of humor.

Someone who can make learning fun.

Someone who is cheerful.

Items Mentioned 30% of the Time

Someone who supports and respects them.

Someone who is intelligent.

Someone who is patient.

Someone who is firm with them.

Someone who is flexible.

Items Mentioned Occasionally (5% to 10% of the Time)

Someone who knows the subject.

Someone who explains things carefully.

Someone who is skilled in group processes.

The teachers and parents chose "knowledge of nature and needs of gifted," "skill in developing self-concept," and "skills in integrating the cognitive, affective, sensory and intuitive abilities" as top priorities in their ranking of professional competencies for teachers of gifted. They listed "understands, accepts, respects, trusts and likes self"; "supports, respects, trusts and is sensitive to others"; and "is open to new ideas, flexible" as the top priorities for personal attributes.

Story (1985) conducted a study to discover the behavioral characteristics necessary for successful teaching of the gifted and found that successful teachers of the gifted:

- Provide for positive and close physical relationships that support learning for gifted children.
- Demonstrate both quality and quantity in verbal interactions with gifted children.
- Are flexible in scheduling their time according to students' needs.
- Are process oriented, with children's creative productivity the ultimate goal.

- Provide appropriate environmental supports based on children's independent study interests.
- Display "gifted behavior" as brought to bear upon their professional responsibilities.

Maddux, Samples-Lachmann, and Cummings (1985) conducted another study that showed that personal-social characteristics are teacher behaviors preferred by gifted students. Gifted students in the seventh, eighth, and ninth grades showed a significant preference for personal-social characteristics over cognitive or classroom-management variables. The top items in each of the categories are: (1) Personal-social—friendly, confidence in students, and sense of humor; (2) Cognitive—knowledge of the subject taught, imaginative, and teaches useful information; and (3) Classroom management—allows open class discussion, treats students as adults, and teaches in an organized way.

Wendel and Heiser (1989) provide support for previous studies in their summary of effective instructional characteristics of junior high school teachers of gifted students. From observations of videotapes, researchers found that effective teachers of gifted learners demand high-quality work, use their sense of humor to demonstrate to their students that they care for and respect them, and stress the students' personal involvement in learning and do so in creative ways. They conduct stimulating discussions using probing questions requiring deeper thought and ask students to think for themselves.

From interviews of teachers of the gifted identified as outstanding or average, Whitlock and DuCette (1989) found that outstanding teachers differed from average teachers in their enthusiasm, self-confidence, role as a facilitator, ability to apply knowledge, achievement motivation, ability to build program support, and commitment.

The qualities mentioned in these studies do make good teachers, and students prefer them. Some of the characteristics may even be unique preferences of gifted students. It is unclear which are desirable for all students and which are necessary only for gifted learners. However, we know that to be effective with gifted learners, teachers will need the knowledge and understanding of:

- Nature and nurture of high levels of intelligence in all of its aspects.
- Cognitive, social, and emotional characteristics, needs, and problems found with gifted students as a result of their atypical development.
- Environment in which gifted learners can feel safe to use their strengths, explore their personal and interpersonal development, risk new areas of thought and action, find and accept challenges, and express their uniqueness and be able to create it.
- Flexible, individualized, differentiated curricula that are appropriate to meeting the unique needs of gifted learners and be able to create and implement it.
- Creativity in all of its aspects and be able to nurture it.
- How to encourage in gifted learners a sense of social awareness of and commitment to humanity and to their environment, and a respect for the worth and dignity of others.

- How to relate positively to colleagues and parents of gifted learners, conduct informational meetings, and advocate for gifted education.

To develop such knowledge and understanding requires an uncommon amount of ability to:

- Empathize and inspire.
- Tolerate ambiguity; be open, flexible, and innovative.
- Share enthusiasm, a love of learning, and a joy of living.
- Be authentic and humane as a deep personal commitment.
- Be alert, knowledgeable, and informed.
- Value intelligence, intuition, diversity, and uniqueness in self and others.
- Value change, growth, and self-actualization for self and others.

The abilities necessary for effectively working with gifted learners provide a base of competency or professional standards toward which teacher educators can instruct and state agencies can certify. Basing a teacher education program, either pre-service or in service, on these standards ensures that those who acquire such an education have at least the basic requirements for providing quality programs for gifted learners. There is no way to ensure success in classrooms; however, opportunities can be provided for teachers to gain an awareness of and experiences with these competencies that have been shown to increase a teacher's effectiveness in gifted programs.

Teacher Education and Certification

An important part of any teacher education program is the ability and attitude of the teacher educator. Those who teach teachers must themselves possess the attributes, knowledge, and skills essential for optimizing learning and developing individual potential. The program should allow all who participate to learn within the structure and with the teaching and evaluation strategies they are being asked to use in their classrooms. The processes we value in gifted education must be modeled in the teacher/learner's classroom. The characteristics and competencies appropriate for a teacher of the gifted must be evident in the teacher of that teacher.

In 1996, the National Research Center on Gifted and Talented (NRC/GT) conducted a national survey to investigate the scope and nature of professional development practices in gifted education used in school districts throughout the country (Westberg, Burns, Gubbins, Reis, Park, & Maxfield, 1998). The findings indicate that professional development in gifted education is limited, some of the most effective practices such as collegial coaching are rarely used, and very few districts provide differentiated experiences for their teachers. The findings include:

- Districts spend only 4% of their total professional development budget on inservice related to gifted education.
- More professional development experiences were found in districts with state mandates to identify and serve gifted students.

- Districts in the South provided significantly more professional development experiences than were provided in a 3-year period in the Northeast, North Central, and West regions of the country.

- Gifted education specialists rarely provided professional development training to other faculty members within their school districts.

- The majority of districts do not evaluate the impact of their professional development practices in gifted education.

There are many ways for teachers to gain the competencies needed to teach gifted students, from district-sponsored workshops and conferences to an intensive involvement in a university teacher education program leading to a credential, a graduate degree, or both. This discussion details two of the many models that could be used and briefly looks at some other alternatives.

College and University Programs: Pre-service and In-service

At least 140 colleges and universities in more than 40 states currently offer some type of program to teachers wishing to specialize in teaching gifted learners (Hultgren, 1981). The programs may offer only one or two courses periodically, or there may be an entire multicourse program leading to a degree or credential in the gifted specialization, with the master's degree programs the most commonly found. Several surveys have indicated that many courses offered do not lead to degrees or credentials, are nearly all at the graduate level of study, and require the candidate to have a teaching credential and some previous teaching experience (Lindsey, 1980).

According to data reported by The Council of State Directors Program for the Gifted (1999), 125 colleges and universities in 30 states offer programs that culminate in one or more graduate degrees in education of gifted learners, and 18 have doctoral programs with majors or concentration in gifted education.

Although some universities and colleges are offering programs focused on the needs of teachers of gifted learners, some further concerns must be noted. A survey of practitioners in the field (Hultgren, 1981) revealed a list of areas not adequately addressed by the university programs they attended. Included in this list were leadership skills, counseling for gifted learners, career options for gifted learners, cultural differences, educational technological developments, the needs of underachievers, and parent/community relations and resources. The university personnel surveyed also were concerned about the lack of opportunities in many of the areas. One of the highest rated deficiencies of preparation programs was the lack of supervised practicum experience. At both the teaching and administrative levels, opportunities for practicum experience were seen to be inadequate or missing in far too many programs.

In 1995, the NAGC adopted standards for graduate programs in gifted education developed by a group of more than 75 educators from widely diverse roles and populations in the field. These concepts, skills, and professional competencies are seen to be essential for persons preparing to provide or direct services for gifted students. The document, available from the NAGC office, was developed to guide institutions preparing educators in the field of gifted education. It is organized into criteria for professional studies and field experiences, student entrance qualifications, composition, assessment, exit criteria, and criteria for the qualifications, composition, and scholarly activity of the professional education faculty delivering the program.

The Course Work. The overall content of courses on education of the gifted is similar in most institutions involved in gifted education programs. Most commonly offered is a course that explores the education and psychology of the gifted individual; introduces the concept of giftedness; and includes definition, identification, characteristics, etiology, and nurture. Many institutions also offer a course in methods and curriculum for teaching gifted learners. Other areas that may be found as part of programs leading to degrees or credentials in education of the gifted include: measurement and testing, leadership principles and practices, affective development, creative behavior, classroom management, advanced studies, research methods, and administrative provisions. Practicum experiences are rated as essential by both practitioners and university trainers; yet 37% of universities offering programs in gifted education offer no practicum experiences in teaching the gifted learner, and 76% offer no administrative practicum (Hultgren, 1981). In the same sample, 61% of the practitioners assessed had no practicum in teaching and 80% had no administrative practicum, although one-third engaged in administration of gifted programs. Universities offering higher degrees, rather than just occasional course work, offered more practicum experience.

It has also been noted that attitudes of teachers are influenced favorably toward gifted learners if they have had even one course in education of the gifted. The major part of the educational experience of most gifted students is planned and implemented by the regular classroom teacher, yet information regarding gifted learners and their needs is rare in the general offerings for teachers. Most of the courses with information on understanding giftedness are offered at the graduate level and to students taking them in pursuit of a higher degree in this area of specialization.

Standards-Based Programs. Standards-based programs use content and performance standards to place the emphasis on what educators should know and be able to do, rather than on what courses they must complete. Additionally, standards-based programs have several advantages: the standards approach is systematic, the standards set clear expectation for student achievement, and the process is designed by and communicated to those in the particular setting. Wiggins and McTighe (1998) call their approach to planning for standards-based programming the backward design process and suggest three basic steps: (1) identify the desired results or outcomes of the program, that is, what they wish the students to achieve or become; (2) determine acceptable evidence to demonstrate understanding of the students' knowledge or skill; and (3) plan learning experiences and instruction to aid the students in their learning. To develop a standards-based program for training teachers of the gifted, this process is most useful. The following steps will make the process more clear:

> STEP 1—Define the knowledge, skills, and attitudes to be achieved. These are the content standards. Three areas in which content standards should be

developed are: what a teacher needs to be, to know, and to be able to do. The unifying theme is the development of understanding.

STEP 2—Determine acceptable evidence that the content standards have been achieved. The forms of evidence must give choice to the students, allowing for a variety of evaluative procedures and products. These are called performance standards. Just as the best way for gifted children to reach their potential is through educational programs that are individualized with varied opportunities, so too should teacher preparation programs be planned to allow teachers to identify and meet their own needs and interests appropriately.

STEP 3—Design alternative strategies, learning experiences, and instruction for helping different students achieve the content standards.

STEP 4—Evaluate the degree to which or level of quality with which the content standards are met. Evaluation rubrics will allow the teacher to provide the student with a clear understanding of the expectations for achievement considering both the quantity and quality. Evaluation is not synonymous with examination, and it has been my experience that far more learning and change occur when a variety of data—student projects, papers, journals, observations, case studies, task sheets, book and journal reviews, media productions—provides the means for the products of evaluation. Feed back the results into all elements of the system.

Rogers (1989) delineates three levels of training needs to be met: Level One—the classroom teacher; Level Two—the cluster/resource teacher of the gifted; Level Three—the gifted program administrator. She identifies knowledge, understanding, and skills to be mastered at each level and allocates time for each level of training (see Table 6.1). This model provides one way of organizing for differentiated training depending on the role of the educator.

Although in-service for teachers has been conducted by university faculties for years, an outcome of the educational reform legislation in many states has been the opportunity for universities to expand the structures and delivery systems of teacher in-service to develop more effective models. Some universities and districts have established cooperative partnerships to allow for more off-campus courses, planned specifically for particular school faculties, to be taught directly on school sites. The modeling, demonstration, and follow-up support can be far more meaningful in the onsite setting. For special populations such as the gifted learner, such onsite partnerships can involve large numbers of school faculty that were not previously available and can improve instruction throughout the school program.

Modules for Gifted Education. Currently, service centers, universities, and the NAGC are structuring modules that can be used to provide needed information for teachers learning to work with gifted students. The modules can be delivered in a variety of time elements (e.g., a combination of evenings and weekends), and can be structured so that the teacher/learner can be allowed to select only those modules that meet their needs. The place and communication medium can also vary, with some modular programs utilizing distance learning using videotape, television, or computers, available at service centers or used to provide choice in university classrooms or district in-services.

Table 6.1 *Levels of Training, Depending on the Role of the Educator*

Level One Training: General Classroom Teachers (GTC) (Approx. 45 Hours)	**Level Two Training: Cluster; Resource, Catalyst Teachers (Approx. 180 Hours)**	**Level Three Training: Program Coordinators, Directors (Approx. 225 Hours)**
Knowledge & Understanding 1. Cognitive and affective differentiating characteristics of gifted learners 2. Educational needs of GCT learners 3. Future studies 4. Creativity, creative thinking strategies 5. Specific instructional materials and curriculum already designed for basic content areas 6. Nature of giftedness, intelligence *Skills & Competencies* A. Instructional modification techniques B. Instructional design strategies C. Teaching strategy selection D. Higher order questioning E. Creative problem-solving F. Futuring G. Group process H. Parent conferencing	A. Completion of Level One Training B. Level Two *Knowledge & Understanding* 1. Knowledge generation 2. Developmental patterns of giftedness 3. Affective, psychological, social needs of the gifted 4. Curriculum development methods and models 5. Individualized teaching/learning techniques 6. Nature of the gifted learner 7. Nature of the learning process 8. Integrated lesson design 9. Models, systems for program development *Skills & Competencies* A. Identification, assessment B. GCT roles C. IEP, GEP General Educational Plan design D. Resource provision E. Interactive/Interpersonal skills F. Counseling G. Presentation for program defense H. Program design, development, implementation, evaluation	A. Completion of Level One Training B. Completion of Level Two Training C. Level Three *Knowledge & Understanding* 1. Major school adaptations 2. Principles, practices of leadership 3. Evaluation procedures for GCT 4. Systems approach to curriculum development 5. Measurement, assessment of giftedness 6. Educational practice, traditions, philosophies 7. Administration *Skills & Competencies* A. Program design B. Program implementation C. Program evaluation D. Presentation E. Interactive/Interpersonal F. Research interpretation G. Staff development in-servicing

Source: From "Training Teachers of the Gifted: What Do They Need to Know?" by K. B. Rogers, 1989, *Roeper Review, II,* (3), pp. 146, 147, 149. Adapted with permission of the *Roeper Review,* PO Box 329, Bloomfield Hills, MI 48303.

Starko and Schack (1989) found that in-service could be improved by strengthening the confidence of teachers in their ability to use particular strategies, because teacher efficacy has a high correlation with the use of new strategies in the classroom. In addition to lectures, they suggest the use of demonstration lessons, simulated class activities, coaching, and micro-teaching opportunities to enhance self-efficacy.

A study of the effects of intervention on the attitudes, beliefs, and practices of pre-service teachers found that the use of workshops and coaching were more effective than workshops alone in preserving novice teachers' positive attitudes for pursuing differentiated teaching with gifted students in the classroom (Moon, Callahan, & Tomlinson, 1999). Before actual classroom teaching, most pre-service teachers were reported as believing that individual student differences should be recognized and accommodated. However, when teaching in classrooms with the diversity of needs now common, their attempts to develop teaching and management skills resulted in loss of enthusiasm and less favorable beliefs in the use of differentiation. They found that providing learning options that allow students to progress at their own level, varying the amount of instruction and practice that students receive, and otherwise working to meet the needs of students in an academically diverse environment became overwhelming. Moon, Callahan, & Tomlinson believe that interventions, such as workshops and coaching can serve as a starting point for supporting and shaping the novice teacher's practice in diverse learning environments and help them to better serve gifted learners.

Other types of inservice provided by universities have been summer institutes, conferences and workshops, demonstration classes, and consulting services. More cooperation among university faculties, district teachers and administrators, and state consultants and directors can only enhance the implementation of quality programs.

Other Forms of In-service

A number of other in-service models have been used in addition to those provided by the universities. Among them have been district- or state-sponsored conferences or workshops, regional service centers, and district or regional consortiums. In planning in-service experiences, the same professional standards and teacher competencies that can be found in more extensive credential and degree programs offered by universities should serve as a basis.

One statewide format for in-service that has evolved over several decades with increasing effectiveness can be found in Illinois (Van Tassel-Baska, 1986b). Having begun as gifted program demonstration centers, the Area Service Centers now include services in computers, math, science, and reading in addition to service in gifted education. This format allows for pooling of strength and resources from many areas in the service of each.

Over the long history of this program, five ideas for ensuring the effectiveness of in-service that can be generalized to other programs have been noted:

1. Real needs as well as perceived needs must be included. Those planning in-service experiences must assess them to determine what is needed to improve the program and what teachers want from in-service.

2. In-service should follow a developmental model. The needs will be different depending on the level of knowledge and experience with gifted programming a district has, and the in-service experiences should build on this growing expertise.

3. Training should be targeted toward specific outcomes for individuals and groups. This type of attention to specific needs has proved more effective than the wider service to large numbers of teachers.

4. Follow-up observation and monitoring are critical to the effectiveness of the in-service.

5. Techniques and ideas for continuing staff development are important for those involved.

These suggestions should add to the effectiveness of any in-service planning and its ability to effect change.

One important outcome of well-planned and well-implemented in-service programs is the increase in the teacher's perception of competence. In a 19-month longitudinal study by Adkins and Harty (1984), these feelings of competence had interesting results for gifted programs. Researchers found that "appropriate, consistent, and timely in-service preparation can provide school staff with the capacity to better monitor and evaluate the degree to which the needs of gifted students are met in a school system" (p. 40). They also found that growing feelings of competence and confidence in applying concepts of gifted education led teachers to support homogeneous-ability classes or groups, releasing pupils to special classes, increased interest in improving gifted education, and promoting quality education for gifted students. Another interesting finding was that, for some teachers, increased knowledge and understanding of the gifted resulted in less enthusiasm about and less interest in teaching gifted learners as they discovered that a truly differentiated curriculum required more work on their part to plan challenging learning experiences. Both results can only strengthen the quality of education available to gifted learners.

Developing Effective In-service

A survey (Tomlinson, 1986) of teacher responses to the effectiveness of techniques used in in-service and staff development workshops resulted in information that could be of benefit to those planning such experiences for teachers. Of most benefit were the group participation and hands-on experiences; lectures used alone were perceived as least beneficial. Consultants should be prepared to make whatever information they share immediately applicable to the teaching situation. Whenever possible, grouping of participants should be by teaching areas, disciplines, and grade levels for maximum benefit. Although it is not suggested that the in-service present material relating only to the desires and perceived needs of participants, it is considered helpful to know what those perceptions are.

Weiss and Gallagher (1986) developed TARGET, a needs-assessment approach to gifted education in-service that proved to be successful. A needs assessment showed the areas in which the teachers perceived they had a need and the areas in which they believed they had knowledge. A training module was designed with these data in mind. Time was allowed between sessions for teachers to try some activities that were related to these areas. They discussed the results of trying these new ideas in class at the beginning of each session. Teachers seemed to have benefited from sharing such information. At the end of the in-service, teachers were asked

University programs can help teachers gain knowledge about gifted learners and build support systems with other teachers.

to identify specific examples of their use of learning from the in-service. At 1-month follow-up, the teachers perceived the results of their in-service as positive, and they continued to use the materials and strategies. The elements of this in-service may be of benefit to others who have the responsibility for planning in-service in gifted education.

Most district conferences and in-service workshops have one abiding weakness: their overemphasis on strategies and "how to's." Teachers need to be aware of effective techniques to use with gifted children. However, if they are never exposed to a deeper understanding of the needs and problems of these children, they will never learn to generate activities appropriate to their style of teaching and to the atypical learning style of the students with whom they work daily. What does a teacher do on the 102nd day after having attended the workshop on "101 Creative Activities for Gifted Learners"? Teachers deserve better than the dependency and confusion that result from total reliance on these workshops and conferences.

Of course, the opposite is also true. In-service programs that give nothing but theoretical background with little or no participation can result in little or no change in the classroom. In-service for classroom teachers should be offered in a total context of theory into practice, designed not only to teach strategies, but also to show in what way the strategies meet the needs of gifted learners. Teachers of the gifted must themselves understand the nature of these learners and the needs they have. The information presented at in-service sessions is too often only at the knowledge level, and it is left to the teacher to find ways to take the information and turn it into something useful in the classroom. Although there may be great enthusiasm for the ideas, actual strategies for incorporating them in a school program as well as fiscal or moral support for such incorporation are too often missing.

It is important to identify the components of effective teaching and learning, to give examples of best practices, and to demonstrate these in the classroom. It must then be possible for teachers to develop that information into a model that works for them, to add to it, and to take from it, with their students' and their own personalities reflected in what is to become the procedure for that particular school. It is most important to have the teachers and the administrators become a community of learners. Imposing models, ideas, and strategies on teachers renders them powerless. If it is detrimental for teachers to do this to their students, then such practices must not be used on teachers. Teachers must be empowered if they are to empower their students.

From my experience with university/district in-service come the following suggested nine steps to make staff development more effective:

1. Develop trust and the perception of control with and among the teachers and administrators.

2. Focus on the teachers' needs. Meaningful staff development that creates change in the classroom will not happen in just one session; it is unlikely to happen in a series of sessions unless the focus is on the teachers and their needs.

3. Expose teachers to many possibilities of what can be learned to improve teaching and learning and then let them choose those they want, while encouraging them to add their own ideas to those suggested. It is unproductive to simply ask teachers what they need from their in-service program; that would be like asking those coming into a new country what they would like to see when they do not even know what is available. One of the first steps in any in-service program must be the development of an awareness on the part of the teachers of the full range of what can be learned to optimize learning and teaching.

4. Help the teachers become aware of what they are already doing that works, and allow time and a structure for them to share their successes. A consultant or a team of colleagues, in consultation with each teacher, should observe the classroom to identify the behaviors that do work and those that do not work that they want to change. Successful in-service education must include the involvement of the learner.

5. Conduct a needs assessment. Once teachers become aware of the new research and strategies for improving learning and teaching and have looked at their own strengths, a needs assessment should be made of what they now wish to learn.

6. Plan the content procedures for the in-service program. This decision-making should be shared with teachers. State these as content and performance standards to support the use of these structures by the teachers in their own classrooms.

7. Include classroom support. In-service education can begin to change teacher behaviors only if there is actual support in the classroom. In-service programs can provide support for change in the classroom by including peer coaching,

demonstration teaching, videotaped examples of teacher behavior to be used by the teacher, and continuing consultations as needed. It is one thing to give information; it is quite another to show how that information can function in the classroom and provide support for its use.

8. Keep in mind the importance of providing continuity, meeting specific identified needs, and presenting practical implications and strategies for all new ideas. In-service education should use and exemplify what we know are good learning procedures.

9. Facilitate continuing self-evaluation and the development of effective teaching. At the end of the project there should exist a community of learners among the faculty who will encourage continued self-growth.

This is exactly the pattern that is found to be most effective in the classroom itself. Students are made aware of content and performance standards as well as a scope and sequence so they know what is possible for them to learn, and they are assessed so that they know what skills they already have developed and which ones they still need to develop. They are given a variety of strategies and methods to choose among and are supported during the learning process. They are then given the opportunity to see how the new skill or information fits into their own lives, with self-evaluation encouraged. Much is known about how to optimize learning. This knowledge and the practices mentioned should be part of all in-service programs if such programs are really going to make learning to teach more effective.

As a further extension of the principle that effective teaching strategies must be used in the education of teachers, Kaplan (1995) suggests that the expectancies held for teachers in their preparation for teaching gifted students should parallel the level of sophistication that is held for the gifted learners themselves. "The scholarliness anticipated by students must generalize to the adults who assumed the role of students during professional development sessions" (p. 34). Not only should the dimensions of acceleration, depth, complexity, and novelty that create a differentiated curriculum for gifted students define the learning experiences of their teachers, but also the definition of the indicators that determine their success during their professional development experiences should be equally clear, consistent, and challenging. Individualized and meaningful learning experiences that allow satisfaction and personal, sustained change require continuous support and opportunities for self-appraisal against well-thought-out and important standards of professional development. Among the performance standards teachers might pursue during their professional in-service, Kaplan suggest active participation during the staff development, integration of new ideas from the in-service into existing practices without extinguishing practices that currently work, and person-alization of the information shared during the professional development experience for use in their own classroom. Using such behaviors as part of the standards on a rubric for successful professional development would provide teachers with appropriate expectations and a way to assess their role in their own professional improvement.

THE IMPORTANCE OF SUPPORT
FOR EFFECTIVE PROGRAMS

When an effective gifted program is found at a school site, the climate and curriculum of the entire school is enhanced. Administrators need to be assured that the education of all the students in their school will be positively affected by any additional programs. Any requests for provisions that take unfair quantities of resources away from the rest of the school, create unrelated and isolated programs, or show concern for only a few teachers, parents, and students should be discouraged. Such practices will only make the administration less willing to support appropriate educational programs for gifted learners.

Provisions for meeting the educational needs of gifted students are difficult to establish and impossible to maintain without strong and committed support systems. Such support systems must include the teaching faculty, the administration, the parents, and the larger community. The members of the support system must understand the nature and nurture of intelligence, how high levels of intelligence create different educational needs for gifted students, current data on teaching and learning, and alternative programs and strategies that have been successful in meeting the educational needs of gifted learners. They must be willing to advocate for these students as part of the entire student population.

Gaining the Support of Teachers

Gaining support from other teachers can be difficult and frustrating, as Jane discovered in our opening vignette. Teachers of the gifted, especially if they are creative, innovative, and effective, will often encounter some unexpected consequences. Many of our more traditional schools resist change, reward conformity, and submit teachers to subtle pressures to maintain the system as it is. In such a system, the person who deviates and does not follow the usual procedures is neither valued nor supported. Innovative teachers would do well to present the changes they wish to make as cooperatively as possible and be aware of any imposition their practices may have on others. Teachers who are not part of the regular faculty, but are hired as a special teacher, have an even more difficult problem. Their very presence says to some teachers, "I am here to do what you cannot. I'm a special teacher." Teachers who find themselves in this position must take care to establish good interpersonal relations with the entire faculty.

There are many ways to gain the support of other teachers:

1. Watch for those teachers who are interested in what you are doing, invite them into your room, share your materials and ideas, and ask them for their opinions.

2. Be sure to take every opportunity to let the entire faculty know they are welcome at any time to visit, participate, share ideas, or have their students work with yours.

3. Discuss what you are doing with the principal and other administrators. Keep administration informed and invite their participation, but be careful of making

presentations before the entire faculty. Many may be there only because they were required to attend and will view the proceeding as a criticism of what they are doing. Unexpected attacks may follow such a presentation, no matter how good it is.

4. Include parents wherever possible. If they are informed, they will provide tremendous support. Parents have the power to establish or shut down a program. Make sure they know your goals and are involved in their implementation.

5. Include custodians in the planning. Custodians and office clerks can provide invaluable support. They have knowledge about systems and how to make them work that can never be learned from those "in charge."

6. Attend workshops, conferences, and university classes that present training in your areas of interest and in innovative approaches. Meet others, exchange phone numbers, and then call them when you need sympathetic, understanding discussions. Near the end of each class I teach, we discuss the problem of support. The students exchange addresses and phone numbers so that they know there are always knowledgeable, caring people out there, should they need them.

Examples of how others, in addition, to Jane, have successfully worked with the teachers in their schools should be helpful. Although the following examples are quite different and the schools diverse in population and geographic settings, the ideas may be helpful at your school.

Sagebrush Elementary School, Colorado

Sagebrush Elementary School is in a suburb of Denver, Colorado. The surrounding area is composed of a growing, largely middle-class community. The school principal and the teachers work together to create excellent educational experiences for all of their students, including gifted learners. For several years they have created in-service opportunities to develop their understanding of new data in teaching and learning and have incorporated them into their practices. They meet regularly as a faculty in working sessions and support each other in planning and implementing a school-wide program to meet their common goals. The teachers are organized into teams of four in cross-graded pods of students.

Planning among the team members provides another level of support for the educational program. The most helpful organizational idea has been establishing every teacher as an expert. Teachers use their interests and talents to become an acknowledged expert in an area. There are teachers who are experts in reading, math, language arts, music, gifted education, remedial education, and so on. It is not unusual for teachers or students to leave the pods to join other pods on a temporary basis, depending on where their talents can best be used or their needs can best be met. Because the planning is school wide and the teams have developed such flexibility within their pods, the needs of the gifted students can be met on a continuous basis within the structure. If outside experts are needed, they fit comfortably into the structure, and any teacher or student can use their expertise without disturbing the program.

It is far easier to gain the support of other teachers for programs that meet the needs of gifted learners when the teachers are knowledgeable about the children and how their needs should be met. Their support is more available when they all have expertise to contribute to such provisions, and when the educational structure of the school supports and allows them to value unique and individual intellectual development in themselves as well as the students.

Wailuku Elementary School, Hawaii

In an elementary school in Wailuku, Maui, Hawaii, a somewhat different structure allows all teachers throughout the school to support gifted learners. In a school-wide meeting, assessment data from all of the students in the school are reviewed. Students who seem to need advanced content or different methods of instruction in specific subjects are identified and assigned for instruction each week to a member of the faculty particularly skilled in the specific subject area. The teachers plan together when the students will be involved in special instruction so that the students will not miss appropriate instruction in their grade-level room and will not have to repeat or engage in inappropriate content. Teachers are given the opportunity to use their expertise in this program and jointly decide the schedule for teaching and learning. Again, it is much easier to establish a support system for gifted learners when their education is the concern of all of the teachers in the school.

Gaining the Support of Parents

Another important member of the education team is the parent. Parents can provide needed information about identification and the best ways to work with their child. They can volunteer to teach, drive on a field trip, or organize classroom tasks. They also can be strong advocates for the program within the school, the district, and the state. Parents can be the program's best supporters, but if they are not kept informed of the goals and practices of the program, they can also be its harshest critics and can even use their influence to shut it down.

Early in my educational career an oversight taught me a very valuable, although difficult, lesson. A teacher in a local elementary school and I were collaborating between his classroom and my course at the university to develop a curriculum and instructional structure for an experimental class for gifted learners. We were using many innovative and creative ideas to motivate the students and make their learning more effective. After only a few weeks, the gains the children were making were quite exciting.

Several months into the project we were informed by the principal at the school that we could no longer conduct the class in the open, flexible structure we were using but had to conform to the more traditional structure and methods. It seemed that a network of parents had been established by one of the student's mothers, who was concerned that her daughter was not really getting an appropriate education in the class we had developed. We were not conducting it as she thought classes should be conducted because her daughter no longer considered her experience at school difficult and unpleasant but was enjoying school, giving her mother the impression that she was only playing and being entertained. The mother called the state department of education and discovered that the educational code required a prescribed number of minutes of instruction in each subject; because we were using an interdisciplinary approach we were, in her mind, violating the law. To protect her daughter's education she contacted other parents with the "problem" and then, with their support, she demanded that the principal shut down the project.

We had made a mistake that my colleague and I would make sure was never repeated: We had not informed the parents before we began the project. They were not given any of the data on which we based our changes, nor were they informed of the goals and methods we planned to use. They had no way to participate in the classroom or to understand the education of their children. We had overlooked the power parents have in the schools and had not allowed them to become advocates for the new ideas we found so exciting. Instead their power was directed toward maintaining a structure and methods with which they were familiar and in which they believed.

Make Parents Part of the Planning

Over the years educators have developed ways to involve parents in educational projects and have observed how others have accomplished this important goal. In the 7-year project that resulted in the development of the Integrative Education Model discussed in Chapter 11, a meeting with the parents was held a week prior to the beginning of each year's summer project. At this meeting the philosophy, goals, and methods of the project were explained using the database from which such ideas were drawn. Examples of the structure and strategies to be used were demonstrated. The expectations of the faculty and the schedule and learning experiences planned for the students were discussed. A number of options for parent participation were explained, including development of learning centers in the classrooms in which parents could instruct the students in their area of expertise (a guide for developing a center was made available). Involvement in community contact committees that would arrange for learning expeditions beyond the classroom for the students, working with the faculty as aides on day or overnight learning expeditions, and participation as drivers, telephone tree members, or classroom newsletter editors and typists were other possible options. Parents were encouraged to ask questions, discuss concerns, and commit to any involvement in which they were willing to engage.

A month later, the parents were invited to individual conferences with the teachers in which they were given an update on their child's educational program and could discuss any additional concerns or request information. Weekly newsletters went home with highlights of the week's activities, and each unit (the school was cross-graded) reported individual happenings. A week prior to the end of the 6-week project a family picnic/open-house was held, and the students presented a program in their units and as a school to give the parents an opportunity to appreciate their talents and achievements. During the final week, a 3-day learning expedition was shared with the families and students. By that time the school had a strong advocacy base of informed parents, many of whom saw themselves as members of the school community who could carry the program forward in their local schools and in their own homes. By the end of the 7-year project, more than two-thirds of the students had attended at least four of the seven summers and many, with their siblings, had been a part of every summer program. The result was a close-knit family of students, parents, and teachers.

Schedule a Lunch Bunch

A colleague who teaches in a highly gifted magnet program has found that meeting with the students and their parents during the weeks before school—in a more personal setting than a group meeting can provide—has helped her to work more successfully with her students during the year. She schedules lunch with three of the students and their mothers, their fathers, and sometimes both, and by the end of 2 weeks she has seen and discussed the next year's activities with all of the class and their families. She is convinced that this use of her time is most valuable because she can get to know both the students and the parents, begin to form networks among the parents, handle any concerns, and solicit the help needed to implement a successful program. In small groups parents are far more likely to volunteer their involvement, raise their concerns, and understand the goals and methods to be used in the class.

The proof of the effectiveness of this approach was seen later at a meeting of the school board. Because of budget problems, the board was looking for ways to cut programs to save money, and one of the programs that was under discussion was the highly gifted magnet program. When the possibility of canceling this program was raised, a large group of parents stood and asked to speak. From personal knowledge they informed the board of the need for and the benefits of the program and encouraged the board to look elsewhere for a way to balance the budget. Their advocacy saved the program—not the administrative reports that showed the achievement and accomplishments of the program, but the enthusiasm and involvement of the parents. The current structure of back-to-school nights that occur weeks after the beginning of school—and are far less personal—are not enough to gain this level of knowledge, commitment, and support.

Include Parents on the Educational Team

One of the most effective ways of bringing parents into the educational community is to include them as part of a team, as was done at a 3-day conference on gifted programs sponsored through my university. The goal was to develop or improve the programs being offered to the gifted students in the participating districts. A small grant funded the conference planning, operation, transportation, housing, food, and materials for each participant. Thirty facilitators and group leaders as well as the major speakers donated their time and talent. Each district that elected to participate was required to send teams consisting of a teacher, an administrator, and a parent. It was hoped that such teams would represent the major power groups that could enhance or inhibit the development of gifted programming in the district. The outcome of the conference was to be a written 3-year plan and timelines for developing or improving the district's gifted program.

The conference was structured so that the entire group attended two or three major input sessions each day. The information given in these sessions concerned the understanding of intelligence and giftedness and their nurture; the characteristics and needs that high levels of intelligence create; new data on teaching and learning; alternative programs that successfully provided for the education of gifted learners; issues of evaluation; and advocacy. After each major session, participants met in small groups (approximately 12) with facilitators to accomplish assigned tasks, which had been planned by the organizing committee after a task analysis of the overall goal of the conference. These small groups were composed of representatives from each of the three power groups (teachers, administrators, and parents) from different districts. Meeting times were also built into the conference for teams from each district to come together, for job-alike groups to meet (all parents, all administrators, all teachers), and for individual contemplation. The speakers and group leaders were available for consultation during the entire conference.

At the end of the 3 days, the success of the teams was amazing. People were reluctant to leave the conference grounds, and many stayed to consult with others for hours after the conference had officially closed. After a year, the participants were contacted to ascertain their progress on their planned timelines and tasks, and more than 85% were still involved with the work they had planned at the conference. Later follow-ups showed long-term commitment, and as much as 3 years later the university was still receiving inquiry and results from this conference.

Gaining the Support of the Administration

As another member of the educational team, the administrator can be any of several people who make major decisions regarding the existence and funding of the program. Each person plays a different role, but the superintendent, the principal, and the coordinator are all critical to the functioning of the program. Also important are the members of the school board, although they are not involved in the actual conduct of the program. Each administration function is important, and support at each level is necessary if a quality program is to remain available to gifted learners. Gaining that support should be an important consideration for anyone planning to implement and maintain quality programs for gifted learners.

In this discussion, we will focus on the principal as the administrator most closely involved with the program, assuming that the coordinator has already expressed a commitment to the principles and goals of gifted education. It must be recognized that their role as administrators often requires principals to accomplish a different set of goals than those of other members of the educational team. Ultimately the educational goals are the same as those pursued by the teachers and the parents, but the tasks required to support those goals are different. Principals must assure the educational community of the resources needed to accomplish their goals and assure the board of education and the superintendent that their directives have been implemented. The principal must implement all federal and state provisions at the local level and give evidence of compliance with all legislative directions and mandates. In addition, most principals feel responsible for the educational climate of the school and for giving the faculty and parents opportunities to become informed about all instructional innovations available. The administrator is often called on to be the mediator, champion, facilitator, and guide for personal and interpersonal matters concerning the teachers, students, and parents and their relationships between and among each other. Balancing these responsibilities with their own educational agendas can be overwhelming and time consuming.

When viewed from this perspective, the approach made to gain the support of the administrator for provisions for gifted students clearly must take into consideration a broader set of concerns than just those that relate to the gifted program. Whatever is proposed must include consideration for the budget, the rules, and the regulations; the requests and requirements of the board of education and the superintendent; and the educational climate of the whole school.

One consideration must be to keep administrators informed in a way that is as sensitive to their time as possible. Many state and national organizations involved in the advocacy of gifted students publish one-page information sheets that could be distributed to the administrators, the school board, and the teachers from time to time to give them background information for decision-making. These organizations also produce monthly and quarterly reports and articles that update the reader on current concerns, methods, and research that could be abstracted and disseminated. A copy of all material that is sent home to inform the parents of the activities of the class and to provide them inservice on the needs of their child should be distributed to administrators to keep them updated regarding the program and give them information regarding gifted education.

If no gifted program exists at your school and you want to start one, you could prepare a packet of information to leave with the different levels of administrators. Starting with your principal, make an appointment and present the proposed program in detail at your meeting. Some of the areas you need to cover include:

- Who gifted learners are and why they need special programs.
- The program experiences you have had or would like to plan.
- What your program offers that is not already being provided.
- How it could be staffed, scheduled, and equipped.
- What it will cost and how it will be funded.
- How it will be evaluated.
- Ways the program will benefit the entire school and district.
- Ways the parents will be involved.
- The steps you plan to follow to plan the program (refer to the "Steps to a Program for Gifted Learners" in Chapter 7).

Finally, find out what the administrator needs from the program and answer any questions remaining.

Many of the activities that you wish to plan for your class may require the approval of the administration. Be sure to research the education code before requesting permission for activities that are not commonly carried out at your school. In your request, give evidence of your knowledge of the enabling legal provisions and submit the appropriate forms to minimize the work of the administrator to allow you to implement your plan. For example, a colleague who teaches in a high school near the university is a wilderness expert and finds learning expeditions off campus, often overnight, very valuable to the understanding of his area of science.

The district had no procedures for allowing students to leave campus, and the administrator was inclined to deny any request for this type of expedition, although he could see the value of the request. The teacher researched the state and district policies, compiled them in writing with all conditions stated, and devised procedures for district approval, insurance and legal compliance, parental participation and permissions, student responsibilities, and the instructional goals and methods. When faced with such careful preparation, the district administration decided to permit a trial expedition to be evaluated before any new policies were adopted. The procedure is now in place, and not only can this teacher use it for future learning expeditions, but all of the teachers in the district can now use the procedures as well.

When you want to start any program or service, be willing to take the time and energy to plan carefully. You may have to volunteer to get a new program started. Be sure that the new provisions are institutionalized as soon as possible, however. Gaining all the permissions and getting the procedures into policy for the school, the district, and the school board will enable the provisions you are making to continue even when you are no longer available to provide the leadership.

Another help to getting more services available to your students is to publicize what you do. Have students or parents make projects out of getting the students' activities into the local paper, or write articles for local, state, and national newsletters and journals with pictures of outstanding or unusual educational experiences. (With the need for pictures in mind, be sure to get photo release forms on file from each member of your class at the beginning of the school year.) Selling your program to the administration is easier if you can show the positive impact that it has.

COUNSELORS AND PSYCHOLOGISTS AS SUPPORT PERSONNEL

Including the school counselor or psychologist as part of the educational team allows the group to benefit from another point of view and service. The other members of the team can benefit from the expertise school counselors and psychologists have in planning and implementing identification procedures, finding solutions to academic and social-emotional concerns, and providing alternative strategies for optimal growth of gifted students.

As with teachers, attitudes of counselors toward gifted students improve when they are aware of the needs and problems common to this population. Unfortunately, school counselors and those who train them have been found to have little awareness of the special needs of gifted students (Ford & Harris, 1995). As a result, there exists a shortage of counseling personnel trained to work with gifted students and their families. Although reported as more favorable in schools with gifted programs, counselors and psychologists are more indifferent and even hostile toward gifted students than any other group of education professionals (Moon, Kelly, & Feldhusen, 1997). In their study to assess the types of counseling services parents, teachers, counselors, and related professionals perceived as important for gifted

Counselors can provide gifted students with tools for self-discovery.

youth and their families, the researchers concluded that a compelling need exists for family counseling with families with gifted children. Need for career interest assessment and educational planning to maximize the unique abilities of gifted students, including college and graduate school or professional training, was also expressed.

Unfortunately, most gifted students, especially those in secondary programs, perceive the counselor only as a program scheduler. Sometimes they experience the counselor as a tester or evaluator. Gifted learners too often are given a very limited view of this educational staff member who could provide them with valuable and, in some instances, critical services.

A number of years ago when he was in junior high, my own son had for several semesters complained about his dull, repetitive math class. I became aware that if something were not done, his interest in math, previously a true fascination, would be completely gone. I phoned the school counselor to arrange an appointment to discuss the problem. After identifying myself and the problem as I perceived it, I asked for consultation time. "I don't recall any problem we have had," said the counselor. "Let me pull his file." After a pause, he returned to the phone to assure me that there was no problem and an appointment would not be necessary.

I repeated my perception of the problem, assuring him that I realized that my son was not a behavior problem, but that I felt he did need help. I suggested that I would agree to let my son attend math classes at the nearby high school if that was considered feasible, but in any case, I would like an opportunity to explore the issue. "Well, we don't use acceleration. Our policy is against it except in rare cases. We have lots of students here as smart as your son. I don't see any purpose in a conference. He is not a problem, is doing excellent work, and his file shows that he is well-adjusted. I'll call you if we see any problem in the future." End of conversation. I was not at all assertive at that point in my life and was unsure of the value of pursuing the matter further. My son did drop his math interest and, although he might have done so in any case, I will always wonder. My work over the years that followed has convinced me that gifted children who are not "problems" very often get little, if any, help from school counselors. But when a counselor or guidance staff member becomes involved in the program for gifted learners, the results and benefits are very exciting, not only to the gifted students but to their teachers and parents as well.

A counselor can provide students with preventive and informational consultation, crisis intervention, and ongoing process or self-discovery counseling. Rather than wait for a problem to occur, the counselor should inform gifted students of such things as graduation needs, career counseling, and alternative choices for future planning. Important issues might include which college or university would be best suited to a student's interests and talents, and even whether to go on to college immediately or work or travel for a year first. The counselor has access to resources that are not known to the student, the teacher, or the parents.

In support for the need gifted students have for counseling services, Ford (1989) reports the views of fifth- and sixth-grade gifted students on a variety of social and emotional issues of significance to them and the impact such perceived problems have on their achievement.

> Throughout the interviews, these youngsters articulated many interpersonal, intrapersonal, social and emotional difficulties that were related to their exceptional abilities or to their placement in special programs. It appears that these children are confused by their abilities, bored with school, burdened with the quantity of work, and distressed by the expectations of their parents and teachers. These youngsters often feel misunderstood, and they are hurt that classmates tease them for being smart. Most of these children set very high standards for themselves and suffer the guilt of failure for anything short of top performance. Yet, they spend countless hours engaged in meaningless tasks that foster intellectual laziness. As a result, they know they have never really done their best.
>
> These youngsters have strong needs to stand out, and yet they yearn to be unnoticed. They experience great responsibilities and suffer the burdens of many things beyond their control. They often feel alien in their classrooms as they get caught up in issues and causes that other students do not see. (p. 134)

From her interviews, Ford concludes that teachers and parents should have workshops that address the social-emotional needs of these children. Teachers must have more information on techniques and curricula that are appropriate for gifted learners. The youngsters need programs in psychological education to better understand themselves, facilitate their leadership roles, and resolve problems they confront in the social and emotional domains. Gifted students have many problems to which they could find their own solutions if given a little help from an effective counselor.

Colangelo (1991) advocates a counseling approach in which the counselors do some therapy and are on call but spend most of their time and energy on establishing a school environment that is conducive to the educational growth of gifted students. He believes that knowledge of the affective and cognitive needs of gifted learners is essential to a counselor who works with gifted students and their parents because the needs of this population are unique and cause differences among these students that must be recognized and honored. As a guide to issues in counseling the gifted learner, Colangelo along with others before him (Gowan & Demos, 1964; Newland, 1976) remind us of the students' need to:

- Discuss what is happening to them in their classroom, in their program, and in their personal lives.
- Find ways to communicate effectively with their teachers and parents.
- Discuss questions of identity, roles, relationships, and self-concept.
- Discover their special abilities and vocational choices, selecting from an over-whelming number of interests and abilities.
- Develop study habits and overcome underachievement patterns.
- Develop effective self-expression and communication.
- Develop personal standards of conduct.
- Discuss frustration over discrepancy between ideals or intellectual conception of performance and physical ability to realize a performance level that is high enough to meet their expectations.

Immediacy of contact is the major element of crisis intervention counseling that must be available. Many students complain that, when they want to get help from a school counselor, the procedure is so cumbersome and time-consuming that they seldom persevere. However, the present situation in many schools must be looked at carefully to make some decisions regarding priorities of services. If gifted students benefit so much from crisis intervention counseling, then they must be able to get it.

Counselors should provide a third service for gifted students—process, or personal growth, consultation. Some programs use small counseling groups that meet weekly for support and discussion of personal problems. The adult counselor facilitates but also encourages students to give their ideas. Group members assist in clarifying problems and presenting solutions. Even if they cannot agree on a solution, having the opportunity to discuss the problem with sympathetic listeners often helps alleviate the crisis, allowing the student to try alternative ideas for coping. Such a group can serve as a peer counselor training experience at the same time. A group session is often more beneficial to the student than an individual session.

In addition to solving problems, a growth group structured as a learning experience can provide a safe place for gifted students to explore areas of communication, self-concept, assertion, and other strategies to facilitate personal and interpersonal growth. Gifted students will be able to interact with other students who have many of the same problems and are more of a peer group than students found at their grade level. Teachers trained and experienced in guidance procedures may provide these functions. Whether through a counselor or a teacher, this type of guidance must be available to the gifted throughout their academic careers.

The Counseling and Personnel Services Clearinghouse (1982) suggests that although every gifted student differs, the following problems and issues are often unique to the gifted population:

- Positive self-concept may be difficult to maintain because of excessive self-criticism and sensitivity to criticism from others. Gifted students may experience a split self-concept because of the conflict between superior ability and the need to be "one of the gang."

- Great frustration may occur in gifted students with subjects or situations they cannot handle. They are unaccustomed to this experience and think they should know all the answers. As a result, they may not know how to ask for help when they need it.

- Greater sensitivity and perceptiveness may result in acute negative responses to lack of genuineness, warmth, and understanding, or to an uncomfortable situation.

- Values and attitudes are likely to be divergent, different from the "norm." This can make it difficult for them to find true peers. It can also complicate career/vocational choices and pursuits.

- Gifted students are not necessarily aware of their own abilities. They may not have had the opportunity to do truly outstanding work because they have not been fully challenged in the classroom. Both academic and career/vocational decisions can be seriously misguided.

- Gifted students may have intense single interests and fail to apply themselves in other areas of school and social life. They may have poor and inefficient study habits.

- Gifted girls often face socialization conflicts and lack good role models. Personal and social problems can result, as well as underachievement in school and career/vocation.

- Gifted cultural and racial minorities may lack family support, appropriate role models, and social/economic access to particular careers or vocations.

- The wider interests and multiple superior abilities of gifted students often require a broader range of career areas for exploration and selection. (p. 2)

Davis and Rimm (1994) find that the problems most frequently requiring counseling with gifted learners are: (1) social relationships, especially conformity pressure, acceptance, and isolation; (2) personal adjustment, such as acceptance of criticism, resistance to authority, excessive competitiveness, uneven development, and poor social skills; (3) academic concerns, such as lack of challenges, repetitious assignments, and poor study habits; and (4) life skills, including career choice among diverse interests and multipotentiality and the establishment of a philosophy of life.

Interactions Among Counselors and Other Educational Team Members

For the teacher of the gifted learner, the counselor may provide help in identification and with assessment profiles. A helpful consulting service would make suggestions for placement and how to meet needs best. A counselor could train teachers to use strategies and procedures they might otherwise not know. Teachers often encounter problems that require professional guidance; they should be able to seek the help of their colleagues.

For the parents of gifted learners, the counselor can provide information, understanding, and guidance. In crisis situations, a counselor can set up one of the most effective approaches ever developed for finding solutions to family problems, the family therapy group. So many student problems can be solved only when all the family members are aware of their responsibility for the problem and the need the student has for their support. Family therapy groups have been extremely productive.

Buescher (1987) offers a curriculum model that can be used to proactively counsel and support the growth of young gifted adolescents. He suggests that use of such a specialized curriculum reflects several important principles that both the counselors and teachers must hold: (1) Effective guidance and counseling occur at a proactive, preventative stage rather than a reactive, intervention stage; (2) the expectations of others—teachers, parents, and peers—coupled with extraordinary self-expectations, can immobilize gifted adolescents; and (3) the multipotentialities and intensity of a gifted adolescent can provide keen insight into the dynamics of adjustment the student is using. Buescher provides three stages of support in the model: perceiving, ideating, and presenting. Although he feels the perception of new information is a step often emphasized in the learning process, he believes that research shows the other steps must follow if a concept is to be gained or a behavior affected and changed. The counseling curriculum can be implemented in several ways: within a course in personal growth and adjustment or literature and writing, or as the content focus for a monthly series of special topical seminars. The model is also suggested for training teachers, counselors, and parents of gifted adolescents.

Among the resources available on guiding gifted students is a book originating from the professional psychological community (Webb, MeckStroth, & Tolan, 1982). The larger community of parents has also become more aware of these needs through an organization founded by James Webb (at the time a Wright State University psychological services professor) known as Supporting the Emotional Needs of the Gifted (SENG). Through SENG, conferences and a national network support parents, gifted students, and educators seeking to understand these demanding emotional needs. Other sources of support are the Counseling and Guidance Division of the National Association for the Gifted, and the research and writing of Linda Silverman, Barbara Kerr, Sylvia Rimm, Gary Davis, and their colleagues.

GAINING THE SUPPORT OF THE COMMUNITY

A Gallup public opinion survey (Larsen & Griffin, 1992) showed that the vast majority of the public is very supportive of education for gifted children. When asked if they would support special funding for a program to provide a more challenging education for the smartest and most gifted children, 84% of the general public and 90% of parents of school-age children responded that they would support funding. Only 15% of the general public and 9% of the parents of school-age children said that they would oppose it. It is good to know that this support is available if you have to confront colleagues who are not supportive of your concerns for gifted learners, an administration that gives low priority to such concerns, school boards and legislators that must be lobbied to provide funding for gifted programs, or a state department of education that gives little leadership to the education of these students.

There are many ways in which a supportive public can help you to provide appropriate educational experiences for your students. A colleague who teaches in a highly gifted second- through fourth-grade magnet uses her community very much like an extended classroom. During a unit on economics, she arranges for the local bank, which is within walking distance, to give the students a tour. The bank also provides simulated credit cards, bank cards, checks, and all of the materials used in banking so that the students can set up their own bank in the classroom. This is a very sophisticated simulation that includes student involvement in merchandise retailing, stock purchasing, researching daily interest for loans and saving accounts, and computing sales tax for state collection. Other local businesses she involves in the unit include restaurants, retail shops, and grocery stores.

Local professionals can also be invited to host students interested in their work in their work places or conduct a seminar for interested students in the classroom. Local hospitals, emergency units, and other service organizations can provide resources and personnel to support the understanding of complex issues and functions. For example, during a study unit of anatomy, self, or any inquiry into human function, surgeons in nearby hospitals are often willing to bring a human brain into the classroom for study.

The community can provide a wealth of resources for research studies, such as answering surveys, contributing to oral history projects, or providing depth to social studies and current events by personal interviews or lectures. Once they become involved, the community's understanding of the needs of gifted students is greatly increased. Interaction with bright minds is the best advocacy effort that can be made in a community. Another advantage for the students that alone would justify the time and effort required to set up such community involvement is the understanding and sense of commitment the students develop about involvement in the solutions of the problems of society. Although walking field trips are not new, they continue to be used very rarely and seldom at the level of complexity and integration of the curriculum from which gifted students could best profit.

By including teachers, parents, administrators, and the community in a support system, a wide variety of services can be planned and implemented for gifted students. Representatives from each group need to be a part of the school planning committee that provides site-based management for the school. This group should develop a philosophy for the school to which all members can subscribe and support. As you move to fulfill your goals, look at the summary of some of the ways that have worked for others to develop their support system in each important constituent group.

To Gain the Support of Other Teachers

- Provide in-service to all of the teachers in the school on the concept of intelligence, the nature and needs of gifted learners, the most current data on teaching and learning, and an array of structures and strategies that could be used to meet gifted needs.

- Include all of the teachers in the school in the planning for provisions to be made for gifted learners.
- Recognize each member of the faculty as an expert in an area or discipline.
- Include teams of teachers, administrators, and parents in the planning of the overall program that will be provided to gifted students.

To Gain Parental Support

- Provide inservice for parents on the concept of intelligence, the nature and needs of gifted learners, the most current data on teaching and learning, and an array of structures and strategies that could be used to meet gifted needs through your school, district, or local university.
- Hold frequent formal and informal meetings with large and small groups of parents to include them in the education of their children.
- Keep parents informed of the activities and achievements of the students through the use of newsletters, conferences, and classroom visits.
- Invite parents to share their expertise with the class in ways that are satisfying and productive.
- Prepare parents for opportunities when they can provide advocacy for the education of their child.

To Gain Administrative Support

- Provide information to the administrators on the concept of intelligence and the nature and needs of gifted learners.
- Share with administrators the most current data on teaching and learning, and an array of structures and strategies that could be used to meet gifted needs through the use of one-page information sheets and abstracts of current research and reports from gifted education journals.
- Provide copies of all materials sent to parents to update the administrator on the activities and achievements of the gifted program.
- Prepare well-researched and well-documented plans for any requests made to provide services that may be unusual or new to the district or the school.
- Institutionalize any new procedures that you find successful so that others in the district and school can benefit from your efforts.
- Show clearly in all evaluation and planning reports how the provisions being made for the gifted learners are benefiting the school and the district as well as meeting the needs of the gifted learners.

To Gain Community Support

- Arrange to have community businesses, professional offices, retail stores, and service providers become an extension of your classroom.

- Invite the professional and lay community to become integral contributors to the learning by providing resources and personnel at appropriate times to add understanding, complexity, and depth to the curriculum.
- Involve the community in advocacy efforts on behalf of the gifted students.

The teacher is the most significant influence on the learning environment at school. In this chapter, general differences between effective and ineffective teachers have been identified. In addition, the abilities every teacher of gifted learners should develop have been reviewed. To develop them, both pre-service and in-service teacher education must be provided.

For classroom teachers to become more effective, especially in situations requiring change and innovation, they will need to establish a support system. To aid in such development, this chapter suggested gaining the support of the faculty, the parents, the administration, and the community. Counselors can provide special kinds of support to gifted students that are often overlooked or underused. Equipping these groups to be advocates for gifted students and including them in the planning and delivery creates strength, continuity, and longevity for the gifted program.

Teachers at home (parents) can be among the most important sources of support and enrichment for the gifted program. They must be encouraged to organize, become informed, and collaborate with the school personnel to provide the best possible education for their children.

QUESTIONS OFTEN ASKED

1. What can you do if your principal doesn't believe in "gifted education"?

Many different ideas have been tried. One teacher sent her principal short articles on a regular basis that showed the advantages of gifted programs to the students and to the school. She then requested a conference with the principal to present her plan for an adjunct program that would benefit the students. From that beginning, she showed how such programs were important to the school and gradually got more adequate programming into the regular schedule. Sometimes parent requests will make a difference. Sometimes it is necessary to work directly with the school board members who share your interests; sometimes it takes legislative mandates. One teacher I knew did all he could, then took administrative courses while trying to make the changes that he could, and finally became a principal of his own school where he developed a strong gifted program. Another teacher

I know asked for a transfer to a school that was more supportive of her interests.

2. If a number of the faculty want to engage in a more shared decision-making model but the principal does not, can anything be done?

You might try collectively discussing the idea with the principal in a cooperative mode, sharing all the advantages of the new model. If you have a plan of how it might happen and its advantages to the school, parents, and students and to the goals for which the principal is most responsible, you could be successful. Most people who hold to the hierarchical model do so because it is the only one they understand and the only one with which they feel comfortable, or they fear they will not get the results they must have with the new model. You should show the principal the advantages and a plan for a clear transition.

3. What if the principal wants to use a participatory management style, but the teachers are unwilling to become involved?

Again, it will be necessary to be sure the teachers understand the advantages to the school, to the students, and especially to themselves and their success as teachers. If the teachers are satisfied with what they are doing, it is hard for them to understand why they should change. They must be shown the benefits of change. Also, there must be a plan that makes the change easy and productive. The teachers must feel supported as the change occurs. It has been my experience that once most teachers have experienced shared decision-making, they do not want to go back to being told what to do in the parental structure of the hierarchical model.

4. Our counselors have a full caseload for scheduling and placement. How can our gifted students get any personal counseling services?

Counseling issues can be built into the curriculum, or special seminars can be developed on a regular weekly basis. Counselors can be invited to group sessions to teach their skills to teachers, parents, or students or to present special topic sessions within the classes. Peer counselors can be trained and scheduled for groups. Because personal counseling is an important goal, creative ways must be found to meet it.

5. If parents want to help but no one from the school asks them, what can they do?

Decide what services you would be willing to provide and then offer your services. Often the need is there but no one has the time to organize to get help. It would be of great service if under the teacher's direction you could organize a group of parents to provide support services.

CHECKING FOR UNDERSTANDING
Follow-Up Activity

Give the assessment instrument (Figure 6.1) to colleagues, teachers, parents, or any group of others in the community and discuss the results with other members of your class. Analyze the results and consider what you might do as an advocacy activity for gifted learners in your community.

SUMMARY

Programs for Gifted Learners Yesterday and Today

1. Organizing a program that will deliver educational services to gifted learners is one of the most complex, most researched, and least clarified areas of gifted education.
2. The provision a state makes in the areas of mandates, funding, and administrative leadership has a direct correlation to the level of services provided to gifted students, with the most critical area being mandates for appropriate services.

Teachers of the Gifted: At School

3. Research shows that those who wish to provide optimal learning situations for gifted students need to be concerned about the characteristics, values, self-concepts, and training of the teachers who implement gifted programs.
4. Attitudes of teachers, counselors, and administrators change favorably toward the gifted when they have participated in some gifted education.
5. Effective teachers of gifted learners demand high-quality work, use their sense of humor

to demonstrate to their students that they care for and respect them, and stress the students' personal involvement in learning and do so in creative ways. They conduct stimulating discussions using probing questions requiring deeper thought and ask students to think for themselves.

Teacher Education and Certification

6. Those who teach teachers must themselves possess the attributes, knowledge, and skills essential for optimizing learning and developing individual potential.
7. Professional development in gifted education is limited, some of the most effective practices such as collegial coaching are rarely used, and very few districts provide differentiated experiences for their teachers.
8. Standards-based programs have several advantages: the standards approach is systematic, standards set clear expectation for student achievement, and the process is designed by and communicated to those in the particular setting.

The Importance of Support for Effective Programs

9. When an effective gifted program is found at a school site, the climate and curriculum of the entire school is enhanced.
10. Provisions for meeting the educational needs of gifted students are difficult to establish and impossible to maintain without strong and committed support of the teaching faculty, the administration, the parents, and the larger community.

Counselors and Psychologists as Support Personnel

11. As with teachers, attitudes of counselors toward gifted students improve when they are aware of the needs and problems common to this population.
12. A counselor can provide students with preventive and informational consultation, crisis intervention, and ongoing process or self-discovery counseling.
13. For the teacher of the gifted learner, the counselor may provide help in identification and with assessment profiles. For the parents of gifted learners, the counselor can provide information, understanding, and guidance.

Gaining the Support of the Community

14. The community can provide a wealth of resources and personnel to support the understanding of complex issues and functions, such as answering surveys; contributing to oral history projects; providing depth to science, social studies, and current events; mentoring; or conducting seminars for interested students in the classroom or in the workplace.
15. Teachers, parents, other school personnel and the community are the most important sources of support and enrichment for the gifted program. They must be encouraged to organize, become informed, and collaborate with each other to provide the best possible education for their children.

Providing a Continuum of Services for Gifted Learners

In this chapter the reader will discover information on:

- Developing a program for gifted learners, including the role of the coordinator.

- Planning and writing a program for gifted learners.

- Choosing among organizational modifications and structures for elementary school, middle school, and high school; their adventages and disadvantages.

The relatively few gifted students who have had the advantage of special programs have shown remarkable improvements in self-understanding and in ability to relate well to others, as well as in improved academic and creative performance. The programs have not produced arrogant, selfish snobs; special programs have extended a sense of reality, wholesome humility, self-respect and respect for others. A good program for the gifted increases their involvement and interest in learning through the reduction of the irrelevant and redundant.

—SIDNEY P. MARLAND, JR.

Linda sat quietly, impressed with the panel that had been assembled to hear the testimony regarding a new federal law that was being written to support gifted education. It was exciting to be a part of this panel, her first, as a professional in the field. She was now a member of the faculty of the local university and had been asked to listen with the rest; then together they would make recommendations to the Commissioner on Education to be read into the Congressional Report and perhaps persuade Congress to pass this important legislation.

All morning they had been hearing testimony from parents, teachers, school board members, school administrators, and other community leaders interested in gifted learners and how to educate them. There were many ideas; however, most of the speakers they had heard seemed to be primarily concerned with the financial arrangements in the bill before Congress. There was disagreement about how the money should be allocated, who should control it, and the best way to spend it. There was disagreement about the service that should be provided for gifted learners. Some speakers were against having special provisions for gifted students in any form and felt that the money was better spent supporting other groups of children that had different needs.

Linda began to wonder how the panel was going to develop a compelling case for these children with so many different ideas being given. There were so many experts with so many conflicting opinions, so little money, and so many needs.

Just then the next speaker came to the microphone. He was so small that someone had to lower the microphone so that he could reach it. He was about 8 or 9 years old, dressed in a suit and tie, and his hair had been slicked back with something to make it lie down. It was obvious that he was having to concentrate very hard to stand still. As the young man began to speak, he tried to give his reasons why gifted programs were important. He started several times only to stop and start again with a somewhat different approach. He was very nervous and wanted very much to impress the panel with the importance of his concern. Suddenly, in mid-sentence, he stopped. He stood very quietly and thoughtfully looked at each of the panel members. As he started again he had everyone's attention.

"Well, you see, the thing is, I just do not flourish in a regular classroom," he stated passionately. Again he looked steadily at each person and then turned and left the microphone. As he started to leave the room he turned back and almost as an afterthought he said, "Do you suppose you could do something about that? Please?"

Linda knew she had just found her compelling case.

DEVELOPING PROGRAMS FOR GIFTED LEARNERS

The primary purpose of the gifted program is to provide opportunities for gifted learners to meet the needs that cannot be met in a regular classroom program. These provisions will help gifted students to grow as integrated people toward their full potential. What is done specifically for each child will depend on assessment data and the continuum of services available. Programs for the gifted do not begin with different curricula or different structures for learning, but with the distinct needs of gifted learners taken into consideration. The gifted program is different only because, and in the same way that, the needs of gifted learners are different.

The level of educational achievement found in any traditional, chronologically age-grouped class can span from 4 to 8 years. The range broadens as children progress from kindergarten to sixth grade. Because the span of achievement can be so vast, most teachers plan the instructional program for the average, at-grade-level learners. Some modification is made for the bottom group and for the top group, but most instruction falls within the normal range. For very slow learners, remedial programs, often mandated by the state and well-financed, are available in most schools. Special educational modifications are provided for the learners in the bottom 2% of the intelligence scale, because the needs of those students for a different learning program are obvious. These provisions are accepted and expected by both parents and educators. For the students with learning problems, part-time resource rooms are available, as well as special tutors or special classrooms where these students participate in appropriate educational programs until they are able to keep pace with the average learner. The time spent in the special educational facility depends on the level of need the student exhibits. The regular classroom is expected to provide for only part of the program this atypical learner needs.

On the other end of the scale, the school's organization may be quite different. The learners in the upper 2% of the intelligence scale need as much special instruction to continue their growth as do students at the lower end. Yet seldom are special classes provided or resource personnel made available. All students must adjust to the average classroom program, but the gifted students lose most (Figure 7.1) because they constantly must restrain their efforts to work within the parameters of the highest level of instruction provided. This situation leads to loss of ability, especially among girls and minority students, as regression toward a more average ability level is the observed outcome. This loss can be prevented by structures that provide opportunities for learning that are appropriate for each child. Such structures must become more available to gifted learners.

Figure 7.1 *Range of Traditional Classroom Instruction*

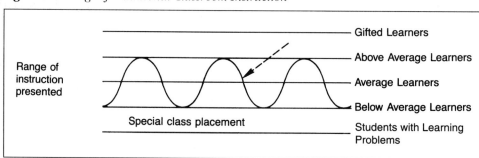

Programming by Level of Involvement

Adopting the programming model used by atypical learners in the same way at the upper end of the intelligence scale, as is done at the lower end, would be a reasonable way to provide programs for gifted learners. There are at least three types of gifted learners—the mildly or moderately gifted, the highly gifted, and the exceptionally or profoundly gifted—that would parallel the categories used for the three levels of learners with disabilities. The educational modifications could then be provided based on how much need the student has for a differentiated program, with the focus on the atypical needs of the gifted learners, not on their IQ scores.

Mildly and moderately gifted students could be clustered in groups of at least five in a regular classroom *if* the teacher is skilled in assessing, differentiating curriculum, working with flexible grouping, and individualizing instruction. A resource room for the gifted learners and a resource teacher to supplement the experiences provided by the regular classroom would add strength to this type of program. Mentorships and, at middle and secondary levels, advanced core-subject placement might provide additional program options.

Highly and exceptionally gifted students are found far less often, but because of their more demanding needs, they require opportunities for more accelerated pacing, more advanced materials, and a higher level of complexity and depth in their work. These needed modifications are most effectively offered by special classes, such as resource or advanced placement classes, or special schools, such as magnet schools or governor's schools. In middle school and high school, academic subjects could be provided in special classes or an academically advanced core, with heterogeneously grouped elective classes added. A few gifted learners are so exceptional that many educators have suggested that schools as they are now organized have little to offer them. Radical acceleration and private tutoring can provide other appropriate programming options in addition to special schools for such students. For some families, homeschooling is a feasible and meaningful alternative.

In Figure 7.2, the concept of the levels of involvement of giftedness is shown as a tower of blocks, with the types of program structures that would be most effective for each level. The programs build on each other, and as the students climb, the demands of higher intelligence create the necessity for more specialized programs.

It is important to note that all programs for gifted learners, regardless of how they are structured, must provide differentiation, flexible grouping, continuous progress, intellectual peer interaction, continuity, and teachers with specialized education for this population if optimal learning is to occur.

Although no single structure can appropriately provide for all atypical learners, there is clearly a parallel need that gifted learners have, just as those with other exceptionalities have, for modifications of educational programs and structures that will allow them to optimize their potential.

Programming in a Full-Inclusion Classroom

Acknowledging the need for program modification is especially necessary if gifted learners are to have any opportunity for appropriate educational experiences in a

Figure 7.2 *Structuring Gifted Programs: Alternatives for Elementary, Middle, and High Schools*

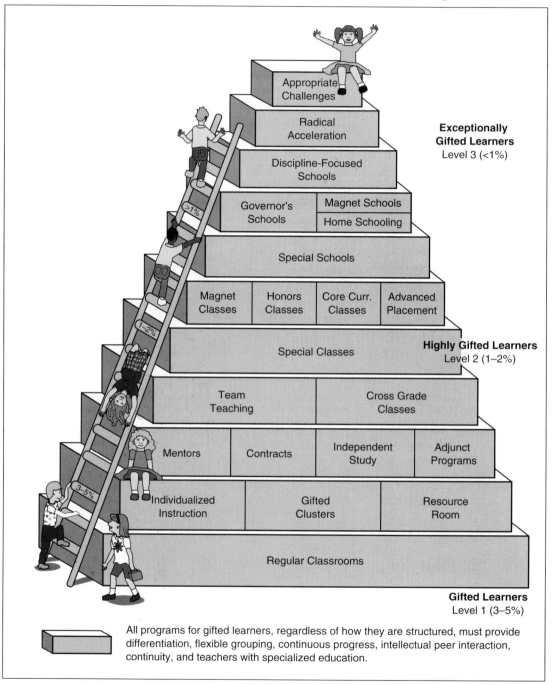

All programs for gifted learners, regardless of how they are structured, must provide differentiation, flexible grouping, continuous progress, intellectual peer interaction, continuity, and teachers with specialized education.

classroom that is inclusive of children of all exceptionalities on a full-time basis. "Inclusionary practices for gifted students and upgraded curriculum for all students have actually caused a decline in the rigor of academic options for able learners" (Delisle, 1999). Delisle notes that practices in gifted education, such as critical thinking strategies, problem-solving opportunities, and self-selection of products, have much to offer to all students, but no program can provide the necessary support for the gifted learner unless there is differentiation, flexible grouping, continuous progress, intellectual peer interaction, continuity, and a teacher that is knowledgeable about meeting the needs of gifted learners. Teachers in full-inclusion classrooms may seek a solution by combining several program options that allow gifted students to have choices of high-end learning in a variety of settings, including:

- Team teaching, with one member of the team knowledgeable regarding gifted needs and planning for appropriate modifications of the regular program.
- Regularly scheduled meetings of the gifted learners to provide support in meeting needs for challenge academically, interaction socially, and a forum for emotional exploration and growth.
- Partial program placement opportunities in higher grade levels during subjects in which the gifted learner is accelerated.
- Community-based or service projects that can be accomplished on an independent or mentored basis.

As long as the administrative philosophy contends that every teacher can and should be responsible for the learning of every student and has all the knowledge and skills necessary to provide for each child's appropriate educational experiences, and as long as equity is interpreted to mean that students of all levels of ability and need must learn together the same material, in the same way, at the same time, very bright students are at risk. Although students at the lower end of the learning curve may have specialists available to support the teacher in meeting their needs, this is less likely to be true for the gifted learners. In these settings, it becomes critical that those who plan programs are aware of the findings from brain research that admonish educators to challenge a learner at the point of growth, because if ability is not used, it can be lost. Inclusion when and where appropriate for all children to meet their academic, social-emotional, and personal learning needs can bring a broader level of understanding to society. However, any such planning must be focused on the learning needs and growth of the child.

Planning a Program for Gifted Learners

The planning necessary to develop a gifted program that will provide the best match for the needs of the students, parents' expectations, the school administration's philosophy, community resources, and the talents and commitment of the school staff is like orchestrating a symphony. There are areas of knowledge to build and skills to perfect; there are personnel and materials to collect, beliefs and abilities to assess, and cooperation to solicit. To put it all together, the timing is crucial.

The Program Coordinator

To ensure that the program for the district's gifted students has an organization plan to coordinate and deliver the agreed upon services, someone must be designated to coordinate it. Some districts give the responsibility to the school principal, others to the special education director. Some add it to the responsibilities of the school counselor, and some hire a part-time teacher for the assignment. In all of these cases, the most well-meaning people may find it difficult to succeed.

Adding such a program to an already overloaded administrator or counselor merely admits its low priority in the district and suggests that both the organizer and the program will have inadequate support for the job. The teacher will find the part-time status detrimental to any relationship with full-time personnel, with parents, and with the students. There is not enough time to develop the personal contacts, the assessment materials, and the type of continuity in the program that is necessary. In many cases, teachers in this position find themselves working full-time for part-time pay. Although such a situation is not uncommon in education, it should not be encouraged. Planning a program based on this type of professional commitment is unfair and can lead to an inadequate program that may be wasteful of the resources expended.

According to Coleman, Gallagher, and Foster (1994), 47 states have a person at the state level who is designated as a consultant or coordinator of education for gifted students. They may be housed within special education, curriculum and instruction, or other areas of the state system. It has been found that in states in which the total time of at least one person is devoted to gifted education, far more students have been adequately served. What is true for state levels can be said also for local levels. Whatever monies are allotted to educating the gifted students in a district, a part would be best spent on a full-time person. If the district is small, it can cooperate with other surrounding districts to establish a full-time position of coordinator of gifted programs.

Some people, especially parents and school boards, may say that the money should not be spent on administering the program; it should be spent on the students. Ultimately, the gifted students will gain more in educational services with a full-time coordinator. When monies are "given to the kids," they are usually spent on materials or experiences that may or may not fit into a planned program. Sometimes undirected money ends up buying library books, reading kits, laboratory equipment, or computers. None of these does any harm, but questions must be asked: Do any of these materials bring the gifted students closer to meeting their needs? How do these materials or experiences provide a continuing, comprehensive program? Who decides which materials or experiences are appropriate? Again, a full-time coordinator seems the best buy.

The district coordinator of gifted programs would do the following:

- Plan the overall structure of the district's gifted program in consultation with the Gifted Advisory Council and its teachers, administrators, and parents.
- Take care of all administrative paperwork inherent in the district program, such as writing proposals for funding, evaluating data, and so forth.
- Interview and recommend teachers for the program for either integrated classes or special classes.

- Conduct teacher in-service in gifted education for identification and implementation of programs and contact professionals with expertise in gifted education for special in-service opportunities.
- Arrange meetings of teachers responsible for the education of the gifted in the district.
- Conduct parent meetings for in-service in gifted education and encourage their active participation in the district program.
- Establish case studies on all students who have been screened for gifted identification.
- Conduct assessments of all students identified as gifted and establish profiles.
- Chair the selection committee for identification of students for the gifted program.
- Organize a mentor program as a part of the opportunities available to the gifted students in the district.
- Arrange for field trips that are needed for the gifted program.
- Contact local colleges, universities, and museums for educational experiences available to gifted students who are advanced in areas not taught within the local school.
- Provide support and resources for teachers with gifted students in their classrooms.
- Teach special classes for gifted students in small districts or occasionally in large districts.
- Evaluate the district program and individual school programs to improve services to gifted students by obtaining data from teachers, students, and parents.
- Provide a liaison between parents and the school; regular teachers and special teachers; and among the administration, the program personnel, and the community at large. Communicate regularly with the school board.
- Serve on administrative committees with general education responsibilities to provide advocacy for gifted learners (such as the textbook selection committee).
- Attend professional workshops and meetings to stay informed about current ideas and practices in gifted education.

It is obvious that anything less than a full-time position for the coordinator would restrict the program. Many opportunities appropriate for gifted students throughout the community cost very little but require someone to ferret them out and make them available.

The selection of an effective coordinator can ensure a successful program for the gifted. It would be wise to choose a person with teaching or counseling experience who is open, is excited about learning, enjoys gifted individuals, and has a very positive view of life. Additional training in gifted education would greatly benefit the position. An experienced educator from the same district would provide a lot of support for the program, although certainly that criterion is not as important as the person's attitudes and background. Having a full-time coordinator for delivery of services in educating gifted students provides many advantages and the potential contributions to the entire district's educational system are endless.

Standards for a Program for Gifted Learners

One of the first steps in planning for a gifted program is the development of the district's program standards. Standards for gifted programs provide a useful guide for developing programs for gifted learners, an incentive for program improvement, and criteria for program evaluation. Standards can be written to reflect the national, state, district, and school programs. At each level they can be made more specific to reflect the philosophy and goals specific to that level. Standards usually are written delineating levels of performance with at least minimal and exemplary standards given.

In 1998, the NAGC adopted a set of Pre-K through Grade 12 Gifted Program Standards with the following organizing principles:

- Standards should encourage but not dictate approaches of high quality.
- Standards represent both requisite program outcomes and standards for excellence.
- Standards establish the level of performance to which all educational school districts and agencies should aspire.
- Standards represent professional consensus on critical practice in gifted education that most everyone is likely to find acceptable.
- Standards are observable aspects of educational programming and are directly connected to the continuous growth and development of gifted learners. (Landrum & Shaklee, 1998)

In this document, the minimum standards delineate the required conditions for acceptable gifted education programming practice and their exemplary standards extend the conditions to include desirable and visionary practices promoting excellence in gifted education programming. The entire document can be obtained from the Office of the National Association for Gifted Children, 1707 L St NW, Ste 550, Washington, DC 20036.

Several states have developed such gifted program standards for their programs and many other states have their standards in progress.

Renzulli (1975) identified seven key features that experts in the field of gifted education agreed were basic to a successful program:

1. The selection and training of teachers.
2. A curriculum that is both systematic and comprehensive.
3. Multiple appropriate screening and identification procedures.
4. A statement of philosophy and objectives that support differential education for the gifted.
5. Staff orientation to promote a knowledgeable and cooperative attitude.
6. A plan of evaluation.
7. A delineation of administrative responsibility.

With these elements in mind, the following 10 basic steps should be helpful in planning a program for gifted learners (Figure 7.3):

Figure 7.3 *Steps to a Program for Gifted Learners*

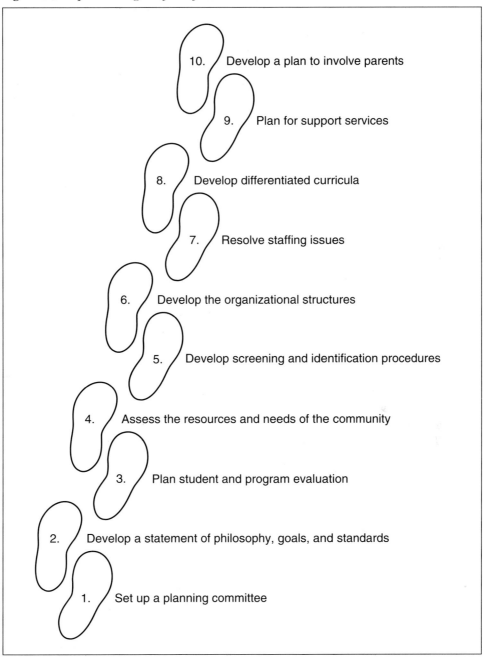

10. Develop a plan to involve parents

9. Plan for support services

8. Develop differentiated curricula

7. Resolve staffing issues

6. Develop the organizational structures

5. Develop screening and identification procedures

4. Assess the resources and needs of the community

3. Plan student and program evaluation

2. Develop a statement of philosophy, goals, and standards

1. Set up a planning committee

Steps to a Program for Gifted Learners

STEP 1: Establish a Gifted and Talented Education (GATE) Advisory Committee chaired by the GATE Coordinator and composed of teachers of gifted students, administrators, parents of gifted students, and community representatives. The committee should be reflective of and responsible to the school and the community. This committee will be most helpful, not only in the planning, but their support will make the implementation of the plan much more effective. It will be important to provide in-service opportunities for this group, including information on the nurture and nature of intelligence, new data on teaching and learning, the needs created by high intelligence, and strategies and structures for meeting these needs. Their work will be much easier if they share this common knowledge base in gifted education.

The GATE Advisory Committee will need to:

STEP 2: Develop and approve a statement of philosophy, a conceptual framework, goals, and standards for the gifted program. Some of the questions that must be answered by the committee as they develop this philosophy and mission statement include:

- What do we believe about the nature and nurture of gifted learners?
- Why do we need to make special provisions for gifted learners? What needs do they have that cannot be met in the regular classroom with the general education curriculum?
- What kind of provisions would meet our needs?
- What are our goals and purposes for such provisions?
- What is our vision for the gifted learners? For the school?
- How will we get there? What steps do we need to take and when?

As the committee considers program goals, they should look at the summary of some of the successful methods others have used to develop their support system in each important constituent group shared in Chapter 6.

STEP 3: Develop a plan to evaluate the program and individual students. Include a strategy for reporting the evaluation data—for example, decide what data are needed; how, when, and by whom they will be collected; and how, how often, and to whom they will be reported (see Chapter 8).

STEP 4: Assess the resources and needs of the school, the staff, the parents, and the community. Knowledge of the discrepancy between what is ideally wanted from the program and what is available and actually exists will allow the plan to be more realistic as to what can be accomplished now and what must be developed for future implementation.

STEP 5: Develop screening and identification procedures based on the population that the district wishes to serve. Intelligence can be expressed in many ways; however, only those students with special needs in areas for which service can be provided should be identified.

STEP 6: Develop organizational patterns, including facilities, structure of classes, and the fiscal and time allocations, that will be used for the delivery of services to the identified population. Figure 7.4 provides some of the alternatives possible in a continuum of services that allow a diversity of students to be served appropriately. The resources at school and in the community should be assessed before developing this part of the plan.

STEP 7: Resolve staffing issues, including criteria for selection of teachers for the program, provision for in-service needs of teachers, and accountability of personnel for meeting the goals and standards.

STEP 8: Develop differentiated curricular opportunities and program options that meet the needs of gifted learners, are articulated with general education, and are an integral part of the school day. For example, a plan for experiences that can accelerate the curriculum and the process of instruction, allow for in-depth study, involve complexity, and present a range of alternatives. The plan should include materials with a range of levels and styles. Groups of teachers, both regular and specialized, should be involved in this part of the plan.

STEP 9: Develop a plan for support services, including counselors, psychometrists, mentors, and consultants.

STEP 10: Develop a plan to involve parents in the planning, implementation, and evaluation of the program.

When producing a written plan the committee must be sure to include a clear and descriptive summary of the program and its elements. The summary should provide a reference that can be used by those interested to answer questions about the goals and operation of the program.

Next we consider the many options for the provisions that can be used for the delivery of services to the individuals who have been selected for the gifted program.

Administrative Provisions

For decades, enrichment, acceleration, and ability grouping have been used in various forms to provide appropriate educational opportunities for gifted learners at school. The evidence is clear that none of these strategies should be used alone in programming for gifted students, because each provides for a different need exhibited by this population. However, because these are traditionally the first provisions considered for programs for gifted students, and they are often separately considered as total programs, they will be briefly described. All program organizations and structures should make these provisions part of their continuum of service.

Enrichment

Enrichment is the administrative provision most used in programs for gifted learners at both the elementary and secondary levels and is often used by a district or school in preference to acceleration. The problem with such a preference is that both enrichment and acceleration are needed options in every program for gifted learners. Enrichment must be well-planned and enhanced by other modifications or it will meet few of the gifted students' needs. Because enrichment succeeds in providing for growth, acceleration may be needed to provide the appropriate level of content and learning experiences.

Enrichment can refer to adding disciplines or areas of learning not normally found in the regular curriculum, using more difficult or in-depth material to enhance the core curriculum, or expanding the teaching strategies used to present instruction. Enrichment, when used alone, is often limited in the time allowed for its implementation and, therefore, causes the least change in the learning opportunities provided for the gifted student. Enrichment may appeal to district administrators and school boards as the most inexpensive way to meet gifted needs, but it may become only more work, sometimes more of the same work. If the problems of limited teacher time, teacher knowledge, availability of resources, and individualized planning are not met, then this provision may be by far the most expensive in its waste of human potential. Enrichment is most effective when the needs of the students are assessed and identified and when it is used as a part of a differentiated curriculum plan.

Enrichment approaches commonly used include teaching Bloom's Taxonomy of Educational Objectives: Cognitive Domain (Bloom, 1956) as a conceptual framework and encouraging gifted students to focus on the upper levels of the taxonomy—analysis, synthesis, and evaluation—in their learning. Teaching research skills, higher level or critical thinking, meta-cognitive skills, and multidisciplinary or thematic connections are examples of enrichment approaches often used in programs for gifted learners.

Acceleration

Acceleration can take many forms, including (1) early entrance to formal schooling, which can occur at kindergarten or university levels, (2) moving through age-graded classes in less time by grade skipping, moving through cross-age grouped or nongraded classes in 2 rather than 3 years, or advanced placement, and (3) moving through curriculum materials and concepts at an accelerated rate by curriculum compacting, telescoping content, or receiving credit by examination. However acceleration is implemented, it should result in student completion of formal schooling in less time than is usually required.

Since the early use of acceleration by Terman in 1947, research in this area has been almost uniformly positive in its results (Alexander & Skinner, 1980; Anderson, 1960; Bish & Fliegler, 1959; Braga, 1969; Brody & Benbow, 1987; Fund for the Advancement of Education, 1957; Gallagher, 1966; Lucito, 1964; Morgan, Tennant, & Gold, 1980; Plowman & Rice, 1967; Pressey, 1955; Reynolds, 1962; Terman & Oden, 1947). Some of the rationales and advantages reported are:

- Gifted students are inclined to select older companions because their levels of maturity are often more similar. Neither the method nor the age of acceleration appears to be of consequence.
- Acceleration can be used in any school.
- Acceleration allows capable students to enter their careers sooner, resulting in more productivity.

- A larger proportion of students who are accelerated in primary and secondary schools attend highly selective colleges than gifted students who are not.

- Because they spend less time in school, gifted students' educational costs are lowered.

- Accelerated students do as well as or often better than the older students in their classes.

- There is less boredom and dissatisfaction for bright students.

- Social and emotional adjustment are generally high, in most reports above average, when accelerated.

- In general, teachers and administrators are opposed to acceleration, whereas parents and students, especially those who have experienced acceleration, are in favor of it. Possible reasons given for the negative attitudes of some educators are the convenience of lockstep, chronological grade placement; ignorance of research; belief in social maladjustment, now largely discredited; and state laws preventing early admission.

- To be successful, acceleration must be continuous and coordinated.

In an attempt to clarify the research findings on acceleration, Kulik and Kulik (1984, 1991) performed a meta-analysis of 26 studies of acceleration effects and concluded that gifted and talented students are able to handle the academic challenge that accelerated programs provide. In support of this finding they reported that:

> First, talented youngsters who were accelerated into higher grades performed as well as the talented, older pupils already in those grades. Second, in the subjects in which they were accelerated, talented accelerates showed almost a year's advancement over talented same-age nonaccelerates. (p. 421) [Author's note: In this study, "talented" is used interchangeably with "gifted" and "gifted and talented."]

Brody and Benbow (1987) report that benefits for students include the opportunity to select an educational program that is challenging and that meets the needs of the individual student. For schools they report that acceleration offers "a way to challenge highly able students without the expense and effort of designing a special curriculum" (p. 109). Even Johnson and Johnson (1987), promoters of heterogeneity and cooperative learning, state that high-achieving students may need to study material far above their grade level and suggest placing them in higher grades for certain subject areas during part of the day or having them study advanced material in homogeneous groups.

Although acceleration should not be used as the total plan for a gifted program, the literature shows very few disadvantages to this provision when used on an individual basis. For highly and exceptionally gifted students, opportunities for acceleration are essential. The work of Stanley at Johns Hopkins University (Nevin, 1977) validates its importance. In a project begun in 1971, Stanley gave students who were highly gifted in mathematics an opportunity to develop their ability at an accelerated pace. Not only has his program met with success among the students, but the results—their contributions to our society—have already been evidenced. The program is described in more detail later in this chapter.

Because one of the most commonly found characteristics of gifted individuals is their ability to learn at a faster rate than more typical learners, acceleration in some form should be available in every gifted program, at both the elementary and secondary levels.

Grouping by Ability or Need

Grouping by ability or need is a provision that allows some students to be separated from the more typical students by some given criterion—in this case, the level of measured intelligence or achievement—so that their learning may be facilitated. Grouping by ability or need may be implemented as clustering within regular classes, special classes or schools, magnet programs, special groups meeting prior to or after school, or summer school enrichment classes. A pull-out or resource room program during school hours in which gifted students are separated for a given period of time and then returned to the regular program is another example. At the secondary level, honors or advanced placement classes are often used to group students into classes based on academic ability. Highly gifted students do well in special classes or magnet class programs.

Grouping in and of itself is insufficient to have significant effects on achievement. The curriculum content and processes also must change to become more appropriate to gifted learners. When this is the case, the longer the gifted students are allowed to be in special programs, the greater will be their gain (Martinson, 1972).

Grouping must be flexible to accommodate the growth of each student. The pace of learning, interest, and commitment of gifted learners make such flexibility necessary. Flexible ability grouping has many advantages. In the 1971 hearings held by the US Department of Health, Education, and Welfare, gifted students expressed preference for programs in which they were separated for part of the day, but not totally segregated from other students. They asked for flexibility in their program and in their curriculum (Marland, 1972).

Cluster Grouping

Clustering gifted learners in an elementary classroom and differentiating their instruction is a grouping arrangement that is growing in popularity as a program option to provide for gifted learners (Schuler, 1997). Of course, these arrangements will assume that all of the conditions have been met for quality gifted programs as seen in Figure 7.2. A majority of schools responding to Schuler's survey defined a cluster as four to six identified gifted students or a group of three to five students of the top 5% of students. Content enrichment, differentiation, and thinking skills were noted as the most used strategies in the clusters found in the surveyed schools. It was reported that cluster members increase in intellectual stimulation, challenge, and level of expectation.

Grouping in any form does not solve problems of poor teaching or inappropriate curriculum, but without grouping the benefits of good teaching and the delivery of an appropriate curriculum will be limited. Educational decision makers are often concerned that clustering or removing gifted students from the regular classroom will be detrimental to other students who do not need such a challenge.

Teachers are sometimes concerned that their slower children will have no incentive, that the "spark" will be gone.

One such argument, often set in a moral tone, is that ability grouping must be abandoned because all students benefit from heterogeneous grouping (students of all levels of ability or achievement in one group) and that to consider grouping students by ability or need would cause grievous harm to those who are less able than others (Oakes, 1985). However, Shields (1995) reports that academically gifted students can be served in homogeneous classrooms (students grouped by like levels of ability or achievement) without detrimental effects to other students in heterogeneous classrooms. Her findings show that "students placed appropriately in regular classes do not suffer socially or emotionally when students identified as academically talented or gifted are served in separate, homogeneous classes. These findings will offer support to educators wanting to provide more than one way to organize students for instructional purposes" (p. 238). Rogers (2001) concludes, "Homogeneous groups are more beneficial academically for all abilities than heterogeneous grouping" (p. 25).

Shield's work also supports other current research that homogeneous grouping for high-ability students has a significant, positive effect on their academic achievement, allowing them to achieve significantly better than when placed in heterogeneously grouped classes (Goldring, 1990). Rogers (1993) also found that "academic gains are substantial for a wide variety of grouping options for gifted learners." (pp. 10–11). Among grouping options mentioned were "full-time placement in special enriched or accelerated gifted programs, regrouping for enriched instruction in specific subjects, cross-grade grouping for specific subjects, pullout grouping for enrichment, cluster grouping within a heterogeneous classroom and within-class ability grouping" (p. 9).

The encouragement to use only heterogeneous grouping in all classrooms came about through sincere concerns that some children were not receiving quality educational experiences and were being penalized by the practices of the educational system. There is no denying that the system, as it is typically organized, fails to serve all students equally well. Students who enter the schooling process without the skills that will allow them to operate as successful learners and who have little support from home often fall further and further behind. Those from the culture of poverty, those who have limited language ability in either their native language or the dominant language of the classroom are often at-risk. Those who are significantly ahead of or behind the designated grade-level curriculum will find learning in the current schooling system difficult. Many who began ahead will find no way to realize the extent of their abilities. A simplistic notion has been advanced to account for the failure of these children. According to a few researchers, the practice of grouping in classrooms is at fault (Johnson & Johnson, 1987; Oakes, 1985).

It is interesting that in the discussions of the problems created by grouping, no mention is made of age-grouping, which is the most inappropriate of any form of grouping. We have long known that age is not related to learning; however, most schools continue to organize classrooms and learning experiences using age as the sole criterion for grouping. Other forms of grouping have been used by educators hoping to alleviate the problems caused by age-grouping. Those who would do away with all of these modifications have not suggested any reorganization to replace age-grouped classes.

Without doubt there have been abuses in the practice of grouping. Grouping students from test scores recorded in their files without observing these students or their specific needs is one abuse. Tracking learners into all advanced classes without consideration for where their talents need advancement is another. Keeping students rigidly in three groups for the entire year, and sometimes year after year, is yet another, as is using grouping without assessment of ability, interest, or pace of learning. The answer is not to discontinue the benefits of grouping but to reveal the abuse and suggest better grouping practices and more alternatives to help students succeed.

However, ability-grouping and tracking are not the same and should not be referred to synonymously (Kulik, 1992). The term tracking is usually reserved for provisions made in high school on the basis of the students' educational goals, such as college preparatory, general, or vocational. It is sometimes used in high school or middle school to designate classes formed on the basis of achievement and IQ tests, such as curricular tracks. When tracking is used in elementary school, it involves assignment of students to groups, especially in reading, that will progress throughout their educational experience together. When tracking is used inflexibly, regardless of the student's individual needs or growth patterns, it is an undesirable way to structure students for learning, and the concern for de-tracking is justified. However, according to Loveless (1998), tracking systems today differ from the rigid placement of previous systems. Track assignments are now usually made on a subject-by-subject basis. Performance more often dictates placement decisions rather than standardized tests, and placement by IQ tests is a thing of the past. Equating the rigid forms of tracking with flexible ability grouping has created much misleading discussion and seriously damaging practices.

In discussing the findings of meta-analyses of ability grouping, Kulik (1992) states:

> If the grouping programs that were eliminated were ones that actually adjusted methods and materials to student aptitude, the damage to student achievement would be greater [than if they all covered the same basic curriculum], and the effects would be felt more broadly. Both higher and lower aptitude students would suffer academically from such detracking. But the damage would be truly profound if, in the name of detracking, schools eliminated enriched and accelerated classes for their brightest learners. The achievement level of such students would fall dramatically if they were required to move at the common pace. No one can be certain that there would be a way to repair the harm that would be done. (p. 42)

Rogers (1991) finds from her analysis of five meta-analyses (Kulik, 1985; Kulik & Kulik, 1982, 1984, 1990; Vaughan, 1990), two best-evidence syntheses (Slavin, 1987, 1990), and one ethnographic/survey research synthesis (Gamoran & Berends, 1987) that:

> While full-time ability grouping (tracking) for regular instruction makes no discernible difference in the academic achievement of average and low ability students . . . it does produce substantial academic gains for gifted students enrolled full-time in special programs for the gifted and talented. (p. x)

Not only achievement but also motivation is affected by heterogeneous grouping. Feldhusen and Moon (1992) found that heterogeneous grouping and cooperative learning in heterogeneously grouped classes lead not only to lowered achievement for gifted learners but also to poorer attitudes toward school and lowered motivation. Kulik and Kulik (1982) report differences in attitudes toward subject content when gifted students are grouped heterogeneously or homogeneously, with homogeneous grouping showing improved attitudes and motivation. Loveless (1998) even reports that low ability students' self-concept is strengthened from ability grouping and tracking.

Slavin and Karweit (1984) concluded from their data that schools can best deal with individual differences in ability by dividing students into smaller groups within classes. Later, Slavin (1987) noted that when the level and pace of instruction were adapted to the achievement level of the group, grouping could be an effective instructional procedure. Although some critics of grouping have cited the Kulik and Slavin reviews to show that gifted students should not be grouped, they have excluded these comments in their work. In support of grouping, a 3-year study by Simpson and Martinson (1961) showed that, regardless of the form of grouping—whether a pullout program or a special class—achievement gains positively correlated with the time the gifted student spent in special grouping.

Those who have focused study on heterogeneous grouping for several years have the following criticisms of this practice (Evans, 1985):

- Less-achieving students experienced more difficulty, because there was more pressure from the pacing and higher thought processes of brighter students.
- Less-achieving students exhibited more difficult behavior.
- Teachers experienced increased management problems.
- Some children showed a return to failure situations that had been remediated by grouping.

Cushenberry and Howell (1974) criticize the use of gifted students as teachers' aides, demonstrators, tutors, or record keepers, roles that seem to result from relying solely on heterogeneous grouping. They consider such arrangements to be violations of gifted students' rights to appropriate education and to healthy social interactions with classmates. From these reports it seems that the special needs of neither high- nor low-ability students were met by abandoning ability grouping.

Quite different results have been reported with both gifted and more typical learners in classes appropriately grouped using flexible ability grouping (Gentry & Owen, 1999; Kulik, 1992; Kulik & Kulik, 1990; Loveless, 1998; Rogers, 1993, 2001; Schuler, 1997).

- Both qualitative and quantitative findings show cluster grouping, when combined with high teacher expectations and appropriate modifications of curriculum and environment, has a positive impact on all children.
- Significant academic gains result when programs are adjusted to student abilities. Grouping alone is insufficient to show differences in achievement of grouped over nongrouped gifted students.
- Attitudes of parents, teachers, and gifted students are generally favorable toward special groups or classes, especially if such grouping is flexible and not totally segregated.

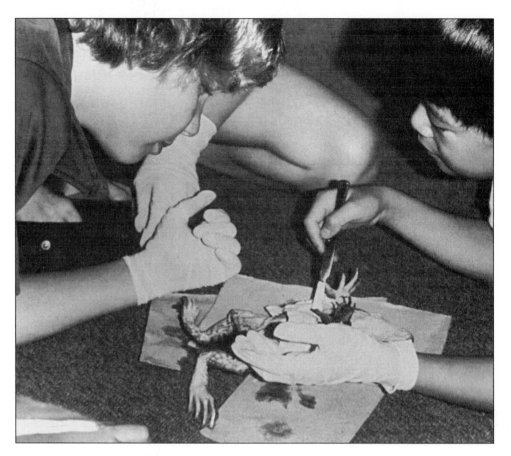

The use of flexible grouping enhances motivation by allowing gifted students to explore advanced concepts and skills as they are ready for them.

- Positive development in self-concept and a sense of well-being result from special group placement.
- The amount of time spent in special groups or classes relates positively to achievement gains of gifted students.
- There is more opportunity for individual expression, in-depth study, acceleration, and freedom from regimentation in ability-grouped classes.
- There are more high achievers and fewer underachievers reported in ability-grouped classes.
- More learning takes place.
- A lack of cliquishness and friction exists among students.
- More trusting relationships are established, allowing students to spend their time and energy in learning, rather than in disruptive behaviors.
- Interest in subject matter increases.

Ability grouping may provide a partial answer to the question of appropriate education for the gifted, but other modifications must be made for the program to succeed. When ability grouping is used, the research recommends the following:

- Recognize that there will still be individual differences. A tremendous range is found within the gifted group; they are not homogeneous. Assess and plan for individualized instruction.
- Avoid complete segregation.
- Select secure, specially trained teachers.
- Encourage growth in all functions of intelligence, not just the cognitive.
- Communicate with all teachers and parents.
- Be informed on research, assessment, and curricula for this population.

The realization that students may be highly capable in different areas and may have needs that differ one from the other forces us to conclude that equal opportunity does not mean the same opportunity.

Homogeneous and heterogeneous grouping practices have made important contributions to teaching and learning and the need for both homogeneous and heterogeneous programs seems evident. We can use homogeneous grouping to:

- Provide peer stimulation. (A peer is defined as one who has like ability in any area of human endeavor, not just a similar age.)
- Support skill development.
- Meet specific needs.

We can use heterogeneous grouping to:

- Develop social skills.
- Introduce new experiences or information needed by the whole class.
- Build a community of learners.

Rogers (2001) notes three new trends occurring in classroom grouping research:

1. The study of high- and low-ability dyads reveals that for socialization dyads work for low-ability students, however for academic achievement, dyads produce no improvement;
2. Studies of academic gain show that like ability groups produce higher academic effects for gifted learners than mixed-ability groups; and
3. All students gain more academically from smaller groupings for instruction than from whole-class instruction.

Among the goals for gifted programming must be: to provide experiences for individuals to continue their own educational progress and to learn from others; to meet their personal needs and to understand the needs of others; to learn to be independent and self-reliant; and to have the skills of working with others. To accomplish such goals, both individualized and grouped learning experiences must be provided for the students.

PROGRAM ORGANIZATIONS AND STRUCTURES FOR GIFTED LEARNERS IN THE ELEMENTARY SCHOOLS

Some researchers have identified giftedness as "asynchronous development in which advanced cognitive abilities and heightened intensity combine to create inner experiences and awareness that are qualitatively different from the norm" (Columbus Group, 1991, cited in Silverman, 1993, p. 3). It is this "being out of sync" that is responsible for many of the problems experienced by gifted children the moment they start school. What if you could think up wonderful stories, but you were not supposed to talk and you could not find any way to write them down because you did not yet know how to write? Or you could read thrilling tales of adventure, but the only books available in the first grade classroom were baby stories? Or you could draw really great cartoons, funny ones and sad ones, exciting ones and silly ones, but the third-grade teacher insisted that you had to write stories instead and there wasn't even a computer? Or you could make up amazing dances in your head and do the steps beautifully, but you were told over and over that you had to sit still now that you were "a big kindergarten girl"?

The idea that all 6-year-old students need to learn the same basic first-grade concepts and skills has been the guiding principle of our schools for nearly 100 years. Then, when you are 7, you are supposed to learn second-grade content and skills, and so on, and so on. By the time middle school rolls around, some children are as much as 4 or 5 years ahead of their age-mates and the curriculum for that grade level, and some even more. These are the children who often find school very frustrating, and unless there are gifted programs available or differentiated curriculum offered, these are the children that will lose the magic of learning, like Julie in the vignette on page 286. These are the young people that could be our most excited and productive students. Our challenge is to find a place for children who may be 6 years old, read like a 10-year-old, write like a 6-year-old, solve math problems like a 12-year-old, talk like a 15-year-old, and handle emotions and hurt feelings like a 4-year-old. It is bewildering for the teacher to relate to such a child, but think what it must be like to be such a child, especially in a setting that is structured for all 6-year-olds to be the same.

Gifted children are not usually identified for special programs or differentiated instruction until the third grade. This is based on the belief that standardized testing will be too unstable and will not prove valid until the student is older. It is true that rapid changes occur in the child's abilities throughout early childhood; however, advanced ability and accelerated thinking will be evident very early, and adjusting the learning experience to the child should not depend on the results of any standardized test.

Unfortunately, as we have seen in Chapter 4, many educational experiences provided for early learners are still limited by the belief that maturation must precede and dictate the child's experience. This belief continues into many kindergarten and first-grade classrooms. Some teachers are even concerned that children will have social-emotional problems if they are allowed to engage in advanced learning experiences. Many are convinced that they will ruin their eyes if they read, their health if they solve hard problems, or their future if they advance too rapidly. As you learned in Chapter 4, Vygotsky, Piaget, eye specialists, and hundreds of successful, happy children and adults will attest to the fact that intellectual stimulation is necessary to healthy growth and development. We are in far more danger of understimulating growing minds than the reverse. As was true in the home, the responsive learning environment, in which the child is the guide for the pace and content of learning, is still the best provision for optimizing learning. Although elementary learners will have many needs in common, it is essential that we acknowledge and provide for their differences.

Organizational Modifications for Gifted Learners in the Elementary Schools

Enrichment, acceleration, and grouping by ability and need are a part of many educational modifications that have been used with young gifted learners. Some of the options are: early admission; nongraded or cross-age grouped classes; individualized instruction; accelerated promotion (i.e., grade-skipping); independent study; mentors; pull-out or resource room programs; grouping by ability or need (e.g., clustering in the regular classroom); field trips; after-school, Saturday, or summer enrichment; special classes; magnet classes; and special schools. The modification chosen will be successful to the degree that differentiation is used and is directly correlated to the time involved in appropriate experiences.

Early Admission

Early admission to kindergarten or first grade is one of the first modifications of the educational experience possible for gifted children. For children who have already mastered school skills such as counting and identifying colors, letters, and letter sounds, and especially for those who are already reading, counting, and categorizing, this would be an important consideration. Although some school personnel are concerned about such an arrangement, there are no data that show negative consequences either cognitively or emotionally for children who begin school early.

Nongraded or Cross-Age Classes

When available, such classes are helpful to gifted students. Combination classes—for example, grades 1 through 3 in one classroom—can allow the student to move at a faster pace, use advanced materials and concepts, and have the stimulation of older students throughout their learning experience. However, if the class is taught in three groups, with first, second, and third graders placed in separate materials and curriculum, then the advantages of this cross-age grouping are lost.

Accelerated Promotion (i.e., Grade-Skipping)

This is another provision that could be made for the advanced gifted learner in elementary school. When differentiation is also a part of the plan, grade-skipping can help meet the needs of a gifted learner who learns rapidly and needs advanced work. School personnel often express the concern that this will cause the student to miss critical basic skills. This need not be the case if appropriate assessment is done of the student's knowledge of the content standards and curriculum frameworks from the previous grades and the instruction and material used are individualized to meet the needs of the child.

Independent Study

Although independent study can include acceleration of material and concepts and can be carried out in a variety of settings, it is most often used to provide enrichment. The outcome of independent study should be a self-directed learner who can investigate real problems, but too often teachers expect gifted students to be self-directed learners from the start. Gifted students often have the curiosity, the interest, and the motivation to pursue a study of their own choosing, but all too often they do not have the skills. Skills such as how to search for primary sources, use professional methods of inquiry, collect and organize raw data, analyze and evaluate data, and form conclusions often need to be taught if the student is to be successful. Doherty and Evans (1981) suggest a three-phase process for using independent study. Phase 1 is teacher led and incorporates learning centers, experimentation, and simulation as the student explores the depth and breadth of the academic area. Phase 2 is the independent study and involves a nine-step process of locating and using data, producing new ideas, and developing a product that is examined by experts:

STEP 1 The student selects a topic that is issue oriented.

STEP 2 The student establishes a schedule.

STEP 3 The student develops five or more questions (first objectives) to direct the research.

STEP 4 The student secures references and seeks sources or raw data.

STEP 5 The student researches the topic, collects raw data, and takes notes.

STEP 6 The student develops five final objectives using Bloom's taxonomy.

STEP 7 The student has a conference with the teacher, who evaluates the depth of knowledge and the idea production.

STEP 8 The student makes a product showing some new ideas.

STEP 9 The student's product is displayed, evaluated with a friend, and examined by an expert. (p. 109)

The final phase is a culminating seminar. This process allows students to build the skills necessary to carry out an investigation that will satisfy their intellectual curiosity and truly enrich their academic lives.

The value of independent study to gifted learners is supported by findings of Stewart (1981): Compared with learning styles of more average students, gifted students seemed to prefer instructional methods emphasizing independence, that is, independent study and discussion. The general population within the study preferred more structured methods such as lectures and projects.

Mentorships and Internships

Mentors share their expertise with gifted learners who are interested in their field and are at a point of development in that field where they can benefit from involvement with an expert. Mentors can be found in many places. Older students can become mentors for younger students, especially if a structure is provided for their contact and some prior training in interpersonal relations is made available. Retirement communities provide an excellent resource for mentors, because many retired persons have the experience and record of achievement to share and the time to share them. Parents of gifted students may become mentors for other students. Practicing professionals in the community should not be overlooked. Although their time may be at a premium, they will often make time for that one bright, inquiring student who finds their field fascinating.

Mentors should not be considered the same as other traditional teachers who need to evaluate, report, and record the progress of the student. In the mentor relationship a more equal partnership is involved, with more emphasis on the guidance aspect of learning. Mentors provide a social contact and sponsorship into the world of the profession being shared. Mutual interest and trust are necessary components of successful mentorships.

The Richardson study (Cox & Daniel, 1983) described some mentor and internship programs. Among them were the Illinois Governmental Internship Program, the Executive High School Internship Association (a national organization), the Executive Assistant Program, the Creative and Performing Arts Program (a Dallas-based program), Texas A&M University's Career Education Model, and other programs found in Texas. Betts (1985) has a strong component of mentorship in his Autonomous Learner Model (discussed later).

Pull-out or Resource Rooms

An often-used modification of the school organization is the pull-out or resource room model. In such a plan, gifted students spend most of their educational experience in the regular classroom and leave for brief visits to a resource room, often as little as 2 hours per week, and then return to their regular classroom. Pull-out or resource rooms can be a part of many types of programs and are typically used to enrich the regular school program. If the pull-out or resource room is the only provision for meeting the needs of gifted learners, the result may be a partial experience lacking continuity and seldom meeting the students' assessed needs and interests. If a resource room is available as part of a well-planned and well-integrated program, it provides a source of enriching experiences and adds to the options available to teachers seeking to develop special interests and special talents.

Many problems are associated with this model, including lack of continuity with the regular program. Such a modification seldom is able to meet the educational needs of the student beyond content enrichment in an area that may not be the student's area of achievement. Other problems involve the visibility of the student as a "special" student and limited involvement with an appropriate pace and level of learning.

One well-known and well-structured example of such a program is the Schoolwide Enrichment Model (SEM) (Renzulli & Reis, 1985), which incorporates earlier work done on the Enrichment Triad (Renzulli, 1977) (see Chapter 10) and Revolving Door Identification models (Renzulli, Reis, & Smith, 1981). The Schoolwide Enrichment Model was designed to provide advanced-level learning and creative productivity to a broad spectrum of the school population by making various types and levels of enrichment available. Two levels of general enrichment are provided to a talent pool representing approximately 15% to 20% of the school population; advanced-level enrichment and curriculum compacting are provided to students from that pool who show evidence of needing such services. The model is rich in procedures and formats to guide and support the teacher in moving theory into practice.

Program Structures for Educating Elementary-Age Gifted Learners

Although providing organizational modifications allows programs to be administered more appropriately for gifted students, the program that is planned must meet the needs of the individual student. The need for complexity, acceleration, advanced and abstract ideas, and depth in the content must be met. The degree of difficulty or ease in delivering these provisions will depend on how the program is structured. This section presents a range of possible structures and their advantages and disadvantages that will provide support for each gifted student.

There are many options for structuring programs for gifted learners. How much progress gifted learners make and how successful they are in fulfilling their unique potential will depend on how many of their needs can be met by the program in which they participate and how much time they are allowed to meet those needs in the program. Figure 7.4 provides an overview of program options for gifted learners. According to a report by Delcourt, Loyd, Cornell, and Goldberg (1994), students in pull-out, separate class, and special school programs showed higher achievement than gifted students who were not in such programs and those who were in programs provided only in the regular classroom.

The structure chosen does not ensure that the needs of gifted learners will be met, only that within the particular structure those needs could be met. Factors other than structure, such as teacher skill and administrative and community support, will determine the quality of the program; however, adoption of less flexible structures will actually limit the ability to meet the potential needs of gifted learners. Research has shown (Delcourt et al., 1994) that the existence of programs for gifted students has no harmful effect on the academic achievement of the nongifted students present in schools with identified gifted students, nor does the type of grouping arrangement influence student perceptions of their social relations for gifted or nongifted students.

Each district should have a wide variety of programs available for the continuum of services needed. No one structure can meet the needs of all the gifted learners in any district; therefore, providing a range of planned services would be the best practice. The choice of structure depends on:

- The level of involvement of the population to be served. As previously discussed, the child's level of giftedness should be considered in program planning. A special class may be most appropriate for a highly gifted learner, but unnecessary and socially limiting for less gifted students. An individualized, cross-graded class-

Figure 7.4 *Summary of Organizational Modifications and Program Structures Elementary and Secondary*

ORGANIZATIONAL MODIFICATIONS	PROGRAM STRUCTURES
ELEMENTARY	
Early Admission	Regular classroom
Nongraded or cross-age grouped classes	– with cluster
Individualized instruction	– with nongraded or
Accelerated promotion (grade skipping)	cross-age grouped classes
Independent study	Individualized classroom
Mentors	Special classes
Pull-out programs/Resource rooms	– with heterogeneously
Grouping by ability or need	grouped classes
Field trips	Special schools
After-school, Saturday school,	Adjunct programs
or summer enrichment	
Special classes	
Magnet classes	
Special schools	
SECONDARY	
Early admission to middle or high school	School-within-a-school
Core academic classes	Governor's schools
Group seminars	Advanced Placement
Honors classes	International Baccalaureate
Minicourses	Secondary Triad
Personalized instruction	Autonomous Learner Program
Early entrance to college	Purdue Secondary Program
	Accelerated College
	Enrollment

room that both clusters gifted learners and provides time in special classes may be the best possible choice for the great majority of youngsters, but may be totally unsuitable and limiting for highly and exceptionally gifted learners.

- The training and skills of the teacher. Although an individualized classroom may best meet learner needs, if the teacher does not have management skills for this degree of complexity, then such a structure will have a very limited chance for success.

- The educational philosophy of the administration. It is difficult at best to develop and deliver appropriate services for the highly unique learners we call gifted. If there is little support from the administration, it can be impossible. Work carefully to get the support needed—physically, financially and, most important, philosophically—from those who make decisions for your program. A team effort is important for the success of the program and the growth of the learners within it.

- The cooperation of the parents and the community at large. Building parent and community support is important. As part of the team, parents can bring a wealth of resources and information to the program. Without their support—or worse, with their opposition—the program has a limited chance of delivering the best service.

Regardless of the program structure chosen for the delivery of services, to successfully produce appropriate, quality education, all programs for gifted learners must provide differentiation, flexible grouping, continuous progress, intellectual peer interaction, continuity, and teachers with specialized education.

In planning a program for gifted learners, the limitations as well as the strengths of the particular setting must be considered. Among the many ways of structuring (see Figure 7.4) the one most suited to the particular situation should be chosen. By being aware of the difficulties that the model could present because of its structure, many of those problems can be prevented. The continuum can range from regular classrooms with cluster grouping, to special schools. Individualized classrooms allow more flexibility for the learner and may be combined with clusters, pullout, and nongraded or cross-age grading with even more effect. Special classes and special schools allow even more needs to be met, especially for the highly gifted students. Other possibilities for providing for gifted learners include adjunct programs, independent study, mentors, tutorials, internships, and resource rooms. Students in any of these programs have higher achievement than do gifted students who are in regular programs or those who are not in programs for gifted students at all. Further strength is added to the advocacy for programs for gifted learners by the findings that after 2 years' participation in programs for gifted learners students show high achievement scores that do not differ significantly across levels of social status nor ethnic groups (Delcourt et al., 1994).

Regular Classrooms

The range of instruction in the regular classroom as traditionally organized (Figure 7.1) is not adequate for gifted education. Such classrooms rely on group instruction and a set curriculum. The instruction is usually by subject, with similar experiences for everyone. Whitmore (1980) comments, "It seems likely that future research could prove that the regular classroom is the most restrictive environment for the gifted child. . . . This finding will be most probable if teachers are not helped to become more able to effectively individualize instruction" (p. 68).

A study of instructional and curricular practices in regular third- and fourth-grade classrooms throughout the United States was conducted to discover the extent of differentiation that is provided to meet the needs of gifted and talented students (Archambault et al., 1993). A companion observational study (Westberg, Archambault, Dobyns, & Salvin, 1993) was conducted to obtain descriptive information regarding these differentiated instructional and curricular practices. It was determined that little differentiation in either instruction or curriculum was provided, and even grouping arrangements or verbal interactions used to meet the needs of these students were seldom found. Of the population of gifted and talented or high-ability students studied, no instructional or curricular differentiation was experienced in 84% of their instructional activities. This becomes of particular concern with the current trend of eliminating programs for gifted learners, making the regular classroom their only educational experience. Other programs for gifted learners may be limited to 1 to 2 hours a week, leaving the regular classroom, again, as the place where their needs must be met. The study found that schools with gifted programs make similarly limited provisions for their gifted students when the students are back in the regular classroom, as do schools without formal programs.

One explanation might be that almost 61% of the regular classroom teachers in the study had received no staff development in the area of gifted education (Archambault et al., 1993). Considering that the study had a large national sample, the author raises concern about other teachers in other regular classrooms across the country.

With Cluster. Clustering gifted students could meet their needs for peer interaction, but usually group teaching does not provide an appropriately differentiated curriculum. Clustering at least five gifted students in the regular classroom gives them a more appropriate learning environment, but only if the teacher is aware of and tries to meet their differentiated needs.

With Cross-Age Grouping or Nongraded. Combining several age-graded classes into one group—for example, first through third grade—provides easy access to materials and a level appropriate to the gifted students' level of development. Use of cross-age grouping enables us to move away from the age-in-grade lockstep that has for years been so limiting to all students. Team teaching provides additional resources, skills, and stimulation for both teachers and learners.

With Pull-out or Resource Room. In a pull-out class, students leave the regular class for a specified amount of time for a resource room or special instruction, and then return to spend most of their time in the regular program.

Advantages. Gifted students may have an opportunity to work at their level of ability and in their area of interest and to interact with other gifted students for at least part of their school time. Upon leaving the regular program, the student may experience seminars, specialized resource rooms, special classes, field trips, or other unique learning situations.

Disadvantages. Most of the time spent in school still does not provide an appropriate learning experience for meeting the needs of gifted students. Often gifted students are asked to do the regular classroom work missed during the time they were not in the classroom, in addition to the special class work. Furthermore, the special class has little time for meeting all of the needs of gifted students, teachers may resent interruption of their program, and other students in the regular classroom may envy and isolate the gifted child because of the special class. Teachers in pull-out or resource room programs must establish good working relations with the regular class teachers if this plan is to benefit the gifted learner.

As a result of data collection over a 4-year period, the Richardson study (Cox, Daniel, & Boston, 1985) recommended against the use of the pull-out structure for delivery of services to the gifted student. Viewing pull-out as a part-time solution to a full-time problem, the researchers suggest a more comprehensive program structure.

Individualized Classrooms

By individualizing a classroom, we can make use of individual, team, and flexible small-group instruction. The curriculum and materials for each student are determined through assessments. The classroom is decentralized to give access to many types of learning. In most cases, individualized classes are cross-age graded and are often team taught. Learning centers are often found in these classrooms.

Advantages. Individualization allows gifted students to work at their own level and pace and helps to ensure that the learning experience is continuous.

Disadvantages. If there are only one or two gifted students, they may feel isolated and have no one with whom to share ideas. An individualized classroom requires a highly competent teacher (or teachers) to avoid becoming unstructured or only partially individualized. The teacher may not have enough resources available to keep up with a gifted learner and 35 others.

Individualized classrooms with cluster and pullout have the same advantages as individualized classrooms, with the additional advantage of more resources available to both the gifted learner and the teacher. This situation avoids the problems created by the pull-out program. If all students are valued and allowed to meet their needs, then no students will feel that they must do what every other person does. The gifted can meet their needs without envy from others. Such a program has continuity and allows each student's needs to be met all through the week.

Moderately and mildly gifted students would need less specialized grouping if classrooms were individualized. In cross-age graded, individualized classrooms, a cluster group of five to seven gifted students could meet the needs of each for peer challenge. When clustering is used in a classroom that is not organized to meet individual needs, when flexible grouping cannot occur, or when different types of ability are not valued and nurtured, gifted students cannot flourish.

Special Classes

The special class structure can provide for all of gifted students' needs and can be used at any level. It is most appropriate for the moderately to highly gifted student. In the special class, if the curriculum is differentiated, gifted students can be challenged to their full potential in every area. They are stimulated rather than tempted to hide their gifts in order to be accepted. Teachers must be specially trained to work with gifted learners for these classes to be effective.

Special Classes Scheduled With Some Heterogeneous Classes. A special class scheduled for part of the day, with heterogeneous classes completing the schedule, is especially appropriate for intermediate, middle, and secondary schools organized by subject. Examples include concurrent enrollment at colleges and high schools, and interdisciplinary academic core classes with electives.

Advantages. Programs and environments can be designed in the special class to meet the needs of the gifted. By working in additional classes other than those with academic subjects, such as the arts, gifted students can learn to appreciate other students for their abilities. The mildly and moderately gifted would find this helpful.

Disadvantages. A special class requires a specially trained teacher, or it can be just as inhibiting as no program. Often these classes are different only in the population attending them and in the added quantity of assignments. It is important to individualize in this setting, because the gifted are quite different from each other. Although gifted students are not highly advanced in every discipline, many secondary schools inappropriately use tracking across all areas.

Special Schools

The special school structure most often is recommended only for highly and exceptionally gifted or talented students and has the advantages and disadvantages of special classes in a more intensified form. Magnet schools for the highly gifted, magnets for technology, math, science, the arts, and so forth, as well as residential schools for math and the sciences, are some of the types of schools that are found in this category. When considering total separation, we might look at the level of the students' involvement in giftedness. All gifted students need to interact with those who can challenge them. For the highly and exceptionally gifted, high-ability grouping would justifiably comprise the major part of their educational experience.

Adjunct Programs

In addition to many of the structures previously mentioned, adjunct programs give additional service to students with special needs. These often are planned at times that provide minimal services for gifted students, such as after school, on Saturdays, or during the summer. They can range from a special-interest group or class with a single subject content to an open, varied experience. Disadvantages of adjunct programs, if used as the total gifted program, are that they do nothing about the student's gifted needs during the entire day, and they usually lack continuity.

Only when they are planned as a part of a well-integrated, full-time program can adjunct programs provide the full value of which they are capable. Adjunct programs should be used as only one component, never the entire gifted program.

Program Limitations

All of these program structures have been and are currently being used in various combinations and with varying degrees of success. Research shows that none is without merit, nor does any one answer all the needs of gifted students.

In using any of the traditional program models, as we have in the past, we are left with some uncomfortable problems. Programs often exist for minimal periods of time throughout the gifted students' educational experience, resulting in little continuity of learning experiences. Often gifted students are faced with having their needs met only during the allotted special program time—one half-day per week, a few weeks per year, or during a 6-week summer program. Not only are they asked to give up their free time so that their special learning needs can be attended to, but it is assumed that during the rest of their school time, these needs do not exist, or if they do, they can be sublimated until the allotted period arrives.

Other problems—labeling and lack of skills in social integration and interpersonal relationships—can result from part-time provisions. It therefore becomes important to find a way to individualize school learning experiences so that gifted individuals can have their atypical needs met continuously throughout their school career. Their differences must become strengths, not the handicaps they often are in a traditional setting. The gifted have a right to pursue learning at their own pace to their own level of capability, with challenges available on a full-time basis and progress encouraged by their learning environment.

PROGRAM ORGANIZATIONS AND STRUCTURES FOR GIFTED LEARNERS IN THE MIDDLE SCHOOL AND HIGH SCHOOL

Even if they were identified and had special programs in the elementary grades, by middle school, gifted learners will often find few special provisions made to modify their programs. During or after sixth grade, most schools departmentalize their curriculum, and the concepts of differentiation and continuous progress are seldom used.

Ken couldn't believe he was doing this! While everyone else was hanging around talking and relaxing, he was picking up the stupid papers in the stupid quad with this stupid stick. He would rather Mr. Benson had assigned him to detention if he really felt he needed to punish him. Oh no! He had to assign "community work." In this case that meant policing the quad every day after lunch for a week. Ken couldn't see what was so bad about what he had done anyway. All he did was correct Mr. Benson when he was wrong about the moon dust thing. Even though Ken had told him that he had "proof" from the latest copy of *Scientific American,* Mr. Benson said that the textbook was right, so obviously Ken was wrong. He supposed that he should have left it at that, but Ms. Collins would not have wanted him to fold so easily. She had always said, when Ken had her in the fourth and fifth grades, "Get your data straight and then make your case." She liked a good debate. Ken remembered loving math and science when he was in her room. Good thing he had her for 2 whole years!

The trouble started in the sixth grade when the new teacher insisted that Ken and all of the gifted cluster from Ms. Collins's room do all of the problems in the sixth-grade arithmetic book. He tried to tell her that they had already done all those kinds of problems years ago. They were already 4 years ahead of that book. But she said they had to do the problems anyway. And to make matters worse, she never even talked about science! The seventh-grade math teacher was a lot like that, too, and Ken thought seventh-grade math was suspiciously like sixth-grade arithmetic. He had told his mom about the problem and she had called the school to suggest that Ken go over to the high school for math, but the counselor said it was against district policy. When she asked for an appointment to discuss the problem Ken was having, the counselor said that it wasn't necessary because Ken wasn't a behavior problem.

Science wasn't any better. The seventh-grade science teacher only read from a book; they never did any experiments like they had in Ms. Collins's room. Now this! It was really embarrassing doing this. But, of course, that was the point. Humiliation was a part of the punishment for "sassing" the teacher. He had never thought of debating as "sassing." Well, he had had it! He had already completed all of his math and science requirements and so he didn't have to take any more classes in either subject. He still loved trying to solve hard problems or exploring things he didn't know, but what was happening in these classes was definitely not math and science. At least, not the exciting part. He could read on his own and play with math at the math club. He really didn't ever have to take another stupid math or science class!

As Ken put the trash in the bin and started to class, he smiled to himself, "Just one more day of punishment, then just coast to the end of the term. I'll never get involved in this stupid kind of math and science again!" With that comforting thought he felt as though he could make it until June.

Often those who plan the gifted program in the district concentrate on the elementary school structure and curriculum. Part of the reason for omitting secondary levels can be explained by the greater flexibility available and the organization of time in the elementary structure. Many of the needs created by the characteristics of gifted learners (e.g., need for continuity, interdisciplinary content, delay of closure, flexible grouping to take advantage of peak learning areas, depth and diversity of interest, alternative learning styles, creative expression) can be more easily met in the elementary school organization. Other reasons are the limitations of the secondary structure in time given to each class and to each student because of the large number of students who must be served each day by each teacher and the limited interaction between faculty of the various disciplines. Although there are ways all of these problems can be resolved to provide appropriate programs for gifted learners, the greatest barrier is the perception that program modification for gifted students is unnecessary in secondary schools. It is assumed that in a departmentalized setting, students can choose learning experiences that will meet their needs from the variety of courses offered. There may even be special honors classes available from which the gifted student can choose.

One often-used practice that needs to be examined is the establishment of one or two advanced classes into which all gifted students are tracked regardless of their needs and abilities. Many high schools use special mathematics or science classes for this purpose. Such classes comprise the entire gifted program, and if students do not do well in mathematics or science, their identification as gifted learners comes under suspicion. The widest range of qualitatively different experiences we can devise must be offered, for this population is the most diverse in ability. Neither tracking systems nor a few special classes comprise a complete program that can meet the needs of secondary gifted learners.

In a review of research and theoretical literature, Hoover and Feldhusen (1987) conclude that the special needs of gifted and talented secondary students must include:

- The development of a knowledge base of concepts and principles in major disciplines and a substantial knowledge in one or two areas.
- The development of skills for in-depth study in specific disciplines.
- Recognition and development of relationships among various disciplines.
- Relation to and interaction with other high-ability students.
- Involvement in advanced studies at a level and pace commensurate with abilities.
- Experience with a variety of cultural and career options.
- Participation in counseling services that provide for their social and emotional needs and concerns.

Silverman (1980) points out that although elementary gifted students may have relatively little involvement in either the identification or the planning procedures used in their program, secondary gifted students should be involved in both. In addition to more commonly used identification procedures, Silverman suggests the use of subject area examinations, preferably college-level assessments; independent study proposals designed by the students; auditions and interviews; and self-nomination and self-selection.

Middle School Reform and Gifted Learners

The middle school has been in the forefront of school reform efforts. The movement for reform was both structural and philosophical. Structurally the change was from the six-grade elementary/three-grade junior high/three-grade senior high (grades 1–6, 7–9, 10–12) to the five-grade elementary/three-grade middle school/four-grade high school (grades 1–5, 6–8, 9–12). Philosophically the focus is on social development needs, interdisciplinary curriculum, critical and higher-level thinking, team teaching, and individualization. In some middle schools, an emphasis has been placed on heterogeneous grouping. Although many of the reforms are clearly aligned with the philosophical beliefs found in gifted education, an overemphasis on support for social development at the expense of academic growth and heterogeneous grouping at the expense of ability grouping or forming groups from need to learn has created problems for gifted learners. However, a study by Coleman, Gallagher, and Howard (1993) showed that it is possible for differentiated services for gifted students to be operated within an authentic middle school philosophy. In all of the schools surveyed as providing strong programs both in middle school and gifted education, some form of ability grouping of students was used to provide a challenging program for the advanced students while continuing to meet all students' needs at their instructional level.

Curiously, many of the very reforms that are intended to improve middle school education for most students can make the goals of appropriate and challenging education for gifted students even more difficult to achieve. To correct for the "dumbing-down" of the learning presented in lower level academic classes, heterogeneously grouped classes are being pursued. The result has been raising the level of expectation and presentation for most of the students, but through lack of flexibility in the implementation, thus "dumbing-down" the curriculum for gifted students (Tomlinson, 1994). Cooperative learning in heterogeneously grouped classes allows many students to gain through joint ventures. However, gifted students too often may be asked to demonstrate mastery in fact-based information that was mastered years before and then to assume the role of teacher in the group. Such practices may result in mediocre performance by them and lack of challenge in their learning. However, Elmore and Zenus (1994) found that when grouped cooperatively with other gifted students in accelerated math classes, gifted students benefited personally and academically. When gifted students are grouped together, cooperative groups can provide a balance between academic and social-emotional development because such groups can allow the academic challenge and acceleration needed by gifted learners.

Gifted students in secondary school can provide leadership in service projects for their schools.

Tomlinson (1994) raises the concern that the middle school focus on achieving competence for most students using strategies and grouping with little flexibility has inevitably lead to under-challenging gifted students.

> A key role of gifted education is to advocate for instruction which invites and encourages excellence at the level of performance of the gifted students rather than accepting definitions of success based upon performance of the norm. To do less is to foster mediocrity for highly able learners. (p. 177)

Add to these concerns the nature of adolescents to seek approval of their peers and compliance with group norms. Excellence for all will not be realized unless middle school teachers can find a way to provide a climate where both social and academic needs are met, and competence and excellence are available at every student's level of learning. The needs of the gifted learner cannot be ignored without a loss of equity and excellence.

Other Limitations in Secondary Educational Structures

In addition to the reform issues, other limitations to learning found in secondary education, such as the limited time elements available to departmentalized programs, the fragmentation of knowledge, and the lack of flexibility in the pace of learning, need to be addressed if optimal learning is to take place.

All of the characteristics and needs of the gifted discussed in Chapter 2 are applicable to secondary as well as elementary students. They have the same need for differentiated and individualized curriculum. If anything, gifted students need differentiation even more during adolescence. During this period they pursue their independence and separate identity from their parents and their childhood values—sorting, testing, and validating their competence (see Chapter 5). Diamond and Hopson (1998) suggest that "an impoverished, unstimulating environment has as much or more impact on the adolescent brain as does deliberate enrichment. The nearly adult brain needs a variety of inputs just to hold its ground" (p. 241).

The philosophy of learning and teaching is also equivalent, as advances in brain/mind research make the same demands for change on the secondary teacher as they make on the elementary teacher. The theories of cognitive development and the curricular models that attempt to facilitate them are still of great importance at the secondary level. Integrating the other functions of feeling, intuition, and physical/sensing are as critical to optimal learning and development in the secondary level as they were at any other point in the growth of the gifted learner.

The TV interviewer and the group of seven identified gifted high school students were about out of time. They had been discussing the problems that the students had with the honors program offered at their school. "Well, I write novels," one of the students said, "and there is no honors class in literature—only in math and science. Even the Advanced Placement classes at the university are in math and science. I'm not really that good in math and yet I have to go to that class because I'm identified."

"Yeah, but that's why we are all in the drama class, Julie. It's the only place that you can really be the Big G," Frank reminded her.

"I'll tell you one thing," Julie responded, "When school is over I'm sure not going to tie up my life with any more classes. I'm going to write and travel and do something that makes sense."

"Doesn't school make any sense to you? Aren't you given an opportunity to master some of the skills you are going to need to write?" the interviewer asked.

The group laughed. "In the sixth grade I read a lot," Trudy explained. "My teacher let me go to the reading lab and set the pacer at whatever speed I wanted, and I got to be a really fast reader. I could read at any level I wanted, too. It was great! I loved seeing how I could get better and better and understand more and more. But when I got to the seventh grade, the teacher wanted me to stay with the rest of the kids. You know, of course, I was already eons ahead of the books they were reading. What kind of sense does that make?"

"Aren't you ever challenged?" the interviewer asked.

"Does homework count?" Jim asked as the rest of the group groaned. "We get a real challenge producing tons and tons of paperwork that is just the same thing over and over. The challenge is having patience and just staying sane."

"And you wanted to know why I don't want to go on to college," Julie commented sarcastically.

The interviewer asked a final question: "OK, if you could design a program that would challenge you and would make sense, what would you do, given the constraints of the budget and resources available at school?"

"Why couldn't you study things in their natural order?" Jeff asked. "You could start out with, say, musicology. That's what I'm interested in. There is a lot of history in music, as well as geography, economics, and politics, and there is the science of sound. You could get into about anything you can think of. I don't see why we don't learn about the connections, you know, the interactions of all these areas. Subjects really aren't separate, but the school treats them as if they are. It's not only uninteresting and senseless, it misses the real meaning of the living ideas. Teachers could just be resources to help us find the information. Not everything is known. The quest is what is interesting, not unrelated facts—as if there really were absolute facts anyway."

The interviewer ended the program with this suggestion. There was nothing he could say that would add to this young man's idea—nothing that would make any better sense.

Organizational Modifications for Gifted Learners in the Middle and High School

A variety of modifications to program organization are being used in middle and high schools to meet the needs of gifted learners. These include early admission, core academic classes, group seminars, honors classes, mini-courses, Personalized Instruction, and early entrance to college. Just as was suggested at the elementary level, field trips; after-school, Saturday, or summer classes; independent study; and mentors are other possible elements of programs that can be provided. At the very least, two interested teachers can combine their blocks of time and their students to create a laboratory setting where individualization, flexible grouping, and some cross-age grouping and interdisciplinary learning can occur.

Once the organization of the school moves to departmentalization, the flexible ability grouping available to elementary teachers disappears. This is especially true in the middle schools where students are heterogeneously grouped and the focus is on their developmental needs over their academic needs (Connors & Irvin, 1989; George, 1988). When grouping is used, it is far more common to find special classes formed by tracking gifted students into designated classes in a few or all of their academic subjects. Some special schools have been formed at the secondary level, such as the Governor's schools and the schools for special talents such as those in Los Angeles and New York City. Thematic and interdisciplinary teaching are additional elements that can provide the flexibility and complexity to challenge bright minds. For highly or exceptionally gifted students, magnet or special classes or schools provide a necessary level of education on the continuum of services.

Early Admission Programs

At middle and high school levels, one of the earliest modifications possible for gifted students is early admission. There is a transition between schools from the fifth grade to middle school and from eighth grade to high school, so this may be a good time for the student who is ready for advanced work to move ahead academically. The student will be entering a new school the next year anyway, and the social transition may present no additional problems.

Core Academic Classes

Within the school program, core academic classes can be organized to alleviate the lack of a multidisciplinary focus and the time limits of classes organized by subjects. This approach allows two or three middle or high school teachers to block out multiple periods, usually two or three each day, for flexible grouping and a cross-subject focus. The usual student/faculty ratio is maintained, but space is provided for the two or three groups that were formerly separate classes to meet as one group, with the two or three teachers forming an instructional team. The remainder of the students' schedules are as before, with electives chosen by the normal scheduling procedure.

Group Seminars

Another possibility for program modification at the middle or high school level is the use of independently planned group seminars. An example of this type of structure for meeting the needs of gifted students at the secondary level is the Teacher/Advisor Model. Students are allowed to ask any faculty member to serve as their gifted advisor. They then sign up for one period of gifted program time and arrange with their advisor how this period will be used. In this highly individualized model the gifted students may do directed independent study, cooperatively designed seminars with their advisor to be conducted by either the student or the advisor, or regular classes. Having a small area set aside as a gifted center helps to make this a socially, as well as academically, successful modification. Teacher acceptance of this plan is unusually high, and it provides for a wide choice of curricula.

Honors Classes

Honors classes are often used to provide advanced content to gifted learners, but they are usually open to all students who choose to enroll. Several cautions should be considered when arranging this type of class. Remember that even though bright students may be grouped together, the material still must be differentiated. Unless the content, materials, and strategies are modified to meet the needs of gifted learners, the practice of grouping the students together will not, by itself, ensure that the class is accomplishing that goal. A practice often experienced by gifted students is that of assigning them to all honors classes offered, whether the subject of the class is in their area of advanced development or not. Remember, gifted learners are not necessarily gifted in every academic area. Placing them in classes in which they can challenge already growing ability and interest is motivating; placing them in honors classes in subjects where their understanding and interest are average can be frustrating.

Mini-course Structure

What would happen if all secondary teachers could teach only what they wanted to teach and the students were allowed to learn just what they wanted to learn? This question formed the basis for an interesting minicourse structure at a Los Angeles area high school when a group of teachers came together to find out.

After securing permission to use a 6-week time block, each teacher listed courses he or she most wanted to teach and how many weeks they would require. These courses were then scheduled under traditional categories such as history, biology, language, and science, with a descriptive, often creative title. Not surprisingly, most teachers found that their favorite themes fell within the area in which they were credentialed to teach. The students were given the list of minicourses and allowed to choose their favorites. To the extent possible, first choices were honored, with second choices used only when classes became too full. Classes not chosen were dropped. These minicourses comprised only a part of each student's schedule and were fitted into the more traditional class schedule, with other periods run as usual.

The results were exciting! The students and the teachers were highly motivated; the classes became far more creative, better attended, and more productive. The next time minicourses were being scheduled, nearly twice as many faculty wanted to participate, and students who had previously not wished to participate in the gifted program requested permission to sign up. The experiment might have eventually encompassed the entire school had there not been a change in administration, with a resulting return to more traditional and "manageable" scheduling procedures.

Personalized System of Instruction

The Personalized System of Instruction (PSI), developed by Keller in 1968, has been one of the most widely investigated and validated methods designed to improve departmentalized teaching for nearly 30 years (Callahan & Smith, 1990). Holding great promise for gifted students in middle school and high school, the system requires teachers to give a clear description of material to be learned, develop individual units to guide student learning, allow students to pace themselves, and provide evaluation procedures with immediate feedback concerning student progress.

Program Structures for Gifted Learners in Middle and High School Grades

Program structures and models being used include: school-within-a-school, Governor's schools, Advanced Placement, and International Baccalaureate, the Secondary Triad Model, the Autonomous Learner Model (ALM), and the Purdue Secondary Model and Accelerated College Enrollment (ACE).

School-Within-a-School

Somewhat like a combination of core curriculum and special school, the school-within-a-school approach allows gifted students to meet in a more flexible, integrated setting for their entire educational experience but uses the regular school facility and resources. Physically the students are located in a wing of the school or in bungalows on school grounds. As a separate unit they can pursue a curriculum that is accelerated and uses processes at a higher level of complexity than the regular middle or high school classroom can provide. Such a setting allows for more community and field experiences and flexibility of grouping without interrupting the overall school schedule. Many districts find such provisions especially attractive for the highly gifted or as a solution to low-achieving gifted groups, because the cost is little more than offering another section of a regular class.

Governor's Schools

Special schools have been successfully implemented at the secondary level. Notable has been the success of various Governor's schools for gifted and talented learners in several states. In some states, the funding for all aspects of the program except transportation is provided by a combination of state and private resources. Most of the programs are located on university campuses for full utilization of campus facilities. In some cases, students are taught by university faculty. Many of the teachers are from secondary schools and are carefully selected. Student/teacher ratios are kept low. In most programs, grades are not awarded and university credit is not granted for completion of these programs.

The programs vary in length from 4 to 6 weeks and generally take place in the summer. They offer enrichment and acceleration in a variety of subject areas, with different programs focusing on different areas. The students in some programs are as young as sixth grade, whereas in others the participation is limited to high school juniors and seniors. All participants are chosen from carefully developed criteria (Karnes & Pearce, 1981).

One exception to the above profile is the Governor's school in North Carolina, opened in September 1980. It was the first public residential high school for highly able students in science and math. The school offers a full range of courses for 11th and 12th graders but emphasizes expanded course offerings in science and mathematics. The state provides the full costs of education and living expenses (Selby, 1980).

Advanced Placement (AP) Program

The Advanced Placement Program, available at approximately 20% of the secondary schools in the nation, is a program of college-level courses and examinations sponsored by the College Entrance Examination Board in New York City. Usually planned for a full year, AP can take the form of an honors class, an advanced course, a tutorial, or an independent study. Such experiences are intended to be challenging, giving greater opportunity for individual progress and accomplishment. They often require more work, take more time, and go into greater depth than the usual high school course. On completion of the course, students earn high school credits. To earn college credits or advanced placement in participating colleges and universities, students must complete AP examinations, given each year in the spring, and receive designated scores. In many universities a full year of college credit can be earned by AP work.

International Baccalaureate (IB) Program

Originating in Geneva, Switzerland, the International Baccalaureate Program program is composed of a 2-year program outline that includes a theory of knowledge course, a creativity, action, and service requirement, a research project, and an academically rigorous set of courses that emphasize second language proficiency. The program concludes with a formal examination requirement. Although it demands a high level of subject mastery, the program is quite flexible and a school is permitted to write its own program based on the strengths and interests of the students involved. It is usually taken during the last 2 years of high school. The resulting diploma is recognized and respected by the major European universities, and many American universities allow full college credit.

Secondary Triad Model

The Secondary Triad Model (Reis & Renzulli, 1986) is essentially a pull-out program using a resource room for presenting enrichment to meet the unique needs of gifted students. From this basis a wide array of goals, services, strategies, and procedures are offered to provide services for secondary gifted students. The model operates from a unique set of assumptions regarding the definition and identification of giftedness. Rather than seeing any individual as gifted or potentially gifted, the model assumes that the concept of giftedness reflects behavior resulting from an interaction among three basic clusters of human traits: above-average general or specific abilities, high levels of task commitment, and high levels of creativity. The model further assumes that gifted behaviors can be developed, that they are not always present, and that service should be provided only when such behaviors are exhibited.

When implemented at the secondary level, the Triad Model begins with the formation of an Interdisciplinary Planning Team that includes faculty members who volunteer to participate from each of the major academic areas. The team, which meets on a regular basis, is responsible for planning and organizing the program goals and activities, curricular compacting options, and schoolwide enrichment opportunities (Reis & Renzulli, 1989).

Autonomous Learner Model (ALM)

The Autonomous Learner Program was designed by Betts (1985) for the departmentalized structure of secondary schools to support the diversified cognitive, emotional, and social needs of secondary students. It is expected that gifted middle school or high school students will progress through its five major dimensions in a 3-year period of special classes, which meet at specified times throughout the week. For more information on this model, see Chapter 10.

Purdue Secondary Model

A comprehensive model of service for secondary departmentalized schools, the Purdue Secondary Model, developed by Feldhusen and Robinson (1986), offers a range of choices and possible structures to meet the diverse cognitive and affective needs of gifted, talented, and high-ability students. Within the model are provisions for counseling services, seminars, advanced placement or honors classes, acceleration, enrichment, cultural experiences, and career education. Saturday school, summer classes, correspondence study, and college classes are viable alternatives for delivery of services in addition to regular classroom instruction.

This comprehensive programming plan offers gifted students many options for meeting their unique needs. The model provides both accelerated and enriched learning experiences as it addresses the broader issue of curriculum development in a secondary setting.

Accelerated College Enrollment (ACE) and Early Entrance Programs

Many universities and colleges have arrangements with high schools that allow advanced high school students to take lower division classes during the summer or during the regular term. For the Pre-Accelerated College Enrollment (PACE) program 7th through 9th grade students are permitted to take one or two classes on Fridays or during the summer. The ACE program allows 10th through 12th grade students to enroll in the university jointly with their high school enrollment. They may take classes for credit and can plan their schedules, attend classes, and be treated like any other university student. Often a special office in the admissions division will handle their enrollment and advisement. According to a study by Brody,

Assouline, and Stanley (1990), most young entrants can be expected to be successful, graduating in a shorter period of time and earning more honors at graduation.

Early entrance programs allow exceptionally advanced students to enter college before the usual age. Most universities and colleges (87%) have provisions to accept such students without a high school diploma and a few (16%) will admit students of pre-high school age (Olszewski-Kubilius & Limburg-Weber, 2000). However, programs that are specifically developed to attract and support early entrants are rare because both educators and parents are cautious about such provisions. Many of the 11 programs now available admit students who simultaneously complete high school course requirements while taking college classes. Three of these programs admit students 3 to 4 years early, whereas most admit students as full-time students 1 or 2 years early. According to the research conducted and surveyed by Olszewski-Kubilius, (1995), in general, the academic performance of early entrants is impressive, their social and emotional maturity and stability were enhanced, they were better adjusted than their high school counterparts, made friends both within the early entrant group and in the general university community, and only a few regretted leaving high school early.

Johns Hopkins' Study of Mathematically Precocious Youth (SMPY)

One program that combines early entrance with content acceleration is the Johns Hopkins acceleration model, first known as the Study of Mathematically Precocious Youth (SMPY) (Stanley, 1979) and now more commonly referred to as the program of the Johns Hopkins Center for Academically Talented Youth (CTY). For more than a decade, SMPY has developed educational opportunities in several areas of radical acceleration (Stanley, 1979). An 8-week, fast-paced accelerated mathematics program was begun in 1977 that offered seventh graders algebra II and plane geometry (Fox, 1981). These classes differed from most homogeneously grouped programs for the gifted in several ways: Students were selected from measures of specific aptitude in mathematics; they were allowed to self-select into the program after being told that the work load was heavy; there was maximum use of academic learning time, that is, the real time in which a student is actually engaged in learning (Berliner, 1979); the material was fast paced and used a high level of abstraction and complexity; no class time was spent on drill or practice; and activities were kept to a minimum. This individualized program demanded intensive self-study. The SMPY acceleration program follows several basic assumptions (Sisk, 1988).

- Learning is a sequential developmental process.
- There are large differences in learning status among individuals at any given age.
- Students proceed through learning sequences at varying rates.
- Effective teaching involves assessing the student's status in the learning process and posing problems slightly exceeding the level already mastered.

In addition to the fast-paced math, a program for accelerated language arts was begun in 1978 at Johns Hopkins University (Durden, 1980) and a tutorial program based on diagnostic testing, followed by prescriptive instruction in math and verbal ability, was piloted in the summers of 1979 and 1980.

In 1979, the Johns Hopkins CTY was created and conducted talent searches throughout the country. Regional talent-search programs for pre-high school students are now found at universities throughout the country (Walsh, 1990). Stanley (1979) admits that these programs are designed to serve highly able, achieving, and motivated students:

> With more than 2,000 mathematically able boys and girls already identified, we do not have time and facilities to look for latent talent or potential achievers, worthy though that pursuit surely is. We leave that to the many persons who prefer to specialize in identification and facilitation of underachievers, "late bloomers," and the "disadvantaged gifted." Aside from some concern about sex differences in mathematical precocity, we have not tried to screen in a set percent of any group. From socioeconomic and ethnic standpoints, however, the high scorers have been a varied lot. (p. 101)

An example of radical acceleration, this program is now available in several states and universities and provides one alternative for a very specific population of highly gifted learners who are achieving far beyond their age-peers.

Consulting these well-developed program models will provide a range of options for planning the continuum of services in a district. Each can provide for a part of the population, and each has procedures that can be adapted for developing a specific structure. The detailed planning that is available with the model, which can be obtained by contacting the originator, will aid in its implementation. Keep in mind that the best use of any model is to adapt it to the specific needs of the district. These models are intended to be organizational take-off points and the professionals in the district must decide how and when to use the structures and their procedures. Although none of these models used alone will provide a total gifted program, each may provide for a part of a plan for a continuum of service.

In addition to the provisions described, other options might include:

Summer university courses, institutes, or programs for gifted learners.

Curriculum acceleration and early graduation through competency testing and fast-paced materials.

Flexible scheduling (less regular class attendance).

Interdisciplinary courses or themes.

Community-based career education and internships.

Special-topic courses.

Exchange student programs.

Special study centers.

Private schools for gifted students.

Student Views of Programs in the Middle and High Schools

Gifted students often find their secondary programs either inadequate or having specific defects. Gifted students from diverse racial, cultural, and socioeconomic backgrounds were selected to make a videotaped series at our university exploring the feelings of gifted students toward their programs. As was mentioned in the vignette, on page 286, the students most commonly complained that they were never challenged to use their abilities. They were often given more work, but usually of the same type used with typical learners. Even in situations where they were grouped with other gifted students for a small part of their program, they felt that the programs remained the same; only the people were different. Occasionally teachers worked with them to set up interesting educational experiences from which they could learn. These were the exceptions, however; and they expressed the belief that most of their teachers found them threatening and resented any special provisions made on their behalf.

The groups had suggestions for improving the situation. Most felt that a more open, flexible approach would have benefited them. One young woman, Trudy, who had experienced an individualized program for a couple of years in a language arts class, told of how much progress everyone had made and how interesting it was. "But the next year we had to go back into basic texts with our new teacher. We could use equipment like the controlled reader, but they set it at 400 words a minute and wouldn't let us change it. We were already reading 800 words per minute, but they didn't care. They said for our grade level, that was where we were supposed to be," she told us. One of the young men, Frank, had just been dropped from the xx track classes for highly gifted students because he felt the work was too boring and refused to do it. He was finding the x track for mildly gifted even worse.

All of these students expressed great appreciation for teachers who treated them like people and seemed to care how they felt. The students who were most pleased with their program came from an intermediate school where they were grouped together for three of their six periods in a cross-graded (fifth through eighth grade), open structure. Their two-teacher team used the responsive learning environment model and taught them all of their basic subjects. They were allowed to choose electives for the remaining periods from classes throughout the school. These students expressed none of the boredom and dissatisfaction of the others we interviewed.

Gifted 14- to 18-year-old students gave the highest priority for their high school goals as preparation for finding a career that would be interesting to them, being able to decide what vocation to follow, and being able to discover what special abilities they had (Stark, 1972). They felt their greatest problem at school was overcoming boredom, and they wanted the chance to participate in a group that could discuss personal problems with an understanding adult. They desired an advanced program in which they could work alongside a professional in the actual environment. They believed that teachers could help them learn if the teachers were more interested in them as individuals.

A study (Tremaine, 1979) comparing the attitudes, accomplishments, and achievements of gifted high school students participating in a gifted program with those of gifted high school students who did not participate reported the following results. The gifted students in a gifted program:

- Earned higher grade point averages.
- Took more advanced classes.

- Scored higher on Scholastic Aptitude Tests.
- Won significantly more scholarships and awards.
- Planned to attend a 4-year university in far greater numbers.
- Expressed more positive attitudes toward school after graduation.
- Were involved in and spent more time in school activities.
- Evaluated their teachers more highly.
- Enjoyed as many friends.

Tremaine feels that the contention that gifted programs result in snobbery, indifference, conceit, or any other negative quality cannot be validated by these data. In fact, the data indicate that gifted programs in the secondary school make significantly positive differences and are well worth the development and implementation effort.

By synthesizing the developmental theories as they apply to gifted adolescents, Leroux (1986) has been able to offer some suggestions to teachers to aid them in their work with these youngsters. The following list is an excerpt:

- Set exams that require creative, imaginative, and open-ended solutions.
- Ask open-ended questions that encourage risk and tolerate ambiguity.
- Consciously remove fear of failure and competitive elements in the teaching process.
- Expect quality but not perfection from highly able students.
- Use peer counseling to discuss emotions, sexual roles, social relations, and self-worth.
- Have students establish their own code of rules for behavior.
- Have students set goals for personal achievement in a subject.
- Develop a community service module for independent study.
- Conduct philosophy seminars to discuss principles of justice and moral reasoning.
- Have students and faculty participate jointly in decision-making.
- Plan group activities which build awareness of personal skills and social responsibility. (pp. 74-76)

In this chapter we have specified programs and problems unique to the education of gifted children from elementary into the adolescent years. If the needs of gifted learners are to be met, then coordinated programs must be planned with continuity. Programs must be open and responsive to the changing individuals, while providing continuous challenge and an adequate diversity of content and process. Although traditional gifted education models may often be used, the community, parents, students, and staff must make the decisions of structure and intent. Some goals can be generalized; others must be specifically set by the teacher, the student, and the parents in a cooperative effort. A gifted program is difficult to implement without a person who will be responsible, one who will give it full-time support. Money spent on a qualified enthusiastic coordinator will be wisely spent, because the returns are abundant.

Society needs the establishment and maintenance of challenging programs for gifted students. The job is not easy. As Drews (1976) comments:

> Clearly, we shall never meet the needs of the gifted by systems of prescribed programming, by behavioral objectives and accountability. The prime characteristic of the gifted is their individuality. The precondition of creativity is spontaneity. The creative moment is an intuitive flash. Those of our students who have this potentiality cannot be made to fit into neat sequences of stages of development, whether of intellect or character, as Piaget or Kohlberg suggests. (p. 27)

But be of courage. Important things are seldom easy.

QUESTIONS OFTEN ASKED

1. Which is better for a gifted learner, acceleration or enrichment?

Gifted students need both acceleration and enrichment, and any gifted program should be designed to provide both. When to use each will depend on the student's needs.

2. Will grouping by ability and need result in elitist groups of gifted students?

If you mean "Will they feel superior?" no, not usually. In fact, research shows that students who are grouped with their age-peers are more likely to feel superior than are those who are grouped with their intellectual peers. We must be sure what we mean when we use that term, however. The word elite actually means "a group chosen because of some special skill or ability." Perhaps we should ask why it is all right to be chosen for a special group for athletics or the arts, but it is not all right to have an advanced group in academics, and especially not to show higher levels of intelligence.

3. Which program structure is best for educating gifted learners?

That will depend on which gifted learners are being served and where they live. The needs of the student and the resources of the school and the community should be considered when deciding what program structure to use. A wide range or continuum of services is best as has been pointed out by the Richardson study and its Pyramid Project (Cox, Daniel, & Boston, 1985). Of course, some structures allow more service than others. An individual-ized classroom, cross-graded and with cluster and pull-out possibilities, provides far more continuity and service than a regular classroom with a pull-out program that provides minimum service for only part of the time. It might also be interesting to note that the Richardson study reports that the pullout format is the least effective and the most expensive option we can use.

4. Shouldn't we spend the funds for the gifted on the children instead of on an administrator?

In programs that have a full-time coordinator to administer the planning and implementation, the quality of the program and the range of services to the students have been found to be far better. When each classroom teacher is responsible for the expenditure of the funds, that teacher's training and knowledge of the needs of the gifted will determine how well the funds will be spent to meet those needs. When you consider that fewer than one out of six teachers who work with gifted students has any training regarding education for the gifted, the likelihood of that arrangement being productive is minimal. In addition to all the other services coordinators provide, they can arrange for many learning experiences for the youngsters that are free or very inexpensive. Teachers may not have the time or knowledge of resources to make this happen.

5. Should we identify the children first and then plan a program to meet their needs, or plan a program first and then identify students to fit it?

This is a bit like the chicken and the egg; both have advantages. This is also one of the reasons for having as wide a continuum of services as possible. Remember, the only reason you are identifying children as gifted is to find appropriate placement and educational experiences for them. If your community has limited resources—for example, no resources for performing arts programs—it would be inappropriate to identify students with performing arts talent as part of your program. Know your resources first; then plan your basic program structure. By allowing flexibility within the structure you will be able to serve most of the students in need of special service.

6. **There has been concern about middle school students being in a period when the brain is between growth spurts. Should middle school programs reflect this by offering only review and no new material?**

The ideas about brain growth occurring in cycles are interesting theories that bear watching; however, even if they are accurate, each person will have a somewhat different time cycle, and gifted students will be the most different. One problem for this age population is that schools reintroduce information already covered in elementary school. There needs to be more communication among elementary programs, middle school programs, and high school programs. It would be far better to individually assess the students using pretesting and posttesting, functional assessment, and individual conferences to find out what they need to learn instead of generalizing about cycles of learning that may or may not be occurring.

7. **Aren't advanced placement and honors classes enough to meet the needs of secondary gifted students?**

These program structures are ways of providing for content needs when they are organized and taught with the needs of the students in mind. However, they do not meet all the other needs noted in Chapter 2 and in this chapter and suffer from the same lack of continuity and communication, limited time, and other limitations, that we have seen in other discussions of the secondary structure. Advanced placement and honors classes should be only a part of an overall plan for the secondary program for gifted and talented students.

CHECKING FOR UNDERSTANDING
Follow-Up Activity

Investigate the gifted program in your district or at your school.

- Is there a gifted program advisory committee?
- Is there a statement of philosophy, program goals, and curriculum standards?
- Is there a coordinator for the gifted program?
- What provision has been made for teacher and staff professional development in gifted education?
- Have the resources and needs of the school and community been assessed?
- Are there screening and identification procedures organized and accessible?
- What organizational modifications are being used?
- What program structures are being used?

- What programs are available for gifted students in the middle school and high school?
- Does the program for gifted learners provide flexible grouping, continuous progress, intellectual peer interaction, continuity, differentiated curricula, and teachers with specialized education in the needs of the gifted learners?
- Is there a plan for student assessment and program evaluation?

Discuss your results with your class. What are your conclusions about the services provided in your district or school?

✿ SUMMARY

Developing Programs for Gifted Learners

1. The primary purpose of the gifted program is to provide opportunities for gifted learners to meet the needs that cannot be met in a regular classroom program.
2. What is done specifically for each child will depend on assessment data and the continuum of services available. Programs for the gifted do not begin with different curricula or different structures for learning, but with the distinct needs of gifted learners taken into consideration.
3. When students are expected to adjust to the average classroom program, the gifted students lose most as they constantly must pull down to work with the highest level of instruction provided. This situation leads to loss of ability, especially among girls and minority students, as regression toward a more average ability level is the observed outcome.

Planning a Program for Gifted Learners

4. All programs for gifted learners, regardless of how they are structured, must provide differentiation, flexible grouping, continuous progress, intellectual peer interaction, continuity, and teachers with specialized education for this population if optimal learning is to occur.
5. Careful planning is necessary to develop a gifted program that will provide the best match for the needs of the students, parents' expectations, the school administration's philosophy, community resources, and the resources and commitment of the school staff.
6. Standards for gifted programs provide a useful guide for developing programs for gifted learners, an incentive for program improvement, and criteria for program evaluation.
7. It has been found that in states in which the total time of at least one person, such as a coordinator, is devoted to gifted education, far more students have been adequately served. What is true for state levels can be said also for local levels.

Program Organizations and Structures for Gifted Learners in the Elementary Schools

8. Our challenge is to find a place for children who may be 6 years old, read like a 10-year-old, write like a 6-year-old, solve math problems like a 12-year-old, talk like a 15-year-old, and handle emotions and hurt feelings like a 4-year-old.
9. As was true in the home, the responsive learning environment, in which the child is the guide for the pace and content of learning, is still the best provision for optimizing learning.
10. Some of the educational modifications used with young gifted learners are: early admission; nongraded or cross-age grouped classes; individualized instruction; accelerated promotion (i.e., grade-skipping); independent study; mentors; pull-out or resource room programs; grouping by ability or need (e.g., clustering in the regular classroom); field trips; after-school, Saturday, or summer enrichment; special classes; magnet classes; and special schools. There can be advantages and limitations to each approach.
11. Grouping in any form does not solve poor teaching or inappropriate curriculum, but without grouping we can limit good teaching and the delivery of an appropriate curriculum.
12. Each district would be advised to have a wide variety of programs available for the continuum of services needed. Because no one structure can meet the needs of all the gifted learners in any district, providing a range of planned services would be the best practice.
13. The continuum can range from regular classrooms with cluster grouping, to special schools. Individualized classrooms allow more flexibility for the learner and may be combined with clusters, pullout, and nongraded or cross-age grouping with even more effect. Special classes and special schools allow even more needs to be met, especially for the highly gifted students. Other possibilities for providing for gifted learners include adjunct programs, independent study, mentors, tutorials, internships, and resource rooms. There can be advantages and limitations to each program structure.
14. Gifted students in any of the program structures listed have higher achievement than do gifted students who are in regular programs or those who are not in gifted programs at all.
15. It is important to find a way to individualize school learning experiences so that gifted individuals can have their atypical needs met continuously throughout their school career.

Program Organizations And Structures For Gifted Learners In Middle And High School Grades

16. Even if they were identified and had special programs in the elementary grades, by middle school, gifted learners will often find few special provisions made to modify their programs. During or after sixth grade, most schools departmentalize their curriculum and the concepts of differentiation and continuous progress are seldom used.

17. An often-used practice at the secondary level that needs to be examined is the establishment of one or two advanced classes into which all gifted students are tracked regardless of their needs and abilities. Neither tracking systems nor a few special classes comprise a complete program that can meet the needs of secondary gifted learners.

18. Gifted students in heterogeneously grouped classes too often may be asked to demonstrate mastery in fact-based information that was mastered years before. Such practices may result in mediocre performance by them and lack of challenge in their learning.

19. Limitations to learning such as the limited time elements available in departmentalized programs, the fragmentation of knowledge, and the lack of flexibility in the pace of learning found in secondary education need to be addressed if optimal learning is to take place for gifted learners.

20. Modifications to program organization used in middle and high schools to meet the needs of gifted learners include, early admission, core academic classes, group seminars, honors classes, minicourses, Personalized Instruction, and early entrance to college.

21. Program structures and models being used include: school-within-a-school, Governor's Schools, Advanced Placement, International Baccalaureate, the Secondary Triad Model, the Autonomous Learner Model, the Purdue Secondary Model, and Accelerated College Enrollment. Just as was suggested at the elementary level, field trips; after-school, Saturday, or summer classes; independent study; and mentors are other possible elements of programs that can be provided.

22. The data indicate that gifted programs in the secondary school make significantly positive differences and are well worth the development and implementation effort.

8 Outreach of Programs and Program Evaluation

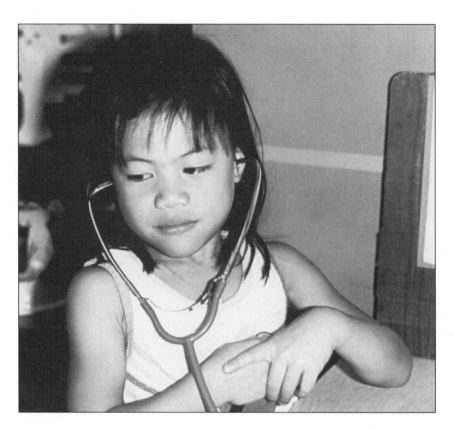

In this chapter the reader will discover information on:

- Career education programs for the gifted learner.
- Rural programs for gifted learners.
- The community as a resource to enrich programs for gifted learners.
- Home schooling—An alternative approach to educating gifted learners.
- Global education.
- The evaluation of programs for gifted learners.

What do you want schools—even families—to accomplish? Do you want to shape adults who will simply repeat what has been done by previous generations? Or do you want individuals who are capable of invention? Those are the real questions. If you want to produce conformists, then the traditional school is perfect. But, if you want original thinkers, you need methods that will permit invention, not simply external reinforcements.

PIAGET (CITED IN WEINHEIMER, 1972, PP. 118, 120)

The interview with the group of highly gifted high school seniors mentioned in Chapter 7 was videotaped for use in a teacher education class. The students had covered most of the usual issues when the interviewer asked, "What do you plan to do when you graduate? What do you think you want to do with your life?" A couple of students mentioned college, although they weren't sure why. It just seemed to be the expected next step. Then Julie, a very pretty young woman, spoke up: "I don't know, the way school is and everything. I'm really not interested in anything we've done. There's such pressure to fit into a mold, especially for women, you know. I just don't know. Maybe I'll travel a year and write. I still like to write, not in English class, but for myself. But right now I just want to get away from school, it's such a drag. I really feel dull and bored."

When you looked at her pretty, young face, so serious, so tired looking, so depressed, you really had to wonder what had disillusioned her, "turned her off" so completely. The group was quiet then, and you could tell they knew what she was feeling. They all wondered what was next, and no one seemed happy about the prospects.

CAREER EDUCATION FOR THE GIFTED LEARNER

The general area of career education for the gifted has drawn the attention of educators, researchers, and government agencies since the National Invitational Seminars on Career Education for Gifted and Talented Students convened at the University of Maryland on October 15, 1972. Hoyt and Hebeler (1974) reported the contributions of this and a subsequent conference. Although we can find a variety of definitions and objectives for career education in the schools, most definitions include these factors:

1. Availability of information about and experience in the world of work to all students K–14 and beyond if desired.

2. Provision of occupational skills and related knowledge and skills.

3. Development of attitudes conducive to occupational responsibility.

4. Development of personal and interpersonal skills, valuing, and communication and decision-making skills.

5. Awareness of consumer issues and consumer rights.

6. Relevance of school studies to preparation for gainful and satisfying employment.

It has been pointed out that career education is not intended to displace liberal arts curricula, but rather to strengthen the student's motivation for pursuing such education. Although some fear that overemphasis on vocational training may subvert the broader goals of education, those espousing career education believe that education that does not contain future goals for the learners becomes irrelevant. It is true that career education and career guidance should be available to all students. However, it is not true that all students should be presented with the same options, asked to process the same information, or proceed through the same decision-making steps. Individualized programming and resources must be made available.

Career development for gifted and talented youth should begin with the parents, continue to be nurtured by educators, and find support in the work settings in which professionals are found. At-risk students from homes where parents do not encourage such development must have additional guidance to be sure that they are exposed to the full range of career possibilities that their abilities would allow (Delisle & Squires, 1989). Most educators believe that the gifted will, because of their ability, be able to easily choose any career and succeed in it. Delisle and Squires find that this belief has caused a variety of problems for these students, including:

- Premature career selection based on someone else's perception of "what a gifted student should become";
- Extended delay in selecting a career path owing to lack of information on the range of career choices available;
- Perceived inability to change career paths owing to the investments of time and money often incurred in career preparation programs; and
- Selection of a career that is beneath one's ability level owing to a lack of role models and/or encouragement from family, school, or society. (pp. 97–98)

In addition, gifted and talented students may encounter the following problems in establishing their careers:

- They find conventional career search programs boring and trivial.
- They possess multiple talents and interests that complicate career choices and tend to make a career search a painful process of focusing on one talent area and rejecting other areas.
- Many become frustrated with the study of science.
- Many are not motivated to succeed but rather to avoid failure at all costs.
- High expectations of parents, teachers, themselves, and society operate as pressures and restrict their choice.
- The length of training for most professional careers preferred by many gifted students is long, requiring an early vocational decision and long-term commitment.
- Gifted individuals tend to regard their work as a means of self-expression and build a life-style around it, becoming consumed by work-related activities.
- Social isolation results from interests that are too different from those of their peers.
- There is a lack of adults in role models who have the intelligence or creative ability of the gifted student in the area of interest.
- Problems faced by women seeking careers in our society are of special concern to nearly all gifted females.

To aid in planning career guidance for gifted and talented students, Kokaska and Brolin (1985) present four stages of development: career awareness; career exploration; career preparation; and career placement, follow-up, and lifelong learning. The following programs have been successful in career education for gifted and talented learners and are presented as a partial resource for planning.

Suggested Programs

The Purdue Model

Feldhusen and Kolloff (1979) suggest a three-stage model of career education that includes instructional activities to enhance and develop creative thinking, problem-solving skills, project abilities, exploratory reading, and independent learning capacity. The model provides a framework for instructional planning for gifted learners. Stage 1 focuses on basic thinking skills and is characterized by short-span activities. The gifted child can begin to explore career possibilities from printed materials and visiting professionals.

Stage 2 introduces creative thinking and problem-solving strategies that stress the process of fact finding, problem finding, idea finding, solution finding, and acceptance finding. Although guidance is still provided by the teacher, the student is involved in implementing the problem-solving process. At this stage, the child begins self-study and is guided toward self-understanding.

At Stage 3 the student gets guidance and encouragement from the teacher, but independently proceeds to research and complete a project. Career mentors provide the next step in career exploration, with in-depth involvement on site, an example of third-level exploration. The mentor relationship is to provide a role model and a guide for meaningful career exploration. The Purdue three-stage model can be used in a regular classroom, in a resource room, or in a special class.

BIASED

Delisle (1984) presents a career education program based on the acronym BIASED. The program for gifted adolescents incorporates these concepts:

B—Basic information about currently available career options and possible future choices based on employment projections.

I—Introspection regarding the personal comforts and disadvantages of selected careers.

A—Adaptation to particular occupations through active involvement in the everyday lives of professionals.

SE—Selection of a career path based on knowledge and insights gained by completing various portions of the above activities.

D—Direction to students who are not yet ready to select a career path or area of professional training.

Enriched Career Search

Willings (1986) offers a seven-module program that can be offered as a 2-year program with one class meeting each week, two 2-week programs held in two consecutive summers, or a 3-week program for teachers and counselors that includes training in administering the program. The programs are available in English and Spanish.

Module 1. Your Career and You. The students explore the theory that in work people are seeking to satisfy two drives—the drive "to be somebody" and the drive "to do something worthwhile." Other issues are discussed, such as moving from fantasy to reality or money in the context of overall satisfaction.

Module 2. Self-Evaluation. Students gain wider insights into themselves by writing and evaluating exercises exploring their career choices to date.

Module 3. Job Study. Students are introduced to the various aspects of job study—the hidden factors, the key and complementary skills, physical skills, job features, requirements for entry, problems of training, difficulties and distastes, and sources of rewards.

Module 4. The Adult World. Students participate in simulations of various situations.

Module 5. Group Roles. The students discover the various roles needed by each group.

Module 6. Ethical Considerations in Work. The codes of ethics of various professionals are discussed, and guidelines are offered on how the students can analyze their personal reactions to ethical situations and, from their reactions, arrive at their personal code of ethics. Willings (1986) feels that no one can or should tell a student what is right and good.

Module 7. Career Strategies and Strategies for Creative Growth. Including values clarification in the study of careers is also a concern of other researchers (Garrison, Stronge, & Smith, 1986; Kerr, 1986). One outcome of the study of values that is of great advantage to the gifted student is identifying the aspects of a career that are personally important. Kerr believes career education must be a search for meaning, not a search for a job. She points out that clarifying values and setting goals based on values have led honors students to change not only their career goals but the way they determine those goals. The frequent occurrence of early eminence among very bright gifted adolescents makes finding a mentor a crucial step in their career development, especially for young women. Mentors not only provide role models; they can support, encourage, and facilitate professional socialization and access to advanced training. An additional phase drawn to our attention by Kerr is the maintenance of productivity. Counselors and those teaching career education can find helpful ideas in Kerr's work.

Competent counseling can direct individuals into new fields that they might not have considered, encourage delaying a decision until major possibilities are known, and help the student to understand parental pressures and to facilitate scholarship opportunities.

Career education for the disadvantaged gifted is an area needing special attention (Dunham & Russo, 1983). Some of the logistics of developing careers today are especially difficult for gifted students from low-socioeconomic homes. Planning for career changes, meeting rising college costs, and finding support available for college tuition may be difficult to manage. Dunham and Russo suggest providing a program of career education that includes realistic job opportunities consonant with the potential of disadvantaged students. Such programs should envision a broad horizon, avoid limited or short-sighted goals, and provide opportunities for adults to work closely and serve as role models in the students' own community.

Singer (1974) finds that the student's image of the future influences the achievement of that student in the present. If the belief in the future is positive, if the student can envision personal success, then academic achievement will be high and school will have meaning for that student. When the future focus is weak or negative, poor achievement, maladaptive behavior, and dropping out of school may result. The study of possible futures can be intriguing to gifted students and can impact their career choices.

Activities to Develop Awareness of Career Possibilities

The following activities can be done in the class or suggested by the career counseling center:

1. Ask students to bring to class the "Help Wanted" section of their newspaper. In small groups, compile the following information:
   * Identify the kinds of job opportunities that now exist.
   * What differences are there in job opportunities for men and for women?
   * What kinds of qualifications and training are required?
   * Discuss.

2. Watch for job roles on television during one week and note the different jobs presented. By whom are they filled (by men, women, older, younger, minorities, etc.)? What kinds of qualifications do you notice the job holders having?

3. Write a list of job categories on the board (e.g., Agricultural, Business, Banking, Communications, Computing and Data Processing, Clerical, Craftsperson, Dental, Drafting, Education, Electronics, Engineering, Florists, Foreign Affairs, Graphic Arts, Health, Home Economics, Hotel/Restaurant, Judicial, Law Enforcement, Politics). Ask students to write down as many names of people who fit in these categories as they can in 3 minutes. Now ask them to go over their lists to see how many are men, women, minorities, and so forth. Discuss.

4. Have students list all advertised positions that interest them personally. Then have them list unadvertised job titles in those interests that describe more specifically what they want to do. These lists can be used by the teacher or counselor to discuss further academic training needed to fill those positions.

5. Using a current issue of a newspaper and working in small groups, list societal problems that are not yet solved. Discuss possible solutions and what jobs these solutions might create. What jobs might no longer exist if the problems are solved? Discuss the group's findings with the class.

RURAL PROGRAMS

In addition to the programming possibilities mentioned in Chapter 7, those planning for gifted learners in rural areas may want to consider mobile enrichment vans, independent study "hot-lines" (access to mentors through a telephone system), itinerant teachers, correspondence courses, summer seminars followed by monthly meetings, and residential summer institutes (Silverman, 1980). Technology networks such as telelearning (Lewis, 1989), electronic bulletin boards, and videotape exchanges (Southern & Spicker, 1989) have been successful in providing opportunities for rural gifted students to exchange information and to receive advanced course work.

Beyond technological developments, Witters and Vasa (1981) consider the most important task in providing educational opportunities for rural gifted students to be the selection and training of teachers who work with these students. Birnbaum (1977) also emphasizes that problems with access to resources, from transportation to materials, may inhibit cultural and intellectual development. Continuous and assertive leadership is necessary to change a number of other factors inhibiting the development of quality gifted programs: poor community understanding, teacher/administrator hostility, and logistical and organizational problems. Cooperatives, consortia of districts, summer programs, and mobile services are suggested as possible solutions.

Administrators developing gifted programs for rural schools will find that advanced planning is a necessary first step that might not be given proper emphasis (Pitts, 1986). At a minimum, giftedness as it will be used must be defined by teachers and administrators, general goals should be set, the program's content should be decided, and an identification procedure should be selected. Because the best teachers are often called on for any new project and undoubtedly will be asked to participate in this program, Pitts believes that, as a second step, these teachers must understand the amount of time and energy the planning process will take and express willingness to take on this new commitment. Third, he cautions those planning the program to be aware that identification procedures are particularly delicate and critical in a small town. He suggests a blind review of the screening data that involves members of the local board of education. Fourth, he feels it is important to start small, and fifth, to use existing resources as much as possible. Sixth, program planners must consider the need for adequate transportation, and finally, they must remember that a local program is to meet local needs to the extent allowed by local resources, not to attempt to duplicate programs designed for other larger or more affluent communities. Planning and implementing a gifted program in a rural community may need extra care to succeed. However, Pitts believes that such a program,

> Can produce a sense of community pride, can open doors of career opportunity and greater academic success for students, and can stimulate enthusiasm and renewed commitment on the part of the teaching staff which make the hours of planning and program development worthwhile. (p. 25).

USING THE COMMUNITY

Many gifted programs have stretched their resources by using facilities and people from the community as part of the teaching process. Community involvement does not just happen by chance. A person has to believe that effort spent in community-related activities will indeed make some difference. Gifted students often have a high degree of idealism, and if allowed to use their abilities to make needed changes in the school or community, such activity will foster future commitment to societal goals. Here are some possible activities:

- Conducting a survey in the school or community that will provide information needed to change something; then doing it.
- Making a place in the school or community more beautiful. Be sure agreement is obtained on what those involved consider more beautiful.
- Working with community groups or organizations for civic improvement.
- Planning money-raising projects for a worthy charity or to buy needed materials for the school.

Class projects can often be made more meaningful by involving students in the larger community. The coordinator of gifted programs might involve the community by:

- Equipping a van or bus as a mobile laboratory to take students into the field for an integrated experience in science, geography, the social sciences, language, mathematics, and interpersonal relations.
- Contacting the nearest retirement community for experts who could serve as mentors to students who are ready for advanced challenges. Some people who would be uncomfortable teaching in a larger group may be willing to work with one or two youngsters.
- Contacting parents to give lessons in their area of interest at their place of business or before groups in the classroom.
- Using the business facilities close to school—stock exchanges, real estate offices, stores, hospitals, pharmacies, insurance companies—for learning opportunities. These facilities are not to be used for one-time-only field trips, but as ongoing or more in-depth contacts. These visits would be especially meaningful to the few students who have special interest in a related field.

- Using tape recorders to direct teams of students on independent searches or explorations of the surrounding area's history, geography, climate, or economic and cultural nature.

The community can also be an amazing source of free materials for the asking. Worth contacting are:

- The telephone company. They have old telephone poles, used equipment, cable spools, and storage containers; some will even set up a communication system in the classroom as a public relations service.
- Electronics companies. They have obsolete electronic parts that can be used for great experiments.
- Construction projects or lumber and hardware stores. Besides the obvious, in their scrap bin they may have old fencing, paint, rope, bricks, and other treasures.
- Billboard companies. Their throwaways are great for signs and displays.
- Rug stores or rug cleaners. If they know it is for kids at school, they often give odds and ends to make a van or classroom really livable.
- Nurseries, agricultural schools, and park departments. They may have plants to donate to science projects and botany buffs.
- Meat packers or meat markets. Check for spare parts to use in biology and anatomy units.

The list is endless; once teachers and their students start thinking this way, they will add many, many more. For very little money a lot of useful items can be purchased from the district, state surplus, local community college, or university warehouse— everything from typewriters and computers to paper cups and newsprint. Hidden treasures are everywhere, sometimes even laying forgotten in the school's storage rooms. If the school will value the items and write a letter specifying that any materials contributed were donated, then teachers may find it very easy to solicit contributions from private families because the donor can claim these donations as a tax deduction. This practice tends to encourage community involvement and support.

HOMESCHOOLING: AN ALTERNATIVE APPROACH

Some children, no matter how supportive the school is, will not benefit from the programs available for gifted learners. These children may learn too rapidly or think at levels of abstractness and complexity that are so advanced that materials are not easily available for them. These may be students who are highly or exceptionally gifted and for whom provisions such as radical acceleration are unavailable. For such students, parents who have the interest and the ability may need to become their teachers at home.

> It's a dream school. Individualized instruction in a responsive learning environment. Integrated curriculum, students traveling at their own pace through material they've selected, small teacher/student ratio. Active involvement in learning, with learning level and style matched to each student. Skiing down tree-covered slopes, horseback riding, chasing newts in a mountain stream, gardening outdoors under the sun, easy

computer access, science exploration in a fully equipped laboratory or rock-hopping at the beach, reading as much and as often as you wish and what you wish without fear of a "pop quiz." Music, painting, and photography (not just on Friday), writing, producing and acting in your own plays. Unlimited resources and community involvement. Pondering, asking questions and seeking answers as you desire. Meeting and interacting with people of all ages, from all places. Dancing and singing your way through the day. (Nidever, 1993, p. 13)

With these words a mother of two highly gifted learners begins her description of their experience with homeschooling. At a time when many schools are experiencing budget cuts, they are also coping with overcrowding, high teacher-student ratios, and an overwhelming diversity of student needs in the classroom. These needs range from a lack of skills to do school work, to inability to focus on school owing to devastating problems in the students' lives, to lack of motivation or discipline. In such conditions, many parents are seeking an alternative approach to public schooling for their children.

Parents of highly gifted learners are especially concerned. Even in schools where student needs are not as serious as those just described, their children are usually 2 to 4 years ahead of the age-graded curriculum of the classes in which they are placed and seldom find intellectual peers among the students with whom they are grouped. The result, through no fault of the teacher, is a lack of the challenge, stimulation, and acceptance necessary to ensure the continued growth and healthy development of bright young minds. Homeschooling may provide a good alternative approach to their education.

Most states have provisions for homeschooling built into their education code. The best known exemptions from compulsory schooling are enrollment in private schools and the provision of a certified tutor. Another approach often written in the code as an alternative is the development of an independent study plan under district supervision. The way in which this provision is implemented by a district varies and ranges widely in the amount of actual supervision the district will require. When built around the types of activities and experiences described above, such independent study programs can offer an exciting and positive learning experience for gifted learners.

Families choose to homeschool their children for a variety of reasons and although religion was once thought to be the primary reason, quality of learning is now more often the motivation. Homeschooling parents may want to provide more challenging coursework for their gifted learners or to focus on subjects that are given little time in school but are of great interest to their children. They may wish to adjust the way learning is presented to better fit the style of their children, changing the pace, the depth, the complexity, or the way the learning can be expressed. Haydock (1997) found that by changing the structure to accommodate for the activity level of her child, his energy, which was previously not appreciated in his classroom, now could be positively used to bring excitement to his learning. Problems with rewards, competition, and socialization that before took much of her son's energy could be refocused and re-examined in a safe environment where he could build intimacy at his own pace.

The structure of homeschooling varies. Some parents, at least at the beginning, use structured curricula either provided by the school system or purchased from publishers. In a method known as unschooling, the child is allowed to pursue personal needs, passions, or curiosities in their learning experiences. Some school districts allow children engaging in homeschooling to be part-time students, enrolling in extra-curricular activities or classes of particular interest like math or science. There are online resources and community facilities and centers that can be incorporated into the structure for homeschooling. The variations and combinations are as numerous as the families participating in this schooling alternative.

There is, according to Schon (1997), an adjustment period that every child who has attended school must work through. Because they have been told when, how, and where to do their studies and what those studies should be—often for many years—they may not know how to cope. Coping strategies and self-reliance may be among the first lessons that they will need. At first, some children may push the boundaries as they redefine who they are and what they can do in this new environment. As Sanchez (1999) explains, homeschooling does not mean that the parents have to be their child's only teachers. There are homeschool support groups that can provide others to teach subjects about which the parent is less informed.

There are many factors that impact the decision when families are considering homeschooling: the characteristics of the learner, including motivation, self-initiation, independence, and drive; the skill of the parent as teacher; and the accessibility of resources. However, when the fit is right, homeschooling can be very successful. Ray and Wartes (1991) report that the average scores of homeschooled students fall in the 65th to 80th percentile on standardized tests, which are higher than the national norm, which averages around the 50th percentile of students who were conventionally schooled. Homeschooled students are found to be better socialized and more mature than public school students as well, evidencing a stronger self-concept and set of values. As Nidever (1991) comments, "The intimacy of the homeschooling situation affords an opportunity to use what works based upon the need of the moment" (p. 13). Clearly this approach can provide the most responsive learning environment.

Comments from a mother who chose homeschooling for her children gives insight into the process and its value:

> This experience caused me to look differently at education. I noticed that what was hindering Nicole and Evan the most was direct instruction. What was most beneficial to them was to allow them to choose their own studies and to proceed in manners that worked best for them . . . However, the most interesting and even eerie discovery was finding that Nicole did indeed have other amazing talents as she had previously claimed . . . Her attitude and hope for the future have dramatically improved. (Staehle, 2000)

Individualization, the ability to meet learners at their individual level and move with their interest at their pace, fosters high levels of learning. Knowledgeable parents have more information about and more interest in the success of their individual learner than any other teacher could. If they know the community well, they can access it for learning experiences. If they can share their love of learning, sustain the excitement of exploration and discovery, accept mistakes as clues to further learning, be comfortable with the risks needed to challenge ideas, and be patient with the struggles to develop self-control and self-esteem, they can help their child profit from the vast possibilities of homeschooling. From Plato to Maslow, the inborn curiosity and natural striving toward growth of the human has been extolled.

When the educator at home can organize to provide for the exploration, experimentation, questioning, and flexibility needed to tap this curiosity and natural striving, the growth and accomplishment of the learner can be truly exemplary, and the learning can be limitless.

For more information on homeschooling, read Colfax and Colfax (1988), Guterson (1992), Kearney (1992), Linehan (1992), Ray and Wartes (1991), and Wallace (1983). There are also periodicals that may be of interest: *Home Education,* Home Education Press, PO Box 1083, Tonasket, WA 98855 and *Growing Without Schooling,* 2269 Massachusetts Ave., Cambridge, MA 02140. You may wish to contact the National Homeschool Association, PO Box 157290, Cincinnati, OH 45215-7290; the National Home Education Research Institution, 5000 Deer Park Drive, SE, Salem, OR 97301; or Isabelle Nidever, 9303 Broadway, Temple City, CA 91780.

GLOBAL EDUCATION

Global education must be considered essential in the preparation of a gifted student for the future. Boyer (cited in King, 1985) identified two objectives for the nation's schools: to make it possible for individual aptitudes and abilities to be discovered, and to discover our connections with each other so that we can live socially, civilly, and spiritually in tune with those about us; "The curriculum must affirm both our independence and our interdependence" (p. 2).

Experiencing the customs of other countries helps us to understand the people better.

VanTassel-Baska and McEachron-Hirsch (1990) see a natural linkage between global education and the education of gifted learners. They point out that gifted education is at a critical juncture regarding curriculum. We must find a way to educate students to become creative scientists and ethical and moral individuals sensitive to human needs. In addition, the characteristics of gifted learners allow them to be an especially logical group for meaningful study of global issues. VanTassel-Baska and McEachron-Hirsch cite the related characteristics as a potential for greater and more profound ethical concerns and insights: a heightened sense of altruism, ability to deal with complex relationships and multidisciplinarity, an affinity to focus on real problems, and effective use of the problem-solving process. Moreover, they suggest that a comprehensive global curriculum can offer such learners a basis for leadership development. Passow (1989) also cites gifted characteristics that make the study of global education imperative for gifted students: unusual potential for intellectual initiative, creativity, critical thinking, social responsibility, empathy, and potential leadership.

Global education as an educational movement is some 30 years old and expands the international studies area, which has included the study of nations, geographic areas, cultures, international organizations, and diplomacy. Students in global education additionally deal with the connections and ties that link individuals and peoples of the world (O'Neil, 1989). Kniep (cited in O'Neil, 1989) has proposed a framework for global education with four organizing areas of study: human values; global systems; global problems and issues; and the history of contacts and interdependence among peoples, cultures, and nations.

The movement to place emphasis on global education is not without controversy (O'Neil, 1989). First, how it should be presented is not in common agreement. Some supporters of the movement want separate courses added to the curriculum with their own content, whereas others believe that we would be better served with an infusion of global information in every course in every discipline. The lack of knowledge of teachers in the complex issues involved is another concern, as is the quality and nature of the materials available to teachers. Some critics suggest that students cannot develop a world perspective and a national, patriotic perspective at the same time, and believe that such studies destroy a commitment to democracy and the American way of life. Developing curricula that allow civic responsibility and global awareness and concern to coexist is the challenge.

Recommendations for implementing a curriculum for global education include offering both courses and programs with an international focus and infusing international issues in all courses. System-wide planning for global education should include cultures education, intercultural relations, and developmental issues. Increasing incorporation of international perspectives in textbooks and expanding study abroad and exchange programs are also important (Hughes-Wiener, 1988). Kniep (1989) suggests a scope and sequence that include the study of systems, human values, persistent issues and problems, global history, and global actors.

> Self-actualization is but one goal of gifted education; self-actualization in service to humankind is the twin goal. To achieve these goals, we need persons who are caring, compassionate, conscientious, committed, and involved and who understand what giftedness means and what obligations to self and society being gifted places on them. (Passow, 1988a, p. 15)

EVALUATING PROGRAMS FOR GIFTED LEARNERS

The word evaluation is for many people, anxiety producing. It has come to mean a judgment: the act of validating or invalidating a person or thing. Often the word is mistakenly used to mean examination or testing. If used properly, it would mean, to ascertain the value of or to get to know about someone or something. Evaluation goes far deeper than testing, although tests may be used as part of the data-collection process. In this discussion, we will consider evaluation as the process of collecting a variety of data to help us understand the gifted program—data that can be used to improve program planning and implementation (Figure 8.1).

Programs for gifted learners tend to be more difficult to evaluate than other school programs, but such evaluations are even more critical owing to the lack of permanence often experienced by these programs. If the program is to last for any length of time, there must be built-in accountability. Those who make decisions about supporting the program for gifted learners must know that the students are benefiting from the program and that the money allotted is being well spent. Those implementing the program also need to know in what ways they must work to improve the program. The parents and the students need information about the program and its impact.

If the evaluation plan for the program is one of the first steps taken by the planning committee, it is far more likely that the program can be justified to those who must provide the resources, and viewed by the staff as needed. The program components adopted after such a plan is established are more likely to be the options that best meet the needs of the students whom the program is meant to serve. A needs assessment will demonstrate that the proposed program can meet needs not

Figure 8.1 *Tips for Evaluating Gifted Programs*

Make sure you:

- Know clearly what each person or group involved in your program needs to know.
- Choose instruments and tools to give you that information.
- Set up collection points throughout the year in addition to your assessment procedure.
- Collect only useful data. If you find state or district forms or procedures that require the collection of irrelevant data, discuss them with people at that level. Tell them what data you have, and inquire into their need for the data they are requesting. You may find that they will be willing to change their procedures into a more meaningful model. Sometimes procedures become institutionalized and continue as they always have only because no one questions their purpose.
- Communicate your information to all concerned persons and groups. It is impossible to get the kind of support your program needs if key people remain unaware of what you are doing. From the student to the board member, keep all persons informed.
- Use your evaluation data to produce growth in the program and with the gifted students. If done properly, evaluation will never be a final judgment.

met by the regular program and clearly stated goals and standards will show how the program plans to meet these needs. Once the program is implemented, a well thought out program evaluation plan can identify the strengths and weaknesses of the many elements and corrections can be made where needed. The evaluation plan should include the major functional areas of the program, such as student selection, teacher training, organization and structure, curriculum differentiation, availability of resources, effectiveness of support services, and program management.

When planning a program evaluation, one of the first questions should be, "Who needs to know what?" What persons are interested in, involved in, or responsible for the gifted program? Included in this group should be, at least, the student, the teacher, the administrator(s), the board members, and the parents. What each of these persons or groups needs or expects to learn from an evaluation must be included in the collection of data. They will all want some information (e.g., data on academic progress and social-emotional growth, gains in decision-making ability and leadership). Some of the groups will need information not required by the others. For example, parents will want information on the effects of home involvement, and the board members will need data on financial issues. It cannot be assumed that what the groups want is known; they should be asked orally or in writing.

In evaluating a program for gifted learners, the planning done at the beginning of the program will provide the reference point. Five basic issues that must be evaluated:

1. Does the implementation of the program support and carry forward the philosophy, conceptual framework, goals, and standards of the program plan?

2. Are the processes used in the program in compliance with the processes described in the program plan, including:
   - the screening and identification process?
   - the fiscal and time allocations?
   - appropriate placement of gifted learners?

3. Does the structure of the learning environment in the program meet the requirements set out in the program plan including:
   - provision of appropriate and adequate physical space?
   - a responsive classroom structure?
   - appropriate and sufficient materials?

4. Are differentiated curricular opportunities available and taught effectively?

5. Are support services adequate and effective?

The program goals are expectations that, ideally, the teacher, the student, the administration, and the parents have cooperatively delineated. The student's file of completed work, teacher observations, parent questionnaires, and the student's self-reports and testing records should be included to discover which of these goals have been reached. Some of the interested groups should visit the program to report their impressions. After reviewing the information, new procedures for meeting the goals of the program may need to be developed, or rethinking and changing the goals might be desirable.

If programs are to evolve into an integral part of the district's educational program, then some policies and standards must be developed and reexamined at regular intervals throughout the program. Policies on grading, textbook selection, quality of homework assignments, and make-up of regular classroom assignments can further the understanding of and support for the gifted program. Standards for such important components of the program as the goals, responsibility for decision-making, monitoring, expenditures, and staff development assure quality within the program and can provide criteria against which evaluation becomes clear and far more useful.

To make the program evaluation as effective and efficient as possible, a plan should be developed that allows information to be cycled throughout the year. The student and the teacher could decide together what form the evaluations should take to show achievement most effectively when the learning goal has been completed. Gifted students do not necessarily show growth against group norms because they are already near the ceiling of many tests. To expect gifted students to raise their test scores or percentile ranks is often not appropriate to measuring their progress.

In addition to information about pupil progress, the learning situation should be evaluated. Are the structure, the time allowed, and the classroom atmosphere conducive to meeting the needs of the gifted students and the goals of the program? Collecting this kind of information will show not only if the program is working, but why. An interesting instrument to use for this purpose is the Class Activities Questionnaire (Steele, 1969). It assesses five areas of the learning environment: lower and higher thought processes (based on Bloom's [1956] taxonomy); classroom focus (the role of the teacher and whether the students play a passive or active role); the classroom climate (attitudes and feelings); and student opinions (about class, about things to change, etc.). Others are useful, such as the interaction analysis procedures developed by Flanders (1960), or a questionnaire could be devised specifically to meet the program's needs.

A practitioner's guide (Callahan & Caldwell, 1995) produced by the NAGC, gives a step-by-step approach to evaluating programs for gifted learners and forms to support the process. In this guide the authors state:

> Those who are advocates of appropriate programs for gifted students have come to recognize that the job is far from over with the establishment of programs. Programs for gifted and talented students are unique in many ways, among which is a general skepticism on the part of many about the benefits of the program. It is not long before questions arise about the identification process, the types of grouping arrangements selected, the curriculum, and the outcomes of a program. If we evaluate our programs appropriately, these questions will not be threatening. A good program evaluation will provide information that leads to sound decision making as the program evolves—decision making which maximizes program effectiveness and the chances of demonstrating that the program is achieving expected outcomes. (p. 1)

In this chapter, the problems and methods of career education have been explored in the hope that gifted adolescents can be helped to discover meaningful and fulfilling roles for their future, which in turn will help form our future. Rural programs for the gifted have special problems in meeting the needs of the gifted learners in their schools. Resources, transportation, and teacher education are only some of the problems that must be solved if such programs are to meet their goals. Continuous evaluation to understand and adjust the gifted program is only one of the tasks involved in assuring its effectiveness no matter what the setting. Once the programs are in place, identification of the students that will benefit from gifted programming becomes our next concern. Chapter 9 will provide different approaches to discovering the gifted learners among us.

QUESTIONS OFTEN ASKED

1. If you live in a small district with few gifted learners, how can you provide a continuum of services?

Although your ability to provide a wide range of services may be less, your ability to involve the community is much greater than would be possible in a large, more impersonal area. By working for continuity, continuous progress, challenge, and personal involvement, you will be able to meet the individual needs of each gifted learner and at the same time provide an enriched experience for all of the students in your area.

2. If we decide to homeschool our daughter, does that mean that she will have to give up playing on the school volley ball team?

Not necessarily. Many districts have policies that allow students in their district to have access to all of the public facilities and organized sports sponsored by the public schools. Schools often have policies that allow students to participate in some of the scheduled classes while involved in homeschooling most of the time. It would be necessary to check with the district and the particular school involved because, while many are very supportive and understanding, there are still some districts and schools that believe strongly that professional teachers and state-approved curriculum are necessary for a quality education.

3. Wouldn't a homeschooled child have trouble socially and in making friends?

Actually, it has been pointed out by numerous parents that school programs never allowed their children to have intimate contact with other children like themselves. After school

and on weekends, homeschooled children can have informal contact with schooled and homeschooled children in whatever time blocks they choose. There are many organized groups that they can join such as sports groups, special interest clubs, Scouts, community events and camps, recreation centers, museum sponsored trips, theater groups, and library events, to name a few. Current data show homeschooled children to be socially mature and socially effective.

4. Wouldn't the achievement of the students be the most important part of evaluating the program?

Student performance would be important, however, the goals of your program would have other components that are important, too. For example, if you set a goal of increasing the diversity of the program, both in subjects taught and in populations included, then you would want to check to see if you were successful in meeting those goals. There would also be information you will need on the other areas of student growth such as social, affective, and perhaps, leadership. The teacher's effectiveness, the impact of the program on the school, and the satisfaction of the families would also be important data to collect.

5. How often is it necessary to evaluate the program?

Program evaluation should be ongoing as one of the purposes is the improvement of the program. Informal narrative comments, portfolios of student work, parent endorsements, awards, student reflections could all be part of the evaluation database. A plan should be in place with a timeline to be sure that all of the information is not left to one overwhelming evaluation period. External evaluation should be conducted at least once every 3 to 5 years, depending on the need of those who will use the information. Each program is different in the reporting needs and when and by whom the information is needed. Planning ahead to meet those needs will ensure evaluations of quality.

CHECKING FOR UNDERSTANDING
Follow Up Activities

There are six sections of this chapter: Career Education, Rural Programs, Using the Community, Homeschooling, Global Education, and Program Evaluation. From your experience, choose three of these issues that had or could have had the most impact on you. Outline your involvement with the issue, and how you benefited or could have benefited from a program in this area. Share your experiences with your classroom group.

Does this reflection give you an idea of how you would develop such a program for your students?

SUMMARY

RURAL PROGRAMS

1. Additional programming possibilities for gifted learners in rural areas are mobile enrichment vans, independent study "hot-lines" (access to mentors through a telephone system), itinerant teachers, correspondence courses, summer seminars followed by monthly meetings, residential summer institutes, and technology networks such as telelearning, electronic bulletin boards, and videotape exchanges.
2. Researchers consider the most important task in providing educational opportunities for rural gifted students to be the selection and training of teachers who work with these students.
3. Problems with access to resources, from transportation to materials, may inhibit cultural and intellectual development.

CAREER EDUCATION FOR THE GIFTED LEARNER

4. Career development for gifted and talented youth should begin with the parents, continue to be nurtured by educators, and find support in the work settings in which professionals are found.
5. It is true that career education and career guidance should be available to all students. However, it is not true that all students should be presented with the same options, asked to process the same information, or proceed through the same decision-making steps. Individualized programming and resources must be made available.
6. Gifted individuals tend to regard their work as a means of self-expression and build a lifestyle around it, becoming consumed by work-related activities.
7. Gifted individuals possess multiple talents and interests that complicate career choices and tend to make a career search a painful process of focusing on one talent area and rejecting other areas.
8. The frequent occurrence of early eminence among very bright gifted adolescents makes finding a mentor a crucial step in their career development, especially for women.

USING THE COMMUNITY

9. Many gifted programs have stretched their resources by using community facilities and people as part of the teaching process.
10. Gifted students often have a high degree of idealism, and if allowed to use their abilities to make needed changes in the school or community, such activity will foster future commitment to societal goals.

HOMESCHOOLING: AN ALTERNATIVE APPROACH

11. Students who are highly or exceptionally gifted and for whom provisions such as radical acceleration are unavailable may learn too rapidly or may think at levels of abstractness and complexity that are so advanced that

placement and materials are not easily available for them. Homeschooling can provide an alternative approach to obtain appropriate education.

12. There are many factors that impact the decision when families are considering homeschooling: the characteristics of the learner, including motivation, self-initiation, independence, and drive; the skill of the parent as teacher; and the accessibility of resources. However, when the fit is right, homeschooling can be very successful.

EVALUATING THE PROGRAM

13. Programs for gifted learners tend to be more difficult to evaluate than other school programs, but such evaluations are even more critical owing to the lack of permanence often experienced by these programs.

14. To make the program evaluation as effective and efficient as possible, a plan should be developed that allows assessment to be ongoing throughout the year. If your assessment procedures are used regularly, data collection becomes relatively easy.

15. The students' growth should be assessed individually, in comparison with their own past achievements and developed criteria only. Gifted students do not necessarily show growth against group norms because they are already near the ceiling of many tests.

Finding Gifted Learners in the Schools

In this chapter the reader will discover:

- Information on the need for identifying gifted individuals in schools.
- Methods and uses of screening for gifted students.
- Tools for the identification of gifted students.
- Procedures for identifying cognitive, academic, creative, leadership, and arts abilities.
- A discussion of identifying the culturally different, disabled, or educationally atypical gifted individual.
- A discussion of labeling and its effects on gifted learners.

The creative and gifted students reach out beyond the amassing and recall of facts. They are at home with the overarching concepts involving the great unitive themes. They strive for a coherent view of themselves, of the world, and of human destiny. Indeed it is by this quality, more than by standardized tests, that we can identify them, for they are ever seeking the interrelations that lead to a higher synthesis.

—ELIZABETH MONROE DREWS

Frank sat quietly listening to his friends in the class discussing giftedness with Ms. Jensen, the coordinator of the highly gifted program that he had been in for the past 3 years. Susan was recalling how she was identified as gifted. He could sure remember the testing that he had been involved in over the years. He really hated tests. He could never decide whether the answer should be true or false. It really depended on the circumstances. It was never as simple as the test givers tried to make it. Hardly anything was just true or false. The multiple-choice questions were no better. They never gave all of the factors that would be involved, and none of the answers ever fit completely.

Suddenly, Frank was aware that Susan had stopped speaking and everyone was looking at him. "Did you say something?" he asked the coordinator.

"I just wondered when you were identified for the program."

"Well, you see, I wasn't gifted in the third grade. I wasn't even gifted in the sixth grade. It wasn't until I was in the ninth grade that I became gifted," Frank responded, grinning. "Of course, I was gifted in language arts all that time, but not in math, so they said that I wasn't really gifted. When I got to the ninth grade, suddenly I was gifted in language arts, in science, and in social sciences. So now I'm in the gifted program."

"How did you know that you weren't gifted in the third and sixth grades?"

"Because I didn't get high enough scores in two subjects."

"What kind of tests did you take? Intelligence tests?"

"That was one kind; I just didn't like all of the pressure and time limits. I could think of a dozen ways to do what they were asking, but by the time I decided which way I was going to do it, we had to go on to something else. Really frustrating! However, the achievement tests were the real problem. I did well on the verbal and reading parts of all of the tests; it was just the math areas I didn't get. You have to be outstanding in at least two areas to get into the program; the two areas they tested were math and language arts. I was outstanding only in one."

"So, what was different in the ninth grade?" Ms. Jensen inquired.

"I don't really know. I had a great teacher and she thought I should be in the program. We talked about it, and I decided to try the exams again. My teacher insisted on putting more than high scores in math and language arts on the identification criteria. She told me not to spend so much time trying to figure out the best answers and just put down what I first thought of. It worked: That time I passed, sort of."

"Why 'sort of'?"

"Well, she added a lot of anecdotal information about me to the file she gave the school psychologist. She got stuff from my parents and the other students in our class, and even included some of my projects. Maybe she wanted to get rid of me," Frank chuckled.

"Has the program been a help to you?" Ms. Jensen inquired.

"Parts of it. I can do a lot more with my writing, and I'm producing one of my plays with the community theater mentor that came to the program. But math is still not my best area. Why do you think they insist that I should be in the math honors class just because I'm in the gifted program? That's the area that nearly kept me out!"

"Most people are not aware that people can be highly gifted in some areas and not in others. I'll see what I can do," promised Ms. Jensen.

DIFFERENT APPROACHES TO DISCOVERING GIFTEDNESS

To provide educational experiences that lead a child to the next level of development, we must be aware of what the child has already accomplished. In schools that provide individualized learning opportunities, that observe, evaluate, and assess as part of the growth experience, and that give access to many levels and types of learning simultaneously, identification is not viewed in the same way that it must be viewed in the more traditional school organization. In schools that use discrete grade placement, primarily determined by chronological age, and that use group instruction almost totally, it may even be necessary to label and isolate atypical learners for at least part of the time. In secondary schools in which departmentalization by subject is the most common way to present the world to a learner, labeling will certainly be necessary. Advanced placement classes and honors sections are often used as the only accommodation to the needs of gifted learners. Such provisions do not take the place of individual assessment, and planning for appropriate experiences for each learner is still necessary.

When public education began in our country, years before testing became available, students often moved through their educational program as their ability allowed. Fewer pupils studied in smaller, multigraded classrooms. Bright children in classrooms where materials were available over a range of grade levels, often as many as eight, could easily learn from older children and become involved in work beyond their own age groups. The early system not only made it possible for students to complete eight grades of schoolwork in a shorter time period, but also encouraged them to do so. The ability to pursue higher levels of education depended on the financial support available to the student. Only bright students had these opportunities, because most families could not economically support their less able students. This was a time when much education stemmed from the home and experience was viewed as a good teacher. It was possible for eminent people such as Thomas Edison, Jessie Benton, and Albert Einstein to be educated by their families when they could not remain in the public educational system.

There are numerous advantages to a similar, more integrated approach to education. For now, let us look at those that affect the educational experience of the gifted child today. Some years ago, I taught a cross-graded class of gifted youngsters in a rural area of one of the Great Plains states. The children were all gifted learners, and the school was committed to providing any resources necessary to further their educational growth. It was possible to develop a program that allowed the children to work at their own level of ability and interest. The program used group instruction, individual conferencing, contracts, and group projects. It made much use of peer and cross-grade tutoring and small-group projects. Students worked with a variety of levels of materials; at times, second graders worked with eighth-grade material for some subject areas and with third-grade material for others. This was true of the third graders and the fourth graders as well. They soon lost sight of what "grade" they were in and dealt with material as they were ready for it. Those exceptionally accomplished in one area dealt with very advanced materials in that area while they worked at less advanced levels in other areas of learning. Some recreation or project work included the entire class, for learning was a joint venture. We had an exciting time.

As a child became ready or approached a new level or interest area, appropriate learning opportunities were available. Their abilities did not need to be identified; they could just "bubble up." We could use materials and school and community resources, including a variety of people, to ensure continued growth. Later, in a similar plan in Illinois, classes of kindergarten children were observed, and those who showed ability in any particular area were given the opportunity to expand their skills and talents as they "bubbled up." Provisions for advanced learning became a normal part of these classroom situations. In both cases, the schools were committed to providing for individual needs and encouraging unique growth. Identification was a continuous occurrence. Special grouping and specialized instruction were normal parts of the classroom routine.

A few years later, working in another area of the country, I experienced a different and, unfortunately, more common way of organizing instruction. This classroom had children all at one grade, with a range of ages not more than 2 years apart. However, their learning abilities were extremely divergent. The students' IQs ranged from 80 to 180, with three children above 130. Several spoke only Spanish. It seemed obvious that this would have to be a very individualized program that would need a wide variety of experiences and an even broader range of materials and learning opportunities. To my dismay, I was expected to teach third-grade reading, to use the state-adopted text at grade level, and to give standardized tests at regular intervals. Using any of the tests to diagnose was not allowed. Whether appropriate to the learner or not, the tests had to be administered and turned in for scoring. Only a printout of the stanines achieved by the students was returned for classroom use. The administration then used the results to compare schools within the district and to make decisions on these comparisons. The room was regularly visited to see that the furniture was in place (fire marshal rules) and that the children were seated and quiet. My final defeat came with the declaration that teachers in first through third grade (this was a third-grade room) would be prohibited from using materials from the upper-grade bookroom and that it would be locked with keys issued only to eligible staff members. This was to prevent children from going ahead of their grades so that they would not be bored when they were given material the following year!

In educational settings such as this, identifying atypical learners becomes a concern. In such rigid situations, the energy necessary to meet the needs of the school administration and still provide meaningful individualized learning for such diverse students is overwhelming. Of course one can try, against all odds, to enrich the learning of children such as the three with bright minds. More likely, the push for conformity will prevail, and any extra energy will be spent trying to bring the children with learning problems up to the pace and norms the school expects. One way to ensure a gifted learner's growth in this situation is by identification and at least partial segregation. Chapter 7 discussed the possibilities of programming for the gifted.

What is known about discovering the gifted in large populations of students? This is indeed a difficult task, for although certain characteristics can be generalized within this population, some gifted individuals may not possess the same characteristics as other gifted individuals or exhibit them in quite the same way. They may not appear to have any physically observable differences. The gleam in their eyes and that extra energy level they seem to possess do not show in many unchallenging educational situations. Depending on how their previous life experiences have dealt with their giftedness, they may even actively attempt to appear quite "ungifted." They may, too willingly, go along with the inappropriate classroom program.

To confound the issue, not all gifted children cooperate in a classroom. Many resist routine, exhibit nonconformist behavior, and may be classified as behavioral problems. Others may be labeled slow learners because they are bored, uninterested in material learned long ago, and nonresponsive to classroom activities. Unless observed in activities of their own choosing, they may even appear to be educationally retarded or emotionally disturbed. Many gifted youngsters are discovered only after their frustration leads them, by teacher request, to the office of a counselor for testing for a learning disability or Attention Deficit and Hyperactive Disorder (ADHD) program. They are just as likely to withdraw into the "good" child syndrome, passively doing only what is required and drawing attention to themselves only for excessive participation in school-approved activities such as reading. This is especially common among girls. Because the very qualities that cause a person to be gifted can be successfully used to hide giftedness, we need to be aware of some identification procedures.

Because not all children and teachers find themselves in situations in which the "bubble-up" method can work and because, even in ideal situations, assessment, profiles, and case studies are extremely valuable, alternative procedures for finding gifted children will be explored.

SEARCH, SCREENING, AND IDENTIFICATION PROCEDURES

In this discussion of identification of gifted and talented students, the categories given in the federal definition will be used to organize the possible expressions of giftedness. Therefore, search, screening, and identification procedures will be viewed from these aspects:

- Intellectual ability—general cognitive intellectual development that is significantly higher than that of chronological peers.
- High achievement—consistently high functioning in academic areas.
- Specific academic ability—consistently high functioning in one academic area.
- Creative ability—high levels of ability in creating unusual, unique, and meaningful contributions and solutions.
- Leadership—unusual ability to inspire, guide, direct, or influence others.
- Visual and performing arts—high levels of ability in origination, performance, and production in any area of the arts.

Smith and colleagues (1990) suggest that a comprehensive identification program should provide the following:

- Evidence that students demonstrate extraordinary ability in relationship to their age-level peers.
- Evidence of the range of capabilities and needs.
- Processes that measure potential as well as achievement.
- Methods that seek out and identify students from varying linguistic, economic, and cultural backgrounds, and special populations.
- Implications for educational planning. (p. 5)

It was stated earlier that gifted children are those who have developed or show evidence of developing high levels of intelligence, with high levels of intelligence being defined as ideas and actions that give evidence of advanced or accelerated whole-brain function. Such children may exhibit any of the characteristic behaviors discussed in Chapter 2. The federal definition is focused on gifted children who show their high levels of intelligence in cognition, academic achievement, specific academic achievement, creativity, leadership or the visual and performing arts. Children who show the potential for such high intelligence receive special attention. Placement of students in gifted programs is recommended when such ability cannot be furthered in the educational program that is ordinarily provided by the schools.

Figure 9.1 illustrates the relationship between the tests used and the Universe of Intelligence (see Figure 2.2). It becomes obvious that intuition is neither tested nor included in programs. Even for the areas outside of the linear, analytic thinking in which tests are available, they are seldom used and service for these areas is seldom provided. Developing an integrated, balanced gifted person becomes difficult when we neither seek the full range of abilities nor educate to enhance such abilities.

Educators and researchers have provided a number of recommendations for the process used in the identification of gifted students (Abeel, Callahan, & Hunsaker, 1994). Among these recommendations:

- The identification procedures be based on a broad and well-defined conception of giftedness to ensure appropriate service to the portion of the gifted population designated for the program.
- Multiple criteria that includes standardized and nonstandardized instruments, process and performance indicators, and multiple sources of data be used in the identification of gifted learners.
- Identification strategies and instrumentation be used that are appropriate for each different area of giftedness that the program is designated to serve.
- The instruments selected for the identification process be reliable and valid for the construct they are expected to measure. For example, Abeel and colleagues suggest that "Although tests of intelligence provide relatively objective, valid and reliable measures of general intellectual ability in the sense of predicting general school achievement, they give little information about specific talents, even in the intellectual domain" (p. 4).

Figure 9.1 *Testing the Universe of Intelligence*

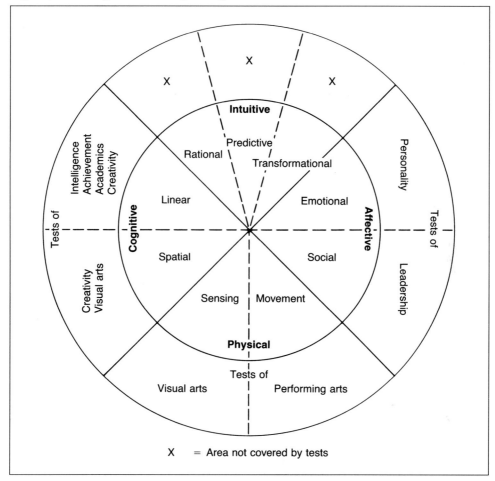

- The limitations of the use of the score of a single test or the summed matrix score as the basis of identification be recognized, leading to a more comprehensive selection of evaluation data.
- Identification and placement be based on student need, rather than on the number of students who can be accommodated by a program or a prespecified percentage of students.
- Appropriate instruments and strategies be used to identify underserved populations that account for the different behavioral aspects of giftedness exhibited in different cultures.

Researchers in the 1970s and 1980s (Hunt & Kirk, 1971; Sternberg, 1981, 1985) perceived a need for a different way of assessing intellectual development. They felt that our reliance on tests comparing people against a standard or norm (decided by taking the average of what many people can do and assigning a score to it) prevented us from developing more useful measures. They believed that we must discover which activities and skills include both cognitive and motivational ability and in what sequence these activities or skills usually appear. From that information, criterion measures could be established that would indicate not only the present level of a child's development, but also which experiences would best challenge further growth. Sternberg (1981) states that the tests used are little better than tests used decades ago and are, in many cases, the same tests. He believes that the weakness of these tests is not the kind of items they contain, but rather their lack of a viable theory base.

Sternberg (1981) and others are working on a theoretical base for intelligence. Setting their work in an information-processing framework, these researchers believe that such a theory base will prove more useful than has the factor-analytic, psychometric base previously used for measuring, understanding, and nurturing intelligence. By delineating the components of giftedness and their functions, all of which point to specific abilities found in learners with high levels of intelligence, we may better understand how to facilitate advanced and accelerated brain development—that is, giftedness.

Currently, the conventional standardized tests measure analytic abilities fairly well but fail to measure synthetic abilities—those allowing for invention, creativity, and personal contribution (Sternberg, 1986).

Measuring Intelligence

The general intellectual ability is the concept most frequently adopted for gifted programs (Abeel, et al., 1994). The measurement of intelligence has often depended on the results of paper and pencil tests, although the limited tasks on such tests narrowly reflect the possibilities for human intellectual growth (see Figure 9.1). Sternberg (1986) feels that traditional tests benefit students who can solve problems quickly in the intermediate range of difficulty and penalize those who can solve very difficult problems, for such problems have been eliminated. Further, he feels that the kind of planning and evaluating needed for good performance in everyday life differs from the kind of planning and evaluating assessed by these traditional tests. Sternberg and other investigators such as Gardner, a Harvard psychologist, and Feldman, from Tufts University, are working to develop tests that they believe will be more sensitive to varying expressions of intelligence.

From Bar-Ilan University in Israel another psychologist-researcher, Reuven Feuerstein (cited in Mohs, 1982), sees an entirely different problem. Feuerstein suggests that conventional IQ tests measure what people already know, which is not as important as what they can learn or where their cognitive deficiencies lie. Feuerstein believes that such additional information allows learners to overcome their deficiencies, such as impulsiveness, lack of precision, and failure to discriminate the important from the unimportant. The real task is to effect change. "We are not interested in providing the child with information or specific skills. We are interested in endowing the child with capacities to benefit from his encounters" (Mohs, 1982, p. 24).

Until more productive measures of intelligence are developed, available measures will continue to be used. It would be wise to supplement their use with other evaluative tools, such as observation of the processes, performance, or products of learning; the results from a variety of measures of achievement and creativity; and input from parents, teachers, peers, and self-reporting.

Individual Tests of Intelligence

Although, as noted, no single test can measure the entire universe of intelligence, the most commonly used individual tests of rational, linear intelligence are the Stanford-Binet Intelligence Scale and the Wechsler Intelligence Scale for Children (WISC). A person's score on both intelligence tests is given as an intelligence quotient or IQ. In the development of intelligence tests, variations in test performance caused by age differences were taken into account. This adjustment led to the idea of IQ, which is computed by dividing the mental age by the chronological age times 100. Standardized on the general population, the tests evolved to set the average IQ at any age at 100. The middle 50% of the population falls between 90 and 110 IQ. On the Stanford-Binet, an IQ of 132 reflects the beginning of the upper 2% of the population, and a score of 68 IQ reaches the top of the lower 2%; on the Wechsler the top 2% begins at 131.

The Stanford-Binet Intelligence Scale was written in 1916 at Stanford University by Lewis Terman and was an adaptation of a test developed in 1906 in France by Binet and Simon. Terman used the test to identify children for his longitudinal study of giftedness that began in 1921. Curiously, it has been used to show "fixed" intelligence, although Binet himself believed that intelligence was dynamic and could be influenced by education. The test was standardized on 1000 children and 400 adults found in and around the Stanford area. The test was revised in 1937 using 3184 native-born white persons ages $1\frac{1}{2}$ to 18 years of age, with equal numbers of males and females. Seventeen communities, both rural and urban in widely separated states, represented the geographical distribution. In 1960 another revision, Form L-M, was made, again with a geographically diverse group. The 1972 revision was undertaken by Thorndike and the 1960 norms were updated.

The Stanford-Binet scale was developed to test general intellectual ability, including verbal adroitness, ability to perceive analogies and abstractions, capacity for problem-solving, ability to find causal relationships, and classification aptitude. It gained wide acceptance because it did just what was expected of it. Those intuitively judged to be highly intelligent did well on the test, whereas those who exhibited subnormal ability, in fact, did poorly on the test. The test was never based on an exact definition of intelligence, nor did it reflect any commitment to a rationale for how we develop intelligence. It was based, rather, on relative performance. Large numbers of people have taken the test, lending stability to it, but its predictive nature is limited to performance in similar activities, such as schoolwork. The predictive validity of such tests ranks highest on performance of school-related tasks, especially for those tested after the age of 5.

The fourth revision was made in 1986 and is not recommended for the identification of gifted children. The upper limit is lower than that of the third edition and produces scores that run 13.5 points lower than Form L-M, resulting in a child previously tested with a 140 IQ now receiving a score of 127 or less. Many students who need to be considered for differentiation of instruction would be easily missed with this new form.

The individual intelligence test most commonly used in schools is the WISC, developed in 1949 by David Wechsler. The test is divided into two scales, the verbal and the performance, and has a total score IQ. It was standardized on only 100 boys and 100 girls who were chosen to represent each age group from 5 to 15 years and reported as white, American children. The test abandons the concept of mental age found in the Stanford-Binet scale and instead uses a score derived from comparing the child with a sample of same-age peers. The sampling of very bright children in the standardization group was quite small.

The WISC-III was developed in 1991, and the standardization group included white, African-American, Hispanic, Puerto Rican, American Indian, and Asian students in about the same proportion as they appear in the American population. This new edition has the same problem that the latest revision of the Stanford-Binet shows: The scores have now been shifted down 8 or 9 points. Neither test revision differentiates well for gifted and highly gifted children.

Other individually given intelligence tests commonly used in schools are the Leiter International Performance Scale, the Peabody Picture Vocabulary Test, and the Slosson Intelligence Test.

Group Intelligence Tests

There are cautions against using IQ scores derived from group tests to make discrete decisions (Borland, 1986). The difference between scores of 128 and 132 may be a function of the test, rather than an accurate representation of the child's ability. Group tests are timed, less reliable than individual tests, especially at high levels, and tend to miss children with diverse ability. However, because they are low in cost and relatively easy to administer in groups, they will continue to be used. When used for screening, as is often done, group intelligence tests can lead to unfortunate distinctions. Harrington (1982) points out that the higher the ability that is tested, the greater will be the discrepancy between the student's group IQ and the individual IQ. Because of such misrepresentation, the common practice of using a group test as a screen for identifying gifted students must be done with an attitude of inclusion, not exclusion. The danger of missing a student in need is very real.

The more commonly used group intelligence tests are the Otis-Lennon School Abilities Test (OLSSAT), the SRA Primary Mental Abilities Tests, the Kuhlman-Anderson Intelligence Tests, the Cognitive Abilities Tests (CogAT), the Slosson Intelligence Test (SIT), and the Henmon-Nelson Test of Mental Ability.

The Nature of the IQ

Unfortunately, many people, including too many educators, believe that the IQ score gives an accurate description of a person's capacity. It does not. Currently, there are no tests of capacity. The most any test will reveal is how well a person can handle certain problems on the test. Because IQ tests were designed to predict success in school and resemble the material covered in formal schooling, performance on these tests will very likely predict how well the child will do in school-related activities. The strengths and weaknesses of each test must be understood before any inferences or predictions about a person's innate abilities or potentials can be made. Much more must be known before decisions about the person's future should be attempted.

Advantages of IQ tests discussed by Pyryt (1996) are their ability to identify exceptionally gifted students and their unique educational needs and students who are underachievers, have low verbal ability, or have handicaps such as learning disabilities, behavioral disorders and visual, hearing or physical impairments. He also points to the usefulness of IQ tests in making legal decisions regarding the eligibility for participation in gifted programs. He acknowledges that they are less useful for determining the most appropriate educational experiences. He suggests a comprehensive assessment that incorporates high-ceiling measures of specialized abilities, motivation, interests, and other factors for individualized educational planning.

According to Goleman (1995), an IQ contributes only 20% to the factors that are responsible for success in life. Goleman suggests that "emotional intelligence" may be as important or even more important to a person's success than is the more familiar IQ. Emotional intelligence can be discussed in five components:

- Awareness of one's own feelings and the ability to use that knowledge in decision making.
- Ability to manage one's feelings to prevent distress from blocking thought processes.
- Ability to motivate one's self despite setbacks; remaining positive, hopeful, and delaying gratification.
- Ability to empathize with others.
- Ability to develop rapport and cooperate with others; handling feelings in relationships.

These abilities show high correlation with success in careers, good relationships, good health, and lower rates of delinquency, violence, and drug use in children. According to Goleman, performing better on achievement tests is also a result of improving emotional skills.

Children with special needs would begin to emerge very early if, from the beginning of their educational experience, all children were allowed to learn at their own rates, pursue ideas and activities to whatever depth possible for their ability, and encouraged to be curious in a rich, responsive environment. An educational program designed to meet each person's needs from the beginning of school can better reveal those children with high intellectual ability than can any single test instrument. Such a program could also be advantageous in continuously building on these strengths. Thus, the problems usually encountered in traditional group-oriented programs would be less inhibiting to the child's development.

Currently, when so many schools are moving in lockstep, using only a group approach to instruction and authoritarian modes of organization, this approach to identification could not possibly be reliable. However, it does have many advantages, and movement could be made in this direction by encouraging those involved in education for the gifted to consider approaches and programs that allow for this type of natural selection.

Were it not so expensive, the quickest way to find a large percentage of cognitively gifted youngsters would be to administer individual intelligence tests. The protocol—the original copy of the test with the actual responses recorded—is a good diagnostic tool. Tests used properly provide much information. Test scores alone give very limited data; without a protocol they can be nearly valueless. For some groups of children, the more commonly given intelligence tests may not provide enough information. For some, the child-rearing practices of their parents, the language they use most, and their past experiences are not reflected in these tests. The scores may give a false picture of the level of their abilities. Binet (Binet & Simon, 1973), in originating the intelligence scales in 1906, and Terman (1916), in revising and popularizing these scales, both warned that they were to be used as only one piece of datum in combination with other important information about the student in any process of educational decision-making. However, such was seldom the case. Even now, the intelligence test looms very large as a selection tool for gifted individuals. Some of the limits of the intelligence test were discussed earlier, but even the weaknesses mentioned are not the main reason that individual intelligence tests are not used as screening devices. The expense of having such a test administered by a licensed school psychologist is prohibitive. Only after the school has some assurance that the child will perform successfully on such tests can they be scheduled. How, then, can that assurance be provided?

For children who express their intelligence through creative thinking, other tests and activities will be indicated. To identify leadership or artistic abilities will require observation and judgment of products or events. What procedure can be devised to find those who are ready to advance in all these areas?

To find and serve children from each of the areas of ability the district has decided to serve will require varied and numerous resources. A school advisory committee should take an inventory of available resources and make some initial recommendations prior to the implementation of any identification procedures:

- What resources (material and personnel) does the school or community have for providing programs for advanced learners?
- Are they adequate to provide for all five areas of ability?
- If not, which areas should be included?

It will be assumed that the cognitive and specific academic ability areas will be included, for these are usually the primary focus of the school. Very probably creative ability should also be included, as abilities in these areas are supportive to the cognitive functions and are not totally separable. Leadership may become an important sub-component of the gifted program in which the learners could choose to participate. Visual and performing arts talent requires very special resources that are significantly different from those for the other ability areas. The school may need to enlist professional artists, musicians, actors, and dancers from the community to supplement the program in this area.

Dirks and Quarfoth (1981) compared two multiple-criteria models for identifying gifted children, one developed for depth (scoring well in one area) and the other for breadth (scoring well in several areas). Children selected for breadth had high classroom grades and were well-thought of by their teachers. Those selected for depth included more children and more promising underachievers than the breadth model. The authors of this study believe the depth model to be more valuable in identification.

Search

The function of the search component is to generate a list of possible gifted students from all school sites while making sure that all students have an equal opportunity to be selected. Figure 9.2 lists classroom behaviors that are typical among gifted children. Nominations should be obtained from teachers, principals, psychologists, parents, peers who observe these behaviors, and the students themselves. Patterns of achievement on standardized tests should be analyzed and student behavior and production observed. Referrals from the search process should be made to the coordinator of gifted programs, who will then initiate and collect information to complete the screening procedures (Figure 9.3).

Screening

The identification process continues by screening for students who show need for a different kind of educational experience. As shown in Figure 9.3, screens that could be used for all areas of ability include:

- Nomination forms—from teachers, principal, counselor, psychologist, and others.
- Teacher reports of student functioning—including intellectual, physical, social, and emotional functioning; learning style and motivation.
- Family history and student background—provided by parents—including historical and developmental data on the student, health and medical records of student and family, educational and occupational background of parents, description of family unit, anecdotes of the student in the home that indicate unusual capacity and early development, family activities and interests, and the child's extracurricular activities and interests.
- Peer identification.
- Student inventory—of self, values, interests, and attitudes toward school and extracurricular activities.
- Student work and achievements.
- Multidimensional screening tests.

For best results, none of these screens should be used alone; instead, all should be used in combination for screening and later as part of the data in the identification process. Screening should be done as early as possible in the child's school career. Early screening can prevent the waste of talent that is all too prevalent. The actual identification of a child as gifted requires the judgment of a selection committee. Identification at the kindergarten level allows the school to provide children an appropriate education throughout their school experience.

According to a recent analysis of state and local policies regarding identification of students for gifted programs (Coleman, Gallagher, & Foster, 1994), some strategies used for *screening* were:

- Screening all student files for indications of giftedness.
- Increasing the ability of teachers to recognize nontraditional gifted students through staff development.

Figure 9.2 *Classroom Behaviors of Gifted Children*

Does the child

- Ask a lot of questions?
- Show a lot of interest in progress?
- Have lots of information on many things?
- Want to know why or how something is so?
- Become unusually upset at injustices?
- Seem interested and concerned about social or political problems?
- Often have a better reason than you do for not doing what you want done?
- Refuse to drill on spelling, math, facts, flash cards, or handwriting?
- Criticize others for dumb ideas?
- Become impatient if work is not "perfect"?
- Seem to be a loner?
- Seem bored and often have nothing to do?
- Complete only part of an assignment or project and then take off in a new direction?
- Stick to a subject long after the class has gone on to other things?
- Seem restless, out of seat often?
- Daydream?
- Seem to understand easily?
- Like solving puzzles and problems?
- Have his or her own idea about how something should be done? And stay with it?
- Talk a lot?
- Love metaphors and abstract ideas?
- Love debating issues?

This child may be showing giftedness cognitively.

Does the child

- Show unusual ability in some area? Maybe reading or math?
- Show fascination with one field of interest? And manage to include this interest in all discussion topics?
- Enjoy meeting or talking with experts in this field?
- Get math answers correct, but find it difficult to tell you how?

- Enjoy graphing everything? Seem obsessed with probabilities?
- Invent new obscure systems and codes?

This child may be showing giftedness academically.

Does the child

- Try to do things in different, unusual, imaginative ways?
- Have a really zany sense of humor?
- Enjoy new routines or spontaneous activities?
- Love variety and novelty?
- Create problems with no apparent solutions? And enjoy asking you to solve them?
- Love controversial and unusual questions?
- Have a vivid imagination?
- Seem never to proceed sequentially?

This child may be showing giftedness creatively.

Does the child

- Organize and lead group activities? Sometimes take over?
- Enjoy taking risks?
- Seem cocky, self-assured?
- Enjoy decision-making? Stay with that decision?
- Synthesize ideas and information from a lot of different sources?

This child may be showing giftedness through leadership ability.

Does the child

- Seem to pick up skills in the arts—music, dance, drama, painting, etc.—without instruction?
- Invent new techniques? Experiment?
- See minute detail in products or performances?
- Have high sensory sensitivity?

This child may be showing giftedness through visual or performing arts ability.

Figure 9.3 *Identification Procedure*

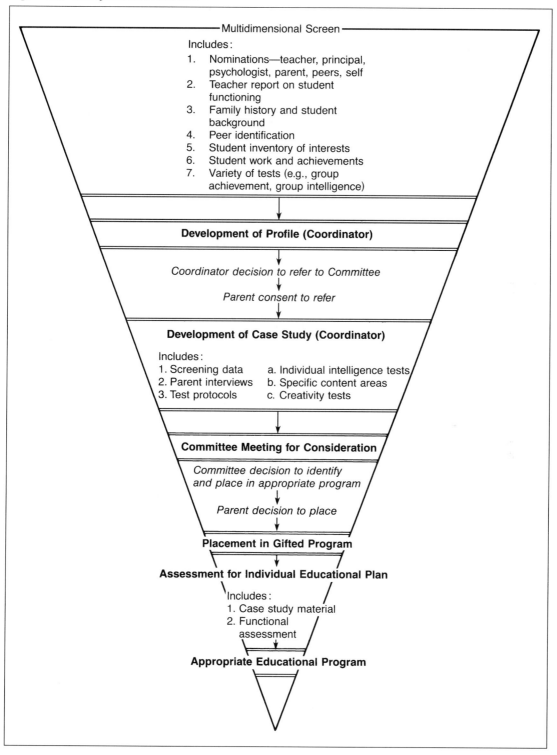

Multidimensional Screen
Includes:
1. Nominations—teacher, principal, psychologist, parent, peers, self
2. Teacher report on student functioning
3. Family history and student background
4. Peer identification
5. Student inventory of interests
6. Student work and achievements
7. Variety of tests (e.g., group achievement, group intelligence)

Development of Profile (Coordinator)

Coordinator decision to refer to Committee

Parent consent to refer

Development of Case Study (Coordinator)
Includes:
1. Screening data   a. Individual intelligence tests
2. Parent interviews   b. Specific content areas
3. Test protocols   c. Creativity tests

Committee Meeting for Consideration

Committee decision to identify and place in appropriate program

Parent decision to place

Placement in Gifted Program

Assessment for Individual Educational Plan
Includes:
1. Case study material
2. Functional assessment

Appropriate Educational Program

- Increasing the ability of teachers to recognize nontraditional gifted students through use of student profiles and case studies.
- Increasing the ability of teachers to recognize nontraditional gifted students through use of autobiographies.
- Increasing the ability of teachers to recognize underachieving gifted students through use of a checklist.
- Referring automatically for further assessment all students who reach a designated score or percentile.

The most commonly used screen is teacher observation and selection of those nominated for testing. Logically, one would believe the teacher to be the one most familiar with the child and best qualified to make such a recommendation. However, one teacher may work with 35 to 45 children during the day; at the secondary level the number can be six-fold greater. The curriculum aimed at the norm may not elicit any obviously brilliant performance. Depending on how many years the child has been in the system, the child may have developed adaptive skills to "fit in." It is known that much of this "adjustment" has already occurred by the third grade, especially among gifted girls.

The particular beliefs and attitudes of the teacher must also be considered. How does the teacher imagine a gifted child? As early as 1959, Pegnato and Birch found that junior high school teachers most often choose children like themselves as gifted. Whatever the teacher values will be the criterion for selection. That is understandable. How can we select those aspects that we do not experience as valuable or good? Often the quiet, well-behaved, well-dressed youngster who gets good grades is a prime target for teacher selection. Unfortunately, although teachers in this study identified only 45% of the children in their classes who were cognitively gifted, only 26% of those they named actually tested high enough to qualify. This problem exists to an even greater extent in lower grades. According to Jacobs (1971), the effectiveness of teacher identification is only 10% identified in kindergarten, compared with 45% identified in junior high.

It cannot be assumed that even the highly gifted are easily identified. Lack of knowledge regarding giftedness causes identification problems. If teachers cannot recognize enough of the gifted in their classes, there may be waste of human potential. However, administering individual intelligence tests is expensive; if teachers select too many students who do not qualify as gifted when tested, the teachers' errors can waste the limited monetary resources designated for the gifted. The dilemma is then to select enough students not to miss those who are gifted, and yet not to select too many who will not test as gifted. Teachers must be both effective—correctly nominating a high percentage of children who are the gifted in their classes, that is, not missing a lot who are gifted—and efficient—having a high percentage of those they nominate identified for the gifted program, that is, not nominating a lot of children who are not gifted. Gear (1978) found that a five-session training program improved the effectiveness of teacher selection without any loss in efficiency. The teachers completing the program were, in fact, twice as effective as were untrained teachers. Borland (1978) showed that teachers can improve their efficiency in selecting cognitively gifted students when given a list of specific behaviors to rate or a list of common characteristics found in gifted learners like the one in Figure 9.2, their ability to predict academic achievement is quite high.

It is important for teachers to be a part of the selection process. First, they have data to offer that are not available to other members of the identification team. Second, they need to become aware of, understand, and support the program for the gifted if it is to succeed. Without some involvement in the selection process, they will be unlikely to cooperate or contribute to any further planning.

Two other screening procedures have yielded results. Parents are very aware of the behavior of their children. When asked relevant questions, they can provide information that is clearly indicative of potential giftedness. Also peers have been extremely helpful in identifying other potentially gifted children for screening. Questions such as "Whom would you choose to help you if you were having difficulty with your arithmetic?" or "If you were planning a learning center on *(subject)*, whom would you choose to be in your group?" or "Who is the smartest person in our room?" form part of a list of identifying questions that can produce important and often otherwise unnoticed information about the students in a class.

The student's work can be useful in screening. Both school and extracurricular activities should be considered. The work done on a hobby or toward solving a unique problem at home often indicates advanced thinking and creative ability. The more information that can be obtained, the greater the likelihood that the screening will be effective in locating gifted students. Just as with Frank in the vignette at the beginning of the chapter, a wide range of sources in a database can validate the existence of gifted needs that testing data may miss.

Identification

The major purpose of identification is to obtain information that will help educators provide the program that is best suited to the development of the gifted student's potential. Actual identification for the purpose of placement in a gifted program is best done by a group of professionals representing a variety of areas of expertise, such as the principal, a teacher, a counselor or psychologist, and the program coordinator. They should develop a case study or profile to aid in the identification decision and also later in program planning for the individual. The report should provide enough information to make good educational planning and placement possible.

All of the materials developed for screening now become a part of the data that provide a background for the identification decision. Data will also be needed that discriminate in the areas the district has chosen to serve. Care must be taken to use tests and procedures that are valid measures both of the skills being sought and for the population being tested. The National Report on Identification, Assessment, and Recommendations for Comprehensive Identification of Gifted and Talented Youth (Alvino, McDonnel, & Richert, 1981), a survey of identification practices now used in gifted and talented education, noted that, "Many tests/instruments are being used for purposes and populations completely antithetical to those for which they are intended and were designed" (p. 128). Such data may serve only to confuse the identification process and the program planning to follow. Richert (1985) noted some of the other problems in identification: Educational equity is being violated in the identification of significant sub-populations; multiple criteria are being combined inappropriately; and instruments and procedures are being used at inappropriate stages of identification (e.g., diagnostic tests used as part of screening).

An analysis of state and local identification policies (Coleman, Gallagher, & Foster, 1994) found that states often rely on multiple criteria to find gifted students. Strategies such as input from parents, teachers, students, and other sources; extra-curricular activities; work samples; products; and creativity are incorporated into the formal identification. Some of the strategies that have been suggested for identification are:

- Establishing child study teams to make placement decisions and coordinate services.
- Documenting giftedness by use of portfolios of student work samples.
- Reevaluating students who show compelling reasons why existing scores underestimate their abilities or who fall within one standard error of measurement below the score needed to qualify for program services.
- Using alternative identification methods with students from special populations.
- Placing students who show potential into the program for a trial period to find out if they would benefit.
- Informing those involved in the identification process about multicultural and nonsexist education and identification of special populations of gifted students.

A wider population of gifted students will be served by: establishing incentives, such as grants, awards, or special honors for districts to include underserved gifted students; encouraging alternative programs for underachieving gifted students; and assisting regular classroom teachers in meeting the needs of bright students not placed in gifted programs and reevaluating later.

Tools for Screening and Identification of Gifted and Talented Learners

Numerous tests, checklists, questionnaires, and inventories have been used to screen and identify students for gifted programs. The tools listed in Table 9.1 and a brief discussion of the possibilities for using such tools in each category of giftedness may clarify the choices available.

Cognitive Ability

Screening. Information collected on students identified in this category may include evidence of high levels or the potential for high levels of abstract reasoning ability, advanced vocabulary, advanced academic performance, an accelerated rate of learning, and/or honors or recognition for outstanding accomplishments. Such evidence may be obtained from an analysis of a group test of cognitive ability, analysis of an individually administered intelligence test, group or individual achievement test results indicating high-level performance, and/or a pattern of advanced academic ability (Smith, et al., 1990).

Table 9.1 *Suggestions for Screening and Identifying Gifted Learners*

Expression of Giftedness	Screening	Identification
Generic	Nomination forms Reports of student functioning Family history and student background Peer identification Student inventories Student work and achievements Multidimensional screen tests (e.g., Kranz; Baldwin; Renzulli and Hartman; Perrone and Male)	
Cognitive	Group intelligence tests (e.g., California Test of Mental Maturity; Lorge-Thorndike Intelligence Test; Henmon-Nelson Test of Mental Ability; Otis-Lennon Mental Ability Test; Pinter General Ability Test; SRA Primary. Mental Abilities Tests; Kuhlmann-Anderson Intelligence Tests) Individual intelligence tests (e.g., Peabody Picture Vocabulary Test; Slosson Intelligence Test; SOI Screening Tests for Gifted and Talented Children)	Stanford-Binet Intelligence Scale Wechsler Intelligence Scales for Children Cognitive Abilities Tests Differential Aptitude Tests Kaufman Assessment Battery for Children
Academic	Student's work Functional assessment of content areas Group achievement tests (e.g., California Test of Basic Skills; Stanford Achievement Tests; Metropolitan Achievement Tests; Iowa Tests of Basic Skills; Sequential Tests of Educational Progress [STEP])	Test in specific areas of content
Creative	Divergent thinking tests (e.g., Torrance Tests of Creative Thinking; Exercise in Divergent Thinking; Wallach & Kogan tests; Guilford tests) The Scale for Rating the Behavioral Characteristics of Superior Students (SRBCSS) Personality inventories (e.g., Preschool & Primary Interest Descriptor; Group Inventory for Finding Talent; Creativity Attitude Survey) Observation of open-ended problem-solving skills	
Leadership	Observation in and out of the classroom Scales on leadership from Kranz; Renzulli and Hartman; Perrone and Male	No formal standardized tests available
Visual and Performing Arts	Observation and recommendations from professional artists Peer nominations	Seashore's Measures of Musical Talents Standardized Tests of Musical Intelligence Horn Art Aptitude Inventory Meier Art Tests On-site task completion Juried student work

Alternative test procedures for identification of gifted and talented children among the students who are atypical, underachievers, from culturally diverse populations, or from low socioeconomic families:
Portfolio assessment procedures
Krantz Talent Identification Instrument
Baldwin Identification Matrix
Torrance's Creative Positives
Raven's Progressive Matrices Test
System of Multicultural Pluralistic Assessment (SOMPA)

To the generic screen in Table 9.1, group intelligence tests (for examples see the table) may be added. Group intelligence testing may be useful as part of the screening procedure; however, a cutoff score of 115 IQ should be used. A higher cutoff will result in many gifted students being missed. Although the Otis-Lennon Mental Ability Test is cited in Abeel and colleagues (1994) as one of the most frequently used group intelligence tests, questions have been raised on its construct validity regarding the identification of giftedness. The Scales for Rating the Behavioral Characteristics of Superior Students (SRBCSS) (Renzulli, Smith, White, Callahan, & Hartman, 1976) is another popular tool used for screening.

Multiple, abbreviated tests can be used as a possible screen. Such testing can reduce the cost of identification, can be administered by untrained examiners, and lacks cultural bias. The pupils also enjoy the tests. Although having advantages as a screen, this abbreviated testing approach should not replace individual testing for identification. The use of matrix systems to compress multiple and varied measures into a single numerical score reduces the sensitivity of the tests and while they could be used for screening, they are seen to be indefensible for identification and placement decisions (Fishkin & Johnson, 1998).

Identification. The standardized tests for individual administration that are most useful in identifying the potentially gifted are those that appraise scholastic aptitude or general cognitive development, such as the Stanford-Binet Tests of Intelligence and the WISC. Shortened versions of individual intelligence tests have been published; although they may be useful for screening, Hagen (1980) warns that they are not suitable for identifying gifted or potentially gifted individuals. She believes that by changing the time limits, content, or directions of the test, the data on reliability, validity, and norms for that test are no longer applicable. The number and variety of cognitive skills appraised by the shortened test are limited also.

Two tests suggested for inclusion in the identification process are the Cognitive Abilities Tests and the Differential Aptitude Tests (Table 9.1). These tests give scores on verbal, quantitative, and nonverbal reasoning. The Otis-Lennon Mental Ability Test gives only one score, cannot be differentiated, and does not appraise high-level thinking skills well (Hagen, 1980).

The Kaufman Assessment Battery for Children (K-ABC) (Kaufman, 1984), is an individually administered measure of intelligence and achievement (Table 9.1) intended for children from $2\frac{1}{2}$ to $12\frac{1}{2}$ years old. Taking its basis from the work in cerebral specialization, the test focuses on the processes of the brain, especially in regard to Sequential Processing, Simultaneous Processing, and a combination of the two, the Mental Processing Composite. The designer believes that this focus on process, rather than content, and de-emphasis on factual knowledge and applied school-related skills makes the test useful in assessing the intelligence and achievement of all children, especially gifted children, gifted minority children, and gifted children with learning problems.

Academic Ability

Screening. Group achievement tests can be added to the generic screen. Functional assessment of just what the child can do would also be most useful. Often knowledge of achievement in subject matter areas is limited within a curricular range deemed appropriate for a particular grade level. If the child has never had an opportunity to show you how high he or she can achieve in reading or math, planning for continuous progress becomes impossible.

Identification. Some sources for evidence in this category include the Stanford Achievement Tests (SAT), the California Tests of Basic Skills (CTBS), the Iowa Tests of Basic Skills, Peabody Individual Achievement Test, the SRBCSS, a representative collection of student schoolwork, tests in content areas, teacher observation, and pupil self-inventories.

> The best single indicator of future academic achievement is the present level of achievement in the area of interest; therefore, data should be obtained on: (1) the level of achievement in general academic skills; (2) the level of achievement in skills and knowledge related to a specific academic area; (3) the level of development of general verbal, quantitative, nonverbal and spatio-visual problem-solving skills; (4) originality; (5) persistent long-term interests; (6) out-of-school time spent on activities related to an academic area; and (7) the trend in complexity of activities that an individual undertakes on his or her own initiative. (Hagen, 1980, p. 10)

Creative Ability

To the generic screen a test measuring divergent thinking ability or a personality inventory may be added. These are often referred to as tests of creativity although, just as with intelligence, no test measures all facets of creativity. The Torrance Tests of Creative Thinking (TTCT) (Torrance, 1966) is the most often used instrument for finding creativity. Torrance (1999) observes, however, that the evidence of 30 years indicates that other factors including motivation, persistence, courage, and loving what one is doing have been shown to be more important than ability. Another frequently-used tool is SRBCSS (Renzulli, et al., 1976), which is used by teachers to rate students on traits that may indicate creative behavior. Observations could be made of a child in an open-ended problem-solving situation, which would provide useful anecdotal material for assessing creative ability.

Caution must be taken about using the data from tests for creativity as the dominant or alternative identification for intelligence or giftedness. Problems often arise when children who do not score well in cognitive testing are placed in gifted programs based on the scores of creativity tests. Unless the program includes methods and content that are designed to include these different skills, the student's abilities may be unfairly compared with the more advanced cognitive skills of the other students in the gifted program. The results may be problematic for the student and that student's self-esteem.

Leadership Ability

Observation of leadership skills in and out of the classroom will provide anecdotal material for screening in this area. The multidimensional scales mentioned in the Generic area include sections related to leadership abilities. Abeel and coworkers (1994) report that the most commonly used measure of leadership is the SRBCSS.

According to Alvino and colleagues (1981), the most significant deficiency in identification of gifted individuals is in the area of leadership. Informal, subjective measures are most commonly used. The sections of the Kranz and Renzulli-Hartman scales provide data in this area. A combination of nominations from the student, peers, and teachers can be used as a predictor of leadership ability (Friedman, Friedman, & Van Dyke, 1984). Of the three, self-nomination was the most powerful predictor, leading the researchers to suggest that a simple, straightforward "volunteer" approach should be tried and its power tested.

Visual and Performing Arts Ability

Little is known about the early indicators of gifted performance in the visual and performing arts. Currently, the best indicator of giftedness in these areas is the ability to perform in the specific area chosen. A panel of experts should be assembled to judge such performances. It is believed that the general level of cognitive skills and achievement in academic areas should receive no weight in these decisions, because no evidence exists that such measures can predict artistic achievement (Hagen, 1980). Hagen finds that even tests of creativity have not demonstrated validity as measures of artistic and musical talent, although Torrance found that students who major in speech, drama, and art attain higher scores on these tests than do other students (cited in Barbe & Renzulli, 1975).

When combined with other data, Seashore's Measures of Musical Talents has been found useful (Kavett & Smith, 1980), as has *Measures of Musical Abilities* (Bentley, 1966). *Gordon's Primary Measures of Music Audiation* (1979) was designed to measure aptitudes in young children.

The Horn Art Aptitude Inventory and the Meier Art Tests (Rubenzer, 1979) are measures used in the field of art. Alexander (1981) has found the Meier Art Tests to be culture-bound and of doubtful value for children younger than 12 years of age. Saunders (1982) suggests several ways to secure artistic screening and identification data—for example, assigning a variety of tasks to 25 to 30 applicants at a time and asking them to complete the tasks on-site in one sitting. The tasks tested were two-dimensional and three-dimensional organization and art problem-solving tasks. Saunders suggested other means for gathering data:

> Take a number from 0 to 9, make an art-work from it. Think of as many ideas as possible, save them, and bring all notes and sketches (to the interview).
>
> Record a dream you remember that had great impact. It does not have to be a recent dream. Draw it in a cartoon form. Include as many elements of the dream as possible, but do not use words.
>
> Using 6 to 10 different found objects (such as screws, a broken wheel, a soda can), construct a three-dimensional portrait of yourself at age 85. Try to use the materials in unusual ways. Try to show not only how you look at that age, but how you might feel. Don't worry about the details, but instead try to suggest the general characteristics, use glue, string, or wire to hold your piece together. The whole piece should be no bigger than $1\frac{1}{2}$ feet by $1\frac{1}{2}$ feet.
>
> Fold a large piece of paper in half. Using a pencil, charcoal, or crayons, do a drawing of the sun on one half, and do a drawing of the moon on the other. Think carefully about their differences and similarities. (p. 9)

Observation and recommendations from professional artists provide excellent additional screening material. Peer nominations have been highly reliable in this area (Kavett & Smith, 1980).

IDENTIFYING CULTURALLY DIVERSE, DISABLED, AND EDUCATIONALLY ATYPICAL GIFTED LEARNERS

As discussed in Chapter 4, giftedness results from an early interaction between the genetic program and a stimulating environment. Family patterns or persons who provide such stimulating interaction can be found in any culture, at any socioeconomic level, and despite many disabling conditions. Such differences, however, may make traditional identification procedures ineffective for discovering such ability.

> The problems of identifying and nurturing talent potential are not resolved by formulating constructs of giftedness solely for minority and economically disadvantaged students that differ from those for the majority populations, or by watering down the criteria or standards for excellence or outstanding performance, or by seeking different areas of talent in various populations . . . The challenge is one of creating paradigms that take culture and context into account in order to enhance the possibilities for identifying potential of many kinds in all populations so that appropriate opportunities and conditions can be provided to nurture potential to talented performance. (Passow & Frasier, 1996)

Screening for Gifted Potential Among Diverse Populations

The screening process can limit or broaden the types of students that will be considered for identification of giftedness. In the case of diverse populations, traditional screening processes such as group testing or behavioral checklists of gifted characteristics may limit from consideration the very students that could most benefit from the opportunities provided by gifted programs. It is important that such students be provided with an approach to screening that uncovers their interests and abilities. Kaplan, Rodriguez, and Siegel (2000) suggest that the screening process use curricular activities rather than instruments to assess the abilities of students, engaging them rather than measuring their outcomes with numerical indices. Such a process would include tasks related to verbal abilities that encourage personal expression, such as thoughtful discussion of open-ended questions and predictions from action pictures; questioning skills and problem-solving strategies; and varying forms of creativity. An example of such a process can be seen in the following scenario:

> The GATE program's administrators decided to change the screening process. They designed a set of curricular activities and placed them in centers to stimulate the students' display of yet uncovered potential through interaction with the materials. Tishandra played the game, "Pick and Tell" at the verbalization center. She chose a card with a face on it and spent her time describing the feelings expressed in the photo with elaborate details. Her verbal skills singled out her potential. Carlos displayed unusual abilities to respond to the "Guess What's in the Bag" activity. He asked many and unusual questions which identified his potential for problem-solving techniques. Both students were referred for testing or further assessment. (p. 21)

Kaplan and colleagues suggest that such a screening process facilitates the inclusion rather than the exclusion of diverse students in the identification process.

Frasier (1987) believes that the nomination or screening phase of the identification of gifted black students would be more successful if it included nominations from community leaders, peers, and self in addition to the teacher. A checklist of learning styles found in African-American populations would be informative. She cites Hilliard's (1976) examples of the learning styles one might find among African-American people:

_____1. Tend to view things in their entirety and not in isolated parts;

_____2. Seem to prefer inferential reasoning to deductive or inductive reasoning;

_____3. Appear to focus on people and their activities, rather than objects;

_____4. Tend to prefer novelty, personal freedom, and distinctiveness;

_____5. Tend to approximate space, number, and time instead of aiming for complete accuracy;

_____6. Have a keen sense of justice and quickly perceive injustice; and

_____7. In general tend not to be "word" dependent, but are proficient in nonverbal as well as verbal communication. (p. 35)

Such checklists may alert teachers to behaviors that are unique to the specific culture and allow teachers to look for giftedness from a new perspective. Frasier (1987) offers the following guidelines:

1. Focus on the diversity within the black population.

2. Gather data from multiple sources, both objective and subjective.

3. Use professionals and nonprofessionals who represent various areas of expertise relevant to your program.

4. Plan identification procedures that occur as early as is possible and are continuous.

5. Pay special attention to the different ways in which children from different cultures manifest behavioral indicators of giftedness. (pp. 174, 175)

These are good guidelines for all of us to follow regardless of the population we are seeking and wish to serve.

Some of the screening tools (Table 9.1) that have been used successfully by districts for some of the students they wish to serve are: the Bella Kranz Multidimensional Screening Device (Kranz, 1978); the Baldwin Identification Matrix (Baldwin, 1980); and the SRBCSS (Renzulli, et al., 1976).

The Problems of Traditional Identification Processes for Culturally Diverse Learners

Traditional Tests

The way IQ tests are constructed has built-in limitations and assumptions that can be unfair to groups who are not closely identified with the dominant culture. First, one assumption of most intelligence tests is that intelligence is a single, unvariable factor. More current data indicate that intelligence is neither a single factor nor a constant one (see Chapter 2). Although our beliefs about the reality of intelligence have changed, our measuring tools still proceed from our previous beliefs.

Another problem results from the choice of items on the tests. From an infinite number of human accomplishments and interests, the items have been restricted to concepts and skills found in school curricula, especially the more basic abilities: reading, language arts, and arithmetic. For this reason, IQ tests tend to be good predictors of success within the school environment. A wide variety of other human activities and abilities that could be well-developed in our atypical learners (e.g., fluency, originality, problem-solving in other than academic areas) are not even represented. To make sure the variation of the growing intellect from younger to older children would not disturb the IQ scores, all items were deleted that did not fit the smooth growth pattern that the tests assumed. Items that displayed bias toward either sex also were deleted. By such limited selection procedures, the tests have become very narrow in their focus.

The population modeled for standardization of any test is important to measure its usefulness. The standardization of most commonly used IQ tests has been done within the major culture. For example, the Stanford-Binet was standardized and its scores for success established on white children of English-speaking parents. It has become known as the "Anglo test." Many believe that such bias makes this test inappropriate as a measure of ability for children reared outside the Anglo culture.

These restrictions have led many educators and psychologists to call for the construction of "culture free" tests. Although many have tried (Cattell, 1949; Davis & Eells, 1953; Leiter, 1951), the results have been disappointing. Jensen (1969) found that blacks not only score higher on conventional tests such as the Stanford-Binet and WISC than they do on "culture free" tests, but that they also score higher on verbal than on nonverbal subtests.

Another possible problem of obtaining valid test results seems to be in the test administration. Katz, Roberts, and Robinson (1965) report that, in several experiments, the race of the test administrator had an effect on the test results of black students. They believe that the white environment in general may be stressful and threatening to black children and can induce inaccurate test results. The effect of examiner variables—bilingualism, ethnic group membership, and style of test administration—on the test performance of Spanish-speaking children was reported by Thomas, Hertzig, and Fernandez (1971).

Verbal versus Non-Verbal Testing

In studies reported by Mercer and Smith (1972), Hispanic-American children performed significantly better on nonverbal than on verbal intelligence tests. The higher performance of these children more adequately reflected their school grade-point average than did the scores they received on verbal scales. Jerison (1977) contends that a nonverbal test of intelligence may be a contradiction in terms because, even if words are avoided, the language and language-related functions of the brain are inevitably dominant in most human performance.

Raven's Progressive Matrices Test (Raven, 1947) attempts to provide measures that do not require the use of verbal symbol systems. There are many questions regarding the advisability of such types of alternative testing, which suggests, among other concerns, that such tests are in many ways dependent on verbal language for administration. School districts have reported increased identification of students from culturally diverse and economically disadvantaged populations that have benefited from gifted programs (Wescott & Woodward, 1981). However, caution is recommended in relying too heavily on the Ravens in any identification process. Its low correlation with achievement measures makes it questionable as a primary selection tool for identifying students for special programs that involved advance academic coursework (Mills & Tissot, 1995). For use as one of several measures and as part of a screening process this test may be of use.

Identification Tools and Procedures Designed and/or Suggested for Diverse Populations

Many alternative tools for assessment are available that educators, psychologists, and researchers have found useful.

Behavioral Identification of Diverse Gifted Students

Behavioral identification has been used with success as an alternative to testing for diverse populations of gifted students. Bruch (1971) was concerned with the problem of finding members of subcultures, primarily black students from the Southeast, who have potential not evidenced on traditional tests. She hypothesized that, by looking at patterns of strength other than those required for the usual IQ tests, otherwise untapped disadvantaged, gifted black children can be found. Some areas of strength she feels need to be considered are visual and auditory figural content as in art and music, memory, convergent production in practical problem-solving situations, awareness of details in descriptions, fluency of ideas, spontaneous categorization and classification of spatial items, and awareness of natural relationships or systems. Her work has led her to develop an abbreviated version of the Stanford-Binet that she feels favors these students and allows the gifted among them to be identified. Her instrument is known as the Abbreviated Binet for the Disadvantaged (ABDA).

The Adaptive Behavior Inventory for Children (ABIC) (Mercer & Lewis, 1977) uses a structured parent interview encompassing family, community, peer relations, nonacademic school roles, earner/consumer status, and self-maintenance. Childs (1981) believes that adaptive behavior can and should be used as part of the identification process, especially because the ABIC showed no significant differences among races or cultures in its standardization sample. As measured by the ABIC, gifted children (1) do more activities related to independence and social responsibility and do them earlier than their chronological peers; and (2) consistently show adaptive behavior superior to that of normal children.

Torrance (1977) believes that, by use of his "creative positives," more talent can be discovered and developed among the culturally diverse and economically disadvantaged. He has developed a system for using his data for nontesting ways of identifying the creative among the gifted in these populations.

Perrone and Male (1981) have developed the GIFTS Talent Identification Procedures, which consist of one or more behavior rating sheets plus scoring and interpretation materials. Raters are asked to rate the child only in the areas of talent they have had the opportunity to observe. Some areas that could be assessed are mathematics, English, music, science, reading, interpersonal relations, and art.

Whitmore (1980) reminds us that "The effective use of behavioral characteristics in the identification process is dependent upon an appropriate environment for observation of superior mental abilities and awareness that a gifted child may excel only in very specific areas or may be underachieving in one or more of the basic skills" (p. 67).

Multidimensional Assessment

Forms of assessment that use multiple sources for the outcomes provide a more comprehensive and broader view of the student than any single dimension could allow. One of the most helpful strategies found in the recent authentic assessment methods is the student portfolio. This method of assessment attempts to demonstrate a relationship between school tasks and those found in the real world. Because of the focus on individual student progress, the use of a student portfolio allows gifted students to better demonstrate their own unique abilities. Although a portfolio can be planned to be multidimensional, it should be used with other measures to assess and identify student potential. More detail regarding the use of the student portfolio can be found in Chapter 10.

Some forms of multidimensional assessment include the entire community. In an effort to develop effective leadership within the American Indian community, a group known as American Indian Research and Development, Inc. (AIRD) was formed (Tonemah, 1987). Because the group has concerns that standardized test scores by themselves cannot measure total achievement, they suggest that the scores not be used as the sole source in evaluating student performance, but that multidimensional assessment be used. In addition to test scores, the group recommends that professionally trained psychometrists, preferably American Indian, administer the evaluation to American Indian students and that group achievement and intelligence tests be developed and normed with American Indian student populations. To gain a tribal perspective of giftedness and talent, AIRD surveyed tribal members, asking them to list the characteristics of their tribe's gifted and talented students. The results are being used as part of the gifted student identification and selection process and will form the basis for a critical look at the curriculum. The goals of AIRD are receiving support from tribal members, and the hope is that their efforts may eventually lead to an American Indian Gifted and Talented Academy.

Another test developed to correct the problems found in traditional testing is the System of Multicultural Pluralistic Assessment (SOMPA). The SOMPA uses three assessment models: (1) the medical model, a deficit model that focuses on pathology; (2) the social system model, which compares the behaviors of the child to the behaviors of those in the social system to which he or she belongs; and (3) the pluralistic model, which assumes that only if factors such as exposure to skills and materials, motivation, and learning experiences are held constant can learning potential be assessed. This use of adaptive behavior and estimated learning potential to identify gifted children from culturally diverse or disadvantaged backgrounds is an approach that shows promise (Mercer & Lewis, 1978).

Bernal (1978) suggests three techniques for identifying gifted Hispanic students: (1) culturally pluralistic assessments, such as those discussed by Mercer and Lewis (1978); (2) Piagetian measures for K–3, that is, looking for advanced schema used in problem-solving on a test such as the Cartoon Conversation Scales, which are available in English and Spanish; and (3) bilingual language proficiency scales whose results showing rapid and advanced growth in language would provide a good indicator of high intelligence.

Dynamic Assessment

Dynamic assessment is a diagnostic procedure that considers the context of the testing situation and the ability of the student to learn from experience in that context. It is essentially a test-intervene-retest format. The focus is on the learning ability of the student rather than the knowledge obtained. Kirschenbaum (1998) suggests the use of this process as a means for assessing economically disadvantaged, disabled, and limited English proficient students who have not demonstrated high ability on traditional tests of intelligence and creativity.

A somewhat related assessment process was developed by Maker (1996) to better identify culturally diverse gifted students too often missed by traditional identification methods. "Tasks believed to be developmentally-appropriate, intelligence-fair, and equally engaging across varying groups of students were devised" (p. 46) and tested. Behaviors of the students shown while completing these tasks initiated the assessment process that could be evaluated through the use of multiple, context-based criteria. Referred to as DISCOVER assessment and curriculum development, Maker reports that, "Collaborative decision-making, curriculum development and diversity are central to its mission. All phases are consistent with the important goal of diversity and can be implemented within the context of existing schools, classrooms, and programs for gifted learners" (p. 48).

The Gifted Among Diverse Populations

A range of explanations have been offered for the low representation of culturally diverse students in gifted programs, including test bias, selective referrals, deficit-based paradigms, and lack of multiple criteria, multiple data sources, and modified selection criteria (Frasier, Garcia, & Passow, 1995). Attempts have been and are being made to develop and use more effective and inclusive procedures. Indeed, nearly all of the Javits Act Projects funded by the federal office in the past decades have been focused on this task. Many of the previous attempts, such as redesigning tests, using alternative criteria, and developing culture-specific rating scales, have produced highly questionable data. Of particular concern is the statistically inappropriate practice of summing scores derived from different tests, scales, and checklists.

The word "underrepresentation" may not be an appropriate term regarding the low participation in gifted programs by all socio-economic and cultural groups in our society. Regardless of the "fairness" of intelligence testing, according to the interactive concept of intelligence, any cultural or family pattern that does not support but, in fact, restricts the growth of intelligence will cause its members to receive low test scores (IQs). We could then find fault not with the test, but rather with the cultural or family patterns that brought about such low performance. The environment was unfair, not the test. Gallagher (1991) concludes from the evidence regarding racial and ethnic differences in performance on commonly used intelligence tests that such differences are not an artifact of the measuring instrument nor test bias, but are real differences between these groups at the time of measurement.

It is important that this segment of the population not be overlooked because children who are truly disadvantaged by their family pattern and circumstances and members of various cultures who are limited by the values and opportunities available within their culture must be provided with more growth-producing alternatives. In a study of alternative screening and identification procedures, Reyes, Fletcher, and Paez (1996) found that students identified as appropriate for participation in the gifted program by the alternative procedure they had designed had similar profiles to those students identified via traditional identification processes.

Delcourt and colleagues (1994) suggest that differences, such as those between two groups of identified gifted that make one group difficult to identify (e.g., culturally diverse students) can be eliminated for students who are identified early and placed in gifted programs. They report that minority students in their study who participated in a gifted program for 2 years were able to overcome significant differences found in achievement of racial and ethnic groups when they were initially identified.

Tests of intelligence are currently being looked at very critically; at the same time, tests sampling other human abilities are being developed. We are learning more about how humans develop high levels of ability and may soon be able to measure all types of abilities more appropriately in a wider range of our human population. Until then we must be cautious about how we use current tests. If they are used as only one bit of information added to many other observations and types of data such as case studies, peer reports, and parent interviews, then intelligence tests have value. By themselves, as the sole criterion for selecting educational experiences for children, they are unnecessarily damaging.

Currently, suggestions for finding ability in culturally diverse people has drawn heavily from the measurement of noncognitive skills. This practice needs close examination. For example, tests of creativity are not the primary tools used in the identification of the major population of cognitively or academically gifted children. How, then, can creativity measures be used for identifying children we include in this population to satisfy our desire to serve diversity? Some data indicate that children with creative ability may be a different population, that they may or may not be cognitively or academically gifted. If we are serving students who are both cognitively and creatively able in our programming procedures, this could be a justifiable practice; however, if we are using only measures of cognitive intelligence and developing our programming for this ability, while just including those few diverse students identified by tests of creativity, then we would be developing an unfair situation. Programs developed for highly cognitive students may not meet the needs of the creative student.

Frasier and Passow (1994) suggest that the identification process will be more effective if we seek the basic intellectual abilities common to all gifted students, regardless of their cultural background and the manner in which they express their abilities, such as:

- A strong desire to learn.
- An intense, sometimes unusual interest.
- Unusual ability to communicate with words, numbers, or symbols.
- Use of effective, often inventive strategies for recognizing and solving problems.
- Exceptional ability to retain and retrieve information, resulting in a large store-house of information.
- Extensive and unusual questions, experiments, and explorations.
- Quick grasp of new concepts, connections; sense of deeper meanings.
- Logical approaches to figuring out solutions.
- Ability to produce many highly original ideas.
- A keen, often unusual sense of humor.

Inequities and ineffectiveness of the identification process should be remedied by comprehensive practices such as:

- Development of consensus on the construct of giftedness in diverse cultures and groups;
- Exploration of components of performance-based designs for assessing the aspects of giftedness that are related to cultural and socioeconomic differences;
- Examination of ways of extending the source of referrals and improving the accuracy of nominations;
- Investigation of the value and validity of data from a variety of sources so that "data from multiple sources" becomes more meaningful;
- Relating the assessment procedures to program and curricula design and vice versa; and
- Development of enriched learning opportunities through which youngsters can actually demonstrate their potential by their performance and products, making self-identification an integral part of the assessment process. (Frasier, Garcia, & Passow, 1995)

It is clear that opportunities for growth must be provided for culturally diverse students, but in so doing, we must guard against changing cultural and family patterns just because they are different. Diversity is the cornerstone of developing potential, and only patterns that inhibit the development of that potential need modification.

Identifying Students With Disabilities

A major problem in finding gifted children among the disabled is a function of the expectation resulting from being labeled *disabled*. Because most special education programs in schools have far more fiscal and human resources at the disposal of the child with disabilities, identification usually is for that program. Once labeled, teachers expect the child's needs and behaviors to fall within those normally found in the identified group. Needs for these children are so often deficit needs that remediation is the primary concern. This climate often obscures evidence of giftedness. So few teachers in the special education setting have been exposed to the characteristic behaviors of gifted children that they may interpret any observed deviations from the norm as being unique to the disabling condition. Even when giftedness is suspected, it is often difficult for a child receiving special services to find a place in a gifted program. The special education teacher may not wish to disrupt the program in the primary area. The teacher in the gifted program may be so limited in time and resources that finding a place for the child may be too difficult. The administration may be under restrictions as to financial and program qualifications. A gifted child who is also blind, deaf, or physically disabled may find it impossible to experience any opportunities for enhancing giftedness at school.

The child who is labeled as learning or educationally disabled has an even more complex problem. Often such a child has extreme ability in one or two areas and remedial needs in others. Such a child may also have a behavioral problem and find working with groups difficult. The tests given to diagnose hyperactivity, disruptive classroom conduct, or extreme withdrawal are often the very tests that spot gifted ability. The excessive energy that creates problems may also be behind the student's achievement in a few areas of interest. Unfortunately, children who cannot cope with the structures of a rigid regular classroom are often put in classes with children with learning disabilities. We have previously discussed the importance of self-concept to the success of the student; the results of a negative view in this situation can be clearly seen.

Suter and Wolf (1987) have identified several characteristics of the gifted population who are disabled, including impaired long-term and short-term memory, visual or auditory processing difficulties, visual-motor integration problems, poor self-concept, high level of self-criticism, withdrawal or aggression behaviors, short attention span, difficulty following directions, and poor peer relations. Suter and Wolf warn that the giftedness of these children often goes unnoticed, because they may use it to mask their learning difficulties or they may be identified as children with learning disabilities and their giftedness be totally overlooked. Several common findings from Suter and Wolf's research with the Wechsler Intelligence Scales for Children-Revised (WISC-R) may help to detect these children. Large verbal-performance discrepancies are frequently seen; subscales that assess verbal reasoning abilities tend to show high scores; and scores on Digit Span, Arithmetic, and Coding tend to be low. These researchers again ask for a multidimensional approach for appropriate identification of gifted children with disabilities.

A study of WISC-R profiles by Schiff, Kaufman, and Kaufman (1981) found that a large discrepancy in scores between the verbal section and the performance section indicated a child with learning disability who might also have a high level of intelligence. A majority of their sample (87%) had higher verbal scores.

Lack of trained school psychologists to interpret test scores poses another problem and can be viewed as one of the difficulties in identifying this population. The training program of all school psychologists and special educators should include some information regarding gifted children.

Most of the identification strategies for culturally diverse, disadvantaged, and gifted individuals with disabilities have focused on cognitive abilities; a few have considered creative behaviors. Is there a need for measures of academic, leadership, or arts abilities that take into consideration the effects of being atypical? Is leadership expressed differently in economically disadvantaged or culturally diverse surroundings? Would an arts audition be different if the artist were culturally diverse or disabled? Perhaps these special talents can be seen when skills of creativity, leadership, and the arts are evaluated; perhaps there is no need for special measures—only a change of attitude and more open-minded observation. Although these are not easy questions to answer, the answers will help us include in our identification all the ways giftedness can be expressed. This area definitely bears investigation.

THE CASE STUDY

Once the data on a child who is being considered for the gifted program have been collected, they must be put into a usable form for the selection committee. A number of plans have been suggested for ranking or quantifying the results of the screening and identification process. Information to include in the data for the committee that will comprise the student's case study should incorporate the following, much of which will have been developed for screening:

- *Family History and Student Background.* Provided by parents, this will include historical and developmental data on the student; health and medical records of student and family; educational and occupational background of parents; description of family unit; anecdotes of the student in the home that indicate unusual capacity and early development; family activities and interests; and the child's extracurricular activities and interests.

- *Teacher Report of Student Functioning.* This report includes observations of intellectual, physical, social, and emotional functioning; learning style; and motivation.

- *Nomination Forms.* These are collected from teachers, principal, counselor, psychologist, and others.

- *Student Inventory.* The student provides an inventory of self, values, interests, and attitudes toward school and out-of-school activities.

- *Test Protocols.* These individual and group tests include scores and the psychologist's interpretation. If other criteria are to be used in lieu of scores, they should be included. For students of separate criteria such as special populations (e.g., disadvantaged gifted, disabled gifted), include all the data necessary for decision-making regarding selection and placement.

- *Student's Work or Achievement Awards.* These include both academic and extracurricular work products and achievements.

After the student has been identified, the parents must be informed of the decision and asked for permission to place their child in whatever program the school provides. The signed permission form will then be placed in the permanent case study file. Administrators should explain to the parents the concept of giftedness and the purpose of the program and clearly invite their participation.

To summarize the identification process, the following recommendations have been drawn from a review of the literature on identification practices done by Abeel, Callahan, and Hunsaker (1994). Experts in the field of gifted education recommend that identification practices:

- Be based on broad conceptions of giftedness.
- Include multiple criteria.
- Include unique instrumentation for different areas of giftedness.
- Include only reliable instruments valid for the program rationale and the definition of giftedness used.
- Avoid identification by a single score.
- Be based on student need.
- Include appropriate instruments for under-served populations.

LABELING GIFTED LEARNERS

Labeling students results in a change in parent and teacher expectations, as well as in the self-concept of the child. Sometimes parents feel suddenly inadequate to guide their child's development once they know their child is "gifted." Sometimes the label results in very unreal expectations. For example, in high schools, labeling a student as gifted can result in placement in every honors class, whether the student is advanced in that particular discipline or not.

Labels create expectations. When using labels such as "gifted" or "honors," the precise meaning of the term must be very clearly stated, not only what it is, but what it is not. Parents deserve more than an announcement of a new label for their child. A parent meeting should be arranged to explain the concept of *giftedness* and answer questions about its development at home and at school. How the school experience will be different for the child after identification should be communicated. Sending out additional information outlining ways the home can be involved in the further growth of the student is important.

The gifted student also needs to know what the label "gifted" means. Chapters 2, 4, and 5 contain information of which all gifted children should be aware, understand, and be allowed to investigate. The lesson on understanding giftedness in Chapter 5 should be an important part of every gifted program. This course structure has been used for children from early elementary through high school and is always one of their favorite topics.

In regard to the impact of labeling, several researchers have looked at the effect of the identification of one family member on the rest of the family. Cornell (1983) reported that the label generally is received by the family as positive, with the child given more status. The question was raised, however, that one effect of the labeling may be disruption, because siblings of gifted learners were reported to be less well-adjusted both emotionally and socially than their counterparts in families without identified gifted siblings. Colangelo and Bower (1987) also concluded that parents need to be concerned, because their review of the literature on the effects of identifying one family member as gifted shows a trend toward adjustment problems for the nongifted siblings. Their study, however, indicates that over the long term, such effects may not remain so negative. Instead it seems to be the gifted student who perceives the negative effects on the family, real or imagined. Although students so labeled enjoyed participating in the gifted program, they felt that neither their siblings nor the family as a whole had a positive attitude toward their label. Colangelo and Bower suggest that attention be given to youngsters at the time they are labeled to prevent disruption within the family or even perceived disruption.

When a school establishes a program for gifted learners, it should include in-service training for the entire faculty and staff regarding the meaning of giftedness and the importance of the new program. For the child's welfare and the success of the program, the school must work as a unit, and all of the personnel must see how the program will fit within the goals and structure of the school. Without such information, misunderstandings, hostility, and unnecessary obstructionism will be focused on the program, the responsible teacher, and the gifted child. As we have seen, teachers, administrators, and counselors in most schools often have very negative attitudes toward gifted students. Yet, by planning a program around the students' needs and purposefully communicating information on the program and on giftedness in general, we can influence these attitudes to become favorable, even supportive. If children are labeled *gifted* to improve their educational experience, then there is an obligation to keep the negative aspects of labeling from becoming the major effect.

In this chapter, the rationales and procedures for selecting gifted children who need special educational provisions to continue their growth have been reviewed. Screening procedures and the problems of screening have been discussed; identification has been viewed from a variety of perspectives, including the importance of assessment and case studies; and the special problems encountered in identifying the atypical, the disabled, and the culturally diverse gifted learner have been seen. But all of this would be meaningless if the programming to meet these special needs was not discussed. In the next chapters, programming will be the focus. The main purpose for identification is to provide special educational experiences that can enhance the continuous growth of every gifted child.

QUESTIONS OFTEN ASKED

1. Why identify gifted children at all? Wouldn't it be better just to improve education for everyone?

Improving education for everyone is the goal for which we all strive; however, while we are doing that we must also make sure the needs of these underserved children are met. Most school systems do not individualize their instruction to the degree that children with special needs can receive an appropriate educational experience. Remember, brain researchers tell us we must use and challenge our brain or we will lose ability. Unless they are specially planned, school experiences seldom challenge bright students. As schools are currently organized and run, identifying children with special needs is the only way to ensure that these needs will be met.

2. How do you identify highly gifted children, and how do they differ from less gifted children?

The highly gifted are usually identified by exceptionally high levels of performance on schoolwork, intelligence tests, or achievement tests. Different districts have different criteria for their identification and even the IQ score used may range from 140 to 165, or even 180. The highly gifted often have intense and abundant energy, high levels of curiosity, advanced concept development, and a large vocabulary that seems to develop very early. They can appear very mature at one moment and typically childlike the next. They differ from less gifted children every bit as much as these children differ from average learners. They have many of the same characteristics and problems of gifted children but to a higher degree. For example, gifted children have difficulty finding peers who think as they do and often choose to be with older children; highly gifted children have even more difficulty and may find that even older children are unable to understand their concerns.

3. Should we identify preschool-age gifted children?

Many of the characteristics and behaviors typical of gifted learners can be observed very early. The only reason to identify them is for appropriate placement and educational planning. As discussed in previous chapters, the early years are the most plastic and should be enriched if we are to allow children to be all that they can be. Currently, there are few early learning programs available that provide well-rounded, integrated, and enriched programs; there are even fewer that provide appropriate programs for young gifted children. With this in mind, I would be more concerned about challenging all children from where they are, allowing continuous progress and enriching experiences, and letting the children guide us to their next steps than I would be about formal identification. Appropriate, stimulating experiences are our best way to nurture giftedness. It is important to let the child be our guide.

4. If a child has high IQ scores but is not highly creative, is this child gifted?

Such a child can be gifted; however, one score is never enough to know if a child has special needs. Certainly a high IQ score is one piece of datum that indicates a need for more information. The biological changes that result in gifted behavior may be expressed in many ways. Creativity may not be the way some children express their giftedness.

5. Should we use the same tests for low–socioeconomic-level students as we do for the others?

Yes, if you are using a wide variety of tests and demonstrations of ability. We once got into trouble when we gave only the standardized intelligence tests to children and then to be more "fair," gave creativity tests to "special criteria" children from very poor communities. We then placed those who scored high in both groups together and gave them the same learning experiences. As a result, we penalized the low–socioeconomic-level children by placing them in an academic setting for which they had no skills. Hopefully, we have learned from our past errors and now offer both groups a wide range of data collection and multidimensional testing for identification and a continuum of services for programs.

6. Aren't "culture free" tests best for identifying culturally diverse students?

Although some tests may be more "culture bound" than others, none are "culture free." Although there is still controversy regarding which tests are best for whom, our safest avenue is to provide multidimensional testing and develop a good profile of the child from which we can make sound educational decisions. Because children will be asked to perform in the mainstream culture, I doubt that we would be doing them a service by providing "culture free" experiences. Sensitivity to their cultural experiences and provision for further opportunities enhancing wider cultural understanding would be more helpful.

7. What is the best identification procedure?

Generally, nominations are requested at the beginning and then multidimensional screening is done, resulting in an educational profile that can be used to decide if further identification is appropriate. If it is, then the profile material is developed into a case study with a variety of more specific and individualized information added. This material then goes before a committee of school personnel for the decision regarding placement. After parent permission is obtained, specific needs are assessed, using the case study information and any additional functional assessments needed. Appropriate placement and an individual educational plan can be developed from this information.

8. Isn't the case study approach too expensive to be practical?

Much of the information used for the case study is available for every child from the school's cumulative records. The additional data will be needed only if the child passes the initial screen. The most expensive parts of the process are the coordinator's time spent collecting the data and the committee's time for considering identification and appropriate placement. Other approaches may be more expensive in that thcy arc cither inefficient if the methods allow too few gifted children to be found or ineffective if the screen allows too many needing further identification. Ultimately, the most expensive proposition would be to lose human potential by inappropriate,

narrow procedures that leave gifted children unserved.

9. What is the biggest problem with labeling a child gifted? Would it be better to call gifted children by another word?

The word gifted does give an unfortunate connotation to the group of children who bear that label. People often think that they were given a gift; that is, they did nothing to earn their ability or talent. In American society we are suspicious of anyone who gets something for nothing. We think that if they did not earn what they have, they probably do not deserve to have it and certainly they should not have more. This line of thinking has been responsible for a lot of misunderstanding about gifted children. However, giving them a different label would still not solve the problems labeling causes nor the needs of the children. We have this label now, so perhaps the best we can do is to be sure everyone, including the gifted child, understands what it means and the importance of nurturing such abilities.

CHECKING FOR UNDERSTANDING
Follow-Up Activity

The following descriptions are very limited case studies of children who are applying for the GATE program in your district. You are a part of the identification committee and are asked to paper screen these children using the data you are being given. Working with a small group of your colleagues, please decide whether you would recommend each child for admission to the gifted program, the highly gifted program, or refuse the request for admission. If the student is to be admitted to the gifted program, designate the area of giftedness in

which you believe the student will have gifted needs (e.g., general intellectual, academic achievement, specific academic achievement, creativity, leadership, or visual and performing arts). Record the reasons for your decision and discuss decisions with other groups in your class. What other information would you have liked to have had when making your decision?

(Hint: Some of these children grew up to be famous adults. Their identities are given following the exercise.)

Case No. 1

Ficticious name: Margaret Howe	Age: 11	Grade Level: 5	
Height: 5'8"	Weight: 98 lbs.	Appearance: Unattractive, homely	
IQ: 110	Social Q: 76	Achievement Q: 82	Creativity Q: 95
Nationality: American	Race: White		

School Adjustment: Seeks attention; at times withdrawn, prefers isolation; fails often; daydreams.

Special skills: Patience with children and elderly or infirm

Vocational goals: None

General physical health: Sickly, bedridden, hospitalized often, wears backbrace from spinal defect.

General emotional health: Bites nails, phobias, attention-seeking behavior, dominates.

Family: Conservative, father alcoholic, parents deceased; father completed B.A., mother high school

Case No. 2

Ficticious name: John Krane   Age: 11   Grade Level: 5

Height: 4'11"   Weight: 142 lbs.   Appearance: Average

IQ: 108   Social Q: 98   Achievement Q: 112   Creativity Q: 104

Nationality: American   Race: White

School Adjustment: Good performer

Special skills: Active in sports, Boy Scouts

Vocational goals: Work in dad's computer sales business

General physical health: Good

General emotional health: Good

Family: Conservative, parents high school graduates, active in church

Case No. 3

Ficticious name: Herman Adler   Age: 9   Grade Level: 4

Height: 5'1"   Weight: 94 lbs.   Appearance: Homely

IQ: 82   Social Q: 74   Achievement Q: 82   Creativity Q: 110+

Nationality: American   Race: White

School Adjustment: Very poor, considered unsociable and disturbed

Special skills: Plays violin, likes to be alone to read

Vocational goals: None

General physical health: Often sickly

General emotional health: Had emotional breakdown and was removed from school temporarily

Family: Parents born in Germany; father self-employed, bankrupt; parents have high school education; family interested in reading and music

Case No. 4

Ficticious name: Pearl Johnson   Age: 16   Grade Level: 10

Height: 5'11"   Weight: 195 lbs.   Appearance: heavy, unattractive

IQ: 138   Social Q: 126   Achievement Q: 149   Creativity Q: 108

Nationality: American   Race: African-American

School Adjustment: Top 5% of her inner-city class

Special skills: Debate team

Vocational goals: Wants to be a lawyer

General physical health: Good

General emotional health: Good, self-confident, ambitious

Family: Conservative, parents high school graduates, father a baptist minister and store clerk, family loves music, plays instruments together

Case No. 1   Eleanor Roosevelt
Case No. 2   Nongifted student
Case No. 3   Albert Einstein
Case No. 4   Barbara Jordan

 **SUMMARY**

DIFFERENT APPROACHES TO DISCOVERING GIFTEDNESS

1. In schools that use discrete grade placement, which is primarily determined by chronological age, and that use group instruction almost totally, it may even be necessary to label and isolate atypical learners for at least part of the time.
2. Many gifted youngsters are discovered only after their frustration leads them, by teacher request, to the office of a counselor for testing for a learning disability or Attention Deficit and Hyperactivity Disorder (ADHD) program.

SEARCH, SCREENING, AND IDENTIFICATION PROCEDURES

3. The general intellectual ability is the concept most frequently adopted for gifted programs.
4. Until more productive measures of intelligence are developed, available measures will continue to be used, but it would be wise to supplement their use with other evaluative tools such as observation of the processes, performance, or products of learning; the results from a variety of measures of achievement and creativity; and self-reporting and reports from parents, teachers, and peers.
5. Unfortunately many people, including too many educators, believe that the IQ score gives an accurate description of a person's capacity. It does not. Currently there are no tests of capacity.
6. One assumption of most intelligence tests is that intelligence is a single, unvariable factor. More current data indicate that intelligence is neither a single factor nor a constant one.
7. Out of an infinite number of human accomplishments and interests, the test items have been restricted to concepts and skills found in school curricula, especially the more basic abilities.
8. IQ tests tend to be good predictors of success within the school environment.
9. Children with special needs would begin to emerge very early if, from the beginning of their educational experience, all children were allowed to learn at their own rate, pursue ideas and activities to whatever depth possible for their ability, and encouraged to be curious in a rich, responsive environment.

Search

10. The function of the search component is to generate a list of possible gifted students from all school sites while making sure that all students have an equal opportunity to be selected.

Screening

11. The identification process continues by screening for students who show need for a different kind of educational experience. To find and serve children from each of the areas of ability the district has decided to serve will take varied and numerous resources.
12. The screening process can limit or broaden the types of students that will be considered for identification of giftedness.

Identification

13. The major purpose of identification is to obtain information that will help educators provide the program that is best suited to the development of the gifted student's potential.
14. Actual identification for the purpose of placement in a gifted program is best done by a group of professionals representing a variety of areas of expertise, such as the principal, a teacher, a counselor or psychologist, and the program coordinator. They should develop a case study or profile to aid in the identification decision and also later in program planning for the individual.

Tools for Screening and Identification of Gifted and Talented Learners

15. There are numerous tests, checklists, questionnaires, and inventories that have been used to screen and identify students for gifted programs.

IDENTIFYING CULTURALLY DIVERSE, DISABLED, AND EDUCATIONALLY ATYPICAL GIFTED LEARNERS

16. Family patterns or persons who provide such stimulating interaction can be found in any culture, at any socioeconomic level, and in spite of many disabling conditions. Such differences, however, may make traditional identification procedures ineffective for discovering such ability.
17. In the case of diverse populations, traditional screening processes such as group testing or behavioral checklists of gifted characteristics may limit from consideration the very students who could most benefit from the opportunities provided by gifted programs.

The Problems of Traditional Identification Processes for Culturally Diverse Learners

18. The way IQ tests are constructed has built-in limitations and assumptions that can be unfair to groups who are not closely identified with the dominant culture.
19. The standardization of most commonly used IQ tests has been done within the major culture.
20. Some culturally diverse groups not only score higher on conventional tests such as the Stanford-Binet and Wechsler than they do on "culture free" tests, but that they also score higher on verbal subtests than on nonverbal subtests.

Identification Tools and Procedures Designed and/or Suggested for Diverse Populations

21. Behavioral identification has been used with success as an alternative to testing for diverse populations of gifted students.
22. Forms of assessment that use multiple sources for the outcomes provide a more comprehensive and broader view of the student than any single dimension could allow.
23. Because of the focus on individual student progress, the use of a student portfolio allows gifted students to better demonstrate their own unique abilities.
24. Dynamic assessment is a diagnostic procedure that considers the context of the testing situation and the ability of the student to learn from experience in that context. It is essentially a test-intervene-retest format.

The Gifted Among Diverse Populations

25. A range of explanations have been offered for the under-representation of culturally diverse students in gifted programs, including test bias, selective referrals, deficit-based paradigms, and lack of multiple criteria, multiple data sources, and modified selection criteria.
26. Regardless of the "fairness" of intelligence testing, according to the interactive concept of intelligence, any culture or family pattern that does not support but, in fact, restricts the growth of intelligence will cause its members to receive low test scores (IQs). We could then find fault not with the test, but rather with the culture or family patterns that brought about such low performance. The environment was unfair, not the test.
27. Authorities believe that racial and ethnic differences in performance on commonly used intelligence tests are not an artifact of the measuring instrument nor test bias, but are real differences between these groups at the time of measurement.
28. The identification process will be more effective if we seek the basic intellectual abilities common to all gifted students, regardless of their cultural background and the manner in which they express their abilities.
29. Opportunities for growth must be provided for culturally diverse students, but, in so doing, we must guard against changing cultural and family patterns just because they are different. Diversity is the cornerstone of developing potential, and only patterns that inhibit the development of that potential need modification.

IDENTIFYING STUDENTS WITH DISABILITIES

30. A major problem in finding gifted children among the disabled is a function of the expectation resulting from being labeled *disabled*. Once labeled, teachers expect the child's needs and behavior to fall within those normally found in the identified group.
31. The tests given to diagnose hyperactivity, disruptive classroom conduct, or extreme withdrawal are often the very tests that spot gifted ability.
32. Because most special education programs in schools have far more fiscal and human resources at the disposal of the child with disabilities than do gifted programs, identification usually is for that program.

33. Needs for children in special education programs are so often deficit needs that remediation is the primary concern. This climate often obscures evidence of giftedness.
34. So few teachers in the special education setting have been exposed to the characteristic behaviors of gifted children that they may interpret any observed deviations from the norm as being unique to the disabling condition. The teacher in the gifted program may be so limited in time and resources that finding a place for the child may be too difficult.

THE CASE STUDY

35. Once the data on a child who is being considered for the gifted program have been collected, they must be put into a usable form for the selection committee.
36. After the student has been identified, the parents must be informed of the decision and asked for permission to place their child in whatever program the school provides.

37. Administrators should explain to the parents the concept of giftedness and the purpose of the program and clearly invite their participation.

LABELING GIFTED LEARNERS

38. Labeling students results in a change in parent and teacher expectations, as well as in the self-concept of the child.
39. Labels create expectations. When using labels such as *gifted* or *honors* the precise meaning of the term must be very clearly stated, not only what it is, but what it is not.
40. When a school establishes a program for gifted learners, it should include in-service training for the entire faculty and staff regarding the meaning of giftedness and the importance of the new program.
41. The main purpose for identification is to provide special educational experiences that can enhance the continuous growth of every gifted child.

Part III

Teaching Gifted Learners

10 Establishing the Foundation for Educating Gifted Learners

In this chapter the reader will discover:

- Curriculum models often used to provide for the needs of gifted learners.

- An introduction to the seven steps for optimizing learning.

- A discussion of the Responsive Learning Environment.

- Strategies for creating the Responsive Learning Environment.

- Ideas for extending learning beyond the classroom.

- Ideas for assessment of individual needs in content, process, and enrichment.

- A discussion of the assessment of knowledge, understanding, and interest.

- Strategies for using authentic, performance-based assessment.

After you understand about the sun and the stars and the rotation of the earth, you may still miss the radiance of the sunset.

—ALFRED NORTH WHITEHEAD

Rocky's mother had brought the tall, gangly 12-year-old to the demonstration school that served 6- to 16-year-old gifted and highly able learners because, as she said, she had heard the school had very good results and she just didn't know what else to do. Although Rocky was profoundly gifted, he had been placed in learning disability classes for the past 2 years because he refused to speak at school. His mother said that Rocky spoke freely at home, but not at all at school. She was so concerned that the director had agreed to accept him on the condition that if the experience had not helped him by the second week, his situation would be discussed further. Although experimental, the school was not equipped for therapeutic counseling and had not been established to work with children who were deeply troubled.

After 2 days there had been no assessment possible, and Rocky refused to speak at this school as well. Each morning the faculty and all 140 students came together to open the day with a quote or saying for the day, a puzzle for the day, and a relaxation before they went to the areas of study they had chosen. On Rocky's third day the quote for the day had something to do with the difference between the educated person and the learned person. To the director's surprise, Rocky raised his hand to speak.

"Yes, Rocky," she said quickly.

Rocky unwound his long legs from the position he had taken on the floor with all of the other children and stood, immediately commanding everyone's attention. "Well, an educated person knows everything about the box. He knows the bottom of the box, the ceiling of the box, the sides of the box, and he even knows all of the space in the box. But the learned person, well he knows all about the box, but he knows how to get out of the box. He knows about the whole universe, and he knows about himself in relation to the universe and . . ." Rocky suddenly stopped and looked down at all of the children looking up at him with amazement clearly visible on their faces. But no one was laughing at him; he could see only surprise and interest, because they had never heard him speak before. So Rocky stood up even taller and continued with his thoughtful and complex thesis. At the end of the opening session he approached the director and very seriously pronounced, "This school is going to be all right."

During the rest of the day the faculty was heard to exclaim to each other, wistfully, with shaking heads, "Do you remember when Rocky didn't talk?" for Rocky was a very verbal youngster.

Later the director learned that Rocky remembered his second-grade teacher saying, "Rocky, do not interrupt. Sit down and be still." And in the third grade, "Young man, you talk too much. Now put down your hand and get to work!" And in the fourth grade and fifth grade he had had more invitations to "Just sit down and shut up!"

Finally Rocky had decided to do just that. He refused to speak at school. The only reason he had spoken again in the demonstration school was because, as he said, "It's safe here. Everyone respects each other. I'm not always wrong here; it's okay to be smart and have lots of questions."

As you begin this chapter, you have already confronted the possible structures for establishing a program that will allow gifted learners to continue to develop their abilities and interests. You have identified ways in which gifted learners express their giftedness and have pondered the complexity of finding gifted learners within the school setting. Teaching the students who are gifted will be our next concern. Several models now in use for organizing the curriculum for gifted learners will be presented with the idea that each has useful concepts and strategies that could benefit a gifted program. The investigation of some of these models may offer some possibilities for meeting the needs of gifted learners.

Regardless of the curriculum model that is used it is important to create conditions that optimize learning in the classroom. A model for optimizing learning will be discussed that is based on the implications from brain research data covered in Chapter 2. The first step is to create a responsive learning environment. Although this step provides a basis for good education for all students, it is one of the basic conditions that facilitates the education of gifted learners. Later in the chapter, there is a discussion of the assessment of the knowledge, understanding, and interest of students that will provide the basis for the differentiation and individualization of curriculum and instruction.

CURRICULUM MODELS OFTEN USED TO EDUCATE GIFTED LEARNERS

A number of conceptualizations of the learning process have influenced the development of curriculum in gifted education. They have provided structures that allow careful consideration of how learning may occur and how experiences may be designed to enhance growth in skills related to thinking and learning. Some of the resulting curriculum models are presented here in abstracted form.

The Taxonomy of Educational Objectives: Cognitive Domain and Affective Domain

One of the conceptualizations often used in gifted education is the *Taxonomy of Educational Objectives: Handbook I: Cognitive Domain,* edited by Bloom (1956). Bloom chaired a committee that presented and clarified a taxonomy that organized how the cognitive thinking process might occur. Educators can use the taxonomy to plan for learning experiences at many levels to meet the needs of a variety of learners. Both average and more able students need to have learning presented at the levels of knowledge, comprehension, application, analysis, synthesis, and evaluation. Opportunities to work at more advanced levels are crucial for the more able student. Because the brain must continue to be stimulated or lose its capability, the fact that the majority of classrooms have been found to present learning experiences only at the lower levels of the taxonomy is of concern to all teachers who wish to optimize learning. Table 10.1 presents and clarifies the taxonomy in ways that have been found useful in curriculum planning. This cognitive taxonomy is often used as a linear model, but it can also be viewed as cyclic, with the highest level, evaluation, seen as producing new information that becomes knowledge and then moves through the entire process (Figure 10.1).

Although one often hears that gifted learners should be working at the top levels of the taxonomy, such a statement can be quite misleading. It would not be possible for gifted students to analyze information that they do not understand. All students need to be exposed to experiences at all levels of the taxonomy. The emphasis in instruction and the time spent on the higher levels makes the difference for

Table 10.1 *Taxonomy of Educational Objectives: Cognitive Domain*

Area of Taxonomy	Definition	What Teacher Does	What Student Does	Process Verbs	
Knowledge	Recall or recognition of specific information	Directs Tells Shows Examines	Responds Absorbs Remembers Recognizes	define repeat list name label	memorize record recall relate
Comprehension	Understanding of information given	Demonstrates Listens Questions Compares Contrasts Examines	Explains Translates Demonstrates Interprets	restate describe explain identify report tell	discuss recognize express locate review
Application	Using methods, concepts, principles, and theories in new situations	Shows Facilitates Observes Criticizes	Solves problems Demonstrates use of knowledge Constructs	translate apply employ use practice shop	interpret demonstrate dramatize illustrate operate schedule
Analysis	Breaking information down into its constituent elements	Probes Guides Observes Acts as a resource	Discusses Uncovers Lists Dissects	distinguish calculate test contract criticize debate question solve analyze	appraise differentiate experiment compare diagram inspect inventory relate examine
Synthesis	Putting together constituent elements or parts to form a whole requiring original, creative thinking	Reflects Extends Analyzes Evaluates	Discusses Generalizes Relates Compares Contrasts Abstracts	compose propose formulate assemble construct set up manage	plan design arrange collect create organize prepare
Evaluation	Judging the values of ideas, materials, and methods by developing and applying standards and criteria	Clarifies Accepts Harmonizes Guides	Judges Disputes Develops criteria	judge evaluate compare score choose estimate predict	appraise rate value select assess measure

Source: From Benjamin S. Bloom, Ed., *Taxonomy of Educational Objectives, Book 1 Cognitive Domain* (pp. 201–207) Copyright © 1984. Adapted by permission by Allyn & Bacon.

Figure 10.1 *Cognitive Taxonomy Circle*

Note: The wheel in Figure 10.1 was developed by my colleague, Barry Ziff, and a class of teachers of gifted students. They found it very useful in curriculum building.

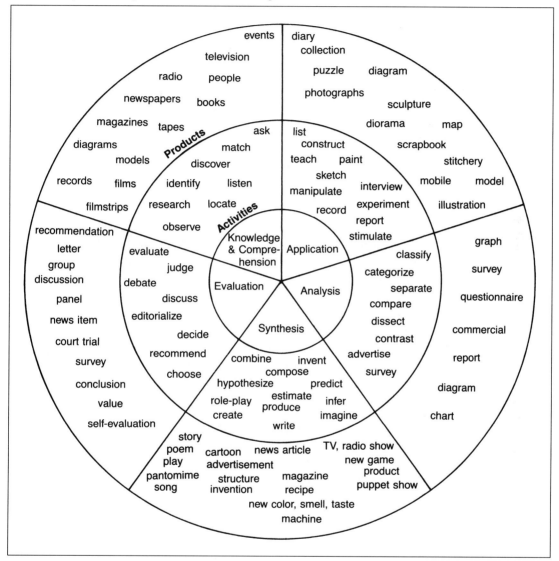

gifted students as they often bring a large amount of knowledge to class with them and can learn new knowledge at a faster pace (see Figure 10.2).

Bloom was also involved in a second committee, chaired by colleague David Krathwohl, that developed a hierarchy of affective learning, the *Taxonomy of Educational Objectives: Handbook II: Affective Domain* (Krathwohl, Bloom, & Masia, 1964). They provided a list of objectives to sequence behaviors that would indicate growth in the emotional areas of function. In Table 10.2 these levels are indicated as

Figure 10.2 *Cognitive Taxonomy Ladder*

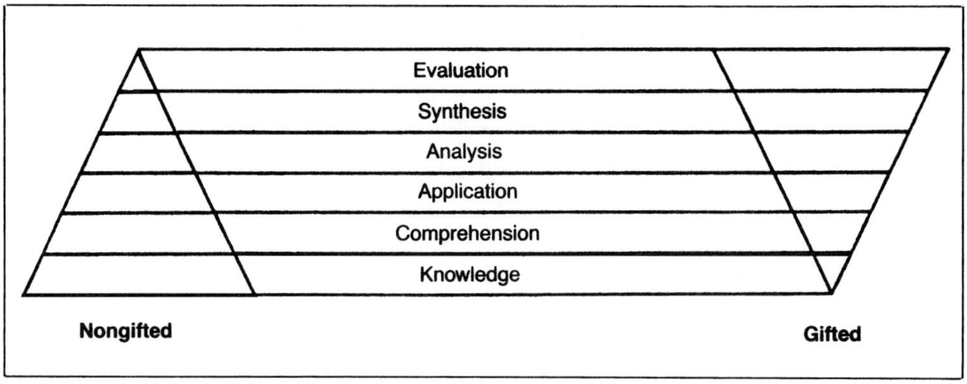

receiving, responding, valuing, organization of a value structure, and characterization by a value.

One of the best things about working with gifted learners is that they enjoy these types of organizers. Not only can teachers find them helpful in curriculum development, but the students themselves, after becoming familiar with the taxonomic structure, can analyze and create experiences at each level.

The Structure of Intellect Model

Another major organizer used for development of curriculum in gifted education is the Structure of Intellect (SOI) Model (Guilford, 1967). The model (Figure 10.3) provided psychology with a multifactor view of intelligence to replace the single-factor view previously held.

A factor analysis of numerous aptitude and ability tests provided the basis for Guilford's SOI Model. The division of intellectual abilities into three dimensions—contents, operations, and products—and their subdivisions gives this model the means to show interrelationships between and among human abilities (Guilford, 1967). Some educators, especially Meeker (1969), extend the use of the SOI Model to serve as a basis for a diagnostic-prescriptive tool in the teaching of thinking skills.

Meeker (1969) asserts that use of the SOI Model provides a theory of intelligence for education where previously none had existed. She believes that, by using the model for curriculum development, we can meet the educational needs of each child more adequately. Meeker has developed assessment techniques that make use of the major tests of intelligence, the Stanford-Binet and the Wechsler. These tests delineate the student's areas of strength and weakness that correspond with specific abilities on the SOI. The resulting profile of the student provides the basis for a curricular plan that may then be implemented with materials developed by Meeker for classroom use.

Meeker's work has made the SOI much more available to the classroom, and the success of her efforts may cause some teachers to restrict their planning to use of just these materials. However, more than just activities of a cognitive nature must be included in a total educational program. After all, the SOI is a theoretical model

Table 10.2 *Taxonomy of Educational Objectives: Affective Domain*

Category	Subdivisions	Student Behavior to Be Attained (Educational Objectives)
1.0 Receiving/ Attending	1.1 Awareness	Observes; recognizes, is aware of; develops sensitivity to
	1.2 Willingness to	Accepts others; develops a tolerance for. Listens carefully; recognizes persons as individuals
	1.3 Controlled and selected attention	Discriminates; appreciates alertness to values; selects reading materials
2.0 Responding	2.1 Acquiescence in responding	Willing to comply; observes rules and regulations
	2.2 Willingness to respond	Voluntarily seeks information, engages in variety of activities. Responds to intellectual stimuli; engages in research
	2.3 Satisfactory in response	Finds pleasure in reading, listening, conversing, art, participation in groups
3.0 Valuing	3.1 Accepting a value	Develops a sense of responsibility, of kinship, of need for worship
	3.2 Preference for a value	Interest in enabling others; examines a variety of viewpoints; assumes active role in politics, literary organizations
	3.3 Commitment	Displays a high degree of certainty, loyalty, faith in the power of reason
4.0 Organization	4.1 Conceptualization of a value	Establishes a conscious base for making choices. Identifies admired characteristics. Analyzes basic assumptions underlying codes of ethics and faith. Forms judgment as to responsibility of society to the individual and environment. Develops personal goals.
	4.2 Organization of a value system According to Edward Spranger, values may be organized around the following: 1. Theoretical 2. Economic 3. Aesthetic 4. Social 5. Political 6. Religious	Examines role of democracy in conserving human and natural resources; accepts own potentialities and limitations realistically; views people as individuals, without prejudice; develops techniques for conflict management. Accepts responsibility for the future.
5.0 Characteriza- tion of a Value	5.1 Generalized set—the basic orientation which enables the individual to act consistently and effectively in a complex world	Readiness to reverse judgments or change behavior in light of evidence; to change one's mind and face facts; confidence in ability to succeed; solves problems in terms of what is, rather than wishful thinking
	5.2 Characterization—one's personal philosophy of life demonstrated in behavior	Develops a code of behavior based on ethical principles consistent with democratic ideals; behavior which is consistent with beliefs

Source: From David R. Krathwohl, Benjamin S. Bloom, and Bertram B. Masia, *Taxonomy of Educational Objectives, Book 2 Affective Domain* (pp. 176–183). Copyright © 1964. Adapted by permission by Allyn & Bacon.

Figure 10.3 *Theoretical Model for Guilford's Structure of Intellect*
Source: From *The Nature of Human Intelligence* (p. 63), by J. P. Guilford, 1967, New York: McGraw-Hill. Copyright 1967 by McGraw-Hill. Reprinted with permission.

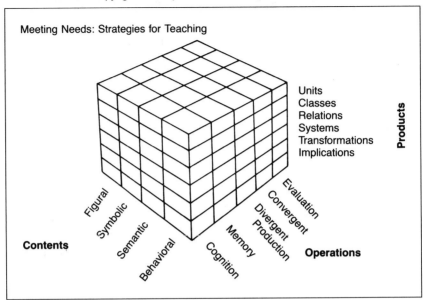

of intellectual abilities that, at best, only partially explains human functioning. Meeker has made a valuable contribution. Nevertheless, when used, the SOI materials should be carefully integrated into a comprehensive educational plan that views cognitive ability as only one area of intellectual functioning.

The Enrichment Triad/Revolving Door Model

The Enrichment Triad/Revolving Door Model (Renzulli, 1977; Renzulli & Reis, 1986) is the most widely known program based on the practice of enrichment. Along with the Secondary Triad Model and the School-wide Enrichment Model, it is, in part, a program model, but it must be examined also as a curriculum model. The model is essentially a pullout program using a resource room for presenting enrichment to meet the unique needs of gifted students. From this basis a wide array of goals, strategies, and procedures are offered to provide services for elementary and secondary gifted students.

The Enrichment Triad/Revolving Door Model operates from a unique set of assumptions regarding the definition and identification of giftedness. Rather than seeing any individual as gifted or potentially gifted, the model assumes that the concept of giftedness reflects behavior resulting from an interaction among three basic clusters of human traits: above-average general and/or specific abilities, high levels of task commitment, and high levels of creativity. The model further assumes that gifted behaviors can be developed, that they are not always present, and that service should be provided only when such behaviors are exhibited.

The Enrichment Triad Model began as an answer to criticism regarding enrichment programs that were not differentiated but seemed to provide good education for all students (Renzulli, 1977). The model has two stated objectives:

- Program Objective No. 1—For the majority of time spent in the gifted programs, students will have complete freedom to pursue topics of their own choosing to whatever depth and extent they so desire; and they will be allowed to pursue these topics in a manner that is consistent with their own preferred style of learning. (p. 307)

- Program Objective No. 2—The primary role of each teacher in the program for gifted and talented students will be to provide each student with assistance in (1) identifying and structuring realistic solvable problems that are consistent with the student's interests, and (2) acquiring the methodological resources and investigative skills that are necessary for solving these particular problems. (p. 312)

As implied in its name, the Enrichment Triad Model identifies the three types of enrichment shown in Figure 10.4. The first two types, General Exploratory Activities and Group Training Activities, are considered appropriate for all learners and provide the basis for overall enrichment. They are intended to provide strategies for expanding student interests and developing the thinking and feeling processes. Type III enrichment, Individual and Small Group Investigations of Real Problems, is

Figure 10.4 *Overview of the Enrichment Triad Model*
Source: From *Systems and Models for Developing Programs for the Gifted and Talented* (p. 275), by J. Renzulli, 1977, Mansfield, CT: Creative Learning Press, Inc. Copyright 1977 by Creative Learning Press. Reprinted with permission.

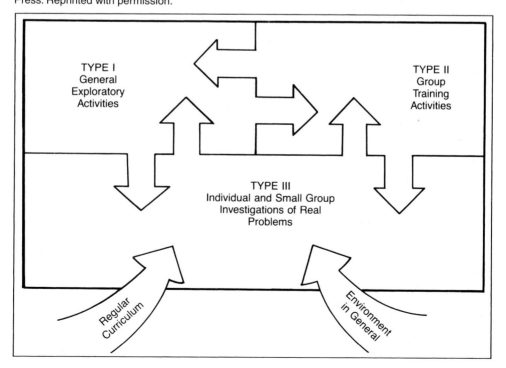

the only one solely appropriate for meeting gifted needs. In Type III enrichment, the student is to focus on real work methods of inquiry to provide first-hand experience in a particular field of interest at an advanced level.

The first two types of enrichment are to be provided by regular classroom teachers, who are given in-service to acquaint them with the methods and strategies identified as part of the model. At these levels, four services may be provided: (1) interest and learning style assessment, (2) curriculum compacting, (3) general exploratory experiences, and (4) group training activities. At the third level, Type III, a specialist provides service for the student (or group of students) who has been identified as ready to pursue an independent project of their own interest.

By use of psychometric, developmental, sociometric, and performance information, students are identified for a Talent Pool that should comprise 15% to 20% of the school population. A step-by-step decision-making format is described for forming the Talent Pool (Renzulli, Reis, & Smith, 1981). This detailed formatting of procedures is one of the strengths of the model; because of these well-thought-out formats, most of the program and curricular operations can be easily followed and adapted to any setting.

It is basic to the operation of the Enrichment Triad/Revolving Door Model that the Talent Pool students be provided with performance-based learning situations in the regular classroom. That will help teachers identify which individuals and small groups should revolve into advanced-level experiences based on their interest in particular topics or problem areas. When a student or group of students shows evidence of interest, need, and commitment to the degree that a special project should be initiated, the students are revolved into the resource room following the appropriate steps and support procedures. The extent to which the student or students remain in the resource room will be individually assessed and planned. A large part of the success of such a pull-out program depends on the cooperation and training of the regular classroom teacher.

Many adaptations have been made of the Enrichment Triad Model, with one of the most recent being the Schoolwide Enrichment Model (SEM) (Renzulli & Reis, 1985). This adaptation emphasizes the schoolwide approach to selection and programming for students with talents and incorporates Types I and II enrichment in every classroom. Other features of the Revolving Door Program are a part of this model.

The model is well-thought-out and extensively used, and it has a large variety of support materials and forms to aid its step-by-step delivery of service at the elementary and secondary levels. The originators of the model hope that all teachers and students at all levels can benefit from this structure and the detailed procedures that have been developed to support it.

The Grid

Some of the models discussed in this chapter provide a structure for developing just parts of a curriculum; however, Kaplan's (1986) model, which she calls the Grid, includes and organizes all the components of a differentiated curriculum. The components of Kaplan's Grid are the content, process (e.g., productive thinking skills, research skills, and basic skills), and products organized around a theme (see Figure 10.5). Affective concerns, descriptions of learning experiences, and activities are also important parts of her model.

The Theme

Kaplan (1986) suggests that we start to plan a differentiated curriculum with a theme, rather than a topic, as the organizing element. When we select only a topic, we may be limiting the learning possibilities of gifted students. Although topics will incorporate parts of the theme's overall knowledge base, a wide variety of topics and the ability to generalize and see relationships are more available to the learner when the larger units of themes are used. Examples of themes are Extinction, Effects of Systems, Knowledge as Power, and Leadership and Followership.

The Content

Kaplan thinks of content as "the knowledge and information defined as useful, important, timely, and interesting for gifted students to acquire as a consequence of their matriculation through an educational program" (p. 185). The relationship of economic, social, personal, and environmental concerns with the needs and interests of individuals, groups, and societies comprise her concept of content worthy of study. She believes that the development of skills and the assimilation of content are interactive, and both must therefore be of importance in planning a lesson. She lists some rules to consider in selecting content:

- It should be referenced to the theme.
- It should be multidisciplinary.
- It should embody information that all students are expected to learn.
- It should be consonant with the needs, interests, and abilities of the gifted students and of particular importance or interest to individual students or groups of students.
- It should allow for the integration of subject areas.
- It should allow a time perspective that includes and relates past, present, and future.

The Processes

Some of the processes Kaplan mentions for consideration are productive thinking skills, basic research skills, learning-to-learn skills, life skills, and the skills of technology. Rather than choose one set of skills, Kaplan suggests the integration of various categories of processes into curriculum planning and implementation.

The Product

Both as a tool for learning and as a verification of learning, the product shows the synthesis and assimilation of both knowledge (content) and skills (processes). Products must be allowed to be communicated in visual, oral, and written formats and

Figure 10.5 *The Grid: An Example*

Source: From "The Grid: A Model to Construct Differentiated Curriculum for the Gifted" by S. Kaplan, in *Systems and Models for Developing Programs for the Gifted and Talented* (p. 184), by J. Renzulli (Ed.), 1986, Mansfield, CT: Creative Learning Press. Copyright 1986 by Creative Learning Press. Reprinted with permission.

Theme—POWER				
Content	Productive Thinking Skills	Research Skills	Basic Skills	Products
Relationship between economic, social, personal displays of power to needs and interests of individuals, groups, and societies	differentiate between fact and opinion	use a retrieval system	identify the main idea	develop an oral presentation
Significance of person-made and natural sources of power to changes in beliefs, life-style and communication	prove or disprove	take notes	write a paragraph	make a graphic representation
Conditions which promote the exercise of power by individuals, organizations, and countries	establish criteria to judge	use fiction and nonfiction	sequence	write an editorial
Value of social forms of power to human rights and environmental usage	substantiate with evidence	use newspapers and journals	classify	debate

result from a variety of production skills such as varied technology and materials, self-determined criteria for evaluation, and identification of formal and informal outlets to share the products.

Kaplan's work is clear and concise, giving many examples to clarify each component. Any of the process models mentioned in this book can be used to develop the process section of the Grid. As a closing comment on planning differentiated curriculum Kaplan states, "Once the curriculum is differentiated, it needs to be individualized for students" (p. 192). Further details on the process of differentiating curriculum for gifted learners can be found in Chapter 12.

The Integrative Education Model

The Integrative Education Model (IEM) (Clark, 1983, 1986, 1997) was developed to synthesize the findings from brain research, the new physics, general systems theory, and psychology as they relate to education and to show the application of these data to teaching and learning. From all of these disciplines comes the concern for connectedness and wholeness. Brain researchers indicate that the complex human brain operates best when all of its functions are integrated. Learning is optimal when thinking (both linear and spatial), feeling, physical/sensing, and intuition are all a part of the learning experience. This is especially important for gifted students as advanced and accelerated learners. They are pushing the limits of learning and need opportunities and processes to ensure their continuous progress.

The IEM is a model of learning and teaching that has a highly complex, flexible structure; is decentralized; and is individualized. It allows variations in pace, level, and grouping. The IEM encourages student choice, participation, and involvement. By better meeting the needs of each learner, the IEM can be used in the regular classroom where it allows for and encourages giftedness. It optimizes learning by offering brain-compatible teaching experiences. In every subject area, the strategies of the IEM combine thinking with feeling, intuition, and physical sensing and movement. Through this model each function of the brain is allowed to support the others, resulting in a very coherent, powerful learning experience. Figure 10.6 shows the integration of these functions in the IEM.

It is important to note that the IEM is inclusive, not exclusive, in nature. It forms a framework that allows all content, all processes, and all products to integrate the four major functions of the brain. Whichever curriculum or program model is chosen, integrative education can be a part of it. In view of the excitement and success that this integrative approach has brought to gifted students of all ages, it deserves to be considered as a fundamental step in planning curriculum for gifted learners.

Components of the IEM include: (1) the responsive learning environment, (2) complex and challenging cognitive activities, (3) empowering language and behavior, (4) choice and perceived control, (5) relaxation and tension reduction, (6) movement and physical encoding, and (7) intuition and integration. Figure 10.6 shows how the IEM creates opportunities for the development of the entire universe of intelligence. Chapter 11 will explore integrative education further and detail strategies and methods for using brain research to support learning in the classroom.

Figure 10.6 *Integrative Education: A Model for Developing Human Potential*

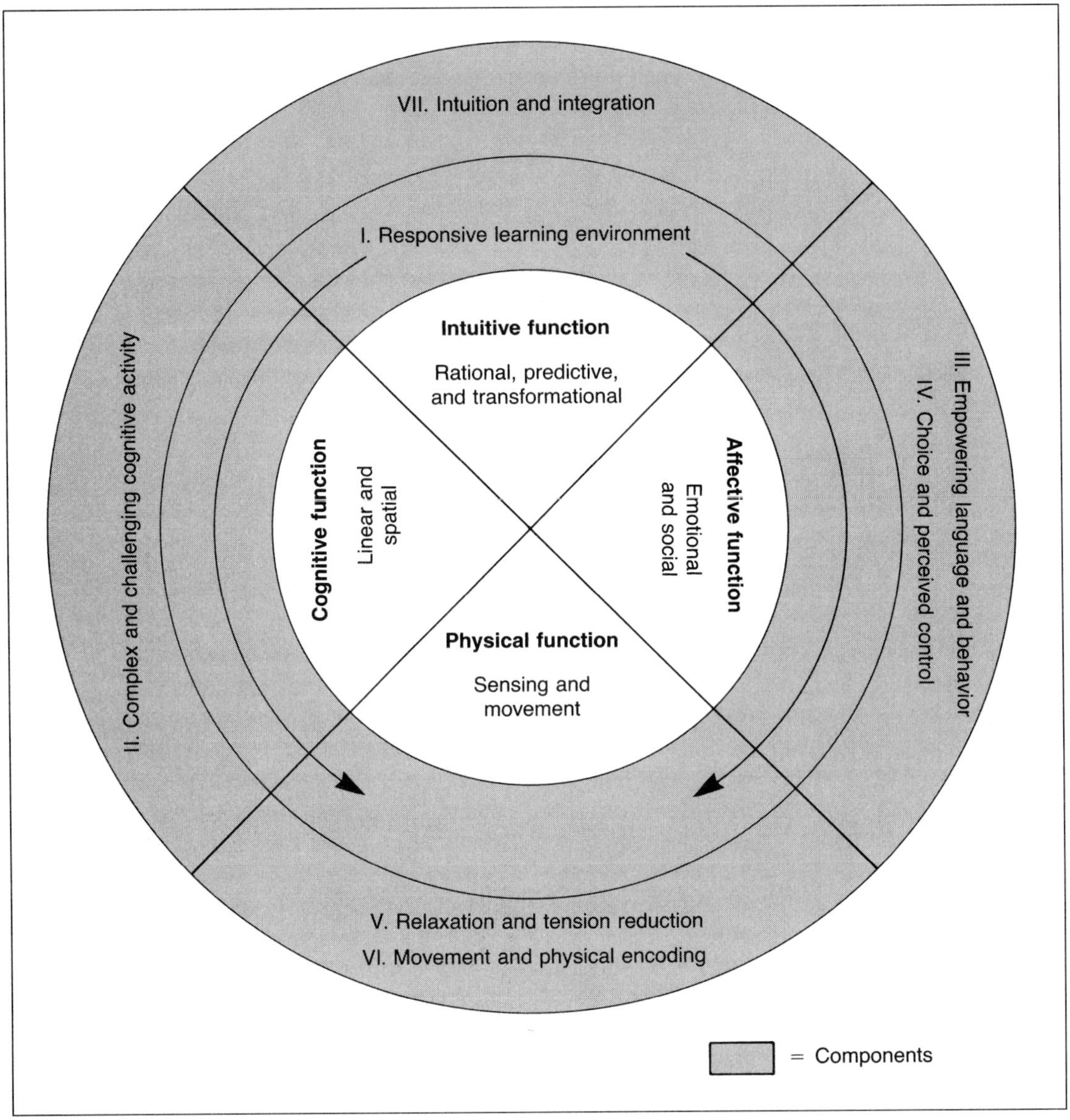

VII. Intuition and integration

I. Responsive learning environment

Intuitive function

Rational, predictive, and transformational

Cognitive function

Linear and spatial

Affective function

Emotional and social

Physical function

Sensing and movement

II. Complex and challenging cognitive activity

III. Empowering language and behavior
IV. Choice and perceived control

V. Relaxation and tension reduction
VI. Movement and physical encoding

= Components

The Autonomous Learner Model

Developed in the late 1970s as a way to meet both the social-emotional and cognitive needs of high school gifted youngsters, the Autonomous Learner Model (ALM), developed by Betts (1999) (Figure 10.7), now serves learners in kindergarten through high school. The elementary classroom teacher can incorporate the model for all learners in the regular classroom while offering an advanced version with identified gifted and talented learners in a pull-out or resource room. For middle

Figure 10.7 *Autonomous Learner Model*

Source: From *The Autonomous Learner Model: Optimizing Ability* (p. 2), by G. Betts and J. K. Kercher, 1999, Greeley, CO: Autonomous Learner. Copyright 1999 by Autonomous Learner Publishing. Reprinted with permission.

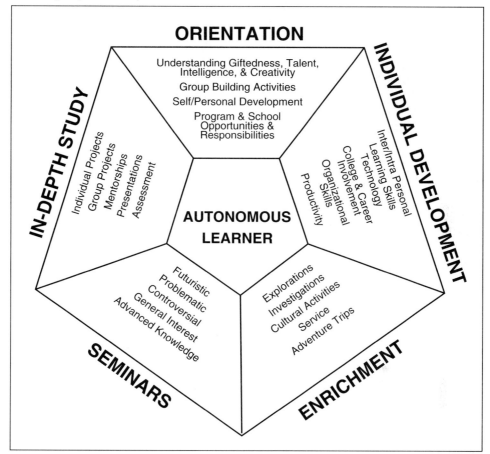

school and high school learners, the model is presented in an elective or special class setting, generally using one period at specified times throughout the week.

The ALM is divided into five dimensions:

1. Orientation—as the name implies, acquaints the students and their parents with the model and its expectations. A foundation of the concepts of giftedness, talent, intelligence, creativity, and the development of potential is built. Opportunities are presented to build group process and interaction skills.

2. Individual Development—stresses the attitudes and concepts necessary to support life-long learning. Skills to promote the use of technology, organization, productivity, and career involvement are the focus.

3. Enrichment—allows students to explore content that is generally not a part of the regular curriculum and to become aware of resources available to them for their use. Differentiation by the teacher and by the student is encouraged in this dimension.

4. Seminar—allows groups of students to pursue topics of their choice through research, then to present their results to a larger group for their own growth through self-evaluation.

5. In-Depth Study—presents students with long-term opportunities to pursue their own areas of interest with small groups or alone.

At this point in the ALM, the learners determine what will be learned, how it will be presented, what will be necessary for their data collection or presentation, what the final product will be, and how the learning will be evaluated.

Detailed forms and planning manuals accompany this model and ALM workshops are available to support the changes needed to incorporate the model into the classroom.

Although ALM is not a total program for gifted learners, it provides essential skills for becoming a life-long independent learner. The model addresses itself to more than just the cognitive needs of the student and encourages independence in the learning setting. It is especially appropriate for the departmentalized structure of secondary schools, as it fills a need usually not meet and ensures opportunities not often provided at this level.

The Multiple Intelligence (MI) Model

In Chapter 2 the multidimensional concept of intelligence (Gardner, 1983), which serves as the basis for this model, was discussed as one of the more recent theories of intelligence. Conceptionalizing intelligence as composed of eight components the model encourages teachers to address multiple expressions of intelligence and ability in the learning process. The components, referred to as "intelligences," are: verbal/linguistic; logical/mathematical; visual/spatial; musical/rhythmic; bodily/kinesthetic; interpersonal; intrapersonal; and naturalistic.

The goals of the MI model are to help students master certain curricular or disciplinary materials and, according to the theory, the students must be taught and assessed in a variety of ways. As Gardner puts it, "Taking human differences seriously lies at the heart of the MI perspective . . . any uniform educational approach is likely to serve only a small percentage of children optimally" (Gardner, 1999, p. 91).

As with several previous models, the MI model can be adapted for all learners at all ages in any subject area. Although not specifically designed to meet the needs of gifted learners, as a process model this model can be used in combination with other models that are specifically able to meet gifted needs. The MI model is used to identify individual differences, plan a curriculum that meets diverse needs, and assess the range of instructional strategies. A wide assortment of classroom materials has been developed based on the MI model.

The Triarchic Componential Model

Sternberg (1981) has advanced an interesting theory that seeks to identify the components of cognitive giftedness for the purpose of improving differentiated curricular planning. His triarchy consists of analytical thinking, creative thinking, and practical thinking. He believes that gifted learners tend to excel in their access to and implementation of the following:

- Decision-making as to just what the problems are that need solving.

- Selection of appropriate components and steps leading to problem solution. Research indicates that when intuitive leaps are necessary for problem solution, most individuals have available in their heads all of the elements necessary for solution; what distinguishes problem solvers is their ability to retrieve these elements.

- Selection of strategies to evolve a plan of action for solving problems.

- Learning ways within a discipline to represent information to be built up to use in problem-solving.

- Decision making regarding allocation of resources.

- Ability to monitor solutions, being flexible in changing plans as needs dictate. This was seen as one of the most important differences between gifted and nongifted learners.

Sternberg's Triarchic Theory of Intelligence suggests that intelligence and the intellectual skills that constitute it are flexible, not fixed, and are forms of developing expertise. Sternberg believes that giftedness can be understood in terms of superior functioning of, activation of, and feedback from information processing components of various kinds, and that the components may be trainable. Research on his work shows that triarchic teaching using the three components of thinking improves achievement at all grade levels, in all subject matter areas examined and with a range of socioeconomic and achievement levels (Sternberg, et al., 2000).

Other Theories and Models

There are several other models used in developing curricula for gifted learners. Among them are Treffinger's (1975) model, which delineates a step-by-step approach for teachers to guide students toward becoming self-directed learners, and Taba's (1966) strategies, which lead students through sequential cognitive tasks to a resolution of conflict that includes the understanding of feelings, attitudes, and values. Taba's rather complex, open-ended structure gives evidence of producing growth in abstract reasoning, which is often declared as a goal in gifted programming.

Another model sponsored by the NAGC (introduced at the NAGC Conference, November, 2000) attempts to give teachers a structure and guide for planning appropriate curricular experiences for gifted students. Called the Parallel Curriculum, the planning model incorporates four parallel or concurrent tracts of development: the Core or Basic Curriculum; the Curriculum of Connections; the Curriculum of Practice; and the Curriculum of Identity. *The Core Curriculum* establishes the knowledge base, understandings, and skills most basic or foundational to the discipline under study. *The Curriculum of Connections* extends the information and skills from the core to allow interactions in various settings, circumstances, and time elements. Opportunities for students to function as professionals in a discipline comprise the content of *The Curriculum of Practice*. Creating experiences from which students can increase their awareness of self and their connections with the discipline under study as they increase their expertise in the field is the purpose of the *Curriculum of Identity*. These four curriculum tracks, when developed together, can provide the learner with a richer learning experience. Appropriate for the enrichment of the curriculum experience of every child, the Parallel Curriculum promises to ensure the depth, novelty, and complexity essential to the education of the gifted student.

During the past two decades, a number of models have been developed that expand the educational focus beyond the cognitive thinking process and its place in curriculum planning and implementation. Although models limited to cognitive thinking strategies remain excellent educational tools for teachers to use as part of their planning for gifted learners, the incorporation of other brain functions into the learning experience will make even these models more effective. The promise is to optimize learning. The use of any of the previously discussed models can be a part of this promise.

SEVEN STEPS TO OPTIMIZING LEARNING

Since the 1960s, research in the neurosciences (see Chapters 2 and 4) has provided support for improving many practices in education. A body of literature has developed that suggests ways of optimizing learning based on such findings (Caine & Caine, 1991, 1997; Clark, 1986; Diamond, 1988, 1998; Hart, 1975; Jensen, 1998; Sylwester, 1986, 1995). A 7-year project was conducted to translate these brain data into strategies for the classroom. By organizing the resulting information into the seven most critical components of the teaching process, a basic structure for optimizing learning resulted (Clark, 1986).

These components must interact to continually improve the effectiveness of each to meet the needs of all learners. For gifted learners, developing this structure can provide the foundation that will ensure an appropriate educational experience. Such an organization of the teaching experience will allow the flexibility and support needed by gifted students and will provide the continuity of intellectual challenges essential to their growth. Gifted learners can flourish in such a structure as it provides continuous progress.

To provide support for learning in any classroom, there are seven components of the teaching process that must be optimally developed. To optimize learning, the teacher must:

1. Create a responsive learning environment.
2. Assess the learner's knowledge, understanding, and interest.
3. Integrate the intellectual processes: The IEM
4. Differentiate the content.
5. Individualize the instruction.
6. Evaluate learning and teaching.
7. Reflect on the entire process and reform the learning plan to incorporate all new insights gained.

For the teacher, this structure provides the security of knowing that his or her program will include appropriate resources and strategies regardless of the number of gifted students in the classroom or the diversity and range of the students' abilities. Attempting to develop a supportive environment and an appropriate curriculum only after the students are in attendance creates pressure and frustration that easily can be avoided. The difficulties of trying to serve gifted students without resources and strategies pre-planned and readily available are daunting. This lack of preparation is the most common reason that gifted students are so often unchallenged and underserved.

The responsive learning environment and the practices of assessment will be discussed in this chapter. In Chapter 11, the integration of the intellectual processes by use of the IEM will be described and discussed. Chapter 12 will focus on the differentiation of the learning experience for gifted students and the individualization necessary for optimal delivery of the curriculum. The final steps of evaluation and reflection ensuring long-range quality programs for gifted learners to be discussed in Chapter 12 will complete the structure to allow optimizing in the classroom.

CREATING THE RESPONSIVE LEARNING ENVIRONMENT

Establishing a classroom environment that is flexible and responsive and allows all students to pursue their own pace and achievement level is a necessary foundation for bringing gifted education into the classroom. Only in such a setting can the unique needs of gifted students be met and their intellectual development challenged (Figure 10.8). The exciting part is that all children benefit from an environment that is cognitively, physically, socially, and emotionally responsive to them. As Gardner states, "Indeed, the 'smarter' the environment and the more powerful the interventions and the available resources, the more proficient people will become, and the less important will be their particular genetic inheritance" (Gardner, 1999, p. 88). Had Rocky, the "silent" student from our opening vignette, had the experience of learning in a responsive learning environment, his strategy of not speaking in the classroom as a way to solve his identity problem would have been unnecessary.

Creating a responsive learning environment is the first step in optimizing learning and the first component in the IEM discussed further in Chapter 11. The responsive learning environment is flexibly structured and presents a complex learning organization for the student. The origins of this organizational plan are deeply rooted in the work of Plato, Socrates, Froebel, Pestalozzi, Dewey, Montessori, Piaget, and numerous other innovative educators. Basically the responsive learning environment strives to provide a unique learning experience for each individual. Participation is seen as necessary to learning, and involvement is encouraged to ensure the assimilation of concepts.

In the responsive learning environment, gifted students can pursue educational requirements and interests in depth and with a minimum of time limitations. They will no longer need to be held to the pace or achievement level of the group, and they can be grouped flexibly with other students as their learning needs require or, when appropriate, they can work individually. Gifted learners can function as

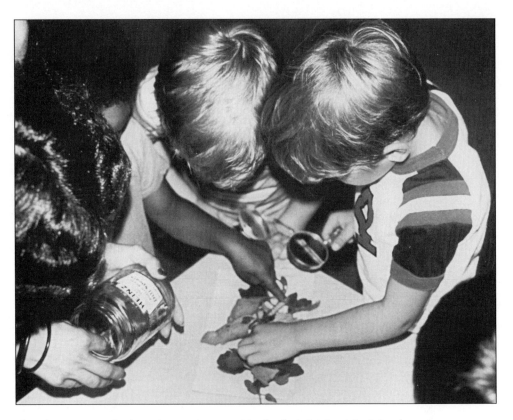

Creating a responsive learning environment is the first step in optimizing learning.

researchers, apprentices, resident experts, teachers, or learning managers. For all students, the classroom becomes a laboratory for learning that is more closely related to the real world. Data collected over several decades (see Clark, 1986) confirm that optimal learning will occur when the environment allows students to:

- Assume some responsibility for their own learning.
- Develop the skills for independent learning.
- Learn at their own pace.
- Learn with material at their own level.
- Learn with strategies that offer multimodalities.
- Be graded in terms of their own achievement.
- Experience a sense of perceived control, achievement, and self-esteem.

The learning environment can influence at least three major conditions for learning: (1) *differences in learning style, pace, and level,* which the brain data indicate are evident in all learners; (2) *motivation,* which can be enhanced or inhibited as a result of participation, shared responsibility, and choice in the learning process; and (3) *challenge and stimulation,* both of which are necessary for optimal learning. The obvious benefits of this more flexible, open approach to learning have been verified

Figure 10.8 *A Responsive Learning Environment Checklist*

You will know that the *physical environment* is responsive when:

1. There is space for students to simultaneously participate in a variety of activities.
2. Students have access to materials with a range of levels and topics.
3. There is space for the students to engage in a variety of instructional groupings, and flexible grouping is used.
4. There are areas supportive of student self-management.
5. Desks are not individually owned.
6. The classroom has a comfortable, inviting ambience supportive of exploration, application, and personal construction of knowledge.

You will know that the *social-emotional environment* is responsive when:

1. The emotional climate is warm and accepting.
2. The class operates within clear guidelines decided upon cooperatively.
3. Instruction is based on each individual student's needs and interests as assessed by the teacher from the student's interaction with the materials and the concepts.
4. Student activities, products, and ideas are reflected around the classroom.
5. Student choice is evident in planning, instruction, and products of evaluation.
6. Building and practicing affective skills are a consistent and valued part of the curriculum and of each teaching day.
7. Students and teachers show evidence of shared responsibility for learning.
8. Empowering language is evident between teacher and student and among students.
9. Students show evidence of becoming independent learners with skills of inquiry and self-evaluation.

by the work in open structures done in the 1970s (Bremer & Bremer, 1972; Hassett & Weisberg, 1972; Silberman, 1971; Stephens, 1974). The importance of this type of experience to gifted students is even more apparent. When offered alternatives, they and their parents overwhelmingly choose an open, flexible model for learning.

The Physical Learning Environment

The classroom, from nursery school to senior high school, needs sufficient "people space" for students to move about and actively participate in their own learning.

Examples: Imagine a classroom with many activity areas and a quiet, comfortable reading and study area. A discussion area is available to students and teacher/student groups. There is a teacher/student conference area and a large group area. Movement is easy because there is a minimum of desks and chairs arranged to facilitate the current lesson. The walls may display alternative activities and materials for self-directed study; closets and cupboard doors may provide media centers.

What has been created in such a setting is a laboratory for learning.

An effective classroom provides space for the students to simultaneously participate in a variety of activities that engage all of the brain functions, including cognitive, affective, physical, and intuitive, discussed in Chapters 2 and 11. The same spaces may be used for different activities at different times.

> **Examples:** Reader's theater; debates; physical encoding of concepts; manipulations of objects for math, language arts, art, or geography; simulations of banks, stores, United Nations' committees, or constitutional conventions; and guided imagery for deeper and more personal understanding of concepts and events.

There should also be space for the students to engage in a variety of instructional groupings.

> **Examples:** Space that allows total-group instruction, small-group instruction or problem-solving, teacher/student interaction, teacher/small-group interaction, peer tutoring or problem-solving, independent study, creative activity, and recreational inquiry or reading.

There should be areas for the students to engage in self-management support

> **Examples:** An assessment table where students can check the answers to their work; areas where students can explore concepts being learned in depth; and areas where students can pursue information, formulate solutions, and design products unique to their level of development and interest.

The space in the classroom will be more flexible and able to be used easily for a variety of activities if there are no individually owned desks. If you create space for students' and teacher's own personal and material storage in baskets, bins, or shelves, it is not necessary to have individually owned desks.

The ambience of the classroom should be comfortable, inviting, and physically supportive of exploration, application, and personal construction of knowledge. Students will need access to materials and resources with a range of levels and topics. The teacher and/or the students can often develop such materials. Color, sound, and other sensory stimuli support learning and should be an important part of the environment.

Gifted individuals often have the ability to integrate and synthesize information from many disciplines to develop new concepts or to enhance their understanding. In a flexibly structured laboratory environment, the opportunity for this type of synthesis should be available and even encouraged.

In a responsive learning environment all types of flexible grouping are possible. Movement in and out of the classroom to the library or other learning centers is not inhibited, and special grouping for specific interests can be formed.

A laboratory environment can be created even in the departmentalized setting still commonly found in middle and secondary schools. If you are responsible for teaching math, you can develop areas that teach the concepts your students must learn in many different ways and with a variety of materials. You can use all types of grouping, from teacher/student conferences to peer tutoring, to small-group activities, to large class lectures and demonstrations.

How to Create Usable Physical Space in the Classroom

To make better use of the space in a classroom, the following ideas might be considered:

Remove Furniture. If students are engaged in a variety of activities, individual desks are unnecessary because there will rarely be a need for everyone to be sitting and writing at the same time.

Carpet Areas of the Room. Carpeted areas provide good group spaces and can easily be used for seating people. Carpet also reduces the noise of movement, causing a room's atmosphere to become more interactive, more pleasant, and less tense. Students seem to show more pride in their surroundings and take better care of a carpeted facility.

Use Floors, Walls, Windows, Closets, and Drawers. For example, a reorganized teacher's desk makes a fine media center. The drawers provide storage space for projectors, films, slides, and filmstrips. The dark knee-hole makes a good projection area, with a white piece of paper located at the far end of the opening for a screen. A small group seated on the floor can participate quite effectively in a self-directed media presentation. When listening posts or headsets are available, such an area can be used at any time, even when the top of the desk is being used for video presentations or computer work for students seated on the opposite side of the desk.

Bring in Comfortable, Movable Furniture. This type of seating is excellent for interactive small-group instruction and makes a significant instructional difference in attention and motivation.

Use Color to Support Learning. Reds, oranges, and yellows (warm colors) stimulate, invigorate, and energize; greens, blues, and violets (cool colors) are restful, soothing, and calming. The use of color as a support for a learning activity enhances the results. Gerard (cited in Meer, 1985) found that even visualizing color has a dramatic impact upon the attitude and well-being of students.

Order Materials at Many Levels in Smaller Numbers. When students are allowed to move at their own pace and work at their appropriate levels of achievement, textbooks can be shared. Planning for students to work more in small groups, you can ensure that all students cover the required concepts without needing one text for each student. It will then be possible to have a range of books and materials available to support learning at different levels without additional cost.

Provide Areas for Designated Activities. To have a variety of activities and a range of levels of difficulty, provide different activities, different materials, and places to work on different projects at the same time. This can be done most easily if the students become familiar with areas of the room that consistently provide the materials and activities necessary for certain uses. For example, quiet, thoughtful areas for reading, writing, and creating ideas; louder, busier areas for construction, practicing debates, working in groups, and peer tutoring might be created.

The Social-Emotional Learning Environment

Once the physical learning environment is supportive of the conditions necessary for optimal teaching and learning, it is easier to develop a safe and caring social-emotional learning environment. In an environment where each student is considered a unique individual, the atypical needs of the gifted student cause no one to feel out of place and a positive self-concept can be developed naturally. Self-esteem can be developed in a realistic perspective, with every person valued for his or her particular qualities. Accomplishments can be shared, and the value of the contributions of others can be experienced. Labels become unnecessary as a result of the system's continuous assessments. Students can learn responsibility and an inner sense of control when expectations and opportunities for choice, sharing responsibility, and self-evaluation are a planned part of their day.

Any problems encountered in learning together as a group can be resolved by the group providing a natural setting for the development of leadership skills. Gifted students can gain recognition without seeming to dominate and strengthen their inner locus of control by continuous encounters with the intrinsic value of learning from their own interest or from real need.

Gifted youngsters have a need to seek out their intellectual peer group. They accomplish this easily when older and younger children can work together in a cross-age grouped classroom, with flexible grouping and freedom of movement.

Building Trust

A trusting environment does not just happen; it is deliberately planned. Classrooms that use the responsive learning environment include use of language and behavior that allow students to feel competent, activities that are more cooperative than competitive, and time for building positive interpersonal interactions. Only when there is trust within the class can students feel safe to take the risk of learning. Trying things you do not know and things at which you may not succeed, making mistakes, and noticing that you learn differently from others all require a safe environment. It may take time to build the trust needed to enhance a learning experience, but the time and effort are well spent. Here are some suggested strategies for building a trusting environment.

Openings and Closings. One way to build community within the classroom and the safety that allows trust to be developed is to begin and end each day (or several periods each week, if you are in secondary schools) with an activity or discussion that is focused on social-emotional issues or community building.

> **Examples:** Discussing possible solutions to a problem either identified by the group or of interest to the group, having a guided imagery or relaxation experience together, or participating in an activity that leads to more open communication among the members of the group are examples of ways to begin classes. Group discussions of what worked during the day, reviewing together the goals that were accomplished, or participating in positive personal feedback (e.g., "What I appreciated most about you today was . . .") are examples of activities that can provide for positive social-emotional growth at the end of

a day or class period. The positive effects of activities focused on social-emotional growth can be extensive and long lasting for students and produce a more productive climate in the classroom.

The Trust Group. Establishment of this strategy in the classroom will allow students a vehicle for resolution of personal and interpersonal problems they encounter in the classroom, at school, or generally in their lives. Begin with everyone, including the teacher, seated in a circle, either on the floor or in chairs. If the students choose the floor, the teacher needs to join them. Next the ground rules must be discussed. The teacher is the facilitator and must ensure the psychological safety of everyone in the group. For that reason, the first agreement must be that only those who feel that they can follow the ground rules of the trust group should participate. The students are given a choice about their readiness to participate each time the group meets. If the teacher has arranged alternative activities or personal planning folders as part of the classroom management, then quiet, self-sustaining activities can be assigned for those who do not wish to participate while the class is involved in the trust group.

Other ground rules that need to be established by consent are:

- What is said in the group remains in the group; to tell what someone said in the group is to break the trust.

- Anyone can call a trust group, to be scheduled by the teacher at the earliest available time.

- Anyone can pass whenever they are not ready to share; however, everyone is expected to listen to the problem and to share their ideas and solutions whenever possible.

- Comments to be shared should be constructive and sensitive to people in the group.

- Problems need to be directed to the person responsible or to the person who can do something about the problem.

Ground rules should be established and agreed to by all members of the group during the first group meeting. The teacher will need to remind the group of the ground rules at the beginning of each session and reestablish their agreement. This will provide a structure for the group that will allow them to explore problems that are sensitive and important to the students or, on occasion, to the teacher. Another opportunity that trust groups provide is the building of self-concept and interpersonal skills. The teacher can introduce a skill, such as use of "I" statements, at the beginning of the trust group and allow the students to discuss and/or apply the strategy or skill in a safe environment.

The Mutual Interview. At the beginning of a new class the mutual interview is a very useful way to begin the process of creating a safe, trusting, and responsive learning environment. All age levels, classroom organizations, and class sizes benefit from this community-building strategy. Ask all of the students to look around the room and find someone they do not know well whom they might like to know better. Each student is to go to that person and find a place to sit. For the next 10 minutes the students are to do three things: share information about themselves with each other, listen as the other person shares, and notice how they feel about the experience. At the end of the 10-minute period, students are asked to introduce this person to the class. In a large class at middle and high school levels, students may introduce their partner to a group formed by three couples. This can become a study group that continues throughout the year.

Younger students may need a list of things they could ask to start the interview. I always remind my students that if they do not want to be the last person chosen they should be the first person to choose. After about 10 minutes, call the partners back into a single group and ask that they close their eyes for a moment. After they close their eyes, ask them to think again about the experience. What do they now know about this person? What did they find interesting or surprising? What would they like others to know about this person? Ask them to gently open their eyes and allow each student to introduce the person they interviewed, sharing the partner's name, something they want everyone to know about the partner, and how they feel about the partner. Students always enjoy this activity, and it quickly establishes a climate of sharing and personal caring that can be built upon during the rest of the term.

Other avenues for establishing a healthy and productive social-emotional learning environment are lowering tension and building choice into the curriculum and the processes of instruction. Both of these issues will be discussed in Chapter 11.

Extending Learning Beyond the Classroom

When learning is extended beyond the classroom into the community or nearby nature areas, integrative education becomes very natural and effective. The Learning Expedition, which is a step beyond the standard field trip, can yield enormous educational benefits and make classroom learning experiences more productive. By planning and participating in such overnight or extended field trips the class becomes a cooperative unit and gains experiences not available in a classroom setting. There are four broad objectives for organizing Learning Expeditions:

1. To support cognitive growth in the content area(s).
2. To further develop and reinforce throughout the experience student thinking skills such as inferring, analyzing, hypothesizing, predicting, verifying, and integrating.
3. To develop an environment in which discussion of values and attitudes is natural and productive.
4. To provide experiential activities that support personal growth, trust, openness, responsibility, independence, interdependence, honesty, integrity, self-confidence, and the personal commitment to excellence.

Allowing students to plan the Learning Expedition from beginning to end gives them an opportunity to experience the natural consequences of their planning and organization. This is learning at its best. Students are also provided with endless opportunities for leadership at all levels and gain self-esteem from having taken

Learning expeditions can provide interdisciplinary study naturally.

responsibilities and personal risks. The success of this endeavor is made possible by allowing students to operate within a high level of trust, interacting openly and honestly. In such an environment it is possible to accomplish impressive goals.

The Critical Role of the Teacher

The teacher is central to the development of the responsive learning environment. The teacher establishes the organization and structure of the lesson and of the classroom, the motivational climate for learning, and the attitude the class will have toward learning and other learners. The teacher helps to clarify the students' personal and class goals and provides the resources necessary to meet those goals. For all of these reasons the role of the teacher is critical to the success of the student in the classroom.

For many years educators explored the importance of self-concept as a factor in the success of students in the classroom. A low concept of self correlated highly to low achievement; a high concept of self showed a high correlation to successful achievement (Purkey, 1970). A surprising finding by Aspy and Bahler (1975) was that although the self-esteem of the students was important to success in the classroom, of even more importance was the self-esteem of the teacher. A teacher's concept of self was significantly related to the achievement of his or her students. Enthusiasm about teaching and excitement as a learner will be among the most important factors in student success.

The teacher who wishes to establish a responsive learning environment will:

- Establish a learning environment that is responsive, flexible, and motivating.
- Create a climate for learning that is warm, accepting, and safe, in which a student can risk changing behavior and sharing new ideas.
- Develop a scope and sequence of what is to be taught.
- Obtain a wide variety of materials with a range of levels of content.
- Plan for student choice.
- Share responsibility for learning with the students.
- Plan learning experiences with students.
- Assess the level of ability, interests, and needs of the students.
- Present a variety of strategies that optimize learning.
- Evaluate a variety of levels and activities using a range of products.

The Student's Role

Students taking part in the responsive learning environment will also need skills if optimal learning is to take place. These students will need to be taught to:

- Plan learning experiences, both independently and with the teacher or a peer.
- Work in a decentralized environment.
- Learn in small groups.
- Learn independently.
- Use resources and appropriate equipment.
- Make choices.
- Self-assess and self-evaluate.
- Conference with the teacher.
- Share the responsibility for learning.

Although gifted education can take place without the support of the responsive learning environment, the development of such an environment will make the job of the teacher and the learner much easier, efficient, and far more effective.

ASSESSMENT OF THE NEEDS AND ABILITIES OF GIFTED LEARNERS

Having identified those students who require differentiated educational experiences, each student's individual gifted needs must now be assessed. In the area of gifted education, a strange phenomenon occurs. Usually most of the differentiated experiences offered to gifted individuals are provided within a minimum amount of time, often outside of the classroom. The advisability of such programming was examined in Chapter 7, but the existence of such practices presents us with a dilemma.

In most special education settings, the word *need* has a connotation of deficiency. In gifted education it means quite the opposite. When gifted individuals are assessed for "needs" for special provisions, these denote areas of strength that cannot be properly nurtured in a regular classroom setting. This is not to say that gifted students would have no need for remedial help in some academic areas, nor does it imply that the gifted individual is equally gifted in all areas. Such is just not the case. However, where special attention or funding is found to meet gifted needs, it is the nurture of advanced ability that is intended, not the remediation of deficits. If attention must be given to deficit needs, then the regular school program should assume that role. Remediation becomes part of a gifted program only if such a program comprises the major portion of the student's educational experience, such as full-day special class placement. When limited part-time programs are used for remediation, children have no opportunity to grow in their areas of gifted need. These are the areas for which no provisions are made in the regular classroom setting and for which these children have been identified. Programs for the gifted learner must focus on these areas.

In Chapter 12 the needs of the gifted learner will provide the basis for how the curriculum is to be differentiated. Once such needs are identified, appropriate programs can be planned. Assessment is not just an activity for the beginning of the year, but must be continued throughout the year if the educational program is to be effective.

Assessing Knowledge, Understanding, and Interest

During the past decade, assessment has become an important and somewhat controversial issue in education. The old reliance on standardized, multiple-choice, paper-and-pencil tests has been challenged. Cizek (1993) believes that among the reasons are an inherent mismatch between the impersonal, mechanistic methods of assessments used in the past and the student-centered orientation of teachers. Also, teachers desire more responsibility for their professional judgment and control over decision-making. He also believes that most teachers have the perception that external and commercially produced tests are not giving information useful to them and do not reflect the classroom learning experience. Hughes (1993) adds that standardized tests often sample only a limited number of skills and fail to assess the students' higher level skills or strategies for problem solving. Newmann (cited in Willis, 1990) finds that multiple-choice tests focus only on low-level cognitive work. The result is that standardized tests have skewed the curriculum toward the teaching of the most easily measured basic skills and isolated facts (Willis, 1990). This teaching-to-the-test approach, with instruction reduced to rote memorization and drill, is evident in too many classrooms.

Gifted students have much to gain from the movement toward authentic, performance-based assessment. The new assessment methods attempt to show a relationship between school tasks and those found in the real world. With a focus on individual student progress, gifted students should be better able to move at their own pace and in their own unique way than was possible with more traditional methods.

In their list of major problems with standardized testing, Poteet, Choate, and Stewart (1993) include the following:

- Misleading information created by people who think the score is an absolute rather than an indicator and who make decisions about action to take and directions for the future based on them.
- Distraction from real social issues, such as overcrowded rooms and lack of instructional materials, when test results are used as measures of accountability and as comparison data to determine which school has a better academic record.
- Expense caused by the cost of materials and time involved in traditional testing when the money could be better used.
- Fostering a one-right-answer mentality, thereby limiting students' thinking processes.

Other reasons given are the broader range of academic and nonacademic competencies that now form educational goals, the need for assessment practices to enhance the learning and teaching processes, and the need for more accurate and useful information regarding the specific knowledge and skills students are mastering (Marzano, Pickering, & McTighe, 1993). Some researchers (Willis, 1990) argue that standardized tests are biased in favor of white middle-income children and are given undue weight in placement and quality of learning decisions.

Assessment has five major purposes: (1) screening and referral; (2) eligibility, placement, and classification; (3) instructional planning; (4) monitoring pupil progress; and (5) evaluating program effectiveness (Hughes, 1993). The National Forum on Assessment would add the advancement of student learning as a primary purpose. In this section, we will be especially concerned about instructional planning and the advancement and monitoring of pupil progress.

The advantages of alternative assessments over traditional testing include the focus on a demonstration of competence as opposed to recognition of correct answers to contrived questions, the teacher's ability to view the process of problem-solving, the ability to elicit real understanding, the promotion of higher-order thinking, the change from fragmented teaching to teaching for coherent understanding, the result seen in greater teacher empowerment, and the higher motivation for students to excel than is found in use of traditional testing (Willis, 1990).

A personal experience convinced me of the difference in the data that can be collected from paper-and-pencil tests and from authentic performance assessment. Some years ago, I was learning to scuba dive and had enrolled in a county course to obtain my certification. At the end of the course a paper-and-pencil test was given over the material covered in the class. The instructor made a big issue of the fact that I had received the highest grade on the test that the county had ever recorded. That experience, along with my persistent efforts in the county pool and at the beach near my house, convinced me that I was ready to demonstrate my competence as a scuba diver.

The class went for a check-out dive at a beach unfamiliar to me and where the surf was far more challenging than any I had yet experienced. My assigned dive buddy for the day was a strong, young man from the class who had not done nearly as well on the "test." As we entered the water the force of the wave turned me around and, try as hard as I could, I was unable to force my way through the surf. After several attempts I finally managed to get beyond the strong surf only to find that I had very little strength left for the swim to the buoy anchored offshore where the dive check-out was to take place. I found that I was unable to stay above the water and swim with the heavy equipment, clear my snorkel to swim more easily, or find and deploy my regulator to swim underwater. I was, in fact, swallowing a lot of water and making little progress in any direction. Later I was to realize that I had been in some danger of drowning.

At that moment the dive master came to my aid, released my weight belt (which was the first thing I should have done and would have marked that procedure on the test correctly), inflated my vest (the second procedure I had "learned"), and took me in to rest on the beach. We were both very disappointed that his star pupil was now a total failure as a diver. Later I completed the course with an ocean dive and spent many years enjoying the sport, but the initial experience made a real impression on me regarding the efficacy of paper-and-pencil testing.

Alternative, Performance-Based, and Authentic Assessment

The discussion of new forms and practices in assessment has created a number of related but different terms and concepts.

Alternative assessment is any way of showing growth, finding out what a student can do, and informing instruction that differs from the standardized or traditional test. This could include performance-based assessment. Poteet and colleagues (1993) find that the major difference is in the response required by the student. In traditional testing, students are asked to select and mark correct answers, whereas in alternative assessments, students are asked to produce, construct, demonstrate, or perform a response.

Authentic assessment requires that the knowledge and process of the content be demonstrated under the conditions in which the achievement would normally occur. That is, demonstrations that give information that shows actual progress toward instructional goals and reflect activities of classrooms and real-life settings are authentic. Some authors suggest that valid, authentic assessment must be worthwhile, significant, and meaningful. Not all performance-based or alternative assessment is authentic. Although the terms alternative assessment, performance-based assessment, and authentic assessment are often used synonymously, they have distinct connotations that differ from each other. For gifted learners these types of assessment can remove the ceiling effect from the testing procedure by allowing them to demonstrate the full extent of their understanding.

Performance-based assessment is a broad term that refers to opportunities given to students that allow them to demonstrate and apply their knowledge and understanding of content and skills being taught. Such tests are designed to assess what the student *can do* with knowledge. These assessments often occur over time and result in a product or an observable performance. An advantage of performance-based assessment is that it measures the thinking curriculum rather than being limited, as multiple-choice testing often is, to the measurement of recognition and retention. Performance-based assessment can take many forms, including observations, journals, group work, class presentations, and/or portfolios.

Standards and Rubrics

Performance-based assessment is a demonstration of what has been learned, and such demonstrations are judged based on a continuum of agreed-upon standards of excellence. Here again is the possibility for confusion. There are several types of standards, including content standards, performance standards, opportunity-to-learn standards, life-long learning standards, and world standards.

Standards require educators to clearly identify what a student should know and what the student should be able to do (Lewis, 1995). To develop such standards school-wide requires some interesting and enlightening discussions in faculty work sessions. Reaching consensus as a faculty on the most important things to know in any subject, let alone how to demonstrate that knowledge and the levels of achievement possible, is not an easy task. But, as Cohen (1995) reminds us, "It is student work that we want to improve, not standards or scholars' ideas about standards" (p. 755).

Content standards, according to Lewis (1995), establish what knowledge and skills should be learned specific to a given discipline or various subject areas. They state important concepts and generalizations and should identify the key elements in content areas. Content standards, sometimes referred to as student outcomes or competencies, lead to the use of a variety of instructional methods. The content standards will remain constant, although they may be expanded for gifted learners or even substituted for remedial students. The instructional methods, however, should vary depending on the need of the learner. The instructional strategies the teacher chooses to use with gifted students may vary to match their level of achievement, pacing, interest, or other special needs.

Appropriate instructional methods will lead the student to the performance standards set by the teacher to demonstrate the mastery of the content standards. There could be a wide range of tasks offered that would appropriately demonstrate this knowledge or skill. The students can more clearly reach their highest achievement when given a choice of acceptable ways to demonstrate their competence than when only one method of evaluation is presented.

Performance standards establish the degree or quality of student performance on the performance tasks selected to give evidence of competency on content standards (National Council on Education Standards and Testing, 1992). Such performance tasks give concrete examples and explicit tasks that can be used to demonstrate the students' knowledge or skill (Linn, 1994). They require an extended period of time to complete and require students to construct new knowledge. They should include real examples of student work from which other students could learn. When presenting performance standards to students, teachers will find it useful to discuss the differences in performance, explaining and offering examples of why one product is at a higher level than another and identifying key elements that make it better.

Rubrics, often developed from levels 1 to 6 (with 6 being high), or stating what is minimum, competent, and exemplary, define the levels of achievement possible for each demonstration or performance. When rubrics are in place and shared, the students can understand the expectations and the level of performance they must meet. This knowledge of expectations leads to a fair and meaningful evaluation of the student's learning. They describe student performance at various levels of proficiency and provide better information on the strengths and weaknesses of students than grades alone could provide. Common rubrics that can be used in many classrooms are being produced by educators and allow shared criteria for what constitutes quality work (O'Neil, 1994).

Opportunity-to-learn standards give the conditions and resources necessary to give students an equal chance to meet the performance standards. Lifelong learning standards are not specific to any one discipline and can be used throughout the student's lifetime. World or world-class standards communicate the expectations held for students in countries worldwide.

Most schools focus on developing content standards, performance standards, and rubrics.

Creating Student Portfolios

One performance assessment strategy that allows gifted students to accumulate evidence of content mastery is the development of a student portfolio. Although it should be used with many other measures to assess student potential, the student portfolio allows students to take more responsibility for their own learning and have more choice and flexibility in how that learning will be demonstrated than would be possible with paper-and-pencil testing.

One approach to the use of student portfolios with gifted learners is found in the Texas Student Portfolio (TSP) developed by Kaplan (1988b). The TSP includes products self-selected by the student from in- and out-of-school settings. It is introduced in the primary grades and continued throughout the school career, with reviews every 6 months. Unlike the performance assessments that focus on skills related to specific disciplines, the TSP focuses on high performance behaviors and assesses all products against the same eight descriptors that can be applied to students at any age or grade level:

1. Presentation of an idea that is unusual.
2. Presentation of an idea that is complex.
3. Presentation of an idea that is organized to communicate effectively.
4. Work that is advanced beyond the student's age or grade level.
5. Understanding of a problem or idea in depth.
6. Use of material that is resourceful and/or clever.
7. Evidence of research support.
8. Evidence of high interest and perseverance.

Kaplan (1988b) suggests that by encouraging students to think about the materials they choose to build their portfolios, teachers are reinforcing attributes of gifted learners, such as persistence, inquiry, and quality production. Therefore, it is very important to provide the teachers involved with professional development on the characteristics of gifted learners and the instructional strategies that enhance their use, thereby empowering the teachers through increased competence and skill at arranging appropriate educational experiences.

Some examples of open-ended activities that would provide high-level performance assessment are:

- To show comprehension of a story, news event, or idea, use past, present, and/or future projections to explore its meaning.
- To show understanding of details and sequences of a biography, historic period, or complex concept, do a progressive drawing: a series of pictures/cartoons on one page that highlight the major events involved.
- To show understanding of the complexity of events, change one element of a historic period, such as "If France had not sold the United States the Louisiana Territory, what would have happened?" Change one character in a story. Change the setting or the time element.

Barton and Collins (1993) suggest a portfolio design that is very useful. For a successful portfolio, include:

- An explicit explanation of the purposes of the portfolio so that learners know what is expected of them before they begin developing their evidence.
- Evidence that establishes a correspondence between academic course work and their experience.
- Multiple sources of evidence to show competency and/or mastery.
- Evidence that shows a direct correspondence with the concepts being learned and classroom instruction.
- Evidence of growth and change in the learner over time. The portfolio should contain a selection of self-selected student work at various points in learning, rather than a sampling of only the student's best work.
- Student choice of evidence and a self-evaluation of that evidence as part of student ownership.
- A multipurpose nature so that the portfolio can be used for more than a single assignment or course.

A portfolio should have at least three distinct parts:

1. Purposes—Explicit statements of essential purposes give direction to the data collection. Each piece of evidence must demonstrate progress toward a purpose. Barton and Collins (1993) suggest a limit of five stated purposes per class.
2. Evidence—This can include documents produced during the normal course work, documents about typical events in the work of the student, documents produced by others about the work of the student, and documents prepared especially for the portfolio. Consider including goal statements, a reflective statement or summary of material to show growth, and statements telling why this evidence

was appropriate to the goals and purposes. Documents can be notes, journal entries, drawings, photographs, audio- and videotapes, models, and computer discs.

3. Assessment Criteria—These can be technical, involving compliance with the criteria for the development of a portfolio; and substantive, how well the student met the purposes and goals.

Barton and Collins believe that the success of students' efforts and the accuracy of teachers' assessments about these efforts depend heavily on the initial clarity of the stated purposes.

Examples of portfolio assessment now being used include the TSP (Kaplan, 1988b) and the Vermont State Portfolio Project (O'Neil, 1993). The data indicate that portfolios have their biggest impact on the improvement of instruction. Students, educators, and parents become more familiar with criteria for good work and have better ability to analyze strengths and weaknesses and participate more meaningfully in the learning process than ever before.

The teacher's role in assessment for gifted students will include:

- Specifying the essential knowledge important for the students to learn in the field of study.

- Understanding the characteristics of gifted students and aligning assessment and curriculum planning to their unique needs.

- Communicating to students the goals of each lesson and unit of study.

- Using assessment continuously to inform and strengthen the planning and delivery of the learning experience.

- Using a variety of assessment strategies, including functional assessment and performance assessment.

- Finding usable ways to demonstrate essential knowledge.

- Linking what is taught within and across courses so that the students' portfolios become reflective of the purposes and goals of the program.

- Teaching the skills of self-assessment and giving opportunities for their use.

Models that have influenced the development of curriculum in gifted education were discussed in this chapter. The philosophies differ, and the structures, time elements, and emphases result in each model offering different ways of meeting the needs of the gifted learner. Districts should be encouraged to find the elements in each model that best fit the conditions and limitations unique to their population and synthesize them into their own district's plan for gifted learners.

Also found in this chapter was an introduction to the concept of seven steps for optimizing learning in the classroom. Such practices provide a basis of effective teaching on which a program for gifted learners could be developed. The first step, creating a responsive learning environment that allows the flexible structure and the complex organization to support the unique needs of gifted students was presented. In such an environment students can pursue their own pace of learning and achievement level, two needs commonly found in programming for gifted learners. The opportunities that can be provided in a complex classroom allow gifted learners to be involved as researchers, apprentices, resident experts, teachers, and/or learning managers. When the classroom is responsive, motivation is found to be higher and choice becomes more prevalent than in a traditionally organized classroom. Suggestions were made for creating both the physical space and the emotional climate that in turn creates the responsive learning environment.

Finally, a discussion of the assessment of knowledge, understanding, and interest of gifted learners (the second step in optimizing learning) completed the ideas for setting the foundation for educating gifted learners. When the focus is on authentic and performance-based assessment, students will find more relevance to their work, become more engaged in the work, and retain the knowledge and skills far longer than with the use of more passive and traditional assessment procedures. Although these tasks are not easy, the promise for involving students in real and meaningful growth and optimal learning more than makes such efforts worthwhile. For gifted students such assessment practices may be the only way to ensure accurate knowledge of the level and depth of their knowledge and understanding.

QUESTIONS OFTEN ASKED

1. If your district is using one model of curriculum development, is it all right to include some ideas from a different model?

You are the professional and know best what will work for you and your students. Most model developers would hope that you will adapt their work so that it is most useful for you. One caution: Be sure the strategies from the second or third model fit your philosophy just as you made sure the original model did. If you are using an overall framework such as Kaplan's Grid, it will be easier to make the appropriate choices and present a unified plan using ideas from many sources.

2. Isn't it difficult to create a responsive learning environment when there are 35 students in the room who are all at different levels?

Yes. It is difficult to create any kind of learning environment for such a varied group of learners. The most successful environment for the learner and the teacher, however, will be a laboratory setting with a range of materials and activities that allows all learners to work at their own pace and level. Unlike in the regular classroom, where the difficulties occur during the instruction, the difficult part in a more complex structure is the preparation. Once the materials and the structure are in place and

the students understand their responsibilities for sharing in their learning and how to operate within the structure, your time can be spent teaching instead of motivating, controlling, and trying to keep each student on task. Although it takes a lot of energy to create a responsive learning environment, it is a lot more exciting and a lot more learning is achieved than in a more traditional, less flexible classroom.

3. How can I find time to build trust in a 45-minute period in secondary school?

The 45-minute block is a difficult time frame for any kind of learning. You may wish to spend a bit more time on trust activities at the beginning of the year with the notion that once trust is built it seems to carry its own momentum. Of course it must be maintained, but once per week for an opening (10 minutes) or a closing (5 to 15 minutes) should help. Using relaxation often and empowering language daily will also help maintain trust in the room. The payoff in real learning is worth the time devoted to it.

4. Which type of classroom is more effective for learning, the teacher-centered or the student-centered classroom?

Neither. A balance of both teacher and student decision-making is the most effective. That is why shared responsibility is such an important part of the responsive learning environment. There are some things that must be the teacher's responsibility and are non-negotiable, just as there are some things the students should be allowed to make decisions about. A balance where everyone feels that they are participating is the most effective for learning.

5. Should gifted students have different standards to meet than other students?

The core content standards for the subject matter being taught should be the same for anyone taking the class and should show continuity through all of the grade levels. However, the difference for gifted students will depend on their level of knowledge, skill, and interest. The modification of content standards that gifted students pursue will depend on the assessment made of their level of progress. In particular subjects the gifted student may need to be working two to four grade levels ahead of the other students and pursuing the content standards that are advanced beyond those of the age-grouped class.

A gifted student might need the opportunity to learn the concepts and skills in ways that are more complex, faster paced, more in depth or through individual research or projects. Gifted students may already have a working knowledge of the material being covered and need to have opportunities to use the information to create, to solve real problems, or to compare with other times, places, or events. Also, there should be different ways that students can meet the content standards and show their mastery of the subject or skill.

6. How can I use portfolio assessment if my district insists on standardized testing?

You do not have to make a choice between testing and portfolio assessment. You can include test data in the portfolio plan. One of the recommendations for the content of a portfolio is to have multiple types of evidence to show mastery. Be sure that in addition to the test data you have performance-based data and you can build a very successful portfolio.

CHECKING FOR UNDERSTANDING
Follow-Up Activity

Assess your classroom regarding the conditions for a Responsive Learning Environment (see Figure 10.8). Then:

Design a classroom or redesign your classroom to meet the conditions on the "Responsive Learning Environment Checklist" in Figure 10.8.

Decide what other conditions you would need to include to meet the needs of gifted students.

Share your ideas with a partner or the class as a whole.

SUMMARY

CURRICULUM MODELS OFTEN USED TO EDUCATE GIFTED LEARNERS

1. Several models now in use for organizing the curriculum for gifted learners have useful concepts and strategies that could benefit a gifted program.
2. During the past two decades, a number of models have been developed that expand the focus beyond the thinking process and its place in curriculum planning and implementation.

CREATING THE RESPONSIVE LEARNING ENVIRONMENT

3. Establishing a classroom environment that is flexible and responsive and allows all students to pursue their own pace and achievement level is a necessary foundation for bringing gifted education into the classroom.
4. The learning environment can influence at least three major conditions for learning: (1) differences in learning style, pace, and level, which the brain data indicate are evident in

all learners; (2) motivation, which can be enhanced as a result of participation, shared responsibility, and choice in the learning process; and (3) challenge and stimulation, both of which are necessary for optimal learning.

The Physical Learning Environment

5. An effective classroom provides space for the students to simultaneously participate in a variety of activities that engage all of the brain functions, including cognitive, affective, physical, and intuitive.

6. The ambience of the classroom should be comfortable, inviting, and physically supportive of exploration, application, and personal construction of knowledge. Students will need access to materials and resources with a range of levels and topics.

The Social-Emotional Learning Environment

7. In an environment where each student is considered a unique individual, the atypical needs of the gifted student cause no one to feel out of place and a positive self-concept can be developed naturally.

8. Students can learn responsibility and an inner sense of control when expectations and opportunities for choice, sharing responsibility, and self-evaluation are a planned part of their day.

9. Any problems encountered in living together as a group can be resolved by the group providing a natural setting for the development of leadership skills.

10. Classrooms that use the responsive learning environment include use of language and behavior that allow students to feel competent, activities that are more cooperative than competitive, and time for building positive interpersonal interactions.

11. Only when there is trust within the class can students feel safe to take the risk to learn.

12. When learning is extended beyond the classroom into the community or nearby nature areas, integrative education becomes very natural and effective.

The Critical Role of the Teacher

13. The teacher establishes the organization and structure of the lesson and of the classroom, the motivational climate for learning, and the attitude the class will have toward learning and other learners.

ASSESSMENT OF THE NEEDS AND ABILITIES OF GIFTED LEARNERS

14. In most special education settings, the word *need* has a connotation of deficiency. In gifted education it means quite the opposite. When gifted individuals are assessed for "needs" for special provisions, these denote areas of strength that cannot be properly nurtured in a regular classroom setting.

15. Where special attention or funding is found to meet gifted needs, it is the nurture of advanced ability that is intended and not the remediation of deficits. If attention must be given to deficit needs, the regular school program should assume that role.

Assessing Knowledge, Understanding, and Interest

16. With a focus on individual student progress, gifted students should be better able to move at their own pace and in their own unique way than was possible with more traditional methods.

17. *Alternative assessment* is any way of showing growth, finding out what a student can do, and informing instruction that differs from the standardized or traditional test.

18. *Performance assessment* is a broad term that refers to opportunities given to students that allow them to demonstrate and apply their knowledge and understanding of content and skills being taught.

19. *Authentic assessment* requires that the knowledge and process of the content be demonstrated under the conditions in which the achievement would normally occur.

20. *Content standards* establish what knowledge and skills should be learned specific to a given discipline or various subject areas. They state important concepts and generalizations and should identify the key elements in content areas. Content standards are sometimes referred to as student outcomes or competencies.

21. *Performance standards* establish the degree or quality of student performance on the performance tasks selected to give evidence of competency on content standards and are set to demonstrate the mastery of the content standards.

22. A *rubric,* often developed from levels 1 to 6 (with 6 being high), or stating what is minimum, competent, and exemplary, defines the levels of achievement possible for each demonstration or performance.

11 *Planning for Integrative Education: Using Brain Research in the Classroom*

In this chapter, the reader will find:

- Components of the Integrative Education Model (IEM)

- Discussion of integrating the cognitive processes and strategies for Integrating Rational-Linear and Spatial-Gestalt Cognitive Functions and developing complex and challenging cognitive activities

- Discussion of integrating the affective processes and strategies for empowering language and behavior; providing choice and perceived control

- Discussion of integrating the physical processes and strategies for relaxation and tension reduction; movement and physical encoding

- Discussion of integrating the intuitive processes and strategies for nurturing intuition and integration

- Sample lessons for integrating intellectual processes

One of the mind's most robust features is its capacity to interconnect a range of processes within its present activity, as well as its functioning across time. Researchers studying diverse aspects of mental life—from social psychology to the neurosciences—have used the term "integration" to refer to the collaborative, linking functions that coordinate various levels of processes within the mind and between people.

—DANIEL J. SIEGEL (1999)

Ann entered the room of Family II, a team-taught class of third- and fourth-grade gifted students. She was there as an observer to see how the teachers were using the ideas on integrative education that she had presented at a workshop a few weeks earlier. As she slid into the nearest chair she looked around at the attractive, colorful room. It was evident that the teachers had taken full advantage of the ideas for creating a responsive learning environment and had added a lot of their own. Every inch of space was being used for learning, either as places that were used for lessons and projects or for displays and materials to add to the learning. A number of areas had been created for different interesting activities, and it all seemed to have a feeling of purpose and warmth. She liked being here and was sure the children did, too.

The children were all seated on a rug at the front of the room, most with their eyes closed, listening to a poem written by their teacher, Ms. Winters. The poem told the story of a boy named Jerry who was about their age, who was spending Saturday afternoon at the movies. The poem was very descriptive and Ms. Winters had asked the children to close their eyes and imagine the afternoon as she described it in words. In the poem, Jerry, was hunting in his pocket for his ticket, then listening to the usher tear it in half. He heard the sounds of the music as he pulled the cold, metal door handle to open the door to the theater. His feet bounced on a plushy carpet as he walked down the aisle, and he felt the soft velvety cushions on the seats as he stepped into his row and found his place to sit. As he settled into his seat, he opened his cellophane sack of lemon drops and as the movie started, he popped one into his mouth . . . As the teacher read, the children imagined each sensory experience and reacted to each of Jerry's actions.

At the end of the poem, Ms. Winters asked the children to open their eyes and discuss with her what they liked about Jerry's experience. They shared similar experiences from their lives. Then Ms. Johnson, the other teacher in the room, passed out small bags of articles as Ms. Winters explained to the children that she was going to read the poem again. This time they were to find items in the bag to help them experience with their senses what Jerry was experiencing. Among the articles in the bags were small paper tickets, pieces of velvet, and a lemon drop wrapped in cellophane.

After reading the poem again and having the children use each of the items in the bag as Jerry went through his adventure, the children were invited to pop the lemon drop into their mouths and return to their tables. As two of the girls passed Ann, she heard one enthusiastically say to the other, "Boy, poems really taste good don't they!" As Ann laughed to herself, she thought there couldn't be a better way to introduce the love for poetry. It was going to be so much fun to spend the day in this room.

INTEGRATING INTELLECTUAL PROCESSES: THE INTEGRATIVE EDUCATION MODEL

A powerful approach to organizing an effective learning process is to develop the areas involved in instruction using the current research on teaching and learning. Connectedness, interrelatedness, and integration are common themes found in many fields of study. As new insights are gained in brain research, cognitive psychology, systems theory, and other diverse fields, they must be reflected in the classroom. Education must take advantage of new information from other fields on how human learning may be enhanced. It was for this purpose of synthesizing current knowledge that the Integrative Education Model (IEM) was developed.

The IEM, a step in optimizing learning, has valuable strategies and practices that can be used in any classroom; it provides for growth in all areas of human ability and all areas of brain development. The interdependence of emotional, cognitive, physical, and intuitive functions allows learners to be effective and efficient when the opportunities are provided for the use of all of these support systems for learning. The integrated use of all of these brain functions give this model power to teach students and to enhance their learning.

The practices described in this chapter can be adapted to accommodate children of diverse needs and teachers of differing strengths and abilities. They are described here because it is the gifted child who needs this approach the most. It is the gifted child who is most underserved in today's schools and who risks the greatest loss of ability in the traditional classroom. And it is the gifted child who is pushing the limits of knowledge and ability and, therefore, can gain the most.

The IEM is inclusive, not exclusive, because it forms a framework that allows the teaching of any content area to be strengthened through the integration of the four major functions of the brain. The components of the IEM include: (1) the responsive learning environment, (2) complex and challenging cognitive activities, (3) empowering language and behavior, (4) choice and perceived control, (5) relaxation and tension reduction, (6) movement and physical encoding, and (7) intuition and integration. These components are organized to support the four major areas/functions of intelligence: the cognitive, the affective (social-emotional), physical (movement and sensing), and the intuitive. Figure 11.1 shows how the IEM creates opportunities for the development of the entire universe of intelligence.

The structure of the IEM is complex, flexible, and decentralized. It encourages individualization by allowing variations in pace, level, and grouping. It promotes student participation, choice, and involvement and creates opportunities for the student to learn and develop in a balanced, brain-compatible way. The Responsive Learning Environment, discussed in Chapter 10, provides the foundation component for the IEM.

INTEGRATING COGNITIVE PROCESSES: COMBINING RATIONAL-LINEAR AND SPATIAL-GESTALT FUNCTIONS OF THE BRAIN HEMISPHERES

The second component of the IEM integrates cognitive processes by including complex and challenging cognitive activities, both rational-linear and spatial-gestalt. Cognition is the most familiar area of brain function for both teachers and students. What may not be as familiar is the way in which this area of function can be

Figure 11.1 *Components of the Integrative Education Model (IEM)*

1. ***Responsive Learning Environment*** This first component requires that the environment be viewed as support for optimizing learning. Within this component is a concern for both the social-emotional environment and the physical environment. The teacher, the parent, and the student are seen to be a team in achieving effective learning. The following can be used as a guide to developing this component:

   - There is an open, respectful, and cooperative relationship among teachers, students, and parents that includes planning, implementing, and evaluating the learning experience.
   - The environment is more like a laboratory or workshop that is rich in materials, with simultaneous access to many learning activities. The emphasis is on experimentation and involvement. Centers may be present.
   - The curriculum is responsive, flexible, and integrative. The needs and interests of the students provide the base from which the curriculum develops.
   - There is a minimum of total group lessons. Most instruction is in small groups among individuals.
   - The student is an active participant in the learning process. Movement, decision-making, self-directed learning, invention, and inquiry are encouraged.
   - Assessment and evaluation are used as tools to aid in the growth of the student.
   - Cognitive, affective, physical/sensing, and intuitive activities are all valued parts of the classroom experience.
   - The atmosphere is one of trust, acceptance, and respect.
   - The environment is flexibly structured and presents a complex organization to meet the needs of each student. There is evidence of individualized activities.
   - Materials at many levels are accessible to the students.
   - The ambience is productive, supportive, and positive.
   - Color, sound, and other sensory stimuli are used to support learning.
   - The physical placement of the furniture, seating of the students, and traffic patterns are planned to support learning.
   - There is evidence of student work and input in the physical appearance of the room.

2. ***Complex and Challenging Cognitive Activities*** Because there are at least two ways to process thinking, opportunities must be provided for learning that allows use of both rational-linear and spatial-gestalt processing. By providing novelty, complexity, variety, and challenge in the classroom as the standard for each lesson, the educational process becomes more brain-compatible. The following can be used as a guide for this component:

   - Pretesting and posttesting are used, and continuous assessment is evident.
   - Lessons are developed at the level of the learner and paced to meet each individual's needs.
   - Tasks used to develop learning are interesting, integrative, and challenging.
   - Students are engaged and motivated to learn.
   - Both rational-linear and spatial-gestalt processes are used in the learning experience.
   - Variety and novelty are a part of the learning experience.
   - The student is given choices and shares the responsibility of planning the learning experience.

3. ***Empowering Language and Behavior*** The brain uses emotions to trigger the production of biochemicals to enhance or inhibit the thinking functions. IEM encourages the use of language and behavior that empowers learners, both between the teacher and the learner and among learners. This component includes strategies to build community and positive interpersonal and intrapersonal communication. The following can be used as a guide for this component:

   - The teacher's language creates for the students a sense of competence, support, closeness, ability, and caring.
   - The teacher uses physical and verbal affirmation, humor, constructive feedback, and "I" messages rather than "You" messages with the students.

Figure 11.1 *continued*

- The teacher uses questions to empower the students and to share the responsibility for learning.
- The teacher avoids the use of *should, shouldn't, must, must not, always,* and *never* and phrases things positively.
- The teacher uses body language that empowers the learner.
- The teacher gives opportunities for self-evaluation.
- The teacher gives students opportunities to share ideas and strategies with each other.
- The teacher helps students gain control over debilitating speech, both inner and oral in nature.

4. ***Choice and Perceived Control*** Choice and perceived control play an important part in the success and continued achievements of the learner. Strategies that build skills of decision-making strengthen the ability to align personal and school goals, and foster alternative thinking and self-evaluation are encouraged. The teacher must include choice in the environment and in the learning experiences if optimal learning is to be achieved. The following can be used as a guide for this component:

- There are choices of activities, timing, and/or ways to learn. Nonnegotiables are known and choices given as to how these can be accomplished.
- The teacher incorporates lessons in decision-making and gives opportunities to practice these skills
- The choices given are real, with no hidden preference on the part of the teacher.
- Students are given the opportunity to develop alternatives, help plan learning experiences, and develop structures and organizations for their learning.
- The teacher avoids giving excessive help and praise or sympathy for easy work that is poorly done.
- The teacher shares the scope and sequence of the content and skills with the students and individually discusses their growth with them.
- The teacher models alternative thinking.
- The teacher values mistakes as learning experiences.
- The students are involved in establishing agreements for appropriate behavior, rather than having the teacher impose rules of behavior.
- The teacher gives the students opportunities to align their goals with the school goals.
- Students are given many alternative coping strategies for solving problems.

5. ***Relaxation and Tension Reduction*** The human brain processes more and retains information longer when tension is reduced. Strategies for reducing tension are important tools for both teachers and learners. The following can be used as a guide for developing this component:

- The ambience of the classroom, including teacher attitude, is calming and stimulating and has a minimum of stress.
- Relaxation techniques are used to support learning and to develop coherence, before testing and during transitions.
- The teacher models a relaxed, centered, calm manner.

6. ***Movement and Physical Encoding*** Because using the physical/sensing function of the brain provides support for learning by increasing understanding and retention of concepts, movement and physical encoding strategies are considered an important part of the teaching process. The following can be used as a guide for developing this component:

- Movement in the room is purposeful.
- Physical sensing, such as touch, smell, and taste, is used to support learning.
- Movement of the body is used to support the development of concepts (i.e., physical encoding).

Figure 11.1 *continued*

---

7. ***Intuition and Integration*** Because intuition, future planning, and creativity are brain processes that are thought to be unique to human beings and may be their most powerful brain functions, inclusion of activities that allow use of these processes is considered essential to optimizing learning. These are highly synthetic functions and require teaching opportunities that are multi-sensory, multidisciplinary, and integrative. The following can be used as a guide for this component:

- The teacher provides experiences in which the child can demonstrate evidence of intuitive processing at three levels:
  Level 1, Rational Intuition: Use of minimum of known information to reorganize, hypothesize, suggest solutions
  Level 2, Predictive Intuition: Use of known information plus hunches to establish probabilities.
  Level 3, Transformational Intuition: Synthesis of many known and unknown sources to create new information, artistic products, and so forth.
- The teacher uses imagery, fantasy, and/or visualization to support the learning experience.
- The teacher uses "what if" and open-ended, future-thinking strategies.
- The teacher uses intuitive stretches
- The teacher uses integrative lessons.
- The teacher encourages creativity.

Students who are taught in this way have been found to be:

- More relaxed, more at ease with themselves and with others.
- More positive, caring, and respectful of each other and their teachers.
- More creative, willing to try more unusual solutions, and able to engage in more alternative and higher level cognitive activities.
- More likely to initiate learning activities.
- More positive and enthusiastic about their learning, more highly motivated.
- More independent and responsible.

---

strengthened by integrating both the rational-linear and the spatial-gestalt processes of both hemispheres of the brain, making learning available through both verbal and visual modes.

In the early 1970s, neuroscientists Sperry (1973), Bogen (1975), and others discovered the specialized functions of the hemispheres of the brain. Their work has been validated over the years by researchers worldwide (Restak, 2000). The left hemisphere is the primary mediator of language and linear, rational processes. The right hemisphere is more involved with the spatial, patterned, gestalt forms of input as it provides support and extension to the processes of the left. With this discovery came the realization that education was focused heavily on the linear, rational, verbal thinking functions and had not taken advantage of the spatial, gestalt, visual thinking functions that are available to support learning. The following strategies give educators examples of how these two important support systems can be used in the classroom and can be adapted for use at the elementary or secondary levels.

Strategies Integrating Rational-Linear and Spatial-Gestalt Cognitive Functions

Visual Thinking

Educators concerned with the development of creative behavior have long used strategies incorporating *visual thinking*. Those in the visual arts have focused on the ability to use visual thinking to create products and solve problems. At Stanford University, McKim (1980) developed a course to teach the skills of visual thinking. These skills provide the basis for including visual thinking in programs for cognitive growth.

To develop the skills of visual thinking, McKim suggests upside-down drawing; drawing lines that express some physical body motion, such as stumbling, dancing, stretching, or exploding; and doodling, covering up the doodle, and then repeating the doodle pattern. McKim believes that visual similes and metaphors help us glimpse the profound reality that lies within each object; for example, having students view an object or a picture and construct a simile that makes a substantial imaginative leap, such as old palm trees becoming broken umbrellas. (McKim, 1980). This associative flexibility allows students to break away from the objectivity that is so carefully taught in most school activities.

Pattern seeking is important in developing visual thinking. A strategy used by Leonardo da Vinci provides practice in developing this skill. With your eyes closed, cover a paper with random lines. Open your eyes and try to identify resemblances to objects, birds, plants, and so forth within the scribbles. Outline any patterns that you find. This technique is used to stimulate creative seeing. Activities of finishing incomplete complex patterns are also useful in developing visual thinking.

Other activities in visual thinking use the ability to imagine. McKim (1980) believes imagination goes beyond the power to be creative; it is all that one has learned or experienced and is central to every perception and act in which one engages. Imagination allows us to ask "How?" or "Why?" and bridges between cause and effect. It enables self-awareness and rules what we choose to see or ignore, to like or dislike. McKim states, "Productive visual thinkers control their inner imagery, manipulate it, transform it, and move it along toward a desired goal. In contrast, worriers are passive victims of negative imaginative ventures that they cannot stop, much less direct" (p. 105).

Instrumental Enrichment

Another learning strategy, *instrumental enrichment,* uses the integration of the cognitive functions embodied in the work of Israeli psychologist Reuven Feuerstein (1978). His theory includes three theoretical aspects:

1. *Structural Cognitive Modifiability*—Feuerstein (1978) describes this concept as "the unique capacity of human beings to change or modify the structure of their cognitive functioning in order to adapt to changing demands of life situations" (p. 1.1). Cognitive changes can be considered structural when they are self-perpetuating—

of an autonomous and self-regulatory nature—and when they show permanence. Human beings are open systems, accessible to change throughout their lives.

2. *Mediated Learning Experiences (MLE)*—Although much is learned through direct experience, most of the structural changes that occur in human cognition are the result of learning experiences that are mediated. Characteristically these experiences are intentional, have the quality of transcendence, have meaning for the learner, mediate behavior, and mediate a feeling of competence.

3. *Learning Potential*—Almost everyone has a great deal more capacity for thought and intelligent behavior than is often exhibited. Assessing this potential requires a dynamic assessment of the learning process, rather than a sampling of previously learned material (e.g., instead of asking "How much does a person know?" the question becomes "How can the person learn what they do not yet know?").

Feuerstein's learning process moves the student from passive dependence to autonomous, independent learning. This, along with the underlying assumptions of Instrumental Enrichment, enable his model to introduce complexity and cognitive challenges. The training that accompanies the use of material developed by Feuerstein includes attention to the students' feeling and attitudes and to relating the information to real-life circumstances.

Suggestopedia

In Bulgaria, Georgi Lozanov (1977), a teacher/researcher, effectively applied gestalt learning principles. By putting together verbal and visual information he developed, through numerous experiments, a system he calls *Suggestopedia,* which accelerates the learning process and dramatically increases the retention factor. Lozanov based the Suggestopedia system on three principles: joy and the absence of tension, oneness of the conscious and unconscious, and suggestive interaction.

To ensure the first principle, Lozanov developed a relaxed ambience using tension reduction and relaxation techniques. Any practice that would produce anxiety, stress, fear of failure, or humiliation for the learner must be discontinued. Students are encouraged to view learning as a pleasant activity, one they will enjoy, with easily obtainable results. The second principle is developed by the use of music (generally classical) chosen for this purpose. Dramatic skits and psychodrama may also be used to heighten the awareness of wholeness or oneness.

The third principle, suggestive interaction, can be met only by a sensitive, nonthreatening, caring teacher. The part the teacher plays and the attitude emanating from this instructor/supporter/facilitator are critical.

The Suggestopedia system has produced some impressive results: Students show significant improvement in memory; they cover material in 2 to 3 months that under former educational methodology and situations took more than a year to learn; and they have a higher level of retention. Research (Racle, 1977) shows that Suggestopedia can be used in every discipline, because the students benefit by feelings of harmony, restfulness, pleasant emotions, and the calling forth and combining of all the mental, physical, and intuitive reserves. Racle reports that this type of instruction is not only "many times more efficacious" than other teaching methods, but "much more humane and much less burdensome for the studying individual" (p. 2).

Many countries, including the United States, and the United Nations Educational Service (UNESCO) are involved in research on the possibilities of this type of accelerated learning. Conferences, workshops, pamphlets, and journal articles disperse information about this exciting new practice. (To learn more, contact the Society for Accelerative Learning and Teaching, Inc., PO Box 1216, Welch Station, Ames, Iowa 50010.)

Mindmapping

Mindmapping (discussed in Chapter 12) is another excellent example of a strategy integrating rational-linear and spatial-gestalt cognitive functions.

Strategies Integrating Cognition With Other Brain Functions

The processes that are most often a part of gifted programs are those of productive or critical thinking, research skills, learning-to-learn skills, and those involving technology. These cognitive processes are important and, when used with other areas of function, will aid gifted students in fulfilling their learning potential. Additional learning power results when cognitive processes are combined with the other brain functions, such as physical/sensing, feeling, and intuition. Although the activities suggested here focus on cognitive development, the other functions will be seen as integrated into this focus, providing accelerated learning, higher retention, and a more complex understanding. All of the strategies that follow can be adapted for use at the elementary or secondary grade levels.

Decision-Making and Alternative Thinking

Gifted students will function in society as innovators, and reconstructionists and agents of change. It is believed that societal problem-solvers will come from this group. By being exposed to many ways of viewing problems, students may find better solutions. Students should be given experiences that allow them to:

- Become aware of bias in thinking, the difference between belief and fact.
- Acknowledge that each conflicting viewpoint may be valid.
- See the importance of sources of information.
- Experience the importance of cooperation and consensus in group action.
- Seek many alternatives before deciding on solutions.

Metacognition

Metacognition is the conscious knowledge of one's cognitive processes and capabilities that allow one to monitor, regulate, and evaluate one's own cognition (Flavell, 1979). By use of the process a student can become a more efficient and flexible learner. Borkowski (1985) viewed metacognition as important in academic achievement because it promotes strategic, thoughtful performance. Using the knowledge that intelligence involves complex internal processes rather than only unidimensional, observable behaviors, Carr and Borkowski (1987) contended that the ability to diverge from the concrete and the obvious is an indicator of intelligence. They believe that explicit training of metacognitive skills may enhance academic achievement, intelligence, and creative problem-solving. For example, when a student has been using manipulatives to understand a mathematical process and then finds that such support is no longer necessary, the student should be asked to verbalize how the process is being thought out internally. This will allow the student to be aware of the way in which the problem is being processed and to clarify and solidify the steps to solution.

Synectics

Another approach to integrating the cognitive function with other functions of the brain is synectics (Gordon & Poze, 1980), which assumes that learning is a combination of focusing, connection making, and application. "To learn, students must respond to subject matter by focusing on important points, internalizing those points, expressing their comprehension, and sometimes creatively applying what they have learned. Effective internalization takes place when students connect the subject matter to something they already know about" (p. 147).

The ways these assumptions are realized in the curriculum or the problem-solving situation follow several steps and use analogy and metaphor as tools for learning. The first step is to discover within the concept to be learned or problem to be solved the paradox that exists at the core. For an example, Gordon showed that the concept of symbiosis has the paradox of double weakness, or that needs when taken together make for strength. Next, the student is asked to develop an analogy for the paradox. Gordon found that the very use of a connective analogy lends clarity and sophistication to expression of the concept. Later, personal analogies are constructed by the students to clarify the concept further, thus allowing children to work at their level of ability; this strategy can be used with a heterogeneously grouped class. Gifted students will produce creative extensions of the process, resulting from connection-making processes that were subliminal, which become conscious, explicit, and within their control.

Research Skills

Gifted students need a way to seek out information and ideas far sooner than more typical learners. They must be able to move efficiently and independently into areas of interest not yet explored. They need to become familiar with the skills of historical research, descriptive research, and experimental research as tools for future learning and thinking.

Other Possibilities

Many other possibilities exist for integrating cognition with the other brain functions.

Integrated Core Classes In small groups (or individually) gifted students could choose a particular period, concept, person, or object and, using it as a central theme, investigate the history, art and music, and social, cultural, economic, and other conditions surrounding the core subject. By actually "living" through the creation of this person, object, period, or concept, the student will understand and appreciate inquiry far more.

Seminar Program A seminar program offers pupil assessment and individualized planning, open curriculum guides, and a variety of resource people. This program can combine the use of independent study, advanced coursework, advanced placement in colleges, and special seminars for gifted students on an individual basis.

Publishing Gifted students should be encouraged to publish their work, either in established journals, magazines, and newspapers or in school- or class-produced publications. Editing for publication teaches far more grammar, punctuation, and spelling skills than do skill drilling and sentence diagramming.

Resident Expert Encourage all gifted students to become resident experts in the one area in which they are most interested. Call upon their expertise; let them help teachers and others in the school with problems that are in their area of knowledge.

Conceptual Frameworks and Systems Expose gifted students to conceptual frameworks that you use to organize your thinking (e.g., Bloom's Taxonomy, Bloom, 1956). Encourage their participation in new problems—yours, theirs, the school's, and the community's—by the development of systems or conceptual frameworks. Be sure the students have a way to share their creations. For example, a group of fifth- and sixth-grade students were studying the land use in their area. They obtained advice from architects, city planners, and engineers who regularly visited their classroom. After several months, one group devised a plan for development that excited them. Their teacher arranged for them to present their plan, with maps and graphs, to the County Planning Board. Later, the students were notified that a portion of their plan had been adopted. They received a commendation from the county for their work.

Studies comparing the learning styles of gifted to nongifted learners (Price, Dunn, Dunn, & Griggs, 1981) indicate that elementary and secondary gifted learners prefer (1) less supervision in the learning setting; (2) manipulative and active, real-life experiences to lectures, discussions, and tapes; and (3) more small group, individual, and self-designed instructional opportunities.

INTEGRATING AFFECTIVE PROCESSES

The brain makes special use of feelings or emotions in the learning process. When learning becomes separated from human values, the persons involved are alienated from each other and from themselves. Emotions are the gateway-triggering mechanism for higher cognitive function.

Strategies for affective development must be integrated into the students' daily activities. Before using any of the activities that follow, the teacher must feel comfortable with them. Of all the areas, the success of the strategies in the affective or feeling area depends most on the attitude and development of the teacher.

The ideas presented not only are useful for gifted students but may be used in heterogeneous groupings. However, as in the cognitive area, the needs of gifted students are different—more intense, with more information on emotions to process. The gifted need opportunities to work with their intellectual peers in groups and, on other occasions, with groups of varying ages and abilities.

It has been said that all major decisions are made at a feeling level. Krathwohl and his committee (1964) organized affective learning into a taxonomy. This taxonomy and the material the committee developed for it may help in organizing an affective curriculum (see Chapter 10, p. 367).

Often students are led to believe that some feelings are "wrong" or "bad." These feelings need to be discussed with the students in an accepting manner—they need to know that feelings just *are*. Once people recognize that they have certain feelings, they can decide what they want to do about the way these feelings affect themselves and others.

Because these techniques concern human beings, there is no limit placed on the ages of the students participating. It will be necessary for teachers to adapt the presentation to their own particular group, whether at the elementary or secondary grade level. Some activities that help students become aware of their emotional life are:

- List every incident and/or person that makes you angry (or happy, or scared, etc.) during one day or a week. Discuss the list.

- Do something nice for someone each day for a week. Tell how you felt doing it, both when they knew and when they did not know that you had done it. List your feelings. Discuss what you found out.

- Write down where in your body you feel it (throat, head, stomach) when you are especially angry (or happy, or anxious, etc.). Discuss.

- Role play different situations while wearing glasses depicting various emotions. Find out how the situation would be different if you felt angry, happy, cared for, lonely, and so forth. Discuss differences in perception.

Empowering Language and Behavior

The third component of the IEM is involved in integrating affective processes. Students must be aware of their real feelings and find a way to communicate them clearly to achieve the goals of empowering language and behavior. Open communication clearly conveys what is being felt and gives clear information to both giver and receiver. Students must also be aware of how active listening affects the communication. To get the feeling and the words to match, the nonverbal and the verbal to convey the same message, is not easy. Students need lots of practice in meaningful situations with the chance to analyze what happened and try again.

One way to contribute to a supportive climate in the classroom would be to affirm the students rather than judge them. Show them that their behavior is the problem, not who they are as people.

Example: Larry noisily enters the room, throws a book on his desk, kicks the chair, and passes loud and profane judgment on the day, the school, and everyone in it.

> Affirming response: Larry, I can see you are really upset. Would you like to step out-side and talk about it or would you rather work awhile now and discuss it later?
>
> Judging response: Larry, you know that kind of behavior is not permitted in this room! What is the matter with you? Can't you grow up? Now sit down and get to work. (Clark, 1986, p. 129)

If students spend their time and energy on defensiveness and resistance, there will be little energy or time for learning.

Open Communication and Back-Off Space

Often teachers and parents are not prepared for gifted students who do not share their views and who challenge their ideas and values. Parents or teachers may consider such differences as disrespectful or as a challenge to their authority. For teachers and parents who want to develop increasing understanding instead of alienation between themselves and the student, back-off space can be a useful tool.

1. The teacher (or student) first shares with the students (or teacher) his or her own weaknesses or moods and discusses how the students (or teacher) can know when this is happening. (For example, (1) some days the student is especially tired or experiencing low energy, and does not want to deal with a lot of extra problems; this is picked up by the teacher through body posture and facial expressions; (2) or a teacher may be annoyed with a student's attitude and not be able to listen further to complaints or "good" reasons and excuses; the student observes this from the teacher's tight lips and abrupt manner.)

2. They agree to allow space for the other person and open communication of problems with dignity and caring—an understanding that when the student (or teacher) is not doing well, he or she will be given "space."

3. When confrontations occur, both parties are committed to discuss, in private, the situation as they see it and to listen to the other person. Open communication respects the feelings of both parties and clarifies the situation.

4. If both parties can arrive at a mutual agreement at that time, they do; if not, both agree to back off, and each gives the other time to cool off. Later discussion may prove more fruitful.

The entire class shares this agreement for open communication and back-off space so that anyone can use it when needed and, at a point of confrontation, the other class members will be aware of the need to allow such a use of time by the teacher and the student. It is important for everyone to agree to participate with a high level of regard and for the technique not to be used punitively.

Group Interaction

The skills of group interaction can make student participation in a group more productive and more satisfying. It appears from Kohn's (1986) research that competition may seem to make teaching easier by use of games that attract and hold the students' attention, but this strategy does not make teaching more effective. It is the gaming that catches the attention, not the competition; cooperative games are

When gifted students confront a problem together, a higher level of thinking is often achieved than any could accomplish alone.

preferred by children over competitive games. Children simply do not learn better when competition dominates the classroom.

Kohn's (1986) review of the evidence found some interesting reasons for competition's failure. Success depends on the ability to use resources efficiently, and competition makes sharing of resources and skills impossible because people have to work against each other, resulting in hostility and suspicion. Competition fails to promote excellence because of its emphasis on trying to win against others. Extrinsic motivators, such as competition, are simply not as rewarding, nor do they call forth the level of excellence as do our own intrinsic structures. Kohn commented: "Years of research have shown that extrinsic motivators not only fail to spur people on to higher achievement but actually undermine intrinsic motivation, the sort that produces better results" (p. 28).

Conversely, cooperation increases motivation, allows more creativity, creates more fluid leadership, and allows everyone to participate actively without fear of censure (Buffington, 1988). Individuals who develop cooperative strategies were found to feel more in control of their life.

For gifted students, there are some cautions regarding learning in cooperative groups that are heterogeneous in composition. When used as an occasional organizer in the classroom, such groups may give gifted students valuable opportunities to appreciate students of varying interests and abilities; when used as a major organizer, gifted students are in danger of serving as tutors to less able learners far too much of the time and missing the challenge of their intellectual peers. When asked about the problems caused for bright students by overuse of cooperative learning groups defined heterogeneously, Roger Johnson, a staunch promoter of cooperative learning groups, replied, "There is a lot of value emotionally for bright kids in cooperative learning groups. They were never meant to be their whole learning experience. They were not designed to challenge them academically" (Johnson, 1988).

Choice and Perceived Control

Researchers in projects throughout the country have found that choice and the resulting perception of control are motivational variables that significantly affect children's academic achievement and their self-concept (Hall, 1987). Children rated as difficult and noncompliant by their nursery school teachers were as obedient as more easy-going youngsters when allowed to control their situation. Interestingly, it is not just the choice or control that is allowed children that makes the difference but their perception of that choice. The possibilities for choice may be in the program, but unless children clearly see those alternatives and believe they can really make a choice that will be acceptable, the positive effect will be missing (see Figure 11.2). For these reasons, choice and perceived control comprise the fourth component of IEM.

One attribute of gifted learners is their early development of an internal locus of control. This means that they often do things for the pure pleasure of it. They can get very excited about learning new information and they derive much satisfaction from discovering the solution to a problem. The term locus of control is used to express the idea that the perceived control can be located either within the child (as when a choice is made from the child's interest) or externally (as when a reward is given for making the choice). This is where gifted children show themselves to be characteristically different from average learners. Gifted children are found to have a greater inner locus of control at a younger age than do average learners. It is one of the notable differences that needs to be considered when planning educational experiences for the gifted. It is important to note that success later in life is in direct correlation to how much inner locus of control the individual has developed. This perception of responsibility for and control over one's life has been recognized from the 1970s as the single most important condition for success, achievement, and a sense of well-being (Bar-Tal, Kfir, Bar-Zohar, & Chen, 1980; Dweck & Goetz, 1978).

Schools use external rewards, such as grades, prizes, gold stars, special privileges, threats, and punishment, without considering whether or not the child is intrinsically motivated. It has been established that the more the environment (either home or school) provides external controls, the greater will be the loss of the inner locus of control (Deci, 1975).

Greene (1974) and others found that an external reward system can be devastating for children who have intrinsic motivation. The child will no longer work for the joy or notice the satisfaction of accomplishment, but will focus on the learning task as a means to a different goal, the reward. Once the reward stops being offered, the task ceases to be worthwhile. For gifted learners this is most important.

Figure 11.2 *Suggestions for Increasing Perceived Control*

- One critical factor is the structure of the program. It must be a complex structure that attempts to give every child alternatives at an appropriate level of choice. A flexible, responsive structure is important at home as well.
- Incorporate lessons in making good choices and in how to develop responsible choices. Children need a lot of practice in choosing.
- The choices must be real; that is, any that are presented are equally acceptable to the teacher (or parents), and there is no hidden preference.
- The situations for choice must come with a procedure for child-developed alternatives to be considered whenever possible. Ask "If you don't find what you want within what we suggest, what do you suggest?"
- Teachers must believe that children can and should make the major part of the decisions about their learning experience. Teachers are there to provide the organizers, the resources, and the structure to help the child be effective. Assignments can be given by teachers or parents, but the order and timing of the completion can be left to the child. It has been found that with even this much control, children complete a significantly higher percentage of their assignments (Wang & Stiles, 1976). Children who participate in activities such as discussion groups, family councils, planning sessions for trips, and committees show far more satisfaction and responsible participation in the class or family (Sharan, 1980; Stipek & Weisz, 1981; Thomas, 1980).
- Children need specific skills to make good choices, such as development of alternative thinking patterns, ability to build personal power through relaxation and tension reduction, imagery, intuitive strategies, and the ability to see and evaluate consequences.
- Each child has irreducible dignity and can be helped to see that quality in oneself and others. Such experiences must be built into a home or school day. Demonstrations of caring cannot be left to chance.
- One of the primary responsibilities of a faculty is to model effective interpersonal relationships and personal power. "If you want to see how it looks to be working toward effective growth." we must say to the child by our actions, "look at us; talk to us; we're trying, too."

Not only do they have more inner control available earlier, they are more sensitive to the demands of the environment. They can, in fact, lose more of their perceived power faster than will the average learner. It then becomes important to plan an environment that builds inner locus and heightens the perception of choice. Development of intrinsic motivation and internal locus of control are important goals for gifted students to help them function positively in society and find personal satisfaction in whatever they choose to do. Care must be taken that unexamined practices of using rewards do not undermine this development.

According to Deci (1985), unless the environment interferes, both teaching and learning are intrinsically motivating for most people. His research shows that both activities are performed most effectively when they are intrinsically motivated. The social environment has an important effect on which type of motivation people will use. Deci stated, "Extrinsic motivation predominates in environments that are controlling, while intrinsic motivation is fostered by environments that support autonomy. Changing the environment can alter the motivational patterns and the results they foster" (p. 52).

Successful experiences are not enough. If children succeed, but believe they were given that success, it does not add to the perceived power. Likewise, failure can be viewed as positive if children believe that by their own effort success would be possible. The world must be seen as able to be acted upon; it must not be viewed as a place where one is helpless and everything just happens to one. This perception is established very early, within the first 2 months of life. It is this perception that is one of the triggering mechanisms for developing higher levels of intelligence (Andrews & Debus, 1978; deCharms, 1976; Gordon, 1977).

Homes and schools must be organized with flexibility and a structure that provides alternatives. Parents and teachers need to see themselves as the resources for ever-widening child-initiated choices. Allowing children to feel comfortable with ambiguity and in novel and open-ended situations is tremendously important. The behavior of all children is significantly influenced by their perceived locus of control. Success, achievement, and well-being come with personal power and the perception of inner control. Helping children develop their power is up to parents and teachers alike. For gifted children it is a matter of survival.

Other Possibilities

Simulation

Simulation develops cognitive abilities and understanding, but it does so by the use of affective involvement. Simulation is the process of exploring a problem or idea by simulating (i.e., by re-creating) the events within the classroom. It requires active participation on the part of the learner. The outcomes are decided by this participation. It has the advantages of:

- Bringing out a high degree of motivation.
- Leading the learner to inquiry and research.
- Using the skills of decision-making, communication, persuasion, and resource allocation.
- Integrating curriculum areas.
- Developing a deeper level of understanding.
- Changing attitudes.
- Enhancing personal growth.

My only caution is in regard to the heavy emotional loading that often occurs. Although teachers may tell their students that they are simulating events, gaming, and role playing, a well-structured simulation may be so real that students will need help leaving their roles and looking at the process skills and information they have gained. For these reasons, the sessions must be debriefed thoroughly.

Among the several types of simulations are board games, such as chess and Stocks and Bonds (3M Company, Minnesota). Paper and pencil exercises can also be designed as simulations. Environmental simulations can be accomplished by use of media equipment.

"Real life" simulations have the most impact (e.g., crises at the United Nations or in the Persian Gulf, power status of socioeconomic classes, or the signing of the Declaration of Independence). Although a number of companies develop and sell simulations, teachers and students can also structure and run them.

Valuing

As individual guides to living, values evolve and mature as experiences evolve and people mature through them. The concern is not with the particular value outcomes of any person's experience, but rather with the process used to develop values. It is important that our values work effectively and lead us to a satisfying, actualizing life. In this way, we form the moral character discussed by Kohlberg (1964, 1972) (see Chapter 5).

Schmidt (1990a) notes that, despite controversy, there is a growing consensus that schools need to teach values. Emphasizing core values and the importance of teachers' skills in conveying them to students seems to be a good approach. Although some schools teach values directly as part of a distinct curriculum, others try to influence the development of values through lessons from the literature or other subjects, through community service, or through greater student involvement in school governance. Schmidt believes that the old concept of values neutrality is no longer a politically safe option.

Valuing begins with the awareness of what values we now hold. Helping students to clarify their own values and to be aware of the values of others is the first step. First, encourage discussion of open-ended problems and positions on controversial issues. The next step provides knowledge of the process of decision-making, knowing that each person is free to choose. The effects of expectations, responsibilities, and consequences must become a part of the information available to students.

Once their values have been affirmed, students need the opportunity to transform them into action, to experience them as an acknowledged part of their life. Change will come only from an examination of their own values and the way these values work for them.

Leadership

Leadership has its beginnings in the patterns being established in very young children. Montagner (cited in Pines, 1984) observed that parents of children who become leaders communicate with their children a great deal; they use mimicry, gestures, and words; and they stoop down to the children's level to talk with them. They ask their children what they want to do, listen to what their children say, and pay attention to any spontaneous behavior. They do not threaten or use aggressive behavior toward their children, nor are they overprotective. Montagner finds their behavior consistently stable.

Roderick (1987) pointed out that even after four decades of interest in leadership as an educational goal there is little agreement on the meaning of the concept and few evaluative studies on the effectiveness of leadership training. Feldhusen and Kennedy (1988) agreed. The elements that find validation in the literature for developing leadership skills seem to be limited to skills that produce a knowledge base in a discipline or skills in a domain of art, and a knowledge level of leadership skill. From a review of theory and developmental efforts, these researchers find the capacity for critical and creative thinking, problem-solving, future study, planning, analysis, synthesis, and evaluative thought to be necessary components for all conceptions of leadership. Feldhusen and Kennedy conclude that leadership skills and theory should be goals in the education of the gifted and should involve an interaction with changes emerging in the society today. As part of the program, they suggest that understanding of the following should be considered: the theories and practices of leadership, self as a potential leader, parliamentary procedures, communication skills, and the skills of group management.

Myers, Slavin, and Southern (1990) demonstrate a relationship between the type of task and the skill demands made on leaders. Highly structured tasks with predetermined leadership and task demands will be more effectively accomplished by task-oriented or authoritarian leaders who have readily applicable skills. As the task becomes less structured, the social and collaborative leadership style emerges as most effective. Groups with authoritarian leadership have less effective and less creative products. Leaders who allow more participation are more successful in enlisting the ideas and the cooperation of the group.

A decade-long study (Roach, 1999) found that youth leadership differs in significant ways from established adult leadership and support the developments in learning theory from cognitive psychology and organizational sociology. "The individual, competitive, incremental model that predominates within adult theories of leadership and many programs conceived according to adult models hold little relevance for today's youth or for future learning demands in organizations" (p. 21). Youth leadership stresses self-knowledge and commitments to relationships that sustain group goals. In youth leadership, skills that are most needed are those that are necessary for constant collection and assessment of information. From her data, Roach admonishes educators to attend less to the traits of individuals to predict leadership and more on learning situations that encourage leadership.

INTEGRATING PHYSICAL PROCESSES

In addition to cognitive and affective development, gifted students must be given opportunities to integrate their minds with their physical bodies. In the past, schools have required the development of the physical body only as a separate entity. This development yields far more when integrated with the other functions.

Relaxation and Tension Reduction

Relaxation and the reduction of tension are key to optimizing the learning process and they comprise the fifth component of the IEM. Far back in recorded history, humans wrote of the need for balance in their life. The ebb and flow of human energy has been central to many belief systems—the yin/yang of ancient China, the *ka* of the ancient Egyptians, the *chi* of the Eastern Indians, the *kaa* of the American

Indians, the *mana* of the Hawaiians, and the circadian and biorhythm cycles of Westerners. We are all affected by the differing amounts of energy available in our lives and by what inhibits or facilitates our energy supply. As early as the 1950s researchers such as Selye (1956) and later Pelletier (1977) presented much information on how stress reduces our energy and on ways to move into energy-producing modes instead. Feldenkrais (1972), Gallwey (1974), Leonard (1975), Masters and Houston (1978), Schutz (1976), and Spino (1976), to name a few, showed us ways to integrate the mind and body, thereby promoting increased function and energy for all human systems. As important as this more holistic view of the human being is to all people, it is even more essential for the gifted person. We have noted that high levels of anxiety reduce access to higher brain functions (Hart, 1981), interrupt the natural flow of information and processing between the hemispheres (Wittrock, 1980b), and inhibit prefrontal cortical functions (Goodman, 1978). Current data confirm and extend these findings (Restak, 2000). If we are to allow students the best education possible, then we must teach tension-reducing techniques to help prevent excessive stress.

Stress is an unavoidable consequence of the challenges of living. As Restak (2000) states, "No matter how fortunate your life circumstances, no one is exempt from stress. A severe or unremitting stress can be devastating to physical and mental health . . . But the most worrying effect of prolonged and inappropriate stress is the harm inflicted on the brain" (p. 138). Stress is inevitable, and the need to keep stress within manageable limits has been recognized by psychologists and medical professionals alike.

Selye (1956, 1979), one of the major theorists in the field, emphasizes that one form of stress—eustress—results from achievement, triumph, and exhilaration. Only when stress becomes distress, producing a sense of loss of security and adequacy, does it become dangerous to one's health and well-being. From Selye's seminal work came the discovery that stress produces chemicals within the brain that shut down the system and, over time, create permanent damage. Although the body reacts to protect the system, prolonged or frequent use of this reaction will, in fact, wear the system out.

Capra (1982) identified stress as "an imbalance of the organism in response to environmental influences" (p. 324). He believed that a certain amount of stress is an essential part of living. Only as temporary stress is prolonged can it become harmful, affecting the body's immune system and playing a significant role in the development of many illnesses.

Stress can affect learning even when the imbalance is not this severe. Hunt (1982) suggested that when under stress we forget things we know well. He explains that part of the reason is that "the stressful input takes up most of the mind's conscious equipment and so impedes the retrieval of information from long term memory" (p. 89).

Of interest to the educator is the finding that higher-level mental faculties are substantially impaired by stress and function more effectively when a person is comparatively calm and not highly aroused. For that reason, Albrecht (1979) and others believe that "one of the most important survival skills for human beings in twentieth-century America is a neurological skill—the ability to physically relax, unwind, and demobilize the body for long enough periods to allow it to recuperate and repair itself" (p. 79). Should anyone believe that the concern over stress is that of just a few researchers, the library of the International Stress Management Association has more than 120,000 publications on stress. You may contact: ISMA at P.O. Box 348, Waltham Cross, EN8 8ZL England or the American Institute of Stress, 124 Park Ave. Yonkers, NY 10703.

Several researchers suggest that instead of trying to avoid stress altogether, the real key is to balance our lifestyle: balanced amounts of work and play, challenge and ease, stress and relaxation, companionship and solitude (Leonard, 1978; Pelletier, 1977; Selye, 1979). Even everyday tasks—driving, teaching, working around the house, or simply walking down the street—involve staying attentive, watchful, and alert. Some of the body's muscles are ready for action, the capillaries constricted to slow down circulation of the blood. The cells in those muscles produce energy, available nutrients are being used up, and the cells excrete toxic wastes. To receive the full benefit of a steady flow of blood, the cells in and around the constricted muscle need to go through their full cycle of tension, release of energy, and relaxation. Unless they complete the cycle, those cells eventually become undernourished and even drugged by the toxins that build up around them. The problem is that many muscles do not complete the cycle but rather operate "at the ready" much of the time, causing the entire body to be in a constant state of tension and thus making it more susceptible to disease.

The first step toward relieving stress is to begin paying closer attention to the physical sensations of our own body. By becoming sensitive to and intimately familiar with the signals from our body, we can prevent stress from becoming distress.

There are many strategies and forms of relaxation that can be employed in the classroom to develop the skill of physically reducing tension.

Progressive Relaxation

Progressive relaxation (Jacobson, 1957) is probably the simplest form of relaxation and involves sitting or lying in a comfortable position with your eyes closed. Concentrate on various muscles in your body, relaxing them one at a time. A systematic sequence is suggested; try starting at the top of the head and progressing to the feet, releasing each of the muscle groups in turn. Imagery may enhance the process (e.g., imagining each area is gradually turning to jelly or sinking into the floor).

Autogenic Training

This relaxation technique from the concept autogenic, meaning self-generating, originated in Germany over 40 years ago (Schultz & Luthe, 1959) and involves the use of tension and release, imagery, and mental concentration. A simple way to experience this form of relaxation is to make a fist with your right hand. As you squeeze your fist shut, push your arm away from your body. Continue pushing and squeezing until you feel discomfort in your arm, then quickly release all tension and allow your arm to hang beside your body. Notice how your hand and arm feel. Be aware that you can relax them even more. Allow your hand and arm to relax more deeply. Notice how that feels. Allow your hand to feel very heavy (it may even begin to feel a little warm). You could relax even more; however, bring your hand and arm back to their normal states by gently moving your fingers and arm. Notice the difference between your right hand and arm and the left hand and arm you have not relaxed. To avoid muscle imbalance, use the same procedure on the left hand and arm. You can use this tension-relaxation procedure on muscles throughout your body.

Mental Rehearsal

Allow your mind to move through anxiety-producing events prior to the actual confrontation. Visualize each step and each detail of the coming event. Picture the place, the people, and possible happenings. See yourself carrying out the task, dealing with any problems or obstacles that arise, and bringing it to a successful completion. Work out alternative ways of handling the event so that you will maximize flexibility when the event occurs. By carefully rehearsing the situation in your mind you can reduce the anxiety you feel and prepare yourself to give your best effort.

Students feel most anxious when faced with an examination. Anxiety interferes with the learning process not only by reducing the amount that can be learned but also by blocking the retrieval of information previously learned. The following exercise is a detailed account of a guided imagery activity to prepare for testing. Toby Manzanares, a high school biology teacher, uses this mental rehearsal to help his students lower their anxiety prior to an examination.

> *Procedure:* The following directions can be given to the class just before an examination. Allow plenty of time for them to react to the instructions. This exercise should not be rushed; the students should have the benefit of approaching an examination with their minds clear and ready. "I need you to take five cleansing breaths. . . . Inhale quietly through your nose. . . . Exhale quietly through your mouth. . . . Each time you exhale imagine that you are blowing tension out of your body. . . . Allow your eyes to close gently. . . . Feel your body soften as the tension leaves your muscles. . . . Allow any sounds that come into the classroom to float through your consciousness and back out again; you need not hold onto any of these sounds. . . . Again, take another deep cleansing breath. . . . And relax. . . . This is a special time for you to find your center. . . . Imagine that you are lying on a hilltop and watching clouds gently drift across a vivid blue sky. . . . Feel the breeze blow through your hair. . . . Feel its coolness. . . . Watch as the clouds move into different shapes. . . . Notice how relaxed your body is . . . and how comfortable you feel. . . . Imagine yourself as you take the exam. . . . Notice the look of confidence on your face, a look that reflects the confidence in your ability to remember. . . . Everything that you've ever heard is permanently recorded year after year in your brain. . . . The more relaxed you can become, the more you can remember and the greater the access to your incredible memory. . . . Notice the smile on your face as you mark the correct answers on your answer sheet, and notice how comfortable your body feels. . . . When you're ready, return to the classroom and open your eyes. . . . Remain relaxed and notice how you feel. . . . You are now in a better mental state to perform well on your exam. . . . Remember that smile of confidence as you begin. If you feel tension building, close your eyes for a moment, take a few cleansing breaths, and blow out the tension as you exhale."

In a study with gifted children involving progressive muscle relaxation and electromyogram (EMG) biofeedback, Roome and Romney (1985) found that both treatment groups showed a significant reduction in anxiety and a shift toward internal locus of control, compared with the untreated control group. Neither treatment was shown to be more effective than the other. Roome and Romney concluded that relaxation training should be considered a routine part of the education of gifted children, especially those who are underachieving, because of the evidence that it facilitates the production of cognitive-emotional states where reality testing is suspended and personal insight, creation of ideas, and inspiration are more likely to occur.

Movement and Physical Encoding

Another way to integrate physical processes into the learning experience is through movement and physical encoding, the sixth component of the IEM. Early in their schooling, gifted children can become bored with the typical physical education curriculum. For many, body coordination does not keep pace with their accelerated mental development, thereby frustrating their expectations of performance. The patience required to drill and practice assures average youngsters of adequate physical performance in games and competitive activities. Youngsters who are more accustomed to moving rapidly through new ideas and challenges often lack that patience. When their physical performance falls short of the standards they set for themselves, when their opportunities for improvement come from repetitive activity, they often choose other alternatives, such as becoming ball monitors, judges, or umpires. They even seek excuses from doctors for such problems as asthma or they find leadership or teaching roles that allow them to use their cognitive ability to advantage.

Movement can improve learning by physically encoding the most complex concepts at all ages.

Not
just
Boys

Immagane
of Tennis
Psychosynthesis
Assist to all
what we call

It is not physical movement but rather the traditional competitive system that creates the problem. Given the opportunity to structure their own physical education class, a group of gifted junior high school students turned to tennis, track events, and various mind/body integrating activities such as Yoga, T'ai-chi Ch'uan, and Aikido with enthusiasm.

Prior to the involvement in physical education classes in school, most gifted children have no problem integrating physical and mental development. A rich fantasy life creates many opportunities for young gifted children to be physically active. They could use this same ability to continue their integrative development. In some schools and in professional sports, the use of fantasy has gained acceptance and is profitably used. Hendricks and Roberts (1977) defined fantasy as "the use of the natural ability of mental imagery to enhance performance or personal growth" (p. 28). The US Olympic ski team, professional baseball and football teams, and highly successful track and field competitors have psychologists instruct them in using fantasy for improving performance. The tennis instruction methods used by Gallwey (1974) exemplify how imagining or fantasizing a correct performance actually changes the physical performance.

Dolle and Bardot (1979) reported confirmation of the importance of physical exercise on cognitive development as a result of their study exploring the influence of physical activity on mastery of cognitive structures in male and female preadolescents (11-year-olds). They made more than six times as much progress as did the controls, who also lacked the depth of understanding shown by the experimental group. The use of judo served as an integrative strategy in teaching the laws of physics. As current researchers learn more about the brain and the biochemical effects of physical exercise, such earlier studies are being validated (Restak, 2000).

When dancers listen to music, their minds very often choreograph the music and they "see" dancers moving with each passage they hear. After experiences with physical encoding, students report that they can "see" ideas physically represented or encoded even when they have not participated in actual movement. Young learners learn through physical activity; it seems curious that such activity is by design denied as a support system soon after the learner enters school. Except in a few disciplines—music, physics, chemistry, and art—learning strategies that promote movement and the physical/sensing function disappear from the curriculum. The following exercises are excellent examples of practical, effective techniques to help students grasp ideas and abstract concepts they might otherwise have problems understanding.

Fractionated Groups

This activity helps learners understand the concept of fractions. Volunteers are asked to form a small group (four to six students), and another student is then asked to use the group to show one-half of the group, one-third, one-fourth, and so forth.

All the students are asked to form groups of various sizes of their choice. They add, subtract, multiply, and divide fraction problems using their group, then work problems with mixed fractions by using their group and other groups.

Example: A group has six members. They are to find one-half of the group. The group must divide themselves in half. A group of five members will notice the difficulty and the need to have a remainder.

Example: Groups are asked to add one-half and one-third. They must first find one-half of one group and one-third of another and then add them together.

A discussion of each problem should be held with the entire class after a group demonstrates a solution. A guided imagery exercise in which the students imagine groups moving could be the next step. This activity precedes pencil and paper work.

INTEGRATING INTUITIVE PROCESSES

The seventh and last component of the IEM integrates the least understood and yet the most powerful area of human brain function, intuition (Figure 11.3). It is probably the area with the greatest promise for the continuance and fulfillment of humankind. All other areas of the brain provide support for and are supported by this area of function. As each area evolves to higher levels, more of the intuitive and creative functions become available (Diamond, 1998, Restak, 2000).

A strange paradox exists in this area of function. According to neurobiologists, the prefrontal cortex is the most uniquely human area of the brain. It is species specific; that is, humans share this area of the brain with no other life form. The functions of this area, however, are those least discussed by researchers, least recognized by educators, and most ridiculed by otherwise intelligent, thoughtful people. One thing is certain: This area of brain function is seldom discussed without some kind of emotional response.

The functions of the prefrontal cortex seem to include future planning, insight, empathy, introspection, and other bases for intuitive thought (MacLean, 1978). It is engaged in firming up intention, deciding on action, and regulating our most complex behaviors (Restak, 2000). Siegel (1999) notes that the prefrontal cortex allows our neural responses to reflect the significance of events. The prefrontal cortex is, in fact, the area that energizes and regulates all other parts: It houses our purpose.

The prefrontal lobes of the cortex play a critical role in high-level intellectual and emotional operations, curiously probing for and monitoring input, analyzing and synthesizing incoming information, excluding the irrelevant, and then referring the new information to memory. Later these areas reconstruct from scraps whole and relevant memories, taking the outward leap of hunches and fantasy, guessing and postulating, carrying the mind into the future, making plans, shaping strategies for goals, forecasting, and then making readjustments to fit new perceptions and new goals. Emotionally these areas will provide empathy and cues to sociability, the basis for a communal spirit, and a moral sense (Loye, 1983). Goodman (1978) specifically placed these functions in the area of the prefrontal cortex. Diamond (1998) observes that a high density of contacts between nerve-cell branches occurs by age 10 years and states that "the early maturing of the prefrontal cortex is one of the hallmarks of human intelligence" (p. 118).

Those most responsible for changing our culture (Plato, Newton, da Vinci, Einstein, etc.); important poets, musicians, and artists (Keats, Mozart, Monet, etc.); philosophers, mathematicians, psychologists, and educators (Pythagoras, Tesla, Jung, etc.); and modern scientists (Bohm, Prigogine, Pribram, etc.) all wrote about

Figure 11.3 *Intuition: Another Way of Knowing*

Intuition is:

- A highly synthetic and dynamic process that integrates all other brain functions.
- Most accessible when one is in a relaxed state of mind and body.
- Inhibited by fear, tension, and stress. The harder we try to grasp it, the less available it becomes. It is the first area of brain function to drop out when anxiety becomes too high.
- Difficult to communicate in a rational, linear mode and is often symbolic in nature. The vocabulary for expressing intuitive experiences is limited.
- Free of the need to see the world in dichotomies, but is a merging of opposites. (E. G., wrong answers are often the best way to learn the correct information. The view of reality includes unity and separation together, self as a part of the world and at the same time apart from the world.)
- A natural process that can be encouraged and developed and that seems to improve with use.
- Productive of insights, creative products and solutions, and affective actions.
- Usually following and based on an accumulation of skill or knowledge.
- Complementary to analytical thinking.
- Instantaneously knowing, complete, and often spontaneous.

(Bruner, 1960; Capra, 1982; Goldberg, 1983; Loye, 1983; Luria, 1973)

Intuition is fostered by:

- A relaxed state.
- Silence.
- Focused attention.
- A receptive, nonjudgmental attitude.
- An ability to synthesize all brain functions.
- Novelty and variety in the environment.
- A teacher who values and encourages intuitive processes; provides opportunities for educated guessing, hypothesis setting, and probability testing; is comfortable with mistakes, both the students' and personal; emphasizes personal discovery over memorization of facts; and models intuitive behavior.

(Bruner, 1960; Galin, 1976; Goldberg, 1983; Loye, 1983; Raudsepp, 1980)

Intuition is inhibited by:

- Focusing on mistakes instead of successes.
- Avoiding change; seeking control and predictability.
- Adhering rigidly to rules and set procedures.
- Anticipating disasters instead of miracles.
- Taking ourselves, our work, and our problems too seriously.

Figure 11.3 *continued*

- Relying heavily on analytic procedures.

(Bruner, 1960; Galin, 1976; Goldberg, 1983; Loye, 1983; Raudsepp, 1980)

Intuitive thinkers:

- Accept and trust the intuitive process.
- Are unconventional and willing to take risks.
- Are confident, secure, and independent.
- Think holistically.
- Enjoy abstract thinking.
- Focus on outcomes, the long-term view.
- Are frequently involved in art, drama, and/or music.
- Read enthusiastically.
- Tolerate ambiguity and change and are flexible.
- Are playful, whimsical, and enjoy humor and informality.

(Goldberg, 1983; Krippner, 1983; Raudsepp, 1980; Wescott, 1968)

Intuitive thinkers prefer:

- Generating possibilities beyond what is present, obvious, or known.
- Generating ideas rather than putting them into action.
- Having their own way of doing things.
- Being patient with complicated details.
- Working best in bursts of energy powered by enthusiasm.
- Being comfortable with open-ended tasks.
- Desiring to achieve important solutions to long-range and important social problems.
- Working continuously when interest is aroused.
- Learning new skills even if not put to use.

(Hanson, Silver, & Strong, 1984)

The teacher's role is to:

- Create a psychologically safe environment.
- Model valuing and using intuitive ability.
- Use imagery, fantasy, and visualization to support learning.
- Develop relaxed attention in the classroom.
- Develop a nonjudgmental and receptive attitude.
- Use "what if" and open-ended future-thinking strategies.
- Use strategies that stretch intuitive ability, such as estimation, prediction, and "best guesses."
- Give students opportunities to engage in creative behavior.
- Encourage students to value their hunches and insights.

the use of intuition in their great discoveries and creative contributions. Although these eminent contributors to our culture highly valued these abilities, schools do nothing to enhance intuitive abilities but rather ignore or actually inhibit their use.

The business community, a group whose organizations and techniques are so often used as models for making schools more efficient and effective, shows interest in intuition, especially the type of intuitive ability that allows prediction and forecasting. This interest is reflected in the increasing number of articles being written by and for the business community regarding the importance of the hunch in making executive decisions and the correlation between success in business and intuitive ability. Screening tests are available to help those hiring at the executive level to know which prospective candidate for an executive position ranks highest in intuitive ability (Goldberg, 1983; Loye, 1983).

Stories of those who have used the intuitive hunch successfully are part of the literature of success in business (Dean, Mihalasky, Ostrander, & Schroeder, 1974). Ray Kroc was advised by his staff, his board, and all those he consulted not to buy a small hamburger chain that he was considering purchasing. He had a nagging hunch that he could not dismiss and, after several days of personal introspection, called his lawyer and ordered him to buy McDonald's. As he said later, "I felt in my funny bone it was a sure thing" (Goldberg, 1983).

Agor (cited in Ferguson, 1986b) contends that top executives have an integrated style and can function both intuitively and analytically. He believes that use of intuition is essential in areas such as marketing, intelligence work, sales, and emergency-care nursing. His work leads him to the conclusion that people can ground and fine-tune their intuition simply by noticing the function more and more.

Cognitive psychologist Arthur Reber (cited in Guillen, 1984) found that people who intuit their way through subtle tasks actually have a competitive edge over those who consciously try to think their way through. He found this to be true of complicated tasks in reading, writing, composing music, and inventing scientific theories. In actual practice, a synthesis of the two modes of learning—analyzing and intuiting—is preferable to use of just one or the other.

The intuitive process seems to be highly synthetic and dynamic, drawing from and integrating all other brain functions. This integrative characteristic allows the intuitive process to be compared with creativity. It is my belief that these two terms may be referring to the same human ability; the processes are quite similar regardless of which term is used. The integration of all of our human functions—thinking, feeling, and sensing—releases intuition, as well as creativity. Restricting any one of these functions restricts intuition and thus creativity. Intuition requires synthesis of all functioning, as well as a spark from another dimension; so does creativity. Creative and intuitive processes seem to be expressions of the highest level of human intelligence. Although this discussion will focus on the intuitive process, the reader should note the similarity to discussions of the concept of creativity. Creativity may, in fact, be a part of the intuitive process.

Defining Intuition

Different investigators find different ways of viewing and defining intuition. Jung (1933) referred to intuition as one of the four basic human functions. Bruner (1960) discussed intuition as an important part of the education process and encouraged its training. Expanding on the work of Loye (1983), and for the purposes of our discussion and the development of implementation strategies, let us think of intuition as occurring on at least three levels: rational, predictive, and transformational.

Rational Intuition

Although this may seem to be a contradiction of terms, rational intuition expresses a level of intuitive behavior that realigns known information in such a way that new insights emerge. We intuit the next step to take in solving a problem, evaluating alternatives, diagnosing a treatment, or resolving a personal crisis. Although we know the facts, we see them in a new light, put them together in a new way, or infer from the past the direction to be taken. This area of intuition relies heavily on the highly synthetic characteristic of the intuition process. By combining all our consciously known information with information we once processed but no longer consciously have available, new alignments and new patterns seem to emerge.

Predictive Intuition

The predictive level enlarges on the processes of the rational level by including new information within existing patterns or sequences. Predictive intuition includes the ability to complete unfinished pictures, see a gestalt from little information, and gain accurate insights not previously available with the given information. This level also builds on the first level by including unknown, or only suspected, information within the synthesis process. This is the level of the hunch, the "best guess," the perception of the whole picture when only the parts can be seen by others. Here an unconscious impression or information from some seemingly unknown source becomes an important part of the new patterns formed, the insights, or the profound conclusions. An individual may arrive at a solution to a problem while remaining unaware of the process involved. Some call this process creativity (Goldberg, 1983).

This type of intuitive process is responsible for many breakthrough discoveries. The "Aha!" experience that comes after perhaps months or years of extensive preparation and that appears when the person is relaxed or involved in an entirely different task is a part of this level of intuition. The experience is euphoric, the solution suddenly absolutely clear. At this level the brain perceives matters with a holistic, gestalt awareness, rather than in a linear, sequential mode.

This level of intuition is responsible for the forecasting of trends and the intuitive leap so valued in business, diplomacy, science, economics, and personal life decisions. Loye (1983) believed that the very best forecasting is done by those who can access all four functions: thinking, feeling, sensing, and intuiting.

Transformational Intuition

This third level of intuitive processing is the most fascinating and the most awesome. When operating on this transformational level, a person seems to be using a different kind of sensing that "picks up information through a means that has defied scientific understanding" (Loye, 1983, p. 52). Those who have received information at this level often report that ideas came to them suddenly, unbidden or in a dream, or that what they wrote came through them as if from an outside source. Brier and Tyminski (1970) concluded that such ability may be common to us all, but for most it is a very weak signal that is usually missed owing to the noise of everyday living.

Another way that this level of intuition may appear is as a coincidence, or what Jung calls synchronicity. These are happenings where events that have no apparent causal connection occur in such a way as to give meaning or significant impact. We seem to be at the right place at the right time, or we think of someone and very soon that person appears.

Finally, this level of intuition can be experienced as transcendence. This level can be observed within the brain as a change in the rate of coherence or the correlation between brain waves from separate regions of the brain. This coherence seems to be at its highest during transcendence (Goldberg, 1983). This highest form of knowing occurs when one knows totally the universe, the self, and the connection between the two. Maslow (1971) began to explore this way of knowing just before his death, and his final work predicted that psychology would become more involved in the transpersonal and in transcendence. Eastern mystics seek this elevated state of knowledge, as do the spiritual of many faiths. Variously known as enlightenment, illumination, ecstasy, or by other similar terms, this form of intuition is the ultimate experience, the drawing together of all other forms of intuitive process.

Intuition has been conceptualized as synonymous with expertise in one view, and with perception in another. Simon (cited in Benderly, 1989) believed that expertise and intuition are not separate phenomena but aspects of the same thing. He further believed that intuition may be an ability that individuals can work toward and organizations can foster. People who seek to become intuitive must master a particular, even if limited, field of knowledge. From such mastery comes a different way of thinking than that used by novices. Experts possess rapid access to and efficient use of an organized body of conceptual and procedural knowledge. Glaser and Chi (cited in Benderly, 1989) expanded this thesis by adding the concept of chunking, the process of bringing large blocks of knowledge out of long-term memory in order to solve problems. This process is possible for experts, say Glaser and Chi, not because of their superior short- and long-term memory but because their expertise allows them to automatize many portions of their skills, thus freeing their resources for greater storage. According to Glaser, expertise is gained when we continually confront new situations in terms of what we already know. The development of intuition will then depend on our ability to perceive large, meaningful patterns as we take on problems that go beyond what we have already mastered and organize information in a way that relates it to specific goals, classifying and reclassifying knowledge as we learn more.

Barrett (1989) uses perception as the process to explain intuition. He views intuition as having perceptual characteristics: pattern recognition, suddenness, illumination, and direct knowledge unmediated by logic or reason. According to Barrett, intuition can work on internal or external objects and things. Synthesis and the phenomenon called holism are involved in all creation. Images play an important part in creating this holism, and imagination is a valuable tool of intuition. Barrett concluded:

> The inventor applies perception and intuition by using the mind's eye to perceive/ intuit WHAT IS POSSIBLE. Rather than seeing things after they exist innovators and inventors perceive them BEFORE they exist. . . . Reason and logic are applied AFTER we have arrived at the discovery, insight or idea in order to check whether it is really as valid as we first felt. (p. 3)

Using Intuition

Intuition is always available to us. Huxley (1962) believed that intuitive ability could be developed and viewed cognition as a conscious, active power and intuition as a complementary, receptive power. "Both kinds of training," he wrote, "are absolutely indispensable. If you neglect either you'll never grow into a fully human being" (p. 255).

Intuition can be quite fascinating to discuss, but what is its value in the classroom? Let us look at history for some possible reasons to include intuitive process skills in our concern for optimal learning. Goldberg (1983) shared the following insights on using intuition:

> In the original manuscript describing his sun-centered cosmos, Copernicus mentioned the possibility that planetary motion might be elliptical rather than circular. He crossed it out. History credits the discovery of Johannes Kepler, who also had turned his back on the idea for three years before accepting it. "Why should I mince my words?" Kepler wrote. "The truth of Nature, which I had rejected and chased away, returned by stealth through the back door, disguising itself to be accepted. Ah, what a foolish bird I have been!" Kepler finally opened the door to elliptical motion, but, in turn, he closed it to universal gravitation, leaving that gem for Newton.
>
> When you find yourself leaning away from an intuitive idea, you may be acting like a "foolish bird." (pp. 195–196)

The physicist Capra (1975) wrote that rational knowing is useless if not accompanied and enhanced by intuitive knowing, equating intuition with new creative insights. Many of those working to include intuition in the classroom believe that the ability to concentrate with unusual clarity on complex tasks is a result of the intuitive function.

Gifted students have been found to be predominantly intuitive in their processing of information and use a high degree of feeling in decision-making (Hanson, Silver, & Strong, 1984).

Fostering Intuition

Clark (1977) gives three basic steps for developing our intuitive abilities: quiet the mind, focus attention, and use a receptive attitude. These simple steps cannot be developed unless teachers regularly allow time for them, practice them, and value the outcomes. This is not a one-time-only exercise or strategy. Creating a space in the room for thinking intuitively is a possibility.

The intuitive process seems to be triggered by a number of practices or skills that can be incorporated into the curriculum, allowing students to release more of their intuition and to become more creative. Students can expect to make impressive gains in the areas of cognition, self-concept, and social-emotional development by using intuition-incorporating strategies. Among the cognitive gains are accelerated learning, higher levels of retention and recall, and higher interest in content. Other areas that will show improvement include the student's sense of competency, pleasure derived from learning, and interpersonal relations, as well as teacher-student rapport (Bordan & Schuster, 1976; Galyean, 1977–1980; Galyean, 1978–1981; Lozanov, 1977; Prichard & Taylor, 1980; Samples, 1975).

As in other integrative work, we begin with relaxation and tension reduction, using any of the relaxation techniques suggested earlier in this chapter. Nervousness, fear, and tension block even learned knowledge. To release intuitive ability, we reduce tension (Assagioli, 1973; Roberts & Clark, 1976). Teaching techniques that reduce tension allow more interaction between the cortical hemispheres and better integration of their specializations. The resulting relaxation allows students to gain access to higher centers of the brain/mind system and to produce biochemical support for the learning process (Hart, 1978; Restak, 1979).

At home, parents can begin by valuing and trusting their own intuition. How many times have you known, really known, how you wanted to do something, but for whatever reason allowed yourself to do it another, possibly more "sensible" way, only to discover later that your original idea would have worked much better? Trusting ourselves to know what is best for us is not easy. We often allow outside pressures to influence any use we might make of this type of knowledge. Begin by demonstrating the usefulness of your knowing as often as possible. Listen to yourself and act on that information more often. Then observe and discover your children's inner rhythms and ideas. Children are more in touch with intuition than are adults. They do not have to work as hard to regain their intuitive power. Find ways to draw out their ideas and show that you respect and value them. The inhibition of this ability begins when children find it ridiculed or devalued by those important to them.

Imagery, Fantasy, and Visualization

The techniques of imagery, fantasy, and visualization are important components in developing intuitive ability. Noted scientists Faraday, Galton, and Einstein reported solving scientific problems in visual images and only afterwards translating their thoughts into words. In current brain research, the terminology for being able to reproduce that which is no longer visible is "working memory" (Restak, 2000). Restak reports that the area of the brain most active in effortful consciousness is the prefrontal cortex.

> In a famous instance of the use of this area, Einstein, unable to reconcile his special theory of relativity with Newtonian physics, pictured a box falling freely down a very long shaft; inside it, an occupant took coins and keys out of his pocket and let them go. The objects, Einstein saw, remained in midair, alongside him, because they were falling at the same rate as he—a situation temporarily identical with being in space, beyond any gravitational field. From this visual construct, Einstein was able to sense some of those seemingly contradictory relationships about movement and rest, acceleration and gravity, that he later put into mathematical and verbal form in his general theory of relativity. (Hunt, 1982, p. 215)

Singer (1976) believed that the foundation for serenity and purpose in our lives may lie in fantasy. He found that those who have trouble using fantasy to enrich their lives or to substitute for aggression have serious problems. Children whose games are lacking in fantasy have trouble recalling facts and integrating events. In adolescence, these children are dependent on the external environment and may engage in antisocial, delinquent, and aggressive acts as a result of their inability to internalize humanistic attitudes. As adults, their problems increase and "their inner experiences seem less insistent than even the most irrelevant physical fact of their immediate environment" (Singer, 1976, p. 34). Alcoholism, obesity, and drug abuse may be the consequences of such an impoverished inner life.

Nurturing the growth of fantasy is easy. Using sound effects and voice changes while reading to children and allowing them to make up plays, to finish open-ended stories, and to play pretending games all provide opportunities for such development. A climate that encourages the sharing of fantasies will allow those fantasies to become the basis for books, reports, poems, and journals.

Meier (cited in Ferguson, 1984) found that college students using mental imagery performed 12% better on immediate recall and 26% better on long-term retention than did those students not using it. He commented, "We all possess the world's finest multi-sensory teaching machine right inside our own heads. . . . We need to give mental imagery the same attention we are giving to sophisticated, computer-driven audiovisual learning devices" (p. 3).

Kosslyn (1985) reports on research that shows successful uses of imagery as (1) a substitute for actual practice in performing some activity; (2) a stand-in for perceptual stimulation, producing effects such as those evoked when subjects actually view a stimulus; and (3) a part of an individual's reasoning skills. It seems that imagery is not a single ability but rather an integration of many abilities.

Imagery represents the process of creating and intellectual problem-solving as much as any other abstract process encouraged by schools. Roodin (1983) suggests the use of imagery in helping children to remember. By establishing vivid images of the items that are to be recalled, their ability to remember is heightened. He asks us to consider that imagery is not restricted to the visual mode alone, but can stimulate sound, taste, smell, and touch. We are reading of more and more musicians, artists, and athletes who make good use of such images. Roodin commented that, "Regardless of the domain, imagery appears useful in the creative process and is, in fact, a major component of flexibility in thinking. . . . In fact, imagery has been reported to provide greater flexibility than verbal techniques in a variety of problem-solving situations" (p. 6).

Imagery can serve the adolescent well as thoughts of future goals and careers begin to be explored. Gifted adolescents are especially able to project the future and to evaluate the emotional satisfactions, personal identity, and specialized roles that a career may involve. Such a tool must become more available in the classroom. The following exercises use mental imagery in three different subject areas.

Spelling Ask the students to gently close their eyes, then ask them to see in their mind's eye something to write on—a chalkboard, a piece of paper, sand, and so forth. Ask them to write (or print, if younger children are involved) each word as you spell it. Ask them to visualize each word clearly. Ask them to gently open their eyes and look at each word as you have written it and compare it with their own image. Later have them see their imagined list of words again. Remind them to check their list image when they are spelling each word as you check for retention.

Math To teach concepts such as diameter, radius, and circumference, ask students to close their eyes and visualize a large, round swimming pool. Ask them to swim around the edge of the pool; they are now swimming the circumference of the pool. Ask them to swim from the side to the middle of the pool; they are now swimming the radius of the pool. Ask them to swim back to the edge and then swim directly from one side of the pool to the other; they are now swimming the diameter of the pool. Ask the students to gently open their eyes and draw each way they just swam. Write the words on the board and ask them to use those words in describing the route they swam.

Composition Galyean (1983) reported that very original and creative compositions can be elicited from students by using their own internal images. For example, ask the students to write about "Things I Like at School" and "Things That Bother Me at School." Begin the lesson by asking the students to close their eyes and imagine themselves as photographers taking pictures of things they like and do not like around the school. After they have had sufficient time to "see" several photos for each topic, ask them to draw and write about their topics using the pictures they just "took" with their mind camera. Galyean found that this intuitive beginning helps students to succeed in their writing.

Alternative Ways of Knowing and Futuristics

Good decision-making and the development of intelligence are highly dependent on our ability to produce and evaluate alternatives. Probability guessing is an activity that brings the intuitive function into the learning process.

For example, when the Westward Movement is the topic of study, the teacher might ask the students to consider the following: What if France had not been willing to sell the Louisiana Territory? What if there had been twice as many Indians living on the Great Plains? What if gold had not been discovered in California and Colorado? This kind of "what if" questioning can lead to some interesting discussions and motivate students to learn more. Once students feel safe in the environment provided and know that teachers value and encourage their intuitive ability, teachers will learn a great deal from them about intuitive functioning. As with all other human abilities, intuition improves with use.

Student-generated scenarios forecasting future events are another natural result of alternative thinking. The field of futuristics—the study of alternative futures (Kauffman, 1976)—is rich in the use of intuitive processing. There is no one future; instead, we have the opportunity to collectively create among a number of possibilities.

The intuitive skill of forecasting is important in the development of future scenarios. Lahe (1985) pointed out that both futuristics and gifted education emphasize higher level thinking skills, creativity, learning beyond the classroom, enrichment, and affective needs, all of which make the classroom for the gifted a good place for this type of program. At the very least, futurists believe that, from the activities involved in looking at alternative futures, gifted children will develop a positive image of the future. This could be very important to how the future will take shape.

If ever a society needed the wisdom and inspiration of intuitive people, it is ours. A growing awareness of the contribution of intuitive and integrative processes in our lives is now taking place.

Studying the Future: Creating an Optimal Reality

Throughout history there have been people and moments that have brought dramatic change to all who followed. It is now becoming increasingly evident that such times are occurring with greater frequency, and the need for gifted people to bring vision to these times is of foremost concern. How can we, who are most concerned with the nurture of gifted people, help provide the experiences and the tools, the attitudes, and the commitment they will need to optimize the future of us all? That is the mission of a group of educators who are increasing in number and organizational strength each year. Their academic discipline, most commonly called future studies, deals with the process of change, alternative thinking, choice, self-concept, values, and the development of optimistic images of the future. A futurist must deal comfortably with uncertainties, open-ended situations, and vastly divergent possibilities. Cornish (1977), a futurist with the World Future Society, believed it imperative that we study the future so that we may:

- Forecast crises so that they may be averted.
- Assist in deciding the future we want.
- Be prepared to live in a changing world.
- Discover a format for working together cooperatively.
- Contribute to and participate in the furtherance of science and thought.
- Encourage more creativity.
- Increase the motivation to learn.
- Provide for the development of a well-balanced and integrated personal value structure and philosophy of life.
- Provide a means for recreation and fun.

In underscoring our need to include the study of the future, Goodlad (cited in Silvernail, 1980) stated, "Other generations believed that they had the luxury of preparing their children to live in a society similar to their own. Ours is the first generation to have achieved the Socratic wisdom of knowing that we do not know the world in which our children will live" (p. 17). Undoubtedly all children will need the attitudes, skills, and information that would result from the future studies curricula, but for gifted students some special benefits and corresponding special responsibilities are involved. One of the most obvious reasons for the involvement in gifted education comes from the needs and characteristics of the gifted themselves. The interdisciplinary nature will appeal to children who think in diverse ways and who see unusual relationships. The higher levels of thinking will meet needs that these children rarely have met in their educational experiences. The challenge of delving into unknown areas will appeal to the gifted of all ages, and the support for self-actualization, creative thinking, and value exploration will further the search for higher values that is characteristic of so many gifted individuals. It seems that the correlation between the needs of the gifted and the goals of programs in future studies is significant and meaningful.

The curriculum of future studies can be quite varied. Silvernail (1980) suggests that a futuristic curriculum contain the following components:

- Basic skills, both the traditional three R's and new skills, such as skill in humanistic processes, cross-disciplinary understandings, computer language, research skills, anticipatory skills of seeing relationships and taking action on evaluated data, skills based on cross-cultural and multi-ethnic insights, and change skills.
- Study of the future that would include examination of the past and emerging issues and developing creative plans for action.
- Self-concept.
- Self-actualization—the exploration and planning for personal futures.
- Valuing.

Torrance's Future Problem Solving Program is a program in future studies that began operation during the early 1970s and by 1981 involved more than 75,000 gifted students in grades 4 through 12 throughout the United States (Torrance, Blume, Maryanopolis, Murphey, & Rogers, 1980; Torrance, 1981). The program consists of a year-long curriculum project and a local, state, and national interscholastic team and individual competition. Its goal is to provide experiences that will allow gifted students to make a constructive difference in the future through development of creative problem-solving skills; through skills of teamwork, cooperation, and communication; through an international sense; and through enlarging, and enriching, more accurate images of the future. The program has established statewide and national networks of interaction among students and teachers interested in future studies and in affecting the world of the future.

Torrance and Torrance (1981) summarized the importance of future studies in the gifted curriculum:

> Perhaps the most important challenge in educating gifted, talented, and creative students for the future is to help them acquire a positive image of the future—especially a positive image of their own future careers. Positive images of the future seem to have a powerful and magnetic force. Our future images draw on us and energize us. They give us the courage and will to take important initiatives to "make a difference" in the future. (pp. 45–46)

Sample Lessons for Integrating Intellectual Processes

The Teacher's Planning Sheet for Integrative Lessons (Figure 11.4) presents a structure or format that can be used over and over to help plan for integrative learning regardless of the subject or content. The sheet serves as a reminder to include all

Figure 11.4 *Teacher's Planning Sheet for Integrative Lessons*

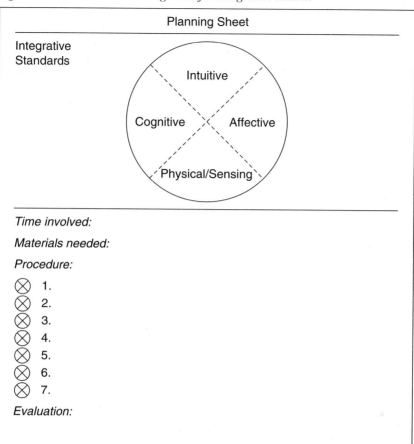

human functions and also allows more effectiveness with less time involved. Teachers can see at a glance what they want the students to learn, what brain functions will be used in that learning, and the strategies that will be used to include them. The five integrative lessons presented in this chapter use this format.

The Integrative Standards section of the lesson or unit is divided into the four areas of the IEM. The brain functions are represented by the dissected circle with four areas of function, designated C (cognitive), P (physical/sensing), A (affective), and I (intuitive). The larger circle will allow a place to state the goal or standard to be achieved in each area of process. Not all lessons or units will be planned to meet standards in all four areas; however, by organizing in this way, the amount of class time spent on each area of growth becomes apparent.

The Time Involved and Materials Needed sections allow for preplanning to aid in the efficiency and effectiveness of the lesson or unit. The Procedure section gives step-by-step directions for implementation and includes strategies that will be used to create optimal learning. By filling in the appropriate area(s) of the smaller circles at the front of each procedure of the learning experience, the teacher indicates the function in which the student will be involved. When one function is overused or another is omitted, it is easy to see and correct. Finally, the Evaluation section of the lesson or unit will depend on the Integrative Standards stated; whatever procedure is designed for evaluation should collect data that directly assesses the level of attainment of these standards.

Integrative Lesson 11.1 helps students learn new words.

Integrative Lesson 11.1 A Personal Word List

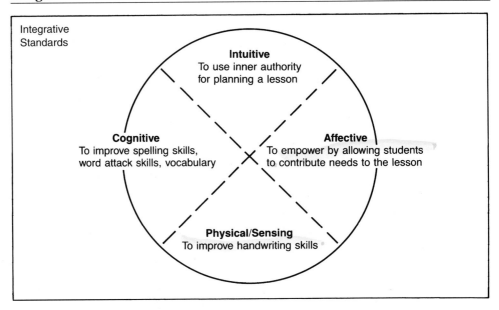

Integrative Standards

Intuitive
To use inner authority for planning a lesson

Cognitive
To improve spelling skills, word attack skills, vocabulary

Affective
To empower by allowing students to contribute needs to the lesson

Physical/Sensing
To improve handwriting skills

Time involved: 15 to 20 minutes

Materials needed: Chalkboard

Procedure:

1. Ask students to find any new or difficult-to-remember words from the new story that was just read.
2. Ask them to gently close their eyes and see three new or difficult words inside their head. "Now open your eyes and let's put them on the board."
3. The teacher writes words on the board as children call them out.
4. The teacher then says, "Notice how you feel about each of these words. If some of them are new or difficult for you, you can borrow them from the person who gave them to us. They can be added to the words on your list."
5. Ask the children to choose one word from their lists; have one child at a time act out a word for the others to guess.

Evaluation: Notice the level of improvement in reading and writing activities.

Integrative Lesson 11.2 gives an example of a self-knowledge lesson on the body (Clark, 1986, p. 198).

Integrative Lesson 11.2 Inner and Outer Space

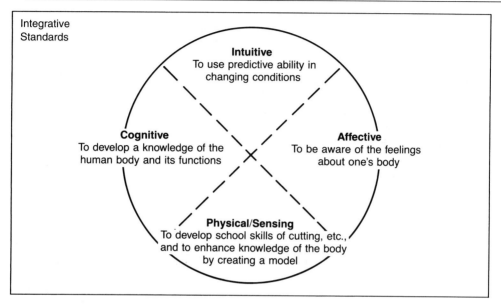

Time involved: 20 to 30 minutes

Materials needed: Butcher paper in a large roll, scissors, colored markers, crayons, paste

Procedure:

1. Invite children to cut a piece of butcher paper large enough for them to lie on. Ask them to estimate the size.

2. Ask the children to lie down on their piece of butcher paper. Trace around their body or allow a partner to do so. Encourage them to lie in any action position they feel good about.

3. Ask the children to cut out their figure and then trace and cut another piece of paper exactly like the first. Attach the two figures at the top of the head.

4. Have the children look into a mirror to help them draw their likeness on one of the papers. They may wish to draw in clothing with their crayons.

5. Now ask the children to close their eyes and imagine the inside of their bodies. Take a fantasy journey through the body, describing the location, shape, and function of each part of the body and its organs.

6. Invite the students to take colored paper or to color paper and cut out organs, such as the heart, the lungs, and the stomach. Ask them to place them inside the body by lifting up the outside paper image and attaching the organs to the second paper figure.

7. Ask the students, "What makes your chest move? Where does the air you breathe go? Can you feel your heart? What does it do? Why is it important? Where does the food go? What does the brain do?" and so on.

8. Hang finished life-size figures around the classroom.

Evaluation: Given a blank schematic of a body and a list of organ names, ask the students to fill in, appropriately, the organs and their names. Then choose one organ and describe its functions.

Integrative Lesson 11.3 addresses measurement and its uses.

Integrative Lesson 11.3 Measuring, Estimating, Graphing

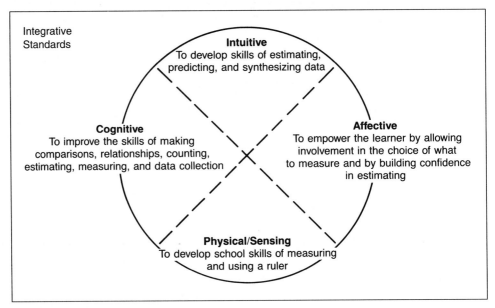

Integrative Standards

Intuitive
To develop skills of estimating, predicting, and synthesizing data

Cognitive
To improve the skills of making comparisons, relationships, counting, estimating, measuring, and data collection

Affective
To empower the learner by allowing involvement in the choice of what to measure and by building confidence in estimating

Physical/Sensing
To develop school skills of measuring and using a ruler

Time involved: 20 to 30 minutes

Materials needed: 10 to 20 "feet" (cardboard cutouts of feet exactly 12″ long); rulers; paste; small containers that hold 1, 2, 3, and 4 cups; containers holding 4 to 6 ounces; rice; cornmeal; gravel; water; paper; crayons; 10″ × 24″ piece of cardboard; 1″ × 10″ strips of construction paper in two colors; clothespins with names of children printed on them; tape to protect edges of board.

Procedure:

Measurement

1. Ask children to choose objects or areas they would like to measure. Show the children a "foot" and ask them to estimate how many feet they think will be in their chosen object or area.

2. Give the children each a "foot" and allow them to measure their chosen object or area.

3. Ask the children to draw their object or area and write the number of "feet" they found it to be.

4. Encourage the children to measure with other things like hands, books, pencils, etc., e.g., "How many books high is the door?"

5. Ask, "How many things did you find that were _____ feet long? How close to your guess was the measurement? Which things are longer? Shorter? The same?"

Estimating

1. Ask the children to predict how many cups can be filled from each container. Have the children write their predictions on a piece of paper in front of the containers.

2. Have the children experiment and check their estimates.

3. Discuss how close the prediction came to the actual measurement. "What did you find? Which container filled the most cups? Is that what you thought would happen? Which containers are largest? Smallest? The same?"

4. "How did you feel when you had more cups than you predicted you would? When you had fewer? When you came very close?"

Graphing

⊗ 1. Ask the children to decide what they would like to find out about their classmates (e.g., their favorite fruit, animals, and colors). Explain that they will survey the class to get that information.

⊗ 2. Have the children decide on two possible choices that the person surveyed could make, (e.g., "Is your favorite color red or blue?") Have them draw or color a picture to represent each category and clip each picture to opposite sides of the cardboard chart.

⊗ 3. Have the children predict which color will get the most votes.

⊗ 4. Using a clothespin to represent each person in the room, have the children conduct their survey and place the clothespins on the appropriate sides of the chart.

⊗ 5. Ask the children to summarize their data. "What did you find out? How many children did you ask? What color was chosen most? What does that mean? Which color do you like best? How do you feel about the class choice?"

Evaluation: Ask each student to use measurement, estimation, and graphing to answer the following question: Are there more boys or more girls in our class that are more than 5 feet tall?

Integrative Lesson 11.4 presents an example of a geography lesson developed in part from a lesson by Beverly Galyean (Clark, 1986, pp. 199–200).

Integrative Lesson 11.4 California (Your State's Name)

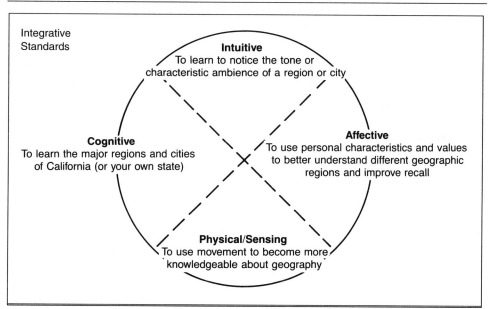

Time involved: 30 to 40 minutes

Materials needed: A large floor map of California, Values Guide Statements (Figure 11.6)

Procedure:

⊗ 1. Ask students to read the section of the text that discusses cities and regions of California

⊗ 2. Write the names of California cities on slips of paper and put them in a bag, then ask the students to draw several slips from the bag (the number depends on the time allowed for this activity). When it is their turn, the children move one at a time to

Figure 11.5 *Values Guide Statements*
Developed by Beverly Galyean.

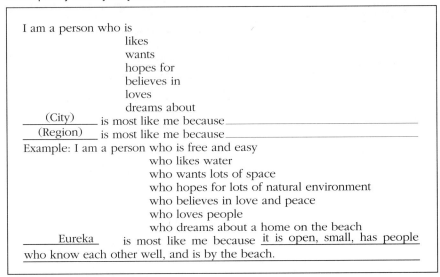

the floor map and walk from their home city to the city on their slip of paper (e.g., if they live in Los Angeles and they have drawn Fresno, they must find both on the map and walk from Los Angeles to Fresno).

3. When each arrives at the destination, ask the class to share all they can remember about the city and the region in which the student now stands.

4. After most of the cities and regions have been described, ask the students to fill out the Values Guide Statements (Figure 11.5).

5. After the students have filled out their individual guides, have them form small groups to discuss their results.

6. As part of the small group discussion, ask the students to predict what will happen to "their" city and region in the next 10 years.

7. Discuss in a total group.

Evaluation: Give each student an unmarked floor map and a list of the major regions and cities of California. Then ask each student to plan a family trip, visiting at least six of the cities and showing the route. Have the students write a tour guide explaining why they chose each site to visit.

Integrative Lesson 11.5 is a sample physiology lesson.

Integrative Lesson 11.5 The Heart and the Human Circulatory System

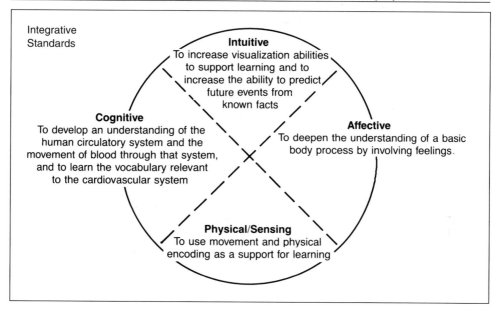

Developed by Tobias Manzanares

Time involved: One 50-minute class period

Materials needed: 30 red and 30 blue cards or pieces of construction paper, movable classroom furniture

Procedure:

1. Ask students to draw the diagram of the circulatory system (see Figure 11.6).

2. Ask the students to visualize the room as a human body, with the desks arranged in the center of the room to represent the four-chambered heart. Ask for volunteers to represent the brain, the lungs, and the digestive tract. Direct them to their appropriate places in the room (body).

3. Distribute one red and one blue card to each of the remaining students. They are now red blood cells. When they reach the lungs and become oxygenated they are to hold up the red card until they reach an organ using oxygen, where they will lower their red card and raise their blue card representing deoxygenated blood. The blue card will be held overhead until they reach the lungs to be recharged with oxygen.

4. With the red card in their right hand and the blue card in their left, have students begin a walk-through of the cycle using the following sequence: right atrium, right ventricle, pulmonary artery, lungs, pulmonary veins, left atrium, left ventricle, aorta, upper body (brain) or lower body (digestive tract), superior vena cava or inferior vena cava, right atrium. This completes the cycle and begins the next trip.

5. Ask for a student volunteer to retrace the 10 sequential steps (assist the student as necessary).

6. Instruct the remaining students to fall in line behind the student leader to begin the first cycle. As the student red blood cells pass, remind the students representing the lungs to raise their right hands (red cards); as the students pass those representing the brain or intestine, remind them to lower the red cards and raise the blue cards. Instruct the student red blood cells to name out loud each of the 10 structures as they pass these locations in the room.

Figure 11.6 *The Heart and Circulatory System*
Developed by Toby Manzanares.

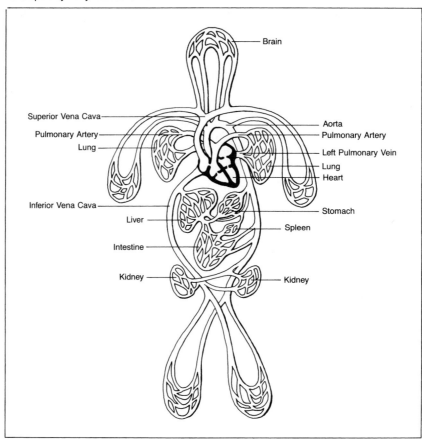

7. Stop the cycle. *HEART ATTACK!!*
8. At this point the brain can control the pace of circulation and the group can play with the various ideas affecting the speed of circulation (running, sleeping, yawning, meditating, watching a scary movie, etc.). Ask for volunteers to replace the students representing the brain, lungs, and intestines so those students can go through the process.
9. Stop the process again and ask how long the students think it will take to go through one complete cycle. Record the guesses on the board and time one cycle. Ask the class to see if they can improve the time while still verbally indicating the name of the structure they are passing. On your mark—get set—go!
10. After the class has returned the room to its usual order, discuss the entire procedure and how it feels to learn in this way.

Evaluation: Write a short essay titled "One Hour in the Life of a Red Blood Cell."

In this chapter, a presentation of the third step to optimizing learning, integrating the intellectual processes, introduced the IEM. Based on brain research and focused on including all of the functions of the brain in the learning experience, the IEM provides a structure for making the curriculum and instruction more brain-compatible.

Strategies were suggested for meeting learning needs in each of the four functional areas of the brain: cognitive (linear/spatial), affective (emotional/social), physical (movement/sensing), and intuitive (rational/predictive/transpersonal).

Chapter 12 will focus on the important fourth step of optimizing learning, differentiating curriculum. This step is one of the most important for providing an appropriate education to gifted learners. Without differentiation, no structure or model can really meet the needs of gifted learners. Steps 5 through 7 will also be discussed as we discover that individualized instruction can be provided to meet the unique needs of gifted students. We will also find that the entire gifted program can be strengthened by evaluation and reflective consideration of what we have accomplished and still wish to achieve.

QUESTIONS OFTEN ASKED

1. Don't you have to have some degree of anxiety or stress in the classroom to keep students motivated?

According to Selye (1956, 1979), there are two types of stress: eustress and distress. Eustress is inevitable and can be motivating, while overstress and the destructive aspects of distress are preventable or at least can be minimized most of the time. The research on learning indicates that a relaxed-alert brain/mind functions best both for initial learning and for retrieval of information. High levels of thought, creativity, and other intuitive processes require conditions of low tension, to at least be available to us.

2. How can we use imagery and intuitive processes in the classroom without upsetting the administration or the parents? Won't they think something strange is going on?

It is most important that you invite the parents to a meeting to explain your purpose and the expected outcomes before you begin working with any new strategies. The meeting should be conducted professionally, and you should explain how brain research provides the biological basis for the changes you plan to make. By involving the parents and the administration from the beginning, you can assure them that you have the same goals for the children as they do. Your belief in the importance of imagery and intuitive processes will communicate this importance to others.

3. How can a teacher find time to include all of the areas of brain function in a lesson?

Substitute activities from the other areas of the brain that you have not been using for some of the activities you are now using, rather than adding more activities. Plan the lesson with activities from each area of function instead of only from the rational, linear cognitive area. The hardest part is that few of us were taught using this approach, and we have to consciously create activities in the other areas of brain function. As you work this way it gets much easier, and the students do so well and retain so much more than with only the cognitive approach that it is well worth the time to change.

4. Should high school teachers be concerned with process when they are really more responsible for teaching specialized content?

It is important that students be introduced to and learn the most content and as many skills as they can during high school, and that is exactly why process is so important. All of the information about process planning allows the teacher to present content and skill development in the most effective and efficient ways possible. Empowering the student by using processes that integrate all of the brain functions, using a variety of materials and methods of teaching, and individualizing instruction ensures a higher level of motivation and attention, a higher rate of acquisition, and longer retention. Without concern for the process that we are using, we will only be covering content; the students will not necessarily be learning it. You need not choose between process and content; they are interdependent and both are important.

CHECKING FOR UNDERSTANDING
Follow-Up Activity

Choose a concept or skill that you might teach to children in your class or to your colleagues. Using the Teacher's Planning Sheet (Figure 11.5) as a guide and the sample Integrative Lessons as examples, plan a lesson that integrates cognitive, affective, physical, and intuitive functions and strategies.

Share your lesson with others in your class.

 SUMMARY

Integrating Intellectual Processes: the Integrative Education Model

1. A powerful approach to organizing an effective learning process is to develop the areas involved in instruction using the current research on teaching and learning.
2. The Integrative Education Model (IEM), a step in optimizing learning, has valuable strategies and practices that can be used in any classroom; it provides for growth in all areas of human ability and all areas of brain development.
3. The interdependence of emotional, cognitive, physical, and intuitive functions allows learners to be effective and efficient when the opportunities are provided for the use of all of these support systems for learning.
4. Components of the IEM include: (1) the responsive learning environment, (2) complex and challenging cognitive activities, (3) empowering language and behavior, (4) choice and perceived control, (5) relaxation and tension reduction, (6) movement and physical encoding, and (7) intuition and integration. These components are organized to support the four major areas/functions of intelligence: cognitive, affective (social-emotional), physical (movement and sensing), and intuitive.

Integrating Cognitive Processes: Rational-Linear and Spatial-Gestalt

5. With the discovery of the specialization of the hemispheres of the brain came the realization that education was focused heavily on the linear, rational, verbal thinking functions and had not taken advantage of the spatial, gestalt, visual thinking functions available to support learning.
6. Educators concerned with the development of creative behavior have long used strategies incorporating visual thinking. These skills

provide the basis for including visual thinking in programs for cognitive growth.

Complex and Challenging Cognitive Activities

7. The processes that are most often a part of gifted programs are those of productive or critical thinking, research skills, learning-to-learn skills, and those involving technology.
8. Gifted students will function in society as change agents, innovators, and reconstructionists. It is believed that societal problem-solvers will come from this group.
9. Gifted students need a way to get to information and ideas far sooner than more typical learners. They must be able to move efficiently on their own into areas not yet explored; therefore, they need to become familiar with the skills of research as tools for future learning and thinking.

Integrating Affective Processes

10. Emotions are the gateway-triggering mechanism for higher cognitive function.
11. Strategies for affective development must be integrated into the students' daily activities.
12. It has been said that all major decisions are made at a feeling level.

Empowering Language and Behavior

13. If students spend their time and energy on defensiveness and resistance, there will be little energy or time for learning.
14. When used as an occasional organizer in the classroom, cooperative learning groups may give gifted students valuable opportunities to appreciate students of varying interests and abilities; when used as a major organizer, gifted students are in danger of serving as tutors to less able learners far too often and missing the challenge of their intellectual peers.

Choice and Perceived Control

15. Choice and the resulting perception of control are motivational variables that significantly affect both children's academic achievement and their self-concept.

16. Gifted children are found to have more inner locus of control at a younger age than do average learners. Success later in life is in direct correlation to how much inner locus of control the individual has developed.

17. It has been established that the more the environment (either home or school) provides external controls, the greater will be the loss of the inner locus of control.

18. Extrinsic motivation predominates in environments that are controlling, whereas intrinsic motivation is fostered by environments that support autonomy. Changing the environment can alter the motivational patterns and the results they foster.

19. The capacity for critical and creative thinking, problem solving, future study, planning, analysis, synthesis, and evaluative thought are necessary components for all conceptions of leadership.

20. Self-actualization is but one goal of gifted education; self-actualization in service to humankind is the twin goal.

Integrating Physical Processes

21. Gifted students must be given opportunities to integrate their minds with their physical bodies.

Relaxation and Tension Reduction

22. Researchers have shown us ways to integrate the mind and body, thereby promoting increased function and energy for all human systems.

23. Stress produces chemicals within the brain that shut down the system and, over time, create permanent damage.

24. Higher-level mental faculties are substantially impaired by stress; they function more effectively when one is comparatively calm and not highly aroused.

Movement and Physical Encoding

25. Research confirms the importance of physical exercise on cognitive development.

26. For many gifted students, body coordination does not keep pace with their accelerated mental development, thereby frustrating their expectations of performance.

27. In some schools and in professional sports, the use of fantasy to promote mastery of physical activity has gained acceptance and is used successfully.

Integrating Intuitive Processes

28. The functions of the prefrontal cortex seem to include future planning, insight, empathy, introspection, and other bases for intuitive thought. This area is engaged in firming up intention, deciding on action, and regulating our most complex behaviors.

29. Those most responsible for changing our culture (Plato, Newton, da Vinci, Einstein, etc.); important poets, musicians, and artists (Keats, Mozart, Monet, etc.); philosophers, mathematicians, psychologists, and educators (Pythagoras, Tesla, Jung, etc.); and modern scientists (Bohm, Prigogine, Pribram, etc.) all wrote about the use of intuition in their great discoveries and creative contributions.

30. Intuition may occur on at least three levels: rational, predictive, and transformational.

31. Intuition is always available to us and can be developed. Cognition is viewed by some as a conscious, active power and intuition as a complementary, receptive power.

32. It is believed by some that rational knowing is useless if not accompanied and enhanced by intuitive knowing.

33. Gifted students have been found to be predominantly intuitive in their processing of information and use a high degree of feeling in decision-making.

34. The techniques of imagery, fantasy, and visualization are important components in developing intuitive ability.

35. The intuitive process seems to be triggered by a number of practices or skills that can be incorporated into the curriculum, allowing students to release more of their intuition and to become more creative. Students can expect to make impressive gains in the areas of cognition, self-concept, and social-emotional development by using intuition-incorporating strategies.

12 Differentiating and Individualizing the Curriculum and Instruction for Gifted Learners

In this chapter, the reader will discover discussions and information regarding:

- The differentiating characteristics of gifted learners that create educational needs and suggestions for meeting those needs.

- The last four of the seven steps for optimizing learning: differentiate the curriculum; individualize the instruction; evaluate learning and teaching; and reflect and reform.

- The process of differentiating the curriculum and instruction and its importance in educating gifted learners.

- A plan for individualizing a differentiated curriculum.

- Structures for developing integrated, differentiated, and individualized curricula.

- Evaluation issues for gifted learners.

- The need for reflective teaching.

Mere critical thinking, without creative and intuitive insights, without the search for new patterns, is sterile and doomed. To solve complex problems in changing circumstances requires the activity of both cerebral hemispheres; the path to the future lies through the corpus callosum.

—CARL SAGAN

A year ago Alice never would have thought of arranging her room this way, let alone teaching this way. Ever since she began teaching in the gifted program and going to classes and conferences focused on gifted learners, Alice had been changing things. She was now trying to arrange the room and the materials to support her as she worked to individualize instruction for the whole class. Some of these ideas were good for both gifted and nongifted students, but gifted students obviously needed this kind of flexibility, and she suspected that without it they would lose far more educationally than other children.

She had replaced the individual desks with tables that allowed a lot more flexibility in grouping because she discovered that her students actually were at many levels of understanding of the basic curriculum. This change had also required access to a wider range of materials. The class library was a big help in this regard. To put together a class library, she had borrowed books from the school, the university, and the city libraries on long-term loan. She had let the Parent-Teacher Organization know of the project and had received a lot of books that families were no longer using. Her visits to yard sales last summer had helped a lot, too—not only with the library, but with materials for many other projects.

As she placed two more completed folders in the file box, she thought what a good idea Claude had had for monitoring the students' progress and giving students more responsibility and direction with these files. He was a resource specialist and had special education students with a variety of learning problems, but his management strategy of putting the goals and rubrics for each subject in a file for each student worked in her class as well. Each student file also contained the current material and directions for the next lessons the student needed. As the students came in, they would go to their individual boxes and pick up their supplies for the morning. They would then get their file out of the file box, look over the material she had corrected, and glance through the assignments for the day. They would put in work they had completed at home, finish something, or start their new work as others were coming in. The file system had cut down on the time she had to spend distributing and collecting material, and she was amazed at how such a simple idea had changed the students' feelings about the class and the responsibility they took for their own work.

As Alice gave the room one last appraisal before she went to call the children in from the yard, she felt very pleased. The room was not only attractive, but functional for the learning plans she had made. Materials stood on the shelves, ready to allow her to go in many different directions when any of the children were ready. Although she had a good plan for the core learning curriculum, with all the optimal learning principles represented, she also had materials and plans that would allow a student to learn more quickly and then move to more sophisticated concepts. She could add more dimensions to the basic curriculum and was prepared to introduce relationships and connections with other disciplines as the students needed more complex ideas. As of last Friday, she even had a list of mentors and specialists that had been put together by a group of the parents. This resource would allow her to tap into the community to support those students who needed more depth or had special interest in parts of the curriculum she would be presenting. Best of all was the new computer program that would give the students an easy way to evaluate where they were in the basic class goals, direct them to choices for their next steps, and provide them with some feedback on their success as they completed basic tasks.

Alice smiled to herself as she thought just how far she had come and how much she enjoyed the excitement of this classroom. As she left the room, she made a mental note to ask Frieda, her next-door colleague, how the assessment workshop had gone this weekend; maybe she could help her figure out some problems she was having with the portfolio assessments she was designing.

DIFFERENTIATING THE CURRICULUM
AND INSTRUCTION FOR GIFTED LEARNERS

The special educational needs of gifted students result from the characteristics that differentiate them from typical learners. Content and instructional strategies that relate clearly to their educational needs meet those needs most effectively and nurture their high-level abilities. As Kaplan (1986) reminds us, "The ultimate goals of a differentiated curriculum are that it recognizes the characteristics of the gifted, provides reinforcement or practice for the development of these characteristics, and extends the recognized characteristics to further levels of development" (p. 182). At its very basic core, differentiation means the modification of the curricular content, process, and products to meet the needs, abilities and interests of learners, in this case gifted learners.

Tomlinson (1995) views differentiation as "consistently using a variety of instructional approaches to modify content, process, and/or products in response to learning readiness and interest of academically diverse students" (p. 80). She considers differentiation to be a philosophy or a way of thinking about the classroom and believes the principles and practices of differentiation are the most effective way to conduct all classrooms (Tomlinson, 2000). Her beliefs are expressed in a set of assumptions that support differentiation in the classroom, including: students of the same age differing so significantly in their learning readiness, style, experiences, and interests that they need differing pace, level of content, and need for support. This is especially true for gifted students. That students need to be challenged with natural learning opportunities beyond what they already know. And that students need to make connections between what they learn and their life experiences. Her view of the central job of the schools is to maximize the capacity of each student. "If a teacher isn't clear about what all students should understand and be able to do when the learning experience ends, he or she lacks the vital organizer around which to develop a powerful lesson" (Tomlinson, 1999, p. 37).

Tomlinson (1995) makes several suggestions for skills that need to be developed by teachers to ensure the success of differentiation in their classrooms. Teachers need to be able to:

- Teach by concept, rather than just covering material.
- Teach with varied resources, rather than a single text.
- Assess learning in varied ways, rather than use a single test or project.
- Manage multiple groups doing the same activity, then move to different groups and individuals working on different activities.

She found that teachers were more successful in ensuring differentiation when they had concrete assistance from other teachers or consultants and when resources such as videotapes and examples of differentiated lessons were available. Teachers found more support when administrators modeled the principles of differentiation with their staff members and worked with them to set common and individual goals and timelines for progress that included pre-assessed teacher readiness, teacher reflection, and dialogue between teachers and consultants. Tomlinson's (1995) case study of a middle school that moved to differentiation for all of its gifted learners provides valuable clues for other school faculty.

The principles of a differentiated curriculum for the gifted as developed by the Curriculum Council of the National/State Leadership Training Institute on the Gifted and the Talented (cited in Kaplan, 1986) provide a framework for appropriately differentiating curriculum for this population:

- Present content that is related to broad-based issues, themes, or problems.
- Integrate multiple disciplines into the area of study.
- Present comprehensive, related, and mutually reinforcing experiences within an area of study.
- Allow for the in-depth learning of a self-selected topic within the area of study.
- Develop independent or self-directed study skills.
- Develop productive, complex, abstract and/or higher level thinking skills.
- Focus on open-ended tasks.
- Develop research skills and methods.
- Integrate basic skills and higher level thinking skills into the curriculum.
- Encourage the development of products that challenge existing ideas and produce "new" ideas.
- Encourage the development of products that use a variety of techniques, materials, and forms.
- Encourage the development of self-understanding, such as, recognizing and using one's abilities, becoming self-directed, appreciating likenesses and differences between oneself and others.
- Evaluate student outcomes by using appropriate and specific criteria through self-appraisal, criterion referenced and/or standardized instruments. (p. 183)

Although a differentiated curriculum really cannot be planned for individual students until the needs of each are known, the standards from the core curriculum can be generally differentiated for gifted learners by modifying the content and performance standards to meet the most commonly found learning needs of gifted students. A review of the characteristics common to gifted learners can provide a basis for planning differentiated curriculum. The possibilities for appropriately differentiating curriculum can be organized by clustering the most common characteristics found among gifted learners into four major areas of need and one area of personal style. Although many other characteristics exist (see Chapter 2, Table 2.1), the focus for differentiation in this chapter will be on the need to differentiate for:

- *Acceleration* in the pace of learning.
- *Complexity* of thought and processing.
- *Depth* of understanding and the level of mastery.
- *Novelty* and uniqueness in personal expression.
- *Intensity* and *idealism* in manner and deed

By designing opportunities to include more complexity and depth, and allowing acceleration and novelty of concepts and materials, an important first step has been taken. It is interesting how these needs reflect the changes found in the brain when appropriate stimulation has occurred and the brain has become more efficient, more integrated, and more advanced in its functions (described in Chapters 2 and 4) as giftedness develops.

After the needs of the students are known, how implementation will occur and how the curriculum will be further modified to meet each student's unique needs and interests must be decided. Kaplan's Grid Model (discussed in Chapter 10) provides an excellent guide for these decisions. Another recent model of differentiation developed by Kaplan (2001), the Layered Curriculum, is an approach to differentiate the core curriculum by emphasizing the acquisition of content. Process and product decisions follow the development of the content through six possible layers. The dimensions that may be added to the core curriculum are layers concerned with theme, generalization, differentiation, and classical and individualized study, each enhancing the study of the core. The Layered Curriculum model was designed to:

- Develop the core curriculum;
- Provide for greater depth and complexity of the core content;
- Introduce classical ideas of the past and correlate the past with the present;
- Allow opportunities to study independently; and
- To make connections within, between, and among areas and disciplines of study using a global theme and related generalizations. (pp. 156–157)

An appropriate curriculum for gifted learners would not only meet their immediate needs but would also be able to show progressive development in both skill and content. It should be increasingly difficult, interdisciplinary, broad based, and comprehensive and should provide for any needed acceleration. One way to ensure that such provisions are made is to plan in advance a scope and a sequence of content standards that reflect the needs of the district as well as the needs of the students.

The scope and sequence give a structure to the curriculum that allows teachers, students, administration, and parents to know the students' progress in learning the skills and in benefiting from the experiences to which they are exposed. The scope and sequence ensure that the content and processes deemed important are taught and learned and that whatever the district will hold students accountable for has been mastered. Planning a scope and sequence should lock neither teachers nor students into limited, inflexible procedures, but should provide continuity and availability of resources. The scope and sequence, when known by students, can provide motivation and empowerment as they see what they have already mastered and discover the possibilities ahead. Such informed students can become partners in the learning process.

It is helpful to understand not only what a differentiated curriculum should include, but also those practices that should not be included if the curriculum is to be effectively differentiated for gifted learners. The guidelines in Figure 12.1 will help to clarify such practices. The Curriculum Criteria Checklist (Figure 12.2)

Figure 12.1 *Differentiated Curriculum Guidelines*

- The curriculum should be planned and sequentially organized to include specific expectations for the acquisition of subject matter, mastery of skills, creation of products, and development of attitudes and appreciation related to self, others, and the environment.
    —The curriculum should not be a potpourri of learning activities that are disjointed and haphazardly selected without reference to specified criteria.
- The curriculum should place emphasis on the interdependence of subject matter, skills, products, and self-understanding within the same curricular structure.
    —The curriculum should not focus on the attainment of cognitive competencies in isolation from the development of affective competencies. Nor should the curriculum focus on affective development without concern for cognitive growth.
- The curriculum should include provisions to meet the need for some type of instructional pacing by any or all of the following means:

    Making it possible to accomplish a range of learning experiences in a shorter span of time using a continuous progress curriculum.

    Assigning students to curricula at levels beyond those expected at the students' age/grade level.

    Eliminating from the curricula what is already learned and substituting curricula more appropriate to student interests, abilities, and needs.
    —The curriculum should not penalize students for being gifted or talented through restricting their opportunities to learn by ignoring those characteristics that define their giftedness.
- The curriculum should allow for the expression of some aspect of the individual's interests, needs, abilities, and learning preferences. The curriculum should be organized to allow for individualization and self-selection.
    —The curriculum should not be without defined expectations and clearly expressed opportunities for both teacher-directed and student-selected learning activities.
- The curriculum should provide opportunities to learn to reconceptualize existing knowledge, to perceive things from various points of view, and to use information for new purposes or in new ways.
    —The curriculum should not stress the accumulation of knowledge or reinforce mastery without simultaneously encouraging students to be productive thinkers.
- The curriculum should provide learning experiences for students to address the unresolved issues and problems of society and apply personal and social data to analyze, clarify, and respond to such issues and problems.
    —The curriculum should not focus only on knowledge of the world as it is, but should encourage development of perceptions of the need to invent in order to restructure the world into what it ideally could be.
- The curriculum should incorporate learning experiences that foster development of the complex thought processes that encourage the creation of unique products and develop strategies of productive thought. The curriculum should teach both fundamental and higher level thinking skills as integral parts of every learning experience.
    —The curriculum should not overemphasize mastery of fundamental basic skills, nor should it exonerate gifted/talented students from mastering these. The curriculum should not ignore the development of fundamental or basic skills for the mastery of higher level thinking skills.
- The curriculum should provide opportunities for students to practice leadership and followership skills and appropriate and varied forms of communication skills and strategies.
    —The curriculum should not be based on the assumption that gifted and talented students can assume positions of leadership without the development of skills and understandings that promote this end.

Although this is a useful guide, educators will always need to assess gifted learners for their particular needs. They are your very best guide to an appropriate curriculum.

Figure 12.2 *A Curriculum Criteria Checklist*

The following criteria are appropriate for all good educational experiences; however, the characteristics found among gifted learners make these criteria especially necessary to a differentiated curriculum. To ensure that your curriculum is appropriate for gifted learners, check to see if it includes provisions for all of these criteria:

1. *Continuity.* A comprehensive set of learning experiences is provided that reinforces specific curricular objectives.
2. *Flexibility.* The scope and sequence of the curriculum are modified to accommodate emerging student and teacher needs.
3. *Responsiveness to learner needs.* Definition of the curriculum is based on an assessment of individual/group abilities, interests, needs, and learning styles.
4. *Diversity.* Alternative means are provided to attain determined ends within a specified curricular framework.
5. *Integration.* The integrative use of all abilities, including cognition, emotion, intuition, and mind/body, is provided in a single curriculum.
6. *Openness.* Present expectations are eliminated that might limit the learnings within the curricular framework.
7. *Independence.* Some types of self-directed learning are provided.
8. *Increasing levels of advanced abstraction and difficulty.* Acceptance of the student's readiness to learn beyond traditional age/grade expectations and provisions for stimulating such readiness are present.
9. *Substantive learning.* Significant subject matter, skills, products, and awareness that are of consequence or of importance to the learner and the disciplines are included.
10. *Decision-making.* Students are able to make some appropriate/relevant decisions regarding what is to be learned and how it can be learned.
11. *Principles of learning.* Teaching practices that allow for motivation, practice, transfer of training, and feedback are included.
12. *Creation/Re-creation.* The creative process is applied to modify and improve one's creations to challenge prevailing thought and offer more appropriate solutions.
13. *Interaction with peers and a variety of significant others.* Students can learn about and meet with individuals who share the same and different expressions of giftedness and talents.
14. *Value system.* Consistent opportunities are available to develop and examine personal and societal values and to establish a personal value system.
15. *Communication skills.* Verbal and nonverbal systems and skills are developed to dialogue, share, and exchange ideas.
16. *Commitment to society.* Provisions are made to understand and relate to the society in which one lives and to find one's place in it.

provides another way of viewing the appropriateness of the curriculum especially designed for meeting the needs of gifted learners. Both figures are based on the work of Clark & Kaplan, 1981.

Providing Differentiation to Meet the Educational Needs of Gifted Learners

Differentiating by Acceleration

As the result of changes in the pace of thought and learning, gifted students often require acceleration in their instruction and advanced and sophisticated materials. The pace of instruction can be accelerated by early entrance to any level of schooling such as kindergarten or college; pre-testing a lesson or unit and receiving instruction on only what has not been learned; self-paced programs of instruction; or other means of tailoring the pace of learning to the student. However the acceleration of the curriculum is accomplished, the result will be that the student moves through the core curriculum in less time than is typical. What will be done with the time gained is a concern, and the following suggestions may help to ensure an appropriate use of the students' time.

Differentiating Characteristics:

Accelerated pace of thought and learning.

Advanced comprehension.

High level of language development and verbal ability.

Extraordinary quantity of information and unusual retentiveness.

High level of visual and spatial ability.

To Meet the Needs Created by Accelerated Learning, Provide Opportunities to:

Learn and work with intellectual peers, including adults and other students with expertise in the student's interest areas.

Compact or telescope content to avoid reteaching material already learned.

Acquire early mastery of basic skills.

Access advanced and/or unusual subject matter, materials, and processes (e.g., speed reading, prediction, brainstorming).

Access new and challenging information about the environment and the culture: aesthetic, economic, political, and social.

Encounter and use increasingly difficult vocabulary, concepts, and information organized with self-checking pretests and posttests and a variety of methods for learning available at each level.

Use mentor programs.

Conference individually.

Form flexible groups.

Use learning centers and individual learning packets.

Use advanced placement and enroll in advanced classes on other campuses.

Individualize deadlines for products.

Teacher's Role:

Know the content and performance standards of the core curriculum and their scope and sequence for the subject being taught.

Assess the student's level of knowledge and skill and document content that has already been learned; teach what is not known.

Make it possible to accomplish a range of learning in a shorter span of time by use of learning packages, peer tutoring, centers, and folders.

Provide a wide range of levels of materials and resources.

Provide self-paced instruction in any learning environment with the use of mentors or tutors, individual contracts, and/or independent study.

Arrange for mentors from higher grade levels, the community, or other resource personnel who possess advanced knowledge and/or skill.

Arrange for advanced instruction.

Teach independent or self-directed study skills.

Provide individualized instruction in the areas of strength.

Provide appropriate group settings with the use of flexible grouping and/or higher grade or age placement.

Combine acceleration with other methods of differentiation.

Evaluate the outcomes of acceleration and provide for self-evaluation.

Example: *Curriculum Compacting.* Renzulli (1977) has developed forms and procedures that make the pre-testing and post-testing of content much easier and lead to a way of making more appropriate use of a gifted student's time. The curriculum compacting system was designed to provide necessary evidence regarding a student's mastery of the skills and concepts required in the regular curriculum. Once the skill or concept has been learned it becomes wasteful to have the student keep reviewing the information or skill again and again. "Curriculum compacting has three major objectives: (1) to create a more challenging learning environment, (2) to guarantee proficiency in the basic curriculum and (3) to 'buy time' for more appropriate enrichment and/or acceleration activities" (Renzulli & Reis, 1986, p. 232). An important part of the services provided by the Enrichment Triad Model (Chapter 9), curriculum compacting is a valuable tool to be used with any curriculum plan as an aid in differentiating the content area.

Differentiating by Use of Complexity

Gifted students often have the ability to broaden their understanding of concepts by making connections with other ideas, seeing the relationship between concepts, and gaining understanding from perspectives other than their own. For these reasons more universal themes and interdisciplinary instruction need to be a part of their educational experiences.

Differentiating Characteristics:

Unusual capacity for processing information.

Flexible thought processes.

Ability to synthesize comprehensively.

Heightened capacity for seeing unusual and diverse relationships and an overall gestalt.

Ability to generate original ideas and solutions.

Early ability to use and form conceptual frameworks.

To Meet the Needs Created by Complexity of Thought, Provide Opportunities to:

Learn through the integration of all intellectual processes (Chapter 11).

Incorporate visual and verbal modes in learning and evaluation.

Access a large variety of ideas at many levels.

Develop skills in identifying data needs, collecting, organizing, and evaluating data.

Develop skills in decision-making.

Use curriculum with themes and interdisciplinary content

Focus on patterns, relationships, and connections.

Learn from a variety of perspectives, including the views of experts.

Recognize the influence of time on change, knowledge, and understanding.

Compare past, present, and future events related to the study topic; include classics, philosophy, and current events.

Design and use conceptual frameworks in information gathering and problem-solving.

Develop original applications of knowledge and understandings, including hypothesizing and hypothesis testing.

Plan and implement solutions to community problems.

Conference individually.

Teacher's Role:

Encourage and accept challenges to established generalizations.

Provide materials from a wide range of disciplines and eras.

Give time and provide structure for independent exploration of varied areas of study.

Provide instruction in the skills and structures needed for independent research.

Present content with interdisciplinary and broad-based issues, themes, and/or problems.

Give experiences that demonstrate interdisciplinary relationships.

Provide experiences with a variety of information and skills.

Integrate higher level thinking skills into the curriculum.

Allow students to choose products and outcome criteria for sharing knowledge and insights.

Example: *Interdisciplinary Instruction* The content standard in the core curriculum is to gain an understanding of the reasons for the westward expansion of the American frontier and how it affected the average citizens of the country. Gifted students are asked to take the perspective of another group or groups, such as women, American Indians, or the hunters and trappers, and discover their relationship to the mainstream settlers, how the westward expansion affected that group, and the effect they had on the outcomes of the movement.

Differentiating by Adding Depth

The curiosity and questioning behavior of gifted learners often create a need to understand the principles and facts that make up generalizations and concepts. This need for depth in thinking allows gifted learners to discover detail, patterns, and trends that can provide the insights that lead to new ideas and products.

Differentiating Characteristics:

An unusual degree of curiosity.

Early ability to delay closure.

Early ability to think in different patterns, in alternatives, and in abstract terms.

Advanced cognitive and affective ability for conceptualizing and solving societal problems.

Early ability to sense consequences, make generalizations, and visualize solutions.

To Meet the Needs Created by Depth of Understanding, Provide Opportunities to:

Develop receptive attitudes and suspend judgment.

Develop skills in research, hypothesizing, and hypothesis testing.

Learn the terms/language of a variety of disciplines.

Use dissonant events to solve problems.

Focus on details and patterns in themes and ideas.

Embellish and elaborate on themes and ideas.

Find trends in events, past, present, and predicting future.

Discover rules and ethics in theories, disciplines, and areas of study and their importance.

Share ideas in depth.

Use a longer incubation time for ideas.

Pursue ideas and unanswered questions; integrate new ideas without forced closure or products demanded.

Conference individually.

Move out into the community for information.

Have flexibility in assignment of deadlines.

Pursue learning from the familiar to the unfamiliar; the concrete to the abstract; the known to the unknown.

Teacher's Role:

Provide a range of materials, including levels of difficulty and complexity, in a variety of disciplines.

Arrange for mentors, using specialized skills and knowledge available from other faculty or community members.

Instruct from the concrete to abstract, familiar to unfamiliar, known to unknown.

Examine topics by determining facts, concepts, generalizations, principles, and theories related to them.

Teach research skills and methods.

Provide time for study of areas of high interest.

Provide flexibility in the assignment of deadlines and cooperative instructional planning through individual conferences.

Develop the use of individual time lines and time management.

Develop the skill of setting priorities.

Help students decide on products or outcomes of study.

Develop student production skills, including planning and organizing.

Example: *Mind Maps* Mind maps, developed by Buzan (1983), allow students to use both hemispheric brain specializations to support and to improve their information processing and retention. This strategy facilitates greater complexity and depth in the writing process. Designed to give students an alternative to the traditional linear mode of organizing information, mind maps ask students to use the multidimensional and pattern-making capabilities of their brains to organize and record unlimited and seemingly unrelated information. Because the brain works primarily with key concepts in an interlinked and integrated manner, Buzan suggests that notes and word relations should be structured in a way that shows these interrelationships as easily as possible. To record information most efficiently Buzan suggests that "one should start from the centre or main idea and branch out as dictated by the individual ideas and general form of the central theme" (p. 91). Buzan gives the following steps for creating a mind map:

1. Print words in capital letters. Printed words are more photographic, more immediate, and more comprehensive when the information is read back.
2. Print words on lines and connect lines to other lines. This gives the mind map a basic structure.
3. Print words in units. This leaves each word to be joined to other thoughts and allows note taking to be more free and flexible.
4. Print the ideas freely and with no concern for order. More will be captured in the mind map when you allow your mind to recall everything as quickly and as freely as possible. Final order will evolve from the map itself.

The importance of the ideas is clearly indicated when main ideas are in the center and the less important ideas are at the edge, making links between concepts immediately recognizable. New information can easily be added, and recall and review are both more effective and more quickly completed.

Figures 12.3 and 12.4 show the results of first a mind map, and then a linear outline. The ideal learning process would make available strategies that use both brain specializations, the linear of the left hemisphere and the spatial of the right hemisphere. Use of both strategies allows students to choose which strategy works best for them to explore an idea or event. Students must be presented with the opportunity to strengthen both the linear-rational and the spatial-gestalt cognitive functions, and then choose which process to use. Using this strategy, the student can discover the details, patterns, and relationships of ideas and events and use this knowledge to make predictions regarding future trends.

Differentiating by Providing Novelty

Gifted students show personal interest and understanding in a wide range of areas and disciplines. They bring to their study a heightened awareness of their individuality and a belief in the value of their own point of view. As they gain a personal understanding of concepts, they can construct unique and individualized meaning if the structure and instruction allow. The resulting products often are exciting innovations and re-creations of old systems and ideas. A higher level of learning can occur when provision is made for this need for personal involvement.

Differentiating Characteristics:

Unusually varied interests.

Heightened self-awareness accompanied by feelings of being "different."

Creativity often apparent in areas of endeavor.

Evidence of risk-taking behavior in developing new ideas and theories.

Willingness to create personal interpretation of established ideas and theories.

Acceptance and expression of high levels of intuitive ability.

Early development of an inner locus of control and satisfaction.

Keen and often unusual sense of humor.

Openness to involvement and interest in intuitive knowing.

To Meet the Needs Created by Novelty, Provide Opportunities to:

Identify and explore one's own emotions, perceptual filters, and defense systems and accept those of others.

Communicate personal expressions and perceptions in a variety of ways.

Continually develop creative abilities.

Work in a classroom with a climate of respect for ideas.

Develop projects of students' choosing that involve communication and exchange of opinions in a variety of ways.

Have unstructured time to physically and mentally explore, examine, and/or alter patterns in existing theories, systems, or areas of study.

Figure 12.3 *Teaching Children to Mind Map—A Mind Map*
Source: Julie Lowerre, Sierra Madre, CA, 1995. Reprinted with permission.

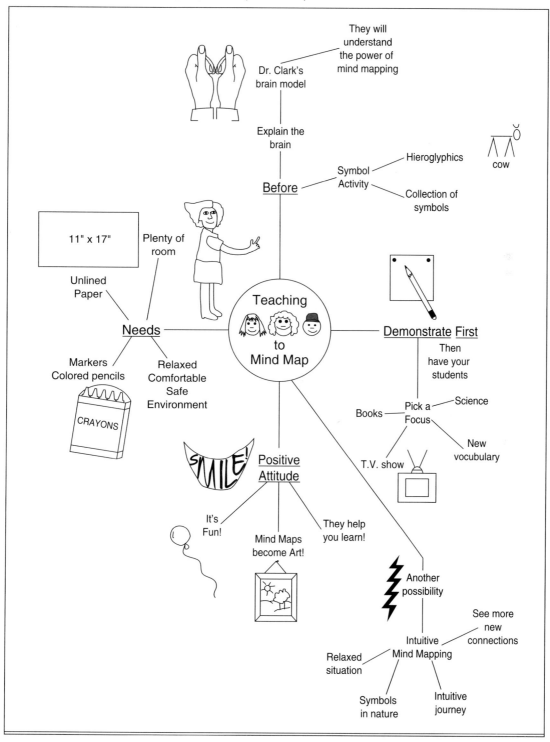

Figure 12.4 *Teaching Children to Mind Map*

  I. Before Teaching the Lesson
    A. Explain the brain using the hand model from Clark (1992)
    B. Discuss the power of mind mapping
    C. Conduct a symbol activity including hieroglyphics and a collection of symbols
  II. Needed for the Lesson
    A. Plenty of room for the students in a relaxed, comfortable, and safe environment
    B. Materials such as unlined paper (11″ × 17″ is best) and colored pencils or crayons
  III. Model and Discuss a Positive Attitude
    A. Mind mapping is fun; smile while working
    B. Mind maps can support learning
    C. Mind maps can become art
  IV. Instruct the Students in Mind Mapping
    A. Demonstrate first
    B. Then have students pick a focus, such as books, science, a TV show, or new vocabulary
    C. Have the children try the strategy and discuss the results
  V. Another Possibility: Intuitive Mind Mapping
    A. Provide a relaxed situation
    B. Help students become aware of the symbols in nature
    C. Guide students on an intuitive journey
    D. Children see more new connections from this experience

---

Integrate knowledge from various areas of their lives into new, divergent, and/or convergent physical and mental structures.

Personally interpret and restate knowledge in areas of study.

Develop original applications of knowledge and understandings, including hypothesizing and hypothesis testing.

Follow divergent paths and pursue strong interests.

Receive guidance in evaluating appropriate uses of creative efforts.

Evaluate personal choices in terms of available data, individual needs and goals, and choice of consequences.

Solve problems in diverse ways.

Develop and conduct original investigations or experiments.

Experience teacher acceptance of unusual products, open-ended assignments, and alternative processes of learning.

Conference individually.

Teacher's Role:

Create a safe learning environment.

Provide choice.

Provide an environment rich and varied in stimulation.

Encourage self-initiated exploring, observing, questioning, feeling, translating, inferring, and predicting.

Allow relaxation and thinking time.

Study problems as opportunities for and encourage novel solutions.

Value the unusual and divergent.

Provide open-ended questions and activities.

Look for new implications among and within disciplines.

Approach areas of study in personalized, individualistic, and nontraditional ways.

Set conditions for divergence to occur and acknowledge the results.

Provide inquiry and exploration into disparate and incongruent patterns of experience that lead to new, often original, reorganized knowledge.

Encourage students to seek original interpretations or restatements of existing information.

Encourage risk-taking, collaboration, and multiple solutions.

Encourage products that challenge existing ideas, produce new ideas, and use a variety of techniques, materials, and forms.

Example: *A Simulation/Inquiry Problem* The following classroom inquiry problem was developed for a fourth-grade social studies unit on Africa. The objective is for the students to bring forth their geographic and climatic knowledge about Africa to discover if they can apply this knowledge in a situation that appears unrelated to their study of Africa. This simulation can be conducted in such a way that it can allow gifted students to interpret knowledge in personal ways and follow their own investigative strategies.

Problem Setting Pretend the year is 2097 and you and your spaceship crew are on a 100-year outer space mission. You have all just awakened from your solar sleep 3 weeks prior to your reentry into Earth's atmosphere and scheduled touchdown. You discover that your radio works, but you cannot communicate with the National Aeronautics and Space Administration (NASA). The lines are dead. You are worried about why NASA doesn't answer, but also you are worried about coordinating landing plans and instruments. Your spaceship has a manual on landing without NASA's help, but it has never been done. To complicate matters, 2 days before reentry you hit a terrific solar storm. Many of your instruments malfunction. Bravely, you and your crew prepare to land on Earth.

Miraculously, the landing was perfect. The crew is safe and alive. However, when you open the door of the spaceship, you realize you are not at the NASA landing strip in Nevada.

All your instruments that tell latitude and longitude, and other important information, broke during the storm. You must discover . . .

Focus Setting: "Where on Earth are we?!"

Structuring: You instruct your crew to make a list of the things they see around them to help decide where they have landed. They agree to meet back at the ship in an hour to compare data.

Here is an example of what was on the lists once they were compiled. You are to use the information to ask more specific questions about the items listed so that you can give opinions about where you are and to develop and prove theories of your location.

The List

1. Landed on flat ground.
2. Miles in the distance emerald green-looking mountains.
3. A small river (20-feet wide) running $\frac{1}{2}$ mile from spaceship.
4. Several large hawks circling above area from time to time.
5. Temperature about 85°F—sunny.
6. A clump of trees near ship that look stunted but have leaves on them; another group of trees that look as if they were planted with their roots in the air instead of having leaves on their tops.
7. Rocky soil, but a lot of scrubby green plant life.
8. Snakes sighted.
9. Doglike paw marks down by the river.
10. A group of small apelike creatures seen in rocky hills $1\frac{1}{2}$ miles from spaceship— probably baboons.
11. Biggest find of all—houses sighted; constructed of materials found in area.
12. People seen through binoculars high up in hills tending sheep.

Accepting, Clarifying: By asking more questions about the list, you should be able to give an idea as to what:

1. Country you landed in.
2. Time of year it is.
3. Time of day it is.
4. Type of life the inhabitants are living.

Inquiry Session Process Debriefing   Through the debriefing period, the students may be helped to see their processes as less or more powerful and to find ways of improving their skills. Students can also be given opportunities to work on separate inquiry skills, such as asking good questions and finding irrelevant data, in short skill-development sessions. Through inquiry, students can become aware that truth still remains to be discovered and information can be personally interpreted.

Differentiating by Supporting Idealism and Acknowledging Intensity

The intensity with which gifted students often pursue their interests allows for high levels of creative and idealistic thinking. An exploration of values and value systems helps them to trust their own ideas and explore them further. Gifted students have concerns for humanity and personal commitment to moral and ethical issues that result in high levels of idealism. Fostering these admirable qualities requires opportunities for their acknowledgement and practice.

Differentiating Characteristics:

Intensity in thought, pursuit of ideas, and concern for others.

Early development of idealism, a sense of justice, and global awareness, including involvement with the meta-needs of society (e.g., justice, beauty, and truth).

Unusual emotional depth and intensity.

Sensitivity to inconsistency between ideals and behavior.

Strong motivation created by self-actualization needs.   *entelechy*

An evaluative approach toward self and others.

Persistent, goal-directed behavior.

Unusual sensitivity to the expectations and feelings of others.

High expectations of self and others, which often lead to high levels of frustration with self, others, and situations.

Accumulation of information about emotions that have not been examined nor analyzed.

Advanced levels of moral judgment.

To Meet the Needs Created by Intensity and Idealism, Provide Opportunities to:

Develop and use intuitive energy and ability.

Use fantasy and imagination.

Investigate ideas of successful, eminent people who had high ethical standards.

Understand the motivations of leaders in the events of historical and political import.

Discuss differing values and ideals across time and cultures.

Explore inconsistencies between ideals and behaviors.

Learn how behaviors affect the feelings and behaviors of others.

Explore, construct, and express personal values and priorities among conflicting values; confront and interact with the value systems of others.

Examine how values and belief systems affect decisions regarding world events.

Use simulations and other activities that emphasize the social cost of various solutions.

Develop the skills of inferring and predicting.

Debate and analyze real problems.

Pursue inquiries beyond allotted time spans.

Experience meaningful involvement in real problems.

Explore issues related to the world community and become aware of personal talents contributing to world issues and to humanity.

Engage in activities with worldwide implications and results.

Access foreign exchange programs and International Baccalaureate.

Engage in future studies.

Engage in leadership training, creating government structures, and organizing and implementing social, cultural, and/or curricular programs.

Find a vocation that provides opportunity for actualization of a student's personal value system as well as an avenue for talents and abilities.

Teacher's Role:

Create a safe learning environment.

Value and model high ethical standards and values.

Address unresolved issues and problems of society.

Treat ideas and inquiries respectfully.

Help students to trust their own senses and feelings.

Provide flexible time modules and individualized instruction.

Give instruction and practice in goal setting and goal evaluation.

Provide for self-evaluation and cooperative evaluation.

Example: *Imagery* The following exercise is an example of the use of imagery in the teaching of grammar: Ask the students to close their eyes and imagine that they are on a hill in summer, lying on their back and watching the clouds floating by in a blue sky. A biplane comes into view and begins to do some skywriting. It is writing their name. After completing the names, the plane continues writing five words around each name to describe them. When the last descriptive word is completed, bring them slowly back into the room and ask them to write the words on a piece of paper. Now ask the students to turn to a neighbor and write five words on the paper describing the neighbor. Give the students a few minutes to share the descriptions they are willing to share with their neighbors, then ask them to close their eyes.

Ask them to see themselves doing something they would feel comfortable doing right then in front of their neighbors. When they have done this, ask them to open their eyes and do what they saw themselves doing, taking turns with their partner. Now ask them each to write five words describing how the partner did whatever he or she did—not *what* the partner did, but *how* the partner did it. Write words on the board given to you by the class: one list of words describing themselves or their partners, another list describing how their partners did the actions requested. Now explain the differences between the lists and introduce the categories of adjectives and adverbs. This is an interesting way to present grammar, and you will find that a high level of understanding and retention follows.

From her work on improving writing through the use of imagery in the classroom, Hess (1987) has found these commonalities:

1. Details and descriptions are vivid.

2. Hints of characters' moods and emotions are present.

3. Choice of words is more evocative than informative, thus creating a clear mental picture in the reader's mind's eye.

4. Stories contain events and scenes that are believable even when imaginary.

5. Individual interpretations are as unique as the writers creating them. (p. 18)

By giving gifted students the opportunity to practice the use of imagery their intensity and idealism has another avenue of expression that will allow both qualities to be exercised in problem-solving and the pursuit of their interests and ideals.

Differentiating Curriculum Content

The determination of what content will be used is a concern of educators, students, parents, and the larger community. Currently, it is difficult to select content that will be basic to everyone's education, because in most disciplines information is burgeoning at such a pace that even our advanced technology cannot keep up with it. Just when a theory seems to be gaining validation, new information requires that a new theory be developed, thus generating a new set of problems. It is also difficult to find solutions by staying within disciplines or by calling on expertise from any one content area, because real world problems increasingly are demanding multidisciplinary study. Single disciplines no longer define a problem; understanding our world requires a view that considers the interdependence and interrelationship of all knowledge. The need is for far more multidisciplinary content areas than schools are often prepared to offer.

When giftedness is shown in a content area, it will be important to assess the level of skill the student has already mastered. Gifted learners are commonly 2 to 4 years ahead of their chronological age peers. Once assessed, the students should participate in individual conferences to acquaint them with their own profile of strength areas, and the scope and sequence that is followed in those areas. This will allow them to see the skills for which they are now ready and the future goals for which they might plan.

The needs of the gifted are not deficit needs, but rather needs for challenge in specific areas of strength. Merely providing more of the same level of content will not fulfill this need; we must find ways to accelerate and enrich the concepts and processes in each content area of strength. Generally, our main goal is to go beyond mastery of the content standards to develop with these students a greater understanding of the concepts underlying the disciplines and fields of study. In both mathematics and science, we often find the computational and rational applications emphasized exclusively, so that the excitement found by the practicing mathematician or scientist is missing. Firing the imagination and creative ability of gifted students requires inclusion of the intuitive aspects of math and science. Only in this way can we help students view such subjects as dynamic, with real problems yet to be solved. These, after all, are the students who will contribute most to the knowledge in these fields and disciplines. We must present them with an expanding, potentially limitless world-view.

Differentiating Language Arts

Expressing oneself and communicating one's ideas to others are among the most basic of our sets of skills. These are also the skills gifted children often develop first, enabling their advancing intellect to be identified. Linguists note that they can predict potential language problems by 3 months of age. Not only can early communication be used to predict future language skills, but also early exposure to language skills, especially allowing the child to read, may actually trigger the development of high levels of intelligence.

Gifted ability in language arts is one of the easiest areas of ability to discover. Children with high ability in this area often use complex sentence structures before 2 years of age. Their conceptual development is reflected in the questions and observations they make and the vocabulary they use at this age. Their memory for events seems unusual, and they have a growing body of information they enjoy sharing even before the age of 3. As an example, a 22-month-old child was talking on the phone to her grandmother and when asked what she was doing said,

"I'm playing with my chalkboard."

"You are?" was the response.

"Yes. I played with it yesterday, too."

"Really," commented the surprised grandmother, upon which the child replied,

"Don't you remember? You gave it to me for my happy birthday last Wednesday."

Reading Often gifted children will come to school reading significantly beyond their age peers. Care must be taken, however, that the scope of material presented is difficult enough to tap the extent of this growth. "Top" reading groups may still be far below the gifted reader's capability. As we saw in Chapter 4, many children have ability, but in age-graded classes, they may not be given the opportunity to show just how capable they are.

Mangieri and Madigan (1984) conducted a survey to find out what schools are doing in the area of reading instruction for gifted learners. They reported five findings as having statistical significance:

1. The major focus of reading programs for gifted learners is enrichment.
2. Teacher recommendation was the major identification tool.
3. The same basal series that was used with the nongifted readers was used with the gifted readers.
4. The regular classroom teachers were responsible for the majority of the instruction, and no staff development was available to upgrade their skills in this area.
5. A high degree of communication was reported between the school and the parents of the gifted students.

Brown and Rogan (1983) noted that, just as you would not expect Olympic-bound athletes to get by on their own, gifted readers are in the greatest need of brilliant coaching or, in this case, special and intensive reading instruction. By keeping these children in the regular basal series, insisting that they adhere to the regular reading program, follow-up, and skill-builder activities, we often frustrate them. This can destroy their belief in school as an interesting, exciting place and in learning and books as the wonderful experiences they thought they were. These researchers point to age-in-grade grouping and the reluctance to provide acceleration or experiences beyond the regular classroom as obstacles to appropriate programming for gifted readers. Allowing young children to read widely, creatively, critically, and with an excellent and motivated teacher is suggested as part of the solution to providing more appropriate language arts instruction.

Savage (1983) suggests solving the basal problem by the use of reading guides. A reading guide is an individual assignment sheet that can be used at any level, including high school, and includes a set of questions and activities that structure a reading lesson. Such a structure allows for creativity, student input on activities and evaluation, and more complex and challenging assignments.

Another strategy for challenging gifted learners is to use reading to help them find deeper understanding, both of subject areas and of themselves. Bibliotherapy is a program that uses books and other reading materials as tools to aid children in solving their problems, whether personal or educational. The strategy has been used to help develop a more positive self-concept, to change attitudes and values, and to promote mental and emotional health. The use of this technique with gifted children has special advantages. It takes some of their strength areas, such as their ability to conceptualize, to generalize, and to abstract, and allows them to use these strengths to support areas of need and personal growth. The use of bibliotherapy in the reading program adds depth to the reading and challenges the reader to make complex analyses and connections to find a deeper understanding of the characters and their relationship to themselves. To begin a bibliotherapy program, the needs of the children to be served are first assessed, then assistance is sought for appropriate books to provide solutions for identified problems. A selection of appropriate alternative readings is made available. A file of such books could be established as the teacher discovers them. Follow-up activities and discussions are an important part of such a program. For resources, the Frasier and McCannon (1981) selection of books covering personal, social, and educational/vocational problems should be considered.

Other Activities That Promote Depth, Complexity and Novelty in Language Arts

A Project on Propaganda and Advertising Students learn the basic techniques of propaganda and then analyze grocery and department store displays, newspaper ads, and television commercials for evidence of propaganda.

Meet the Author After reading and discussing the works of authors, the class could invite these authors to teach a seminar on writing with a group of interested students.

Personal Words Integrative Lesson 11.1 in Chapter 11 shows how the reading of a new story can become an integrative lesson while expanding the student's vocabulary (Clark, 1986).

Differentiating Mathematics

Ancient mathematicians were also mystics (e.g., Pythagoras); more recently, important mathematicians and physicists (e.g., Einstein) who communicated in math symbols wrote about the solutions to mathematical problems that they found in images. Currently, schools treat the study of math as though there is no mystery, no insight, and no wonderful visions involved. Inspired, enthusiastic teachers who value the beauty of math keep this often sterile teaching area alive. But for too many students, especially gifted girls, math is only computational rather than conceptual, only analytic, seldom visual, and almost always fraught with anxiety. Most basic math skills taught today allow students to do little more than machines and computers can already do. The goals for school mathematics today must be appropriate for the demands of a global economy in an age of information.

Findings from studies conducted by the National Research Council, the National Council of Teachers of Mathematics, and the American Association for the Advancement of Science (cited in Steen, 1990) agree on many basic new directions that educators must take. Among them are raising expectations for achievement; increasing the breadth of offerings to include estimation, chance, symmetry, and exploration of data; engaging students; demonstrating connections; and reducing fragmentation. For gifted learners, researchers advise us to diagnose the level and pace of instruction needed; group by need; encourage advanced students to use synthesis and evaluation; combine subject matters; and use puzzles, math centers, and contracts (Wolfle, 1988). To allow gifted students to engage in problem-solving using estimation, exploration of connections, and abstract thinking, the following math challenges are presented.

Brain Games*

1. Can you split 100 into four parts so that when you add 4 to one part, you get the same answer as when you multiply 4 by another part, or subtract 4 from another part, or divide the last part by 4?

2. Can you put the digits in for the letters in the following statement so that the addition makes sense in numbers, too? All the o's must be replaced by the same digit, all the n's by the same digit, and so on.

Easy		Difficult	
	one		forty
	_one		ten
	two		_ten
			sixty

3. Mazes Amaze!!! Over 75 years ago, a maze similar to the one in Figure 12.5 stirred considerable interest at the 1926 World's Fair. A person entered the maze after purchasing a ticket. The ticket was punched with the numbers of the gates that the person passed through in attempting to get to the center. In the center of the maze was a small building with the number 138 over the entrance. Anyone holding a card with six numbers (one for each gate) that added up to 138 won a prize. See if you can figure a winning route through the gates to the center. Only six gates can be used, and the total must be 138. For example, if a person went through the gates that have the numbers of 25, 20, 1, 50, 10, and 2, then the total would be 108. Too bad. Can you do it? (Loomis, 1977)

4. The idea is to connect A with A, B with B, and C with C in Figure 12.6 so that no lines cross each other. Lines must stay inside the big rectangle, and they may not go through the small rectangles in which the letters have been placed. (Loomis, 1977)

*See Figure 12.8, p. 471, for answers.

Figure 12.5 *Maze*

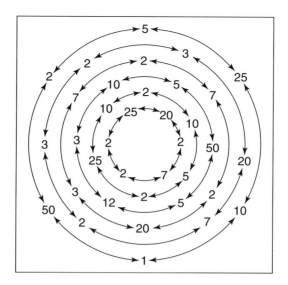

Figure 12.6 *Connect the Boxes*

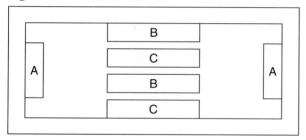

Tessellation Tessellation, a technique for interrelating geometric forms and natural shapes, was first in evidence in Moorish mosaics and then explored in detail by M. C. Escher. Gifted students are fascinated by the intricate relationships that are possible in the construction of tessellated designs, and the technique fills their need for complexity and visual thinking. Figure 12.7 shows procedures that can be used to create the tessellation. Each tessellation is based on an underlying grid of identical triangles, quadrilaterals, or hexagons.

Differentiating Science

More than any other area, science has had an explosion of knowledge to assimilate. And more than any other area, this knowledge has affected the daily lives of us all. Understanding science concepts allows us to understand our world, indeed our inner and outer universe. Gifted children are intensely curious about the questions of science long before they can understand the structure of the discipline. How can

Figure 12.7 *Creating Tessellations*

1. Modify and Translate

2. Modify and Translate

Winged Horse

Figure 12.8 *Answers to Brain Games*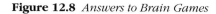

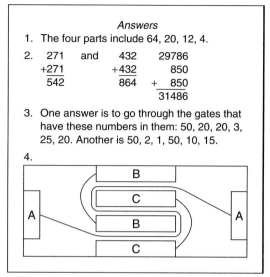

we keep that interest alive? How can we encourage the wonder and awe that the study of our physical and biological worlds creates as these bright children continue through school? Whether or not a career in science is chosen, lifelong learning in this area is necessary if they are to make informed decisions about their futures. And for those who choose to pursue their life's work in this area, how can we help them to be humane and caring in the new worlds they are about to discover? From the very beginning the study of science must be an integrative, multidisciplinary search.

For example, during the 21st century an interplanetary multi-mission program, known as the Outer Planets Program, will explore our solar system and the systems beyond. Included in the missions will be one that places an orbiter around Neptune and another that will drop off a probe on Titan, one of the moons of Saturn, as it speeds on to explore the outer planets. New spacecraft equipped with components at the cutting edge of technology are being designed for these missions by a team of scientists from around the world. The project is being coordinated by and housed at the Jet Propulsion Laboratory (JPL) in Pasadena, California. The following exercise is part of the educational outreach material available to teachers from this project. This and other science project information can be obtained from NASA, Jet Propulsion Laboratory, California Institute of Technology, MS 301-250D, 4800 Oak Grove Dr., Pasadena, CA 91109. This exercise was adapted from material written by Richard Shope (1994), Curriculum Development Lead, JPL.

An Exercise on Interplanetary Distances The astronomical unit is useful within our solar system to aid in our understanding of the vast distances involved between planetary bodies. This activity is designed to give a common frame of reference for relative distances in our solar system.

Divide the class into teams of five to seven in a group or have the cluster group of gifted students complete this exercise and demonstrate the results for the class. Using the information from The Astronomical Unit table (Figure 12.9), have each team choose an arbitrary distance to represent an astronomical unit (for instance, a team member with arms outstretched). Each team has the task of creating a scale model of the relative distances of the solar system in the hall, on the playground, or in a nearby park area. Each team member acts as one of the objects in the solar system.

Variations

1. With chalk, mark the positions of each planetary body.
2. Work out the orbital path of each planetary body, and mark it with chalk, string, or rope.
3. Set the solar system in motion with these calculations.
4. Consider distances beyond the solar system. If Pluto is across the playground from the sun, how far away is Alpha Centauri, the next nearest star?

Research Questions

1. Since its discovery in 1930, Pluto has only moved about one-quarter of its orbit around the sun. How do we observe, predict, and refine our understanding of its orbital path?
2. What other units of measurement can we use within the solar system?

Going Into Depth

1. The relative distances of the visible planets were observed and recorded by ancient skywatchers. What naked eye observations are necessary to determine the distance of the visible planets?
2. The absolute distance between the sun and Earth was not fully calculated until recent times. What observations and basic principles allowed astronomers to calculate this value?

The Astronomical Unit (AU) For interplanetary distances the astronomical unit, or AU, is used. It is a handy ruler that corresponds to the average distance between the sun and Earth, about 93 million miles or 150 million kilometers (Figure 12.10).

Other Activities That Promote Depth, Complexity, and Novelty in Science

Weather Prediction By keeping records and consulting past records of weather and climatic conditions, students can use the laws of probability to predict the weather.

Planning and Developing a Planetarium By careful study of known astronomical data, gifted students can design and build models of the planetary system that can be used for programs they conduct. Mentors in this field could provide the advanced level of thought and depth desired by many gifted learners.

Figure 12.9 *The Astronomical Unit*

Source: From Exercise 1: Interplanetary Distances, *Pluto Express Preproject Curriculum Guide* (p. 2) by R. Shope, 1994. Copyright 1994 by R. Shope. Reprinted with permission.

Interplanetary distance can be expressed in Astronomical Units or A.U., as follows: (Figures represent AVERAGE distance)	
OBJECT	DISTANCE FROM SUN
Sun	0 A.U.
Mercury	0.4 A.U.
Venus	0.7 A.U.
Earth	1.0 A.U.
Mars	1.5 A.U.
Asteroid belt	2.8–3.0 A.U.
Jupiter	5.2 A.U.
Saturn	9.5 A.U.
Chiron	13.7 A.U.
Uranus	19.2 A.U.
Neptune	30 A.U.
Pluto	39 A.U.

Differentiating Social Sciences

By its very nature, the area of the social sciences is multidisciplinary. It is the study of systems past and present, human and political. As we combine this area with science, math, and the language arts, powerful concepts about our world emerge. Again we must be aware of the need to conceptualize, to bring past, present, and future into the overall conceptualization, and to reach for the larger themes. A few approaches follow.

City Redevelopment Project With outside consultative help, students can plan solutions for some of the city problems and present their ideas to appropriate government bodies.

Land and Mountain Measurement Instruction and field trips with a licensed land surveyor give students a new view of math, geology, and land-use planning and development.

Academic areas such as mathematics, science, and social studies (including psychology, sociology, anthropology, economics, etc.) can be made exciting and appropriate for gifted learners by use of integrative experiences, the community, and outside experts. Encouraging research, survey, and field study techniques can make each discipline dynamic. It is the larger concepts, peopled by real participants, not just the involvement with the facts, that stimulates and challenges gifted learners. Allowing students to develop their own curriculum after they have been given conceptual frameworks, such as Bloom's (1956) taxonomy, is a good way to ensure that they will be able to pursue their own interests, as well as those the district considers necessary.

Differentiating Visual and Performing Arts

To develop abilities in the visual and performing arts, the strategies must be specific to the art skill being developed and should be planned and implemented by an accomplished artist. Although all children can benefit from exposure to enrichment in this area, only those teachers with advanced skills will be able to guide a student who shows giftedness through artistic ability.

Although children who show their giftedness through expression in the visual arts are difficult to detect at the elementary level, such identification is important if the proper encouragement is to occur. A strategy suggested by Chetelat (1981) to use for nurturing gifted artists within the classroom is the station learning experience, in which a child can investigate visual arts concepts with an emphasis on exploring in an individual, independent, and accelerated manner. One such station devised by Chetelat contained three 18-in. × 24-in. wooden panels containing on each side reproductions of drawings and paintings of landscapes by great artists, statements concerning advanced concepts to be read and studied, and art history books. One panel contained a landscape by Van Gogh, the other side a landscape by Cezanne. The directions read:

> Look at landscape drawings by Van Gogh and Cezanne to discover ways that the artist used line to represent surface qualities found in nature. Use oil pastels to create a drawing of scenes in your community. Use line direction to emphasize contours of observed surfaces and use line to create textures and patterns on the surfaces of various objects in your drawing. (p. 156)

Chetelat found his students to be enthusiastic about the station learning experience and advises that when supervised by an art specialist, such an experience can be an effective way of providing for gifted artists within the classroom.

Some art educators believe that the most important thing a teacher can do for artistically gifted children is to encourage them to maintain a sketchbook (Szekely, 1982). Such a book can serve to record observations, try out new ideas, develop technical skills, facilitate fanciful play, and most of all provide the growing artist with a place of privacy and freedom that has neither time pressures nor continuity. It is important that the sketchbook be chosen and retained by the artist as personal property. If there is to be an assigned format, it should be in a different book, one to be shared. Encouraging your students to keep their own sketchbooks is encouraging them to be their own art educators, encouraging the freedom, independence, and personal commitment of the accomplished artist.

To help students move from the consumer role in the arts to a creator role and to aid in the identification of those who are most able, programs must be developed to give experiences and understanding of how artistic products are created. An interdisciplinary thematic model, *Arts From the Inside Out*, designed by Cohen (1981) includes all areas of the arts. The program focused the first year on opera and included visiting artists, singers, and production personnel; visits to the orchestra, to cast rehearsals, and to performances behind the scenes; tours; workshops; and in-class projects. The children designed and built sets and props and worked on stage lighting. Some took parts in productions at theaters in the area. All learned firsthand about every aspect of opera production. *Arts From the Inside Out* demonstrated what is possible when children, artists, and teachers work cooperatively together.

Mary Hunter Wolf (1981), a long-time leader in arts programs for gifted learners, suggested that unusual talent can be uncovered by the use of exercises aimed at:

- Learning how to enter and share a learning community.
- Exploring and sharpening individual powers of concentration.
- Learning to own, release, and actualize one's imagination.
- Developing and sharpening environmental awareness.

A specialized curriculum will not, according to Passow (1981), develop poets, musicians, and so forth, but should "activate and motivate the commitment and the development of the competencies and affective behaviors required for nurturing such talents" (p. 6).

Academics and the Arts

The term multidisciplinarity usually refers to the study of the relationships among academic subjects. It is time to include the arts in this integration—not just as a follow-up enrichment activity but as a full partner in the enterprise of learning. On several occasions I have had this art-academic role brought to my attention—from students, from readings and, most powerfully, from events. At a conference for educators interested in serving gifted learners, I had an opportunity to see a performance of a group of students from a local high school for the performing arts. The performance piece they had selected was entitled "Metamorphosis" and told the story in drama, chant, dance, and song of an adolescent's transformation from a self-conscious, confused teenager to a resolute, self-confident, independent young adult. It was well-written and magnificently performed. At the end, it occurred to me that this was indeed a powerful learning experience for the audience. It was not possible to be present at this event and not be changed, in attitude, in point of view or, at the very least, be put in touch with one's own past. From this experience I realized that the arts could have a dynamic place in the transmission of academic knowledge. Such a performance would make many other topics, such as immigration, more meaningful and, therefore, more understandable. Inclusion of such experiences in our academic teaching would be more effective than lecture and would carry understanding to the level of change in the learner.

A biochemist, Robert Root-Bernstein (cited in Ferguson, 1985), proposed much the same idea.

> It's time the contributions of the fine arts to science and technology are recognized and used. . . . [With them] we can provide tools for educating the eye of the mind more fully, or we can [continue] to send students into the world blinkered or blind. It all depends on what kind of science we want to foster. (p. 1)

Root-Bernstein sees the creative process as the unifier of art and science. He believes that the arts embody rational techniques that can be used as organizers for information.

Biologically there are two paths to cognitive processing. By acquainting ourselves with the structure and underlying principles of each specialization we may come to a powerful unified thinking process. Nonverbal forms of thought, especially visual thinking, are at least as important to scientists as verbal forms. Scientific and artistic problem-solving may indeed involve a similar process; physicists Murray Gell-Mann, Victor Weisskopf, and Robert Wilson (cited in Ferguson, 1985) think so. Mathematics and music may have parallel and similar complex systems sharing the same rules and patterns; mathematician Ralph Abraham thinks so (cited in Ferguson, 1985). Root-Bernstein postulated, "The ability to translate between modes of intelligence may be a key" (p. 2). Through the integration of these processes we may be able to develop the power of which each of the academicians is speaking.

Wilson (cited in Cary, 1987), a neurologist, found that music holds fascinating keys to understanding the brain. This belief, in combination with his close relationship with the American Music Conference, has convinced Wilson that music educators must stop isolating music as a separate field and teach it in the core of academic subjects. Music, he suggests, enables students to work toward unpredictable outcomes that are similar to discoveries made from scientific inquiry. Kean (1989) believes that now more than ever the arts have important contributions to make to education. Examples of our moral and ethical traditions can be found in our art. Through the arts we may be trained to see more clearly, hear more acutely, and feel more sensitively—skills now seen to be essential to surviving with civility and joy.

INDIVIDUALIZING INSTRUCTION

Once the environment has been made responsive to the teacher and the student, integrative lessons have been planned, the curriculum and the materials have been differentiated, and the students have been assessed to determine which pattern of modification will be needed, individualized instruction is the natural and logical next step. This is not one-on-one teaching, but rather instruction that uses the flexibility of the environment and the range of grouping patterns, materials, content, and strategies to deliver curriculum that meets the assessed needs of the students. Continuous progress is ensured when instruction results from such careful planning.

Individualization can be defined as a way of organizing learning experiences so that the pace of instruction, content, complexity of activities, and depth of exploration available to all students stem from their assessed achievement, needs, and interests. Varying degrees, or levels, of individualization are possible:

Level 1. The teacher assesses each student's needs, resulting in an individualized level and pace of instruction.

Level 2. The instruction becomes more personalized when, in addition to individualized level and pace, the student becomes involved in the selection of goals.

Level 3. Once Levels 1 and 2 have been achieved, the student can begin to incorporate self-directed or independent study skills, as well as the responsibility to self-select learning activities and materials.

Level 4. Total individualization allows teacher and student to cooperatively assess and select goals, learning materials, activities, and instructional techniques. This also allows the student to self-pace, self-level, and self-evaluate, using the teacher as a consultant and resource.

Optimum learning occurs when the environment allows students to:

- Assume some responsibility for their own learning.
- Learn at their own pace.
- Learn by way of material related to their own style.
- Learn on a level appropriate to their abilities.
- Be graded in terms of their own achievement.
- Experience a sense of perceived control, achievement, and self-esteem.
- Become independent learners.

We can understand the importance of individualizing the curriculum for each learner through the eyes of a child in a classroom where everyone learns in the same way, with the same material, at the same time. Keeping in mind what brain researchers tell us about the need gifted children have for high levels of stimulation, which if not supplied results in self-generated stimulation blocking all external input, a teacher's remembrance from her childhood has poignant insight:

I'm a night exploding fireflowers; rockets and shrieking shimmers split my sky!	Now a giant clam on a reef with showers of fishes rainbowing by.	A hungry, hungry polar bear on a slippery, tippy chunk of ice.	Who? Me? No, teacher; I'm not bored. I think your class is nice.

(A. G. Thompson, 1987)

Comparing the instruction of persons who achieved exceptional accomplishment of international note with the instruction of those who made less significant contributions, Bloom and Sosniak (1981) found that the early instruction and much of the later instruction in their field of accomplishment had been individualized.

A number of strategies can help to individualize instruction:

1. *Programmed learning* offers students a way to move at their own pace through skill-level learning. It includes individual assessment and allows students continuous feedback on work that is done at their own level. Programmed learning frees the teacher from much unnecessary drill work and allows students to learn materials basic to higher learning or research by a self-checking procedure.

2. *Learning activity packages* provide a way for students to work individually or in small groups and to take charge of their learning. A learning activity package includes an assessment or pre-test procedure that permits students to discover their own level of need, multisensory resources and activities, and a self-evaluation or post-test component. The package gives students a way to move through basic materials and new information. It should be self-paced and allow students to correct all their own mistakes prior to the teacher's evaluation of the learned information or skill.

3. *Learning contracts* can be as simple as a statement of need or intent by the student, a description of what will be needed for accomplishing such a goal, and the agreed-on evaluation procedures or criteria for deciding when the project or learning goal has been completed. Or it can be very complex, depending on its use and the student's ability to be self-directed. Usually the teacher and the learner cooperate in negotiating the learning contract; negotiation may even include the parents. Contractual decisions should be made after substantial assessment has been completed and its results have been discussed with the student. The teacher and the student (and sometimes the parents) cooperatively decide on the goals, resources to be used, possible activities, reporting alternatives, and evaluation procedures for both self-assessment and teacher assessment. Although contracts give a mutually agreed-on base for beginning, they must always remain negotiable. Many factors such as detours and side investigations can cause the original plan to need modification.

The Power of Choice

In developing an individualized program, one of the most critical areas of concern is motivation. A very important way to bring out the motivation of students is to make them aware of their own power and to allow them to exercise it. Any way that a program or course can be structured to give more choice to the student enhances that power.

Not all gifted students make choices easily. The choices must be structured for those who have difficulty in order to guide them gradually into their own power. Others will be ready for responsible freedom; they should be given independence immediately. The following ideas have been found to work in allowing responsible choice:

- The non-negotiables, whether mandated by the state, the district, or the school, should be known. The students must understand the real consequences to the teacher and to themselves of choice related to these non-negotiables. For example, if the state requires the completion of a certain course of study, how that can be accomplished and what will happen if it is not should be discussed. Information and choices should be given to students in whatever areas are possible. One teacher found that by telling the students what the class requirements were and what other things could be done when they finished, she and the students worked out a schedule that got the required work completed in time to pursue other materials and projects. Previously, students in her classes had moved slowly and unwillingly through only the required work.

- If tests are used for evaluation, a choice can be given between objective and subjective examination, between teacher-written or student-written tests. Often, even though the same previously used tests are to be given, the element of choice creates more willing, more motivated students.

- If tests are not required, then contracts can be initiated with students allowing a choice over a wide range of possible products and evaluation criteria. Portfolios would provide a useful organizational tool for assessment.

- Many ways of reaching the same learning goal can be established. At the secondary level, classrooms for English can become learning labs just as well as classrooms for chemistry. In the elementary class, the possibilities are limited only by the teacher's creativity.

- Cross-grading can be accomplished, even in traditionally structured schools, by developing a relationship between different-age classes or nearby schools and allowing students extended passes to work with these other students in their classrooms.

- Off-school sites can be made available for those interested in working independently.

- The requirements for entry into the colleges and universities that students will likely attend should be made public and accessible. The students and their parents can then make choices about which of these sets of requirements best meet the students' needs.

Gifted students are interested in current topics that involve them and their personal welfare. Any new information, such as discoveries in brain research or physics, that can be shown to affect them and their world is of great interest, especially if presented with all the unanswered questions and future challenges. Allowing choice of such topics when the content standard is to teach skills such as analyzing and synthesizing information increases their motivation for learning the skill.

Secondary educators might consider using an open, individualized approach that would allow more subject areas to be taught at higher levels. One school with a small faculty can offer 5 years of all basic languages, plus any number of other languages (e.g., Latin, Russian, and Japanese) by teaching in an individualized pattern. Students can sign up for the language of their choice at their appropriate level. The individualization model allows them to receive instruction while others pursue their own choices during the same period. One period of typing or computer processing could be individualized to accommodate many levels and instructional goals. A business teacher in my university class developed a programmed typing manual to help her individualize her class. This method of presenting instruction would work for all subject areas.

Interdisciplinary presentations are most requested by gifted students. One teacher with the proper background or a team from differing disciplines can make this approach available. Be aware that what the students are asking for is not tandem teaching, with one instructor then the other, but a real team situation in which the students can be a part of an interaction between disciplines.

One of the best approaches to individualizing I have discovered was presented by Dunn and Dunn (1975). See Figure 12.10 for their step-by-step approach

Figure 12.10 *A Step-by-Step Approach to Individualizing the Classroom*
(Taken from the work of Dunn & Dunn, 1975)

---

1. Give students opportunities to build the skills needed for participation in individualized learning to:
   a. Make choices (choosing wisely offers many options; choosing less wisely allows fewer options, and only consequences can determine the value of the choice)
   b. Self-evaluate
   c. Share
2. Teach students the skills of learning in small groups:
   a. Role playing
   b. Peer teaching
   c. Group analysis
   d. Discussion
3. Establish instructional areas that will support individualized learning:
   a. Interest centers
   b. Learning stations
   c. Media center
   d. Game area
   e. Quiet reading and study area
   f. Assessment center
4. Develop student independence:
   a. Knowledge of resources, location, and use
   b. Alternative thinking in activities and in reporting
5. Carefully assess students, curricula, and resources.
6. Help class learn skills of cooperative assessment, goal setting, and evaluation.
7. Let class assume more responsibility for planning and implementing the program.

---

to individualizing a classroom successfully. These steps are not easy. They require time and effort to be used successfully. However, if the goal is independent, stimulated learners, then the efforts will be well-rewarded.

Developing the Individual Educational Plan for Gifted Students

One way some states have chosen to ensure that their gifted students' needs for individualized planning are met is to modify the Individuals with Disabilities Education Act (IDEA) (PL 94–142)*, a federal law requiring that all students with disabilities receive an annual Individual Educational Plan (IEP). By legislative action, several states have included gifted learners as children with special needs along with learners with disabilities. As a result, individualized planning has been mandated for gifted learners in those states.

An IEP would be easy to plan from the student's profile suggested when the assessment for identification was developed. In addition to the profile data,

---

*PL 94–142 was originally enacted in 1975 under the name Education for All Handicapped Children Act.

objectives must be identified that reflect the needs shown by the profile; activities planned to meet them, including a time line for implementation; and an evaluation of the child's progress toward these objectives developed. It is important to be realistic but not adhere to minimum limits when planning these objectives. One advantage of the IEP system is the planning conference at which the parents, the teacher, the gifted specialist, and the school psychologist and other appropriate school personnel meet to discuss the educational plan and its implementation. If done in a cooperative spirit, the team effort can have very positive outcomes for all concerned, especially for the child.

The secondary teacher is asked to look again at Chapters 10 and 11 with a view to adapting and translating the models and suggestions to fit gifted learners. The description of the IEM and its use of brain/mind research in the classroom does not change, nor does the environment in which it can best be implemented, whether at the elementary or at the secondary level. What does change is the way the implementation looks. Just as a decentralized laboratory setting in language arts looks different from this type of environment in science, so the individualized setting looks different when a school has a core curriculum or a six-period day. The appearance may be different, but the same rules apply.

Individualizing the secondary experience for students is within reach of teachers, even in the traditional departmentalized setting with 35 students per period and at least 175 different students every day.

Beginning an Individualized Education Plan

The plan and step-by-step procedures in Figures 12.11 and 12.12 are beginning activities for individualizing. They have been successful in a high school class in which the teacher who uses them, Toby Manzanares, averages 170 students each 8-hour day. He begins the individualizing process the first week of the new semester. The process will last the entire year but will be modified, improving as the students provide input. One advantage secondary teachers have is the ability of their students to assume a partnership role in individualizing their learning. When given the opportunity, students can share the responsibility.

Manzanares feels that the process of individualizing a classroom begins with getting to know each student as a unique individual. He believes that as he comes to know his students during the semester, he learns from each of them what they care about, what they are interested in, their strengths, what they want to improve, and where they want to go in life. He pays careful attention to what they tell him and uses these data to connect the content of the course to the individual student in a meaningful way. By the end of the semester, he has gotten to know most of his students well. He believes his life is richer for knowing them, and they benefit from knowing each other. The entire learning experience becomes more personal.

Later in the course, Manzanares continues the individualization process with Customized Term Projects and Learning Expeditions. (For a step-by-step plan and support material for the Learning Expedition, see Chapter 4, pp. 85–108 in *Optimizing Learning,* [Clark, 1986].) Manzanares believes that with the attitude that it is possible to individualize the secondary classroom, the reality can be achieved step by step. Empowering learners gives them greater skill at making choices. Planning

Figure 12.11 *The Individual Inventory*

Source: Developed by Tobias Manzanares, Schurr High School, Montebello, California, 1986.

STEP 1 The class participates in a lecture/discussion of an educational concept that operates from the premise that, "Each individual in this room has knowledge that, once shared, will be valuable to the teacher-learner and, just as importantly, to each student as a learner-teacher."

STEP 2 The class is asked to consider things of value that can be shared with the group. (A typical comment at this point is, "Like what?" which leads nicely to the introduction of the inventory sheet.)

STEP 3 The inventory sheet is examined and the questions discussed (see Figure 12.12). Students are instructed to scan the room looking for people they don't know. Students are instructed to stand up and select one of these unknown students for a partner. At this point the teacher may add, "Should any of you have a concern about not being picked as a partner, then be the first to move to make a selection."

STEP 4 The teacher helps the few students remaining form dyads and works with the last student should there be an odd number present.

STEP 5 Instructions for the dyads are:
   a. Write your partner's name in the space provided on the inventory sheet.
   b. Interview your partner using the questions on the sheet and note your partner's answers as you go. Take turns answering questions as you work down the sheet. At the end of 10 minutes, you will introduce your partner to the class and your partner will introduce you, sharing with the group two or three unique qualities you've discovered about each other.

STEP 6 Instructions to the class before the sharing session: "On your data sheet (see Figure 12.12) record the name of the person being introduced and one of the unique qualities he or she possesses. Also record at least one observation of your own as you attend to the person being introduced."

STEP 7 The teacher now invites a dyad to begin by introducing each other.

STEP 8 As students introduce each other, the teacher can record relevant personal data for each individual on the reverse side of the class roster. By the end of the session the teacher will have the beginnings of a data bank on each student. In addition, the teacher can collect the papers from the group and will then have 34 student perceptions of each individual in the room.

---

a curriculum with choices available individualizes the classroom as students learn to personally select more meaningful learning activities.

A Format for Differentiated, Integrative, and Individualized Content

The following format was developed to allow teachers to include a wide range of content, processes, and products as a part of the planning of all lessons. By changing the format to meet your particular needs and style of planning, you may find it useful as you differentiate the curriculum for your students.

Figure 12.12 *Inventory and Data Sheets*
Source: Developed by Tobias Manzanares, Schurr High School, Montebello, California, 1986.

Period: _____ Name: _____

PERSONAL INVENTORY BY INTERVIEW

1. If you could go anywhere in the world, where would you go and why would you go there? _____

2. Who is the person you admire the most and why? _____

3. What is your favorite book? _____
4. What is your favorite song? _____
5. Are you extreme, liberal, conservative, or otherwise? _____

6. What is your favorite sport (as a participant)? _____
7. What is your favorite sport (as a spectator)? _____
8. What is your favorite pastime? _____
9. What is your favorite class and why? _____
10. What is your favorite animal and why? _____
11. What would you do with $115,000? _____
12. What is the funniest thing that ever happened to you? _____

13. What is the greatest thing that has ever happened to you? _____
14. What is the strangest thing that has ever happened to you? _____
15. What are your special talents? _____
16. What makes you unique? _____
17. Additional questions: _____

DATA SHEET 1—INDIVIDUAL INVENTORY

1. Name: _____
   Notes and Observations: _____

2. Name: _____
   Notes and Observations: _____

3. Name: _____
   Notes and Observations: _____

4. Name: _____
   Notes and Observations: _____

5. Name: _____
   Notes and Observations: _____

6. Name: _____
   Notes and Observations: _____

7. Name: _____
   Notes and Observations: _____

The Student's Integrative Education Planning Sheet (Figure 12.13) can be used to present curriculum choices to help students become more responsible for their own learning. Allowing students to participate in the learning process at the planning level makes them feel empowered.

In the upper left corner of the planning sheet is printed "*Nonnegotiable." This tells students that asterisked items are not negotiable and must become a part of their plan of study. Under the heading "Content Standards," the teacher lists all of the knowledge and/or skills involved in the lesson being taught, with nonnegotiables listed first. The teacher may then list a number of other areas of content or skills that could be studied but that are not required. For example, in a lesson on the westward movement in the United States, the nonnegotiable content might be the geography of the westward movement, the dates involved, and the major events leading to this movement. Other areas of content that might be interesting to study, but which would not be required, could include the economic climate of the times, the role of women, or an in-depth study of the cultures of the people involved. Students use the box on the right of the teacher's listing of content to list the choices of knowledge or skill they wish to put in their study plan.

In the "Performance Standards: Ways to Learn" section, are four subcategories: Cognitive, Affective, Physical, and Intuitive. Using the westward movement example, some cognitive activities could be "Read the text pp. 22 to 115," "Read and report on four sources other than your text," or "Collect a series of maps showing the westward movement." An asterisk indicating required reading would precede the text reading. The affective area might have suggestions such as, "Participate in a class simulation of the westward movement," "Prepare a monologue revealing the feelings of a Plains Indian as the land of these people began to be invaded by the pioneers," or "Read the open-ended vignettes about life in the covered wagons and discuss with one or two classmates the possible resolutions to the problems posed." The physical category could include, "Develop a salt and flour map of the territories explored during the westward movement," "Collect and display items for a museum on this historical period," or "Demonstrate a skill pioneers would have needed that is no longer common today." The intuitive area might read, "Participate in a class fantasy trip back in time to the days of the movement west," "Write a short essay on what would have changed if there had been no mountains in the West," or "Imagine the outcome if there had been thousands more Indians in the West and write what you think it would be like then and now." Again the students choose ways to learn that they prefer, writing them in the "Your Choice" box to the right of the teacher's list. Students must list one activity from each subcategory.

The "Products" section lists suggested outcomes and the criteria the teacher will use to evaluate them. Using the same westward movement example, some products might be "An examination," "A filmstrip of life in the West," "A study center on women of the West," "A portfolio giving evidence of knowledge of both negotiable and nonnegotiable knowledge and skills," with asterisks again communicating which products are nonnegotiable. Students are free to add ideas that are agreeable to the teacher to any of the sections.

The "Time Line" in the lower right-hand corner of Figure 12.13 allows both the student and the teacher to project the deadline dates for different areas of study.

Figure 12.13 *Student's Integrative Education Planning Sheet*

*Nonnegotiable Content/Skills Standards
- *
- *
- *

Your Choice
- *
- *
- *
- Other:

Performance Standards: Ways to Learn
- *Cognitive
- *Affective
- *Physical
- *Intuitive

Your Choice

*Choose at least one from each

- Other:

Products
- *
- *

Evaluation Criteria

Your Choice
- *
- *
- Other:

Your Plan:

Content/Skills	Ways to Learn	Products	Evaluation
	Cog.		
	Aff.		
	Phys.		
	Int.		

Time Line

Task				Dates							

EVALUATING LEARNING AND TEACHING

The information in Chapter 10 on assessment of knowledge, understanding, and interest also applies to the evaluation of learning and teaching. The evaluation process should include strategies that parallel the instruction. Strategies such as student inquiry, collaboration, and reflection may be used as a means of collecting information about student knowledge, understanding, and skill mastery. Standardized or specially constructed tests, rating scales, questionnaires, interview schedules, or observation techniques can be used. The students' growth should be assessed individually and compared with their own past achievements and developed criteria.

If the assessment procedures (discussed in Chapter 10) are used regularly, then data collection becomes relatively easy. Evaluation should be ongoing throughout the year. When additional data are needed which the usual assessment procedure overlooked, the procedure should be expanded to include such information. When used properly, evaluation data become part of the total assessment package.

Evaluation of gifted learners is made more difficult by the system of age-grouped classes, which may have inadequate content and performance standards. The instruments used for evaluating learners also presents difficulties if only normative data are used.

However, the most difficult issue is assigning grades to the achievements of gifted students. Although performance assessment, especially the use of portfolios, will be far more useful in learning about their progress and ability, in many school settings, grades are required.

You are attending a commencement program at a local high school. The senior class valedictorian, a lovely young woman, gives a pleasant but not very insightful address. As the scholarships from local service organizations are announced, you notice that the students you know well from the Honors and Advanced Placement classes receive only a few awards. After the ceremony, you inquire of one of the students about the identity of the valedictorian, someone you had not known before. "Oh, she took a lot of home economics courses," you are told. "Her grade point average was higher than any of ours because we took all those accelerated classes." To your dismay, you discover this is also the reason the gifted students did not receive more of the service club special awards and scholarship money.

Grading Gifted Learners

To understand the problems of grading encountered by gifted students, we must first understand the problems inherent in the practice of grading itself. Grading began as our society moved toward the goal of mass education. When it became impossible for school personnel to know each student and that student's ability, a system was devised to give a symbol—the grade—for each student's achievement. Individual ability disappeared into a more manageable, numerically manipulatable representation of academic ability. Grades have been an integral part of schooling, indeed the major part, for more than half a century. Now it is difficult to conceive of schools functioning without them. Grading does not, however, contribute to the learning process, and in many ways it inhibits and impedes learning. Whatever reasons are given for continued use of grading, it must be recognized as a force external to the student. These reasons are given for using grades (not evaluations, but grades):

- They provide a convenient communication of the student's academic progress to parents, administrators, other teachers, and the student.
- They provide motivation for performance.
- They help the school gain the cooperation of the parents in pursuing educational goals.
- They establish an overall academic pattern of the student for other teachers, counselors, and administrators.
- They establish data for educational research.

Grades Have No Inherent Stable Meaning and Low Reliability

Grades are usually based on tests, observations, and performance as rated by the teacher. The teacher almost always subjectively constructs tests, even when they are given and scored in an objective manner. Few teachers take the time needed or have learned the skills necessary to construct valid tests. Observations made over time provide far more data than test scores. However, many teachers have not developed adequate observational skills, and the observations they make tend to be influenced by such things as their personal feelings about the student and the student's behavior, appearance, status, previous academic record, label, and so on (LaBenne & Greene, 1969; Reichstein & Pipkin, 1968).

Teachers differ significantly in their interpretations of grades and in the standards they use. Even the philosophy of grading varies from teacher to teacher. Some believe grades should show student effort, others grade on how much success a student has had in meeting a goal, and still others grade against an outside criteria set up for the entire class or grade level. Many teachers grade according to a distribution dictated by the statistical representation of a normal population ("grading on the curve"). Although statisticians will quickly point out that the size of most classes makes the use of the curve technique totally inappropriate, it is, nevertheless, quite commonly used, especially in secondary and higher educational systems. Even with adaptations, this method of grading can be very unfair to the students and results in arbitrary and capricious grades (LaBenne & Greene, 1969).

Leiter and Brown (1985) have shown that teacher expectations and bias affect grades. The student's reputation, label, special placement, behavior, previous grades, and even race and social class may, in part, determine the grades received. With such a range of philosophies and beliefs possible, Leiter and Brown believe that grading as a standard for comparison is worthless.

Engleberg and Evans (1986) found that using grades for comparative purposes is of even less value in classrooms of exceptional performers. Grades do not reveal creativity, internal motivation, or special talents and interests. These researchers found that high-achieving students are less likely than lower achieving students to view grades as either an expected or necessary part of school and they do not believe that grades are a good source of feedback.

Researchers have noted the variation in interpretation and its effect on grading in a number of studies in which teachers from different classes, in some cases from different schools, were asked to grade the same papers. The range of grades on a single paper was extreme. Some defensive teachers blamed the results on the material used, and they believed that the outcome would be different if papers and examinations from the more precise disciplines of math and science were used. If anything, the range in grades was even greater in math and science. Even when graders have received intensive training to ensure reliability, they disagree significantly. Such factors as fatigue and personal values, as well as students' neatness, organization, and showing or not showing calculations, all influence grading. Over a 2-month period, teachers have been found to be inconsistent in re-marking the same paper. Thus, it seems that variability in marks is not a function of the subject, but rather of the grader. When analyzing the meaning of grades, we should mention that some teachers even use testing and test grades for punishment, for example, the "pop quiz" to punish those who might not have studied (Rosenthal & Jacobsen, 1969; Temple University, 1968).

Grades Do Not Predict Success in Careers, Living, or Level of Ability

Numerous studies continue to show little or no correlation between grades received in high school or college and future success in the world of work. Only moderate correlation exists between test scores and grades with long-range academic performance and none with postacademic performance. Even in professions that are highly dependent on skills (e.g., engineering, teaching, physics), there is little relationship between grades and later career success. The type of schools attended, the number of years of education, and the teachers and student peers encountered all seem to have a greater correlation with success. The only predictive ability grades seem to have is on the basis of entry screening, in which the grade point average (GPA) is used for hiring, placement, or further study; but beyond this use as a screen, little correlation with job performance has been found. It has been pointed out that the GPA is an average or mean figure that flattens any high levels of achievement, thereby leaving outstanding abilities hidden in some cases (Drews, 1972; Hoyt, 1965; Lavin, 1965; Wright, 1965).

For Most Students, Grades Do Not Motivate Learning

For a few successful students, grades provide external motivation toward greater effort and achievement. A student who has repeatedly experienced success may be motivated to perform for grades. Even with these students, there is the risk for lessening their intrinsic motivation and creating a reward situation that makes learning only a means, not a fulfilling or exciting pursuit in its own right. For less successful students, grades serve only to demean and debilitate their self-concept further. The research shows that downgraded students continue to fail.

From their interviews with high-achieving students, Perrone and Male (1981) found that they "frequently dislike doing assignments and perceive a good grade not as recognition for what was produced but rather as payment for having endured such a painful or dull experience. Good grades may in fact lead good students to resent formal learning, while poor grades combined with a dislike of the learning task may lead poor achievers to abhor formal learning" (pp. 69–70). Both those who are failing and others whose performance is mediocre sometimes resort to failure-avoiding strategies such as false effort, academic cheating, or acting out in class to gain peer approval (Covington & Beary, 1976).

Intellectual ability may not be the determiner for categorizing students by grading. Under the threat of grades, bright students balk at venturing into the unknown or trying any area in which they are not sure they will succeed. Boredom, irrelevant assignments, repetition, meaningless or unrealistic subject matter, and lack of opportunity to build skills all contribute to low grades. Researchers have shown grades to be poor indicators of student learning. Short-term memorization, cheating, and other coping strategies result directly from grading practices; learning does not (Fala, 1968; Knowlton & Hamerlyneck, 1967; LaBenne & Greene, 1969). Others (Bidwell, 1973; Covington & Beary, 1976) have found that the excessive reliance on extrinsic rewards, the atmosphere of continual evaluation, and the fact that standards for success or failure are set by someone other than the student result in a breakdown in commitment and in self-regulated learning. When performance is exchanged for grades, many high-achievers learn shortcuts to achievement rewards and learn to regard out-of-class learning as unrewarding (Doyle, 1978). Maehr and Stallings (1972) provide evidence that continuing motivation may be directly affected by the nature of evaluation procedures. They found that external evaluation, even though used to maintain or increase performance in the classroom, does so while producing negative effects on continued motivation.

Evaluation Without Grades Facilitates the Learning Process

Allowing students the knowledge of their strengths and weaknesses while giving them support and opportunities to develop their skills is important to learning. Providing an environment where mistakes are valued as clues to the next needed learning experiences promotes exploration and increases areas of knowledge. Reducing anxiety promotes long-term retention and higher quantities of knowledge gained.

Evaluation, as a continuous process, can use many sources for data collection. In evaluating, the teacher is the facilitator who helps the students discover their strengths and weaknesses and their interests and abilities and guides their growth toward greater fulfillment of their potential.

> The question is not how many of the "right" things the student remembered, what the student did to the subject, or how well he compared with others. It is rather how well did the student do in the things the teacher and student agreed were important, what the subject did to the student, and how he compared to his own goals and objectives. (LaBenne & Greene, 1969, p. 87)

Gifted students in pull-out classes often encounter grading practices that penalize them for missing class sessions while they attend their special classes. One junior high student related that his math teacher held him responsible for material covered during the classes he missed, although he was working on second-year algebra in his gifted class. Even worse, he would explain assignments for the week and how he wanted them done while the student was out of the room. When he returned and asked for the information, the teacher said, "You're gifted. Figure it out." One of the reasons for the criticism by gifted students and their parents of special classes and honor programs is the inequitable grading.

As evidenced in our vignette, students in high schools find scholarships, honors at graduation, and even membership in honor societies based on their GPA. I have, on several occasions, noted the frustration of gifted students who were passed over for special awards because of their attendance in the honors classes. In an attempt to correct the situation, some schools have adopted a grading policy that requires accelerated classes to give all students A's, or extra points for the class that will appear on their transcripts; however, these directions can also create problems.

Parents have often been the reason schools keep or revert to grading practices. In many schools, teachers and administrators are pleased by the conference method of evaluating. Although it may require more work, many teachers feel it more clearly reflects the student's achievements and is far more diagnostic in nature. However, they complain that the parents insist on knowing how their children compare to other children, rather than what their strengths and weaknesses are, and what grade they received, rather than in what areas they should be guided.

In a statewide survey taken of parents and teachers by a California advocacy group, the following questions produced some interesting answers:

1. *What grading practices are used in honors classes in your district or your school?*
   - In one district program no grades are given.
   - A normal curve or traditional grading is used in 70% of the districts, and several parents complained that grades are used as motivators and require more work to obtain than the same grade in a regular class.
   - Special provisions such as narrative reporting with grades, counseling during day-to-day evaluation, and detailed reporting of data from projects used for grades are made for 30% of the districts.

2. *Do you feel that grading practices are a major consideration in whether students enroll in these classes?*
   - More than half of the teachers and parents believed this to be a factor.

3. *If you feel grading practices penalize gifted students or discourage involvement in honors classes, what provisions are being made to remedy the situation?*
   - In half the cases it was reported that either the local parent group or the individual parent recommended a change to the local school board, with no results.
   - Others had made no attempt to change the policy.

4. *What would you recommend be done locally or statewide to alter grading procedures?*
   - Some suggestions offered were: self-evaluation, grading on an individualized basis, conferencing, no grades in honors classes, weighted grades for honors classes, in-service for parents and teachers on grading practices and policies, use of more comments, and special notation of honors courses on the transcript.

Grades are quickly read, easy-to-manipulate symbols. In our ever-growing school system, they provide a quick way to categorize and group children. However, grades are also unfair, misleading, meaningless in most cases, and damaging to the self-concept of both bright and less bright children. They create pressures and anxieties for both teachers and students. They neither motivate nor contribute to learning. They communicate information on a par with chance estimates; at best, what they say is neither explicit nor constructive. But for many parents and teachers, grades are the most important part of the school's responsibility.

Syphers (1972) wrote of a teacher who wanted a different use to be made of the students' work and devised a way for students to do their own diagnoses. She displayed a checklist of common weaknesses and had the students organize and file sets of their papers. At regularly designated times, the students examined their papers to discover which mistakes they repeatedly made and why (owing to carelessness, haste, lack of skill, misreading directions, etc.). She found that self-diagnosis created involvement on the part of the students in their own improvement and did not impose the stifling effects of grading. It also saved her a great deal of time. Even when a grade must ultimately be recorded, self-evaluation can be an important part of the process. It is possible to evaluate constructively and, if learning is our goal, the effort is really worth it.

Gifted students present special problems in the process of assigning grades. On objective tests they are often at the top of the testing scale or the stanine chart at the beginning of the class. Their progress is difficult to record on standardized or norm-referenced tests. Criterion-referenced tests are often set more appropriately for the nongifted students at grade level, thus presenting the gifted learners, especially those who are highly gifted, with a ceiling beyond which they cannot register. Their motivation for achieving high test scores may be very low, because rather than experiencing new learning opportunities, they may be re-learning previously mastered work. By establishing content and performance standards that reflect a differentiated curriculum based on their level of knowledge, understanding, and skill and by including self-evaluation, a more appropriate and realistic evaluation plan can be developed for the gifted learner.

REFLECT AND RE-FORM

Six of the seven steps to optimizing learning have now been discussed: creating a responsive learning environment; integrating the intellectual processes; assessing the knowledge, understanding, and interest; differentiating the curriculum; individualizing instruction; and evaluating learning and teaching. The seventh reviews all of the other six, reflects on how they were planned and implemented, and considers what changes need to occur to re-form the lessons, unit, and/or program to make it more effective. The seventh step brings the reader full circle and ensures that the program will be dynamic and growth producing.

In this chapter, differentiation of the curriculum, allowing the content to become more appropriate for gifted learners, was discussed. Frameworks and checklists were presented to help organize this most important method of modifying teaching and learning. Five clusters of common learning characteristics found in populations of gifted learners—acceleration, complexity, depth, novelty, and intensity and idealism—were highlighted as ways to meet the needs created by such characteristics were explored. Formats for differentiating content were presented, as were suggestions for activities in each content area. Individualization was seen as a natural next step in modifying learning and teaching to meet needs of gifted students. Grading still presents problems to educators, and for the gifted learner the problem is magnified. Reflection on how all of the seven steps and the issues they raise can best be utilized in the classroom can lead to re-forming education. For gifted students this can mean making their learning experience more challenging and more meaningful. Ideas and strategies discussed in Chapters 10 and 11 should provide a starting place to accomplish these seven steps for optimizing learning. Students allowed to meet their needs in such a classroom will move closer to the goal of realizing their unique potential.

QUESTIONS OFTEN ASKED

1. Why is knowing characteristics of gifted learners important to differentiating the curriculum?

It is from the characteristics of gifted learners that we can get a general idea of what their needs may be. As we plan to meet those needs, this knowledge will give us a way to prepare and a place to start. If we know that certain behaviors are characteristic of gifted children, then we will not be surprised or concerned when some of those behaviors are expressed. Many times teachers and parents who have heard these characteristics for the first time comment, "Oh, that's why he does that!" or "I thought she was just being weird."

2. What is the difference between differentiation and individualization?

Differentiation for gifted learners is the preparation that is made for the curriculum to respond to their characteristic needs, such as allowing for a faster pace of learning and choosing themes and content that allow for more complex investigation. Individualization for gifted learners is the process of adapting that curriculum to the needs and interests of a particular gifted student. A program for gifted learners requires both to be most successful.

3. If I have content that is required by the district, how can I differentiate the curriculum for the gifted students in my classroom?

Content or skills that are required for all children can be put into the context of a more complex theme or can be enriched by broader inquiry. For example, a study of prehistoric times can be included in the theme of Effects of Change or the question of the relationship of past to present to future. It is also possible to include a range of different processes and products in your planning that will allow the gifted learners in your classroom to make choices and to meet their needs more appropriately while meeting the district requirements. It is also possible to consider compacting, a strategy that Renzulli (1977) detailed with procedures and forms in his Enrichment Triad Model. As long as the student can show evidence of having learned the required content, the time can then be planned more appropriately.

4. Why is individualized instruction so important for gifted learners?

It is important for all learners; however, learners with special needs find it essential. Gifted students are so different from each other, as well as from less able students, that they do not fit into any norms. They do not achieve at high levels in all of the content areas. It then becomes important to know just where they are and allow them to move from there.

5. How can I individualize instruction when I have 35 students in my classroom?

With 35 students and only one teacher in a classroom, any instructional strategy will be harder to manage. It is important that you plan your classroom environment to work for you. By building flexibility into the schedule and the room arrangement, providing a range of materials available, and having a number of designated areas already set up, your job becomes easier. If you have already planned opportunities for acceleration, complexity, in-depth study, novelty, and intensity and idealism, then you can draw on those materials and use those strategies on a moment's notice and more easily meet the needs of all of the students. Actually, working in this way is easier than trying to keep everyone in the same material all of the time and much more productive.

6. Individualization, flexible grouping, multidisciplinary teaching, responsive environments—these all sound good, but how can we do any of these with only 40 minutes per class?

A 40-minute time block is very difficult to work with. You might want to try to find another teacher or two who want to team for at least part of the day. That would allow you to put two or three time blocks together, teach in a multidisciplinary fashion (if the other teacher was from a different discipline), and use flexible grouping. Even in a single time block you can get closer to these ideas if you create an environment that is supportive and more like a learning lab. If neither of these is possible, you then must become very creative to include as much as you can from the research information that results in optimal learning, much as Manzanares does in the Individual Inventory

(Figure 12.11). You have identified one of the greatest barriers to making the secondary system more effective, the short blocks of time in which the teachers and students try to operate.

7. If a teacher is not "enthusiastic" about math and only follows the textbook, what can he or she do to meet the needs of students gifted in math?

No one is great at everything. That is why it is so helpful to team with those who have other interests and skills. If you choose not to team-teach, you may wish to take a workshop or two from a very enthusiastic math specialist. Mentors can be of help here—parents, professionals, or older students with high levels of ability in math. None of us will be really enthusiastic about everything, so we must be able to facilitate getting the child to someone who is. By using the integrative approach to teaching math as described in Chapter 11, you may find that you become enthusiastic.

8. If you have to give grades, how can you do it with the least problem for the student?

Developing a procedure that involves the student in planning and evaluation makes a big difference in the effect grading can have. Student contracts, criteria for evaluation (sometimes developed by the student), and student conferences to work with the teacher on turning the work done into a representative grade are some ways to alleviate the problems of grading.

9. Why is there concern about grading anyway? We are certainly evaluated in the real world.

Evaluation is not the problem; grading is. There are many ways to evaluate a process or product that can be very constructive for the student. As you can see from the discussion in this chapter, the research shows nothing constructive about grading practices.

CHECKING FOR UNDERSTANDING
Follow-Up Activity

Using the following format, differentiate an example of the content, process and product from a lesson that you have taught or might plan to teach. You may refer to any of the examples or charts in the chapter for guidance. This activity may be done with a colleague or a small group planning together or as an individual activity.

CONTENT	PROCESS	PRODUCT
State one content standard from your lesson that is part of the core curriculum.	State one performance standard from your lesson that is part of the core curriculum.	State the evaluation tool that would commonly be used as part of the core curriculum.
State a content standard that is accelerated, more complex, more in-depth, or that allows novelty that is related to the core curriculum standard.	State a performance standard that is accelerated, more complex more in-depth, or that allows novelty that is related to the core curriculum standard.	State evaluation tools that you would accept to give evidence of the mastery of the related standard.

 ## SUMMARY

Differentiating the Curriculum and Instruction for Gifted Learners

1. At its basic core, differentiation means the modification of the curricular content, process, and products to meet the needs, abilities and interests of learners, in this case gifted learners.

2. Although a differentiated curriculum really cannot be planned for each student until the needs of each are known, the standards from the core curriculum generally can be differentiated for gifted learners by modifying the content and performance standards to meet the most commonly found learning needs of gifted students, acceleration, complexity, depth, novelty, intensity, and idealism.

3. The scope and sequence give a structure to the curriculum that allows teachers, students, administration, and parents to know the students' progress in learning the skills and in benefiting from the experiences to which they are exposed. The scope and sequence ensure that the content and processes deemed important are taught and learned and that whatever the district will hold students accountable for has been mastered.

Providing Differentiation to Meet Educational Needs of Gifted Learners

Differentiating by Acceleration

4. As the result of changes in the pace of thought and learning, gifted students often require acceleration in their instruction and advanced and sophisticated materials.

5. The pace of instruction can be accelerated by early entrance to any level of schooling such as kindergarten or college; pre-testing a lesson or unit and receiving instruction on only what has not been learned; self-paced programs of instruction; or other means of tailoring the pace of learning to the student.

6. However the acceleration of the curriculum is accomplished, the result will be that the student moves through the core curriculum in less time than is typical.

Differentiating by Use of Complexity

7. Gifted students often have the ability to broaden their understanding of concepts by making connections with other ideas, seeing the relationship between concepts, and gaining understanding from perspectives other than their own.

Differentiating by Adding Depth

8. The curiosity and questioning behavior of gifted learners often create a need to understand the principles and facts that comprise generalizations and concepts. This need for depth in thinking allows gifted learners to discover detail, patterns, and trends that can provide the insights that lead to new ideas and products.

Differentiating by Providing Novelty

9. Gifted students bring to their study a heightened awareness of their individuality and a belief in the value of their own point of view. As they gain a personal understanding

of concepts, they can construct unique and individualized meaning if the structure and instruction allow.

Differentiating by Supporting Idealism and Acknowledging Intensity

10. The intensity with which gifted students often pursue their interests allows for high levels of creative and idealistic thinking. They often have concerns for humanity and personal commitment to moral and ethical issues that result in high levels of idealism.

Differentiating Curriculum Content

11. The needs of the gifted are not deficit needs, but rather needs for challenge in specific areas of strength. Merely providing more of the same level of content will not fulfill this need; we must find ways to accelerate and enrich the concepts and processes in each content area of strength.
12. Generally, our main goal is to go beyond mastery of the content standards to develop with these students a greater understanding of the concepts underlying the disciplines and fields of study.

Individualizing Instruction

13. Once the environment has been made responsive to the teacher and the students, integrative lessons have been planned, the curriculum and the materials have been differentiated, and the students have been assessed to determine which pattern of modification will be needed, individualized instruction is the natural and logical next step.
14. This is not one-on-one teaching, but rather instruction that uses the flexibility of the environment and the range of grouping patterns, materials, content, and strategies to deliver curriculum that meets the assessed needs of the students.
15. Continuous progress is ensured when instruction results from such careful planning.
16. Individualization can be defined as a way of organizing learning experiences so that the pace of instruction, content, complexity of activities, and depth of exploration available to all students stem from their assessed achievement, needs, and interests.

The Power of Choice

17. A very important way to bring out the motivation of students is to make them aware of their own power and to allow them to exer-

cise it. Any way that a program or course can be structured to give more choice to the student enhances that power.

Developing the Individual Educational Plan (IEP) for Gifted Students

18. An IEP would be easy to plan from the student's profile suggested when the assessment for identification was developed. In addition to the profile data, objectives must be identified that reflect the needs shown by the profile; activities planned to meet them, including a time line for implementation; and an evaluation of the child's progress toward these objectives.

Evaluating Learning and Teaching

19. The evaluation process should include strategies that parallel the instruction. Strategies such as student inquiry, collaboration, and reflection, may be used as a means of collecting information about student knowledge, understanding, and skill mastery.
20. The students' growth should be assessed individually, in comparison with their own past achievements and developed criteria.
21. Evaluation should be ongoing throughout the year.

Grading Gifted Learners

22. Grades have no inherent stable meaning and low reliability.
23. Grades do not predict success in careers, living, or level of ability.
24. For most students, grades do not motivate learning.
25. By establishing content and performance standards that reflect a differentiated curriculum based on their level of knowledge, understanding, and skill and by including self-evaluation, a more appropriate, and realistic evaluation plan can be developed for the gifted learner.

Reflect and Reform

26. The seventh step to optimizing learning considers what changes need to occur to re-form the lessons, unit, and/or program to make it more effective and ensures that the program will be dynamic and growth-producing for all gifted learners.

13 *Understanding the Diversity of Cultures and Giftedness*

In this chapter, the reader will discover discussions and information regarding:

- The meaning of culture
- Multicultural education

- Gifted females
- Racially and ethnically diverse gifted learners
- Economically disadvantaged or low–socioeconomic-status gifted students

Culture is so much a part of us that we do not realize that we might behave differently from others . . . Culture imposes order and meaning on all our experiences. It allows us to predict how others will behave in certain situations. On the other hand, it prevents us from predicting how people from a different culture will behave in the same situation. Misunderstanding cultural cues between teachers and students can inhibit learning in a classroom.

—Donna M. Gollnick and Philip C. Chinn

This chapter discusses and disseminates information on cultural issues and the concerns of diversity, especially those reflected in gifted females, racially and ethnically diverse gifted learners, and gifted learners who are economically disadvantaged. These populations pose special challenges for educators of gifted children. Included are suggestions for meeting the needs created by these issues and the students they affect. There are always more questions than answers, and no single idea or strategy will be successful with every student. However, by acknowledging the complexity of the challenge, optimizing learning for every student can remain an exciting and important part of gifted education. Through reviewing the issues and what is now known, a clearer understanding emerges and possible solutions may become more apparent.

CULTURAL DIVERSITY AND GIFTEDNESS

Giftedness at the highest level can be found in every cultural group. The incidence of giftedness varies from group to group as a result of differing values, attitudes, and opportunities. Cultural groups differ on availability of support systems, attitudes toward development of giftedness, provision of resources, priority given to certain kinds of talent, individual initiative, and leadership, among other factors, depending on what the culture values. What is valued by the culture is produced by the culture.

It is important that when the issues and concerns regarding culturally diverse students are considered the term culture is understood to mean more than racial or ethnic groups. Any group of people who share a common value structure, belief system, language, and/or world view may be said to be a cultural group. Often the cultural heritage is confused with the biological heritage. The cultural heritage is learned and is not innately based on the culture in which one is born. For example, children from middle-income, fourth-generation Chinese-American families will have many different values and behaviors than children from families who have recently immigrated to the United States. However, because of the lack of understanding of culture, these same children may often be treated as Asian-Americans, with Asian cultural values, by those unaware of their cultural heritage. Even more subtle is the plight of the middle-class African-American child who is assumed to understand and share the values of the low–socioeconomic-status African-American child living in poverty. Although both may be gifted, their knowledge base, values, and needs may be very different.

"Culture provides the blueprint that determines the way an individual thinks, feels, and behaves in society. We are not born with culture, but learn it through enculturation and socialization." (Gollnick & Chinn, 1990, p. 32). Rather than being restricted to the ethnic and racial heritage, cultural identity is influenced by religion, gender, age, socioeconomic level, primary language, geographical region, disabilities, and any other exceptional conditions. In reality, these many influences can be seen as changing, enriching, or comprising microcultures, indicating that they share distinctive cultural patterns while sharing some cultural patterns with all members of a macroculture, in this case the United States. Figure 13.1 makes this relationship more clear and can be applied to everyone in society. So in our discussion, this complex relationship must be foremost in our thinking if we are to understand how to best serve culturally diverse gifted students.

Further confusion arises from use of the terms economically disadvantaged, low-socioeconomic status (SES), and culturally diverse. Although these terms are often used interchangeably in program reports, informational articles, and research

Figure 13.1 *Cultural Identity of an American*

Source: From *Multicultural Education in a Pluralistic Society* (3rd ed.) (p. 15) by D. M. Gollnick and P. C. Chinn, 1990, Upper Saddle River, NJ: Merrill/Prentice Hall. Reprinted by permission of Pearson Education, Inc.

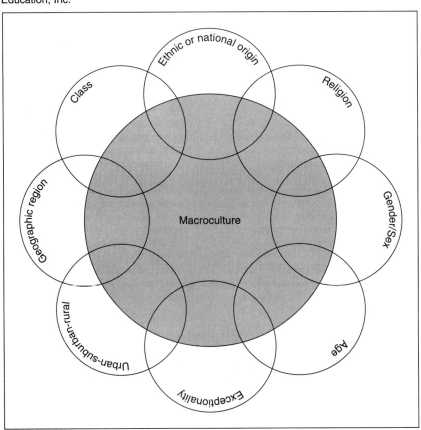

reports, there are important differences. Some children of low-socioeconomic status are also ethnically or racially diverse; however, it is important to remember that many are not, and yet both groups are culturally diverse. Economically disadvantaged students can also be referred to as low-SES students, and these children are being reared by poor, low-SES parents out of the economic (rather than ethnic or racial) mainstream. This population seems characterized by the values and attitudes often found as a result of poverty, which include a victim orientation, survival thinking, short-term planning, and dependency. Culturally diverse students, on the other hand, are those being reared in any group that differs significantly in values and attitudes from the dominant culture. When the two conditions are found together, the result can be overwhelming for the children and can require thoughtful planning in their educational experiences. You will recall that how or if giftedness is expressed depends both on the genetic patterns and anatomical structure of the individual and on the support and opportunities provided by that individual's environment. Stimulating environments significantly change the brain, allowing the accelerated, complex, and integrated function that we are referring to as giftedness. It is this dynamic nature and origin of intelligence that must be kept clearly in mind as we pursue the issues of cultural diversity. Whatever beliefs and practices support and enrich the growth of the child's potential can be viewed as positive and essential; whatever beliefs and practices inhibit and diminish the growth of the child's brain's functioning, thereby denying potential development, must be seen as negative and in need of change.

In too many cases, our educational system may penalize children who are raised with significantly different values and attitudes from those found in the dominant culture. Cultural groups can create conditions for their members that can be facilitating to the growth of intelligence and supportive of achievement or limiting to both in many ways. The amount of support from the cultural group can enable children to reach outstanding achievement or prevent the emergence of their innate talents.

In cultural groups that give the school the total responsibility for the education of their children and for the provision of models of adult achievement, painful disappointments cannot be avoided. The problems, and therefore the solutions, seem to lie partly within the family and its representation of the culture, partly with the dominant society expressed through the people of the mainstream culture, and partly with the school as a translator of the dominant society's values and attitudes. Banks and Banks (1993) suggest that the main danger we face as teachers is that the programs that we provide for culturally diverse children may only address the expressive side of their cultural heritage, such as their customs and aesthetic aspects, and miss the important issue that these children must go out into a pluralist world and compete with others for their very living.

The United States has taken pride, in the past, in being a "melting pot" for all nationalities and ethnic and racial groups and as a haven for all religions. Our laws have become progressively more protective of rights to ensure the equality of diverse groups and move us toward a pluralist society. The establishment of the Office of Civil Rights (OCR) reflects that trend (Karnes, Troxclair, & Marquardt, 1997). The primary purpose of OCR is to investigate school districts' compliance with federal legislation. Discrimination is prohibited on the basis of race, color, and national origin (Title VI of the Civil Rights Act of 1964), sex (Title IX of the Education Amendments of 1972), disability (Section 504 of the Rehabilitation Act of 1973), and age (Age Discrimination Act of 1975). They also respond to complaints filed under any legislation protecting the civil rights of individuals. Between 1992 and 1995, the alleged discrimination and/or placement in gifted programs was the subject of 38 of the investigations conducted by OCR. The cases involved culturally diverse students, either disabled or racially and ethnically diverse.

The rights of culturally diverse students are of concern at many levels, and equity and excellence are issues in education today. Yet the attitudes of the people are not always so open or so accepting. Often people are considered inferior, when actually they are only different. We have a long way to go to reach our goal of valuing each individual for his or her uniqueness, and yet the dream is there, and that, after all, is what can make it happen.

MULTICULTURAL EDUCATION AND GIFTED LEARNERS

Multicultural education has as its intention to realize the dream of recognizing an individual's value regardless of culture. Multicultural education as a concept incorporates cultural diversity and provides equality in schools. The basic assumptions of multicultural education are:

- Promoting cultural diversity is valuable
- Schools need to be models of respect for cultural differences and individual human rights
- Curricula must teach and model social justice and equality for all people
- Schools can and should promote the attitudes and values of a democratic society
- Schools can and should provide the knowledge, dispositions, and skills for the redistribution of power among cultural groups
- Educators can create an environment supportive of multiculturalism (Gollnick & Chinn, 1994)

Banks and Banks (1993) suggest that there are different levels of involvement in multicultural education that are found in schools today. At the most frequently used *Contribution Level* educators focus on holidays, eminent people, traditions, music, and other artifacts of the culture that require little study, thought, examination of values, or in-depth understanding of the culture. At the *Additive Level* some concepts, books, and perspectives of the culture are represented, but little time, effort, or rethinking is required of the student or the teacher. Students are still not required to view society from diverse perspectives or to understand the interconnections between cultures. At the *Transformational Level* the structure of the curriculum changes and students are asked to view concepts, issues, and events from other perspectives, enabling them to better understand the world view of the culture studied. The *Social Action Level* requires the student to make decisions on important social issues and take action to help solve them. Self-examination is an integral part of this level as the student acts to change a condition faced by another culture. A very useful matrix has been developed to use the levels with the Bloom's taxonomy to plan curricular experiences for a gifted classroom (Ford & Harris, 2000).

Educators who develop successful multicultural learning experiences are found to be self-aware and understanding, socially responsive and responsible, and culturally sensitive (Sue, Arrendondo, and McDavis, 1992).

Although it is common to consider students with racial and ethnic diversity as the major recipients of multicultural programs, examining the challenges faced by gifted learners who are involved in other forms of cultural groups is necessary for a full understanding of this issue. The limitations placed on gifted females by society is a cultural issue that requires serious consideration.

GIFTED FEMALES

Jane stood at the board between Tommy and her best friend Doris. As the teacher pronounced each word, they wrote it on the board, carefully covering their work until everyone was finished. When all the chalk was returned to the chalk tray, the teacher spelled the words so that they could check their own work. Doris had missed two already, and this time Tommy misspelled the word. Jane noticed that the two of them nodded to each other and, although she wasn't sure, she felt that they were excluding her. Four more words, and Doris missed another one. Tommy missed the next one. Now it was obvious that she was being excluded as Doris and Tommy exchanged gestures and looks of "I know how you feel" and "Jane thinks she's so smart." Jane felt really uncomfortable. She really liked Doris and Tommy; why did they have to act like that? There were only two words left on the test when Jane decided that they would like her better if she missed some words, too.

"Receive," said the teacher.

Jane carefully wrote r-e-c-i-e-v-e. Not too obvious, she thought. It wouldn't help if they thought she missed on purpose. Everyone stood back. Tommy spelled it just as she did. When the teacher read the right answer, Tommy noticed hers was wrong and grinned at her encouragingly. She felt much better.

"Commitment," said the teacher.

C-o-m-m-i-t-t-m-e-n-t wrote Jane. Tommy got this one right. Both he and Doris looked sympathetically at Jane. Jane felt even better.

"For those who have 100% on their test today," the teacher was saying, "I've got a special treat. The rest of you take out paper and pencil and write correctly the words you missed 100 times." The teacher took the "good students" in tow, and off they went down the hall. Jane wanted to go too. After all, she knew those words. She wanted to tell Miss Jennings why she missed them, but that was silly. She'd never understand. After everyone left, Tommy and Doris began talking to her; she was obviously in their favor now. She thought a moment about the treat and wondered what it was, but as she heard comments around the room about the "smarty alecks," and the "prissy britches" who had just left, and as she looked again at her friends happily chatting with her included, she thought it was really worth it.

Only in the last 25 years has there been interest and effort spent on understanding the problems encountered by the gifted female in our society. The January 1977 supplement of the National/State Leadership Training Institute Bulletin featured attitudes of the past toward gifted women. Let us look at profiles of some of those noted.

After 29 American medical schools rejected her, **Elizabeth Blackwell** (1821–1910) was accepted by New York's Geneva College because the study body voted in the "hen-medic" as a lark. She graduated at the head of the class. Barred from practicing in city hospitals, she opened a one-room dispensary in a New York slum that became the New York Infirmary for Women and Children.

Because "her presence would distract the male students" (p. 1), **Belva Lockwood** (1830–1917) was refused admittance to law school for 2 years. When she did complete the course, she had to petition the school's honorary president, US President Ulysses S. Grant, to get her diploma. When denied access to federal courts to try cases, she persuaded Congress to pass a special bill. In 1879, she became the first woman to practice law before the US Supreme Court.

Founder of ecology as a science, with specialties in water pollution, home economics, and consumer rights, **Ellen Swallow Richards** (1842–1911) was the first woman graduate of the Massachusetts Institute of Technology (MIT). Also the first female faculty member at MIT, she was denied a doctorate by the narrow policies of the school. Smith College made her an honorary Doctor of Science at the age of 69, just 1 year before her death.

One would like to think the experiences of these women would be ridiculous now and that they simply could not happen; however, in 1972 it was said that if a woman wanted to become a college president she should become a nun, because only 1% of college presidents were women and almost all of them were nuns. By 1975, there were 148 women chief executive education officers at US colleges and universities, and by 1992 that figure had more than doubled to 348 (American Council on Education, Office of Women in Higher Education, 1992, cited in Taeuber, 1996).

Although in some areas women have made progress toward equality, the progress has been very slow. For example, in higher education, during 1987 as few as 26% of the faculty positions in the United States were filled by women (Reis, 1987); by 1994, this figure had risen to only 27% (DiMona & Herndon, 1994). This seems even more inadequate when it is noted that women comprise 55.9% of college students and earn 52% of all college degrees. Although 44% of law school students are women, only 7% of law school deans are women (American Bar Association, Commission on Women in the Profession, cited in DiMona & Herndon, 1994). Women who do get an academic job are likely to be assigned a lower rank and salary than their male counterparts. The breakdown by rank of the increase in the percentage of women in academic jobs provides a basis for other interesting questions regarding equality of opportunity. Within the 27% of the faculty positions that are filled by women, only 12.8% of the faculty at the professor rank are women, 26.4% of the associate professor rank, and 39.5% of the assistant professor rank. However, more than half (56.5%) of the faculty at the instructor level are women. It was also found that 46% of the women in faculty positions had tenure in 1975 and that figure had remained at 46% in 1990, whereas among men on the faculty 64% had been granted tenure in 1975, increasing to 68% by 1990.

In 1972, it was reported that 13% of all doctoral degrees granted went to women, and by 1993 the figure had increased to only 25% (Taeuber, 1996). Although women earn 29% of the bachelor of science degrees in science and engineering, only 18% of all scientists and engineers employed are women. Women account for less than 10% of the physicists and engineers. Between 1986 and 1994, there was a

50% decrease in the numbers of women pursuing degrees in computer science. The gap is reported to be greater at the doctoral level in the sciences than at the bachelors' degree level (Fox, Engle, & Sooler, 1999).

Although the percentage of doctorates awarded to women has increased during the past decade, unemployment rates for women with doctoral degrees are two to five times higher than for their male counterparts. These data provided the basis for a study of the bias in hiring in academia conducted by Geis and colleagues at the University of Delaware (cited in McLeod, 1984). Identical resumes with a male or female name were sent to university department heads. Those with male names earned the rank of associate professor, whereas the same information from female applicants received the lower ranking of assistant professor. Geis found that studies of actual rankings of men and women show the same discrepancy. Salaries of male faculty members exceeded those of women by 15%, even when rank, tenure, publications, and type of institution were equivalent.

The master's degrees earned by women in business increased from 4.9% in 1973 to 34.9% in 1991 (American Assembly of Collegiate Schools of Business, cited in DiMona & Herndon, 1994). Women were granted only 9% of all doctorates in mathematics in 1974, and by 1993 earned 28%. They received 4% of all doctoral degrees in engineering in 1974 (National Science Foundation, 1990), and by 1995 earned 29% (DiMona & Herndon, 1994).

Even after receiving their diplomas, women's salaries do not equal the salaries of men. Upon graduation, men with MBA degrees earn 12% more than women, and in 1986 women held only 19 of the 4012 highest positions in business (Hymowitz & Schellhardt, 1986). Among Fortune 500 companies in 1989, less than 2% of top executives were female, and the higher women advanced, the larger was the wage gap. Women at the vice-presidential level and above earned 42% less than their male peers (Wallis, 1989). Overall, a college-educated woman earns only a little more than a man with a high school education (American Association of University Women, 1995). The more female-dominated a profession is the lower salaries are likely to be.

The number of women in elected office at the local level had more than tripled by 1989 compared with 1975, although their presence changed only slightly in the US Congress (Wallis, 1989). In 1989 there were 2 women senators, and by 2001 there were 87 male and 13 female members in the US Senate. In the House of Representatives in 1993 there were 388 men and 47 women seated. Although women are 52% of the population, they comprise only 10% of Congress.

In 1960, 34.8% of women were in the workforce; by 1989 there were 57.8%, with the numbers of female lawyers and judges climbing from 7500 to 180,000, female doctors from 15,672 to 108,200, and female engineers from 7,404 to 174,000 (Wallis, 1989). However, women comprised only 13% of lawyers, 13% of doctors, 7% of architects, 5% of executive positions in US corporations, and no top positions in the top five US orchestras (Reis & Callahan, 1989). Women who worked full-time earned only 68 cents to the men's dollar, only 12 cents better than 1969 figures (Taeuber, 1996).

It is important to note that some additional factors keep women from enjoying the achievements of men. In what has been called the second shift, typically women come home from work to do 75% of the household tasks (Wallis, 1989). There is some evidence that women's issues are slowly being noticed. Legislation addressing these issues is more often being discussed and more business organizations for women are being formed, from the film industry to construction. Still much remains to be done if gifted women are truly going to be able to actualize their potential as full societal members with choice.

The famous Terman study of gifted children becoming adults (Terman & Oden, 1959) followed the progress of only the men for information on careers, because not enough women were expected to become professionals to make collection of data from them necessary. Later, when the women were not restricted from the reports, it was found that 11% of the women were working in a professional job, whereas 45% of the men were so engaged. Although 70% of both men and women graduated from college, 13.8% of the men (compared with only 4% of the women) had taken a doctorate. Of the men, 47.7% earned more than $10,000 a year, whereas only 6% of the women did so. The median earnings for the men were $9640; and for the women, $4875.

Kerr (1985a) points to another interesting finding in the Terman and Oden (1959) data. As a group, the participants lost an average of 9 IQ points during adolescence, but the loss for the girls was five times greater than for the boys; girls scored 13 IQ points lower and boys less than 3 IQ points lower. Interestingly, the grades for both groups continued to be high. Could a sudden dramatic genetic change have occurred? Were the tests significantly altered? Kerr suggests that the girls may possibly have decided not to try on the IQ test or that the label gifted may, during adolescence, have become unacceptable. They may have decided to begin denying their giftedness.

The importance of helping young gifted women pursue career goals can be seen in the reports from women who were part of the Terman study and who were resurveyed in their 70s (Holahan, 1984). The majority of our gifted girls of today will become members of the workforce tomorrow, and these data clearly make opportunities to enhance their choice of careers necessary.

In the Terman study, some data raised questions about the loss of contributions of the gifted and talented women to society. Seven of the most talented writers in Terman's gifted group of children were girls, yet practically all the eminent adult writers were men. Carroll (1940) observed a similar contradiction in a follow-through study of artistic ability. Although nearly all the eminent artists were men, the gifted girls, as a group, had been superior to the boys in artistic ability.

Why does this happen? If females have outstanding ability at one point in their lives, why not at another? To understand, we must look at society's expectations for women, the type of encouragement that is given, and the consequences of achievement for women. One clue comes from the factors that set eminent women apart from women in general and from gifted women who do not achieve (Kerr, 1994) (Figure 13.2).

Barriers to Equity

At Home

In our dominant culture, and even more intensely in many other cultures, girl babies have an entirely different experience as a member of the family and the larger community than do boys. Evidence exists that one of the most consistent determinants

Figure 13.2 *Factors That Set Eminent Women Apart from Women in General and Gifted Women Who Do Not Achieve*

Source: From *Smart Girls Two: A New Psychology of Girls, Women, and Giftedness* by B. Kerr, 1994, Dayton, OH: Ohio Psychology Press. Copyright 1994 by Ohio Psychology Press. Adapted with permission.

- They fell in love with ideas.
- They had time alone.
- They spent unusual amounts of time gaining information and experiences through reading.
- They felt different or special, in positive and negative ways.
- They received individualized instruction as children, often in their later area of eminence.
- They were often educated in a same-sex environment.
- They often experienced an awkward and socially difficult adolescence.
- They seem capable of connectedness in relationships without giving up personal identities and goals.
- They believe their convictions and values to be of value and choose to be guided by their own actions and beliefs.
- They often make primary relationships aligned to the passion for their work.
- They assume an equality with men, even in the face of resistance.
- Most have had mentors who nurtured their talents and provided access to professional involvement.
- They were often impatient with mediocrity or either railed against it or withdrew from it.
- They chose to integrate many roles and tasks into their lives (e.g., wife, mother, professional, etc.) and sought to excel at all of them.

of parental expectations, perceptions, and organizers of behavior is the sex of their infant. This difference in expectation is evident even before the child is born. Parents prefer male offspring across a wide variety of cultures (Arnold et al., 1975; Poffenberger & Poffenberger, 1973). Hoffman (1977) found that in the United States there was a 2 to 1 preference for boys over girls. Among men the preference was 4 to 1. Couples are more likely to continue having children just to get a boy, partly because primarily only the boy carries on the family name in Western culture. Boys have a larger number of different toys and twice as many toys as do girls (Rheingold & Cook, 1975). The colors and the volume of sound surrounding them, the type of material used to clothe them, the toys given to them, the activities they are allowed to engage in, as well as the way they participate, are all very different.

From the beginning, girls are taught to be passive, accepting, nurturing. They are expected to enjoy quieter games and activities and not to take risks. They receive these messages from many places and many people in our society. Mothers encourage daughters to stay close by, to work with them. They buy irons and ironing boards, miniature kitchens, doll houses, tiny brooms, and baby dolls with cradles and bathinettes for them, so they can imitate and learn the woman's role. Little boys are discouraged from playing with these "sissy" toys and, even when dolls are included for boys, they are male action figures or stuffed animals.

Little boys learn to cope with stress and switch to an independent mode by the age of 2. Passivity and a dependent orientation toward adults appear consistently in girls into adulthood as a result of being kept from learning to cope by having stress-related situations mediated to the point of overprotection (Dowling, 1981).

You can guess the sex of a baby just by walking into the nursery of most middle-class or upper-class homes. The wallpaper, the mobiles, the choice of pictures and colors differ for boys and girls. The babies also receive different treatment within the nursery. Researchers have discovered that fathers and mothers both turn boy infants out toward the world and push them; little girls more often get hugged up close, face-to-face (Serbin & O'Leary, 1975).

Rubin, Provenzano, and Luria (1974) report interesting results from a study in which parents were asked to describe their newborn first child within the first 24 hours. The infants were nearly identical in length and weight, and all were healthy. The parents were given a list of opposite words and asked to choose ones that best described their infant. Baby boys were believed to be better coordinated, more alert, more attentive, bigger, and stronger. If a girl, the description included softer, finer featured, littler, and less attentive. Although the descriptions contradict the fact that physiologically girls are less vulnerable, nonetheless the stereotype held in every case.

In spite of their greater sturdiness and developmental maturity, female babies are handled less vigorously than are boy babies (Hoffman, 1972). The caregiver responds differently to crying from boys and girls. Because they are comforted less and their crying is less often attended to, boy babies learn to become their own emotional caregiver, whereas girls learn to rely on others to meet their needs. Because her cries are often met with anxiety and concern, a girl learns to doubt her own competence.

This is the point at which parents begin inculcating their small daughters with the idea that so far as risk-taking and the evaluation of their own safety are concerned, they should not trust themselves (Dowling, 1981). Risk-taking, self-trust, and independence are necessary to the development of high levels of intelligence. Studies show that bright girls consistently underestimate their own ability. The brighter the girl, the less expectation she has for intellectual success (Crandall, Katkovsky, & Preston, 1962).

Differences in ability between men and women may be rooted in biological differences that are established in the brain during prenatal life, shown in later differences in brain organization, and enhanced by hormones throughout the life span (Levy, 1980). How the sexes differ genetically in the way their brains develop, how the outside environment modifies this development, and how much we as parents and educators can affect the development of brain organization are questions now being asked and studied by those in the neurosciences. Some of the differences were summarized by Block (cited in Nova, 1980) into seven major areas:

1. *Aggression*. Males are far more aggressive, as expressed in play, in fighting behavior, in preference for more adventurous and aggressive films and stories, and in greater competition.

2. *Activity.* Males play outside more, more actively, and with more variety, and they find it harder to stay still.

3. *Curiosity and exploratory behavior.* Males want to know how things work, and they engage in more exploratory activities than females.

4. *Impulsivity.* Males find it more difficult to resist temptation, distractions, risk-taking, and becoming involved in dangerous situations.

5. *Importance of social relationships.* Females are more nurturing from an early age and express concern for the welfare of the group, cooperate and compromise more, and are more emphatic. Females have fewer, but more intimate, intense relationships.

6. *Self-concept.* Males view themselves as more powerful and having more control over events in the world, and they believe that they make a difference. They see themselves as more effective, more ambitious, more assertive, and more able to make things happen.

7. *Achievement-related behaviors.* Males expect to do better than females and set higher levels of aspiration for themselves. Females tend to underestimate their performances and are less confident. Males blame failure on external circumstances and take credit for their successes; females reverse this view.

Kerr (1994) summarized previously conducted research to develop a profile of gifted females. Her key points are shown in Figure 13.3. From her concern for the negative effects that these profiles show, Kerr has developed guidelines for parents and teachers that follow gifted girls from preschool through their emergence as gifted women in the workplace. These suggestions for changing the limiting conditions into enhancing conditions for the lives of gifted females are quite valuable.

At School

As children enter school subtle, and some not so subtle, clues inculcate their role expectation. Preschool teachers reinforce the same types of behavior noted in the home. Little girls are allowed to stay near and are patted and spoken to quietly, whereas little boys are given directions for independent activity and sent on their way. Boys get more attention when they actively misbehave, and teachers are more active in controlling them.

A report from the American Association of University Women (AAUW) (1992) points to the early education environment as the beginning of the schools' educational neglect of girls. Such environments often concentrate on areas in which girls already are competent and fail to provide the investigatory and experimental activities that would develop needed skills so critical to their development. The AAUW report concludes that boys in school are consistently given more instructional time and more teacher attention. Boys are called on more often than girls and are allowed, even encouraged, to call out answers for which they receive acknowledgment. In groups, their participation is actively sought by the teacher, whereas girls are ignored if they do not voluntarily participate. Callahan (1992) suggests that the learned helplessness exhibited by many girls in later years of schooling may begin from being ignored in these early school experiences. Detailed

Figure 13.3 *Profile of Gifted Females*

Source: From *Smart Girls Two: A New Psychology of Girls, Women, and Giftedness* by B. Kerr, 1994, Dayton, OH: Ohio Psychology Press. Copyright 1994 by Ohio Psychology Press. Adapted with permission.

Regarding younger gifted girls,

- Many gifted girls are superior physically, have more social knowledge, and are better adjusted than are average girls, although more highly gifted girls are not as likely to seem well-adjusted.
- Highly gifted girls are often second-born females.
- Highly gifted girls have high academic achievement.
- In their interests, gifted girls are more like gifted boys than they are like average girls.
- Gifted girls are confident in their opinions and willing to argue for their point of view.
- By age 10 gifted girls express wishes and needs for self-esteem and are interested in fulfilling needs for self-esteem through school and club achievements, although highly gifted girls are often loners without much need for recognition.
- Gifted girls are more strongly influenced by their mothers than are gifted boys.
- Actual occupations of parents do not affect gifted girls' eventual career choices.
- Gifted girls have high career goals, although highly gifted girls aspire to careers having moderate rather than high status.

Regarding adolescent females,

- Gifted girls' IQ scores drop in adolescence, perhaps as they begin to perceive their own giftedness as undesirable.
- Gifted girls are likely to continue to have higher academic achievement as measured by grade point average.
- Gifted girls take less rigorous courses than gifted boys in high school.
- Gifted girls maintain a high involvement in extracurricular and social activities during adolescence.
- Highly gifted girls do very well academically in high school; however, they often do not receive recognition for their achievements.
- Highly gifted girls attend less prestigious colleges than highly gifted boys, a choice that can lead to lower-status careers.

---

and precise feedback, praise, criticism, and remediation greet the participation of boys, whereas such useful teacher behaviors are seldom experienced by girls. The AAUW report cites numerous studies that suggest that these concerns and differences in teacher behavior toward boys and girls are far greater at the highest levels of achievement, among those scoring in the top 10% to 20% of the school population.

From the first years of school, girls learn to conceal their talents by imitating the behavior of the children with whom they are placed (Silverman, 1993). As they easily pretend to be less capable, they are rewarded and taught to show less of their intellectual abilities to receive more social acceptance. One is reminded of the brain research from Chapter 2 that shows that we are only as intelligent as we need to be

Figure 13.3 *continued*

- Between 12 and 14 years of age gifted girls experience a change in values related to love and belonging needs and a steep decline in self-esteem and confidence in opinions.
- Gifted girls fear having to choose between career and marriage, although most integrate both into their lives.

Regarding college women,

- The self-esteem of gifted young women is at a low point upon entrance to college.
- Some lower their self-estimate of their intelligence by the sophomore year of college.
- Often the campus peer system rewards a woman's "romantic achievements" while disregarding her intellectual ones.
- Inequities exist in and out of the classroom for gifted young women.
- Women's colleges provide the recognition for giftedness, identification with fields of study, chances for leadership, and the mentors that gifted women need to succeed; however, few women choose these colleges.

Regarding gifted women,

- Gifted women's academic and vocational achievement, compared with that of gifted men, continues to decline, particularly during childbearing years.
- Salaries of gifted women have been much lower than those of gifted men in occupations at the same level. The salaries of highly gifted men have averaged almost twice those of highly gifted women.
- Single, working, childless gifted women, looking back on their lives, are highly satisfied as a group.
- Gifted women engaged in income-producing work are more satisfied with their lives than are those who are not.
- Age 40 may mark another critical change in lifestyle values for gifted women, when esteem needs become highly important and the urge for self-actualization may be great.
- Gifted women who integrate homemaking and career receive more satisfaction from their work than do women who pursue either area alone.

in our environment, and troubled by the predictable results in the warning, "use it or lose it."

Boys actually learn more than girls because the teacher explains how things work and encourages them to try out toys and materials. Girls are shown passively, because the teacher usually does the manipulation. Boys can explore and get involved in games and activities that are considered too rough for girls and from which they are protected (Serbin & O'Leary, 1975).

From my childhood I distinctly recall my father's aversion to my involvement in tree climbing. Our neighborhood was predominantly male, so my playmates were all tree climbers. There were dire consequences, both natural, as when I fell, and inflicted, as when I got caught, for my participation in this activity. Although I did not always escape undetected, I must admit that I was the best tree climber in the neighborhood. I could not only go higher, probably because I weighed less, but I also mastered the chicken house, the garage, and the neighbor's grape arbor. I never did think prohibiting me, while letting all those boys climb without any discouragement, was really fair. They did not worry at all about getting caught.

Serbin and O'Leary (1975) discovered that girls' actions have far less effect on their environment than do the actions of boys. The kind of help each receives—encouraging action for boys, passivity for girls—also seems to influence the development of their spatial and analytic reasoning. Boys learn to manipulate the environment openly, whereas girls must sit passively by and watch, manipulating covertly out of frustration.

The preprimers and beginning readers given to school children express this same attitude. A student in our program surveyed the preprimers and beginning readers adopted for use in California schools to look for sexist materials. The results were amazing. She converted the especially biased pages into slides, and for more than 20 minutes our class watched page after page build a stereotype of females that was demeaning, unrelentingly insipid, and totally incompetent. We watched Jane and Mother make lemonade to take out to Dick and Mike, who were building a doghouse. We saw Mother get ready to go on a shopping trip and put on earrings that did not match, an act that was discovered by Dick and Father with the comment, "Silly, silly Mother." At each crisis, we found we had to wait with Mother and Jane until Father came home to solve the problem. The final blow came when my student showed a slide of a page of occupations Dick was considering when he grew up. There were six columns of small print covering the page with a wide range of possible jobs. The next page was for Jane and showed the choices available to her. There were three very short columns with very large print. The first column read, "Nurse, Teacher, Mother, Secretary." The two other columns were equally unimaginative.

Guttentag (1975) found that by age 5, most children are already sexist. They are convinced that boys are strong and fine and can do all sorts of interesting jobs, but that girls are weak and silly and best kept at home. By the fifth grade, it did not matter for boys whether their mother was a homemaker or a doctor; the peer group pressures and media influences outweighed the example they got at home. Girls were not affected the same way. They responded to a course given in the fifth grade on sex roles by accepting the idea that women can enter a wide variety of jobs and combine work and family. The course also resulted in an increase in self-esteem for the older girls. Boys expressed traditional opinions more freely.

Gifted children tend to develop more quickly than more typical children, and gifted girls usually develop even more quickly in the first few years. Connelly (1977) points out that this may cause devastating loneliness for sensitive girls of high potential. This loneliness may persist through their adult lives or lead to an eventual disconnection between their actual lives and their untapped abilities. When, as youths, these girls try to show their ability, they are accused of being bossy, unfeminine, and show-offs, so they tend to withdraw. Gifted girls are often considered aloof, conceited, and totally self-sufficient, and others do not feel comfortable with them. For this reason they may go through life with very few friends. Average ability classmates and teachers who have not had a course in gifted education perceive gifted girls more negatively than they do gifted boys (Solano, 1977).

To determine if the sexism observed in the classroom in the 1970s had disappeared, the Sadkers (1985) did a study involving more than 100 elementary classrooms and found that, unfortunately, it had not. Among their findings were:

1. If a boy calls out in class, he gets the teacher's attention, whereas a girl calling out is told to raise her hand. Support for this observation comes from data reported by Bouman (1986) that response opportunities given to males are ninefold greater than those given to girls.
2. Teachers praise boys more than girls.
3. Teachers give boys more academic help than girls.
4. Boys' comments are accepted more than those of girls.
5. Boys dominate classroom communication by a ratio of 3 to 1.
6. Teachers give boys dynamic, precise, and effective responses; girls receive bland, diffuse reactions.

On a positive note, the researchers found that these patterns can be eliminated. After only 4 days of training to establish equity in classroom interactions, not only were the teachers able to eliminate the patterns, they improved their overall teaching effectiveness as well.

Although Siegle and Reis (1994/1995) found that girls are clearly perceived by classroom teachers as working harder and producing higher quality work than boys, these same teachers give boys the same grades as girls in all content areas except language arts. The result may, in part, be the reason for the confidence gifted boys show over gifted girls in their abilities in mathematics, social studies, and science. As the researchers ponder, "If teachers really believe gifted girls are producing higher quality work in these areas than the boys, why do they not receive higher grades?" The answer could be most enlightening.

Another problem creating such lowered evaluations may be the limitations that females impose on themselves. The report from the AAUW (1992) stated that by sixth grade, girls report more concern about being popular and well-liked than being perceived as independent and competent. Boys reverse the priority of these concerns. In addition, the decline of self-esteem and self-confidence begins for girls at the onset of adolescence (Callahan, 1992).

As early as junior high school, the career expectations of gifted boys and girls differ. More than 98% of the boys and only 46% of the girls expect to have a full-time career. Many of the girls expect to be involved in careers only until they marry or have children, or only part-time, or with interruptions to have children (Fox, Tobin, & Brody, 1981). Up to 94% of a group of very gifted girls wanted to have careers; however, 71% either did not plan to work or planned to work only part-time.

Evidence from a meta-analysis and process analysis conducted by Linn and Hyde (1989) shows the nature and size of gender differences in cognitive, psychosocial, and physical tasks and their implications for mathematics and science. Although gender differences in cognitive skills have declined, with those remaining largely explained by differences in experience, massive discrepancies are still reported between men and women in career access and earning power. The researchers suggest that the tendency of women to follow social conventions may be a part of the problem. Such skills as learning shortcuts and estimation techniques useful for solving complex problems quickly, aggressive argumentation, confidence, and expectation of success may be inhibited. Confronting traditional perspectives in male-dominated fields may be even more difficult without such skills.

Linn and Hyde (1989) suggest that schools focus on situations that minimize gender differences. They must establish environments that instill confidence in all participants by providing support for students in devising procedures to solve problems and acquiring new skills, encourage sharing of ideas, self-evaluation, and extensive feedback to reflect the need for confidence, high-level cognitive skills, and expectations of success.

From these summaries, it is evident that differences in expectations and results—whether caused primarily by biological differences, environmental differences, or an interaction of both—do not favor independent, successful achievement for females.

One of the barriers to gifted women becoming more involved in nontraditional careers is their lack of mathematics preparation. A study of 1324 children in grades 2 through 12 found no significant differences between boys and girls in reported enjoyment of mathematics (Ernest, 1976). However, Ernest (1980) acknowledges that when mathematics becomes an optional course of study in high school, few girls enroll. From extensive study of the causes of attrition from the science preparation pipeline, Hanson (1996) concludes that high school courses in mathematics and physics are the gatekeepers for careers in the sciences. Interestingly, women make up 50% of undergraduate majors in mathematics, but are poorly represented in engineering and computer science. Fox, Engle, and Soller (1999) point out that this presents a double bind for women. Damaging myths will persist about the abilities of women to pursue careers in science and technology as long as this under-representation continues, and the myths will serve to reinforce the under-representation of women in these fields.

Luchins and Luchins (1980) may have some of the reasons. Interviews of 350 female members of the Association for Women in Mathematics and a smaller number of male mathematicians found that three times as many women reported being discouraged by teachers or advisers than did men, with the most marked discouragement occurring at the graduate level. As students, the women mathematicians experienced stereotypic behaviors and comments. They were told that boys do not like or are afraid of girls who are smart. They found that girls received less support than boys; expectations were lower for girls; they were advised to go into more traditional fields; their competence was questioned; and they often were not taken seriously. When the female mathematicians applied for jobs, they encountered fewer offers, lower salaries, and less advancement potential than equally or less qualified males. The women in this study had some suggestions for change if women are to be encouraged to pursue mathematics as a career. Teachers, counselors, and/or parents should:

1. Increase emphasis on precollege mathematics education for girls.

2. Encourage, not discourage, interest.

3. Treat girls as equal to boys in this area of study.

4. Provide female role models.

5. Provide awareness of career opportunities.

6. Change the conception of mathematics as a masculine domain.

7. Stress intuitive recreational mathematics throughout school to dispel fear of the subject.

Rekdal (1984) showed that fewer than 12% of women entering the University of California system have the high school math prerequisites that would allow them to participate in 80% of the majors offered by that system. According to Rekdal, gifted females do not pursue math majors even when they express levels of interest in math and perform as well as males. Gifted females take fewer demanding high school math and science courses (Benbow, 1992). Compared with males, fewer (40% to 72%) major in math or science in college or (24% to 56%) consider math or science related careers.

The problem seems to start in the first years of school. Few gender differences in locus-of-control exist until the sixth or seventh grade. In a study of sixth to eleventh grade students and their parents, Jacobs and Weisz (1994) found that girls already hold more negative beliefs about their abilities in mathematics, even when they consistently earn the highest grades in the class. A study by Marsh and Hocevar (1985) found that fifth grade girls had a more positive self-concept than boys only in reading, although they also had better grades in math.

Girls seem to attribute any success they have in math or sciences to external factors, whereas they believe their failures are the result of their own lack of talent (Heller & Ziegler, 1996); the attribution is just the opposite for boys. These gender differences increase with higher ability levels and result in unrealistically low expectations for success among highly gifted females. They tend to give up more readily after failure, which they attribute to their low ability.

This difference seems to mirror findings that the parents attributed their daughters' successes to diligence and effort and their sons' successes to special abilities or talents. Similar attribution patterns were found in teachers. In a study of the problem of low self-concept of mathematical abilities among gifted girls, Dickens and Cornell (1993) found that it would be advisable for educators and counselors to study the expectation of the parents and the effect that expectation has on the development of such concepts. Parents should become aware of how their expectations may be influenced by their own successes and failures in mathematics and how these influences may be impacting upon the expectations they hold for their daughters.

The findings of Heller and Ziegler (1996) lead them to believe that gender-related attribution patterns develop, in part, as a result of learning and, therefore, are subject to modification by attributional retraining techniques. Although they found some success with their program of retraining, they advise that it is best to combine such techniques with other interventions that improve knowledge. Their work demonstrated that it was possible to reduce gender differences in math and science performance, which they suggest should not be attempted with children younger than 10 years of age. Prospects for success, they report, would be more favorable for preventive measures at a much earlier age.

Silverman (1993) suggests that one area in which gifted girls need special help is in goal setting. From middle school on, gifted girls need to have their aspirations raised and to be taught effective strategies for reaching these higher goals.

One day in a freshman honors class that I taught at the university, the students were sharing their visions for their future career goals. One young man, Steven, informed us that he was planning to get his degree in political science, go to law school, and then begin his political career. He stated confidently, "I plan to be president of the United States." A young woman, Rosa, near him spoke next and quietly said that she thought she would take more math courses because she "really liked to play with math ideas." She thought she would probably be a bookkeeper or something. Steven exploded! "You like to play with math and you just think you'll be a bookkeeper!" he shouted. "Why not shoot for a think tank, or be an astronaut, or a CEO for some big company? People who like to 'play with math' are in demand you know. There aren't many of you and you could really name your price!" Rosa smiled shyly and looked surprised. Although she thought the idea was interesting, she did not think it was very realistic for her.

Role models, internships, mentorships, speakers, professionals willing to be shadowed, films, and biographies can be used to change the level of aspirations and teach the strategies needed to achieve the higher goals appropriate for gifted girls. Silverman, (1993) among numerous researchers, asks that same-sex schools be considered for their educational experience because such settings promote leadership and higher achievement in girls.

In Society

The literature on need achievement should provide some clues as to why girls start out so well, only to achieve in very small numbers. However, such clues are not provided for the simple reason that, in the impressive and theoretically consistent body of data about the achievement motive, Horner (1969) discovered that women have been excluded altogether. In the few studies that included women, the results were so contradictory or confusing that they omitted women from future consideration. The need to achieve has been defined as an internalized standard of excellence, motivating the individual to do well in any achievement-oriented situation involving intelligence and leadership ability. We do know that women get higher test-anxiety scores than men, probably because a woman who is motivated to achieve directly contradicts the role expectation of femininity. Horner stated, "A bright woman is caught in a double bind. In testing and other achievement-oriented situations she worries not only about failure, but also about success" (p. 38). The solution for most women is to inhibit achievement motivation. Horner (1968) has researched what she has termed the motive to avoid success. The results were most interesting:

1. Success inhibits social life for women; it enhances social life for men.
2. Women will fully explore their intellectual potential only when they do not need to compete.
3. Women block achievement even more when in competition with men.
4. Society holds the belief that it is not ladylike to be too intellectual.
5. Most men treat the intelligent woman who pursues a career with distrustful tolerance at best, and outright prejudice at worst.

Horner found that the women in her study also equate intellectual achievement with loss of femininity. They respond to success in one of three ways, by (1) showing anxiety about becoming unpopular, unmarriageable, and lonely; (2) feeling guilt and despair and doubting their femininity or normality; and (3) denying the possibility that a mere woman can be successful.

Horner's initial studies began in 1964, and in the 1970s she re-examined these issues, using as her population the "liberated" young women of the new women's movement era. She found an even higher portion of women showing fear of success, coping poorly or avoiding competition, and lowering their career expectations. The negative attitudes expressed by women had increased from 65% in 1964 to 88.2% in 1970 (Horner, 1972). This fear of success has been shown to intensify as girls move from seventh to tenth grade (Lavach & Lanier, 1975).

Girls seem to believe that if they succeed, it is luck; if they fail, it is their fault. Boys reverse this view for their successes and failures. It has been shown that teachers have contributed significantly to these views (Dweck, Davidson, Nelson, & Enna, 1978). In the study by Dweck and colleagues, whenever a girl's work was evaluated negatively, it was always pointed out that the failure resulted from intellectual inadequacy; however, the feedback the boys received attributed failures to nonintellectual aspects of their performance, such as lack of motivation or effort.

Noting the continuing lack of adult creative productivity in women, and the prevailing attitudes that continue to support this occurrence, Reis (1987) has drawn our attention to attitudes held by women that may be contributing to self-sabotage. Gifted women often believe that they must excel in every role they play and they must play every role assigned. High energy is expended by such women to simultaneously maintain their femininity; succeed as a wife; have an outstanding career; be a perfect parent; have an attractive body; and run a beautiful, well-managed home. This perfection complex causes women not only to set impossible goals but also to continually strive to achieve at ever-higher levels. Reis believes it is important to teach gifted girls that they cannot possibly be perfect in everything they do and that they must make choices about careers, marriage, and children. When bright women do achieve success, their self-sabotage continues to work. They attribute their success to factors other than their own efforts and see their outward image of success as undeserved or accidental. Bright men, on the other hand, attribute their success to their own efforts. Hollinger and Fleming (1984) believe that the well-documented fear of success so often demonstrated by women may be playing a part in this phenomenon of self-sabotage and is even more prevalent in gifted women than in the nongifted because the possibility of success is greater.

Expectations of society also enter into career decisions. To resolve the home/career conflict, women may choose to delay their education or the pursuit of appropriate career placement until after the family's needs have been mostly met and the children are less dependent; thus, they are beginning their career at an older age. Or they may choose an occupation, such as teaching or nursing, that is more compatible with the approved female role. These careers also meet the need of availability in most localities, because the primary decision of where the family will live usually hinges on the husband's career. If a woman chooses a more male-dominated career, she might work only part-time and choose specializations that are more compatible with the female role expectations (Wolleat, 1979). As with achievement motivation research, career development theory is derived almost entirely from research on males (Mattheis, 1974).

In a study of high school valedictorians, Denny and Arnold (cited in Conroy, 1989) discovered that, even though they outperformed men in college, few women pursued doctoral degrees, and they performed at lower levels than men in the work world. Arnold stated, "We're losing the talents of some of our best women, and if this is happening to those who have everything going for them, who have every conceivable credential, one can only imagine the handicaps and barriers that women in general face" (p. 20). The researchers suggest that women's colleges may be one solution. Sadker (cited in Conroy, 1989) stated, "When girls go to single-sex schools, they stop being the audience and become players" (p. 20). Although this may not be the answer for every woman, the statistics show that alumnae of women's colleges are six times more often found on the boards of Fortune 500 companies, seven times more likely to be named as an outstanding graduate, twice as likely to pursue doctoral degrees, and six times more likely to be on *Business Week's* list of top corporate women (Conroy, 1989).

Although gifted adolescent girls agree with less than a 5% difference among themselves that women should enjoy gender equality in vocational and intellectual pursuits, ambivalence in their attitudes still exists toward gender equality in social and emotional roles. Competition in educational and occupational arenas is acceptable; competing for power in relationships is not (Bakken, Hershey, & Miller, 1990).

Society helps to establish these mixed expectations by expressing attitudes that give mixed messages. Women should fill a supportive nurturing role, but they are expected to assertively develop their own talent. Girls are rewarded by teachers and parents for good grades and high performance in school, but society—as expressed in the media, in books and textbooks, and through peer groups—relays the message that intellectual pursuits are unfeminine. With these mixed expectations and few successful women role models to follow, it is easy for gifted girls to become confused about how to pursue a truly satisfying future (Garrison, et al., 1986). Garrison and coworkers suggested some goals and strategies for career programs for gifted females:

- Information should be presented which dispels the myth of a forced choice between career and family and the myth of irreversible life planning.
- Men as well as women should be counseled about the redistribution of family responsibilities when this is a desirable solution.
- Experiences should be provided which help girls develop their autonomy, self-esteem, self-confidence, tolerance for ambiguity, willingness to compete, and assertiveness.
- Information and role models should be provided which illustrate a variety of possible satisfying lifestyles.
- Gifted girls should be encouraged to engage in appropriate career planning and be taught how to incorporate interruptions and delays for childraising into their career plans. (p. 102)

Society places girls at risk through preferences in their behaviors (Kline & Short, 1991). As early as the middle school years, values of intimacy and empathy are preferred over all other agendas for girls, compared with the male values of competitiveness and individualism. Gifted girls are urged to become all they can be and pursue career goals as high as they can, while at the same time remaining selfless, nurturing, giving, passive, dependent, and "feminine." As adults they are expected by society to skillfully manage a household, fulfill themselves through motherhood, and subjugate their goals to those of their spouses and family, resulting in loss of goals, dreams, expectations, and the inability to see how their future can encompass their uniqueness. Such contradictory expectations can place gifted females emotionally at risk.

What Can Be Done?

Silverman (1993) calls for societal support to make development of gifted girls' talents a priority. In this support, she would include use of nonsexist childrearing and teaching practices; use of nonsexist language in every classroom, with sexist terms such as "bossy" resisted; elimination of the emphasis on processing speed in standardized testing; funding of support for assistance to girls in math in the same proportion as there is for boys in reading; and availability of special counseling assistance in developing self-esteem and in career planning.

Kerr (1994) has some specific suggestions to parents for helping gifted girls through the school years.

At the preschool age: Dress your child for active play; choose nonsexist toys and/or balance the selection; allow practice in developing a sense of mastery and self-worth; choose childcare that integrates girls and boys and has challenging activities for every child; take your child to work with you, explain your job to her, and explain the work of the other people she sees; and take time to answer her questions.

During the elementary years: Buy books of many types, including those that portray women in many roles; let her read all she wants and help her when she asks; give her math puzzles and problems to play with; buy a computer; whatever her interests, supply the materials to pursue them; broaden her knowledge of the world by exploring, going to museums, and traveling with her; don't overschedule her—allow time for imagination and fantasy; watch for signs of boredom at school, such as withdrawal, daydreaming, and lack of class participation; provide role models; support her emotionally; and help her feel unique and special by acknowledging her abilities.

During middle school: Allow her need to be "like everyone else"; continue to encourage her efforts to self-actualize; insist that she get a good background in math and science; encourage exploration of careers, such as doing volunteer work in appropriate settings; and discuss relationships with boys and the need to withstand societal pressure to subvert her own personality and goals to theirs.

During high school: Reinforce interests in academics and careers; help her find information on colleges and scholarships; talk about college and postgraduate education; be sure she has an adequate math background; help her understand her choices in romantic feelings and relationships; clearly show your admiration for her; provide accurate sex education; help her manage her time to avoid becoming overextended; and discuss future plans with her.

During college: Consider an all-women's college or find an academically oriented coed institution with tenured female faculty in good numbers; encourage her to find a female mentor; help her to become assertive in her academic life; help her keep her romantic relationships in perspective; initiate values-centered discussions; and make your home a safe haven.

> During postgraduate or professional school: Be interested in her work and give her emotional support; help her financially as much as she will permit to let her engage in educational opportunities even if the cost is beyond her present means; encourage her to expect a rightful amount of remuneration for various positions; and continue to believe in her and hold high expectations as she faces discouragement and self-doubt . . .

As Kerr further comments,

> The best programs use a combination of individual assessment, individual counseling, and group counseling. Bright girls need to fantasize about their future, to learn about their unique interests, needs, and values, and to set specific goals for their future. Only by establishing goals based on their most deeply held values can gifted girls find a meaningful path to their future. (p. 216)

Suggestions for teaching methods to remediate the gender gap in the US include: more emphasis on authentic curriculum (Kreinberg, & Wahl, 1997); use of active learning and the applications of science and technology to solve real problems, and the integration of science and mathematics curriculum material with social studies and language arts (Fox, Engle, & Soller, 1999); and the exposure to women in science-career role models from middle school through graduate school (Seymour, 1995).

To remove educational barriers to progress for gifted girls, Higham and Navarre (1984) have suggested:

- Awareness programs for parents where gender differences and influences of the parents' beliefs and actions on the achievement and career patterns of their daughters can be explored.
- Educational and career counseling where the under-representation of gifted girls in science, mathematics, and other male-dominated courses can be discussed and broader career choices for females can be made known.
- Selection of role models and mentors from nontraditional and interesting careers.
- Single-sex classes or schools in secondary and higher education where gifted females may find advantages.

Higham and Navarre found that schools are not adequately addressing the issues of gender differences in measures of achievement, in learning and teaching styles, in behavior, and in selection of courses of study and career.

Grau (1985) listed eight psychosocial barriers to the career achievement of gifted girls:

1. The psychological construct of femininity being inconsistent with achievement.
2. Women's self-sabotage.
3. The socialized need for affiliation.
4. Female reliance on external sources of control and praise.
5. The motherhood mandate.
6. The home and hearth mandate.
7. Male or female labeling of occupations and professions.
8. Lack of nontraditional female role models.

Grau's suggestions for dealing with these barriers to free the achievement possibilities include becoming well-read about these issues, understanding the barriers, and being prepared to deal with them. Support groups and available role models also aid in meeting these needs.

Callahan (1980) suggested that the curriculum could do the following:

- Provide activities that require females to practice visual-spatial problem solving from a young age.
- Provide role models of gifted women engaging in successful problem-solving activities.
- Provide activities that teach gifted girls the impact they can have on their own destinies (i.e., help them develop an internal locus of control).
- Provide opportunities for gifted females to interact with successful, attractive feminine role models in a variety of professions.
- Provide activities that encourage women to establish their own personal goals.
- Set equivalent standards and criteria for reinforcement for males and females. (p. 20)

Silverman (1991) considers eight areas essential to the development of the potential of gifted girls: parent education, early identification, gifted peers, early entrance, teacher inservice, special programs, career counseling, and conferences for gifted girls. Her specific suggestions for the facilitation of each area are valuable.

A recent model (Noble, Subotnik, & Arnold, 1999) provides a structure for further consideration of the possible dilemmas and solutions involved in female talent development. Synthesized from studies originating in psychology and education the model has three major interactive components:

1. Individual and demographic traits, such as personality, family background, protective factors and distance from the mainstream;
2. Opportunities (actual, perceived, and acted upon) interact with a talent domain (e.g., arts letters, sciences); and
3. Spheres of influence that form expressions of women's giftedness, such as the personal domain (self and community) and the public domain (leadership in organizations, institutions, communities and professions; and eminence).

Interesting concepts included in the model are the consideration of women's distance from the centers of power as a variable in their achievement; the exploration of resilience as protective factors in the development of talent; and the acceptance of a wide range of expressions of talent as indicators of success. Noble, Subotnik, and Arnold note three strands of data that differentiate gifted women from gifted men: the devaluing of their accomplishments and discounting of their potential; the role of women as minorities in high-level, male-dominated achievement settings; and the affect of the career-family balancing often required in professional choices. The purpose of such a model is to aid in the understanding of the issues involved in women's talent development and to help in the identification and actualization of women's talents and gifts.

A model of leadership that is based on traits associated with female thinking is proposed by Seney (cited in Checkley, 2000). He contends that most models of leadership reflect the way men think, so he is suggesting that a new model:

- Reject the top-down model of authority.
- Value connectedness and responsibility over separation and competition.
- Encourage teaming and the sharing of leadership.
- Advocate development of networks and other support groups.
- Value and develop intuitive thinking.
- Recognize the importance of authentic conversation.

Seney believes that the field of leadership is moving from the transactional to the transformational and, if they are not to be left behind in the competitive information age, organizations must shift from emphasizing control to providing opportunities for people to fulfill their potential. This will require that effective leaders understand and embrace traits once attributed only to women.

Both Kitano (1994/1995) and Kerr (1994) suggest that the research on mainstream gifted women may not necessarily generalize to gifted women from other ethnic and racial groups. The values and customs of each diverse group may overlie the issues found in this discussion with more contradictory concerns and barriers for these women to overcome. Further research is needed to provide the understanding and the strategies that can allow the gifted girls found among these populations to become achieving and fulfilled adults. Although the issues of gifted females are continuing to find advocates and the understanding of these issues is growing owing to continuing research, many questions and limitations to the development of the potential of gifted women still exist. There is much still to be done.

RACIALLY AND ETHNICALLY DIVERSE GIFTED POPULATIONS

Rosa is a lovely, dark-haired girl who has lived with her Hispanic family in the barrio all of her life. Her parents were raised in Mexico and came to Southern California to find a higher standard of living. They hold the traditional values of their culture and have found adapting to American values difficult. Throughout her high school career, Rosa has noticeably grown into a first-rate student—curious, intelligent, constantly pursuing ideas and problems to ferret out original and creative solutions. She totally enjoys her scholastic ability. Rosa is quiet, poised, and self-confident. Her family provides her with strength and love and values her as a woman of their culture.

At the beginning of her senior year, the gifted coordinator suggested that she apply for scholarships to major universities throughout the country. She wrote to Stanford, Harvard, Yale, University of California-Berkeley, and Columbia. When she received her scholarship offer from Stanford, everyone at school was excited. Then, when Harvard, Yale, and Berkeley also offered excellent scholarships, the entire faculty and all her friends were ecstatic. They all were anxious to see which one she would choose. What a fantastic opportunity! But then the gifted coordinator got the word that Rosa's father refused to allow her to go to college, any college. It was not right for women to be away from home unless they were married, and her place was with her family. Besides, what did she need a college degree for? She must start her family soon. Women had no business running around getting ideas put in their heads. The gifted coordinator talked to Rosa's father, and the principal and the family priest also talked to him, but to no avail.

Then one day in May, Rosa came to school very disturbed and asked to see the gifted coordinator and one of her favorite teachers. As they sat down together, Rosa quietly, almost in whispers, with tears brimming in her eyes and spilling softly down her cheeks, said that her father had issued an ultimatum. If she persisted in her foolishness of wanting to go to college, she would no longer be considered his daughter. She would have to move out of the house and never come back. Her beloved family would no longer claim her. He would forbid her mother, her brothers and sisters, even her grandmother and other relatives, to contact her or to receive her ever again. As far as the family would be concerned, she would not exist.

Rosa now sat looking very small as she lowered her head, and the momentary pause gave the others a chance to take in the finality and enormity of what she had said. Before anyone else could speak, she said, "I will leave this weekend." Now everyone spoke at once. Graduation was still a month away, and the scholarships would not begin for 3 months after that. Where would she go; how would she live? Rosa sat looking very lost. Although she had thought of the questions herself, she had not worked out any answers. She only knew she had to be free to make her own choice. She had to decide for herself what her life was to be. To do that, she must leave home this weekend. The teacher, with her own daughter in her mind, spoke first. "You will come live with me until you decide." And so it was that Rosa, who loved her family and loved the marvelous ability of her mind, was forced to give up one to have the other. Whether her father could be persuaded or time might change his resolve was known only to the future. For now, her loss was almost too great to bear.

Differences in Attitudes and Skills Among and Between Racial and Ethnic Cultures

What responsibilities to the child's dreams of the future do the families within diverse racial and ethnic cultures have? The attitudes and skills for thinking and learning are established in the family, a base that forms the future of the children. Every cultural group instills both advantages and limiting attitudes in their children before they enter school. Families who want to help their children to develop more of their potential talents and allow others the same rights need to be aware of any self-limiting practices so they can reduce them as much as possible. There is no reason to weaken the ties the child has with the culture if there is awareness of what facilitates and what inhibits growth. It is the responsibility of the family, cultural group, and school to engage in attitudes and practices known to bring out the highest levels of intelligence and ability unique to each child.

Racially and ethnically diverse gifted children differ in many respects, but they do hold certain mental traits in common (Gallagher & Kinney, 1974):

- The ability to meaningfully manipulate some symbol system held valuable in the subculture.
- The ability to think logically, given appropriate information.
- The ability to use stored knowledge to solve problems.
- The ability to reason by analogy; and

- The ability to extend or extrapolate knowledge to new situations or unique applications. (p. 16)

Frasier (1991) believes that goals for identifying such diverse learners should include identifying the traits associated with giftedness and investigating the way in which such learners express giftedness in different groups.

Information about the contributions various ethnic and racial groups make to the educational development of their children is generalized and oversimplified, because it is the family unit that makes the decisions as to how the values and beliefs of these groups are to be interpreted and practiced. However, such generalizations can be helpful to show trends that may help parents and teachers to be more aware of the preparation that must be made for these children. All researchers in this field repeatedly warn against generalizing attributes in decision-making processes even within racial or ethnic groups, because a great deal of variation exists. Also, the data originate from studies of ethnically and racially diverse gifted children and may not be applicable to those who, in addition to their cultural difference, must deal with the limitations of poverty.

Strengths in some cultures could improve the functioning of others. For example, the achievement orientation of the Asian-American culture combined with the cooperative spirit of the Hispanic culture would enrich both. The practical, solution orientation of the dominant culture of the United States combined with the concerned respect for nature and the intuitive understanding of the American Indian culture could preserve the earth's fragile ecosystems. The possibilities are fantastic when we let go of the view of superior or inferior groups and notice that we have all just learned to experience life differently.

Baldwin (1985) noted that the literature available on racially and ethnically diverse students has focused more on deficits than on strengths. Baldwin discusses definition, goal-setting, and effective instructional systems and their evaluation and bases her discussion on three basic assumptions:

1. Giftedness exists in all human groups, and the way that this giftedness is expressed cannot be genetically ascribed to that group. Culture and environment play important roles in the development of certain abilities and skills, but highly specific behaviors cannot be seen as innate capacities of that group.

2. Techniques other than usual standardized tests can be used to identify gifted learners.

3. Behaviors that may be unique or special to a cultural group can serve as accurate indicators of high-level capacity to conceptualize and organize phenomena.

According to Baldwin, certain factors may influence the functioning level of racially and ethnically diverse children when they are raised in lower SES homes:

- Parents' inability to speak English does not allow them to foster English language skills;

- Home environments that lack toys and other playthings may not stimulate cognitive and developmental skills;

- Homes lacking in conversation may deny the opportunity to listen to the discussion of topics and to learn the art of dialogue; and

• The type of discipline may not encourage the development of inner locus of control, self-motivation, and problem-solving skills.

Baldwin concludes that planners for such populations need to be concerned with positive attitudes toward cultural differences, awareness of ethnic and racial history and traditions, resources related to the population, flexibility in programs, and knowledge of behavioral expressions of conceptual capability.

The identification of culturally diverse gifted children has been recognized as a problem and has been a major focus of the Javits Grants for the Study of Gifted and Talented students since their inception. A variety of models and strategies for identification of learners from racially and ethnically diverse groups are currently being researched. Past solutions have included adjusting the entrance criteria by use of less predictive instruments, such as self-nominations, behavioral rating scales, and creativity tests, or by allowing entry to programs based on the rank of the students within their particular group (Lynch & Mills, 1990). Neither process has resulted in equal representation and, in many cases, the results have led to unfair competition for these students.

Loury (1986–1987) believes that some children simply are not prepared for demanding course work. Efforts need to be focused in early preparation, taking advantage of early levels of plasticity of brain cells and the impact of early learning. In response to this problem, the Johns Hopkins' CTY Program began in 1985 to develop a Skills Reinforcement Program (SRP) to explore and resolve problems that result in a lower proportion of minority students being involved in gifted programs. At the end of the project it was found that the students showed a higher level of function in terms of content knowledge, discussion, and attention span than they had previously shown (Lynch & Mills, 1990).

It seems clear that certain ethnic groups have cognitive styles that are distinct from those of other groups. These style preferences result from socialization practices, culture, and the ecology of the group's environment. The cognitive style from which children operate affects their view of themselves in relationship to others and their sense of being a separate self, which is associated with field independence, or not being separate, which is associated with field dependence, (Figure 13.4). A sense of separateness or field independence results in reduced reliance on external sources of guidance and an ability to break up an organized perceptual field, whereas field dependence results in heavy reliance on external guidance, acceptance of the prevailing field, and inability to separate an item from its context.

Although it is evident that learners from some racial and ethnic groups are not well-represented in the gifted population, the reasons for this are complex. Among those suggested are traditional IQ-based definitions and theories of giftedness, inadequate identification practices, inadequate attention to different ways of expressing giftedness, limited belief systems of teachers regarding potential among diverse learners, and inadequate opportunities for intellectual development (De Leon, 1983; Ford, 1994; Frasier, 1991; Lynch & Mills, 1990). A brief overview of some of the attitudes and abilities relevant to learning in some of the diverse cultures will help to identify the range of opportunities that educators must develop to meet the needs of these populations.

Figure 13.4 *Characteristics of Field-Dependent and Field-Independent Students*

Source: From "Cognitive Style Difference and the Underrepresentation of Mexican Americans in Programs for the Gifted," by J. De Leon, 1983, *Journal for the Education of the Gifted, 6*(3), 167–177.

Field dependents

- Are superior in the incidental learning of social stimuli.
- Are affected more by negative reinforcement.
- Prefer a spectator approach.
- Do better on verbal tasks of intelligence tests than on analytic tasks.
- Learn materials more easily that have human, social content and that are characterized by fantasy and humor.
- Are sensitive to the opinions of others.
- Perform better when authority figures express confidence in their ability.
- Are more cooperative.

Field independents

- Prefer discovery learning.
- Do best on analytic tasks.
- Learn material that is inanimate and impersonal more easily.
- Are not greatly affected in their performance by the opinions of others.
- Are more competitive.

African-American Culture

Many African-American gifted children continue to confound those who attempt to identify and nurture their talents. The educational strengths or problems found in this population seem to be more a function of the socioeconomic status of the student than of the ethnic culture. As the only group to have been involuntarily removed from their root culture and then systematically prohibited from continuing or furthering their cultural traditions, this population shows more clear alignment to the behaviors of the socioeconomic status level than any other group discussed. One third of the population of African-American families are prospering, and the number of professionals rose 50% in the past decade. The vast majority of the population are far from realizing their potential, with alarming numbers dropping out of school, becoming teenage parents, involved in the penal system, or dying at an early age (Los Angeles Times, 1990). The gifted among this section of the population find very limited opportunities within either the schools or the professional world. For them, poverty is indeed creating a generation of lost children.

Ford (1994) suggests guidelines for recruiting and retaining African-American students in gifted programs that include identifying and serving them early; involving parents and extended family members early, consistently, and substantively in the process; and providing comprehensive services to increase the belonging and ownership in gifted programs.

Middle and higher SES African-Americans accept as valid the values and attitudes of the dominant society's middle class, resulting in a valuing of education from early years, with a variety of experiences provided and high parental expectations.

Cooley, Cornell, and Lee (1991) found that despite some differences in achievement and social status, high ability African-American students are accepted by other high ability peers and share a comparable level of self-concept and academic self-esteem with them.

Researchers (Baldwin, 1989; Bowman, 1993; Ford, 1994; Frasier, 1989; Maker & Schiever, 1989a) have found that children in this population are often resourceful, self-sufficient, and people oriented. They seem to learn quickly and show good retention, when opportunities for physical action and experience are part of the learning. They have been found to often add rich imagery to language and project imagination and humor.

Learning Opportunities Educators Should Consider:

- Using small groups for instruction, building trust and belonging.
- Providing structure by use of contracting, clear goals, and individualization.
- Providing mentors and role models.
- Emphasizing use of oral language, providing many opportunities for debate, discussion, and oral presentations.
- Providing for visual learning experiences, manipulative materials, and active real-life experiences in learning.

American Indian Culture

The gifted American Indian child has now gained the attention of Indian tribes, organizations, and communities as they seek to provide for the improvement of educational opportunities. More than 177 different tribes are recognized by the US government, each unique in its culture and language. More than 1.5 million American Indians, Eskimos, and Aleuts were recorded in the 1980 US census, with more than half living on federal reservations. More than 75% of the children attend public schools, and, interestingly, a higher percentage of these children enroll in and receive baccalaureate degrees from college than do children from Hispanic-American or African-American populations (Maker & Schiever, 1989b). As with many other racially and ethnically diverse populations, a large number of American Indians fall within the low-SES group, but important cultural factors support these children and create a potential for identification of gifted learners among them.

Bradley (1989); Davidson, (1992); Maker & Schiever (1989a); Montgomery (1989); and Pfeiffer (1089) all contributed observations to the picture of the American Indian learner. These researchers find that they often work well in groups, are good mediators, and communicate effectively. These children are found to accept the responsibility and discipline of leadership and can be quite resourceful. They have often been taught to value oral traditions and can create stories, poems, and legends. Such practices result in well-developed intuitive ability, excellent memory, and good spatial ability. They understand design and symbols as communication and are often talented in visual arts. Their attitudes toward nature and natural resources are personal and conservationist. They seem to learn best holistically and often have long attention spans.

Learning Opportunities Educators Should Consider:

- Using storytelling, metaphor, and myths as media for delivering information.
- Developing personal and group goals relevant to those of the tribal community as well as the student.
- Providing visual and spatial experience.
- Teaching from whole to details.
- Exploring and honoring belief in collective tribal self as an alternative world view; use intuitive ability in learning experiences.

Asian-American Culture

Curiously, the image of the Asian-American student as a model achiever in the schools works against the appropriate service needed by many gifted children in this population. Although the majority of Asian-American students give credence to the stereotype, there are students from families of low socioeconomic status, who have problems similar to those we have seen in other culturally diverse populations in poverty conditions. Far from a homogeneous group, the Asian-American community includes a wide variety of origins, beliefs, and languages. Given this great variety of Asian-Americans and those who come from low socioeconomic conditions, traditional measures for identification of the gifted are unlikely to be appropriate for all (Chen, 1989; Kitano, 1989).

Those studying this population (Chen, 1989; Kitano, 1989; Maker & Schiever, 1989a; Tanaka, 1989) have suggested some common attitudes and abilities that affect the learning experience. Asian-American children often have a serious and caring attitude toward their families, and respect for their teachers and other adults. The families are usually very supportive of their children's achievements. The children are found to have a high degree of self-discipline and self-motivation. They value academic achievement and have learned a strong work ethic. There is often evidence of excellent problem-solving ability and ability to listen and follow directions, resulting in high test scores. These children live with and are familiar and comfortable with the use of the intuitive in their learning and thinking.

Learning Opportunities Educators Should Consider:

- Giving opportunities to learn in teams and small groups.
- Giving opportunities to use intuition in learning.
- Providing visual learning experiences.
- Encouraging expressions of feelings, verbally and in writing.
- Including creative expression in the learning experience.

Hispanic-American Culture

The Hispanic-American population is increasing rapidly and is predicted to be the nation's largest ethnic group in the 21st Century. This population is also heavily immersed in the culture of poverty, with all of its inherent physical and intellectual deprivation. As with the other racial and ethnic diverse populations, the Hispanic-American population includes a variety of groupings. The population does, however, share strong cultural beliefs, a common language, and similar traditions. These very factors make it essential that we avoid stereotypes as we plan for the needs of the gifted Hispanic-American child.

In a well-documented discussion of culturally related differences in cognitive styles, De Leon (1983) presents a thoughtful rationale for the lack of success Hispanic-American students have with current identification procedures that result in their low representation in gifted programs. Through a review of the literature, De Leon finds that Hispanic-American children have consistently been shown to be more field dependent than Anglo children, and family socialization practices that do not encourage autonomy are seen as the main reason. In other words, the traditional Hispanic-American cultural attitudes and values related to family cohesiveness have been associated with the lack of development of a separate sense of identity. Field-dependent children are as proficient in concept attainment as field independents, but they express themselves in different ways (see Figure 13.4). De Leon concludes that these children differ only in the type of information each processes most effectively and in the situation which aids such processing. He cautions that unless the concept of giftedness, the identification procedures, and the range of activities for learning to include other cognitive styles is changed, other modes of interacting that can be as valuable as the current dominant mode will never be discovered.

Studies (Aragon & Marquez, 1975; Bernal, 1973; Ewing & Yong, 1992; Laudenslager & Valdez, 1986; Maker & Schiever, 1989b; Nazzaro, 1981) have found that the strengths in the learning attitudes and abilities of the Hispanic-American learner include a facility to learn a second language and fluent communication with peers and within their community. The children are very cooperative and share their parents' value of education. Families are supportive of their children, affectionate, and eager for them to succeed. The children often show unusual maturity and responsibility for their age and seem eager to try new ideas. The oral tradition is valued as is history of family and community.

Learning Opportunities Educators Should Consider:

- Using cooperative intellectual peer groups for learning and encouraging independent production.
- Providing visual and kinesthetic learning experiences.
- Providing extensive experience with both English and Spanish.
- Using successful Hispanic Americans as mentors.
- Including the family as part of the educational team.

Choosing Teachers for Racially and Ethnically Diverse Gifted Learners

Among those who want to improve the educational experience for racially and ethnically diverse gifted learners, requests are heard for teachers who deeply and intimately understand the culture of a particular group. At the same time, the same people often desire integrated classrooms, expressing a need for cultural pluralism and exposure to the values of the dominant culture. Such contradictory demands place teachers in an impossible position. Few people have the experience or information to understand the values and attitudes of the dominant culture and even one additional racial or ethnic culture intimately.

If we select a teacher for an integrated class because of upbringing in one racial or ethnic group, how will the teacher relate to others in the class from other racial or ethnic groups? Wouldn't it be better to select teachers on the basis of their sensitivity, openness, self-esteem, desire to work with culturally diverse children, and excellence of teaching skill? Focusing on the qualities that create student success in a classroom seems a far better rationale for teacher selection than is race or ethnic membership. To create racial and ethnic diversity in a classroom, a team of teachers from differing backgrounds might be formed. The children can then truly benefit from seeing and experiencing a model interface of cultures. Think what both teachers and learners could gain from such experiences.

Raising the awareness of all teachers and parents to the differing needs of children from diverse backgrounds should concern every teacher and inservice education program. Grantham and Ford (1998) suggest that all learning materials should be representative of racial and cultural groups and concepts of cultural diversity should be a part of every subject area studied.

Optimizing Learning for Racially and Ethnically Diverse Gifted Learners

Research suggests that some of the important issues that parents, counselors, and teachers need to help students from racially and ethnically diverse cultures deal with are the development of questioning skills and introspective attitudes and the remediation of any areas of skill that are lacking, especially limited language skills. As they begin to succeed, they will need help coping with peer pressures *not* to succeed, when they exist, and the alignment of their cultural values with those of the dominant culture. Finally, they will need help exploring opportunities in a variety of career options, understanding and exploring the problems they may face as they become upwardly mobile, and developing their own individuality and establishing their personal cultural identity.

In addition, many will need help in dealing with the excessive pressures to succeed as they are perceived to be models for others. As Grantham and Ford (1998) point out, after being identified as gifted, students may be faced with superhuman expectations to be a role model, a spokesperson, and a leader for other students. They comment on the experience of a subject of their study: "Danisha is expected to be a high achiever and an outstanding citizen as a student, and to lead social change amongst her African-American peers" (p. 99). Yet the student feels powerless to influence social problems that are beyond her control. She wants to successfully integrate within her gifted classes yet not sacrifice her close ties with her African-American friends. She is in danger of being misunderstood by both groups, because accommodating to either is likely to distance the other. Like so many other students, they will need to learn to value all persons, regardless of cultural or gender identity, and to understand and value the strengths of each culture and the importance of unity for all people. There are few bigger, more difficult, nor more important teaching tasks facing educators today.

ECONOMICALLY DISADVANTAGED OR LOW–SOCIOECONOMIC–STATUS (SES) GIFTED STUDENTS: THE CULTURE OF POVERTY

If the circumstances of poverty are added to cultural differences, the growing child risks alienation and very limited intellectual development. The overlying problems of poverty on the cultural characteristics makes it difficult to assess the potential achievements of the children involved. Unfavorable socialization, unequal school opportunities, and occupational discrimination work together to lower motivation and achievement. According to research begun in the 1960s (Bloom, Davis, & Hess, 1965; Dreger & Miller, 1960; Pettigrew, 1964), such children attend school less regularly and drop out in greater numbers. These conditions continue the restriction of a stimulating interaction with the environment, and student talents are often lost.

Low SES alone can be the most debilitating factor in the circumstances of a child, and where it exists enormous amounts of potential can be lost. A report for the US Department of Education (Alamprese & Erlanger, 1989) revealed that students from low-income backgrounds comprised 20% of the student population. During their school experience, such students are less than half as likely to qualify for and participate in gifted and talented programs. They were much less likely to be enrolled in academic programs that could open the access to college enrollment. The report recommended identification procedures, including the use of a preselection process wherein students are encouraged to develop and display their skills and abilities over an extended period of time. Such a process could increase the opportunities for the children to show advanced abilities appropriate for admission into a gifted program. As in many other studies, the use of multiple criteria for identification was also recommended.

VanTassel-Baska (1989b) found that the family's role in the success of low-SES gifted learners was most important. The families of successful students from this population encourage and monitor progress, communicate high expectations and standards for academic achievement, and view socioeconomic circumstances as motivators to succeed. These families were perceived as a major source of encouragement and influence.

In the matter of self-concept, the findings of a study by VanTassel-Baska, Olszewski-Kubilius, and Kulieke (1994) indicated that some differences in self-concept and social support in gifted students were based on ethnicity and gender, but most differences occurred between lower and higher SES groups. The authors suggest that disadvantagement should be viewed not as a generic condition but as a pattern specific to each disadvantaged child. They did, however, find differentiating traits between disadvantaged achievers and nonachievers. Some of the traits favoring the economically disadvantaged achievers were a strong sense of identity; supportive, inspiring relationships; a question orientation; awareness of alternative paths; and risk-taking capacity. The authors concluded that economically disadvantaged gifted students perceived that they have less support from classmates, friends, parents, and teachers than do advantaged students; that they are less scholastically competent; and that they are less correct in social conduct than are advantaged gifted students.

An interest has been found in understanding the characteristics and behaviors of children who withstand difficult circumstances and succeed despite the problems they encounter; they are known as *resilient* children. For these children, certain personal characteristics have been noted as protective factors, such as high ability, sense of humor, and support from an adult or family (Zetlin, 1998). The school can also be a supportive force. Zetlin suggests that schools with high expectations for student achievement, challenging curricula and instructional activities, a clear sense of mission, nurturing and supportive teachers, and strong administrative support can be associated with resilience.

> "Schools must seek ways to build upon and strengthen the enabling role of families in fostering competence and school success; schools must become resource centers for families and proactively encourage home-school connections that support and reinforce ongoing family efforts . . . educators must recognize the crucial nature of their roles as models, mentors, and nurturant supporters" (p. 155)

Even with such an obvious need, Patton, Prillaman, and VanTassel-Baska (1990) found that only slightly more than 30% of the states reported the use of low SES to any great degree in the identification process, and more than 34% reported no use at all. The best chance such children have to show their abilities is by the use of multiple tests, especially nontraditional tests. However, over 90% of the states use norm-referenced tests to some extent in their identification of economically disadvantaged students, and less than 40% indicated use of nontraditional approaches. The authors conclude that although states have been philosophically committed to providing for the low-SES gifted students, they have been slow in incorporating equity and pluralism into the definitional and funding structures of their gifted programs. Differentiated curricula, mentorships, counseling, and special tutorials are suggested provisions if the students from low-SES backgrounds are to have a chance of success.

Characteristics of Low-SES Gifted Learners

The first task is to make parents, teachers, principals, and boards of education aware that gifted learners can be found in low-SES homes; then they must know how to identify them. Chapter 9 reviewed the problems and alternative possibilities for identifying these gifted learners. Some traits of low-SES gifted learners that help with their identification (where testing often fails) are observations of:

- High mathematical abilities
- Alertness, curiosity
- Independence of action
- Initiative and eagerness to do new things
- Fluency in nonverbal communication

- Imagination in thinking
- Flexibility in approach to problems
- Learning quickly through experience
- Retaining and using ideas and information well
- Showing a desire to learn in daily work
- Originality and creativity in thinking
- Responding well to visual media
- Leadership ability in peer group
- Responsible social behavior
- Varied interests
- Ability to generalize learning to other areas and to show relationships among apparently unrelated ideas
- Resourcefulness; the ability to solve problems by ingenious methods
- Entrepreneurial ability; readily making money on various projects or activities
- Imaginative storytelling, using language rich in imagery
- Mature sense of humor
- Responsiveness to the concrete (Baldwin, 1973; Farrell, 1973; McMillin, 1975; Torrance, 1964)

Once identified as gifted, these low-SES learners may be grouped with more advantaged gifted students. Such grouping will aid them in many ways, but only if the teacher is aware that their needs may be quite different.

Family Patterns

Some important work from the 1960s (Rohrer & Edmonson, 1960) suggests some important differences in family structures and values between low- and middle-SES families that put the low-SES learner at a disadvantage. Four major family patterns—Middle Class, Matriarchy, Gang, and Nuclear—were identified that provided varying support for students. These profiles give insights that could be used to guide programs toward better serving students today.

Middle Class families hold values that view education as an important aspect of life. When low-SES families identify with this group and become upwardly mobile, these values take precedence over earlier religious, family, or political affiliations. However, if the pattern of *Matriarchy*—mother and daughter aligned against the world—is adhered to, there is a strong female dependency and male alienation that is not conducive to intellectual growth or independent thinking. The equivalent male pattern, the *Gang,* fosters aggressive independence, group secrecy and loyalty, and exaggerated masculinity. Because educational achievement is seen by the gang as a feminine characteristic, alignment with such a pattern inhibits intellectual development. The *Nuclear* family, as defined in the study, develops respect for parenthood, reliable employment, and family support. However, it is also characterized by suspicion and distrust of the outside world. Education is favored so long as it supports the family unity. If, as often is the case in higher education, discovery of different ideas and values brings the possibility of a different world view to the student, education may then be rejected. Any of these last three patterns would be antithetical to the development of giftedness.

In a study of the role played by the family in the success of low-SES gifted learners, VanTassel-Baska (1989b) reports that families of successful students encourage and monitor progress, communicate high expectations and standards for academic achievement, and view socioeconomic circumstances as motivators to succeed. Successful students in the study perceived their families as a major source of encouragement and influence. The message they received from their families was, "You must work hard, get an education, and achieve what your parents and grandparents did not, even though they too were bright and eager. You will have the chance that we did not have. Don't waste it" (pp. 34–35).

Learning Differences

According to Sisk (1973), the most serious deficiencies for low-SES children are reported to be in cognitive functioning (e.g., the ability to observe and state sequences of events, to perceive cause-and-effect relationships, and to categorize); language skills (e.g., limited vocabularies, nonstandard-English grammar); and reading. "The variations in responses are due in part to the individual's motivation and in part to the availability of adequate adult mediators who can help the child develop concepts with which to interpret his environment" (p. 5). These deficits may result in classroom behavior we seldom associate with gifted students: negative attitudes toward school, toward teachers, and toward their own achievement; inability to focus on long-term goals; and the use of violence in resolving problems. Baldwin (1973) notes that low-SES gifted students have seldom been exposed to books and magazines at home and have been "starved for verbal encounters" (p. 11). She also notes that, as with most underachievers, low-SES gifted students exhibit an external locus of control. Other differences in learning styles include spatial rather than temporal; physical rather than aural; content centered rather than form centered; and inductive rather than deductive. The importance of planning with alternative activities when low-SES children are in the program is evident.

Intervention

A major problem encountered in providing for gifted students among the low-SES population is the attitude, shared by teachers and parents alike, that giftedness cannot exist in this population. For parents living in poverty, development of facilitating conditions for nurturing giftedness is not easy, but it is possible. Review again the activities suggested in Chapters 4 and 5 and notice how many could be achieved in homes that have limited resources.

The literature contains many suggestions to consider when planning and implementing services for low-SES gifted learners. Renzulli (1973) cited two major factors to consider: the characteristics of the teacher and the relevancy of the curriculum. Teachers must enjoy working with these children and experience real personal satisfaction with their achievements and growth for the program to be successful. The curriculum must be involved with the immediate lives of the students. Renzulli defined a relevant curriculum as "a set of experiences which deal with topics and issues that youngsters would talk about if given a free choice" (p. 443). When structured properly, these issues can be used to teach all the process skills and content information, while eliciting far more motivation and interest.

Edmonds (1980) believed that schools can be developed to overcome the limitations of impoverished family environments. He and his Harvard colleagues have identified five elements as the keys to urban, low–socioeconomic-area school success: (1) a school's leadership, (2) its instructional emphasis, (3) overall climate, (4) how teachers imply what they expect, and (5) how administrators use standardized testing results. These elements have all been found to affect student achievement. After conducting a needs assessment of a school, the Edmonds project provided help to bring it into positive alignment with the five elements for success. Through this procedure he improved the quality of many inner-city New York schools.

Alamprese and Erlanger (1989) reported from projects for low-SES gifted students these successful practices:

For Instruction of Students:

- Extend the time students spend learning by providing after-school, weekend, and summer enrichment and accelerated courses.
- Offer special programs to prepare students for acceptance into gifted programs.
- Provide advanced courses at local universities.
- Use hands-on learning techniques.
- Provide community programs designed to enhance students' cultural and intellectual development, such as those in museums and with mentors in business and industry.

For Support of Students:

- Set external goals.
- Provide career awareness programs.
- Provide social-emotional support.
- Encourage parent participation.

Alamprese and Erlanger offer other recommendations to school districts in the administration and management of programs.

A research project begun in response to concerns that minority low-SES students were being referred for identification for gifted programs less frequently, and large numbers of those who were in gifted programs were withdrawing after experiencing academic difficulties, will provide an example of one structure of multicultural education (Sisk, 2000). The information gained from such a study can provide strategies and procedures that can be used in regular and special classrooms to better meet the needs of gifted children from diverse cultures.

A research project called STEP UP (Systematic Training for Educational Programs for Underserved Pupils) was organized incorporating economically disadvantaged students from Arizona, Arkansas, Florida, and Texas (Sisk, 2000). The goal was "to establish a system for identifying minority economically disadvantaged students with gifted potential and to provide these students a transitional curriculum of study to meet their educational needs and enhance their potential" (p. 44). Recommendations for the identification process include: use teacher judgment after they have been informed of the strengths of low-SES children; establish an assessment baseline from a number of tests and other sources of data; use appropriate criteria for low-SES students; use the pretest-teach-posttest strategy of dynamic assessment; analyze strengths of child and sub-tests; locate model schools in low-SES areas. The success of the project added new information of the needs of this population and among these were the need for:

- Encouragement to pursue and integrate ideas without forced closure
- Development of higher level productive thinking skills and problem solving skills
- Exposure to alternatives, abstractions, consequences of choices, making and testing generalizations
- Strategies for clarifying feelings and expectations of others
- Awareness of how their behavior affects the feelings and behavior of others
- Strategies for transcending negative reactions of teachers, parents, and students
- Establishment of personal purpose and direction
- Realistic goal setting

Although the low representation of racially and ethnic low-SES students in gifted programs is sometimes attributed to inappropriate testing, it is evident that the learning skills often must be built and the experience and knowledge bases broadened if these students are to benefit from opportunities in gifted programs. By including the strengths and special needs of low-SES gifted learners in the curricular planning, these children can have of a better chance to develop their giftedness.

To increase the probability that identified gifted students from poverty are successful in gifted programs, Slocumb and Payne (2000) suggest that the programs must move from pull-out programs that offer part-time services for full-time needs to full-time programs. "Of all of the program designs, the one that is least defensible for gifted students from poverty is the pullout program " (p. 161). Teachers who work with children from poverty should not assume that the low level of readiness often exhibited by these students means that they have no school skills. It is very possible that they just do not know how to tranfer their skills to the school setting. For that reason, instead of outside projects and products, Slocumb and Payne suggest that class time be used for such products so that resources and support will be available. An emphasis needs to be placed on teaching the value of academics to broaden the students' perspective and motivation. Of high priority to the child from poverty, at every age, is the need for significant relationships. Positive relationships with fellow students make learning more possible; with the school such relationships are also important; but with the teacher a positive accepting relationship is crucial to this child's success.

In this chapter, we have briefly explored populations of gifted learners who present educators with special concerns: culturally diverse gifted learners including gifted females, racially and ethnically diverse gifted students, and economically disadvantaged gifted learners. Although we are learning more about working successfully with these gifted students, questions continue to arise and more research is needed. This limited discussion was meant to create an awareness of some of the problems in these areas in the hope that such an awareness might foster increased efforts toward solutions, both in the home and at school.

QUESTIONS OFTEN ASKED

1. As a teacher I feel so inadequate in the face of all the diversity in my classroom. How can I ever know enough about all of the cultures to help all of the children in my class?

The most important thing you can do is to get to know each child in your class. It is always helpful to understand as much as possible about the effects of culture on the children; however, each child in any culture has individual traits and ideas. Let the children teach you about themselves and the perspectives they have of their cultures. Take some time in the class to implement activities that help the children know each other and you. These relationships are very important to how well they will learn and support each other. Emotional and social safety have an amazingly positive effect on academic success.

2. Do culturally diverse students require a separate curriculum?

A separate curriculum is not necessary when the instruction is individualized and the curriculum is differentiated. What is important, however, is that the teacher and others involved in gifted programs in which cultural diversity exists hold positive attitudes toward cultural differences. It is also important that lots of resources related to diverse populations be made available, and that the program be flexible and responsive to each child's needs. An awareness of cultural and ethnic history and traditions helps to understand the child's view of his or her world.

3. Why do gifted females not show as high a rate of success when they become women as they did as girls, but the rate of success between boys and men does not seem to change?

There are differences in the rate of development, learning styles, and hemispheric maturation between males and females, but the differences in parental, educational, and societal expectations and practices from childhood through adulthood contribute most heavily to this pattern. Even succeeding becomes a problem for many women because they have learned to fear success. They believe they will be less feminine, less desirable, and less likely to be happy if they are too successful, even though research shows that women who achieve closer to their potential are more fulfilled and satisfied with their lives.

4. If gifted children can come from all racial and ethnic groups, why are some groups better represented in gifted programs than other groups?

There are many factors responsible for the low representation of gifted children from some racial and ethnic groups. Many find that the identification procedures are restricting to some of these children and a great deal of research has been and is being done on how to better structure such procedures so that they better represent a broader range of diversity of thought and achievement. Others point to the lack of opportunities of some children to develop school skills and the rational thinking processes that are so closely related to the American experience. A growing body of research in brain development shows that the brain requires stimulation from conception throughout life if children are to develop the most of the potential encoded in their genes. Issues of poverty often overlie cultural diversity and limit the amount and type of stimulation some children can access. Cultural values, such as the emphasis placed on education, and the way the children are or are not encouraged to express themselves may be a part of the answer. All of these factors are of concern and need our consideration as we seek to understand this important discrepancy.

5. How does poverty affect the development of intelligence?

Because adequate nutrition and appropriate stimulation are necessary to the development of intelligence, limitations of these factors inhibit such development. Too often such limitations are a part of the syndrome of poverty. Add to these problems the attitudes of victimization, hopelessness, and frustration, and any expression of intelligence can be seriously curtailed. Retardation shows a statistically significant high correlation to poverty; giftedness a very low correlation. There are many reasons to work to eliminate the culture of poverty, the suppression of intelligence is a very important one.

 ## CHECKING FOR UNDERSTANDING
Follow-Up Activity

Choose three cultural groups and list at least five culturally supported attitudes or abilities that children from that group might bring to the learning setting which would be facilitating and five which would be limiting. What impact would these have on the gifted program? What could you do to use these differences to enhance learning? This activity can be done individually or in groups.

SUMMARY

Cultural Diversity and Giftedness

1. Giftedness at the highest level can be found in every cultural group. The incidence of giftedness differs from group to group as a result of differing values, attitudes, and opportunities.
2. Cultural groups differ on availability of support systems, attitudes toward development of giftedness, provision of resources, priority given to certain kinds of talent, individual initiative, and leadership, among other factors, depending on what the culture values. What is valued by the culture is produced by the culture.
3. Any group of people who share a common value structure, belief system, language, and/or world view may be said to be a cultural group.
4. The cultural heritage is learned and is not innately based on the culture in which one is born.
5. Rather than being restricted to the ethnic and racial heritage, cultural identity is influenced by religion, gender, age, socioeconomic level, primary language, geographical region, disabilities, and any other exceptional conditions.
6. Some children of low-socioeconomic status (SES) are also ethnically or racially diverse; however, it is important to remember that many are not, and yet both groups are culturally diverse.
7. Economically disadvantaged students, also referred to as low-SES students, are being reared by poor, low-SES parents out of the economic (rather than ethnic or racial) mainstream. This population seems characterized by the values and attitudes often resulting from poverty, which include a victim orientation, survival thinking, short-term planning, and dependency.
8. Culturally diverse students are those being reared in any group that differs significantly in values and attitudes from the dominant culture. Too often, our educational system penalizes children who are raised with significantly different values and attitudes from those found in the dominant culture.
9. Cultural groups can create conditions for their members that can be facilitating to the growth of intelligence and supportive of achievement or limiting to both in many ways.
10. Our laws have become progressively more protective of rights to ensure the equality of diverse groups and move us toward a pluralist society.

Multicultural Education and Gifted Learners

11. Multicultural education as a concept incorporates cultural diversity and provides equality in schools.
12. Educators who develop successful multicultural learning experiences are found to be self-aware and understanding, socially responsive and responsible, and culturally sensitive.

Gifted Females

Barriers to Equity—At Home

13. In our dominant culture, and even more intensely in many other cultures, girl babies have an entirely different experience as a member of the family and the larger community than do boys. There is evidence that one of the most consistent determinants of parental expectations, perceptions, and organizers of behavior is the sex of their infant.

14. Studies show that bright girls consistently underestimate their own ability. The brighter the girl, the less expectation she has for intellectual success.

15. How the sexes differ genetically in the way their brains develop, how the outside environment modifies this development, and how much we as parents and educators can affect the development of brain organization are questions now being asked and studied by those in the neurosciences.

Barriers to Equity—At School

16. The early education environment is the beginning of the schools' educational neglect of girls. Such environments often concentrate on areas in which girls already are competent and fail to provide the investigatory and experimental activities that would develop needed skills so critical to their development.

17. From the first years of school, girls learn to conceal their talents by pretending to be less capable as they are rewarded and taught to show less of their intellectual abilities to receive more social acceptance.

18. Boys actually learn more than girls because the teacher explains how things work and encourages them to try out toys and materials.

19. Girls' actions have far less effect on their environment than do the actions of boys.

20. It is evident from research that differences in expectations and results, whether caused primarily by biological differences, environmental differences, or an interaction of both, do not favor independent, successful achievement for females.

Barriers to Equity—In Society

21. Women equate intellectual achievement with loss of femininity.

22. Girls seem to believe that if they succeed, it is luck; if they fail, it is their fault. Boys reverse this view for their successes and failures.

23. Gifted women often believe that they must excel in every role they play and they must play every role assigned. High energy is expended by such women to simultaneously maintain their femininity; succeed as a wife; have an outstanding career; be a perfect parent; have an attractive body; and run a beautiful, well-managed home.

24. As with achievement motivation research, career development theory is derived almost entirely from research on males.

25. Because of society's mixed expectations that women should fill a supportive nurturing role but also assertively develop their own talent and with few role models of successful women to follow, it is easy for gifted females to become confused about how to pursue a truly satisfying future.

Racially and Ethnically Diverse Gifted Populations

26. The attitudes and skills for thinking and learning are established in the family, a base that forms the future of the children. Every cultural group instills both advantages and limiting attitudes in their children before they enter school.

27. It is the responsibility of the family, cultural group, and school to engage in attitudes and practices known to bring out the highest levels of intelligence and ability unique to each child.

28. Information about the contributions various ethnic and racial groups make to the educational development of their children is generalized and oversimplified, because it is the family unit that makes the decisions as to how the values and beliefs of the ethnic or racial group are to be interpreted and practiced.

29. It has been noted that the literature available on racially and ethnically diverse students has focused more on deficits than on strengths.

Economically Disadvantaged or Low–Socioeconomic–Status (SES) Gifted Students: The Culture of Poverty

30. Low SES alone can be the most debilitating factor in the circumstances of a child, and where it exists enormous amounts of potential can be lost. If the circumstances of poverty are added to cultural differences, then the growing child risks alienation and very limited intellectual development.

31. Studies have found that the family's role in the success of low-SES gifted learners was most

important. They encouraged and monitored progress, communicated high expectations and standards for academic achievement, and viewed socioeconomic circumstances as motivators to succeed.

32. Children who withstand difficult circumstances and succeed despite the problems they encounter are known as *resilient* children.

33. The most serious deficiencies for low-SES children are reported to be in cognitive functioning (e.g., the ability to observe and state sequences of events, to perceive cause-and-effect relationships, and to categorize); language skills (e.g., limited vocabularies, non-standard-English grammar); and reading.

Intervention

34. A major problem encountered in providing for gifted students among the low-SES population is the attitude—shared by both teachers and parents—that giftedness cannot exist in this population.

35. By including the strengths and special needs of low-SES gifted learners in the curricular planning, these children can be ensured of a better chance to develop their giftedness.

Supporting Gifted Learners with Special Needs

In this chapter, the reader will find information
and programs to assist:

- Underachieving gifted students
- Gifted learners with disabilities

The various school adjustment problems not only tend to obscure any signs of giftedness, but also distract the teacher from suspecting that giftedness exists. The need to remediate deficits becomes a greater concern than the need to nurutre special talents in children . . . The symptoms of the handicap are so distracting that they divert attention from any sign of giftedness.

—Abraham J. Tannenbaum and Lois J. Baldwin

Rich attends a large integrated high school where the majority of students come from middle-class families. The school is in the suburbs of a large city. Rich is athletic, good looking, and always well-dressed and well-groomed. His family has fairly traditional values and aspirations of achievement for their children. Rich, the third of five children, has an older brother and sister who were both high academic achievers. His father was a high school dropout, but has worked his way from a dock loader to an office job with his firm. His mother was a college graduate, and her family is from a decidedly higher social stratum than her husband's.

Although Rich has been identified as a gifted learner, he does not belong to the group of school leaders and achievers who determine school activities. Instead, he has chosen a peer group of underachievers like himself among whom he is considered a leader.

Rich is known to be very good at sports and is probably one of the best tennis players in his school, although he refuses to try out for the school tennis team.

Rich has been placed in advanced classes, although he maintains about a C average. His teachers often comment that he is not living up to his capability. Part of the reason for his low grades is his habit of putting off all assignments to the last minute and then doing only enough to get by. He is a good reader, has an exceptional vocabulary, and reads extensively in books unrelated to his school subjects. When Rich "tunes in" to a class, which is rare, he can pull an A without any problem. But that occurs only when he gets excited about the class or the subject, as when he got into government last year and became so involved with politics, political systems, and strategies that he spent hours before and after school questioning the teacher about everything he knew. He was chosen to attend a model government conference in the state capital last summer but now, with his new classes, he has "tuned out" again.

Although Rich is outgoing and open with his peers, he is extremely nervous and uncomfortable around authority figures, such as teachers. He lacks confidence in himself and is not very self-accepting. Once he was allowed to contract cooperatively with his teacher for a project in which he felt he would be interested. He set unrealistically high standards for himself, even though the teacher insisted that she would settle for far less. He procrastinated for weeks and then gave up the entire project saying, "If I can't do a good job on something, I just won't do it."

In trying to understand Rich and help him with his underachieving pattern, one of his teachers met with him and his family several times in his home. Although his father expressed the desire for Rich to attend college, he seemed to have a very negative attitude toward education. His father was very insistent on his son's strict obedience to the rules, seeing each act of compliance as a minor victory for himself and a defeat for his son. There was an obvious emotional gap between the father and son. Rich's father seemed to express only two attitudes toward his son, indifference or hostility. He seemed totally incapable of responding to any of Rich's achievements, no matter how excellent. The teacher's effort to discuss the accomplishments Rich had made in the government class were met with stony silence. It seemed as if there were actually a competition between the two, wherein the father hid his fear of losing behind demands for perfection and a refusal to recognize perfection should his son approach it. Thus, for Rich to attempt any new task meant risking almost certain reaffirmation of his inabilities, his self-perceived worthlessness, and that would be even more traumatic should his efforts actually produce less than average grades or results. Thus, failure became the one thing Rich could not allow. To quote Rich, "If I can't do a good job on something, I just won't do it."

UNDERACHIEVING GIFTED STUDENTS

Underachievement in gifted children is one of the most baffling, most frustrating problems parents or teachers can face. You can see the child's possibilities, occasionally you are given a glimpse of the brilliance, but then it is gone, replaced by a wall of apathy or apparent unconcern. But all of this may be just a facade, because the underachiever may be even more frustrated than we are.

The problem, unfortunately, is growing. Nationwide, Seeley (1993) estimates that 15% to 40% of identified gifted students may become involved with significant underachievement. Robertson (1991) reported that between 18% and 25% of gifted and talented students drop out of high school each year and *US News & World Report* (August, 1983) claimed that 18% of all high school dropouts are gifted students.

At least two types of underachievers have been designated, situational underachievers and chronic underachievers. Situational underachievers are those who underachieve only on occasion, such as when a particularly difficult home problem erupts or a clash occurs with one particular teacher. They generally cause little real concern beyond getting help with the immediate problem.

The chronic underachiever, whose pattern recurs again and again, presents a problem particularly resistant to remediation. In discussing this type of underachiever, keep in mind that the underachievement must be assessed by running the proper diagnostic tests for physical problems to ensure that it is not of organic origin. If these measures do not indicate causation, then there are other places to look. There is a growing body of data regarding the underachievement problem that should be considered.

In this text, the underachieving gifted student is defined as someone who has shown exceptional performance on a standardized test of intellectual ability or achievement and who, nevertheless, does not perform as well as expected on school-related tasks as evidenced by grades or teacher reports.

Although this is a limited definition of gifted underachievement, the commonly used definition of "not performing up to capability or potential" has no basis and cannot be used in good conscience when there are no measures of capacity or potential, innate or otherwise. To indicate underachievement, the measure of performance on standardized achievement or intelligence tests and the evidence of performance on school-related tasks should show a considerable amount of discrepancy and be evident over time. Underachievement becomes especially clear when you observe a student over time and find a noticeable pattern—when you see the special moments, the brilliance. To use any other criterion would create an unmanageable number of underachievers that would certainly include most of the gifted population, because they are so rarely challenged to use their ability. Whitmore (1980) reported that under this definition underachievers may account for 15% to 50% of the gifted population, although she feels that if the scores of all gifted students on individual aptitude tests were compared with their level of performance, as many as 70% may be underachieving.

In a larger sense, every one of us is underachieving, because we continue to use only a small percentage of our brain's potential. Therefore, although we surely expect more from gifted third-grade students than we do from typical third-grade students, those who do not at least perform at the average level will be designated as underachieving.

Characteristics of Underachievers

What is known about underachievers? What are they like? The traits or characteristics of underachievers have been reported in many studies, although no one student would be expected to have all or even more than a few traits from this compilation. To further complicate our identification of these children, it has been noted that such children may be aggressive and act out their frustration by seeking attention negatively, or they may withdraw and quietly allow their talents to waste away (Whitmore, 1980).

Misbehavior may be a way some underachieving gifted students attempt to prove that they are not so smart. They may also use it to cope with a lack of social comfort and competence with age peers and/or an inappropriate curriculum and instruction in the regular classroom. Focusing on prevention, Delisle, Whitmore, and Ambrose (1987) reminded us that:

> Gifted students generally do not develop behavior problems when they are: (a) placed with a teacher who enjoys teaching gifted children and learning with them; (b) afforded frequent opportunities to learn with intellectual peers; (c) actively engaged in learning that is appropriately complex, challenging, and meaningful; and (d) provided guidance in how to understand and cope with their giftedness in society. (p. 38)

The characteristic behaviors of underachieving gifted students are varied and have been studied extensively since the 1950s. As early as the Terman studies in the 1940s, characteristics such as lack of self-confidence, inability to persevere, and lack of goal-setting were reported. Figure 14.1 summarizes this population's characteristics that continue to be discussed in results of studies conducted during the past two decades. They seem to fall into categories of personal, family, social, and school-related behaviors. Still, most commonly mentioned are evidence of a low self-concept, lack of motivation and interest in classroom activities and assignments, and social immaturity. Underachieving gifted students are reported to attribute success to ability and not see the relationship to effort. Anger, frustration, hostility, and rebelliousness are too often present. Poor study habits, lack of persistence, dependency, and impulsiveness often are part of the profile. Although underachievement is difficult to reverse, it is most easily remediated in elementary school; underachievement resists reversal when left to secondary intervention.

Causes for Underachievement

Reasons for underachievement are quite complex and must be individually assessed for each learner. Some patterns of possible causation have been reported to correlate highly with underachievement and seem to occur with great frequency. Causes for underachievement can be found in the personality of the child, the home or the behavior of the parents, or in the classroom, especially in the curriculum and instruction.

Figure 14.1 *Characteristics of Underachieving Gifted Students*

Sources: Davis & Rimm, 1994; Frey, 1989; Janos & Robinson, 1985; Karnes & Pearce, 1981; Laffoon, Jenkins-Friedman, & Tollefson, 1989; Redding, 1990; Rimm, 1986; Whitmore, 1980.

1. Have low self-concept: negative evaluations of self; feelings of inferiority demonstrated by distrust, indifference, lack of concern, and/or hostility toward others.
2. Are socially more immature than achievers; lack self-discipline, procrastinate, refuse tasks deemed unpleasant; highly distractible; highly impulsive; unwilling to face realities and consequences.
3. Have feelings of rejection; believe no one likes them; feel that parents are dissatisfied with them.
4. Have feelings of helplessness; may externalize conflict and problems, avoid challenges.
5. Do not see the relationship between their efforts and subsequent achievement outcomes; negate personal responsibility for failures.
6. Are irresponsible, rebellious; feelings of being victimized; have poor personal adjustment.
7. Have few hobbies or strong interests.
8. Are unpopular with peers, hold lower status in class, have few friends.
9. Are hostile toward adult authority figures; distrust adults in general.
10. Are resistant to influence from teacher or parent.
11. Have lower aspirations for future; lack future plans or career goals; resist goals that have been set for them.
12. May withdraw in classroom situations and be less persistent, less assertive.
13. Lack study skills and academic curiosity; have weak motivation for academic tasks.
14. Dislike school and teachers; choose companions who also have negative attitudes toward school.
15. Often leave schoolwork incomplete; frequently nap during study time; often test phobic.
16. Perform at higher levels on tasks that require synthesizing than on detailed, computational, or convergent problem-solving tasks that require precise and analytic information processing.

The Personality of the Child

Whitmore (1980) has done a thorough job of bringing together the findings that aid us in understanding the gifted underachiever. She admits that the research findings indicate that the personality of underachievers as described by the traits listed in Figure 14.1 is strongly involved in the problem of why they underachieve. However, she believes that such traits are only a part of the reason. According to Whitmore, certain internal pressures influence the observed behaviors, such as the gifted person's supersensitivity, deficiency in social skills, and need for perfectionism. There are also external factors that may be equally at fault in creating this problem. From outside sources may come society's pressure to isolate a person who is different—even if that difference would be beneficial to the group—and the pressure of societal expectations. These pressures intensify the problems of sensitivity and perfectionism found within the gifted learner. To all of these we may too often add inappropriate educational provisions, which include an inappropriate curriculum, a counterproductive instructional style and philosophy of the teacher, and the punitive social climate created by classroom peers. Whitmore writes of how these pressures, both internal and external, intensify the gifted learner's vulnerability and how the very characteristics typical of their high level of intelligence make it easy for them to feel rejected and valueless. She reported that parents and teachers often admit that children who learn quickly and think creatively tend to make them feel uncomfortable and that the children's endless questioning and verbalization cause them to feel irritated.

There are some indications that underachievement is a different problem for girls than for boys. Male underachievers begin getting lower grades than achievers in first grade, with underachievement becoming significant by third grade and more apparent each following year. Female underachievers exceed achievers in first through fifth grade and begin their decline in sixth grade. The difference becomes most apparent in ninth grade. For both groups, the data demonstrate that the problem of underachievement worsens each year between third and twelfth grades. In all the studies reported, the incidence of underachievement in boys was at least twice that found in girls. Whitmore (1980) reported that 90% of all referrals for placement in her underachieving gifted program were boys. It has been suggested that this results from the different expectations and opportunities provided by our society for females. Some gifted students, especially adolescent girls, feel that they risk unpopularity if they reveal their high academic ability. In many high school settings, academic achievement is not valued; conformity is the yardstick of success.

Another cause of underachievement unique to gifted learners stems from their varied and numerous interests. They may, without proper guidance, extend their interests in too many areas, engage in too many activities, and be unable to set appropriate priorities. It is possible for gifted students to get involved in so many things that they do nothing well.

Gifted students who underachieve in the culturally diverse populations present many possible causes; however, generally the factors that distinguish them from achievers in their groups is the lack of a strong belief in self and the resilience to overcome negative experiences (Reis & McCoach, 2000). Many learners who are gifted and disabled underachieve in school. However, Reis and McCoach warn that it is critically important to distinguish between chronic underachievement and processing deficits, learning disabilities, or attention deficits because the appropriate interventions for these subgroups may be radically different.

The Home and/or Parents

Since the early 1960s, the literature has indicated that many of the causes for underachievement can be found in the personality of the gifted child, in the home, and/or in the interaction between the children and the parents (Bricklin & Bricklin, 1967; McGillivray, 1964; Ralph, Goldberg, & Passow, 1966; Shaw & Black, 1960). The families of underachievers differ in many ways from those of achieving students.

In Families of High-Achieving Students, Often

- Parents are interested in their children.
- Fathers are important life influences.
- Mothers are responsible and independent.
- Parents have high educational aspirations for their children.

- Parents are well-educated.
- Families are small.
- Children are often the first born or only child.

In Families of Underachieving Students, Often

- Children are dependent on mothers.
- Fathers are rejecting and domineering and give little warmth or affection.
- Relationships between fathers and daughters or fathers and sons are negative or nonexistent.
- Parents set unrealistic goals for their children, and the children imagine that they are only as valuable or "good" as their accomplishments.
- Parents allow achievement to go unrewarded.
- Children do not identify with their parents.
- Deep social and emotional problems are present in the family.
- Parents are not active in their children's schools.
- Parents are not supportive of their children.
- Children's achievements present a threat to the parents and their adult superiority.
- Parents do not share ideas, affection, trust, or approval.
- Parents are restrictive and severe in their punishment.

The structure of the environments established by families of underachievers are reported to be disorganized, with unclear guidelines about behavior and academic performance; lack of cohesion and parental agreement regarding parenting; and often present the child with emotional distance. The environment is filled with mixed messages regarding the value of achievement and there is a lack of or inconsistent modeling of achievement behavior (Baker, Bridger, & Evans, 1998).

A Stanford study (cited in Report on Education Research, 1986) found that the parental style most conducive to academic achievement entailed setting clear standards while recognizing children's rights, expecting mature behavior, and fostering a healthy share of discussion and dissent. The researchers found an association between low grades and authoritarian parenting, which included attempts to shape, control, and evaluate the behaviors and attitudes of their children in accord with an absolute set of standards. Such parents placed a heavy emphasis on obedience, respect for authority, and the preservation of order, discouraging any open communication between themselves and their children. This parenting style and the resulting grades correlate across ethnic boundaries. The study showed that placing too much emphasis on either punishing or rewarding children for grades makes students less motivated internally toward schoolwork and leads to lower school performance.

Although parenting style has repeatedly been found to be a factor, Rimm and Lowe (1988) concluded from their studies that the style used is less important than consistency in the environment and within the approach provided.

In some cases, the entire neighborhood devalues education. This has caused some researchers to observe that low-achieving, low-socioeconomic students seem to fail not because of an initial lack of motivation to learn, but because basic learning processes used in their own communities are not contiguous with those required for academic success (Bricklin & Bricklin, 1967; Brown, 1971; Fine, 1967).

The School

Schools may be not only a principal cause of underachievement, but one that is most likely to yield to remediation (Whitmore, 1980). By changing the unproductive patterns traditionally found in many classrooms, we may prevent a large amount of the underachievement that we now observe.

> Regardless of the extent to which innate personality characteristics may contribute to the development of the underachiever's problems, it seems much more useful for educators to examine how the environment might contribute to the child's difficulty and thereby be modified to help eliminate the problem.
>
> The actual causes of underachievement are a mixture of the student's characteristics . . . and a social environment that does not meet the personal needs of the child. Factors of the social environment that can contribute to the development of negative attitudes and underachieving behavior include external pressures of unrealistic expectations; emphasis on conformity and convergent thinking; a lack of rewards or the existence of social penalties for creativity and initiative; rigidity and inflexibility; excessive competition and criticism; and personally unrewarding curriculum and required activities. (pp. 190–191)

In Whitmore's study, the students identified lack of respect for the individual, a competitive social climate, inflexibility, stress on external evaluation, and an unrewarding curriculum as elements of their previous classroom environments that they believed contributed significantly to the development of their underachievement. Whitmore (1986) advised that it is important for the parent to develop a sense of partnership with school personnel. Wherever the problem exists it can best be solved if all members of the team are working together. "The caring adult's role is to provide encouragement, guidance, affirming support and unconditional acceptance" (p. 69).

Davis and Rimm (1994) view the school environment in relationship to the dynamics of underachievement to understand how it is reinforced. Inflexibility and rigidity in classrooms are demonstrations of the lack of respect for the individual child and are attributes that allow the needs of the gifted child to go unmet. The heavily competitive classroom contributes to underachievement by emphasizing extrinsic rewards that detract from the intrinsic rewards of learning and creativity so highly correlated to achievement. Negative expectations, unrewarding curricula, and inappropriate goals may also cause or support underachievement.

Predominant in this causal cluster is the incompetent or insecure teacher. Teachers known to contribute to underachievement are teachers who:

- Must maintain superiority in the field of knowledge.
- Impose unrealistic goals and standards (the perfectionist).
- Use threats, ridicule, warnings, and ultimatums and rarely show warmth or acceptance; are cold and impersonal.
- Are too easy; do not present a challenge.
- Have predictable, routine schedules and do not present a stimulating environment. (Evans, 1965)

Prevention and Remediation of Underachievement

Underachievement is a learned behavior and, therefore, can be prevented or un-learned. Prevention is better than any form of remediation. Often underachievement can be a conscious decision that is seen by the student as the best way of coping with a painful situation. Children who find that their endeavors are always seen as inadequate may decide that doing nothing is less painful and far less disappointing than is constant criticism. Children like Rich who find their work constantly compared with work done by other family members or classmates may decide that they can deter comparisons by producing no work at all. For others whose self-image is not secure, producing nothing prevents the mistakes that they are fearful of making and allows them to entertain the possibility that they could do fantastic things if they wanted to.

Whitmore (1986) cautioned that, "Adults have a tendency to demand that a child be disciplined to work diligently even if the task is unrewarding" (p. 67). Even when the child is willing to spend the effort, the reward may be an assign-ment of additional work that is equally unstimulating, typically unchallenging, and largely unsatisfying. When the child begins to show lack of motivation, the use of some of Whitmore's suggestions may help. The sooner the pattern is interrupted, the better.

1. Clearly assess the problem and, to the extent possible, its causes. Observe the child in a variety of settings (e.g., in the home, at school, among intellectual peers) to discover what motivates and is interesting to the child.

2. Communicate your observations with the child, hypothesizing about the problem behavior and the cause as you observe it. Share your understanding of the prob-lem using your own personal experiences, and invite the child to share his or her perceptions of the problem. Only if the child sees the situation as personally un-satisfactory or if there is discomfort with present conditions will the desire for change be forthcoming. The child must desire change before the third step can occur.

3. Develop a partnership with the child and include the parents or teacher if possible. Actively seek solutions to the perceived problem by problem-solving together.

Whitmore advised that it is important for parents to develop a sense of partnership with school personnel. Wherever the problem exists, it can best be solved if all members of the team are working together. "The caring adult's role is to provide encouragement, guidance, affirming support and unconditional acceptance" (p. 69). Whitmore believed that chronic underachievement by gifted students can be pre-vented by educational programs that allow these students to meet their needs. She also concluded that early patterns of underachievement can be reversed through the development of effective classrooms in elementary school.

Laffoon and colleagues (1989) reported the importance of a strong internal locus of control as a key dimension in academic achievement that is more important than school, teacher, or family. Underachievers do not attribute either success or failure to internal causes. To achieve more internal locus of control, these re-searchers suggested that students be taught to make realistic attributions and to learn from their failures. Students should be taught to be self-monitoring and to use self-instructions to change their orientation to one that is more persistent and less helpless.

As early as 1972, Martinson warned that gifted children placed in regular classrooms may regress to the achievement level of their classmates, may develop discipline problems as a result of boredom, and/or may withdraw to their own interests. She cited evidence that students in the highest range of intellectual ability may have the greatest difficulty with adjustment in the regular classroom. Supplee (1989) also suggested that boredom and inadequate academic programming be considered a factor in underachievement. Prevention would demand a better match between the needs of the student and the curricular and instructional requirements.

Teachers, although unintentionally, may contribute to underachievement in other ways: holding too low expectations; or alternately creating undue pressure for high achievement, and by having unfair grading practices for gifted students. Peers may create a climate where gifted students underachieve to allow them to better fit in. This is especially true with middle and high school students when peer relationships assume a higher priority than learning (Clinkenbeard, 1991). Finally, previous success may also create a background for underachievement among students who have had unchallenging curricular experiences throughout elementary and even into middle school. As they enter high school and find specialization demands, they encounter problems from their undeveloped study skills created by years of effortless academic success (Baker, Bridger, & Evans, 1998). Sometimes this confrontation with undeveloped study skills will not occur until college, where it can be especially damaging. Teaching such skills must be approached within the context of high interest meaningful, self-directed activities if they are to be remediated.

From the projects, the investigations, and the observations of teachers and parents come the following suggestions for those who are concerned about gifted underachievers.

If You Are a Parent,

1. Provide an intellectually stimulating, curiosity-producing atmosphere in your home.
2. Establish a close, mutually respectful relationship with your child.
3. Become a role model of behavior you desire your child to have.
4. Be interested in your child's activities at home and at school.
5. Do not compare siblings; each child is unique.
6. Help your child establish effective time priorities.
7. Guide your children toward goals of their interest; do not set goals for them.
8. Make your demands and rules reasonable and mutual.
9. Show your affection, trust, and approval.
10. Support your child; get involved.

If You Are a Teacher or a Counselor,

1. Value achievements of high-ability students.

2. Assess each student regularly, beginning in elementary school; know your students' profiles.

3. Provide opportunities for students to build their self-concept.

4. Create a responsive learning environment, one that is open, accepting, warm, and intellectually challenging.

5. Give the underachiever an opportunity to focus on an area of ability (e.g., music, art, athletics).

6. Be available when help is needed; be sure to have conferences periodically about personal as well as academic matters.

7. Arrange group sessions with peers and with family.

8. Look for ways to meet individual needs (e.g., a place to study, tutorial help).

9. Involve parents in school activities.

10. Offer college and vocational guidance early.

If more than 15% of the gifted learners in a school are seriously underachieving, then the program must be carefully reviewed.

Counseling Approaches to Remediation

Since the late 1950s, group counseling has been reported as a successful intervention strategy. Broedel (1958) showed that adolescent gifted students who participated in group counseling made greater gains in reducing inappropriate behavior and raising grade point averages and in standardized achievement tests than uncounseled students. Baymur and Patterson (1960) found that group counseling showed the most favorable results, compared with individual counseling or one-time-only pep talks.

Family counseling has been reported as successful at treating under-achievement (Colangelo, 1991; Rimm & Lowe, 1988; Satir, 1972). Often, changing the behavior of the student only creates more problems unless the family understands and adjusts to provide the support needed by the student. When the family has been involved in creating the problem, it is essential that the pattern be understood and changed if the remediation is to be a lasting one. As with Rich in the opening vignette, unless his father changes his attitude and the relationship becomes less competitive, the counseling Rich receives will be of limited use.

Curricular and Classroom Organizational Change

Underachieving gifted pupils enrolled in homogeneously grouped gifted classes were found to have made greater gains in academics, creativity, and perceived peer acceptance than underachieving gifted students enrolled in heterogeneously grouped classes (Whitmore, 1980). Davis and Rimm (1994) suggest that schools currently may be teaching gifted children to underachieve by abolishing homogeneous ability grouping and emphasizing cooperative learning in forms that minimize challenge and appreciation for personal success.

A successful program (Supplee, 1989) that showed significant gains in affective and cognitive areas included multiage, cross-graded grouping, and individualized instruction. Academic components were built around student interests and advanced and creative thinking skills, cooperative sports, and trust-building activities. Conflicts were resolved through consensus seeking, and parent training was viewed as an important part of the program.

Baum, Renzulli, and Hebert (1995) found that effective curricular approaches to remediating underachievement have important provisions in common; they tend to be child-centered, focus on student strengths, value student interests, stress the process of learning as well as the product, use active learning strategies, and provide choice.

Rimm's TRIFOCAL Model

A remediation model for underachievement that involves the collaboration of school and family (Davis & Rimm, 1994) has six steps that are implemented simultaneously and are patterned after the steps included in the change process of achievers who had previously been underachievers.

STEP 1 *Assessment of skills, abilities, reinforcement contingencies, and types of under-achievement.* It is suggested that the assessment should include an individual intelligence test, individual achievement tests, a creativity test, and parent and student interviews. Observations of the process of testing will be important, such as the student's attention, perseverance, problem-solving approaches, and so forth.

STEP 2 *Communication.* Discussion between parents and teachers regarding assessed abilities, achievements, and formal and informal evaluations of both affective and cognitive characteristics of the student is an important component.

STEP 3 *Changing the expectations of important others.* High intelligence test scores, anecdotal information, examples of the child's unique work, and specific descriptions of unusual strengths are evidence of giftedness. These can be used to change the expectations of parents, teachers, peers, siblings, and the students themselves.

STEP 4 *Model identification.* The discovery of an achieving model for identification may be a critical turning point for the underachieving student. It is suggested that the model possess characteristics of nurturance and openness, be of the same sex, have similarities to the student, be willing to give time, and display a sense of positive accomplishment.

STEP 5 *Correcting skill deficiencies.* Tutoring of a specified duration with specific goals is recommended. Because the student is gifted, the skill deficiencies may be overcome rapidly.

STEP 6 *Modification of reinforcements at home and school.* The reinforcements must be meaningful to the student, within the value system and range of possibility for the givers, and as small as possible yet still effective in motivating behavior. They may be based on activities completed or on the quality of the activity. Other reinforcements might include acceleration by subject or grade, participation in special projects or clubs, and encouragement of the student's strong interests.

These steps have been reported to be successful with numerous underachieving students, regardless of the cause of the underachievement. More serious involvement with underachievement that includes such factors as drugs and depression may require the help of professional psychologists.

The Prism Metaphor for Reversing Underachievement

The prism metaphor was selected to create a focus on the transformation that occurs when a complex set of enrichment experiences is made available to meet the unique needs of underachievers, thereby causing the students to deviate from the pattern of underachievement (Baum, et al., 1995). In this model, students are allowed to become producers of creative products through the collection of raw data, use of advanced level problem-solving techniques, and the application of research strategies or artistic procedures used by firsthand investigators within various fields of study. Underachievement was reversed for 80% of the study population, regardless of the cause of underachievement. Opportunities to build a positive relationship with the teacher, use self-regulation strategies, investigate personal issues of underachievement, work in an area of interest, and interact with an appropriate peer group supported this change process. The largest gains were experienced by students working with teachers who took time building the relationship with the student, accepted the student, provided time and resources needed, encouraged investigations with a real-world purpose, saw the reversal of the underachievement as a dynamic process, and consistently believed in the student.

There are many common elements in all of the intervention programs. The approaches that were more successful were student-centered, accentuated student strengths, and valued student interests. In these approaches the process of learning was active rather than passive, and students had choice in their learning (Baum, Renzulli, & Hebert, 1995). Optimizing learning in every classroom by following the suggested structures and practices described in Chapter 11 would create these conditions and reduce the underachievement now found in our schools.

GIFTED LEARNERS WITH DISABILITIES

Mike sat staring off into space, munching on a stick of high protein that was given in his class as a "reinforcer." He was seated at a desk alone, or as alone as one can be with 15 students, two teachers, and three teacher aides. The room was arranged so that each student was comparatively isolated, sometimes achieving this with the use of cardboard dividers between the desks. Rock music played in the background. This was a special class, and Mike had been sent here at the beginning of the year—7 months, 4 days, and 2 hours ago. He was selected because he was learning disabled—"passive-aggressive," the psychologist had said. He supposed he was; he sure wouldn't do the work in those dumb junior high classes, partly because the teachers were so "stupid" and partly because he'd already done all that stuff for about 3 years running. Once, he remembered, in third grade there was this neat teacher who had let them all make a movie about a story by Shakespeare and had let some of the kids use her trig book for their math lessons. That was his best year, Mike thought.

"What are you doing, Mike?" came a voice close by.

"Huh! Oh, nothin'," Mike responded.

"Well, it will be checkup time in 5 minutes and I don't see much student behavior going on."

Mike grunted at the teacher, shifted his slouch to a forward lean and picked up his pencil. The "task" before him, the completion of which would show "student behavior," was a work page out of a seventh-grade workbook on basic science. Oh, they had taken it out of the book and clipped off the identifiers so that Mike, an eighth grader, wouldn't know it was baby work, but he knew. "Boy, they must think I'm really stupid," he groused, looking over the low-level questions on the page. But he didn't bother to put in the answers; instead he reached over to a plant near his desk and deposited his protein stick wrapper in its pot.

"Take that out of there, Mike," came the voice again.

"It's OK," Mike answered, "It's really an ash tray." Actually, it was. Last month one of the "creativity projects" was to take a bunch of old ashtrays the teacher brought in and papier-mâché them into pots for these new plants. Of course

Mike realized he was stretching it a bit, but he was right.

"I said take it out, now," said the voice.

Mike did and then made an elaborate and very grand passage to the wastebasket and back to deposit the wrapper, which took fully 3 of the remaining minutes before checkup time. On the way back, Mike managed very cleverly to start a fight between two other boys, who each thought the other responsible for the jabs and bumps they received. Mike looked the soul of innocence. One quickly executed swipe of his pencil completely dislocated the mast of a model ship the boy two tables back was assembling; then he slid back into his seat.

A little bell rang, checkup time was announced, and the teachers and aides hurried through the room giving check marks on cards presented by the students to redeem later that day for protein sticks, puzzles, and other prizes. One of the aides approached Mike, who now was sitting straight, feet on the floor, the perfect model of the attentive student. "You get one check for following directions," referring, Mike supposed, to his wastebasket trip, "and one check for behaving like a student." Mike wasn't sure how she arrived at that assessment. "But Mike, I can't give you a check for work completed. You have another half hour now before lunch to finish your task." As she moved away, Mike slid back down into his seat, eyes glassy, staring off into space, and quietly began munching on another protein stick.

Oh yes, they all knew Mike tested around 165 IQ, but the gifted class wouldn't take him until he learned to behave like a student. In the regular classroom he was too disruptive and never accomplished anything, so here he was, and they were going to have him complete his work successfully if it killed them.

Gifted learners appear in every population of students with disabilities, with the obvious exceptions of the mentally retarded and severely developmentally disabled. Special classes for students who are visually impaired, communication disordered, hearing impaired, behavior disordered, emotionally disturbed, physically disabled, and learning disabled very often have among their students children who are also gifted. Although Davis and Rimm (1994) estimated that there are 120,000 to 180,000 gifted students with disabilities in public schools, Whitmore (1981) suggested that the figure may be as high as 540,000. Minner (1990) estimates that the majority of these students are learning disabled.

Only in the past decade has concern been shown for these gifted and disabled children beyond the remediation of their disabling condition. Children who are gifted and disabled need special educational programming that can remediate any deficits in learning caused by their disability. This will require that schools accommodate the learning experience to minimize the impact of the disability (the condition with which the child was born) and any handicap (the degree to which the disability is allowed to interfere with the child's growth and function) it has created. In particular, they must provide opportunities for development of the students' special abilities and challenge them to fuller use of their potential. Unfortunately, gifted programs often are unprepared to handle the gifted learner with disabilities.

The focus of special education teachers is often on the remediation needed by the child because of the presence of a disability. The amount of time spent on remediation in special education programs may effectively preclude any support or instruction toward development of higher cognitive abilities, if indeed such abilities are recognized at all.

In a report of the Retrieval and Acceleration of Promising Young Handicapped and Talented (RAPYHT) Program for young gifted and talented children with disabilities, Karnes, Shwedel, and Lewis (1983) showed the benefits of early identification and programming for young gifted and talented children with disabilities. Even with the success of the program, they believe even more gains would have been made if in-service training had been available to help elementary teachers program more appropriately for the children. They recommended that such training be conducted for all regular and all special education teachers. Further, the parents of young gifted and talented children with disabilities need to become effective advocates for their children. It should be noted that the RAPYHT Program provided the young gifted and talented children that it served with skills, attitudes, and habits that were reflected in above-average school progress during their elementary school attendance.

Overcoming Teacher Attitudes

In-service training is needed even at the awareness level, as found in a study on teacher attitude toward gifted children with disabilities (Minner, Prater, Bloodworth, & Walker, 1987). Teachers at 68 public schools were randomly assigned to one of three groups and given vignettes briefly describing a gifted child. The descriptions were exactly the same except that one-third were labeled "learning disabled", one-third were labeled "physically handicapped," and one-third were nonlabeled. The teachers were asked, based on the information they were given, to make a decision regarding the referral of each child for a gifted class. There were essentially no differences in the referrals made from the nonlabeled or the physically handicapped groups; however, the learning disability label had a negative effect on the teachers' recommendations.

Because learning disability is the largest of the special education populations and has within it many gifted children, efforts must be made to inform teachers of the nature of the learning-disabled (LD) gifted child. It has been suggested that all teachers develop: knowledge of student abilities and disabilities and how these individual differences affect learning; methods of disability-related compensation; strategies for curricular modifications; and awareness of the counseling needs of gifted students with disabilities and these students' social skills and relationships with both normal and disabled peers.

Characteristics of Gifted Children with Disabilities

Silverman (1989) discovered that, when comparing lists of characteristics of underachieving gifted children and LD gifted children, the key characteristics are identical, including: evidence of lack of social skills, social isolation, unrealistic self-expectations, perfectionistic tendencies, distractibility, frustration in response to school demands, low self-esteem, and failure to complete assignments. Both populations are usually identified by the discrepancy between aptitude and achievement. Silverman asked, "When we look at a student who won't do the work, how do we know we aren't actually seeing a child who can't do the work?" (p. 37).

It seems increasingly possible that LD gifted students either may be identified only for the LD class, with the giftedness masked by the learning disability, or may be using giftedness to compensate for the learning disability so successfully that both go undetected and the student continues functioning at or near grade level. Suter and Wolf (1987) suggested that teachers look for performance characterized by considerable variability across tasks, low motivation and low task completion, impaired long-term and short-term memory, visual or auditory processing difficulty, poor self-concept, high levels of self-criticism, withdrawal or aggression, short attention span, difficulty following directions, and poor peer relations.

Baum and Owen (1988) suggested that LD gifted students show some of the characteristics of LD students but in other areas show learning characteristics that are typical for gifted students. They may be aggressive, disruptive, careless, frequently off task, and deficient in tasks emphasizing memory and perceptual abilities, as would be found with LD nongifted students. They may also excel in abstract thinking and problem-solving, express creativity, and show extraordinary abilities, even becoming highly motivated when engaged in challenging tasks. Confusion about this contradiction of ability and deficit may lead to feelings of helplessness and frustration.

The children within this group, whom Crawford and Snart (1994) call gifted/learning disabled (GLD), give evidence of high verbal expressive ability and good conceptual understanding concurrently with significant academic underachievement, frustration, and lack of motivation. The metacognitive performance of this population resembles that of gifted students more than that of LD students (Hannah & Shore, 1995). From case studies, Vespi and Yewchuk (1992) found that the powerful fear of failure, inconsistent social skills, and fluctuating self-image are other examples of the unique characteristics of this population. They conclude that LD gifted students resemble the LD nongifted students in negative academic characteristics and gifted students in positive emotional characteristics. They are primarily internally motivated, share the gifted children's trait of independence, and accurately interpret and communicate with nonverbal communication. Like the LD nongifted child, they show frustration and anxiety about academic tasks, avoid or hurry through such tasks, and have difficulty concentrating. However, they are not as rejected by their peers nor have they learned helplessness.

The term *paradoxical learners* (Tannenbaum & Baldwin, 1983) hints at another of the distinguishing characteristics of this population. Self-efficacy, according to Bandura (1986), is a person's perception of the ability of self to organize and complete an action. It is self-efficacy or belief in self that determines academic performance and career choice. It is this very quality that is found to be significantly lower in the LD gifted child. These children may fail easier items on a test and then pass far more difficult ones. As Silverman (1989) stated, "The harder the task, the better they do; it's the easy work they can't master" (p. 39).

Twice-exceptional is another term used to identify students who are gifted and mild to moderately disabled (LD, communication disordered, and/or behavior disordered). A project, jointly sponsored by the University of New Mexico, the Department of Special Education, and the Albuquerque Public Schools, was established to identify, serve, and evaluate the progress of twice-exceptional students (Nielsen, Higgins, Hammond, & Williams, 1993). The development of a detailed screening and identification model has led to a high rate of referral and identification—over 80% of the children identified as exceptional were found to be gifted and learning disabled or communication disordered. The students attend general education, special education, and gifted education classes in a blended program design. Teachers are better prepared to meet the diverse needs of these children because of their ongoing training as part of the project.

However, according to Minner (1990), many classroom teachers, including teachers of gifted students, have stereotypical views of LD and gifted students. Because of this bias, they may not even consider children with learning disabilities to be eligible for placement in a program for gifted learners.

LD and emotionally disturbed students have diverse problems that reflect the wide array of characteristics under these designations. Problems of attention, perception, and ability to evaluate adequately are the most commonly found.

Another group of LD children that have characteristics in common with gifted students is the population referred to as Attention Deficit/Hyperactivity Disorder (ADHD) students. Both have high levels of energy; however, the energy of the gifted child is focused, directed and intense, whereas the energy of the hyperactive child is diffuse, random, and erratic. Although both challenge authority, the challenge from gifted children may be from the curiosity and questioning that is part of their nature, and the challenge from hyperactive children has been observed to be more hostile and aggressive in manner (Mendaglio, 1995). Similarly, both groups can disrupt the school environment. Again the cause is different; for gifted children the cause is often boredom with an unchallenging curriculum, whereas for ADHD children it could result from any or all of the ADHD core symptoms (inattention, impulsivity, and hyperactivity). When these symptoms are combined with understimulation, oppositional behaviors commonly result among children in this population. When these characteristics of giftedness and ADHD combine in one child, there is a heightened sense of alienation, sensitivity, and overraction (Mendaglio, 1995).

Students who are blind and visually impaired seem to be capable of the same ability levels as the sighted, but they attain their maximum levels later. These students often show deficits in meaningful verbal memory (Maker, 1977).

Identification of Gifted Children With Disabilities

Identification of the gifted learner with disabilities follows many of the same procedures of screening and multiple data collection that produce the best results in the gifted population (Chapter 9). However, some special considerations created by the disability must be made to alleviate the masking of the ability. These children are often able to use their superior abilities, especially in the areas of predictive ability, vocabulary, conceptual ability, and verbal expression, to compensate for areas of weakness (Crawford & Snart, 1993).

Obstacles to identification of LD gifted students, such as stereotypical expectations held about gifted children, developmental delays that may occur with these children, lack of information available about the child, and the fact that existing programming for students with learning disabilities limits the opportunities for the students to demonstrate superior mental abilities, have been reported by Reis, Neu, and McGuire (1995). Characteristics of the children, such as learned helplessness, lack of motivation, disruptive classroom behavior, lack of organizational skills, and hyperactivity, also create difficulties for the identification of these children as gifted learners and mask all of the characteristics of gifted learners that they also show.

The limited life experiences and environmental interactions owing to the restricted mobility of physically disabled children may make it difficult to find their abilities. The usual tests often register depressed scores, and performance tests or nonverbal testing may be just as limiting. For children with physical disabilities, unless the condition is also related to mental retardation, the rate and type of cognitive processing is comparable to the range of a normal population.

Speech- and language-impaired children cannot adequately respond to tests that require verbal responses, and for hearing and visually impaired children, modifications in the identification process is in even more necessary. Although there are standardized tests that may be used to assess the cognitive abilities of students with physical disabilities, these tests and the way in which they are used often result in information to build a profile of areas of needed improvement rather than of high abilities. Informal assessments, a positive classroom atmosphere, classes structured for individualization, advanced work, and an emphasis on achievement are recommended as necessary components to make identification and development of high ability, physically disabled children more possible (St. Jean, 1996).

Guidelines suggested by Silverman (1989) for identifying gifted children with disabilities include:

1. Distribute lists of characteristics of gifted children with disabilities to teachers and parents.

2. Look for discrepancies in performance including passing hard items and failing easier ones.

3. Assess oral presentations of material and compare with assessments of material read; compare math analysis skills with math computation skills; use timed and untimed assessments.

4. When evaluating for disability, look for unusual abilities.

5. Observe the adaptations children make; note special strengths and difficulties.

Programming for Gifted Children With Disabilities

Strategies and programs developed for children with disabilities have tended to assume cognitive limits and often fail to provide opportunities for self-directed learning, creative self-expression, and exploration of the sciences and the arts—all of which are areas critical to programming for gifted learners (Whitmore, 1981). More collaboration between teachers of children with disabilities and teachers of gifted children will be needed to make the goals of both programs available to gifted learners with disabilities.

In recent years, growing attention has been given to the LD gifted student. To meet the special needs of this population, an increasing number of books and journal articles provide resources previously unavailable to teachers. It is interesting to note that many of the articles and studies discuss the inability of the remediation model used in special education to meet the needs of these gifted students.

Approaches to remediation and enrichment are traditionally in opposition in form and content; most remediation is provided through noncontextual learning, which is focused on isolated basic skills; and the interests and strengths of students are often misused in remedial settings. But does this model of remediation as it is now used in special education provide the best approach for even LD students, not to mention LD gifted students? Perhaps a program using many of the elements of the Responsive Learning Environment as described in Chapter 11 could incorporate both needs, with integrative learning empowering the learner to grow in both need areas.

Rather than placing these children in traditionally organized regular classrooms, gifted programs, or remedial resource rooms, Suter and Wolf (1987) suggested forming a class for students with dual exceptionalities. This would allow the kind of ongoing support such children need and would provide the multidimensional approach that is necessary to develop both areas of need.

> Successful programming for gifted/LD children must be based on individual needs of each child and the setting in which services are provided. Important components include instruction in compensation strategies, exposure to higher level concepts and materials, and a counseling program for students and parents. (p. 235)

In attempting to plan programs that will address the needs of the LD gifted learner, another problem may be encountered. Remediation for the LD student usually is based on structuring learning into manageable tasks to ensure success. For a gifted learner, accomplishing such simple, routine tasks may be neither viewed as a challenge nor considered a success as seen with Mike, the gifted learner in the vignette that opened this section of the chapter. The LD gifted learner needs the same kinds of challenging learning experiences as other gifted learners (Baum & Owen, 1988).

The intervention found to be most often used with ADHD is medication (usually methylphenidate [Ritalin-AE]). Although medication may be successful in controlling behavior, it has been found to inhibit creativity and intellectual curiosity in bright children (Baum, Olenchak, & Owen, 1998). "The most serious concern is that gifted behavior is sacrificed for more manageable behavior in some creative, bright students who are medicated for ADHD" (p. 98). Those working in this area recommend highly structured individualized school environments with challenging and meaningful curricula for successful intervention (Leroux & Levitt-Perlman, 2000). "If every gifted/ADHD child would have a flexible environment in which to thrive, have social and emotional needs met, and strengths used to construct knowledge in a stimulating, respected way, perhaps instead of focusing on deficits, they would be known to have selective attentional gifts" (p. 175).

Those who work with gifted students need to become aware of what can be done and is being done to promote services for the gifted learners with disabilities, so that their educational experience can work not only toward keeping the disability from becoming handicapping but also toward actualizing the high potential of these students. Vespi and Yewchuk (1992) emphasize the need for attention to fostering competency in social relationships and enhancing peer acceptance, developing coping skills for maintaining a commitment to tasks, and including social/emotional needs in any program for LD gifted children. Sah and Borland (1989) reported evidence showing that structuring home activities and the participation of the child's family improve behaviors of gifted learning-disabled children who have organizational deficits.

Maker (1977) interviewed some visually and hearing-impaired gifted people for their ideas in how to improve their programs. Their suggestions included a desire for involvement in less protective, more integrated educational environments and more opportunities to explore the environment using their other, more operable senses. Maker noted a slower rate of development and difficulty dealing with abstractions among the deaf. Her deaf interviewees praised special separate schools.

There are special problems that people who are both disabled and gifted have in developing a positive self-concept. When the low self-esteem that develops around the disabling condition is combined with the often unrealistic expectations of the gifted learner, a level of dissonance between the real and ideal self can occur, which contributes significantly to the inability of the child with a disability to relate and succeed (Maker, 1977).

Reis, McGuire, & Neu (2000) studied successful LD gifted postsecondary students and found that all of the students reported using study and performance strategies, such as note taking, time management, and weekly and monthly organizers; cognitive/learning strategies, such as mnemonics and chunking information;

and compensation supports, such as word processing and books on tape. Individualized strategies were also used, such as interviewing professors, comparing notes with friends in class, taking reduced class loads, and extending time for examinations. By carefully developing good work habits and other support systems, these students were able to succeed in rigorous university settings. These compensation strategies were learned in the university setting because few found that in neither their learning disability programs nor their gifted programs were these skills taught. Reis and colleagues recommend that instruction in compensatory strategies and self-advocacy be incorporated in the elementary school setting.

In 1985, Whitmore and Maker predicted the emergence of a new field of education for gifted students with disabilities. They saw the field engaged in the development of five major goals:

1. Increasing the accuracy of the identification and diagnostic process.
2. Increasing the amount of research-and-development activity directed toward expanding the body of knowledge and instructional technology.
3. Implementing the necessary major changes in the preparation of service personnel.
4. Increasing the sense of shared responsibility for the total development of gifted/disabled children among professionals and parents.
5. Preparing gifted/disabled students for lifelong satisfaction in careers and self-selected avocations.

Although their vision has not been totally actualized, the trend toward provisions for services for gifted children with disabilities includes:

- More generic training for special education teachers so that they will be able to identify and plan for the gifted in their disability populations.
- Implementation of mainstream placement and the concurrent in-service in special education of general education teachers, making them more aware of the needs of gifted learners.
- Strong advocacy for gifted education from organizations whose historical role has been primarily associated with children who are disabled, such as the Council for Exceptional Children.
- Sponsorship of national conferences for the study of problems of the gifted by such groups, such as a conference on the culturally diverse gifted conducted by the Foundation for Exceptional Children.
- National conferences devoted to the problems of gifted students with disabilities.
- The establishment in institutions of higher learning of programs to train leadership and teaching personnel in gifted education within the departments of special education.
- Specialized graduate programs in the area of gifted children with disabilities.
- Programs for young gifted learners with disabilities that explore early intervention, identification procedures, and programming strategies, such as the RAPYHT Program conducted at Chapel Hill, North Carolina.

The concern for gifted learners with disabilities gives educators an opportunity to appreciate the value of working in an interdependent, cooperative, collaborative style, because these children can be served in no other way. The skills of the regular classroom teacher, the special educator, the educator of the gifted, the parents, the counselor/psychologist, the administrator, and the researcher are needed if these children are to actualize their potential abilities (see Figure 14.2).

This chapter has reviewed the work of researchers and practitioners in the areas of underachievement and disability as they relate to the identification and education of gifted learners. These are areas of concern that have just begun to identify concepts, structures, and strategies that work for these children.

Figure 14.2 *Effective Practices for Finding and Serving Gifted Students with Disabilities*
Based on the results of a study by Willard-Holt (1994).

1. Actively seek gifted students among those with disabilities.
2. Learn the student's symbol system to accurately read intended meanings.
3. Check for understanding of the student's messages.
4. Allow time for communication of messages from students.
5. Make students an active part of the class.
6. Facilitate social interactions first and then allow classmates to take over.
7. Encourage cooperation in learning tasks and change partners often.
8. Modify instruction as needed, but no more than is necessary.
9. Provide many different types of learning experiences through many modalities.
10. Individualize pace and choice of learning activities.
11. Hold high expectations for students with disabilities.

QUESTIONS OFTEN ASKED

1. If gifted students are underachieving, is it better to place them with other underachieving gifted students in a special class or keep them with the regular class where they will have better role models?

Actually the students could have the advantage of both a special class for part of their work and placement in a regular class for work they are better able to do. The concept of mainstreaming asks that we consider the least restrictive environment. Each student will have a different cluster of needs, and the decision as to placement must take into account those needs, what the special class provides, and what can be provided by the regular class. The students' individual programs will dictate where and how often they are placed for the best advantage. The teacher's skills, the parents' wishes, and the school's resources all must be considered in this decision. Don't forget to assess the children's feelings and information on possible choices; these could be very valuable and allow them to participate in their own learning.

2. If a child is bored with school, doesn't want to do the work, and really doesn't even want to be there, what can the parents do?

It is very important that you ask for a team meeting with the teacher, yourselves, and the child. Try to find out what everyone thinks is happening and what might happen. Offer to help with whatever plan the teacher feels will help, and if possible offer the child several choices of ways to change the situation. At the very least, get the child's perspective and be sure the child understands the expectations and the consequences for doing or not doing what is planned. Above all, don't just let it continue, thinking it will pass. Learning patterns are formed in this way that can lead to underachievement patterns that will be hard to break later. What may only be a misunderstanding or lack of information now could be a difficult problem later.

3. How can we identify gifted students who are compensating for a disability and do not show their giftedness?

This is a very difficult issue and we probably have a large number of children in classes who are highly able in some areas but their struggles with the disability do not alert either the teacher or even the child to that ability. One suggestion that has been made is to look for large discrepancies in the tests that have been given. If either the verbal or performance score exceeds the other by a large margin, with one or the other in the superior range, this could be an indicator. A variety of types of testing may also give a suspicious pattern. Open-ended activities with observation of the problem-solving strategies being used by the child may bring out abilities that testing does not. Knowing the child and being aware of the characteristic traits of gifted learners will be important to discovering giftedness within the disabling or underachieving patterns.

CHECKING FOR UNDERSTANDING
Follow-Up Activity

These activities can be done individually or in groups.

1. Give three reasons that a gifted student would consciously choose to underachieve. For each situation, how could you as a teacher or parent change this pattern?

2. Identify three types of disability and discuss how they could affect learning. How could you modify the curriculum or learning setting to support a child with each of these disabilities?

SUMMARY

Underachieving Gifted Students

1. The underachieving gifted student is defined as someone who has shown exceptional performance on a standardized test of intellectual ability or achievement and who, nevertheless, does not perform as well as expected on school-related tasks as evidenced by grades or teacher report. To indicate underachievement, the measures should show a considerable amount of discrepancy and be evident over time.

2. At least two types of underachievers have been designated, situational underachievers (those who underachieve only on occasion) and chronic underachievers (whose pattern recurs repeatedly).

3. The underachievement must be assessed by administering the proper diagnostic tests for physical problems to ensure that it is not of organic origin.

4. Gifted students generally do not develop behavior problems when they are: (a) placed with a teacher who enjoys teaching gifted children and learning with them; (b) afforded frequent opportunities to learn with intellectual peers; (c) actively engaged in learning that is appropriately complex, challenging, and meaningful; and (d) provided guidance in how to understand and cope with their giftedness in society.

5. The most commonly mentioned traits of underachieving gifted students are evidence of a low self-concept, lack of motivation and

interest in classroom activities and assignments, and social immaturity. Poor study habits, lack of persistence, dependency, and impulsiveness often are part of the profile.

6. Although underachievement is difficult to reverse, it is most easily remediated in elementary school; underachievement resists reversal when left to secondary intervention.

7. Causes of underachievement can be found in the personality of the child, the home or the behavior of the parents, or in the classroom, especially in the curriculum and instruction.

8. Schools not only may be a principal cause of underachievement but one that is most likely to yield to remediation.

9. Underachievement is a learned behavior and, therefore, can be prevented or unlearned. Prevention is better than any form of remediation.

10. Teachers, although unintentionally, may contribute to underachievement by holding too low expectations; or alternately creating undue pressure for high achievement, and by having unfair grading practices for gifted students.

11. Gifted students who have had unchallenging curricular experiences throughout elementary and middle school may develop underachievement patterns when they enter high school and find specialization demands that they cannot meet because of problems they encounter from their undeveloped study skills created by years of effortless academic success.

12. Group and family counseling have been successful in treating underachievement.

13. Underachieving gifted pupils enrolled in homogeneously grouped gifted classes made greater gains in academics, creativity, and perceived peer acceptance than underachieving gifted students enrolled in heterogeneously grouped classes.

14. The approaches that were more successful in remediating underachievement in gifted learners were student-centered, accentuated student strengths, and valued student interests. In these approaches, the process of learning was active rather than passive and students had choice in their learning.

Gifted Learners With Disabilities

15. Gifted learners appear in every population of students with disabilities, with the obvious exceptions of the mentally retarded and severely developmentally disabled.

16. Children who are gifted and disabled need special educational programming that can remediate any deficits in learning caused by their disability. This will require that schools accommodate the learning experience to minimize the impact of the disability (the condition with which the child was born) and any handicap (the degree to which the disability is allowed to interfere with the child's growth and function) it has created. In particular, they must provide opportunities for development of their special abilities, and challenge them to fuller use of their potential.

17. The focus of special education teachers is often on the remediation of the gifted child with disabilities, and the amount of time spent on remediation may effectively preclude any support or instruction toward development of higher cognitive abilities, if indeed such abilities are recognized at all.

18. When we look at a student who will not do the work, we may actually be seeing a child who cannot do the work because the key characteristics of underachieving gifted children and learning-disabled (LD) gifted children are identical, including evidence of lack of social skills, social isolation, unrealistic self-expectations, distractibility, frustration in response to school demands, low self-esteem, and failure to complete assignments. Both populations are usually identified by the discrepancy between aptitude and achievement.

19. LD gifted students either may be identified only for the LD class, with the giftedness masked by the learning disability, or may be using giftedness to compensate for the learning disability so successfully that both go undetected and the student continues functioning at or near grade level.

20. The LD gifted child may fail easier items on a test and then pass far more difficult ones. The harder the task, the better they do.

21. Many classroom teachers, including teachers of gifted students, have stereotypical views of LD gifted students and as a result they may not even consider children with learning disabilities to be eligible for placement in a program for gifted learners.

22. Another group of LD children who have characteristics in common with gifted students is the population referred to as Atten-

tion Deficit/Hyperactivity Disorder (ADHD) students.

23. Because learning disability is the largest of the special education populations and has within it many gifted children, efforts must be made to inform teachers of the nature of the LD gifted child.

24. Informal assessments, a positive classroom atmosphere, classes structured for individualization, advanced work, and an emphasis on achievement are recommended as necessary components to enhance the identification and development of high-ability, physically disabled children.

25. Strategies and programs developed for children with disabilities have tended to assume cognitive limits and often fail to provide opportunities for self-directed learning, creative self-expression, and exploration of the sciences and the arts—all of which are areas critical to programming for gifted learners.

26. Approaches to remediation and enrichment are traditionally in opposition in form and content. More collaboration between teachers of children with disabilities and teachers of gifted children will be needed to make the goals of both programs available to gifted learners with disabilities.

27. When the low self-esteem that develops around the disabling condition is combined with the often unrealistic expectations of the gifted learner, a level of dissonance between real and ideal self can occur that adds greatly to the inability of the child with a disability to relate and succeed.

28. Those who work with gifted students need to become aware of what can be and is being done to promote services for gifted learners with disabilities, so that their educational experience can work not only toward keeping the disability from becoming handicapping but also toward actualizing the high potential of these students.

29. The skills of the regular classroom teacher, the special educator, the educator of the gifted, the parents, the counselor/psychologist, the administrator, and the researcher are needed if children who are gifted and disabled are to actualize their potential abilities.

EPILOGUE

Education of Gifted Learners: A Predictor of Future Possibilities for Society

The opportunity that I was given to work with the educational leaders of Kyrgyzstan, a country returned to sovereignty at the demise of the former Union of Soviet Socialist Republic, remains in my mind as a strong warning. I share it with you to fulfill a promise to these educators that what had happened in their country would not happen in ours.

It was the end of a week-long workshop on educational reform; the last 3 days specifically focused on educating gifted learners. This was one of the first such meetings that had ever been held in Kyrgyzstan. Now that its inhabitants were independent again, with the freedom to form their own concept of government, they felt that there was much to learn. The conference was being sponsored by a large international foundation whose mission was to improve the welfare of the global society and who saw one of the important steps to such improvement the revitalizing of the educational system.

The large group of educational leaders attending from throughout the country had become good friends. They represented many ethnic groups and several languages, and yet they had the same goal; to reform their educational system and thereby strengthen their country's economic and political future. They had been a part of a communist country for the past 70 years, and before that they were a nomadic people, so they had no precedent and no previous pattern to use as a guide for their development. They were very sure they did not want to use any of the structures or philosophies of the past 70 years, so now they were about the business of inventing their system of education, economics, and political life. It was an exciting, but daunting task. I had been invited to share the seven steps to optimizing learning, and I found this a most attentive and eager audience.

As the final session was drawing to a close, one of the participants who served as an administrator of a school district far from the capital city stood to gain the attention of the group. Although I could not understand the language he spoke, my interpreter stood next to me translating instantaneously to English, as he had throughout the conference, so it was as if I heard in my language the very moment he spoke in his. As he began, the speaker told me of his appreciation for my ideas and practices, then he turned to the group and passionately exhorted them to take every idea for nurturing their brightest children into their schools and use them. He expressed his concern for the immediacy of change: change of programs, change of practices, change of attitudes, and change of beliefs.

"For 70 years we have treated all of our children the same. We have convinced them and ourselves that they are all the same, that they have the same abilities, the same intelligence, the same talents. They believed us and their parents believed us.

And soon they were the same; none were brighter than the others, none were different from the others. We had no leaders, we had no creators, we had no gifted children. We taught them together, all the same."

At this point I noticed that tears were flooding his eyes, dampening his cheeks, and his voice began to break as he continued more loudly and insistently than before.

"If we are to survive as a country we must again find our leaders in our children. We must find the gifted among them and value these children. We must nurture their talents and celebrate their differences. All children must be loved, but they are not alike and they will not have the same destiny. They need us to help them and we need them to help us. For too long we have been without the joy of gifted children. We must help our children find their highest abilities and treasure their differences. We must do this now!"

He sat down again and the room was silent as his passionate appeal reached deep into all of us. I found my eyes wet with tears, for his words heightened my concerns and validated my fears. In my country, there were those who were opposed to the concept of giftedness, who would relegate it to unimportance, who see it as politically wrong, or who deny it altogether. Current popular theories were trying to suggest that all children were the same, must be treated the same, and have opportunities to learn that should always be the same. From this man's words I could see the result of this thinking; the potential of this interpretation of egalitarianism.

As I spoke again to the group, I acknowledged my thoughts and thanked them for the insights they had given me and the lessons I had learned in their country. I promised that I would take their message home with me and share it with my country's educators so that we might learn from them and not allow ourselves to abandon our gifted children. It is with this incident from my life that I wish to end this book with the hope that within these pages you will find the ideas and practices you need to find the highest abilities of our children and nurture them. And because of you, as my far-away colleague has said, we will never be without the joy of gifted children.

REFERENCES

Abeel, L., Callahan C., & Hunsaker, S. (1994). *The use of published instruments in the identification of gifted students.* Washington, DC: National Association for Gifted Children.

Adkins, D., & Harty, H. (1984). Longitudinal view of teacher-leaders' reactions toward gifted education. *Roeper Review, 7*(1), 36–40.

Alamprese, J., & Erlanger, W. (1989). *No gift wasted: Effective strategies for educating highly able, disadvantaged students in mathematics and science (Vol. I: Findings).* Final report prepared for the U.S. Department of Education, Office of Planning, Budget and Evaluation under Contract No. 300-87-0152. Washington, DC: Cosmos.

Albert, R. S. (1998). Letters from the field. *Roeper Review 21*(1), 78–80.

Albert, R. S., & Runco, M. A. (1986). The achievement of eminence: A model on a longitudinal study of exceptionally gifted boys and their families. In R. J. Sternberg & J. E. Davidson (Eds.), *Conceptions of giftedness* (pp. 332–357). New York: Cambridge University Press.

Alexander, P., & Skinner, M. (1980). The effects of early entrance on subsequent social and academic development: A follow-up study. *Journal for the Education of the Gifted, 3*(3), 147–150.

Alexander, R. (1981). An historical perspective on the gifted and talented in art. *Studies in Art Education, 22*(2), 38–48.

Allport, G. (1955). *Becoming.* New Haven, CT: Yale University Press.

Alvino, J., McDonnel, R., & Richert, S. (1981). National survey of identification practices in gifted and talented education. *Exceptional Children, 48*(2), 124–132.

Amabile, T. M. (1983). *The social psychology of creativity.* New York: Springer-Verlag.

Amabile, T. M. (1986). The personality of creativity. *Creative Living, 15*(3), 12–16.

Amabile, T. M. (1989). *Growing up creative.* New York: Crown.

Amabile, T. M. (1990). Within you, without you: Towards a social psychology of creativity, and beyond. In M. A. Runco & R. S. Albert (Eds.), *Theories of creativity* (pp. 61–91). Newbury Park: Sage.

American Association of University Women. (1992). *How schools short-change girls.* Washington, DC: AAUW Educational Foundation.

American Association of University Women. (1995). Education and training: The path out of poverty for women. *Outlook, 89*(2), 19–24.

Anderson, K. (Ed.). (1960). *Research on the academically talented student.* Washington, DC: National Education Association.

Anderson, V. V., & Kennedy, W. M. (1932). *Psychiatry in education.* New York: Harper.

Andrews, G., & Debus, R. (1978). Persistence and the causal perception of failure: Modifying cognitive attributions. *Journal of Educational Psychology, 70,* 154–166.

Aragon, J., & Marquez, L. (1975). Spanish-speaking component. In J. Miley, et al. (Eds.), *Promising practices: Teaching the disadvantaged gifted.* Ventura, CA: Ventura County Superintendent of Schools.

Archambault, F. X. Jr., Westberg, K. L., Brown, S. W., Hallmark, B. W., Emmons, C. L., & Zhang, W. (1993). *Regular classroom practices with gifted students: Results of a national survey of classroom teachers.* Research Monograph 93101. Storrs, CT: National Research Center on the Gifted and Talented.

Arlin, M., & Whitley, T. (1978). Perceptions of self-managed learning opportunities and academic locus of control: A causal interpretation. *Journal of Educational Psychology, 70,* 988–992.

Armitage, S. (1980). Newborns can learn to call for mother's voice and prefer it. *Brain/Mind Bulletin, 5*(17), 1.

Arnold, R., Bulatao, R., Buripakdi, C., Chin, B., Fawcett, J., Iritani, T., Lee, S., & Wu, T. (1975). *The value of children: Introduction and comparative analysis (Vol. 1).* Honolulu: East-West Population Institute.

Aspy, D., & Bahler, J. (1975). The effect of teachers' inferred self concept upon student achievement. *Journal of Educational Research, 68,* 386–389.

Aspy, D., & Roebuck, F. (1972). An investigation of the relationship between student levels of cognitive functioning and the teacher's classroom behavior. *Journal of Educational Research, 65*(8), 365–368.

Assagioli, R. (1973). *The act of will.* New York: Viking.

Association for the Gifted. (1989). *Standards for programs involving the gifted and talented.* Reston, VA: Council for Exceptional Children.

Ausubel, D. P. (1967). Cognitive structure: Learning to read. *Education, 87,* 544–548.

Baer, J. (1994). Performance assessments of creativity: Do they have long-term stability? *Roeper Review, 17*(1), 7–11.

Bailin, S. (1988). *Achieving extraordinary ends: An essay on creativity.* Boston: Kluwer Academic Publishers.

Baker, J. A., Bridger, R., & Evans, K. (1998). Models of underachievement among gifted preadolescents: The role of personal, family, and school factors. *Gifted Child Quarterly, 42*(1), 5–14.

Bakken, L., Hershey, M., & Miller, P. (1990). Gifted adolescent females' attitudes toward gender equality in educational and intergender relationships. *Roeper Review, 12*(4), 261–264.

Baldwin, A. (1973, March). *Identifying the disadvantaged.* Paper presented at the First National Conference on the Disadvantaged Gifted, Ventura, CA.

Baldwin, A. (1985). Programs for the gifted and talented: Issues concerning minority populations. In F. Horowitz & M. O'Brien (Eds.), *The gifted and talented developmental perspectives.* Washington, DC: American Psychological Association.

Baldwin, A. (1989). The purpose of education for gifted black students. In J. Maker & S. Schiever (Eds.), *Critical issues in gifted education (Vol. II): Defensible programs for cultural and ethnic minorities* (pp. 237–245). Austin, TX: Pro-Ed.

Banks, J. A., & Banks, C. M. (1993). *Multicultural education* (2nd ed.). Boston: Allyn & Bacon.

Barbe, W. (1954). Differentiated guidance for the gifted. *Education, 74,* 306–311.

Barbe, W. (1955). Evaluation of special classes for gifted. *Exceptional Children, 22,* 60–62.

Barnett, M., & Kaiser, D. (1978). The relationship between intellectual-achievement responsibility attributions and performance. *Child Study Journal, 8,* 209–215.

Barrett, D. (1989). Intuition and creative thinking. *Human Intelligence Newsletter, 10*(1), 1–3.

Barrett, H. (1957). The intensive study of thirty-two gifted children. *Personnel and Guidance Journal, 36,* 192–194.

Bar-Tal, D., Kfir, D., Bar-Zohar, Y., & Chen, M. (1980). The relationship between locus of control and academic achievement, anxiety, and level of aspiration. *British Journal of Educational Psychology, 50,* 53–60.

Barton, J., & Collins, A. (1993). Portfolios in teacher education. *Journal of Teacher Education, 44*(3), 200–210.

Baum, S. M., Olenchak, F. R., & Owen, S. V. (1998). Gifted students with attention deficits: Fact and/or fiction? Or, can we see the forest for the trees? *Gifted Child Quarterly, 42*(2), 96–104.

Baum, S., & Owen, S. (1988). High ability/learning disabled students: How are they different? *Gifted Child Quarterly, 32*(3), 321–326.

Baum, S., Renzulli, J., & Hebert, T. (1995). Reversing underachievement: Creative productivity as a systematic intervention. *Gifted Child Quarterly, 39*(4), 224–235.

Baumrind, D. (1989). Rearing competent children. In W. Damon (Ed.), *Child development today and tomorrow* (pp. 349–378). San Francisco: Jossey-Bass.

Bayley, N. (1968). Behavioral correlates of mental growth: Birth to thirty-six years. *American Psychologist, 23,* 1–17.

Bayley, N., & Schaefer, E. S. (1964). Correlations of maternal and child behaviors with the development of mental abilities: Data from the Berkeley Growth Study. *Monographs of the Society for Research in Child Development, 29* (6, Whole No. 97).

Baymur, F., & Patterson, C. (1960). Three methods of assisting underachieving high school students. *Journal of Counseling Psychology, 7,* 83–90.

Begley, S. (1993, June 28). The puzzle of genius. *Newsweek,* 46–53.

Benderly, B. (1989, September). Everyday intuition. *Psychology Today,* 35–40.

Benbow, C. P. (1992). Academic achievement in mathematics and science of students between ages 13 and 23: Are there differences among students in the top one percent of mathematical ability? *Journal of Educational Psychology, 84,* 51–61.

Benedersky, M., & Lewis, M. (1994). Environmental risks, biological risks, and developmental outcome. *Developmental Psychology, 30,* 484–494.

Bentley, A. (1966). *Measures of musical abilities.* London: Harrap.

Berg, P., & Singer, M. (1992). *Dealing with genes: The language of heredity.* Mill Valley, CA: University Science Books.

Berlinger, D. (1979). Tempus educare. In P. Peterson & H. Walberg (Eds.), *Research on teaching: Concepts, findings, and implications* (pp. 120–135). Berkeley: McCutchan.

Bernal, E. (1973, March). *Mexican-American perceptions of child giftedness in three Texas communities.* Paper presented at the First National Conference on the Disadvantaged Gifted, Ventura, CA.

Bernal, E. (1978). The identification of gifted Chicano children. In A. Baldwin, G. Gear, & L. Lucito (Eds.), *Educational planning for the gifted.* Reston, VA: Council for Exceptional Children.

Bernal, E. M. (1980). *Methods of identifying gifted minority students.* (ERIC Report 72). Princeton, NJ: Educational Testing Service.

Betts, G., & Kercher, J. (1999). *Autonomous Learner Model: Optimizing ability.* Greeley, CO: ALPS.

Bidwell, C. (1973). The social psychology of teaching. In R. Travers (Ed.), *Second handbook of research on teaching.* Chicago: Rand McNally.

Binet, A. (1969). The education of intelligence. In P. Torrance & W. White (Eds.), *Issues and advances in educational psychology.* Itasca, IL: Peacock.

Binet, A., & Simon, T. (1973). *The development of intelligence in children (the Binet-Simon Scale)* (E. Kite, Trans.). New York: Arno Press. (Original work published 1916).

Birch, H., & Gussow, J. (1970). *Disadvantaged children.* New York: Harcourt, Brace & World.

Birnbaum, M. (1977). Educational problems of rural education for the gifted. In B. Johnson (Ed.), *Ideas for urban/rural gifted/talented.* Ventura, CA: Office of the Ventura County Superintendent of Schools, National/State Leadership Training Institute on the Gifted/Talented.

Bish, C., & Fliegler, L. (1959). Summary of research on the academically talented student. *Review of Educational Research, 39,* 408–450.

Blakemore, C. (1974). Developmental factors in the formation of feature extracting neurons. In F. O. Schmidt & F. G. Warden (Eds.), *The neurosciences: Third study program* (pp. 31–41). Cambridge, MA: MIT Press.

Bloom, B. (Ed.). (1956). *Taxonomy of educational objectives. Handbook I: Cognitive domain.* New York: David McKay.

Bloom, B. (1964). *Stability and change in human characteristics.* New York: Wiley.

Bloom, B. (1982). The role of gifts and markers in the development of talent. *Exceptional Children, 48*(6), 510–522.

Bloom, B., Davis, A., & Hess, R. (1965). *Compensatory education for cultural deprivation.* New York: Holt, Rinehart & Winston.

Bloom, B., & Sosniak, L. (1981). Talent development vs. schooling. *Educational Leadership, 39*(2), 86–94.

Bodmer, W., & Cavalli-Sforza, L. (1970). Intelligence and race. *Scientific American, 223*(4), 19–29.

Bodrova, E., & Leong, D. J. (1995). *Tools of the mind: The Vygotskian approach to early childhood education.* Upper Saddle River, NJ: Merrill/Prentice Hall.

Bordan, R., & Schuster, D. (1976). The effects of suggestion, synchronized breathing and orchestrated music on the acquisition and retention of Spanish words. *SALT Journal, 1*(1), 27–40.

Borkowski, J. (1985). Signs of intelligence: Strategy generalization and metacognition. In S. Yussen (Ed.), *The development of reflection in children.* New York: Academic Press.

Borland, J. (1978). Teacher identification of the gifted: A new look. *Journal for the Education of the Gifted, 2*(1), 22–32.

Borland, J. (1986). IQ tests: Throwing out the bathwater, saving the baby. *Roeper Review, 8*(3), 163–167.

Bouman, L. (1986). Gender expectations and student achievement in math. *The Calculator, 27* (1), 1, 3.

Bower, R., Broughton, J., & Moore, M. (1970). Assessment of intention in sensorimotor infants. *Nature, 228,* 679–681.

Bowman, B. (1993). Early childhood education. In L. Darling-Hammond (Ed.), *Review of research in education (Vol. 19)* (pp. 101–134). Washington, DC: American Educational Research Association.

Bradley, C. (1989). Give me the bow, I've got the arrow. In C. J. Maker & S. W. Schiever (Eds.), *Critical issues in gifted education: Defensible programs for cultural and ethnic minorities* (pp. 133–137). Austin, TX: Pro-Ed.

Braga, J. L. (1969). Analysis and evaluation of early admission to school for mentally advanced children. *Journal of Educational Research, 63,* 103–106.

Branscomb, A. (Chair). (1980, May). *Commerce Technical Advisory Board recommendations on learning environments for innovation* (Report of the CTAB to Jordan J. Baruch, Assistant Secretary for Productivity, Technology and Innovation). Washington, DC: U.S. Department of Commerce.

Brazelton, T. B., & Als, H. (1979). Four early stages in the development of mother-infant interaction. *Psychoanalytic Study of the Child, 34,* 349–369.

Bremer, J., & Bremer, A. (1972). *Open education: A beginning.* New York: Holt, Rinehart & Winston.

Bricklin, B., & Bricklin, P. (1967). *Bright child—poor grades: The psychology of underachievement.* New York: Delacorte.

Brier, C., & Tyminski, W. (1970). PSI applications: Parts I and II. *Journal of Parapsychology, 34,* 1–36.

Brierley, J. (1976). *The growing brain.* Windsor, Great Britain: NFER.

Briggs, D. (1970). *Your child's self-esteem: The key to his life.* Garden City, NY: Doubleday.

Brody, L., Assouline, S., & Stanley, J. (1990). Five years of early entrants: Predicting successful achievement in college. *Gifted Child Quarterly, 34*(4), 131–142.

Brody, L., & Benbow, C. (1987). Accelerative strategies: How effective are they for the gifted? *Gifted Child Quarterly, 3*(3), 105–110.

Broedel, J. (1958). *A study of the effect of group counseling on the academic performance and mental health of underachieving gifted adolescents.* Ann Arbor: University of Michigan Press.

Brolin, D. (1995). *Career education for handicapped individuals.* Upper Saddle River, NJ: Merrill/Prentice Hall.

Brookover, W. (1969, February). *Self and school achievement.* Paper presented at the annual meeting of the American Educational Research Association, Los Angeles.

Brown, J. L., & Pollitt, E. (1996, February). Malnutrition, poverty, and intellectual development. *Scientific American,* 38–43.

Brown, C., & Rogan, J. (1983). Reading and young gifted children. *Roeper Review, 5*(3), 6–9.

Brown, E. (1971, February). *Underachievement— A case of inefficient cognitive processing.* Address to the American Educational Research Association, New York.

Brown, G. (1971). *Human teaching for human learning: An introduction to confluent education.* New York: Viking.

Bruch, C. (1971). Modification of procedures for identification of the disadvantaged gifted. *Gifted Child Quarterly, 15*(4), 267–272.

Bruner, J. (1960). *The process of education.* Cambridge, MA: Harvard University Press.

Bruner, J. (1968). *Toward a theory of instruction.* New York: Norton.

Buell, S., & Coleman, P. (1981). Quantitative evidence for selective dendritic growth in normal human aging but not in senile dementia. *Brain Research, 214*(1), 23–41.

Buescher, T. (1987). Counseling gifted adolescents: A curriculum model for students, parents, and professionals. *Gifted Child Quarterly, 31*(2), 90–94.

Buffington, P. (1987). Perfection: Impossible dream? *Sky, 16*(8), 31–34.

Buffington, P. W. (1988, December). Competition vs. cooperation. *Sky,* 22–25.

Burns, F. (1983). Sex differences—A silent message? A comparison study of parents' assessment and junior high school students' self-assessment of learning strengths and interests. *Journal for the Education of the Gifted, 6*(3), 195–212.

Buzan, T. (1983). *Use both sides of your brain.* New York: Dutton.

Caine, R., & Caine, G. (1991). *Making connections: Teaching and the human brain.* Alexandria, VA: Association of Supervision and Curriculum Development.

Caine, R. N., & Caine, G. (1997). *Education on the edge of possibility.* Alexandria, VA: Association for Supervision and Curriculum Development.

Callahan, C. (1980). The gifted girl: An anomaly? *Roeper Review, 2*(3), 16–20.

Callahan, C. M. (1991). The assessment of creativity. In N. Colangelo & G. Davis, *Handbook of gifted education* (pp. 219–235). Boston: Allyn & Bacon.

Callahan, C. M. (1992). How schools short-change girls: Implications for parents and educators of gifted girls. *Communicator, 22*(4), 1, 35–38.

Callahan, C. M., & Caldwell, M. S. (1995). *A practitioner's guide to evaluating programs for the gifted.* Washington, DC: National Association for Gifted Children.

Callahan, C. M., & Smith, R. (1990). Keller's personalized system of instruction in a junior high gifted program. *Roeper Review, 13*(1), 39.

Callaway, W. R. (1969). A holistic conception of creativity and its relationship to intelligence. *Gifted Child Quarterly, 13,* 237–241.

Calsyn, R. (1973). *The causal relationship between self-esteem, a locus of control and achievement: A cross-lagged panel analysis.* Unpublished doctoral dissertation, Northwestern University, Evanston, IL.

Campbell, F. A., & Ramey, C. T. (1995). Cognition and school outcomes for high-risk African-American students at middle adolescence: Positive effects of early intervention. *American Educational Research Journal, 32*(4), 743–772.

Cancro, R. (Ed.). (1971). *Intelligence: Genetic and environmental influences.* New York: Grune & Stratton.

Capra, F. (1975). *The Tao of physics.* Berkeley: Shambhala.

Capra, F. (1982). *The turning point: Science, society, and the rising culture.* New York: Simon & Schuster.

Carew, J. (1976, April). *Environmental stimulation: A longitudinal observational study of how people influence the young child's intellectual development in his everyday environment.* Paper presented at the annual meeting of the American Educational Research Association, San Francisco.

Carr, M., & Borkowski, J. (1987). Metamemory in gifted children. *Gifted Child Quarterly, 31*(1), 40–44.

Carroll, H. (1940). *Genius in the making.* New York: McGraw-Hill.

Cary, E. (1987). Music as a prenatal and early childhood impetus to enhancing intelligence and cognitive skills. *Roeper Review, 9*(3), 155–158.

Cassel, R., & Haddox, G. (1959). Comparative study of leadership test scores for gifted and typical high school students. *Psychological Report, 5,* 713–717.

Cattell, R. (1949). *The culture-free intelligence test.* Champaign, IL: Institute for Personality Assessment and Testing.

Cattell, R. (1971). The structure of intelligence in relation to the nature-nurture controversy. In R. Cancro (Ed.), *Intelligence: Genetic and environmental influences.* New York: Grune & Stratton.

Chamberlain, D. (1993). Babies are not what we thought: Call for a new paradigm. *International Journal of Pre- and Peri-Natal Studies, 4,* 1–17.

Chance, P., & Fischman, J. (1987). The magic of childhood. *Psychology Today, 21*(5), 48–58.

Chansky, N. (1964). A note of the grade point average in research. *Educational and Psychological Measurement, 24,* 95–99.

Chapman, J. (2000, July 10). Stress in pregnancy may harm your baby. *London Daily Mail,* 19.

Checkley, K. (2000). Changing the way we think: A new model of leadership. *Education Update 4*(8), 3.

Chen, J. (1989). Identification of Asian-American students. In J. Maker & S. Schiever (Eds.), *Critical issues in gifted education (Vol. II): Defensible programs for cultural and ethnic minorities* (pp. 154–162). Austin, TX: Pro-Ed.

Chetelat, F. (1981). Visual arts education for the gifted elementary level art student. *Gifted Child Quarterly, 25*(4), 154–158.

Childs, R. (1981). A comparison of the adaptive behavior of normal and gifted five- and six-year-old children. *Roeper Review, 4*(2), 41–43.

Chomsky, N. (1966). *Cartesian linguistics.* New York: Harper & Row.

Chukovsky, K. (1966). *From two to five.* Berkeley: University of California Press.

Cizek, G. (1993). Alternative assessments: Yes, but why? *Educational Horizons, 72*(1), 36–40.

Clark, B. (1979). *Growing up gifted.* Upper Saddle River, NJ: Merrill/Prentice Hall.

Clark, B. (1983). *Growing up gifted* (2nd ed.). Upper Saddle River, NJ: Merrill/Prentice Hall.

Clark, B. (1986). *Optimizing learning: The Integrative Education Model in the classroom.* Upper Saddle River, NJ: Merrill/Prentice Hall.

Clark, B. (1988). *Growing up gifted* (3rd ed.). Upper Saddle River, NJ: Merrill/Prentice Hall.

Clark, B. (1992). *Growing up gifted* (4th ed.). Upper Saddle River, NJ: Merrill/Prentice Hall.

Clark, B., & Kaplan, S. (1981). *Improving differentiated curricula for the gifted talented.* Los Angeles: California Association for the Gifted.

Clark, F. (1977). Building intuition. In G. Hendricks & T. Roberts (Eds.), *The second centering book.* Englewood Cliffs, NJ: Merrill/Prentice Hall.

Clarke-Stewart, K. (1973). Interactions between mothers and their young children: Characteristics and consequences. *Monographs of Society for Research in Child Development, 38*(No. 153).

Clinkenbeard, P. (1989). The motivation to win: Negative aspects of success at competition. *Journal for the Education of the Gifted, 12*(4), 293–305.

Clinkenbeard, P. R. (1991). Unfair expectations: A pilot study of middle school students' comparisons of gifted and regular classes. *Journal for the Education of the Gifted, 15,* 56–63.

Cohen, D. (1995). What standards for national standards? *Phi Delta Kappan, 76*(10), 751–757.

Cohen, E. (1981). The arts from the inside out Developing a performing arts curriculum. *G/C/T, 20,* 38–42.

Colangelo, N. (1991). Counseling gifted students. In N. Colangelo & G. A. Davis (Eds.), *Handbook of gifted education* (pp. 273–284). Boston: Allyn & Bacon.

Colangelo, N., & Bower, P. (1987). Labeling gifted youngsters: Long-term impact on families. *Gifted Child Quarterly, 31*(2), 75–78.

Colangelo, N., & Davis, G. A. (Eds.). (1991). *Handbook of gifted education.* Boston: Allyn & Bacon.

Colangelo, N., & Kelly, K. (1983). A study of student, parent, and teacher attitudes toward gifted programs and gifted students. *Gifted Child Quarterly, 27*(3), 107–110.

Colangelo, N., & Lafrenz, N. (1981). Counseling the culturally diverse gifted. *Gifted Child Quarterly, 25*(1), 27–30.

Colangelo, N., & Zaffrann, R. (1981). Special issues in counseling the gifted. *Counseling and Human Development, 11*(5), 1–12.

Coleman, J., Campbell, E., Hobson, C., McPartland, J., Mood, A., Weinfeld, F., & York, R. (1966). *Equality of educational opportunity.* Washington, DC: U.S. Government Printing Office.

Coleman, M. R., Gallagher, J. J., & Foster, A. (1994). *Updated report on state policies related to the identification of gifted students*. Chapel Hill, NC: University of North Carolina.

Coleman, M. R., Gallagher, J. J., & Howard, J. (1993). *Middle school site visit report: Five schools in profile*. Chapel Hill, NC: University of North Carolina.

Coleman, L. J., Sanders, M. D., & Cross, T. L. (1997). Perennial debates and tacit assumptions in the education of gifted children. *Gifted Child Quarterly, 41*(3), 105–111.

Colfax, D., & Colfax, M. (1988). *Homeschooling for excellence*. New York: Warners.

Colvin, S. (1915). What infant prodigies teach educators. *Illustrated World, 24,* 47–52.

Combs, A. W. (1969). *Florida studies in the helping professions* (Social Science Monograph, No. 37). Gainesville: University of Florida Press.

Comer, J. (1980). *School power: Implication of an intervention program*. New York: Free Press.

Confessore, G., & Confessore, S. (1981). Attitudes toward physical activity among adolescents talented in the visual and performing arts. *Journal for the Education of the Gifted, 4*(3), 261–269.

Conlan, R. (Ed.). (1993). *Journey through the mind and body: Blueprint for life*. Alexandria, VA: Time-Life Books.

Connelly, M. (1977). Gifted girls and gifted women. *Roeper City and County School Quarterly, 12,* 12–13.

Connors, N., & Irvin, J. (1989). Is "middle-schoolness" an indicator of excellence? *Middle School Journal, 20*(5), 12–14.

Conroy, M. (1989, April). Where have all the smart girls gone? *Psychology Today,* 20.

Contenta, S. (1988, February). Working class kids short-changed: High schools need complete overhaul Ontario study says. *The Toronto Star,* A1.

Cook, J. (1982). How long till equality? *Time 120*(2), 20–29.

Cooley, D., Chauvin, J., & Karnes, F. (1984). Gifted females: A comparison of attitudes by male and female teachers. *Roeper Review, 6*(3), 194–197.

Cooley, M., Cornell, D., & Lee, C. (1991). Peer acceptance and self-concept of black students in a summer gifted program. *The Journal for the Education of the Gifted, 14*(2), 166–177.

Cornell, D. (1983). Gifted children: The impact of positive labeling on the family system. *American Journal of Orthopsychiatry, 53,* 322–335.

Cornell, D., & Grossberg, I. (1987). Family environment and personality adjustment in gifted program children. *Gifted Child Quarterly, 31* (2), 59–64.

Cornell, D. G., Pelton, G. M., Bassin, L. E., Landrum, M. Ramsay, S. G., Cooley, M. R., Lynch, K. A., & Hamrick, E. (1990). Self-concept and peer status among gifted program youth. *Journal of Educational Psychology, 82,* 456–463.

Cornish, E. (1977). *The study of the future*. Washington, DC: World Future Society.

Council of State Directors of Programs for the Gifted. (1999). *The 1998–1999 State of the States Gifted and Talented Education Report*. Denver, CO: Council of State Directors of Programs for the Gifted.

Counseling and Personnel Services Clearinghouse. (1982, Winter). Counseling gifted students. *Highlights*. Ann Arbor: University of Michigan.

Covington, M., & Beary, R. (1976). *Self-worth and school learning*. New York: Holt, Rinehart & Winston.

Cox, C. (1926). The early mental traits of three hundred geniuses. In L. Terman (Ed.). *Genetic studies of genius* (Vol. 2). Stanford: Stanford University Press.

Cox, J., & Daniel, N. (1983, September/October). The role of the mentor. *G/C/T,* 1–8.

Cox, J., Daniel, N., & Boston, B. (1985). *Educating able learners: Programs and promising practices*. Austin, TX: University of Texas Press.

Craig, G. (1980). *Human development* (2nd ed.). Englewood Cliffs, NJ: Merrill/Prentice Hall.

Crandall, V., Katkovsky, W., & Preston, A. (1962). Motivational and ability determinants of young children's intellectual achievement behaviors. *Child Development, 33,* 643–661.

Crawford, S., & Snart, F. (1994). Process-based remediation of decoding in gifted LD students: Three case studies. *Roeper Review, 16*(4), 247–252.

Crick, F. (1994). *The astonishing hypothesis: The scientific search for the soul*. New York: Scribners.

Cropley, A. J. (1999). Creativity and cognition: Producing effective novelty. *Roeper Review, 21*(4), 253–259.

Cross, T. L. (1997). Psychological and social aspects of educating gifted students. *Peabody Journal of Education, 72*(3&4), 180–200.

Cross, J., & Dobbs, C. (1987). Goals of a teacher training program for teachers of the gifted. *Roeper Review, 9*(3), 170–171.

Csikszentmihalyi, M. (1993). *The evolving self: A psychology for the third millennium*. New York: Harper Collins.

Csikszentmihalyi, M. (1995). *Creativity: Flow and the psychology of discovery and invention*. New York: Harper Collins.

Csikszentmihalyi, M. (1998). Letters from the field. *Roeper Review 21*(1), 80–81.

Csikszentmihalyi, M., & Larson, R. (1987). *Being adolescent: Conflict and growth in the teenage years*. New York: Basic Books.

Csikszentmihalyi, M., & Robinson, R. E. (1986). Culture, time, and the development of talent. In R. J. Sternberg & J. Davidson (Eds.), *Conceptions of giftedness* (pp. 264–284). New York: Cambridge University Press.

Cushenberry, D., & Howell, H. (1974). *Reading and the gifted child*. Springfield, IL: Thomas.

Dabrowski, K. (1972). *Psychoneurosis is not an illness*. London: Gryf.

Dabrowski, K., & Piechowski, M. M. (1977). *Theory of levels of emotional development*. Oceanside, NY: Dabor.

Dahlberg, W. (1992). Brilliance—The childhood dilemma of ususual intellect. *Roeper Review, 15*(1), 7–10.

Dalzell, H. J. (1998). Giftedness: Infancy to adolescence: A developmental perspective. *Roeper Review, 20*(4), 259–264.

Daniels, R. (1988). American Indians: Gifted, talented, creative, or forgotten? *Roeper Review, 10*(4), 241–244.

Dansky, J., & Silverman, I. (1980). Make-believe: A mediator of the relationship between play and associative fluency. *Child Development, 51*, 576–579.

Darwin, C. (1859). *On the origin of species*. London: Murray.

Davidson, K. L. (1992). A comparison of Native American and white students' cognitive strengths as measured by the Kaufman Assessment Battery for children. *Roeper Review, 14*(3) 111–115.

Davis, A., & Eells, K. (1953). *Davis-Eells games*. New York: Harcourt, Brace & World.

Davis, G. A. (1995). Identifying the creatively gifted. In J. L. Genshaft, M. Bireley, & C. L. Hollinger (Eds.), *Serving gifted and talented students: A resource for school personnel* (pp. 67–82). Austin, TX: Pro-Ed.

Davis, G. A., & Rimm, S. B. (1994). *Education of the gifted and talented* (3rd ed.). Needham Heights, MA: Allyn & Bacon.

Dean, D., Mihalasky, J., Ostrander, S., & Schroeder, L. (1974). *Executive ESP*. Englewood Cliffs. NJ: Merrill/Prentice Hall.

deCharms, R. (1976). *Enhancing motivation: Change in the classroom*. New York: Halsted.

Deci, E. (1975). *Intrinsic motivation*. New York: Plenum.

Deci, E. (1985). The well-tempered classroom. *Psychology Today, 19*(3), 52–53.

Delcourt, M., Loyd, B., Cornell, D., & Goldberg, M. (1994). *Evaluation of the effects of programming arrangements on student learning outcomes*. Charlottesville, VA: The National Research Center on the Gifted and Talented.

De Leon, J. (1983). Cognitive style difference and the underrepresentation of Mexican Americans in programs for the gifted. *Journal for the Education of the Gifted, 6*(3), 167–177.

Delisle, J. (1984). The BIASED model of career education and guidance for gifted adolescents. *Journal for the Education of the Gifted, 8*(1), 95–106.

Delisle, J. (1998). Gifted children: The heart of the matter. *MCGT News, 20*(1), 1, 4–6.

Delisle, J. (1999). For gifted students, full inclusion is a partial solution. *Educational Leadership, 57*(3), 80–83.

Delisle, J., & Squires, S. (1989). Career development for gifted and talented youth: Position statement of Division on Career Development (DCD) and The Association for the Gifted (TAG). *Journal for the Education of the Gifted, 13*(1), 97–104.

Delisle, J., Whitmore, J., & Ambrose, R. (1987). Preventing discipline problems with gifted students. *Teaching Exceptional Children, 19*(4), 32–38.

Delp, J., & Martinson, R. (1974). *The gifted and talented: A handbook for parents*. Reston, VA: Council for Exceptional Children.

Dennis, W. (1960). Causes of retardation among institutional children: Iran. *Journal of Genetic Psychology, 96*, 47–59.

Dennis, W., & Dennis, M. (1955). The effect of restricted practice upon the reaching, sitting and standing of two infants. *Journal of Genetic Psychology, 47*, 21–29.

Dennis, W., & Najarian, P. (1957). Infant development under environmental handicap. *Psychology Monograph, 71*(7, Whole No. 436), 1–13.

Dettmer, P. (1985). Attitudes of school role groups toward learning needs of gifted students. *Roeper Review, 7*(4), 253–257.

Deutsch, C., & Deutsch, M. (1968). Brief reflections on the theory of early childhood enrichment programs. In R. Hess & R. Bear (Eds.), *Early education*. New York: Aldine.

Diamond, M. (1986, February). *Brain research and its implications for education*. Speech presented at the 25th Annual Conference of the California Association for the Gifted, Los Angeles.

Diamond, M. (1988). *Enriching heredity.* New York: Free Press.

Diamond, M., & Hopson, J. (1998). *Magic trees of the mind.* New York: Dutton.

Dickens, M., & Cornell, D. (1993). Parent influences on the mathematics self-concept of high ability adolescent girls. *Journal for the Education of the Gifted, 17*(1), 53–73.

Diessner, R. (1983, May/June). The relationship between cognitive abilities and moral development. *G/C/T.* 15–17.

DiMona, L., & Herndon, C. (Eds.). (1994). *Women's sourcebook.* Boston: Houghton Mifflin.

Dirks, J., & Quarfoth, J. (1981). Selecting children for gifted classes: Choosing for breadth vs. choosing for depth. *Psychology in the Schools, 18*(4), 437–449.

Dobzhansky, T. (1964). *Heredity and the nature of man.* New York: New American Library.

Doherty, E., & Evans, L. (1981). Independent study process: They can think, can't they? *Journal for the Education of the Gifted, 4*(2), 106–111.

Dolle, J., & Bardot, A. (1979). Learning judo and cognitive development: Understanding the laws of physics through judo. *Psychologie Française, 24*(2), 97–109.

Domino, G. (1969). Maternal personality correlates of son's creativity. *Journal of Consulting and Clinical Psychology 33,* 180–109.

Douglass, J. (1969, April). *Strategies for maximizing the development of talent among the urban disadvantaged.* Paper presented at the annual meeting of the Council for Exceptional Children, Denver.

Dowling, C. (1981). *The Cinderella complex.* New York: Summit Books. Simon & Schuster.

Doyle, W. (1978). Classroom tasks and student abilities. In P. P. Peterson & H. Walbert (Eds.), *Conceptions of teaching.* Berkeley: McCutchan.

Dreger, R., & Miller, K. (1960). Comparative psychological studies of Negroes and whites in the United States. *Psychological Bulletin, 57,* 361–402.

Drews, E. M. (1964, 1965, 1966). *The creative intellectual style in gifted adolescents* (Vols. 1, 2, & 3). E. Lansing, MI: Michigan State University.

Drews, E. M. (1972). *Learning together: How to foster creativity, self-fulfillment and social awareness in today's students and teachers.* Englewood Cliffs, NJ: Merrill/Prentice Hall.

Drews, E. M. (1976). Leading out and letting be. *Today's Education, 65,* 26–28.

Drews, E. M., & Lepson, L. (1971). *Values and humanity.* New York: St. Martin's Press.

Dreyer, A., & Wells, M. (1966). Parental values, parental control in young children. *Journal of Marriage and Family, 28,* 83–88.

Dudek, S. Z., & Cote, R. (1994). Problem finding revisited. In M. A., Runco (Ed.). *Problem finding, problem solving, and creativity,* Norwood, NJ: Ablex.

Dunham, G., & Russo, T. (1983). Career education for the disadvantaged gifted: Some thoughts for educators. *Roeper Review, 5*(3), 26–28.

Dunn, B. (1969). *The effectiveness of teaching early reading skills to two-to-four-year-old children by television.* Unpublished doctoral dissertation, University of California, Los Angeles.

Dunn, R., & Dunn, K. (1975). *Educator's self-teaching guide to individualizing instructional programs.* West Nyack, NY: Parker.

Durden, W. (1980). The Johns Hopkins program for verbally gifted youth. *Roeper Review, 3*(2) 34–37.

Durkin, D. (1966). *Children who read early.* New York: Teachers College Press.

Dweck, C., Davidson, W., Nelson, S., & Enna, B. (1978). Sex differences in learned helplessness. *Developmental Psychology, 14,* 268–276.

Edmonds, R. (1980, November 12). Inner-city schools can be effective. *Report on Education Research.*

Elmore, R., & Zenus, V. (1994). Enhancing social-emotional development of middle school gifted students. *Roeper Review, 16*(3), 182–185.

Engleberg, R. A., & Evans, E. D. (1986). Perceptions and attitudes about school grading practices among intellectually gifted, learning-disabled, and normal elementary school pupils. *The Journal of Special Education 20,* 91–101.

Epstein, H. (1978). Growth spurts during brain development: Implications for educational policy and practice. In J. Chall & A. Mirsky (Eds.), *Education and the brain: The seventy-seventh yearbook of the National Society for the Study of Education,* Part II (pp. 343–370). Chicago: University of Chicago Press.

Erikson, E. H. (1950). *Childhood and society.* New York: Norton.

Erikson, E. (1968). *Identity, youth and crisis.* New York: Norton.

Ernest, J. (1976). Mathematics and sex. *American Mathematical Monthly, 83*(8), 595–614.

Ernest, J. (1980). Is mathematics a sexist discipline? In L. Fox, L. Brody, & D. Tobin (Eds.), *Women and the mathematical mystique.* Baltimore: Johns Hopkins University Press.

Evans, E. (1965). Pupil underachievement, Are we responsible? *Instructor, 75,* 25–42.

Evans, J. (1985). *Teaching in transition: The challenge of mixed ability groupings.* England.

Ewing, N., & Yong, F. (1992). A comparative study of the learning style preferences among gifted African-American, Mexican-American, and American-born Chinese middle grade students. *Roeper Review, 14*(3), 120–123.

Ewing, T., & Gilbert, W. (1967). Controlled study of the effects of counseling on the scholastic achievements of students of superior ability. *Journal of Counseling Psychology, 14,* 235–239.

Fadiman, J. (1976). *The mind can do anything.* Presentation at the Mind Can Do Anything Conference, San Rafael, CA.

Fala, M. (1968). *Dunce cages, hickory sticks and public evaluations: The structure of academic authoritarianism.* Madison, WI: The Teaching Assistant Association, University of Wisconsin.

Falbo, T., & Cooper, C. (1980). Young children's time and intellectual ability. *Journal of Genetic Psychology, 137*(2) 299–300.

Fantz, R. (1961). The origin of form perception. *Scientific American, 204,* 66–72.

Fantz, R. (1965). Visual perception from birth as shown by pattern selectivity. *New Issues in Infant Development, New York Academy of Sciences Annals, 118*(21), 793–814.

Farrell, P. (1973). *Teacher involvement in identification.* Paper presented at the First National Conference on the Disadvantaged Gifted, Ventura, CA.

Feldenkrais, M. (1972). *Awareness through movement.* New York: Harper & Row.

Feldhusen, J., Denny, T., & Condon, C. (1965). Anxiety, divergent thinking and achievement. *Journal of Educational Psychology, 56,* 40–45.

Feldhusen, J. F., & Kennedy, D. M. (1988). Preparing gifted youth for leadership roles in a rapidly changing society. *Roeper Review, 10*(4), 226–230.

Feldhusen, J., & Kolloff, M. (1979). An approach to career education for the gifted. *Roeper Review, 2*(2), 13–16.

Feldhusen, J. F., & Moon, S. M. (1992). Grouping gifted students: Issues and concerns. *Gifted Child Quarterly, 36*(2), 63–67.

Feldhusen, J., & Robinson, A. (1986). Purdue Secondary Model for Gifted and Talented Youth. In J. Renzulli (Ed.), *Systems and models for developing programs for the gifted and talented.* Mansfield Center, CT: Creative Learning Press.

Feldman, D. H. (1979). The mysterious case of extreme giftedness. In A. H. Passow (Ed.), *The gifted and the talented: Yearbook of the National Society for the Study of Education.* Chicago: University of Chicago Press.

Feldman, D. H. (1988). Creativity: Dreams, insights, and transformations. In R. J. Sternberg (Ed.), *The nature of creativity* (pp. 271–277). Cambridge, MA: Cambridge University Press.

Feldman, D. H. (1990). Extreme giftedness: As a bit less mysterious—An editorial. *Roeper Review, 10*(2), 72–74.

Feldman, D. H., & Goldsmith, L. T. (1986). *Nature's gambit: Child prodigies and the development of human potential.* New York: Basic Books.

Fergusen, M. (1993). Frustration response traced to patterns in infancy. *Brain/Mind Bulletin, 18* (7), 1, 6.

Ferguson, M. (1984). Federally funded study shows imagery boosts learning, recall. *Brain/Mind Bulletin, 10*(2), 1, 3.

Ferguson, M. (1985). Arts enhance scientific intelligence, study says. *Brain/Mind Bulletin, 10* (12), 1–2.

Ferguson, M. (1986a). Growing old can mean getting better, experts say. *Brain/Mind Bulletin, 12*(2), 1–2.

Ferguson, M. (1986b). Weston Agor on logic of intuitive decision-making. *Brain/Mind Bulletin 12*(2), 1, 3.

Feuerstein, R. (1978). *Learning potential assessment device.* Baltimore: University Park Press.

Fine, B. (1967). *Underachievers—How they can be helped.* New York: Dutton.

Fishkin, A. S., & Johnson, A. S. (1998). Who is creative? Identifying children's creative abilities. *Roeper Review, 21*(1), 40–46.

Flavell, J. (1979). Metacognition and cognitive monitoring: A new area of cognitive-developmental inquiry. *American Psychologist, 34,* 906–911.

Flescher, I. (1963). Anxiety and achievement of intellectually gifted and creatively gifted children. *Journal of Psychology, 56,* 251–268.

Ford, D. (1994). *The recruitment and retention of African-American students in gifted education programs: Implications and recommendations.* Storrs, CT: National Research Center on the Gifted and Talented.

Ford, M. A. (1989). Students' perceptions of affective issues impacting the social emotional development and school performance of gifted/talented youngsters. *Roeper Review, 1*(3), 131–134.

Ford, D. Y., Grantham, T. C., & Harris, J. J., III. (1996). Multicultural gifted education: A wake-up call to the profession. *Roeper Review, 19*(2), 72–78.

Ford, D. Y., & Harris, J. (1995). Exploring university counselors' perceptions of distinctions between gifted black and gifted white students.

Journal of Counseling and Development, 73, 443–450.

Ford, D. Y., & Harris, J. J. III. (2000). A framework for infusing multicultural curriculum into gifted education. *Roeper Review, 23*(1), 4–10.

Foster, W. (1981). Leadership: A conceptual framework for recognizing and educating. *Gifted Child Quarterly, 25,* 17–25.

Fowler, W. (1962). Teaching a two-year-old to read: An experiment in early childhood learning. *Genetic Psychology Monograph, 66,* 181–283.

Fowler, W. (1963). The concept of the gifted child and the preschool years. *Gifted Child Quarterly, 7,* 102–105.

Fox, L. (1977). Sex differences: Implications for program planning for the academically gifted. In J. Stanley, W. George, & C. Solano (Eds.), *The gifted and the creative: A fifty-year perspective.* Baltimore: Johns Hopkins University Press.

Fox, L. (1981). Instruction for the gifted: Some promising practices. *Journal for the Education of the Gifted, 4*(3), 246–254.

Fox, L., Engle, J., & Sooler, J. (1999). The math-science mystique. *Understanding Our Gifted, 11*(2), 3–7.

Fox, L., Pasternak, S., & Peiser, N. (1976). Career-related interests of adolescent boys and girls. In D. Keating (Ed.), *Intellectual talent: Research and development.* Baltimore: Johns Hopkins University Press.

Fox, L., Tobin, D., & Brody, L. (1981). Career development of gifted and talented women. *Journal of Career Education, 7,* 289–298.

Fox, L., & Turner, L. (1981). Gifted and creative females in the middle school years. *American Middle School Education, 4*(1), 17–23.

Frasier, M. (1979). Counseling the culturally diverse gifted. In N. Colangelo & R. Zaffrann (Eds.), *New voices in counseling the gifted.* Dubuque, IA: Kendall/Hunt.

Frasier, M. (1987). The identification of gifted black students: Developing new perspectives. *Journal for the Education of the Gifted, 10*(3), 155–180.

Frasier, M. (1989). Identification of gifted black students: Developing new perspectives. In J. Maker & S. Schiever (Eds.), *Critical issues in gifted education (Vol. II): Defensible programs for cultural and ethnic minorities* (pp. 213–225). Austin, TX: Pro-Ed.

Frasier, M. (1991). Disadvantaged and culturally diverse gifted students. *Journal for the Education of the Gifted, 14*(3), 234–245.

Frasier, M., Garcia, J. H., & Passow, A. H. (1995). *A review of assessment issues in gifted educa-tion and their implications for identifying gifted minority students.* Research Monograph 95204. Storrs, CT: National Research Center on the Gifted and Talented.

Frasier, M., & McCannon, C. (1981). Using bibliotherapy with gifted children. *Gifted Child Quarterly, 25*(2), 81–85.

Frasier, M., & Passow, A. H. (1994). *Toward a new paradigm for identifying talent potential.* Research Monograph 94112. Storrs, CT: National Research Center on the Gifted and Talented.

Freeman, J. (1994). Some emotional aspects of being gifted. *Journal for the Education of the Gifted, 17*(2), 180–197.

Frey, C. P. (1989). Giftedness and underachievement. *Gifted Education Press Newsletter, 3*(1), 3–4.

Friedman, P., Friedman, R., & Van Dyke, M. (1984). Identifying the leadership gifted: Self, peer, or teacher nominations? *Roeper Review, 7*(2), 91–94.

Frierson, E. (1965). Upper and lower status gifted children: A study of differences. *Exceptional Children, 32,* 83–90.

Fromm, E. (1959). The creative attitude. In H. H. Anderson (Ed.). *Creativity and its cultivation.* New York: Harper & Row.

Fuchs-Beauchamp, K., Karnes, M., & Johnson, L. (1993). Creativity and intelligence in preschoolers. *Gifted Child Quarterly, 37*(3), 113–117.

Fund for the Advancement of Education. (1957). *They went to college early.* (Education Report No. 2). New York: Author.

Galin, D. (1976). Educating both halves of the brain. *Childhood Education, 53*(1), 17–20.

Gallagher, J. (1966). *Research summary on gifted child education.* Springfield, IL: Office of the Superintendent of Public Instruction.

Gallagher, J. (1991). Editorial: The gifted: A term with surplus meaning. *Journal for the Education of the Gifted, 14*(4), 353–365.

Gallagher, J., Aschner, M., & Jenne, W. (1967). Productive thinking of gifted children in classroom interaction. *CEC Research Monograph Series, B, B-5,* 1–103.

Gallagher, J., & Kinney, L. (Eds.). (1974). *Talent delayed—talent denied, the culturally different gifted child—A conference report.* Reston, VA: The Foundation for Exceptional Children.

Gallagher, R. M. (1983). Identification of minority gifted. *Illinois Journal for the Gifted, 1,* 3–5.

Gallwey, W. (1974). *The inner game of tennis.* New York: Random House.

Galton, F. (1869). *Hereditary genius: An inquiry into its laws and consequences.* London: Macmillan.

Galyean, B. (1976). *Language from within*. Los Angeles: Prism.

Galyean, B. (1977–1980). *The confluent teaching of foreign languages*. (ESEA Title IV-C project year-end reports). Los Angeles: Los Angeles City Unified Schools.

Galyean, B. (1978–1981). *A confluent language program for K-3. NES LES students* (ESEA Title IV-C project, year-end reports). Los Angeles: Los Angeles City Unified Schools.

Galyean, B. (1983). *Mind sight*. Long Beach, CA: Center for Integrative Learning.

Gamoran, A., & Berends, M. (1987). The effects of stratification in secondary schools: Synthesis of survey and ethnographic research. *Review of Educational Research, 57,* 415–435.

Gardner, H. (1983). *Frames of mind*. New York: Basic Books.

Gardner, H. (1993). *Creating minds*. New York: Basic Books.

Gardner, H. (1999). *Intelligence reframed*. New York: Basic Books.

Gardner, J. (1971). *The development of object identity in the first six months of infancy*. Paper presented at the Biennial Meeting of the Society of Research in Child Development, Minneapolis.

Garrison, L. (1989). Programming for the gifted American Indian student. In J. Maker & S. Schiever (Eds.), *Critical issues in gifted education (Vol. II): Defensible programs for cultural and ethnic minorities* (pp. 116–127). Austin, TX: Pro-Ed.

Garrison, V., Stronge, J., & Smith, C. (1986). Are gifted girls encouraged to achieve their occupational potential? *Roeper Review, 9*(2), 101–104.

Gazzaniga, M. (1992). *Nature's mind: The biological roots of thinking, emotions, sexuality, language, intelligence*. New York: Basic Books.

Gear, G. (1978). Effects of training on teachers' accuracy in the identification of gifted children. *Gifted Child Quarterly, 22*(1), 90–97.

Gentry, M., & Owen, S. V. (1999). An investigation of the effects of total school flexible cluster grouping in identification, achievement, and classroom practices. *Gifted Child Quarterly, 43*(4), 224–243.

George, P. (1988). Tracking and ability grouping: Which way for the middle school? *Middle School Journal, 20*(1), 21–28.

Gesell, A., Halverson, H., Thompson, H., Ilg, F., Castner, B., Ames, L., & Amatruda, C. (1940). *The first five years of life: A guide to the study of the preschool child*. New York: Harper.

Getzels, J., & Jackson, F. (1961). Family environment and cognitive style: A study of the sources of highly intelligent and highly creative adolescents. *American Sociological Review, 26,* 351–359.

Gibran, K. (1960). *The Prophet*. New York: Knopf.

Goertzel, V., & Goertzel, M. (1962). *Cradles of eminence*. Boston: Little, Brown.

Goldberg, P. (1983). *The intuitive edge*. Los Angeles: Tarcher.

Goldring, E. B. (1990). Assessing the status of information on classroom organizational frameworks for gifted students. *Journal of Educational Research, 83*(6), 313–326.

Goldsmith, L. T. (1990). Girl prodigies: Some evidence and some speculations. *Roeper Review, 10*(2), 74–82.

Goleman, D. (1995). *Emotional intelligence*. New York: Bantam.

Golemen, D., Kaufman, P., & Ray, M. (1992). *The creative spirit*. New York: Dutton.

Gollnick, D. M., & Chinn, P. C. (1994). *Multicultural education in a pluralistic society* (4th ed.). New York: Merrill.

Goodall, K. (1972). Tie line: Who's bright, two approaches. *Psychology Today, 5*(11), 24–26.

Goode, E., & Burke, S. (1990). How infants see the world. *U.S. News and World Report, 109*(8), 51–52.

Goodman, D. (1978). Learning from lobotomy. *Human Behavior, 1,* 44–49.

Gordon, D. (1977). Children's beliefs in internal-external control and self-esteem as related to academic achievement. *Journal of Personality Assessment, 41,* 383–386.

Gordon, E. (1979). Primary measures of music audiation. Chicago: GIA.

Gordon, W., & Poze, T. (1980). SES Synectics and gifted education today. *Gifted Child Quarterly, 24*(4), 147–151.

Gottfried, A. E., & Gottfried, A. W. (1996). A longitudinal study of academic intrinsic motivation in intellectually gifted children: Childhood through early adolescence. *Gifted Child Quarterly, 40*(4), 179–183.

Gould, S. J. (1981). *The mismeasure of man*. New York: Norton.

Gowan, J. C. (1965). What makes a gifted child creative? *Gifted Child Quarterly, 9,* 3–6.

Gowan, J. C. (1972). *Development of the creative individual*. San Diego: Knapp.

Gowan, J. C. (1974). *The development of the psychedelic individual*. Buffalo, NY: Creative Education Foundation.

Gowan, J. C. (1975). *Trance, art, and creativity*. Buffalo, NY: Creative Education Foundation.

Gowan, J. C. (1981). Introduction. In J. Gowan, J. Khatena, & E. P. Torrance (Eds.), *Creativity: Its educational implications* (2nd ed.). Dubuque, IA: Kendall/Hunt.

Gowan, J. C. (1980). *Operations of increasing order*. Westlake Village, CA: Author.

Gowan, J. C., & Demos, G. D. (1964). *The education and guidance of the ablest*. Springfield, IL: Thomas.

Grantham, T. C., & Ford, D. Y. (1998). A case study of the social needs of Danisha: An underachieveing gifted Aftican-American female. *Roeper Review 21*(2), 96–101.

Grau, P. N. (1985). Counseling the gifted girl. *Gifted Child Today, 38,* 8–11.

Greene, D. (1974). *Immediate and subsequent effects of differential reward systems on intrinsic motivation in public school classrooms*. Unpublished doctoral dissertation, Stanford University, Stanford, CA.

Greenspon, T. S. (2000). The self experience of the gifted person: Theory and definitions. *Roeper Review, 22*(3), 176–181.

Griggs, S., & Dunn, R. (1984). Selected case studies of the learning style preferences of gifted students. *Gifted Child Quarterly, 28*(3), 115–119.

Griggs, S., & Price, G. (1980). A comparison between the learning styles of gifted versus average suburban junior high school students. *Roeper Review, 3*(1), 7–8.

Gross, M. (1993a). *Exceptionally gifted children*. New York: Routledge.

Gross, M. U. M. (1993b). Nurturing the talents of exceptionally gifted individuals. In K. A. Heller, F. J. Monks, & A. H. Passow (Eds.), *International handbook of research and development of giftedness and talent,* (pp. 473–490). Oxford: Pergamon.

Gross, M. U. M. (1999). Small poppies: Highly gifted children in the early years. *Roeper Review, 21*(3), 207–214.

Groth, N. (1975). Success and creativity in male and female professors. *Gifted Child Quarterly, 19,* 328–335.

Gruber, H. E., & Davis, S. N. (1988). Inching our way up Mount Olympus: The evolving systems approach to creative thinking. In R. J. Sternberg (Ed.), *The nature of creativity* (pp. 247–263). Cambridge, MA: Cambridge University Press.

Grunwald, L. (1993, July). The amazing minds of infants. *Life,* 46–60.

Guilford, J. P. (1956). The structure of intellect. *Psychological Bulletin, 53,* 267–293.

Guilford, J. P. (1959). Three faces of intellect. *American Psychology, 14,* 469–479.

Guilford, J. P. (1967). *The nature of human intelligence*. New York: McGraw-Hill.

Guillen, M. (1984). The intuitive edge. *Psychology Today, 18*(8), 68–69.

Gunnar, M. R. (1990). The psychobiology of infant temperament. In J. Colombo & J. Fagen (Eds.), *Individual differences in infancy: Reliability, stability, prediction* (pp. 387–409). Hillsdale, NJ: Erlbaum.

Guterson, D. (1992). *Family matters: Why homeschooling makes sense*. New York: Harcourt Brace Jovanovich.

Guttentag, M. (1975). *Undoing sex stereotypes*. New York: McGraw-Hill.

Haggard, E. (1957). Socialization, personality and academic achievement in gifted children. *School Review, 65,* 388–414.

Hall, E. (1987, November). All in the family. *Psychology Today,* 54–60.

Halpin, G., Payne, G., & Ellett, C. (1973). Biographical correlates of the creative personality: Gifted adolescents. *Exceptional Children, 39,* 652–653.

Hannah, C. L., & Shore, B. M. (1995). Metacognition and high intellectual ability: Insights from the study of learning-disabled gifted students. *Gifted Child Quarterly, 39*(2), 95–109.

Hanson, J. R., Silver, H., & Strong, R. (1984). Research on the roles of intuition and feeling. *Roeper Review, 6*(3), 167–170.

Harrington, D. (1980). Creativity, analogical thinking, and muscular metaphors. *Journal of Mental Imagery, 4*(2), 13–23.

Harrington, R. G. (1982). Caution: Standardized testing may be hazardous to the educational programs of intellectually gifted children. *Education, 103,* 112–117.

Hart, L. (1975). *How the brain works*. New York: Basic Books.

Hart, L. (1978). The new "brain" concept of learning. *Phi Delta Kappan, 59*(6), 393–396.

Hart, L. (1981). Brain, language, and new concepts of learning. *Educational Leadership, 39,* 443–445.

Hassett, J., & Weisberg, A. (1972). *Open education: Alternative within our tradition*. Englewood Cliffs, NJ: Merrill/Prentice Hall.

Haydock, D. (1997). Homeschooling the gifted: A personal introduction. *Understanding Our Gifted, 9*(2), 16–19.

Haynes, H., White, B., & Held, R. (1965). Visual accommodation in the human infant. *Science, 148,* 528–530.

Hayward, A. (1985). *Early learners*. Los Angeles: The Education Institute.

Heath, D. (1983). The maturing person. In R. Walsh & D. Shapiro (Eds.), *Beyond health and normality: Explorations of exceptional psychological well-being* (pp. 152–205). New York: Van Nostrand Reinhold.

Hegeman, K. (1981). *A position paper on the education of gifted-handicapped children.* Paper presented to the Committee for the Gifted-Handicapped of the Association for the Gifted. Council for Exceptional Children, Reston, VA.

Heller, K. A., & Ziegler, A. (1996). Gender differences in mathematics and the sciences: Can attributional retraining improve the performance of gifted females? *Gifted Child Quarterly, 40*(4), 200–210.

Hendricks, G., & Roberts, T. (1977). *The second centering book.* Englewood Cliffs, NJ: Merrill/Prentice Hall.

Hess, K. (1987). *Enhancing writing through imagery.* New York: Trillium Press.

Higham, S., & Navarre, J. (1984). Gifted adolescent females require differential treatment. *Journal for the Education of the Gifted, 8*(1), 43–58.

Higham, S. J., & Buescher, T. M. (1987). What young gifted adolescents understand about feeling different. In T. M. Buescher (Ed.), *Understanding gifted and talented adolescents: A resource guide for counselors, educators, and parents* (pp. 26–30). Evanston, IL: Center for Talent Development, Northwestern University.

Hobson, J. (1979). High school performance of underage pupils initially admitted to kindergarten on the basis of physical and psychological examinations. In W. George, S. Cohn, & J. Stanley (Eds.), *Educating the gifted: Acceleration and enrichment.* Baltimore: Johns Hopkins University Press.

Hoffman, L. (1972). Early childhood experiences and women's achievement motives. *Journal of Social Issues, 28,* 129–155.

Hoffman, L. (1977). Changes in family roles, socialization and sex differences. *American Psychologist, 32,* 644–658.

Hoffman, M., & Hoffman, L. (Eds.). (1966). *Review of child development research* (Vol. 2). New York: Russell Sage Foundation.

Hoge, R. D., & Renzulli, J. S. (1993). Exploring the link between giftedness and self-concept. *Review of Educational Research, 63,* 449–465.

Holahan, C. K. (1984). The relationship between life goals at thirty and perceptions of goal attainment and life satisfaction at seventy for gifted men and women. *International Journal of Aging and Human Development, 20*(1), 21–31.

Hollinger, C. L. (1985). Understanding the female adolescent's self perceptions of ability. *Journal for the Education of the Gifted, 9*(1), 59–80.

Hollinger, C. L., & Fleming, E. S. (1984). Internal barriers to the realization of potential: Correlates and interrelationships among gifted and talented female adolescents. *Gifted Child Quarterly, 28*(3), 135–139.

Hollingworth, L. (1926). *Gifted children.* New York: Macmillan.

Hollingworth, L. (1942). *Children above 180 IQ.* Yonkers-on-Hudson, NY: World Books.

Hoover, S., & Feldhusen, J. (1987, Spring). Integrating identification, school services, and student needs in secondary gifted programs. *AGEM, 8*–16.

Hopson, J. (1984). A love affair with the brain: PT conversation with Marian Diamond. *Psychology Today, 18*(11), 62–73.

Horner, M. (1968). *Sex differences in achievement motivation and performance in competitive and noncompetitive situations.* Unpublished doctoral dissertation, University of Michigan, Ann Arbor.

Horner, M. (1969). Fail: Bright women. *Psychology Today, 3*(6), 36–38, 62.

Horner, M. (1972). Toward an understanding of achievement related conflicts in women. *Journal of Social Issues, 28,* 157–175.

Howard, P. (1994). *The owner's manual for the brain: Everyday applications from mind-brain research.* Austin, TX: Leornian Press.

Hoyt, K., & Hebeler, J. (Eds.). (1974). *Career education for gifted and talented students.* Salt Lake City: Olympus.

Hoyt, P. (1965). *The relationship between college grades and adult achievement* (ACT Research Report No. 7). Iowa City, IA: American College Testing Program.

Hughes, S. (1993). What is alternative/authentic assessment and how does it impact special education? *Educational Horizons, 72*(1), 29–35.

Hughes-Wiener, G. (1988). An overview of international education in the schools. *Education and Urban Society, 20*(2), 139–158.

Hunsaker, S., & Callahan, C. (1995). Creativity and giftedness: Published instrument uses and abuses. *Gifted Child Quarterly, 39*(2), 110–114.

Hunt, J. McV. (1961). *Intelligence and experience.* New York: Ronald.

Hunt, J. McV., & Kirk, G. (1971). Social aspects of intelligence: Evidence and issues. In R. Cancro (Ed.), *Intelligence: Genetic and environmental influences.* New York: Grune & Stratton.

Hunt, M. (1982). *The universe within.* New York: Simon & Schuster.

Huttunen, M., & Niskanen, P. (1978). Prenatal loss of father and psychiatric disorders. *Archives of General Psychiatry, 35,* 429–431.

Huxley, A. (1962). *Island*. New York: Harper & Row.

Hymowitz, C., & Schellhardt, T. (1986, March 24). The glass ceiling: Why women can't seem to break the invisible barrier that blocks them from top jobs. *Wall Street Journal*, 1.

Improving America's Schools Act, Title X, Part B, 1994.

Jackson, N., Famiglietti, J., & Robinson, H. (1981). Kindergarten and first grade teachers' attitudes toward early entrants, intellectually advanced students and average students. *Journal for the Education of the Gifted, 4*(2), 132–142.

Jacobs, J., & Weisz, V. (1994). Gender stereotypes: Implications for gifted education. *Roeper Review, 16,* 152–155.

Jacobson, E. (1957). *You must relax*. New York: McGraw-Hill.

Jamison, K. (1993). *Touched with fire: Manic depressive illness and the artistic temperament*. New York: Free Press.

Janos, P., & Robinson, N. (1985). Psychosocial development in intellectually gifted children. In F. Horowitz & M. O'Brien (Eds.), *The gifted and talented: Developmental perspectives* (pp. 149–195). Washington, DC: American Psychological Association.

Jeffrey, W. (1980). The developing brain and child development. In M. Wittrock (Ed.), *The brain and psychology*. New York: Academic Press.

Jellison, J., & Harvey, J. (1976). Give me liberty: Why we like hard positive choices. *Psychology Today, 9*(10), 47–49.

Jensen, A. (1969). How much can we boost IQ and scholastic achievement? *Harvard Educational Review, 39*(1), 1–24.

Jensen, E. (1998), *Teaching with the brain in mind*. Alexandria, VA: Association for Supervision and Curriculum Development.

Jerison, H. (1977). Evolution of the brain. In M. Wittrock (Ed.), *The human brain*. Englewood Cliffs, NJ: Merrill/Prentice Hall.

Jersild, A. (1952). *In search of self*. New York: Bureau of Publications, Teachers College, Columbia University.

Johnson, D., & Johnson, R. (1987). *The achieving student in heterogeneous cooperative learning groups*. Paper developed for a workshop at the University of Minnesota.

Johnson, D. W., & Johnson, R. T. (1989). What to say to parents of gifted students. *The Cooperative Link, 5*(2), 1.

Johnson, G., & Kirk, S. (1950). Are mentally handicapped children segregated in regular grades? *Exceptional Children, 17,* 65–68.

Johnson, R. T. (1988, November). Personal discussion, Our Common Future Conference, Oaxtepec, Mexico.

Johnson, R. T., & Johnson, D. W. (1988). Cooperative learning and the gifted science student. In P. Brandwein & A. H. Passow (Eds.), *Gifted young in science* (pp. 321–330). Washington, DC: National Science Teachers Association.

Jones, K., & Day, J. D. (1996). Cognitive similarities between academically and socially gifted students. *Gifted Child Quarterly, 18*(4), 270–273.

Jourard, S. (1964). *The transparent self: Self-disclosure and well-being*. Princeton, NJ: Van Nostrand.

Jung, C. (1933). *Psychological types*. New York: Harcourt.

Justman, J., & Wrightstone, J. (1956). Expressed attitudes of teachers towards special classes for intellectually gifted children. *Educational Administration and Supervision, 42,* 141–148.

Kagan, J. (1971). *Change and continuity in infancy*. New York: Wiley.

Kagan, J., & Freeman, M. (1963). Relation of childhood intelligence, maternal behaviors, and social class to behavior during adolescence. *Child Development, 34,* 899–911.

Kagan, J., & Moss, H. (1962). *Birth to maturity: A study in psychological development*. New York: Wiley.

Kandel, E., & Schwartz, J. (1991). *Principles of Neural Science* (3rd ed.). New York: Elsevier.

Kaplan, S. (1986). The Grid: A model to construct differentiated curriculum for the gifted. In J. Renzulli (Ed.), *Systems and models for developing programs for the gifted and talented* (pp. 182–193). Mansfield Center, CT: Creative Learning Press.

Kaplan, S. (1988). *The Texas student portfolio*. Developed with funding provided by the U.S. Department of Education Javits Grant #R206 A00070.

Kaplan, S. (1995). Differentiated professional development. *Communicator, 26*(3), 1, 34–35.

Kaplan, S. (2001). Layering differentiated curriculum for the gifted and talented. In F. A. Karnes, & S. M. Bean. *Methods and materials for teaching the gifted* (pp. 133–158). Waco, TX: Prufrock.

Kaplan, S., Rodriguez, E., & Siegel, V. (2000). Nontraditional screening. *Communicator, 31*(2), 20–21.

Karnes, F., & Pearce, N. (1981). Governor's honors programs: A viable alternative for the gifted and talented. *G/C/T, 18,* 8–11.

Karnes, M. B., & Johnson, L. J. (1988). Encouraging gifts and talents of Head Start children. *Educating Able Learners, 13*(1), 4–5, 14.

Karnes, M., & Shwedel, A. (1987). Differences in attitudes and practices between fathers of young gifted and fathers of young non-gifted children: A pilot study. *Gifted Child Quarterly, 31*(2), 79–82.

Karnes, M., Shwedel, A., & Lewis, G. (1983). Long-term effects of early programming for the gifted/talented handicapped. *Journal for the Education of the Gifted, 6*(4), 266–278.

Karnes, M., Shwedel, A., & Steinberg, D. (1984). Styles of parenting among parents of young gifted children. *Roeper Review, 6*(4), 232–235.

Karnes, F. A., Troxclair, D. A., & Marquardt, R. G. (1997). The Office of Civil Rights and the gifted: An update. *Roeper Review, 19*(3), 162–165.

Kathnelson, A., & Colley, L. (1982). *Personal and professional characteristics valued in teachers of the gifted.* Paper presented at California State University, Los Angeles.

Katz, I., Roberts, S., & Robinson, J. (1965). Effects of difficulty, race of administrator and instructions on Negro digit-symbol performance. *Journal of Personality and Social Psychology, 70*, 53–59.

Kauffman, D. (1976). *Teaching the future: A guide to future-oriented education.* Palm Springs, CA: ETC.

Kaufman, A. (1984). K-ABC and giftedness. *Roeper Review 7*(2), 83–88.

Kaufmann, F. (1976). *Your gifted child and you.* Reston, VA: Council for Exceptional Children.

Kavett, H., & Smith, W. (1980). Identification of gifted and talented students in the performing arts. *G/C/T, 14,* 18–20.

Kean, T. (1989). The 'imperative' of arts education. *Education Week, 8*(23).

Kearney, K. (1992). When promising practices go wrong. *Understanding Our Gifted, 5*(2), 16.

Kennell, J., & Klaus, M. (1979). Early mother-infant contact: Effects on the mother and the infant, *Bulletin of the Menninger Clinic, 43*(1), 69–78.

Kerr, B. (1985a). *Smart girls, gifted women.* Columbus, OH: Ohio Psychology Publishing.

Kerr, B. (1985b). Smart girls, gifted women: Special guidance concerns. *Roeper Review, 8*(1), 30–33.

Kerr, B. (1986). The career development of creatively gifted adults. In J. V. Miller & M. L. Musgrove (Eds.), *Issues in adult career counseling* (New Directions for Continuing Education, No. 32, pp. 59–69). San Francisco: Jossey-Bass.

Kerr, B. (1994). *Smart girls two: A new psychology of girls, women, and giftedness.* Dayton, OH: Ohio Psychology Press.

Kerr, B., Colangelo, N., & Gaeth, J. (1988). Gifted adolescents' attitudes toward their giftedness. *Gifted Child Quarterly, 32*(2), 245–247.

King, D. (1985, Summer). Foreign language, international studies, and business ally to combat our appallingly parochial curriculum. *ASCD Curriculum Update,* 1–8.

Kirschenbaum, R. J. (1998). Dynamic assessment and its use with underserved gifted and talented populations. *Gifted Child Quarterly, 42*(3), 140–147.

Kitano, M. (1989). Critique of "Identification of Gifted Asian-American students." In J. Maker & S. Schiever (Eds.), *Critical issues in gifted education (Vol. II): Defensible programs for cultural and ethnic minorities* (pp. 163–168). Austin, TX: Pro-Ed.

Kitano, M. K. (1994/1995). Lessons from gifted women of color. *The Journal of Secondary Gifted Education, 6*(2), 176–187.

Kline, B., & Short, E. (1991). Changes in emotional resilience: Gifted adolescent females. *Roeper Review, 13*(3), 118–121.

Klineberg, O. (Ed.). (1944). *Characteristics of the American Negro.* New York: Harper.

Kniep, W. M. (1986, September). Global education as school reform. *Educational Leadership,* 43–45.

Knowlton, J., & Hamerlyneck, L. (1967). Perception of deviant behavior: A study of cheating. *Journal of Educational Psychology, 58,* 379–385.

Koestler, A. (1964). *The act of creation.* New York: Macmillan.

Kohlberg, L. (1984). *The psychology of moral development.* New York: Harper & Row.

Kohn, A. (1986). How to succeed without even vying. *Psychology Today, 20*(9), 22–28.

Kohn, A. (1987, October). It's hard to get left out of a pair. *Psychology Today,* 53–57.

Koppel, D. (1991, June). What it's like to raise a genius. *Redbook, 51,* 57–58.

Kosslyn, S. (1985). Stalking the mental image. *Psychology Today, 19*(5), 23–28.

Kranz, B. (1978). *Multi-dimensional screening device for the identification of gifted/talented children.* Grand Forks, ND: Bureau of Educational Research and Services, University of North Dakota.

Krashen, S. (1975). The left hemisphere. *UCLA Educator, 17*(2), 17–23.

Krathwohl, D., Bloom, B., & Masia, B. (1964). *Taxonomy of educational objectives. Handbook II: Affective domain.* New York: McKay.

Krech, D. (1969). Psychoneurobiochemeducation. *Phi Delta Kappan, L,* 370–375.

Krech, D. (1970). Don't use the kitchen sink approach to enrichment. *Today's Education, 59,* 30–32.

Kreinberg, N., & Wahl, E. (Eds.) (1997). *Thoughts and deeds: Equity in mathematics and science education.* Washington, DC: American Association for Advancement of Science.

Krippner, S. (1967). The ten commandments that block creativity. *Gifted Child Quarterly, 11,* 144–151.

Krippner, S. (1968). Consciousness and the creative process. *Gifted Child Quarterly, 12*(3), 141–157.

Krippner, S. (1983). A system approach to creativity based on Jungian topology. *Gifted Child Quarterly, 27*(2), 86–89.

Krishnamurti, J. (1963). *Life ahead.* Wheaton, IL: Theosophical Pub. House.

Krishnamurti, J. (1964). *Think on these things.* New York: Harper & Row.

Kulik, C.-L. C. (1985). *Effects of inter-class ability grouping on achievement and self-esteem.* Paper presented at the annual convention of the American Psychological Association, Los Angeles.

Kulik, J. A. (1992). *An analysis of the research on ability grouping: Historical and contemporary perspectives.* Storrs, CT: National Research Center on the Gifted and Talented.

Kulik, J. A., & Kulik, C. C. (1991). Research on acceleration. In N. Colangelo & G. A. Davis (Eds.), *Handbook of gifted education* (pp. 190–191). Boston: Allyn & Bacon.

Kulik, J. A., & Kulik, C.-L. C. (1982). Effects of ability grouping on secondary school students: A meta-analysis of evaluation findings. *American Educational Research Journal, 19,* 415–428.

Kulik, J. A., & Kulik, C.-L. C. (1984). Effects of accelerated instruction on students. *Review of Educational Research, 54,* 409–425.

Kulik, J. A., & Kulik, C.-L. C. (1990). Ability grouping and gifted students. In N. Colangelo & G. A. Davis (Eds.), *Handbook of gifted education* (pp. 178–196). Boston: Allyn & Bacon.

Kurtzman, K. (1967). A study of school attitudes, peer acceptance, and personality of creative adolescents. *Exceptional Children, 34*(3), 157–162.

LaBenne, W., & Greene, B. (1969). *Educational implications of self-concept theory.* Pacific Palisades, CA: Goodyear.

Laffoon, K. S., Jenkins-Friedman, R., & Tollefson, N. (1989). Causal attributions of underachieving gifted, achieving gifted, and nongifted students. *Journal for the Education of the Gifted, 13*(1), 4–21.

Lahe, L. (1985). Sharing images of the future: Futuristics and gifted education. *Teaching Exceptional Children, 17*(3), 177–182.

Lamaze, F. (1970). *Painless childbirth: Psychoprophylactic method* (L. Celestin, Trans.). Chicago: Henry Regnery.

Landrum, M., & Shaklee, B. (Eds.). (1998). *Pre-K–grade 12 gifted program standards.* Washington, DC: National Association for Gifted Children.

Larsen, M. D., & Griffin, N. S. (1992). *Public opinion regarding support for special programs for gifted children.* Research submitted for publication. Gallup Organization, Education Research Division, Lincoln, NE.

Larson, R., Ham, M., & Raffaelli, M. (1989). The nurturance of motivated attention in the daily experience of children and adolescents. *Advances in Motivation and Achievement: Motivation Enhancing Environments, 6,* 45–80.

Lashaway-Bokina, N. (2000). Recognizing and nurturing intrinsic motivation: A cautionary tale. *Roeper Review, 22*(4), 225–227.

Laudenslager, J., & Valdez, A. (1986). *Identifying first generation rural Mexican-American gifted.* Paper presented at the National Association for Gifted Children Convention, Las Vegas.

Lavach, J., & Lanier, H. (1975). The motive to avoid success in 7th, 8th, 9th and 10th grade high-achieving girls. *Journal of Educational Research, 68,* 216–218.

Lavin, D. (1965). *The prediction of academic performances.* New York: Russell Sage Foundation.

Laycock, F., & Caylor, J. (1964). Physiques of gifted children and their less gifted siblings. *Child Development, 35,* 63–74.

Leaverton, L., & Herzog, S. (1979). Adjustment of the gifted child. *Journal for the Education of the Gifted, 2*(3), 149–152.

LeBoyer, F. (1975). *Birth without violence.* New York: Random House.

Lehman, E., & Erdwins, C. (1981). The social and emotional adjustment of young, intellectually gifted children. *Gifted Child Quarterly, 25*(3), 134–137.

Leiter, J., & Brown, J. (1985). Determinants of elementary school grading. *Sociology of Education, 58,* 166–180.

Lenneberg, E. (1967). *Biological foundations of language.* New York: John Wiley & Sons.

Leonard, G. (1978). *The silent pulse*. New York: Dutton.

Lerner, G., & Libby, W. (1976). *Heredity, evolution, and society*. San Francisco: Freeman.

Leroux, J. (1986). Making theory real: Developmental theory and implications for education of gifted adolescents. *Roeper Review, 9* (2), 72–76.

Leroux, J. A. (1994). As asset or a liability? Voices of gifted women. In K. A. Heller & E. A. Hany (Eds.), *Competence and responsibility* (pp. 181–189). Proceedings from the Third European Conference of the European Council for High Ability, Munich, Germany: Hogrefe & Huber.

Leroux, J. A., & Levitt-Perlman, M. (2000). The gifted child with attention deficit disorder: An identification and intervention challenge. *Roeper Review, 22*(3), 171–176.

Levine, S. (1957). Infantile experience and resistance to physiological stress. *Science, 126,* 405.

Levine, S. (1960). Stimulation in infancy. *Scientific American, 202,* 80–86.

Levy, J. (1980). Cerebral asymmetry and the psychology of man. In M. Wittrock (Ed.), *The brain and psychology*. New York: Academic Press.

Levy, J., & Reid, M. (1975). Work reported in right-hemisphere language function may exist only in split-brain subjects. *Brain/Mind Bulletin, 1*(2), 1.

Lewis, A. (1995). An overview of the standards movement. *Phi Delta Kappan, 76*(10), 744–750.

Lewis, G. (1989). Telelearning: Making maximum use of the medium. *Roeper Review, 11*(4), 195–198.

Lewis, M., & Rosenblum, L. (1974). *The effect of the infant on its caregiver*. New York: Wiley.

Liberty, P., Jones, R., & McGurie, C. (1963). Agemate perception of intelligence, creativity and achievement. *Perceptual Motor Skills, 16,* 194.

Linehan, P. (1992). Homeschooling for gifted primary students. *Understanding Our Gifted, 5*(1), 1, 8–10.

Lindsey, M. (1980). *Training teachers of the gifted and talented*. New York: Teachers College Press.

Linn, M., & Hyde, J. (1989). Gender, mathematics, and science. *Educational Researcher, 18*(8), 17–27.

Linn, R. (1994). Performance assessment: Policy promises and technical measurement standards. *Educational Researcher, 23*(9), 4–13.

Lipsitt, L., Mustaine, M., & Zeigler, B. (1976). Effects of experience on the behavior of the young infant. *Neuropadiatrie, 8,* 107–133.

Loeb, R., & Jay, G. (1987). Self-concept in gifted children: Differential impact in boys and girls. *Gifted Child Quarterly, 31*(1), 9–14.

Loomis, A. (1977). *Math is fun—Materials for task cards*. Montebello, CA: Montebello Unified School District.

Los Angeles Times. (1990, September 2). Editorials of the Times, M6.

Loury, G. (1986–1987). Dimensions of excellence in a pluralistic society. *The College Board Review, 142,* 14–17, 41–42.

Lovecky, D. V. (1992). Exploring social and emotional aspects of giftedness in children. *Roeper Review, 15*(1), 18–25.

Lovecky, D. (1994). Exceptionally gifted children: Different minds. *Roeper Review, 17*(2), 116–120.

Loveless, T. (1998). *The tracking and ability grouping debate*. A policy paper produced for the Thomas B. Fordham Foundation.

Loye, D. (1983). *The sphinx and the rainbow*. Boulder, CO: Shambhala.

Lozanov, G. (1977). A general theory of suggestion in the communications process and the activation of the total reserves of the learner's personality. *Suggestopaedia-Canada, 1,* 1–4.

Luchins, E., & Luchins, A. (1980). Female mathematicians: A contemporary appraisal. In L. Fox, L. Brody, & D. Tobin (Eds.), *Women and the mathematical mystique*. Baltimore: Johns Hopkins University Press.

Luftig, R. L., & Nichols, M. N. (1991). An assessment of the social status and perceived personality and school traits of gifted students by nongifted peers. *Roeper Review, 13*(3), 148–153.

Luria, A. R. (1973). *The working brain: An introduction to neuropsychology* (B. Haigh, Trans.). New York: Basic Books.

Lynch, S., & Mills, C. (1990). The skills reinforcement project (SRP): An academic program for high potential minority youth. *Journal for the Education of the Gifted, 13*(4), 364–379.

Maccoby, E. (1966). *The development of sex differences*. Stanford, CA: Stanford University Press.

Maccoby, E., & Jacklin, C. (1974). *The psychology of sex differences*. Stanford, CA: Stanford University Press.

MacKinnon, D. (1964). The creativity of architects. In C. W. Taylor (Ed.), *Widening horizons in creativity*. New York: Wiley.

MacKinnon, D. (1965). Personality and the realization of creative potential. *American Psychologist, 20,* 273–281.

MacLean, P. (1978). A mind of three minds: Educating the triune brain. In J. Chall & A. Mirsky

(Eds.), *Education and the brain: The seventy-seventh yearbook of the National Society for the Study of Education,* Part II. Chicago: University of Chicago Press.

Maddux, C., Samples-Lachmann, I., & Cummings, R. (1985). Preferences of gifted students for selected teacher characteristics. *Gifted Child Quarterly, 29*(4), 160–163.

Maehr, M., & Stallings, W. (1972). Freedom from external evaluation. *Child Development, 43,* 177–185.

Maggio, E. (1971). *Psychophysiology of learning and memory.* Springfield, IL: Thomas.

Maker, J. (1977). *Providing programs for the gifted handicapped.* Reston, VA: Council for Exceptional Children.

Maker, C. J. (1996). Identification of gifted minority students: A national problem, needed changes, and a promising solution. *Gifted Child Quarterly, 40*(1), 41–48.

Maker, J., & Schiever, S. (Eds.). (1989a). *Critical issues in gifted education (Vol. II): Defensible programs for cultural and ethnic minorities.* Austin, TX: Pro-Ed.

Maker, J., & Schiever, S. (1989b). Hispanics. In J. Maker & S. Schiever (Eds.), *Critical issues in gifted education (Vol. II): Defensible programs for cultural and ethnic minorities.* Austin, TX: Pro-Ed.

Mallinson, T. (1972). *Gifted underachievers.* Toronto: Ontario Board of Education, Research Department.

Manaster, G. J., Chan, J. C., Watt, C., & Wiehe, J. (1994). Gifted adolescents' attitudes toward their giftedness: A partial replication. *Gifted Child Quarterly, 38*(4), 176–178.

Mangieri, J., & Madigan, F. (1984). Reading for gifted students: What schools are doing. *Roeper Review, 7*(2), 68–70.

Mann, H. (1957). How real are friendships of gifted and typical children in a program of partial segregation? *Exceptional Children, 23,* 199–201.

Marano, H. (1981). Biology is one key to the bonding of mothers and babies. *Smithsonian, 11*(11), 60–68.

Marland, S., Jr. (1972). *Education of the gifted and talented.* Report to the Congress of the United States by the U.S. Commissioner of Education. Washington, DC: U.S. Government Printing Office.

Marsh, H. W., & Hocevar, D. (1985). The application of confirmatory factor analysis to the study of self-concept: First and higher order factor structures and their invariance across age group. *Psychological Bulletin, 97,* 562–582.

Martindale, C. (1975). What makes creative people different? *Psychology Today, 9*(2), 44–50.

Martinson, R. (1961). *Educational programs for gifted pupils.* Sacramento: California State Department of Education.

Martinson, R. (1972, March). Research on the gifted and talented: Its implications for education. In S. Marland, Jr., *Education of the gifted and talented.* Report to the Congress of the United States by the U.S. Commissioner of Education. Washington, DC: U.S. Government Printing Office.

Martinson, R. (1974, June). *The identification of the gifted and talented.* Ventura, CA: Office of the Ventura County Superintendent of Schools.

Marzano, R., Pickering, D., & McTighe, J. (1993). *Assessing student outcomes.* Alexandria, VA: Association for Supervision and Curriculum Development.

Maslow, A. (1959). Creativity in self-actualizing people. In H. H. Anderson (Ed.), *Creativity and its cultivation.* New York: Harper & Row.

Maslow, A. (1968). *Toward a psychology of being* (2nd ed.). New York: Van Nostrand Reinhold.

Maslow, A. (1971). *The farther reaches of human nature.* New York: Viking.

Masters, R., & Houston, J. (1978). *Listening to the body.* New York: Delacorte.

Matheny, K., & Edwards, C. (1974). Academic improvement through an experimental classroom management system. *Journal of School Psychology, 12,* 222–232.

Mattheis, D. (1974). Career education: What it is and what it seeks to accomplish. Paper presented at Career Education Conference, Edmund, OK, 1972. In K. Hoyt & J. Hebeler (Eds.), *Career education for gifted and talented students.* Salt Lake City: Olympus.

May, R. (1953). *Man's search for himself.* New York: Norton.

May, R. (1959). The nature of creativity. In H. H. Anderson (Ed.), *Creativity and its cultivation.* New York: Harper & Row.

May, R. (1967). *Psychology and the human dilemma.* Princeton, NJ: Van Nostrand.

Maynard, F. (1970, January). How to raise a more creative child. *Woman's Day,* 33–68.

McConnell, F., Horton, K., & Smith, B. (1969). Language development and cultural disadvantagement. *Exceptional Children, 35,* 597–606.

McGillivray, R. (1964). Differences in home background between high-achieving and low-achieving gifted children: A study of one hundred grade eight pupils in the City of Toronto

Public Schools. *Ontario Journal of Educational Research, 6,* 99–106.

McGuffog, C., Feiring, C., & Lewis, M. (1990). The diverse profile of the extremely gifted child. *Roeper Review, 10*(2), 82–88.

McKenna, A. (1978). The role of the adult in infant speech. *Enfance, 1,* 5–12.

McKim, R. (1980). *Experiences in visual thinking* (2nd ed.). Boston: PWS.

McLeod, B. (1984). Learning: Crosstalk, *Psychology Today, 18*(11), 14.

McMillin, D. (1975, May). *Separate criteria: An alternative for the identification of disadvantaged gifted.* Paper presented at the National Teacher Institute on Disadvantaged Gifted, Los Angeles.

McNeill, D. (1966). Developmental psycholinguistics. In F. Smith & G. Miller (Eds.), *The genesis of language.* Cambridge, MA: MIT Press.

Mead, M. (1954). The gifted child in the American culture today. *Journal of Teacher Education, 5*(3), 211–214.

Meador, K. (1992). Emerging rainbows: A review of the literature on creativity in preschoolers. *Journal for the Education of the Gifted, 15*(2), 163–181.

Mednick, S., & Mednick, M. (1967). *Examiner's manual: Remote Associates Test.* Boston: Houghton Mifflin.

Meeker, M. (1969). *The structure of intellect: Its use and interpretation.* Columbus, OH: Merrill.

Meer, J. (1985). The light touch. *Psychology Today, 19*(9), 60–67.

Mendaglio, S. (1995). Children who are gifted/ADHD. *Gifted Child Today, 18,* 37–40.

Mercer, J., & Lewis, J. (1977). *Parent interview manual: System of multicultural pluralistic assessment.* New York: Psychological Corporation.

Mercer, J., & Lewis, J. (1978). Using the System of Multicultural Pluralistic Assessment (SOMPA) to identify the gifted minority child. In A. Baldwin, G. Gear, & L. Lucito (Eds.), *Educational planning for the gifted.* Reston, VA: Council for Exceptional Children.

Mercer, J., & Smith, J. (1972). *Subtest estimates of the WISC full scale IQs for children.* Rockville, MD: National Center for Health Statistics.

Miliora, M. T. (1987). The creative attitude. In D. G. Tuerch (Ed.), *Creativity and liberal learning* (pp. 131–146). Norwood, NJ: Ablex.

Miller, N. B., Silverman, L. K., & Falk, R. F. (1994). Emotional development, intellectual ability, and gender. *Journal for the Education of the Gifted, 18*(1), 20–38.

Mills, B. (1973). Attitudes of decision-making groups toward gifted children and public school programs for the gifted. *Dissertation Abstract International, 34,* 1739–1740.

Mills, C. J., & Tissot, S. L. (1995). Identifying academic potential in students from under-represented populations: Is using the Ravens Progressive Matrices a good idea? *Gifted Child Quarterly, 39*(4), 209–217.

Minner, S., Prater, G., Bloodworth, H., & Walker, S. (1987). Referral and placement recommendations of teachers toward gifted handicapped children. *Roeper Review, 9*(4), 247–249.

Minner, S. (1990). Teacher evaluations of case descriptions of LD gifted children. *Gifted Child Quarterly, 34*(1), 37–39.

Mitchell, P., & Erickson, D. (1978). The education of gifted and talented children: A status report. *Exceptional Children, 45*(1), 12–16.

Mohs, M. (1982, September). I.Q.: New research shows that the Japanese outperform all others in intelligence tests. Are they really smarter? *Discover,* 18–24.

Montgomery, D. (1989). Identification of giftedness among American Indian people. In J. Maker & S. Schiever (Eds.), *Critical issues in gifted education (Vol. II): Defensible programs for cultural and ethnic minorities* (pp. 79–90). Austin, TX: Pro-Ed.

Moon, T. R., Callahan, C. M., & Tomlinson, C. A. (1999). The effects of mentoring relationships on preservice teachers' attitudes toward academically diverse students. *Gifted Child Quarterly, 43,* (2), 56–62.

Moon, S. M., Kelly, K. R., & Feldhusen, J. F. (1997). Specialized counseling services for gifted youth and their families: A needs assessment. *Gifted Child Quarterly, 41*(1), 16–25.

Moore, O. K. (1961). Orthographic symbols and the preschool child. In E. Torrance (Ed.), *Creativity.* Minneapolis: University of Minnesota Press.

Moore, O. K. (1967). Personal letter to J. S. Chall. In J. S. Chall, *Learning to read: The great debate.* New York: McGraw-Hill.

Morelock, M. J. (1996). On the nature of giftedness and talent: Imposing order on chaos. *Roeper Review, 19*(1), 4–12.

Moustakas, C. (1967). *Creativity and conformity.* New York: Van Nostrand Reinhold.

Mumford, M. D. (1998). Creative thought: Structure, components, and educational implications. *Roeper Review, 21*(1), 14–19.

Mumford, M., Baughman, W., Costanza, D., Uhlman, C., & Connelly, M. (1993). Developing creative capacities in gifted and talented children. *Roeper Review, 16*(1), 16–21.

Mumford, M., Connelly, M., Baughman, W., & Marks, M. (1994). Creativity and problem solving: Cognition, adaptability, and wisdom. *Roeper Review, 16*(4), 241–246.

Murphy, J., Dauw, D., Horton, R., & Friedian, A. (1976). Self-actualization and creativity. *Journal of Creative Behavior, 10,* 39–44.

Myers, M., Slavin, M., & Southern, W. T. (1990). Emergence and maintenance of leadership among gifted students in group problem solving, *Roeper Review, 12*(4), 256–260.

Nash, J. M. (1997, February 3). Fertile minds. *Time,* 49–56.

National Council on Education Standards and Testing. (1992). *Raising standards for American education.* Washington, DC: U.S. Government Printing Office.

National Science Foundation. (1990). *Women and minorities in science and engineering.* Washington, DC: Author.

National/State Leadership Training Institute on the Gifted and Talented. (1977, January). *Gifted female supplement. National/State Leadership Training Institute Bulletin.* Los Angeles: Author.

Nazzaro, J. (Ed.). (1981). *Culturally diverse exceptional children in school.* Reston, VA: Council for Exceptional Children.

Neihart, M. (1998). Creativity, the arts, and madness. *Roeper Review, 21*(1), 47–50.

Nielsen, M. E., Higgins, L. D., Hammond, A. E., & Williams, R. A. (1993). Gifted children with disabilities. *Gifted Child Today, 16*(5), 9–12.

Neimark, E. (1975). Longitudinal development of formal operational thought. *Genetic Psychology Monograph, 91,* 175–225.

Nevin, D. (1977). Seven teenage math prodigies take off from Johns Hopkins on the way to advanced degrees. *Smithsonian, 8*(7), 76–82.

Nichols, R. (1964). Parental attitudes of mothers of intelligent adolescents and creativity of their children. *Child Development, 35,* 1041–1049.

Nidever, I. (1993). Homeschool: Where present and future meet. *Communicator, 23*(3), 13–14.

Noble, K. D., Subotnik, R. F., & Arnold, K. D. (1999). To thine own self be true: A new model of female talent development. *Gifted Child Quarterly, 43*(3), 140–149.

Nova. (1980, September). *The pinks and the blues.* Broadcast by Public Broadcasting System.

Oakes, J. (1985). *Keeping track: How schools structure inequality.* New Haven, CT: Yale University Press.

Ohnmacht, F. (1966). Achievement, anxiety, and creative thinking. *American Educational Research Journal, 3,* 131–138.

Olszewski-Kubilius, P. (1995). A summary of research regarding early entrance to college. *Roeper Review, 18*(2), 121–126.

Olszewski, P., Kulieke, M., & Buescher, T. (1987). The influence of the family environment on the development of talent: A literature review. *Journal for the Education of the Gifted, 8,* 9–23.

Olszewski-Kubilius, P., Kulieke, M., & Krasney, N. (1988). Personality dimensions of gifted adolescents: A review of the empirical literature. *Gifted Child Quarterly, 32*(4), 347–352.

Olszewski-Kubilius, P., & Limburg-Weber, L. (2000). Here comes high school: Understanding and planning for your child's educational future. *Gifted Education Press Quarterly, 14* (3), 2–7.

O'Neil, J. (1989, January). Global education: Controversy remains, but support growing. *ASCD Curriculum Update,* 1–8.

O'Neil, J. (1993). The promise of portfolios. *ASCD Update, 35*(7), 1, 5.

O'Neil, J. (1994). Making assessment meaningful. *ASCD Update, 36*(6), 1, 4, 5.

Oram, G. D., Dewey, D. G., & Rutemiller, L. A. (1995). Relations between academic aptitude and psychosocial adjustment in gifted program students. *Gifted Child Quarterly, 39*(4), 236–244.

Ornstein, R. (1991). *The evolution of consciousness: The origins of the way we think.* New York: Simon & Schuster.

Owen, R. (1984). *Language development.* Columbus, OH: Merrill.

Parke, B. N., & Ness, P. S. (1988). Curricular decision-making for the education of young gifted children. *Gifted Child Quarterly, 32* (1), 196–199.

Parker, W. D., & Adkins, K. K. (1995). Perfectionism and the gifted. *Roeper Review, 17*(3), 173–176.

Parnes, S. (1967). *Creative behavior guidebook.* New York: Scribner.

Passow, A. (1980). *Education for gifted children and youth: An old issue—a new challenge.* Ventura, CA: Office of the Ventura County Superintendent of Schools.

Passow, A. (1981). The four curricula of the gifted and talented: Toward a total learning environment. *G/C/T, 20,* 2–7.

Passow, A. H. (1988). Educating gifted persons who are caring and concerned. *Roeper Review, 11*(1), 13–15.

Passow, A. H. (1989, May/June). Designing a global curriculum. *Gifted Child Today,* 24–26.

Passow, A. H., & Frasier, M. M. (1996). Toward improving identification of talent potential among minority and disadvantage students. *Roeper Review, 18*(3), 198–202.

Patlak, M. (1989, April 10). Cornerstones of conversation: Researchers study the formation of speech. *Los Angeles Times,* Part II, 3.

Patton, J., Prillaman, D., & VanTassel-Baska, J. (1990). The nature and extent of programs for the disadvantaged gifted in the United States and territories. *Gifted Child Quarterly, 34*(3), 94–96.

Pelletier, K. (1977). *Mind as healer, mind as slayer.* New York: Delacorte.

Perkins, J., & Wicas, E. (1971). Group counseling bright underachievers at 9 Florida high schools. *Gifted Child Quarterly, 18,* 273–278.

Perrone, P., & Male, R. (1981). *The developmental education and guidance of talented learners.* Rockville, MD: Aspen.

Pettigrew, T. A. (1964). *A profile of the Negro American.* Princeton, NJ: Van Nostrand.

Pfeiffer, A. (1989). Purpose of programs for gifted and talented and highly motivated American Indian students. In J. Maker & S. Schiever (Eds.), *Critical issues in gifted education (Vol. II): Defensible programs for cultural and ethnic minorities* (pp. 102–106). Austin, TX: Pro-Ed.

Piaget, J. (1952). *The origins of intelligence in children* (M. Cook, Trans.). New York: International Universities. (Original work published 1936)

Piaget, J. (1954). *The construction of reality in the child.* New York: Basic Books.

Piaget, J. (1965). *The moral judgment of the child* (M. Gabin, Trans.). New York: Free Press. (Original work published 1932)

Piechowski, M. M. (1991). Emotional development and emotional giftedness. In N. Colangelo & G. A. Davis (Eds.), *Handbook of gifted education* (pp. 285–306). Needham Heights, MA: Allyn & Bacon.

Piechowski, M. M. (1991). Emotional development and emotional giftedness. In N. Colangelo & G. A. Davis (Eds.), *Handbook of gifted education* (pp. 285–306). Needham Heights, MA: Allyn & Bacon.

Piechowski, M. M., Silverman, L., & Falk, F. (1985). Comparison of intellectually and artistically gifted on five dimensions of mental functioning. *Perceptual and Motor Skills, 60,* 539–549.

Piirto, J. (1998). *Understanding those who create.* Scottsdale, AZ: Gifted Psychology.

Pines, M. (1979 September). A head start in the nursery. *Psychology Today, 13*(4), 56–68.

Pines, M. (1984). Children's winning ways. *Psychology Today, 18*(12), 58–65.

Pitts, M. (1986). Suggestions for administrators of rural schools about developing a gifted program. *Roeper Review 9*(1), 24–25.

Plowman, P., & Rice, J. (1967). *Final report: California Project Talent.* Sacramento: California Department of Public Instruction.

Plucker, J. A., & Runco, M. A. (1998). The death of creativity measurement has been greatly exaggerated: Current issues, recent advances, and future directions in creativity assessment. *Roeper Review, 21*(1), 36–39.

Podgoretskaya, N. (1979). A study of spontaneous logical thinking in adults. *Soviet Psychology, 17*(3), 70–84.

Poffenberger, T., & Poffenberger, S. (1973). The social psychology of fertility in a village in India. In J. Fawcett (Ed.), *Psychological perspectives on population.* New York: Basic Books.

Popspisil, J. (1994). Creativity: An evolving construct. *AGATE, 8*(2), 23–31.

Poteet, J., Choate, J., & Stewart, S. (1993). Performance assessment and special education: Practices and prospects. *Focus on Exceptional Children, 26*(1), 1–20.

Powell, P., & Haden, T. (1987). The intellectual and psychosocial nature of extreme giftedness. *Roeper Review, 6*(3), 131–133.

Power, T., & Chapieski, L. (1986). Childrearing and impulse control in toddlers: A naturalistic investigation. *Developmental Psychology, 22*(2), 271–275.

Prescott, J. (1979). Alienation of affection. *Psychology Today. 13*(7), 124.

Pressey, S. (1955). Concerning the nature and nurture of genius. *Science, 31,* 123–129.

Pressey, S. (1964). The nature and nurture of genius. In J. French (Ed.), *Educating the gifted child.* New York: Holt, Rinehart & Winston.

Pribram, K. (1977). Primary reality may be frequency realm. *Brain/Mind Bulletin. 2,* 1–3.

Price. G., Dunn. K., Dunn. R., & Griggs, S. (1981). Studies in students learning styles *Roeper Review 4*(2), 38–40.

Prichard, A., & Taylor, J. (1980). *Accelerating learning: The use of suggestion in the classroom.* Novato. CA: Academic Therapy Publications.

Purkey, W. (1966). Measured and professed personality characteristics of gifted high school students and analysis of their congruence. *Journal of Educational Research, 3,* 99–103.

Pyryt, M. (1996). IQ: Easy to bash, hard to replace. *Roeper Review, 18*(4), 255–258.

Racle, G. (1977). Documents: Research Institute of Suggestology, Sofia, Bulgaria, 1971. *Suggestopaedia-Canada, 2,* 1–3.

Rakic, P., Bourgeois, J. P., & Goldman-Rakic, P. S. (1994). Synaptic development of the cerebral cortex: Implications for learning memory and mental illness. *Progress in Brain Research, 102,* 227–243.

Ramaseshan, P. (1957). *The social and emotional adjustment of the gifted.* Unpublished doctoral dissertation, University of Nebraska, Lincoln.

Ralph, J., Goldberg, M., & Passow, A. (1966). *Bright underachievers.* New York: Teachers College Press.

Raspberry, W. (1976). What about elitist high schools? *Today's Education, 65,* 36–39.

Raudsepp, E. (1980). Intuition: A neglected decision making tool. *Machine Design, 52,* 91–94.

Raven, J. (1947). *Raven's progressive matrices test.* London: Lewis.

Ray, B., & Wartes, J. (1991). The academic achievement and affective development of home-schooled children. In J. Van Galen & M. Pittman (Eds.), *Home schooling: Political, historical, and pedagogical perspectives* (pp. 43–62). Norwood, NJ: Ablex.

Raymond, C. (1991a, January 23). Cross-cultural study of sounds adults direct to infants shows that "baby talk" can be serious communication. *The Chronicle of Higher Education,* A5, A7.

Raymond, C. (1991b, January 23). Pioneering research challenges accepted notions concerning the cognitive abilities of infants. *The Chronicle of Higher Education,* A5–A7.

Redding, R. (1990). Learning preferences and skill patterns among underachieving gifted adolescents. *Gifted Child Quarterly, 34*(2), 72–75.

Reichstein, K., & Pipkin, R. (1968). A study of academic justice. *The Law and Society Review, 2,* 259–276.

Reis, S. (1987). We can't change what we don't recognize: Understanding the special needs of gifted females. *Gifted Child Quarterly, 31*(2), 83–89.

Reis, S. M., & Callahan, C. (1989). Gifted females: They've come a long way—or have they? *Journal for the Education of the Gifted, 12*(2), 99–117.

Reis, S. M., Neu, T., & McGuire, J. (1995). *Talents in two places: Case studies of high ability students with learning disabilities who have achieved.* Research Monograph 95114. Storrs, CT: The National Research Center on Gifted and Talented.

Reis, S. M., & McCoach, D. B. (2000). The underachievement of gifted students: What do we know and where do we go? *Gifted Child Quarterly, 44*(3), 152–170.

Reis, S. M., McGuire, J. M., & Neu, T. W. (2000). Compensation strategies used by high-ability students with learning disabilities who succeed in college. *Gifted Child Quarterly, 44*(2), 123–134.

Reis, S., & Renzulli, J. (1986). The secondary triad model. In J. Renzulli, *Systems and models for developing programs for the gifted and talented.* Mansfield Center, CT: Creative Learning Press.

Reis, S., & Renzulli, J. (1989). The Secondary Triad Model. *Journal for the Education of the Gifted, 13*(1), 55–77.

Rekdal, C. K. (1984). Guiding the gifted female through being aware: The math connection. *G/C/T, 35,* 10–12.

Renzulli, J. (1968). Identifying key features in programs for the gifted. *Exceptional Children, 35,* 217–221.

Renzulli, J. (1973). Talent potential in minority group students. *Exceptional Children, 39*(6), 437–444.

Renzulli, J. (1977). *The Enrichment Triad Model: A guide for developing defensible programs for the gifted and talented.* Mansfield Center, CT: Creative Learning Press.

Renzulli, J. (1978). What makes giftedness? Reexamining a definition. *Phi Delta Kappan, 60,* 180–184, 261.

Renzulli, J. (1985). Are teachers of the gifted specialists? A landmark decision on employment practices in special education for the gifted. *Gifted Child Quarterly, 29*(1), 24–28.

Renzulli, J. S. (1992). A general theory for the development of creative productivity through the pursuit of ideal acts of learning. *Gifted Child Quarterly, 36*(4), 170–181.

Renzulli, J. S., & Reis, S. M. (1985). *The Schoolwide Enrichment Model: A comprehensive plan for educational excellence.* Mansfield Center, CT: Creative Learning Press.

Renzulli, J., & Reis, S. (1986). The enrichment triad/revolving door model: A schoolwide plan for the development of creative productivity. In J. Renzulli (Ed.), *Systems and models for developing programs for the gifted and talented.* Mansfield Center, CT: Creative Learning Press.

Renzulli, J., Reis, S., & Smith, L. (1981). *The Revolving Door Identification Model.* Mansfield Center, CT: Creative Learning Press.

Renzulli, J., Smith, L., White, A. J., Callahan, C. M., & Hartman, R. (1976). *Scale for rating the behavioral characteristics of superior students.* Mansfield Center, CT: Creative Learning.

Report on Education Research. (1986, April). Stanford study links parents' approach with children's grades, p. 3.

Restak, K. (1979). *The brain: The last frontier.* New York: Doubleday.

Restak, R. (1985). The human brain: Insights and puzzles. *Theory Into Practice, 24*(2), 91–94.

Restak, R. (1986). *The infant mind.* Garden City, New York: Doubleday.

Restak, R. (1991). *The brain has a mind of its own.* New York: Crown.

Restak, R. (1994). *The modular brain.* New York: Scribners.

Restak, R. (2000). *Mysteries of the mind.* Washington, DC: National Geographic Society.

Reyes, E. I., Fletcher, R., & Paez, D. (1996). Developing local multidimensional screening procedures for identifying giftedness among Mexican-American border population. *Roeper Review, 18*(3), 208–211.

Reynolds, M. (Ed.). (1962). *Early school admission for mentally advanced children.* Reston, VA: Council for Exceptional Children.

Rheingold, H., & Cook, K. (1975). The contents of boys' and girls' rooms as an index of parent behavior. *Child Development, 46,* 459–463.

Richert, S. (1985). Identification of gifted children in the United States: The need for pluralistic assessment. *Roeper Review, 8*(2), 68–72.

Rimm, S. (1986). *Underachievement syndrome: Causes and cures.* Watertown, WI: Apple.

Rimm, S. B. (1996). Parenting for achievement. *Roeper Review, 19*(1), 57–59.

Rimm, S., & Davis, G. (1976). GIFT: An instrument for the identification of creativity. *Journal of Creative Behavior, 10*(3), 178–182.

Rimm, S. & Lowe, B. (1988). Family environments of underachieveing gifted students. *Gifted Child Quarterly, 32,* 353–359.

Roach, A. A. (1999). Leadership giftedness: Models revisited. *Gifted Child Quarterly, 43*(1), 13–24.

Roberts, T., & Clark, F. (1976). Transpersonal psychology in education. In G. Hendricks & J. Fadiman (Eds.), *Transpersonal education.* Englewood Cliffs, NJ: Merrill/Prentice Hall.

Robertson, E. (1991). Neglected dropouts: The gifted and talented. *Equity & Excellence, 25,* 62–74.

Robinson, A. (1990). Does that describe me? Adolescents' acceptance of the gifted label. *Journal for the Education of the Gifted, 13*(3), 245–255.

Robinson, N. (1993). *Parenting the very young, gifted child.* Research-Based Decision Making Series No. 9308. Storrs, CT: The National Research Center on the Gifted and Talented.

Roderick, J. (1987). Painful questions about leadership. *Leadership Network Newsletter, 2*(2), 1–2.

Roedell, W. (1984). Vulnerabilities of highly gifted children. *Roeper Review, 6*(3), 127–130.

Roedell, W. C., Jackson, N. E., & Robinson, H. B. (1980). *Gifted young children.* New York: Teachers College Press.

Roeper, A. (1992). Characteristics of gifted children and how parents and teachers can cope with them. *Roeper Review, 11,* 31–32.

Rogers, C. (1959). Toward a theory of creativity. In H. H. Anderson (Ed.), *Creativity and its cultivation.* New York: Harper & Row.

Rogers, C. (1961). *On becoming a person.* Boston: Houghton Mifflin.

Rogers, C. (1969). *Freedom to learn.* Upper Saddle River, NJ: Merrill/Prentice Hall.

Rogers, K. (1989). Training teachers of the gifted: What do they need to know? *Roeper Review, 11*(3), 145–150.

Rogers, K. (1991). *The relationship of grouping practices to the education of the gifted and talented learner.* Storrs, CT: National Research Center on the Gifted and Talented.

Rogers, K. (1993). Grouping the gifted and talented: Questions and answers. *Roeper Review, 16*(1), 8–12.

Rogers, K. (2001). Grouping the gifted: Myths and realities. *Gifted Education Communicator, 32*(1), 20–25, 34–35.

Rohrer, J., & Edmondson, M. (Eds.). (1960). *The eighth generation.* New York: Harper & Row.

Roodin, P. (1983). Imagery: An overlooked ability among the gifted. *Roeper Review, 5*(4), 5–6.

Roome, J., & Romney, D. (1985). Reducing anxiety in gifted children by inducing relaxation. *Roeper Review, 7*(3), 177–179.

Rose, S. (1972). Environmental effects on brain and behavior. In K. Richardson & D. Spears (Eds.), *Race, culture and intelligence.* Baltimore: Penguin.

Rosenthal, R. (1968). *Pygmalion in the classroom: Teacher expectation and pupil's intellectual development.* New York: Holt, Rinehart & Winston.

Rosenthal, R., & Jacobsen, L. (1969). *Pygmalion in the classroom: Self-fulfilling prophecies and teacher expectations.* New York: Holt, Rinehart & Winston.

Rosenzweig, M. (1966). Environmental complexity, cerebral change and behavior. *American Psychologist, 21,* 321–332.

Ross, P. O. (1993). *National excellence: A case for developing America's talent.* Washington, DC: U.S. Government Printing Office.

Rothenberg, A. (1990). *Creativity & madness: New findings and old stereotypes.* Baltimore: Johns Hopkins University Press.

Rubin, J., Provenzano, F., & Luria, Z. (1974). The eye of the beholder: Parents' views on sex of newborns. *American Journal of Orthopsychiatry, 44,* 512–519.

Runco, M. (1992). Creative thinking in the fifth grade. In J. F. Wakefield, *Creative thinking: Problem-solving skills and the arts orientation,* (pp. 13–26). Norwood, NJ: Ablex Publishing.

Runco, M. A. (1995). New dimensions in creativity. *Understanding our Gifted, 7*(5), 1, 12–15.

Runco, M., & Nemiro, J. (1994). Problem finding, creativity, and giftedness. *Roeper Review, 16* (4), 235–240.

Runions, T. (1980). The Mentor Academy Program: Educating the gifted/talented for the 80's. *Gifted Child Quarterly, 24*(4), 152–157.

Sadker, M., & Sadker, D. (1985). Sexism in the schoolroom of the '80s. *Psychology Today, 19*(3), 54–57.

Sagan, C. (1974). *Broca's brain.* New York: Random House.

Sagan, C. (1977). *The dragons of Eden.* New York: Random House.

Sah, A., & Borland, J. (1989). The effects of a structured home plan on the home and school behaviors of gifted learning-disabled students with deficits in organizational skills. *Roeper Review, 12*(1), 54–57.

Samples, B. (1975). Learning with the whole brain. *Human Behavior, 4,* 18–23.

Samples, B. (1976). *The metaphoric mind: A celebration of creative consciousness.* Reading, MA: Addison-Wesley.

Samples, B. (1977). Mind cycles and learning. *Phi Delta Kappan, 58,* 688–692.

Sanchez, A. (1999). As is. *Understanding Our Gifted, 11*(2), 21–22.

Sapon-Shevin, M. (1995, Dec./Jan.). Why gifted students belong in the inclusive schools. *Educational Leadership,* 64–70.

Satir, V. (1972). *Peoplemaking.* Palo Alto, CA: Science & Behavior Books.

Savage, J. (1983). Reading guides: Effective tools for teaching the gifted. *Roeper Review, 5*(3), 9–11.

Schaefer, E., & Aaronson, M. (1972). Infant education pre-school project: Implementation and implications of a home tutoring program. In R. Parker (Ed.), *The pre-school in action: Exploring early childhood programs.* Boston: Allyn & Bacon.

Scheibel, A. (1993, July). *Review of how the brain operates: Application and implications.* A presentation at The Developing Brain: New Frontiers of Research Conference, University of California, Los Angeles.

Scheibel, M., & Scheibel, A. (1964). Some neural substrates of postnatal development. In M. Hoffman & L. Hoffman (Eds.), *Review of child development research* (Vol. 1). New York: Russell Sage Foundation.

Schiff, M., Kaufman, A., & Kaufman, N. (1981). Scatter analysis of WISC-R profiles for learning disabled children with superior intelligence. *Journal of Learning Disabilities, 14,* 400–404.

Schmidt, P. (1990a). Despite controversy, consensus grows on the need to teach values in schools. *Education Week, 9*(20), 1, 10.

Schmidt, P. (1990b). Web of factors said to influence children's views on moral issues. *Education Week, 9*(20), 1,–11.

Schon, K. (1997). When children come home: The process of deschooling. *Understanding Our Gifted, 9*(3), 20–23.

School Staffing Survey, 1969–70. Washington, DC: Department of Health, Education, and Welfare, U.S. Office of Education.

Schuler, P. A. (1997, Winter). Cluster grouping coast to coast. *The National Research Center on the Gifted and Talented Newsletter,* 11–15.

Schultz, J., & Luthe, W. (1959). *Autogenic training: A psychophysiological approach to psychotherapy.* New York: Grune & Stratton.

Schutz, W. (1976). Education for the body. In G. Hendricks & J. Fadiman (Eds.), *Transpersonal education: A curriculum for feeling and being.* Englewood Cliffs, NJ: Merrill/Prentice Hall.

Scott, J. (1962). Critical period in behavioral development. *Science, 138*(3544), 949–953.

Seagoe, M. (1974). Some learning characteristics of gifted children. In R. Martinson, *The identification of the gifted and talented.* Ventura, CA: Office of the Ventura County Superintendent of Schools.

Seeley, K. R. (1993). Gifted students at risk. In L. K. Silverman (Ed.), *Counseling the gifted and talented* (pp. 263–276). Denver: Love.

Selby, C. (1980). Science as the 'Fourth R'—Basic and also beautiful. *Science Digest, 88*(3), 44–47.

Selye, H. (1956). *The stress of life.* New York: McGraw-Hill.

Selye, H. (1979). Foreword. In K. Albrecht, *Stress and the manager* (pp. v–vii). Englewood Cliffs, NJ: Merrill/Prentice Hall.

Serbin, L., & O'Leary, K. (1975). How nursery schools teach girls to shut up. *Psychology Today, 9,* 57–58, 102–103.

Seymour, E. (1995). The loss of women from science, mathematics, and engineering undergraduate majors. *Science Education 79*(4), 437–473.

Sharan, S. (1980). Cooperative learning in small groups: Recent methods and effects on achievement, attitudes, and ethnic relations. *Review of Educational Research, 50*(2), 241–271.

Shaw, M., & Black, D. (1960). The reaction to frustration of bright high school underachievers. *California Journal of Educational Research, 11,* 120–124.

Sheely, A. R., & Silverman, L. K. (2000). Defining the few. *Communicator, 31*(4), 1, 36–37.

Shields, C. (1995). A comparison study of student attitudes and perceptions in homogeneous and heterogeneous classrooms. *Roeper Review, 17* (4), 234–238.

Shope, R. (1994). Exercise 1: Interplanetary distances. *Pluto Express Preproject Curriculum Guide 1*(1), 2.

Shostrom, E. (1964). An inventory for the measurement of self-actualization. *Educational and Psychological Measurement, 24,* 207–218.

Siegel, D. J. (1999). *The developing mind.* New York: Guilford.

Siegle, D., & Schuler, P. A. (2000). Perfectionism differences in gifted middle school students. *Roeper Review, 23*(1), 39–44.

Silberman, C. (1971). *Crisis in the classroom,* New York: Random House.

Silberstein, D. (1995). *Interview with my brother.* Unpublished paper, California State University, Los Angeles.

Siegle, D., & Reis, S. (1994/1995). Gender differences in teacher and student perceptions of student ability and effort. *The Journal of Secondary Gifted Education, 6*(2), 86–92.

Silverman, L. (1980). Secondary programs for gifted students. *Journal for the Education of the Gifted, 4*(1), 30–42.

Silverman, L. (1986). Giftedness, intelligence and the new Stanford-Binet. *Roeper Review, 8* (3), 168–171.

Silverman, L. K. (1990, February). *The plight of the highly gifted.* Paper presented at the California Association for the Gifted Annual Conference, Fresno, CA.

Silverman, L. K. (1991). Helping gifted girls reach their potential. *Roeper Review, 13*(3), 122–123.

Silverman, L. K. (Ed.). (1993). *Counseling the gifted & talented.* Denver: Love.

Silverman, L. K. (1994). The moral sensitivity of gifted children and the evolution of society. *Roeper Review, 17*(2), 110–116.

Silverman, L. K. (1995). *The universal experience of being out-of-sync.* Keynote address for the 11th World Conference on Gifted and Talented Children, Hong Kong.

Silvernail, D. (1980). Gifted education for the 80's and beyond: A futuristic curriculum model for the gifted child. *Roeper Review, 2*(4), 16–18.

Singer, B. (1974). The future-focused role image. In A. Toffler (Ed.), *Learning for tomorrow.* New York: Vintage.

Singer, J. (1976). Fantasy: The foundation of serenity. *Psychology Today, 10*(2), 32–37.

Simonov, P. (1970). Emotions and creativity. *Psychology Today, 4*(3), 51–55, 77.

Sisk, D. (1973, March). *Developing teacher mediators/teacher training for disadvantaged gifted.* Paper presented at the First National Conference on the Disadvantaged Gifted, Ventura, CA.

Sisk, D. (1987). *Creative teaching of the gifted.* New York: McGraw-Hill.

Sisk, D. (1988). The bored and disinterested gifted child: Going through school lockstep. *Journal for the Education of the Gifted, 11*(4), 5–18.

Sisk, D. (2000). Maximizing the potential of minority economically disadvantaged students. *Illinois Association for Gifted Children Journal,* 44–47.

Skeels, H. (1966). Adult status of children with contrasting early life experiences. *Monographs of the Society for Research in Child Development, 31*(3).

Skeels, H., & Dye, H. (1959). A study of the effects of differential stimulation on mentally retarded children. *Proceedings of American Association of Mental Deficiency, 44,* 114–136.

Skeels, H., Updegraff, R., Wellman, B., & Williams, H. (1938). A study of environmental stimulation: An orphanage preschool project. *University of Iowa Studies in Child Welfare, 15*(4), 28, 264.

Skodak, M., & Skeels, H. (1949). A final followup study of one hundred adopted children. *Journal of Genetic Psychology, 74–75,* 85–125.

Slavin, R. (1987). Ability grouping and student achievement in elementary schools: A best-evidence synthesis. *Review of Educational Research, 57*(3), 293–336.

Slavin, R. (1990). Achievement effects of ability grouping in secondary schools: A best-evidence synthesis. *Review of Educational Research, 60,* 471–499.

Slavin, R., & Karweit, N. (1984, April). *Within-class ability grouping and student achievement.* Paper presented at the annual meeting of the American Educational Research Association, New Orleans, LA.

Slavkin, H. (1987, February). *Science in the 21st century.* Speech presented at the 25th Annual Conference of the California Association for the Gifted, Los Angeles.

Slocumb, P. D., & Payne, R. K. (2000). *Removing the mask: Giftedness in poverty.* Highlands, TX: RFT.

Smith, R. (1965). *The relationship of creativity to social class*. (United States Office of Education Cooperative Research Project No. 2250). Pittsburgh: University of Pittsburgh.

Smith, S., Dean, S., Kaplan, S., Phelan, P., Russell, S., & Spelman, C. (1990). *Assessing and identifying students for gifted and talented programs: Recommended procedures*. Canoga Park, CA: California Association for the Gifted.

Snowden, P. L., & Christian, L. G. (1999). Parenting the young gifted child: Supportive behaviors. *Roeper Review, 21*(3), 215–221.

Solano, C. (1977). Teacher and pupil stereotypes of gifted boys and girls. *Talents and Gifts, 19*, 4–8.

Sontag, L., Baker, C., & Nelson, V. (1958). Mental growth and personality development: A longitudinal study. *Monograph of Sociological Research in Child Development*, 1958, *23* (2, Whole No. 68).

Southern, W., & Spicker, H. (1989). The rural gifted on line: Bulletin boards and electronic curriculum. *Roeper Review, 11*(4), 199–202.

Sperry, R. W. (1973). Lateral specialization of cerebral function in the surgically separated hemispheres. In F. McGuigan (Ed.), *The psychophysiology of thinking*. New York: Academic Press.

Spino, M. (1976). *Beyond jogging: The innerspaces of running*. Millbrae, CA: Celestial Arts.

St. Jean, D. (1996, Spring). Valuing, identifying, cultivating, and rewarding talents of students from special populations. *The National Research Center on the Gifted and Talented Newsletter*, 12–15.

Staehle, D. (2000). Taking a different path: A mother's reflections on homeschooling. *Roeper Review, 22*(4), 270–271.

Standing, E. (1966). *The Montessori revolution in education*. New York: Schocken.

Standford study links parents' approach with children's grades. (1986, April 9). *Report on Education Research*, p. 3.

Stanley, J. (1979). The case for extreme educational acceleration of intellectually brilliant youths. In J. Gowan, J. Khatena, & E. P. Torrance (Eds.), *Educating the ablest. A book of readings* (2nd ed). Itasca, IL: F. E. Peacock.

Stanley, J., Keating, D., & Fox, L. (Eds.). (1974). *Mathematical talent: Discovery description, and development*. Baltimore: Johns Hopkins University Press.

Stark, M. (1972). *Results of a questionnaire given to 152 high school gifted students*. Paper presented at California State University, Los Angeles.

Starko, A., & Schack, G. (1989). Perceived need, teacher efficacy, and teaching strategies for the gifted and talented. *Gifted Child Quarterly, 33*(3), 118–122.

Steele, J. (1969). *Instructional climate in Illinois gifted classes*. Springfield, IL: Illinois State Office of the Superintendent of Public Instruction, Department of Program Planning for Gifted.

Steen, L. A. (1990, April). Making math matter. *Instructor*, 21–23.

Stern, D. N. (1990, Aug. 20). Diary of a baby. *U.S. News & World Report*, 54–59.

Sternberg, R. (1981). A componential theory of intellectual giftedness. *Gifted Child Quarterly, 25*(2), 86–93.

Sternberg, R. (1985). *Beyond IQ: A triarchic theory of human intelligence*. Cambridge, MA: Cambridge University Press.

Sternberg, R. (1986). Identifying the gifted through IQ: Why a little bit of knowledge is a dangerous thing. *Roeper Review, 8*(3), 143–147.

Sternberg, R. (1996). Neither elitism nor egalitarianism: Gifted education as a third force in American education. *Roeper Review, 18*(4), 261–263.

Sternberg, R. J. (1998). Letters from the field. *Roeper Review, 21*(1), 87.

Sternberg, R., & Lubart, T. (1993). Creative giftedness: A multivariate investment approach. *Gifted Child Quarterly, 37*(1), 7–15.

Sternberg, R., Grigorenko, E. L., Jarvin, L., Clinkenbeard, P., Ferrari, M., & Torff, B. (2000, Spring). The effectiveness of triarchic teaching and assessment. *The National Research Center on the Gifted and Talented Newsletter*, 3–8.

Stewart, E. (1981). Learning styles among gifted/talented students: Instructional technique preferences. *Exceptional Children, 48*(2), 134–138.

Stipek, D., & Weisz, J. (1981). Perceived personal control and academic achievement. *Review of Educational Research, 51*(1), 101–137.

Stollak, G. (1978). *Until we are six*. Huntington, NY: Academic Press.

Story, C. (1985). Facilitator of learning: A microethnographic study of the teacher of the gifted. *Gifted Child Quarterly, 29*(4), 155–159.

Strop, J. (2000). Meeting the needs of highly gifted students in a large, comprehensive public high school. *Understanding Our Gifted, 12* (2), 17–20.

Suchman, J. R. (1962). *The elementary school training program in scientific inquiry*. Urbana, IL: University of Illinois Press.

Sue, D. W., Arrendondo, P., & McDavis, R. J. (1992). Multicultural counseling competencies and standards: A call to the profession. *Journal of Counseling and Development, 70,* 477–486.

Supplee, P. (1989). Students at risk: The gifted underachiever. *Roeper Review, 11*(3), 163–166.

Suter, D., & Wolf, J. (1987). Issues in the identification and programming of the gifted/learning disabled child. *Journal for the Education of the Gifted, 10*(3), 227–237.

Sylwester, R. (1995). *A celebration of neurons: An educator's guide to the human brain.* Alexandria, VA: Association for Supervision and Curriculum Development.

Sylwester, R., & Cho, J.-Y. (1993, Dec.). What the biology of the brain tells us about learning. *Educational Leadership, 51*(4), 46–50.

Syphers, D. (1972). *Gifted and talented children: Practical programming for teachers and principals.* Arlington, VA: Council for Exceptional Children.

Szekely, G. (1981). The artist and the child—A model program for the artistically gifted. *Gifted Child Quarterly, 25*(2), 67–72.

Szekely, G. (1982). Creative learning and teaching of the gifted through sketchbooks. *Roeper Review, 4*(3), 15–17.

Taba, H. (1966). *Teaching strategies and cognitive functioning in elementary school children* (U.S. Office of Education Cooperative Research Project #2404). San Francisco: San Francisco State College.

Taeuber, C. (Ed.). (1996). *Statistical handbook on women in America.* Phoenix: Oryx Press.

Tammi, L. (1990, February 14). Programs for the gifted are not "elitist." *Education Week,* Commentary, 44.

Tanaka, K. (1989). A response to "Are we meeting the needs of gifted Asian-Americans?" In J. Maker & S. Schiever (Eds.), *Critical issues in gifted education (Vol. II): Defensible programs for cultural and ethnic minorities* (pp. 174–178). Austin, TX: Pro-Ed.

Tannenbaum, A. (1962). *Adolescent attitudes toward academic brilliance.* New York: Bureau of Publications, Teachers College, Columbia University.

Tannenbaum, A. (1983). *Gifted children.* New York: Macmillan.

Tannenbaum, A. J., & Baldwin, L. J. (1983). Giftedness and learning disability: A paradoxical combination. In L. H. Fox, L. Brody, & D. Tobin (Eds.), *Learning-disabled/gifted children: Identification and programming* (pp. 11–36). Baltimore: University Park Press.

Tan-Willman, C., & Gutteridge, D. (1981). Creative thinking and moral reasoning of academically gifted secondary school adolescents. *Gifted Child Quarterly, 25*(4), 149–153.

Tardif, T. Z., & Sternberg, R. J. (1988). What do we know about creativity? In R. J. Sternberg (Ed.), *The nature of creativity* (pp. 429–440). New York: Cambridge University Press.

Tarjan, G. (1970). Some thoughts on sociocultural retardation. In H. C. Haywood (Ed.), *Socio-cultural aspects of mental retardation.* New York: Appleton-Century-Crofts.

Tassi, F., & Schneider, B. H. (1997). Task-oriented versus other-referenced competition: Differential implications for children's peer relations. *Journal of Applied Social Psychology, 27,* 1557–1580.

Taylor, C. W. (1959). Identifying the creative individual. In E. P. Torrance (Ed.), *Creativity: Proceedings of the second Minnesota conference on gifted children.* Minneapolis: Center for Continuation Study.

Taylor, C. W. (1985). Multiple talents. *Journal for the Education of the Gifted, 8*(3), 187–198.

Taylor, C. W., & Williams, F. E. (1966). *Instructional media and creativity.* New York: Wiley.

Taylor, L., & Bongar, B. (1976). *Clinical applications in biofeedback therapy.* Los Angeles: Psychology Press.

Taylor, L., Tom, G., & Ayers, M. (1981). *Electromyometric biofeedback therapy.* Los Angeles: Biofeedback and Advanced Therapy Institute.

Tegano, D. W., Sawyers, J. K., & Moran, J. D. (1989). Problem-finding and solving in play: The teacher's role. *Childhood Education, 66,* 92–97.

Temple University. (1968). *Report of the college of education ad hoc committee on grading systems.* Philadelphia: Author.

Terman, L. (1916). *The measurement of intelligence.* Boston: Houghton Mifflin.

Terman, L. (1925). Mental and physical traits of a thousand gifted children. In L. Terman (Ed.), *Genetic studies of genius* (Vol. I). Stanford, CA: Stanford University Press.

Terman, L. (1954). The discovery and encouragement of exceptional talent. *American Psychologist, 9,* 221–230.

Terman, L., & Oden, M. (1947). The gifted child grows up. In L. Terman (Ed.), *Genetic studies of genius* (Vol. IV). Stanford, CA: Stanford University Press.

Terman, L., & Oden, M. (1959). The gifted group at mid-life; thirty-five year's follow-up of the superior child. In L. Terman (Ed.), *Genetic studies of genius (Vol. V).* Stanford, CA: Stanford University Press.

Teyler, T. (1977). An introduction to the neurosciences. In M. Wittrock (Ed.), *The human brain*. Englewood Cliffs, NJ: Merrill/Prentice Hall.

Thistlewaite, D. (1958). How the talented student evaluates his high school. *School Review, 66,* 164–168.

Thomas, A., Hertzig, I., & Fernandez, P. (1971). Examiner effect in IQ testing of Puerto Rican working-class children. *Measurement and Evaluation in Guidance, 4*(3), 172–175.

Thomas, J. (1980). Agency and achievement: Self-management and self-regard. *Review of Educational Research, 50*(2), 213–240.

Thorndike, R. L. (1975). Mr. Binet's test 70 years later. *Educational Researcher, 4*(5), 3–6.

Thorndike, R. L., & Hagen, E. (1983). *The Cognitive Abilities Tests.*

Tolan, S. S. (1992). Only a parent: Three true stories. *Understanding Our Gifted, 4*(3), 1, 8–10.

Tomer, M. (1981). Human relations in education—A rationale for a curriculum in interpersonal skills for gifted students—grades K-12. *Gifted Child Quarterly, 25*(2), 94–97.

Tomlinson, C. (1994). Gifted learners: The boomerang kids of middle school? *Roeper Review, 16*(3), 177–181.

Tomlinson, S. (1986). A survey of participant expectations for inservice in education of the gifted. *Gifted Child Quarterly, 30*(3), 110–113.

Tomlinson, C. A. (1995). Deciding to differentiate instruction in middle school: One school's journey. *Gifted Child Quarterly, 39*(2), 77–87.

Tomlinson, C. A. (1999). *The differentiated classroom.* Alexandria, VA: Association for Supervision and Curriculum Development.

Tomlinson, C. A. (2000). Reconcilable differences? Standards-based teaching and differentiation. *Educational Leadership, 58*(1), 6–11.

Tonemah, S. (1987). Assessing American Indian gifted and talented students' abilities. *Journal for the Education of the Gifted, 10*(3), 181–194.

Torrance, E. P. (1963). *Education and the creative potential.* Minneapolis: University of Minnesota Press.

Torrance, E. P. (1964). *Rewarding creative behavior.* Englewood Cliffs, NJ: Merrill/Prentice Hall.

Torrance, E. P. (1966). *Torrance Tests of Creative Thinking: Norms—Technical manual.* Princeton, NJ: Personnel Press.

Torrance, E. P. (1969). Creative positives of disadvantaged children and youth. *Gifted Child Quarterly, 13*(2), 71–81.

Torrance, E. P. (1978). Ways of discovering gifted Black children. In A. Baldwin, G. Gear, & L. Lucito (Eds.), *Educational planning for the gifted: Overcoming cultural, geographic and socioeconomic barriers.* Reston, VA: Council for Exceptional Children.

Torrance, E. P. (1981). Cross-cultural studies of creative development in seven selected societies. In J. Gowan, J. Khatena, & E. P. Torrance (Eds.), *Creativity: Its educational implications* (2nd ed.) (pp. 89–97). Dubuque, IA: Kendall/Hunt.

Torrance, E. P. (1999). The millennium: A time to reflect and a time to project. *Understanding Our Gifted, 12*(1), 16–18.

Torrance, E. P., Blume, B., Maryanopolis, J., Murphey, F., & Rogers, J. (1980). *Teaching scenario writing.* Lincoln, NE: Future Problem Solving Program, Nebraska Department of Education.

Torrance, E. P., & Torrance, J. P. (1981). Educating gifted, talented and creative students for the future. *American Middle School Education, 4*(1), 39–46.

Treffinger, D. (1975). Teaching for self-directed learning: A priority for the gifted and talented. *Gifted Child Quarterly, 19*(1), 46–59.

Treffinger, D. (1986). Research on creativity. *Gifted Child Quarterly, 30*(1), 15–19.

Tremaine, C. (1979). Do gifted programs make a difference? *Gifted Child Quarterly, 23*(3), 500–517.

Trotter, R. (1971). Self-image. *Science News, 100,* 130–131.

Trotter, R. (1987, May). You've come a long way, baby. *Psychology Today,* 34–45.

Trowbridge, A. (1978). Evolution of triune brain consciousness. *Man-Environment Systems, 8*(3), 105–112.

Tucker, R. (1986). Breaking through with your ideas. *Creative Living, 15*(3), 2–8.

Tucker, B., & Hafenstein, N. L. (1997). Psychological intensities in young gifted children. *Gifted Child Quarterly, 41*(3), 66–75.

Udvari, S. J., & Schneider, B. H. (2000). Competition and the adjustment of gifted children: A matter of motivation. *Roper Review, 22*(4), 212–216.

Urban, K. K. (1995, August). *Creativity: A componential approach.* Paper presented at the Post Conference Meeting of the 11th World Conference on Gifted and Talented Children, Beijing.

Uzgiris, I. (1989). Issue: Infant intelligence test arouses controversy. *ASCD Update, 31*(5), 4–5.

Vallerand, R. J., Gagne, F., Senecal, C., & Pelletier, L. G. (1994). A comparison of the school intrinsic motivation and perceived competence of gifted and regular students. *Gifted Child Quarterly, 38*(4), 172–175.

VanTassel-Baska, J. (1986). Lessons from the history of teacher inservice in Illinois: Effective staff development in the education of gifted students. *Gifted Child Quarterly, 30*(3), 124–126.

VanTassel-Baska, J. (1989a). Counseling the gifted. In J. Feldhusen, J. VanTassel-Baska, & K. Seely (Eds.), *Excellence in educating the gifted* (pp. 299–314). Denver: Love.

VanTassel-Baska, J. (1989b). The role of the family in the success of disadvantaged gifted learners. *Journal for the Education of the Gifted, 1,* 22–36.

Van Tassel-Baska, J. (1997). Excellence as a standard for all education. *Roeper Review, 20*(1), 9–12.

Van Tassel-Baska, J. (2000). *The talent development process: What we know.* Presented at the Utah Association for the Gifted Midwinter Conference, January 29, Salt Lake City, Utah.

VanTassel-Baska, J., & McEachron-Hirsch, G. (1990). Global education for the gifted: A curriculum focus for the 21st century. *Gifted International, 6*(1), 35–45.

VanTassel-Baska, J., Olszewski-Kubilius, P., & Kulieke, M. (1994). A study of self-concept and social support in advantaged and disadvantaged seventh and eighth grade gifted students. *Roeper Review, 16*(3), 186–191.

Vasconcellos, J. (1990). *Toward a state of esteem.* Sacramento: Office of State Printing.

Vaughan, V. L. (1990). *Meta-analysis of pull-out programs in gifted education.* Paper presented at the annual convention of the National Association for Gifted Children, Little Rock, AR.

Vernon, P. (1979). *Intelligence: Heredity and environment.* San Francisco: Freeman.

Verny, T. (1981). *The secret life of the unborn child.* New York: Summit Books.

Vespi, L., & Yewchuk, C. (1992). A phenomenological study of the social/emotional characteristics of gifted learning disabled children. *Journal for the Education of the Gifted, 16*(1), 55–72.

Vygotsky, L. (1962). *Thought and language* (E. Hanfmann & G. Vakar, Eds. and Trans.). New York: Wiley.

Vygotsky, L. (1974). The problem of age-periodization of child development (M. Zender & B. Zender, Trans.). *Human Development, 17,* 24–40.

Vygotsky, L. S., & Luria, A. (1994). Tool and symbol in child development. In R. van der Veer & J. Valsiner (Eds.), *The Vygotsky Reader.* Oxford: Blackwell. (Original published in Russian in 1984).

Wachs, T. (1976). Utilization of a Piagetian approach in the investigation of early experience effects: A research strategy and some illustrative data. *Merrill-Palmer Quarterly, 22,* 11–30.

Walberg, H. (1969). Physics, femininity, and creativity. *Developmental Psychology, 1,* 47–54.

Walker, J. L. (1988). Young American Indian children. *Teaching Exceptional Children, 20*(4), 50–51.

Wallace, N. (1983). *Better than school: One family's declaration of independence.* New York: Larson.

Wallas, G. (1926). *The art of thought.* London: Watts.

Wallis, C. (1989). Onward, women! *Time, 134*(23), 80–89.

Walsh, M. (1990). Interest in college talent-search programs for young students is continuing to grow. *Education Week, 9*(37), 1, 26.

Wang, M., & Stiles, B. (1976). An investigation of children's concept of self-responsibility for their school learning. *American Educational Research Journal, 13,* 159–179.

Webb, J. T. (1994). *Nurturing the social emotional development of gifted children.* (Report N. EDOEC-93-10). Reston, VA: Council for Exceptional Children.

Webb, J., Meckstroth, E., & Tolan, S. (1982). *Guiding the gifted child.* Columbus, OH: Ohio Psychology Publishing.

Webb, R. (1974). Concrete and formal operations in very bright six to eleven year olds. *Human Development, 17,* 292–300.

Weiner, J. (1968). Attitudes of psychologists and psychometrists toward gifted children and programs for the gifted. *Exceptional Children, 34,* 354.

Weiner, N., & Robinson, S. (1986). Cognitive abilities, personality and gender differences in math achievement of gifted adolescents. *Gifted Child Quarterly, 30*(2), 83–87.

Weinheimer, S. (1972, March). How to teach your child to think: A conversation with Jean Piaget, the "giant in the nursery." *Redbook,* 96–97, 118, 120.

Weiss, P., & Gallagher, J. (1980). The effects of personal experience on attitudes toward gifted education. *Journal for the Education of the Gifted, 3*(4), 194–197.

Weiss, P., & Gallagher, J. (1986). Project TARGET: A needs assessment approach to gifted education inservice. *Gifted Child Quarterly, 30*(3), 114–118.

Wellman, B. (1940). Iowa studies on the effects of schooling. *Yearbook of the National Society on Studies in Education, 39,* 377–399.

Wendel, R., & Heiser, S. (1989). Effective instructional characteristics of teachers of junior high school gifted students. *Roeper Review, 11*(3), 151–153.

Wescott, G., & Woodward, J. (1981). Locating the not so obvious gifted. *G/C/T, 20,* 11.

Wescott, M. (1968). *Toward a contemporary psychology of intuition.* New York: Holt, Rinehart & Winston.

Westberg, K. L., Burns, D. E., Gubbins, E. J., Reis, S. M., Park. S., & Maxfield, L. R. (1998). *Development practices in gifted education: Results of a national survey.* Storrs, CT: University of Connecticut National Research Center on Gifted and Talented.

Westberg, K. L., Archambault, F. X., Jr., Dobyns, S. M., & Salvin, T. J. (1993). *An observational study of instructional and curricular practices used with gifted and talented students in regular classrooms.* Storrs, CT: The National Research Center on the Gifted and Talented.

White, B., & Watts, J. (1973). *Experience and environment* (Vol. I.) Englewood Cliffs, NJ: Merrill/Prentice Hall.

Whitlock, M. S., & DuCette, J. (1989). Outstanding and average teachers of the gifted: A comparative study. *Gifted Child Quarterly, 33*(1), 15–20.

Whitmore, J. (1980). *Giftedness, conflict, and underachievement.* Boston: Allyn & Bacon.

Whitmore, J. (1981). Gifted children with handicapping conditions: A new frontier. *Exceptional Children 48*(2), 106–114.

Whitmore, J. (1986). Understanding a lack of motivation to excel. *Gifted Child Quarterly, 30*(2), 66–69.

Whitmore, J., & Maker, J. (1985). *Intellectual giftedness in disabled persons.* Rockville, MD: Aspen.

Wiggins, G., & McTighe, J. (1998). *Understanding by design.* Alexandra, VA: Association for Supervision and Curriculum Development.

Willard-Holt, C. (1994). Recognizing talent: *Cross-case study of two high potential students with cerebral palsy.* Storrs, CT: National Research Center on the Gifted and Talented.

Willis, S. (1990). Transforming the test. *ASCD Update, 32*(7), 3–6.

Willis, S. (1993, November). Teaching young children: Educators seek "Developmental appropriateness." *ASCD Curriculum Update,* 1–8.

Wills, C. (1993). *The runaway brain: The evolution of human uniqueness.* New York: Basic Books.

Wilson, R. (1986). Risk and resilience in early mental development. In S. Chess & A. Thomas (Eds.), *Annual progress in child psychiatry and child development* (pp. 69–85). New York: Brunner/Mazel.

Witters, L., & Vasa, S. (1981). Programming alternatives for educating the gifted in rural schools. *Roeper Review, 3*(4), 22–24.

Wittrock, M. C. (1993, July). *The developing brain: Application and implications.* Presented at The Developing Brain: New Frontiers of Research Conference, University of California, Los Angeles.

Witty, P. (1940). Some considerations in the education of gifted children. *Educational Administration and Supervision, 26,* 512–521.

Wolf, M. (1981). The CTTE approach to innovative education. *Roeper Review, 4*(2), 33–34.

Wolfle, J. (1988). Mathematically gifted third graders—A challenge in the classroom. *Roeper Review, 10*(4), 235–238.

Wolleat, P. (1979). Guiding the career development of gifted females. In N. Colangelo & R. Zaffrann (Eds.), *New voices in counseling the gifted.* Dubuque, IA: Kendall/Hunt.

Wright, P. (1965). *Enrollment for advanced degrees* (E-5401-63, Circular No. 786). Washington, DC: Office of Education, U.S. Department of Health, Education and Welfare.

Wright, P. B., & Leroux, J. A. (1997). The self-concept of gifted adolescents in a congregated program. *Gifted Child Quarterly, 41*(3), 83–94.

Yarrow, L. (1968). Research in dimensions of early maternal care. *Merrill-Palmer Quarterly, 9,* 101–114.

Zetlin, A. G. (1998). School success: Top students in an inner-city school. *Educational Horizons, 76*(3), 151–155.

NAME INDEX

McDonnel, R., 335
McEachron-Hirsch, G., 312
McGillivray, R., 544
McGuffog, C., 65
McGuire, J., 556, 558-559
McKenna, A., 131
McKim, R., 92, 405
McLeod, B., 503
McMillin, D., 531
McNeill, D., 130
McTighe, J., 226, 390
Mead, M., 194
Meador, K., 87
Meckstroth, E., 175, 246
Mednick, M., 93
Mednick, S., 93
Meeker, M., 366, 368
Meer, J., 383
Mendaglio, S., 555, 556
Mercer, J., 343, 344, 345, 346
Mihalasky, J., 425
Miliora, M. T., 82-83, 84, 85-86
Miller, K., 529
Miller, N. B., 190-191
Miller, P., 516
Mills, B., 196
Mills, C., 344, 523
Minner, S., 553, 555
Mitchell, P., 215
Mohs, M., 326
Montessori, M., 35, 37
Montgomery, D., 525
Moon, S. M., 202, 241, 268-269
Moon, T. R., 229
Moore, O. K., 131
Moran, J. D., 92
Morelock, M. J., 27, 34, 50
Moss, H., 40
Moustakas, C., 79
Mumford, M. D., 78, 90, 92
Murphey, F., 434
Mustaine, M., 111
Myers, M., 417

Najarian, P., 38
Nash, J. M., 117, 196
Navarre, J., 518
Nazzaro, J., 527
Neihart, M., 83
Neimark, E., 200
Nelson, S., 515
Nelson, V., 40
Nemiro, J., 84, 85, 93, 97
Ness, P. S., 145
Neu, T., 556, 558-559
Nevin, D., 265

Nichols, M. N., 171
Nichols, R., 87
Nidever, I., 308-309, 310, 311
Nielsen, M. E., 555
Niskanen, P., 115
Noble, K. D., 519
Nova, 506-507

O'Leary, K., 506, 509, 510
O'Neil, J., 312, 393, 395
Oakes, J., 267
Oden, M., 40, 169, 264, 504
Olenchak, F. R., 558
Olszewski, P., 152
Olszewski-Kubilius, P., 170, 292, 529
Oram, G. D., 171
Ornstein, R., 56
Ostrander, S., 425
Owen, R., 135
Owen, S., 269, 544, 558

Paez, D., 347
Park, S., 224
Parke, B. N., 145
Parker, W. D., 175
Parnes, S., 78, 84
Passow, A., 312, 341, 346, 347-348, 476, 544
Patlak, M., 131
Patterson, C., 549
Patton, J., 530
Payne, G., 91
Payne, R. K., 534
Pearce, N., 290, 543
Pelletier, K., 418, 419
Pelletier, L. G., 172
Perrone, P., 337, 344-345, 489
Pettigrew, T. A., 529
Pfeiffer, A., 525
Piaget, J., 35, 39, 116, 135-136, 137, 200, 272-273, 296, 301
Pickering, D., 390
Piechowski, M. M., 79, 138, 171, 191
Piirto, J., 77, 87, 89
Pines, M., 416
Pipkin, R., 487
Pitts, M., 306, 307
Plowman, P., 264
Plucker, J. A., 96, 97
Podgoretskaya, N., 136
Poffenberger, S., 505
Poffenberger, T., 505
Pollitt, E., 118

Popspisil, J., 79-80
Poteet, J., 390, 391
Powell, P., 56
Power, T., 134
Poze, T., 408
Prater, G., 553
Prescott, J., 48
Pressey, S., 109-110, 155, 264
Preston, A., 506
Pribram, K., 28, 56
Price, G., 201, 409
Prichard, A., 430
Prillaman, D., 530
Provenzano, F., 506
Purkey, W., 172, 179, 387
Pyryt, M., 329

Quarfoth, J., 330

Racle, G., 406
Raffaelli, M., 134
Rakic, P., 45
Ramaseshan, P., 171
Ramey, C. T., 134
Raph, J., 544
Raudsepp, E., 424, 425
Raven, J., 343
Ray, B., 310, 311
Ray, M., 86, 98-99
Raymond, C., 116, 117, 127, 131
Reber, A., 426
Redding, R., 543
Reichstein, K., 487
Reid, M., 56
Reis, S., 224, 275, 290, 291, 368, 370, 454, 502, 503, 511, 515, 544, 556, 558-559
Rekdal, C. K., 513
Renzulli, J., 26-27, 32, 33, 77, 78, 82, 93, 183, 218, 260, 275, 290, 291, 338, 339, 342, 368, 369, 370, 372, 454, 492, 532-533, 550, 551
Restak, K., 28, 48, 49, 122-123, 430
Restak, R., 56, 113, 116, 117, 123, 129-130, 404, 418, 422, 423, 430
Reyes, E. I., 347
Reynolds, M., 264
Rheingold, H., 505
Rice, J., 264
Richards, E. S., 502
Richert, S., 335-336

SUBJECT INDEX